Robert Greene

A Joost Elffers Book

PENGUIN BOOKS

PENGUIN BOOKS
Published by the Penguin Group
Penguin Group (USA) Inc., 375 Hudson Street, New York, New York 10014, U.S.A.
Penguin Group (Canada), 90 Eglinton Avenue East, Suite 700, Toronto,
Ontario, Canada M4P 2Y3 (a division of Pearson Penguin Canada Inc.)
Penguin Books Ltd, 80 Strand, London WC2R 0RL, England
Penguin Ireland, 25 St Stephen's Green, Dublin 2, Ireland (a division of Penguin Books Ltd)
Penguin Group (Australia), 250 Camberwell Road, Camberwell, Victoria 3124, Australia
(a division of Pearson Australia Group Pty Ltd)
Penguin Books India Pvt Ltd, 11 Community Centre, Panchsheel Park,
New Delhi–110 017, India
Penguin Group (NZ), 67 Apollo Drive, Mairangi Bay, Auckland 1311, New Zealand
(a division of Pearson New Zealand Ltd)
Penguin Books (South Africa) (Pty) Ltd, 24 Sturdee Avenue, Rosebank,
Johannesburg 2196, South Africa

Penguin Books Ltd, Registered Offices:
80 Strand, London WC2R 0RL, England

First published in the United States of America by Viking Penguin,
a member of Penguin Putnam Inc. 2001
Published in Penguin Books 2003

20

THE LIBRARY OF CONGRESS HAS CATALOGUED THE HARDCOVER EDITION AS FOLLOWS:
Greene Robert.
The art of seduction / Robert Greene.
p. cm.
"A Joost Elffers book."
ISBN 0-670-89192-4 (hc.)
ISBN 0 14 20.0119 8 (pbk.)
1. Sexual excitement. 2. Sex instruction. 3. Seduction. I. Title.
HQ31 .G82 2001
306.7—dc21
2001025868

Printed in the United States of America
Set in Bembo
Designed by Jaye Zimet with Joost Elffers

Grateful acknowledgment is made for permission to reprint excerpts from the following copyrighted works:

Falling in Love by Francesco Alberoni, translated by Lawrence Venuti. Reprinted by permission of Random House, Inc.

Seduction by Jean Baudrillard, translated by Brian Singer, St. Martin's Press, 1990. Copyright © New World Perspectives, 1990. Reprinted by permission of Palgrave.

The Decameron by Giovanni Boccaccio, translated by G. H. McWilliam (Penguin Classics 1972, second edition 1995). Copyright © G. H. McWilliam, 1972, 1995. Reprinted by permission of Penguin Books Ltd.

Warhol by David Bourdon, published by Harry N. Abrams, Inc., New York. All rights reserved. Reprinted by permission of the publisher.

Behind the Mask: On Sexual Demons, Sacred Mothers, Transvestites, Gangsters and Other Japanese Cultural Heroes by Ian Buruma, Random House UK, 1984. Reprinted with permission.

Andreas Capellanus on Love by Andreas Capellanus, translated by P. G. Walsh. Reprinted by permission of Gerald Duckworth & Co. Ltd.

The Book of the Courtier by Baldassare Castiglione, translated by George Bull (Penguin Classics 1967, revised edition 1976). Copyright © George Bull, 1967, 1976. Reprinted by permission of Penguin Books Ltd.

Portrait of a Seductress: The World of Natalie Barney by Jean Chalon, translated by Carol Barko, Crown Publishers, Inc., 1979. Reprinted with permission.

Lenin: The Man Behind the Mask by Ronald W. Clark, Faber & Faber Ltd., 1988. Reprinted with permission.

Pursuit of the Millennium by Norman Cohn. Copyright © 1970 by Oxford University Press. Used by permission of Oxford University Press, Inc.

Tales from The Thousand and One Nights, translated by N. J. Dawood (Penguin Classics, 1955, revised edition 1973). Translation copyright © N. J. Dawood, 1954, 1973. Reprinted by permission of Penguin Books Ltd.

Emma, Lady Hamilton by Flora Fraser, Alfred A. Knopf, 1987. Copyright © 1986 by Flora Fraser. Reprinted by permission.

Evita: The Real Life of Eva Peron by Nicolas Fraser and Marysa Navarro, W. W. Norton & Company, Inc., 1996. Reprinted by permission.

The World's Lure: Fair Women, Their Loves, Their Power, Their Fates by Alexander von Gleichen–Russwurm, translated by Hannah Waller, Alfred A. Knopf, 1927. Copyright 1927 by Alfred A. Knopf, Inc. Reprinted with permission.

The Greek Myths by Robert Graves. Reprinted by permission of Carcanet Press Limited.

The Kennedy Obsession: The American Myth of JFK by John Hellman, Columbia University Press 1997. Reprinted by permission of Columbia University Press.

The Odyssey by Homer, translated by E. V. Rieu (Penguin Classics, 1946). Copyright © The Estate of E. V. Rieu, 1946. Reprinted by permission of Penguin Books Ltd.

The Life of an Amorous Woman and Other Writings by Ihara Saikaku, translated by Ivan Morris. Copyright © 1963 by New Directions Publishing Corp. Reprinted by permission of New Directions Publishing Corp.

"The Seducer's Diary" from *Either/Or, Part 1* by Søren Kierkegaard, translated by Howard V. Hong and Edna H. Hong. Copyright © 1987 by Princeton University Press. Reprinted by permission of Princeton University Press.

Sirens: Symbols of Seduction by Meri Lao, translated by John Oliphant of Rossie, Park Street Press, Rochester, Vermont, 1998. Reprinted with permission.

Lives of the Courtesans by Lynne Lawner, Rizzoli, 1987. Reprinted with permission of the author.

The Theatre of Don Juan: A Collection of Plays and Views, 1630–1963 edited with a commentary by Oscar Mandel. Copyright © 1963 by the University of Nebraska Press. Copyright © renewed 1991 by the University of Nebraska Press. Reprinted by permission of the University of Nebraska Press.

Don Juan and the Point of Horror by James Mandrell. Reprinted with permission of Penn State University Press.

Bel-Ami by Guy de Maupassant, translated by Douglas Parmee (Penguin Classics, 1975). Copyright © Douglas Parmee, 1975. Reprinted by permission of Penguin Books Ltd.

The Arts and Secrets of Beauty by Lola Montez, Chelsea House, 1969. Used with permission.

The Age of the Crowd by Serge Moscovici. Reprinted with permission of Cambridge University Press.

The Tale of Genji by Murasaki Shikibu, translated by Edward G. Seidensticker, Alfred A. Knopf, 1976. Copyright © 1976 by Edward G. Seidensticker. Reprinted by permission of the publisher.

The Erotic Poems by Ovid, translated by Peter Green (Penguin Classics, 1982). Copyright © Peter Green, 1982. Reprinted by permission of Penguin Books Ltd.

The Metamorphoses by Ovid, translated by Mary M. Innes (Penguin Classics, 1955). Copyright © Mary M. Innes, 1955. Reprinted by permission of Penguin Books Ltd.

To the memory of my father

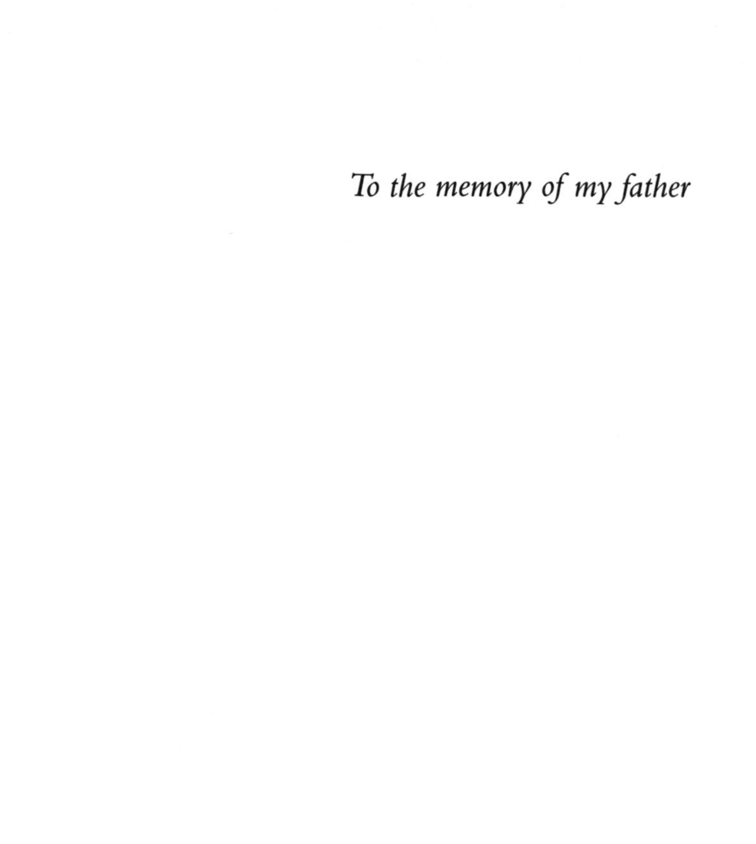

Acknowledgments

First, I would like to thank Anna Biller for her countless contributions to this book: the research, the many discussions, her invaluable help with the text itself, and, last but not least, her knowledge of the art of seduction, of which I have been the happy victim on numerous occasions.

I must thank my mother, Laurette, for supporting me so steadfastly throughout this project and for being my most devoted fan.

I would like to thank Catherine Léouzon, who some years ago introduced me to *Les Liaisons Dangereuses* and the world of Valmont.

I would like to thank David Frankel, for his deft editing and for his much-appreciated advice; Molly Stern at Viking Penguin, for overseeing the project and helping to shape it; Radha Pancham, for keeping it all organized and being so patient; and Brett Kelly, for moving things along.

With heavy heart I would like to pay tribute to my cat Boris, who for thirteen years watched over me as I wrote and whose presence is sorely missed. His successor, Brutus, has proven to be a worthy muse.

Finally, I would like to honor my father. Words cannot express how much I miss him and how much he has inspired my work.

Contents

Phase Three: The Precipice—Deepening the Effect Through Extreme Measures

Phase Four: Moving In for the Kill

Preface

Thousands of years ago, power was mostly gained through physical violence and maintained with brute strength. There was little need for subtlety—a king or emperor had to be merciless. Only a select few had power, but no one suffered under this scheme of things more than women. They had no way to compete, no weapon at their disposal that could make a man do what they wanted—politically, socially, or even in the home.

Of course men had one weakness: their insatiable desire for sex. A woman could always toy with this desire, but once she gave in to sex the man was back in control; and if she withheld sex, he could simply look elsewhere—or exert force. What good was a power that was so temporary and frail? Yet women had no choice but to submit to this condition. There were some, though, whose hunger for power was too great, and who, over the years, through much cleverness and creativity, invented a way of turning the dynamic around, creating a more lasting and effective form of power.

These women—among them Bathsheba, from the Old Testament; Helen of Troy; the Chinese siren Hsi Shi; and the greatest of them all, Cleopatra—invented seduction. First they would draw a man in with an alluring appearance, designing their makeup and adornment to fashion the image of a goddess come to life. By showing only glimpses of flesh, they would tease a man's imagination, stimulating the desire not just for sex but for something greater: the chance to possess a fantasy figure. Once they had their victims' interest, these women would lure them away from the masculine world of war and politics and get them to spend time in the feminine world—a world of luxury, spectacle, and pleasure. They might also lead them astray literally, taking them on a journey, as Cleopatra lured Julius Caesar on a trip down the Nile. Men would grow hooked on these refined, sensual pleasures—they would fall in love. But then, invariably, the women would turn cold and indifferent, confusing their victims. Just when the men wanted more, they found their pleasures withdrawn. They would be forced into pursuit, trying anything to win back the favors they once had tasted and growing weak and emotional in the process. Men who had physical force and all the social power—men like King David, the Trojan Paris, Julius Caesar, Mark Antony, King Fu Chai—would find themselves becoming the slave of a woman.

In the face of violence and brutality, these women made seduction a

Oppression and scorn, thus, were and must have been generally the share of women in emerging societies; this state lasted in all its force until centuries of experience taught them to substitute skill for force. Women at last sensed that, since they were weaker, their only resource was to seduce; they understood that if they were dependent on men through force, men could become dependent on them through pleasure. More unhappy than men, they must have thought and reflected earlier than did men; they were the first to know that pleasure was always beneath the idea that one formed of it, and that the imagination went farther than nature. Once these basic truths were known, they learned first to veil their charms in order to awaken curiosity; they practiced the difficult art of refusing even as they wished to consent; from that moment on, they knew how to set men's imagination afire, they knew how to arouse and direct desires as they pleased: thus did beauty and love come into being; now the lot of women became less harsh, not that they had managed to liberate themselves entirely from the state of oppression to which their weakness condemned them; but, in the state of perpetual war that continues to exist between women and men, one has seen them, with the help of the caresses they have been able to invent, combat ceaselessly, sometimes vanquish, and often more skillfully take advantage of the forces directed against them; sometimes, too, men have turned against women these weapons the women had forged to combat them, and their slavery has become all the harsher for it.

—Choderlos de Laclos, *On the Education of Women*, translated by Lydia Davis, in *The Libertine Reader*, edited by Michael Feher

sophisticated art, the ultimate form of power and persuasion. They learned to work on the mind first, stimulating fantasies, keeping a man wanting more, creating patterns of hope and despair—the essence of seduction. Their power was not physical but psychological, not forceful but indirect and cunning. These first great seductresses were like military generals planning the destruction of an enemy, and indeed early accounts of seduction often compare it to battle, the feminine version of warfare. For Cleopatra, it was a means of consolidating an empire. In seduction, the woman was no longer a passive sex object; she had become an active agent, a figure of power.

With a few exceptions—the Latin poet Ovid, the medieval troubadours—men did not much concern themselves with such a frivolous art as seduction. Then, in the seventeenth century came a great change: men grew interested in seduction as a way to overcome a young woman's resistance to sex. History's first great male seducers—the Duke de Lauzun, the different Spaniards who inspired the Don Juan legend—began to adopt the methods traditionally employed by women. They learned to dazzle with their appearance (often androgynous in nature), to stimulate the imagination, to play the coquette. They also added a new, masculine element to the game: seductive language, for they had discovered a woman's weakness for soft words. These two forms of seduction—the feminine use of appearances and the masculine use of language—would often cross gender lines: Casanova would dazzle a woman with his clothes; Ninon de l'Enclos would charm a man with her words.

Much more genius is needed to make love than to command armies.

—Ninon de l'Enclos

At the same time that men were developing their version of seduction, others began to adapt the art for social purposes. As Europe's feudal system of government faded into the past, courtiers needed to get their way in court without the use of force. They learned the power to be gained by seducing their superiors and competitors through psychological games, soft words, a little coquetry. As culture became democratized, actors, dandies, and artists came to use the tactics of seduction as a way to charm and win over their audience and social milieu. In the nineteenth century another great change occurred: politicians like Napoleon consciously saw themselves as seducers, on a grand scale. These men depended on the art of seductive oratory, but they also mastered what had once been feminine strategies: staging vast spectacles, using theatrical devices, creating a charged physical presence. All this, they learned, was the essence of charisma—and remains so today. By seducing the masses they could accumulate immense power without the use of force.

Menelaus, if you are really going to kill her, \ Then my blessing go with you, but you must do it now, \ Before her looks so twist the strings of your heart \ That they turn your mind; for her eyes are like armies, \ And where her glances fall, there cities burn, \ Until the dust of their ashes is blown \ By her sighs. I know her, Menelaus, \ And so do you. And all those who know her suffer.

—Hecuba speaking about Helen of Troy in Euripides, *The Trojan Women*, translated by Neil Curry

Today we have reached the ultimate point in the evolution of seduction. Now more than ever, force or brutality of any kind is discouraged. All areas of social life require the ability to persuade people in a way that does not offend or impose itself. Forms of seduction can be found everywhere, blending male and female strategies. Advertisements insinuate, the soft sell dominates. If we are to change people's opinions—and affecting opinion is basic to seduction—we must act in subtle, subliminal ways. Today no political campaign can work without seduction. Since the era of John F. Kennedy, political figures are required to have a degree of charisma, a fascinating presence to keep their audience's attention, which is half the battle. The film world and media create a galaxy of seductive stars and images. We are saturated in the seductive. But even if much has changed in degree and scope, the essence of seduction is constant: never be forceful or direct; instead, use pleasure as bait, playing on people's emotions, stirring desire and confusion, inducing psychological surrender. In seduction as it is practiced today, the methods of Cleopatra still hold.

No man hath it in his power to over-rule the deceitfulness of a woman.

—Marguerite of Navarre

People are constantly trying to influence us, to tell us what to do, and just as often we tune them out, resisting their attempts at persuasion. There is a moment in our lives, however, when we all act differently—when we are in love. We fall under a kind of spell. Our minds are usually preoccupied with our own concerns; now they become filled with thoughts of the loved one. We grow emotional, lose the ability to think straight, act in foolish ways that we would never do otherwise. If this goes on long enough something inside us gives way: we surrender to the will of the loved one, and to our desire to possess them.

Seducers are people who understand the tremendous power contained in such moments of surrender. They analyze what happens when people are in love, study the psychological components of the process—what spurs the imagination, what casts a spell. By instinct and through practice they master the art of making people fall in love. As the first seductresses knew, it is much more effective to create love than lust. A person in love is emotional, pliable, and easily misled. (The origin of the word "seduction" is the Latin for "to lead astray.") A person in lust is harder to control and, once satisfied, may easily leave you. Seducers take their time, create enchantment and the bonds of love, so that when sex ensues it only further enslaves the victim. Creating love and enchantment becomes the model for all seductions—sexual, social, political. A person in love will surrender.

It is pointless to try to argue against such power, to imagine that you are not interested in it, or that it is evil and ugly. The harder you try to resist the lure of seduction—as an idea, as a form of power—the more you will find yourself fascinated. The reason is simple: most of us have known the power of having someone fall in love with us. Our actions, gestures, the things we say, all have positive effects on this person; we may not completely understand what we have done right, but this feeling of power is intoxicating. It gives us confidence, which makes us more seductive. We may also experience this in a social or work setting—one day we are in an elevated mood and people seem more responsive, more charmed by us. These moments of power are fleeting, but they resonate in the memory with great intensity. We want them back. Nobody likes to feel awkward or timid or unable to reach people. The siren call of seduction is irresistible because power is irresistible, and nothing will bring you more power in the modern world than the ability to seduce. Repressing the desire to seduce is a kind of

This important side-track, by which woman succeeded in evading man's strength and establishing herself in power, has not been given due consideration by historians. From the moment when the woman detached herself from the crowd, an individual finished product, offering delights which could not be obtained by force, but only by flattery . . . , the reign of love's priestesses was inaugurated. It was a development of far-reaching importance in the history of civilization. . . . Only by the circuitous route of the art of love could woman again assert authority, and this she did by asserting herself at the very point at which she would normally be a slave at the man's mercy. She had discovered the might of lust, the secret of the art of love, the daemonic power of a passion artificially aroused and never satiated. The force thus unchained was thenceforth to count among the most tremendous of the world's forces and at moments to have power even over life and death. . . . • The deliberate spell-binding of man's senses was to have a magical effect upon him, opening up an infinitely wider range of sensation and spurring him on as if impelled by an inspired dream.

—Alexander von Gleichen-Russwurm, *The World's Lure*, translated by Hannah Waller

hysterical reaction, revealing your deep-down fascination with the process; you are only making your desires stronger. Some day they will come to the surface.

The first thing to get in your head is that every single \ Girl can be caught—and that you'll catch her if \ You set your toils right. Birds will sooner fall dumb in \ Springtime, \ Cicadas in summer, or a hunting-dog \ Turn his back on a hare, than a lover's bland inducements \ Can fail with a woman. Even one you suppose \ Reluctant will want it.

—OVID, *THE ART OF LOVE*, TRANSLATED BY PETER GREEN

To have such power does not require a total transformation in your character or any kind of physical improvement in your looks. Seduction is a game of psychology, not beauty, and it is within the grasp of any person to become a master at the game. All that is required is that you look at the world differently, through the eyes of a seducer.

A seducer does not turn the power off and on—every social and personal interaction is seen as a potential seduction. There is never a moment to waste. This is so for several reasons. The power seducers have over a man or woman works in social environments because they have learned how to tone down the sexual element without getting rid of it. We may think we see through them, but they are so pleasant to be around anyway that it does not matter. Trying to divide your life into moments in which you seduce and others in which you hold back will only confuse and constrain you. Erotic desire and love lurk beneath the surface of almost every human encounter; better to give free rein to your skills than to try to use them only in the bedroom. (In fact, the seducer sees the world as his or her bedroom.) This attitude creates great seductive momentum, and with each seduction you gain experience and practice. One social or sexual seduction makes the next one easier, your confidence growing and making you more alluring. People are drawn to you in greater numbers as the seducer's aura descends upon you.

The combination of these two elements, enchantment and surrender, is, then, essential to the love which we are discussing. . . . What exists in love is surrender due to enchantment.

—JOSÉ ORTEGA Y GASSET, *ON LOVE*, TRANSLATED BY TOBY TALBOT

Seducers have a warrior's outlook on life. They see each person as a kind of walled castle to which they are laying siege. Seduction is a process of penetration: initially penetrating the target's mind, their first point of defense. Once seducers have penetrated the mind, making the target fantasize about them, it is easy to lower resistance and create physical surrender. Seducers do not improvise; they do not leave this process to chance. Like any good general, they plan and strategize, aiming at the target's particular weaknesses.

What is good?—All that heightens the feeling of power, the will to power, power itself in man. • What is bad?—All that proceeds from weakness. • What is happiness?—The feeling that power increases—that a resistance is overcome.

—FRIEDRICH NIETZSCHE, *THE ANTI-CHRIST*, TRANSLATED BY R. J. HOLLINGDALE

The main obstacle to becoming a seducer is this foolish prejudice we have of seeing love and romance as some kind of sacred, magical realm where things just fall into place, if they are meant to. This might seem romantic and quaint, but it is really just a cover for our laziness. What will seduce a person is the effort we expend on their behalf, showing how much we care, how much they are worth. Leaving things to chance is a recipe for disaster, and reveals that we do not take love and romance very seriously. It was the effort Casanova expended, the artfulness he applied to each affair that made him so devilishly seductive. Falling in love is a matter not of magic but of psychology. Once you understand your target's psychology, and strategize to suit it, you will be better able to cast a "magical" spell. A seducer sees love not as sacred but as warfare, where all is fair.

Seducers are never self-absorbed. Their gaze is directed outward, not inward. When they meet someone their first move is to get inside that person's skin, to see the world through their eyes. The reasons for this are several. First, self-absorption is a sign of insecurity; it is anti-seductive. Everyone has insecurities, but seducers manage to ignore them, finding therapy for moments of self-doubt by being absorbed in the world. This gives them a buoyant spirit—we want to be around them. Second, getting into someone's skin, imagining what it is like to be them, helps the seducer gather valuable information, learn what makes that person tick, what will make them lose their ability to think straight and fall into a trap. Armed with such information, they can provide focused and individualized attention—a rare commodity in a world in which most people see us only from behind the screen of their own prejudices. Getting into the targets' skin is the first important tactical move in the war of penetration.

The disaffection, neurosis, anguish and frustration encountered by psychoanalysis comes no doubt from being unable to love or to be loved, from being unable to give or take pleasure, but the radical disenchantment comes from seduction and its failure. Only those who lie completely outside seduction are ill, even if they remain fully capable of loving and making love. Psychoanalysis believes it treats the disorder of sex and desire, but in reality it is dealing with the disorders of seduction. . . . The most serious deficiencies always concern charm and not pleasure, enchantment and not some vital or sexual satisfaction.

—Jean Baudrillard, *Seduction*

Seducers see themselves as providers of pleasure, like bees that gather pollen from some flowers and deliver it to others. As children we mostly devoted our lives to play and pleasure. Adults often have feelings of being cut off from this paradise, of being weighed down by responsibilities. The seducer knows that people are waiting for pleasure—they never get enough of it from friends and lovers, and they cannot get it by themselves. A person who enters their lives offering adventure and romance cannot be resisted. Pleasure is a feeling of being taken past our limits, of being overwhelmed—by another person, by an experience. People are dying to be overwhelmed, to let go of their usual stubbornness. Sometimes their resistance to us is a way of saying, Please seduce me. Seducers know that the possibility of pleasure will make a person follow them, and the experience of it will make someone open up, weak to the touch. They also train themselves to be sensitive to pleasure, knowing that feeling pleasure themselves will make it that much easier for them to infect the people around them.

Whatever is done from love always occurs beyond good and evil.

—Friedrich Nietzsche, *Beyond Good and Evil*, translated by Walter Kaufmann

A seducer sees all of life as theater, everyone an actor. Most people feel they have constricted roles in life, which makes them unhappy. Seducers, on the other hand, can be anyone and can assume many roles. (The archetype here is the god Zeus, insatiable seducer of young maidens, whose main weapon was the ability to assume the form of whatever person or animal would most appeal to his victim.) Seducers take pleasure in performing and are not weighed down by their identity, or by some need to be themselves, or to be natural. This freedom of theirs, this fluidity in body and spirit, is what makes them attractive. What people lack in life is not more reality but illusion, fantasy, play. The clothes that seducers wear, the places they take you to, their words and actions, are slightly heightened—not overly theatrical but with a delightful edge of unreality, as if the two of you were living out a piece of fiction or were characters in a film. Seduction is a kind of theater in real life, the meeting of illusion and reality.

Finally, seducers are completely amoral in their approach to life. It is all a game, an arena for play. Knowing that the moralists, the crabbed repressed types who croak about the evils of the seducer, secretly envy their power, they do not concern themselves with other people's opinions. They do not deal in moral judgments—nothing could be less seductive. Everything is

Should anyone here in Rome lack finesse at love-making, \ Let him \ Try me—read my book, and results are guaranteed! \ Technique is the secret. Charioteer, sailor, oarsman, \ All need it. Technique can control \ Love himself.

—OVID, *THE ART OF LOVE*, TRANSLATED BY PETER GREEN

pliant, fluid, like life itself. Seduction is a form of deception, but people want to be led astray, they yearn to be seduced. If they didn't, seducers would not find so many willing victims. Get rid of any moralizing tendencies, adopt the seducer's playful philosophy, and you will find the rest of the process easy and natural.

The Art of Seduction is designed to arm you with weapons of persuasion and charm, so that those around you will slowly lose their ability to resist without knowing how or why it has happened. It is an art of war for delicate times.

Every seduction has two elements that you must analyze and understand: first, yourself and what is seductive about you; and second, your target and the actions that will penetrate their defenses and create surrender. The two sides are equally important. If you strategize without paying attention to the parts of your character that draw people to you, you will be seen as a mechanical seducer, slimy and manipulative. If you rely on your seductive personality without paying attention to the other person, you will make terrible mistakes and limit your potential.

Consequently, *The Art of Seduction* is divided into two parts. The first half, "The Seductive Character," describes the nine types of seducer, plus the Anti-Seducer. Studying these types will make you aware of what is inherently seductive in your character, the basic building block of any seduction. The second half, "The Seductive Process," includes the twenty-four maneuvers and strategies that will instruct you on how to create a spell, break down people's resistance, give movement and force to your seduction, and induce surrender in your target. As a kind of bridge between the two parts, there is a chapter on the eighteen types of victims of a seduction—each of them missing something from their lives, each cradling an emptiness you can fill. Knowing what type you are dealing with will help you put into practice the ideas in both sections. Ignore any part of this book and you will be an incomplete seducer.

The ideas and strategies in *The Art of Seduction* are based on the writings and historical accounts of the most successful seducers in history. The sources include the seducers' own memoirs (by Casanova, Errol Flynn, Natalie Barney, Marilyn Monroe); biographies (of Cleopatra, Josephine Bonaparte, John F. Kennedy, Duke Ellington); handbooks on the subject (most notably Ovid's *Art of Love*); and fictional accounts of seductions (Choderlos de Laclos's *Dangerous Liaisons*, Søren Kierkegaard's *The Seducer's Diary*, Murasaki Shikibu's *The Tale of Genji*). The heroes and heroines of these literary works are generally modeled on real-life seducers. The strategies they employ reveal the intimate connection between fiction and seduction, creating illusion and leading a person along. In putting the book's lessons into practice, you will be following in the path of the greatest masters of the art.

Finally, the spirit that will make you a consummate seducer is the spirit in which you should read this book. The French writer Denis Diderot once wrote, "I give my mind the liberty to follow the first wise or foolish idea that presents itself, just as in the avenue de Foy our dissolute youths follow close on the heels of some strumpet, then leave her to pursue another, attacking all of them and attaching themselves to none. My thoughts are my strumpets." He meant that he let himself be seduced by ideas, following whichever one caught his fancy until a better one came along, his thoughts infused with a kind of sexual excitement. Once you enter these pages, do as Diderot advised: let yourself be lured by the stories and ideas, your mind open and your thoughts fluid. Slowly you will find yourself absorbing the poison through the skin and you will begin to see everything as a seduction, including the way you think and how you look at the world.

Most virtue is a demand for greater seduction.

—Natalie Barney

the art of Seduction

Part One

the Seductive Character

We all have the power of attraction—the ability to draw people in and hold them in our thrall. Far from all of us, though, are aware of this inner potential, and we imagine attractiveness instead as a near-mystical trait that a select few are born with and the rest will never command. Yet all we need to do to realize our potential is understand what it is in a person's character that naturally excites people and develop these latent qualities within us.

Successful seductions rarely begin with an obvious maneuver or strategic device. That is certain to arouse suspicion. Successful seductions begin with your character, your ability to radiate some quality that attracts people and stirs their emotions in a way that is beyond their control. Hypnotized by your seductive character, your victims will not notice your subsequent manipulations. It will then be child's play to mislead and seduce them.

There are nine seducer types in the world. Each type has a particular character trait that comes from deep within and creates a seductive pull. *Sirens* have an abundance of sexual energy and know how to use it. *Rakes* insatiably adore the opposite sex, and their desire is infectious. *Ideal Lovers* have an aesthetic sensibility that they apply to romance. *Dandies* like to play with their image, creating a striking and androgynous allure. *Naturals* are spontaneous and open. *Coquettes* are self-sufficient, with a fascinating cool at their core. *Charmers* want and know how to please—they are social creatures. *Charismatics* have an unusual confidence in themselves. *Stars* are ethereal and envelop themselves in mystery.

The chapters in this section will take you inside each of the nine types. At least one of the chapters should strike a chord—you will recognize part of yourself. That chapter will be the key to developing your own powers of attraction. Let us say you have coquettish tendencies. The Coquette chapter will show you how to build upon your own self-sufficiency, alternating heat and coldness to ensnare your victims. It will show you how to take your natural qualities further, becoming a grand Coquette, the type we fight over. There is no point in being timid with a seductive quality. We are charmed by an unabashed Rake and excuse his excesses, but a halfhearted Rake gets no respect. Once you have cultivated your dominant character trait, adding some art to what nature has given you, you can then develop a second or third trait, adding depth and mystery to your persona. Finally the section's tenth chapter, on the *Anti-Seducer,* will make you aware of the opposite potential within you—the power of repulsion. At all cost you must root out any anti-seductive tendencies you may have.

Think of the nine types as shadows, silhouettes. Only by stepping into one of them and letting it grow inside you can you begin to develop the seductive character that will bring you limitless power.

the Siren

A man is often secretly oppressed by the role he has to play—by always having to be responsible, in control, and rational. The Siren is the ultimate male fantasy figure because she offers a total release from the limitations of his life. In her presence, which is always heightened and sexually charged, the male feels transported to a world of pure pleasure. She is dangerous, and in pursuing her energetically the man can lose control over himself, something he yearns to do. The Siren is a mirage; she lures men by cultivating a particular appearance and manner. In a world where women are often too timid to project such an image, learn to take control of the male libido by embodying his fantasy.

The Spectacular Siren

In the year 48 B.C., Ptolemy XIV of Egypt managed to depose and exile his sister and wife, Queen Cleopatra. He secured the country's borders against her return and began to rule on his own. Later that year, Julius Caesar came to Alexandria to ensure that despite the local power struggles, Egypt would remain loyal to Rome.

One night Caesar was meeting with his generals in the Egyptian palace, discussing strategy, when a guard entered to report that a Greek merchant was at the door bearing a large and valuable gift for the Roman leader. Caesar, in the mood for a little fun, gave the merchant permission to enter. The man came in, carrying on his shoulders a large rolled-up carpet. He undid the rope around the bundle and with a snap of his wrists unfurled it—revealing the young Cleopatra, who had been hidden inside, and who rose up half clothed before Caesar and his guests, like Venus emerging from the waves.

Everyone was dazzled at the sight of the beautiful young queen (only twenty-one at the time) appearing before them suddenly as if in a dream. They were astounded at her daring and theatricality—smuggled into the harbor at night with only one man to protect her, risking everything on a bold move. No one was more enchanted than Caesar. According to the Roman writer Dio Cassius, "Cleopatra was in the prime of life. She had a delightful voice which could not fail to cast a spell over all who heard it. Such was the charm of her person and her speech that they drew the coldest and most determined misogynist into her toils. Caesar was spellbound as soon as he set eyes on her and she opened her mouth to speak." That same evening Cleopatra became Caesar's lover.

Caesar had had numerous mistresses before, to divert him from the rigors of his campaigns. But he had always disposed of them quickly to return to what really thrilled him—political intrigue, the challenges of warfare, the Roman theater. Caesar had seen women try anything to keep him under their spell. Yet nothing prepared him for Cleopatra. One night she would tell him how together they could revive the glory of Alexander the Great, and rule the world like gods. The next she would entertain him dressed as the goddess Isis, surrounded by the opulence of her court. Cleopatra initiated Caesar in the most decadent revelries, presenting herself as the incarnation of the Egyptian exotic. His life with her was a constant game, as challenging as warfare, for the moment he felt secure with her she

In the mean time our good ship, with that perfect wind to drive her, fast approached the Sirens' Isle. But now the breeze dropped, some power lulled the waves, and a breathless calm set in. Rising from their seats my men drew in the sail and threw it into the hold, then sat down at the oars and churned the water white with their blades of polished pine. Meanwhile I took a large round of wax, cut it up small with my sword, and kneaded the pieces with all the strength of my fingers. The wax soon yielded to my vigorous treatment and grew warm, for I had the rays of my Lord the Sun to help me. I took each of my men in turn and plugged their ears with it. They then made me a prisoner on my ship by binding me hand and foot, standing me up by the step of the mast and tying the rope's ends to the mast itself. This done, they sat down once more and struck the grey water with their oars. • We made good progress and had just come within call of the shore when the Sirens became aware that a ship was swiftly bearing down upon them, and broke into their liquid song. • "Draw near," they sang, "illustrious Odysseus, flower of Achaean chivalry, and bring your ship to rest so that you may hear our voices. No seaman ever sailed his black ship past this spot without listening to the sweet tones that flow from our lips . . ." • The lovely voices came to me across the water, and my heart was filled with such a longing to listen that with nod and frown I signed to my men to set me free.

—Homer, *The Odyssey*, Book XII, translated by E.V. Rieu

would suddenly turn cold or angry and he would have to find a way to regain her favor.

The weeks went by. Caesar got rid of all Cleopatra's rivals and found excuses to stay in Egypt. At one point she led him on a lavish historical expedition down the Nile. In a boat of unimaginable splendor—towering fifty-four feet out of the water, including several terraced levels and a pillared temple to the god Dionysus—Caesar became one of the few Romans to gaze on the pyramids. And while he stayed long in Egypt, away from his throne in Rome, all kinds of turmoil erupted throughout the Roman Empire.

When Caesar was murdered, in 44 B.C., he was succeeded by a triumvirate of rulers including Mark Antony, a brave soldier who loved pleasure and spectacle and fancied himself a kind of Roman Dionysus. A few years later, while Antony was in Syria, Cleopatra invited him to come meet her in the Egyptian town of Tarsus. There—once she had made him wait for her—her appearance was as startling in its way as her first before Caesar. A magnificent gold barge with purple sails appeared on the river Cydnus. The oarsmen rowed to the accompaniment of ethereal music; all around the boat were beautiful young girls dressed as nymphs and mythological figures. Cleopatra sat on deck, surrounded and fanned by cupids and posed as the goddess Aphrodite, whose name the crowd chanted enthusiastically.

The charm of [Cleopatra's] presence was irresistible, and there was an attraction in her person and talk, together with a peculiar force of character, which pervaded her every word and action, and laid all who associated with her under its spell. It was a delight merely to hear the sound of her voice, with which, like an instrument of many strings, she could pass from one language to another.

—Plutarch, *Makers of Rome*, translated by Ian Scott-Kilvert

Like all of Cleopatra's victims, Antony felt mixed emotions. The exotic pleasures she offered were hard to resist. But he also wanted to tame her—to defeat this proud and illustrious woman would prove his greatness. And so he stayed, and, like Caesar, fell slowly under her spell. She indulged him in all of his weaknesses—gambling, raucous parties, elaborate rituals, lavish spectacles. To get him to come back to Rome, Octavius, another member of the Roman triumvirate, offered him a wife: Octavius's own sister, Octavia, one of the most beautiful women in Rome. Known for her virtue and goodness, she could surely keep Antony away from the "Egyptian whore." The ploy worked for a while, but Antony was unable to forget Cleopatra, and after three years he went back to her. This time it was for good: he had in essence become Cleopatra's slave, granting her immense powers, adopting Egyptian dress and customs, and renouncing the ways of Rome.

The immediate attraction of a song, a voice, or scent. The attraction of the panther with his perfumed scent . . . According to the ancients, the panther is the only animal who emits a perfumed odor. It uses this scent to draw and capture its victims. . . . But what is it that seduces in a scent? . . . What is it in the song of the Sirens that seduces us, or in the beauty of a face, in the depths

Only one image of Cleopatra survives—a barely visible profile on a coin—but we have numerous written descriptions. She had a long thin face and a somewhat pointed nose; her dominant features were her wonderfully large eyes. Her seductive power, however, did not lie in her looks—indeed many among the women of Alexandria were considered more beautiful than she. What she did have above all other women was the ability to distract a man. In reality, Cleopatra was physically unexceptional and had no political power, yet both Caesar and Antony, brave and clever men, saw none of this. What they saw was a woman who constantly transformed herself before their eyes, a one-woman spectacle. Her dress and makeup changed from day to day, but always gave her a heightened, goddesslike appearance.

Her voice, which all writers talk of, was lilting and intoxicating. Her words could be banal enough, but were spoken so sweetly that listeners would find themselves remembering not what she said but how she said it.

Cleopatra provided constant variety—tributes, mock battles, expeditions, costumed orgies. Everything had a touch of drama and was accomplished with great energy. By the time your head lay on the pillow beside her, your mind was spinning with images and dreams. And just when you thought you had this fluid, larger-than-life woman, she would turn distant or angry, making it clear that everything was on her terms. You never possessed Cleopatra, you worshiped her. In this way a woman who had been exiled and destined for an early death managed to turn it all around and rule Egypt for close to twenty years.

From Cleopatra we learn that it is not beauty that makes a Siren but rather a theatrical streak that allows a woman to embody a man's fantasies. A man grows bored with a woman, no matter how beautiful; he yearns for different pleasures, and for adventure. All a woman needs to turn this around is to create the illusion that she offers such variety and adventure. A man is easily deceived by appearances; he has a weakness for the visual. Create the physical presence of a Siren (heightened sexual allure mixed with a regal and theatrical manner) and he is trapped. He cannot grow bored with you yet he cannot discard you. Keep up the distractions, and never let him see who you really are. He will follow you until he drowns.

of an abyss . . . ? Seduction lies in the annulment of signs and their meaning, in pure appearance. The eyes that seduce have no meaning, they end in the gaze, as the face with makeup ends in only pure appearance. . . . The scent of the panther is also a meaningless message—and behind the message the panther is invisible, as is the woman beneath her makeup. The Sirens too remained unseen. The enchantment lies in what is hidden.

—Jean Baudrillard, *De la Séduction*

The Sex Siren

Norma Jean Mortensen, the future Marilyn Monroe, spent part of her childhood in Los Angeles orphanages. Her days were filled with chores and no play. At school, she kept to herself, smiled rarely, and dreamed a lot. One day when she was thirteen, as she was dressing for school, she noticed that the white blouse the orphanage provided for her was torn, so she had to borrow a sweater from a younger girl in the house. The sweater was several sizes too small. That day, suddenly, boys seemed to gather around her wherever she went (she was extremely well-developed for her age). She wrote in her diary, "They stared at my sweater as if it were a gold mine."

The revelation was simple but startling. Previously ignored and even ridiculed by the other students, Norma Jean now sensed a way to gain attention, maybe even power, for she was wildly ambitious. She started to smile more, wear makeup, dress differently. And soon she noticed something equally startling: without her having to say or do anything, boys fell passionately in love with her. "My admirers all said the same thing in different ways," she wrote. "It was my fault, their wanting to kiss me and hug me. Some said it was the way I looked at them—with eyes full of passion. Others said it was my voice that lured them on. Still others said I gave off vibrations that floored them."

We're dazzled by feminine adornment, by the surface, \ All gold and jewels: so little of what we observe \ Is the girl herself. And where (you may ask) amid such plenty \ Can our object of passion be found? The eye's deceived \ By Love's smart camouflage.

—Ovid, *Cures for Love*, translated by Peter Green

He was herding his cattle on Mount Gargarus, the highest peak of Ida, when Hermes, accompanied by Hera, Athene, and Aphrodite delivered the golden apple and Zeus's message: "Paris, since you are as handsome as you are wise in affairs of the heart, Zeus commands you to judge which of these goddesses is the fairest." • "So be it," sighed Paris. "But first I beg the losers not to be vexed with me. I am only a human being, liable to make the stupidest mistakes." • The goddesses all agreed to abide by his decision. • "Will it be enough to judge them as they are?" Paris asked Hermes, "or should they be naked?" • "The rules of the contest are for you to decide," Hermes answered with a discreet smile. • "In that case, will they kindly disrobe?" • Hermes told the goddesses to do so, and politely turned his back. • Aphrodite was soon ready, but Athene insisted that she should remove the famous magic girdle, which gave her an unfair advantage by making everyone fall in love withthe wearer. "Very well," said Aphrodite spitefully. "I will, on condition that you remove your helmet—you look hideous without it." • "Now, if you please, I must judge you one at a time," announced Paris. . . . Come here, Divine Hera! Will you other two goddesses be good enough to leave us for a while?" • "Examine me conscientiously," said Hera, turning slowly around, and displaying her magnificent figure, "and remember that if you judge me the fairest, I will make you lord of all Asia, and the richest man alive." • "I am not to be bribed my Lady . . . Very well, thank you. Now I have seen all that I need to see. Come, Divine Athene!" • "Here I am," said Athene, striding purposefully forward. "Listen, Paris, if you have enough common sense to award me the prize, I will make you victorious in all your battles, as well as the handsomest and wisest man in the world." • "I am a humble

A few years later Marilyn was trying to make it in the film business. Producers would tell her the same thing: she was attractive enough in person, but her face wasn't pretty enough for the movies. She was getting work as an extra, and when she was on-screen—even if only for a few seconds—the men in the audience would go wild, and the theaters would erupt in catcalls. But nobody saw any star quality in this. One day in 1949, only twenty-three at the time and her career at a standstill, Monroe met someone at a diner who told her that a producer casting a new Groucho Marx movie, *Love Happy*, was looking for an actress for the part of a blond bombshell who could walk by Groucho in a way that would, in his words, "arouse my elderly libido and cause smoke to issue from my ears." Talking her way into an audition, she improvised this walk. "It's Mae West, Theda Bara, and Bo Peep all rolled into one," said Groucho after watching her saunter by. "We shoot the scene tomorrow morning." And so Marilyn created her infamous walk, a walk that was hardly natural but offered a strange mix of innocence and sex.

Over the next few years, Marilyn taught herself through trial and error how to heighten the effect she had on men. Her voice had always been attractive—it was the voice of a little girl. But on film it had limitations until someone finally taught her to lower it, giving it the deep, breathy tones that became her seductive trademark, a mix of the little girl and the vixen. Before appearing on set, or even at a party, Marilyn would spend hours before the mirror. Most people assumed this was vanity—she was in love with her image. The truth was that image took hours to create. Marilyn spent years studying and practicing the art of makeup. The voice, the walk, the face and look were all constructions, an act. At the height of her fame, she would get a thrill by going into bars in New York City without her makeup or glamorous clothes and passing unnoticed.

Success finally came, but with it came something deeply annoying to her: the studios would only cast her as the blond bombshell. She wanted serious roles, but no one took her seriously for those parts, no matter how hard she downplayed the siren qualities she had built up. One day, while she was rehearsing a scene from *The Cherry Orchard*, her acting instructor, Michael Chekhov, asked her, "Were you thinking of sex while we played the scene?" When she said no, he continued, "All through our playing of the scene I kept receiving sex vibrations from you. As if you were a woman in the grip of passion. . . . I understand your problem with your studio now, Marilyn. You are a woman who gives off sex vibrations—no matter what you are doing or thinking. The whole world has already responded to those vibrations. They come off the movie screens when you are on them."

Marilyn Monroe loved the effect her body could have on the male libido. She tuned her physical presence like an instrument, making herself reek of sex and gaining a glamorous, larger-than-life appearance. Other women knew just as many tricks for heightening their sexual appeal, but what separated Marilyn from them was an unconscious element. Her background had deprived her of something critical: affection. Her deepest need was to feel loved and desired, which made her seem constantly vulnerable, like a little girl craving protection. She emanated this need for love before the camera; it was effortless, coming from somewhere real and deep inside. A look or gesture that she did not intend to arouse desire would do so doubly powerfully just because it was unintended—its innocence was precisely what excited a man.

The Sex Siren has a more urgent and immediate effect than the Spectacular Siren does. The incarnation of sex and desire, she does not bother to appeal to extraneous senses, or to create a theatrical buildup. Her time never seems to be taken up by work or chores; she gives the impression that she lives for pleasure and is always available. What separates the Sex Siren from the courtesan or whore is her touch of innocence and vulnerability. The mix is perversely satisfying: it gives the male the critical illusion that he is a protector, the father figure, although it is actually the Sex Siren who controls the dynamic.

A woman doesn't have to be born with the attributes of a Marilyn Monroe to fill the role of the Sex Siren. Most of the physical elements are a construction; the key is the air of schoolgirl innocence. While one part of you seems to scream sex, the other part is coy and naive, as if you were incapable of understanding the effect you are having. Your walk, your voice, your manner are delightfully ambiguous—you are both the experienced, desiring woman and the innocent gamine.

> *Your next encounter will be with the Sirens, who bewitch every man that approaches them. . . . For with the music of their song the Sirens cast their spell upon him, as they sit there in a meadow piled high with the moldering skeletons of men, whose withered skin still hangs upon their bones.*
>
> —Circe to Odysseus, *The Odyssey*, Book XII

Keys to the Character

The Siren is the most ancient seductress of them all. Her prototype is the goddess Aphrodite—it is her nature to have a mythic quality about her—but do not imagine she is a thing of the past, or of legend and history: she represents a powerful male fantasy of a highly sexual, supremely confident, alluring female offering endless pleasure and a bit of danger. In today's world this fantasy can only appeal the more strongly to the male psyche, for now more than ever he lives in a world that circumscribes his aggressive instincts by making everything safe and secure, a world that offers less chance for adventure and risk than ever before. In the past, a man had some outlets for these drives—warfare, the high seas, political intrigue. In the sexual realm, courtesans and mistresses were practically a social institu-

herdsman, not a soldier," said Paris. . . . "But I promise to consider fairly your claim to the apple. Now you are at liberty to put on your clothes and helmet again. Is Aphrodite ready?" • Aphrodite sidled up to him, and Paris blushed because she came so close that they were almost touching. • "Look carefully, please, pass nothing over. . . . By the way, as soon as I saw you, I said to myself: 'Upon my word, there goes the handsomest young man in Phrygia! Why does he waste himself here in the wilderness herding stupid cattle?' Well, why do you, Paris? Why not move into a city and lead a civilized life? What have you to lose by marrying someone like Helen of Sparta, who is as beautiful as I am, and no less passionate? . . . I suggest now that you tour Greece with my son Eros as your guide. Once you reach Sparta, he and I will see that Helen falls head over heels in love with you." • "Would you swear to that?" Paris asked excitedly. • Aphrodite uttered a solemn oath, and Paris, without a second thought, awarded her the golden apple.

—Robert Graves, *The Greek Myths*, volume 1

tion, and offered him the variety and the chase that he craved. Without any outlets, his drives turn inward and gnaw at him, becoming all the more volatile for being repressed. Sometimes a powerful man will do the most irrational things, have an affair when it is least called for, just for a thrill, the danger of it all. The irrational can prove immensely seductive, even more so for men, who must always seem so reasonable.

If it is seductive power you are after, the Siren is the most potent of all. She operates on a man's most basic emotions, and if she plays her role properly, she can transform a normally strong and responsible male into a childish slave. The Siren operates well on the rigid masculine type—the soldier or hero—just as Cleopatra overwhelmed Mark Antony and Marilyn Monroe Joe DiMaggio. But never imagine that these are the only types the Siren can affect. Julius Caesar was a writer and thinker, who had transferred his intellectual abilities onto the battlefield and into the political arena; the playwright Arthur Miller fell as deeply under Monroe's spell as DiMaggio. The intellectual is often the one most susceptible to the Siren call of pure physical pleasure, because his life so lacks it. The Siren does not have to worry about finding the right victim. Her magic works on one and all.

First and foremost, a Siren must distinguish herself from other women. She is by nature a rare thing, mythic, only one to a group; she is also a valuable prize to be wrested away from other men. Cleopatra made herself different through her sense of high drama; the Empress Josephine Bonaparte's device was her extreme languorousness; Marilyn Monroe's was her little-girl quality. Physicality offers the best opportunities here, since a Siren is preeminently a sight to behold. A highly feminine and sexual presence, even to the point of caricature, will quickly differentiate you, since most women lack the confidence to project such an image.

Once the Siren has made herself stand out from others, she must have two other critical qualities: the ability to get the male to pursue her so feverishly that he loses control; and a touch of the dangerous. Danger is surprisingly seductive. To get the male to pursue you is relatively simple: a highly sexual presence will do this quite well. But you must not resemble a courtesan or whore, whom the male may pursue only to quickly lose interest in her. Instead, you are slightly elusive and distant, a fantasy come to life. During the Renaissance, the great Sirens, such as Tullia d'Aragona, would act and look like Grecian goddesses—the fantasy of the day. Today you might model yourself on a film goddess—anything that seems larger than life, even awe inspiring. These qualities will make a man chase you vehemently, and the more he chases, the more he will feel that he is acting on his own initiative. This is an excellent way of disguising how deeply you are manipulating him.

The notion of danger, challenge, sometimes death, might seem outdated, but danger is critical in seduction. It adds emotional spice and is particularly appealing to men today, who are normally so rational and repressed. Danger is present in the original myth of the Siren. In Homer's *Odyssey*, the hero Odysseus must sail by the rocks where the Sirens, strange

To whom can I compare the lovely girl, so blessed by fortune, if not to the Sirens, who with their lodestone draw the ships towards them? Thus, I imagine, did Isolde attract many thoughts and hearts that deemed themselves safe from love's disquietude. And indeed these two—anchorless ships and stray thoughts—provide a good comparison. They are both so seldom on a straight course, lie so often in unsure havens, pitching and tossing and heaving to and fro. Just so, in the same way, do aimless desire and random love-longing drift like an anchorless ship. This charming young princess, discreet and courteous Isolde, drew thoughts from the hearts that enshrined them as a lodestone draws in ships to the sound of the Sirens' song. She sang openly and secretly, in through ears and eyes to where many a heart was stirred. The song which she sang openly in this and other places was her own sweet singing and soft sounding of strings that echoed for all to hear through the kingdom of the ears deep down into the heart. But her secret song was her wondrous beauty that stole with its rapturous music hidden and unseen through the windows of the eyes into many noble hearts and smoothed on the magic which took thoughts prisoner suddenly, and, taking them, fettered them with desire!

—GOTTFRIED VON STRASSBURG, *TRISTAN*, TRANSLATED BY A. T. HATTO

female creatures, sing and beckon sailors to their destruction. They sing of the glories of the past, of a world like childhood, without responsibilities, a world of pure pleasure. Their voices are like water, liquid and inviting. Sailors would leap into the water to join them, and drown; or, distracted and entranced, they would steer their ship into the rocks. To protect his sailors from the Sirens, Odysseus has their ears filled with wax; he himself is tied to the mast, so he can both hear the Sirens and live to tell of it—a strange desire, since the thrill of the Sirens is giving in to the temptation to follow them.

Just as the ancient sailors had to row and steer, ignoring all distractions, a man today must work and follow a straight path in life. The call of something dangerous, emotional, unknown is all the more powerful because it is so forbidden. Think of the victims of the great Sirens of history: Paris causes a war for the sake of Helen of Troy, Caesar risks an empire and Antony loses his power and his life for Cleopatra, Napoleon becomes a laughingstock over Josephine, DiMaggio never gets over Marilyn, and Arthur Miller can't write for years. A man is often ruined by a Siren, yet cannot tear himself away. (Many powerful men have a masochistic streak.) An element of danger is easy to hint at, and will enhance your other Siren characteristics—the touch of madness in Marilyn, for example, that pulled men in. Sirens are often fantastically irrational, which is immensely attractive to men who are oppressed by their own reasonableness. An element of fear is also critical: keeping a man at a proper distance creates respect, so that he doesn't get close enough to see through you or notice your weaker qualities. Create such fear by suddenly changing your moods, keeping the man off balance, occasionally intimidating him with capricious behavior.

Falling in love with statues and paintings, even making love to them is an ancient fantasy, one of which the Renaissance was keenly aware. Giorgio Vasari, writing in the introductory section of the Lives about art in antiquity, tells how men violated the laws, going into the temples at night and making love with statues of Venus. In the morning, priests would enter the sanctuaries to find stains on the marble figures.

—LYNNE LAWNER, *LIVES OF THE COURTESANS*

Siren is Physical

The most important element for an aspiring Siren is always the physical, the Siren's main instrument of power. Physical qualities—a scent, a heightened femininity evoked through makeup or through elaborate or seductive clothing—act all the more powerfully on men because they have no meaning. In their immediacy they bypass rational processes, having the same effect that a decoy has on an animal, or the movement of a cape on a bull. The proper Siren appearance is often confused with physical beauty, particularly the face. But a beautiful face does not a Siren make: instead it creates too much distance and coldness. (Neither Cleopatra nor Marilyn Monroe, the two greatest Sirens in history, were known for their beautiful faces.) Although a smile and an inviting look are infinitely seductive, they must never dominate your appearance. They are too obvious and direct. The Siren must stimulate a generalized desire, and the best way to do this is by creating an overall impression that is both distracting and alluring. It is not one particular trait, but a combination of qualities:

faces not Perfect

The voice. Clearly a critical quality, as the legend indicates, the Siren's voice has an immediate animal presence with incredible suggestive power. Perhaps that power is regressive, recalling the ability of the mother's voice to calm or excite her child even before the child understood what she was saying. The Siren must have an insinuating voice that hints at the erotic, more often subliminally than overtly. Almost everyone who met Cleopatra commented on her delightful, sweet-sounding voice, which had a mesmerizing quality. The Empress Josephine, one of the great seductresses of the late eighteenth century, had a languorous voice that men found exotic, and suggestive of her Creole origins. Marilyn Monroe was born with her breathy, childlike voice, but she learned to lower to make it truly seductive. Lauren Bacall's voice is naturally low; its seductive power comes from its slow, suggestive delivery. The Siren never speaks quickly, aggressively, or at a high pitch. Her voice is calm and unhurried, as if she had never quite woken up—or left her bed.

Body and adornment. If the voice must lull, the body and its adornment must dazzle. It is with her clothes that the Siren aims to create the goddess effect that Baudelaire described in his essay "In Praise of Makeup": "Woman is well within her rights, and indeed she is accomplishing a kind of duty in striving to appear magical and supernatural. She must astonish and bewitch; an idol, she must adorn herself with gold in order to be adored. She must borrow from all of the arts in order to raise herself above nature, the better to subjugate hearts and stir souls."

A Siren who was a genius of clothes and adornment was Pauline Bonaparte, sister of Napoleon. Pauline consciously strove for a goddess effect, fashioning hair, makeup, and clothes to evoke the look and air of Venus, the goddess of love. No one in history could boast a more extensive and elaborate wardrobe. Pauline's entrance at a ball in 1798 created an astounding effect. She asked the hostess, Madame Permon, if she could dress at her house, so no one would see her clothes as she came in. When she came down the stairs, everyone stopped dead in stunned silence. She wore the headdress of a bacchante—clusters of gold grapes interlaced in her hair, which was done up in the Greek style. Her Greek tunic, with its gold-embroidered hem, showed off her goddesslike figure. Below her breasts was a girdle of burnished gold, held by a magnificent jewel. "No words can convey the loveliness of her appearance," wrote the Duchess d'Abrantès. "The very room grew brighter as she entered. The whole ensemble was so harmonious that her appearance was greeted with a buzz of admiration which continued with utter disregard of all the other women."

The key: everything must dazzle, but must also be harmonious, so that no single ornament draws attention. Your presence must be charged, larger than life, a fantasy come true. Ornament is used to cast a spell and distract. The Siren can also use clothing to hint at the sexual, at times overtly but more often by suggesting it rather than screaming it—that would make you seem manipulative. Related to this is the notion of selective disclosure, the revealing of only a part of the body—but a part that will excite and stir the imagination. In the late sixteenth century, Marguerite de Valois, the infamous daughter of Queen Catherine de Médicis of France, was one of the first women ever to incorporate décolletage in her wardrobe, simply because she had the most beautiful breasts in the realm. For Josephine Bonaparte it was her arms, which she carefully always left bare.

Movement and demeanor. In the fifth century B.C., King Kou Chien chose the Chinese Siren Hsi Shih from among all the women of his realm to seduce and destroy his rival Fu Chai, King of Wu; for this purpose, he had the young woman instructed in the arts of seduction. Most important of these was movement—how to move gracefully and suggestively. Hsi Shih learned to give the impression of floating across the floor in her court robes. When she was finally unleashed on Fu Chai, he quickly fell under her spell. She walked and moved like no one he had ever seen. He became obsessed with her tremulous presence, her manner and nonchalant air. Fu Chai fell so deeply in love that he let his kingdom fall to pieces, allowing Kou Chien to march in and conquer it without a fight.

The Siren moves gracefully and unhurriedly. The proper gestures, movement, and demeanor for a Siren are like the proper voice: they hint at something exciting, stirring desire without being obvious. Your air must be languorous, as if you had all the time in the world for love and pleasure. Your gestures must have a certain ambiguity, suggesting something both innocent and erotic. Anything that cannot immediately be understood is supremely seductive, and all the more so if it permeates your manner.

Symbol: *Water.*
The song of the Siren is liquid and enticing, and the Siren herself is fluid and ungraspable. Like the sea, the Siren lures you with the promise of infinite adventure and pleasure. Forgetting past and future, men follow her far out to sea, where they drown.

Dangers

No matter how enlightened the age, no woman can maintain the image of being devoted to pleasure completely comfortably. And no matter how hard she tries to distance herself from it, the taint of being easy always follows the Siren. Cleopatra was hated in Rome as the Egyptian whore. That hatred eventually lead to her downfall, as Octavius and the Roman army sought to extirpate the stain on Roman manhood that she came to represent. Even so, men are often forgiving when it comes to the Siren's reputation. But danger often lies in the envy she stirs up among other women; much of Rome's hatred for Cleopatra originated in the resentment she provoked among the city's stern matrons. By playing up her innocence, by making herself seem the victim of male desire, the Siren can somewhat blunt the effects of feminine envy. But on the whole there is little she can do—her power comes from her effect on men, and she must learn to accept, or ignore, the envy of other women.

Finally, the intense attention that the Siren attracts can prove irritating and worse. Sometimes she will pine for relief from it; sometimes, too, she will want to attract an attention that is not sexual. Also, unfortunately, physical beauty fades; although the Siren effect depends not on a beautiful face but on an overall impression, past a certain age that impression gets hard to project. Both of these factors contributed to the suicide of Marilyn Monroe. It takes a genius on the level of Madame de Pompadour, the Siren mistress of King Louis XV, to make the transition into the role of the spirited older woman who continues to seduce with her nonphysical charms. Cleopatra had such an intellect, and had she lived long enough, she would have remained a potent seductress for many years. The Siren must prepare for age by paying attention early on to the more psychological, less physical forms of coquetry that can continue to bring her power once her beauty starts to fade.

the Rake

A woman never quite feels desired and appreciated enough. She wants attention, but a man is too often distracted and unresponsive. The Rake is a great female fantasy figure—when he desires a woman, brief though that moment may be, he will go to the ends of the earth for her. He may be disloyal, dishonest, and amoral, but that only adds to his appeal. Unlike the normal, cautious male, the Rake is delightfully unrestrained, a slave to his love of women. There is the added lure of his reputation: so many women have succumbed to him, there has to be a reason. Words are a woman's weakness, and the Rake is a master of seductive language. Stir a woman's repressed longings by adapting the Rake's mix of danger and pleasure.

The Ardent Rake

For the court of Louis XIV, the king's last years were gloomy—he was old, and had become both insufferably religious and personally unpleasant. The court was bored and desperate for novelty. So in 1710, the arrival of a fifteen-year-old lad who was both devilishly handsome and charming had a particularly strong effect on the ladies. His name was Fronsac, the future Duke de Richelieu (his granduncle being the infamous Cardinal Richelieu). He was impudent and witty. The ladies would play with him like a toy, but he would kiss them on the lips in return, his hands wandering far for an inexperienced boy. When those hands strayed up the skirts of a duchess who was not so indulgent, the king was furious, and sent the youth to the Bastille to teach him a lesson. But the ladies who had found him so amusing could not endure his absence. Compared to the stiffs in court, here was someone incredibly bold, his eyes boring into you, his hands quicker than was safe. Nothing could stop him, his novelty was irresistible. The court ladies pleaded and his stay in the Bastille was cut short.

Several years later, the young Mademoiselle de Valois was walking in a Paris park with her chaperone, an older woman who never left her side. De Valois's father, the Duke d'Orléans, was determined to protect her, his youngest daughter, from all the court seducers until she could be married off, so he had attached to her this chaperone, a woman of impeccable virtue and sourness. In the park, however, de Valois saw a young man who gave her a look that set her heart on fire. He walked on by, but the look was intense and clear. It was her chaperone who told her his name: the now infamous Duke de Richelieu, blasphemer, seducer, heartbreaker. Someone to avoid at all cost.

A few days later, the chaperone took de Valois to a different park, and lo and behold, Richelieu crossed their path again. This time he was in disguise, dressed as a beggar, but the look in his eye was unforgettable. Mademoiselle de Valois returned his gaze: at last something exciting in her drab life. Given her father's sternness, no man had dared approach her. And now this notorious courtier was pursuing her, instead of all the other ladies at court—what a thrill! Soon he was smuggling beautifully written notes to her expressing his uncontrollable desire for her. She responded timidly, but soon the notes were all she was living for. In one of them he promised to arrange everything if she would spend the night with him; imagining it was

[After an accident at sea, Don Juan finds himself washed up on a beach, where he is discovered by a young woman.] • TISBEA: *Wake up, handsomest of all men, and be yourself again.* • DON JUAN: *If the sea gives me death, you give me life. But the sea really saved me only to be killed by you. Oh the sea tosses me from one torment to the other, for I no sooner pulled myself from the water than I met this siren—yourself. Why fill my ears with wax, since you kill me with your eyes? I was dying in the sea, but from today I shall die of love.* • TISBEA: *You have abundant breath for a man almost drowned. You suffered much, but who knows what suffering you are preparing for me? . . . I found you at my feet all water, and now you are all fire. If you burn when you are so wet, what will you do when you're dry again? You promise a scorching flame; I hope to God you're not lying.* • DON JUAN: *Dear girl, God should have drowned me before I could be charred by you. Perhaps love was wise*

impossible to bring such a thing to pass, she did not mind playing along and agreeing to his bold proposal.

Mademoiselle de Valois had a chambermaid named Angelique, who dressed her for bed and slept in an adjoining room. One night as the chaperone was knitting, de Valois looked up from the book she was reading to see Angelique carrying her mistress's nightclothes to her room, but for some strange reason Angelique looked back at her and smiled—it was Richelieu, expertly dressed as the maid! De Valois nearly gasped from fright, but caught herself, realizing the danger she was in: if she said anything her family would find out about the notes, and about her part in the whole affair. What could she do? She decided to go to her room and talk the young duke out of his ridiculously dangerous maneuver. She said good night to her chaperone, but once she was in her bedroom, the words she had planned were useless. When she tried to reason with Richelieu, he responded with that look in his eye, and then with his arms around her. She could not yell, but now she was unsure what to do. His impetuous words, his caresses, the danger of it all—her head was whirling, she was lost. What was virtue and her prior boredom compared to an evening with the court's most notorious rake? So while the chaperone knitted away, the duke initiated her into the rituals of libertinage.

Months later, de Valois's father had reason to suspect that Richelieu had broken through his lines of defense. The chaperone was fired, the precautions were doubled. D'Orléans did not realize that to Richelieu such measures were a challenge, and he lived for challenges. He bought the house next door under an assumed name and secretly tunneled a trapdoor through the wall adjoining the duke's kitchen cupboard. In this cupboard, over the next few months—until the novelty wore off—de Valois and Richelieu enjoyed endless trysts.

Everyone in Paris knew of Richelieu's exploits, for he made it a point to publicize them as loudly as possible. Every week a new story would circulate through the court. A husband had locked his wife in an upstairs room at night, worried the duke was after her; to reach her the duke had crawled in darkness along a thin wooden plank suspended between two upper-floor windows. Two women who lived in the same house, one a widow, the other married and quite religious, had discovered to their mutual horror that the duke was having an affair with both of them at the same time, leaving one in the middle of the night to be with the other. When they confronted him, the duke, always on the prowl for something novel, and a devilish talker, had neither apologized nor backed down, but proceeded to talk them into a ménage à trois, playing on the wounded vanity of each woman, who could not stand the thought of him preferring the other. Year after year, the stories of his remarkable seductions spread. One woman admired his audacity and bravery, another his gallantry in thwarting a husband. Women competed for his attention: if he did not want to seduce you, there had to be something wrong with you. To be the target of his attentions became a great fantasy. At one point two ladies

to drench me before I felt your scalding touch. But your fire is such that even in water I burn. • TISBEA: *So cold and yet burning?* • DON JUAN: *So much fire is in you.* • TISBEA: *How well you talk!* • DON JUAN: *How well you understand!* • TISBEA: *I hope to God you're not lying.*

—TIRSO DE MOLINA, *THE PLAYBOY OF SEVILLE*, TRANSLATED BY ADRIENNE M. SCHIZZANO AND OSCAR MANDEL

Pleased with my first success, I determined to profit by this happy reconciliation. I called them my dear wives, my faithful companions, the two beings chosen to make me happy. I sought to turn their heads, and to rouse in them desires the strength of which I knew and which would drive away any reflections contrary to my plans. The skillful man who knows how to communicate gradually the heat of love to the senses of the most virtuous woman is quite certain of soon being absolute master of her mind and her person; you cannot reflect when you have lost your head; and, moreover, principles of wisdom, however deeply engraved they may be on the mind, are effaced in that moment when the heart yearns only for pleasure: pleasure alone then commands and is obeyed. The man who has had experience of conquests nearly always succeeds where he who is only timid and in love fails. . . . • *When I had brought my two belles to the state of abandonment in which I*

fought a pistol duel over the duke, and one of them was seriously wounded. The Duchess d'Orléans, Richelieu's most bitter enemy, once wrote, "If I believed in sorcery I should think that the Duke possessed some supernatural secret, for I have never known a woman to oppose the very least resistance to him."

In seduction there is often a dilemma: to seduce you need planning and calculation, but if your victim suspects that you have ulterior motives, she will grow defensive. Furthermore, if you seem to be in control, you will inspire fear instead of desire. The Ardent Rake solves this dilemma in the most artful manner. Of course he must calculate and plan—he has to find a way around the jealous husband, or whatever the obstacle is. It is exhausting work. But by nature, the Ardent Rake also has the advantage of an uncontrollable libido. When he pursues a woman, he really is aglow with desire; the victim senses this and is inflamed, even despite herself. How can she imagine that he is a heartless seducer who will abandon her when he so ardently braves all dangers and obstacles to get to her? And even if she is aware of his rakish past, of his incorrigible amorality, it doesn't matter, because she also sees his weakness. He cannot control himself; he actually is a slave to all women. As such he inspires no fear.

The Ardent Rake teaches us a simple lesson: intense desire has a distracting power on a woman, just as the Siren's physical presence does on a man. A woman is often defensive and can sense insincerity or calculation. But if she feels consumed by your attentions, and is confident you will do anything for her, she will notice nothing else about you, or will find a way to forgive your indiscretions. This is the perfect cover for a seducer. The key is to show no hesitation, to abandon all restraint, to let yourself go, to show that you cannot control yourself and are fundamentally weak. Do not worry about inspiring mistrust; as long as you are the slave to her charms, she will not think of the aftermath.

wanted them, I expressed a more eager desire; their eyes lit up; my caresses were returned; and it was plain that their resistance would not delay for more than a few moments the next scene I desired them to play. I proposed that each should accompany me in turn into a charming closet, next to the room in which we were, which I wanted them to admire. They both remained silent. • "You hesitate?" I said to them. "I will see which of you is the more attached to me. The one who loves me the more will be the first to follow the lover she wishes to convince of her affection. . . ." • I knew my puritan, and I was well aware that, after a few struggles, she gave herself up completely to the present moment. This one appeared to be as agreeable to her as the others we had previously spent together; she forgot that she was sharing me [with Madame Renaud]. . . . • [When her turn came] Madame Renaud responded with a transport that proved her contentment, and she left the sitting only after having repeated continually: "What a man! What a man! He is astonishing! How often you could be happy with him if he were only faithful!"

—The Private Life of the Marshal Duke of Richelieu, translated by F. S. Flint

The Demonic Rake

In the early 1880s, members of Roman high society began to talk of a young journalist who had arrived on the scene, a certain Gabriele D'Annunzio. This was strange in itself, for Italian royalty had only the deepest contempt for anyone outside their circle, and a newspaper society reporter was almost as low as you could go. Indeed well-born men paid D'Annunzio little attention. He had no money and few connections, coming from a strictly middle-class background. Besides, to them he was downright ugly—short and stocky, with a dark, splotchy complexion and bulging eyes. The men thought him so unappealing they gladly let him mingle with their wives and daughters, certain that their women would be safe with this gargoyle and happy to get this gossip hunter off their hands. No, it was not the men who talked of D'Annunzio; it was their wives.

Introduced to D'Annunzio by their husbands, these duchesses and marchionesses would find themselves entertaining this strange-looking man, and when he was alone with them, his manner would suddenly change. Within minutes these ladies would be spellbound. First, he had the most magnificent voice they had ever heard—soft and low, each syllable articulated, with a flowing rhythm and inflection that was almost musical. One woman compared it to the ringing of church bells in the distance. Others said his voice had a "hypnotic" effect. The words that voice spoke were interesting as well—alliterative phrases, charming locutions, poetic images, and a way of offering praise that could melt a woman's heart. D'Annunzio had mastered the art of flattery. He seemed to know each woman's weakness: one he would call a goddess of nature, another an incomparable artist in the making, another a romantic figure out of a novel. A woman's heart would flutter as he described the effect she had on him. Everything was suggestive, hinting at sex or romance. That night she would ponder his words, recalling little in particular that he had said, because he never said anything concrete, but rather the feeling it had given her. The next day she would receive from him a poem that seemed to have been written specifically for her. (In fact he wrote dozens of very similar poems, slightly tailoring each one for its intended victim.)

His very successes in love, even more than the marvellous voice of this little, bald seducer with a nose like Punch, swept along in his train a whole procession of enamoured women, both opulent and tormented. D'Annunzio had successfully revived the Byronic legend: as he passed by full-breasted women, standing in his way as Boldoni would paint them, strings of pearls anchoring them to life—princesses and actresses, great Russian ladies and even middle-class Bordeaux housewives—they would offer themselves up to him.

—Philippe Jullian, *Prince of Aesthetes: Count Robert de Montesquiou*, translated by John Haylock and Francis King

A few years after D'Annunzio began work as a society reporter, he married the daughter of the Duke and Duchess of Gallese. Shortly thereafter, with the unshakeable support of society ladies, he began publishing novels and books of poetry. The number of his conquests was remarkable, and also the quality—not only marchionesses would fall at his feet, but great artists, such as the actress Eleanor Duse, who helped him become a respected dramatist and literary celebrity. The dancer Isadora Duncan, another who eventually fell under his spell, explained his magic: "Perhaps the most remarkable lover of our time is Gabriele D'Annunzio. And this notwithstanding that he is small, bald, and, except when his face lights up with enthusiasm, ugly. But when he speaks to a woman he likes, his face is transfigured, so that he suddenly becomes Apollo. . . . His effect on women is remarkable. The lady he is talking to suddenly feels that her very soul and being are lifted."

In short, nothing is so sweet as to triumph over the Resistance of a beautiful Person; and in that I have the Ambition of Conquerors, who fly perpetually from Victory to Victory and can never prevail with themselves to put a bound to their Wishes. Nothing can restrain the Impetuosity of my Desires; I have an Heart for the whole Earth; and like Alexander, I could wish for New Worlds wherein to extend my Amorous Conquests.

—Molière, *Don John or The Libertine*, translated by John Ozell

At the outbreak of World War I, the fifty-two-year-old D'Annunzio joined the army. Although he had no military experience, he had a flair for the dramatic and a burning desire to prove his bravery. He learned to fly and led dangerous but highly effective missions. By the end of the war, he was Italy's most decorated hero. His exploits made him a beloved national figure, and after the war, crowds would gather outside his hotel wherever in Italy he went. He would address them from a balcony, discussing politics, railing against the current Italian government. A witness of one of these speeches, the American writer Walter Starkie, was initially disappointed at the appearance of the famous D'Annunzio on a balcony in Venice; he was short, and looked grotesque. "Little by little, however, I began to sink under the fascination of the voice, which penetrated into my consciousness. . . .

Never a hurried, jerky gesture. . . . He played upon the emotions of the crowd as a supreme violinist does upon a Stradivarius. The eyes of the thousands were fixed upon him as though hypnotized by his power." Once again, it was the sound of the voice and the poetic connotations of the words that seduced the masses. Arguing that modern Italy should reclaim the greatness of the Roman Empire, D'Annunzio would craft slogans for the audience to repeat, or would ask emotionally loaded questions for them to answer. He flattered the crowd, made them feel they were part of some drama. Everything was vague and suggestive.

The issue of the day was the ownership of the city of Fiume, just across the border in neighboring Yugoslavia. Many Italians believed that Italy's reward for siding with the Allies in the recent war should be the annexation of Fiume. D'Annunzio championed this cause, and because of his status as a war hero the army was ready to side with him, although the government opposed any action. In September of 1919, with soldiers rallying around him, D'Annunzio led his infamous march on Fiume. When an Italian general stopped him along the way, and threatened to shoot him, D'Annunzio opened his coat to show his medals, and said in his magnetic voice, "If you must kill me, fire first on this!" The general stood there stunned, then broke into tears. He joined up with D'Annunzio.

When D'Annunzio entered Fiume, he was greeted as a liberator. The next day he was declared leader of the Free State of Fiume. Soon he was giving daily speeches from a balcony overlooking the town's main square, holding tens of thousands of people spellbound without benefit of loudspeakers. He initiated all kinds of celebrations and rituals harking back to the Roman Empire. The citizens of Fiume began to imitate him, particularly his sexual exploits; the city became like a giant bordello. His popularity was so high that the Italian government feared a march on Rome, which at that point, had D'Annunzio decided to do it—and he had the support of a large part of the military—might actually have succeeded; D'Annunzio could have beaten Mussolini to the punch and changed the course of history. (He was not a Fascist, but a kind of aesthetic socialist.) He decided to stay in Fiume, however, and ruled there for sixteen months before the Italian government finally bombed him out of the city.

Among the many modes of handling Don Juan's effect on women, the motif of the irresistible hero is worth singling out, for it illustrates a curious change in our sensibility. Don Juan did not become irresistible to women until the Romantic age, and I am disposed to think that it is a trait of the female imagination to make him so. When the female voice began to assert itself and even, perhaps, to dominate in literature, Don Juan evolved to become the women's rather than the man's ideal. . . . Don Juan is now the woman's dream of the perfect lover, fugitive, passionate, daring. He gives her the one unforgettable moment, the magnificent exaltation of the flesh which is too often denied her by the real husband, who thinks that men are gross and women spiritual. To be the fatal Don Juan may be the dream of a few men; but to meet him is the dream of many women.

—Oscar Mandel, "The Legend of Don Juan," *The Theatre of Don Juan*

Seduction is a psychological process that transcends gender, except in a few key areas where each gender has its own weakness. The male is traditionally vulnerable to the visual. The Siren who can concoct the right physical appearance will seduce in large numbers. For women the weakness is language and words: as was written by one of D'Annunzio's victims, the French actress Simone, "How can one explain his conquests except by his extraordinary verbal power, and the musical timbre of his voice, put to the service of exceptional eloquence? For my sex is susceptible to words, bewitched by them, longing to be dominated by them."

The Rake is as promiscuous with words as he is with women. He chooses words for their ability to suggest, insinuate, hypnotize, elevate, infect. The words of the Rake are the equivalent of the bodily adornment of the Siren: a powerful sensual distraction, a narcotic. The Rake's use of language is demonic because it is designed not to communicate or convey information but to persuade, flatter, stir emotional turmoil, much as the serpent in the Garden of Eden used words to lead Eve into temptation.

The example of D'Annunzio reveals the link between the erotic Rake, who seduces women, and the political Rake, who seduces the masses. Both depend on words. Adapt the character of the Rake and you will find that the use of words as a subtle poison has infinite applications. Remember: it is the form that matters, not the content. The less your targets focus on what you say, and the more on how it makes them feel, the more seductive your effect. Give your words a lofty, spiritual, literary flavor the better to insinuate desire in your unwitting victims.

> *But what is this force, then, by which Don Juan seduces? It is desire, the energy of sensuous desire. He desires in every woman the whole of womanhood. The reaction to this gigantic passion beautifies and develops the one desired, who flushes in enhanced beauty by his reflection. As the enthusiast's fire with seductive splendor illumines even those who stand in a casual relation to him, so Don Juan transfigures in a far deeper sense every girl.*
>
> —Søren Kierkegaard, *Either/Or*

Keys to the Character

At first it may seem strange that a man who is clearly dishonest, disloyal, and has no interest in marriage would have any appeal to a woman. But throughout all of history, and in all cultures, this type has had a fatal effect. What the Rake offers is what society normally does not allow women: an affair of pure pleasure, an exciting brush with danger. A woman is often deeply oppressed by the role she is expected to play. She is supposed to be the tender, civilizing force in society, and to want commitment and lifelong loyalty. But often her marriages and relationships give her not romance and devotion but routine and an endlessly distracted mate. It remains an abiding female fantasy to meet a man who gives totally of himself, who lives for her, even if only for a while.

This dark, repressed side of female desire found expression in the legend of Don Juan. At first the legend was a male fantasy: the adventurous knight who could have any woman he wanted. But in the seventeenth and eighteenth centuries, Don Juan slowly evolved from the masculine adventurer to a more feminized version: a man who lived only for women. This evolution came from women's interest in the story, and was a result of their frustrated desires. Marriage for them was a form of indentured servitude; but Don Juan offered pleasure for its own sake, desire with no strings attached. For the time he crossed your path, you were all he thought about. His desire for you was so powerful that he gave you no time to think or to worry about the consequences. He would come in the night, give you an unforgettable moment, and then vanish. He might have conquered a thousand women before you, but that only made him more interesting; better to be abandoned than undesired by such a man.

The great seducers do not offer the mild pleasures that society condones. They touch a person's unconscious, those repressed desires that cry out for liberation. Do not imagine that women are the tender creatures that some people would like them to be. Like men, they are deeply attracted to the forbidden, the dangerous, even the slightly evil. (Don Juan ends by going to hell, and the word "rake" comes from "rakehell," a man who rakes the coals of hell; the devilish component, clearly, is an important part of the fantasy.) Always remember: if you are to play the Rake, you must convey a sense of risk and darkness, suggesting to your victim that she is participating in something rare and thrilling—a chance to play out her own rakish desires.

To play the Rake, the most obvious requirement is the ability to let yourself go, to draw a woman into the kind of purely sensual moment in which past and future lose meaning. You must be able to abandon yourself to the moment. (When the Rake Valmont—a character modeled after the Duke de Richelieu—in Laclos' eighteenth-century novel *Dangerous Liaisons* writes letters that are obviously calculated to have a certain effect on his chosen victim, Madame de Tourvel, she sees right through them; but when his letters really do burn with passion, she begins to relent.) An added benefit of this quality is that it makes you seem unable to control yourself, a display of weakness that a woman enjoys. By abandoning yourself to the seduced, you make them feel that you exist for them alone—a feeling reflecting a truth, though a temporary one. Of the hundreds of women that Pablo Picasso, consummate rake, seduced over the years, most of them had the feeling that they were the only one he truly loved.

The Rake never worries about a woman's resistance to him, or for that matter about any other obstacle in his path—a husband, a physical barrier. Resistance is only the spur to his desire, enflaming him all the more. When Picasso was seducing Françoise Gilot, in fact, he begged her to resist; he needed resistance to add to the thrill. In any case, an obstacle in your way gives you the opportunity to prove yourself, and the creativity you bring to matters of love. In the eleventh-century Japanese novel *The Tale of Genji*, by the court lady Murasaki Shikibu, the Rake Prince Niou is not disturbed by the sudden disappearance of Ukifune, the woman he loves. She has fled because although she is interested in the prince, she is in love with another man; but her absence allows the prince to go to extreme lengths to track her down. His sudden appearance to whisk her away to a house deep in the woods, and the gallantry he displays in doing so, overwhelm her. Remember: if no resistances or obstacles face you, you must create them. No seduction can proceed without them.

The Rake is an extreme personality. Impudent, sarcastic, and bitingly witty, he cares nothing for what anyone thinks. Paradoxically, this only makes him more seductive. In the courtlike atmosphere of studio-era Hollywood, when most of the actors behaved like dutiful sheep, the great Rake Errol Flynn stood out in his insolence. He defied the studio chiefs, engaged in the most extreme pranks, reveled in his reputation as Hollywood's supreme seducer—all of which enhanced his popularity. The Rake needs a backdrop of convention—a stultified court, a humdrum marriage, a conservative culture—to shine, to be appreciated for the breath of fresh air he provides. Never worry about going too far: the Rake's essence is that he goes further than anyone else.

When the Earl of Rochester, seventeenth-century England's most notorious Rake and poet, abducted Elizabeth Malet, one of the most sought-after young ladies of the court, he was duly punished. But lo and behold, a few years later young Elizabeth, though wooed by the most eligible bachelors in the country, chose Rochester to be her husband. In demonstrating his audacious desire, he made himself stand out from the crowd.

Related to the Rake's extremism is the sense of danger, taboo, perhaps even the hint of cruelty about him. This was the appeal of another poet Rake, one of the greatest in history: Lord Byron. Byron disliked any kind of convention, and happily played this up. When he had an affair with his half sister, who bore a child by him, he made sure that all of England knew about it. He could be uncommonly cruel, as he was to his wife. But all of this only made him that much more desirable. Danger and taboo appeal to a repressed side in women, who are supposed to represent a civilizing, moralizing force in culture. Just as a man may fall victim to the Siren through his desire to be free of his sense of masculine responsibility, a woman may succumb to the Rake through her yearning to be free of the constraints of virtue and decency. Indeed it is often the most virtuous woman who falls most deeply in love with the Rake.

Among the Rake's most seductive qualities is his ability to make women want to reform him. How many thought they would be the one to tame Lord Byron; how many of Picasso's women thought they would finally be the one with whom he would spend the rest of his life. You must exploit this tendency to the fullest. When caught red-handed in rakishness, fall back on your weakness—your desire to change, and your inability to do so. With so many women at your feet, what can you do? You are the one who is the victim. You need help. Women will jump at this opportunity; they are uncommonly indulgent of the Rake, for he is such a pleasant, dashing figure. The desire to reform him disguises the true nature of their desire, the secret thrill they get from him. When President Bill Clinton was clearly caught out as a Rake, it was women who rushed to his defense, finding every possible excuse for him. The fact that the Rake is so devoted to women, in his own strange way, makes him lovable and seductive to them.

Finally, a Rake's greatest asset is his reputation. Never downplay your bad name, or seem to apologize for it. Instead, embrace it, enhance it. It is what draws women to you. There are several things you must be known for: your irresistible attractiveness to women; your uncontrollable devotion to pleasure (this will make you seem weak, but also exciting to be around); your disdain for convention; a rebellious streak that makes you seem dangerous. This last element can be slightly hidden; on the surface, be polite and civil, while letting it be known that behind the scenes you are incorrigible. Duke de Richelieu made his conquests as public as possible, exciting other women's competitive desire to join the club of the seduced. It was by reputation that Lord Byron attracted his willing victims. A woman may feel ambivalent about President Clinton's reputation, but beneath that ambivalence is an underlying interest. Do not leave your reputation to chance or gossip; it is your life's artwork, and you must craft it, hone it, and display it with the care of an artist.

Symbol: *Fire.*
The Rake burns with a desire that enflames the woman he is seducing. It is extreme, uncontrollable, and dangerous. The Rake may end in hell, but the flames surrounding him often make him seem that much more desirable to women.

Dangers

Like the Siren, the Rake faces the most danger from members of his own sex, who are far less indulgent than women are of his constant skirt chasing. In the old days, a Rake was often an aristocrat, and no matter how many people he offended or even killed, in the end he would go unpunished. Today, only stars and the very wealthy can play the Rake with impunity; the rest of us need to be careful.

Elvis Presley had been a shy young man. Attaining early stardom, and seeing the power it gave him over women, he went berserk, becoming a Rake almost overnight. Like many Rakes, Elvis had a predilection for women who were already taken. He found himself cornered by an angry husband or boyfriend on numerous occasions, and came away with a few cuts and bruises. This might seem to suggest that you should step lightly around husbands and boyfriends, especially early on in your career. But the charm of the Rake is that such dangers don't matter to them. You cannot be a Rake by being fearful and prudent; the occasional pummeling is part of the game. Later on, in any case, at the height of Elvis's fame, no husband would dare touch him.

The greater danger for the Rake comes not from the violently offended husband but from those insecure men who feel threatened by the Don Juan figure. Although they will not admit it, they envy the Rake's life of pleasure, and like everyone envious, they will attack in hidden ways, often masking their persecutions as morality. The Rake may find his career endangered by such men (or by the occasional woman who is equally insecure, and who feels hurt because the Rake does not want her). There is little the Rake can do to avoid envy; if everyone was as successful in seduction, society would not function.

So accept envy as a badge of honor. Don't be naive, be aware. When attacked by a moralist persecutor, do not be taken in by their crusade; it is motivated by envy, pure and simple. You can blunt it by being less of a Rake, asking forgiveness, claiming to have reformed, but this will damage your reputation, making you seem less lovably rakish. In the end, it is better to suffer attacks with dignity and keep on seducing. Seduction is the source of your power; and you can always count on the infinite indulgence of women.

the Ideal lover

Most people have dreams in their youth that get shattered or worn down with age. They find themselves disappointed by people, events, reality, which cannot match their youthful ideals. Ideal Lovers thrive on people's broken dreams, which become lifelong fantasies. You long for romance? Adventure? Lofty spiritual communion? The Ideal Lover reflects your fantasy. He or she is an artist in creating the illusion you require, idealizing your portrait. In a world of disenchantment and baseness, there is limitless seductive power in following the path of the Ideal Lover.

The Romantic Ideal

One evening around 1760, at the opera in the city of Cologne, a beautiful young woman sat in her box, watching the audience. Beside her was her husband, the town burgomaster—a middle-aged man and amiable enough, but dull. Through her opera glasses the young woman noticed a handsome man wearing a stunning outfit. Evidently her stare was noticed, for after the opera the man introduced himself: his name was Giovanni Giacomo Casanova.

The stranger kissed the woman's hand. She was going to a ball the following night, she told him; would he like to come? "If I might dare to hope, Madame," he replied, "that you will dance only with me."

The next night, after the ball, the woman could think only of Casanova. He had seemed to anticipate her thoughts—had been so pleasant, and yet so bold. A few days later he dined at her house, and after her husband had retired for the evening she showed him around. In her boudoir she pointed out a wing of the house, a chapel, just outside her window. Sure enough, as if he had read her mind, Casanova came to the chapel the next day to attend Mass, and seeing her at the theater that evening he mentioned to her that he had noticed a door there that must lead to her bedroom. She laughed, and pretended to be surprised. In the most innocent of tones, he said that he would find a way to hide in the chapel the next day—and almost without thinking, she whispered she would visit him there after everyone had gone to bed.

So Casanova hid in the chapel's tiny confessional, waiting all day and evening. There were rats, and he had nothing to lie upon; yet when the burgomaster's wife finally came, late at night, he did not complain, but quietly followed her to her room. They continued their trysts for several days. By day she could hardly wait for night: finally something to live for, an adventure. She left him food, books, and candles to ease his long and tedious stays in the chapel—it seemed wrong to use a place of worship for such a purpose, but that only made the affair more exciting. A few days later, however, she had to take a journey with her husband. By the time she got back, Casanova had disappeared, as quickly and gracefully as he had come.

Some years later, in London, a young woman named Miss Pauline noticed an ad in a local newspaper. A gentleman was looking for a lady lodger to rent a part of his house. Miss Pauline came from Portugal, and was of the nobility; she had eloped to London with a lover, but he had been

If at first sight a girl does not make such a deep impression on a person that she awakens the ideal, then ordinarily the actuality is not especially desirable; but if she does, then no matter how experienced a person is he usually is rather overwhelmed.

—Søren Kierkegaard, *The Seducer's Diary*, translated by Howard V. Hong and Edna H. Hong

A good lover will behave as elegantly at dawn as at any other time. He drags himself out of bed with a look of dismay on his face. The lady urges him on: "Come, my friend, it's getting light. You don't want anyone to find you here." He gives a deep sigh, as if to say that the night has not been nearly long enough and that it is agony to leave. Once up, he does not instantly pull on his trousers. Instead he comes close to the lady and whispers whatever was left unsaid during the night. Even when he is dressed, he still lingers, vaguely pretending to be fastening his sash. • Presently he raises the lattice, and the two lovers stand together by the side door while he tells her how he dreads the coming day, which will keep them apart; then he slips away. The lady watches him go, and this moment of parting will remain among her most charming memories. • Indeed, one's attachment to a man depends largely on the elegance of his leave-taking. When he jumps out of bed, scurries about the room, tightly fastens his trouser sash, rolls up the sleeves of his court cloak, overrobe, or hunting costume, stuffs his belongings into the breast of his robe and then briskly secures the outer sash—one really begins to hate him.

—THE PILLOW BOOK OF SEI SHONAGON, TRANSLATED AND EDITED BY IVAN MORRIS

forced to return home and she had had to stay on alone for some while before she could join him. Now she was lonely, and had little money, and was depressed by her squalid circumstances—after all, she had been raised as a lady. She answered the ad.

The gentleman turned out to be Casanova, and what a gentleman he was. The room he offered was nice, and the rent was low; he asked only for occasional companionship. Miss Pauline moved in. They played chess, went riding, discussed literature. He was so well-bred, polite, and generous. A serious and high-minded girl, she came to depend on their friendship; here was a man she could talk to for hours. Then one day Casanova seemed changed, upset, excited: he confessed that he was in love with her. She was going back to Portugal soon, to rejoin her lover, and this was not what she wanted to hear. She told him he should go riding to calm down.

Later that evening she received news: he had fallen from his horse. Feeling responsible for his accident, she rushed to him, found him in bed, and fell into his arms, unable to control herself. The two became lovers that night, and remained so for the rest of Miss Pauline's stay in London. Yet when it came time for her to leave for Portugal, he did not try to stop her; instead, he comforted her, reasoning that each of them had offered the other the perfect, temporary antidote to their loneliness, and that they would be friends for life.

Some years later, in a small Spanish town, a young and beautiful girl named Ignazia was leaving church after confession. She was approached by Casanova. Walking her home, he explained that he had a passion for dancing the fandango, and invited her to a ball the following evening. He was so different from anyone in the town, which bored her so—she desperately wanted to go. Her parents were against the arrangement, but she persuaded her mother to act as a chaperone. After an unforgettable evening of dancing (and he danced the fandango remarkably well for a foreigner), Casanova confessed that he was madly in love with her. She replied (very sadly, though) that she already had a fiancé. Casanova did not force the issue, but over the next few days he took Ignazia to more dances and to the bullfights. On one of these occasions he introduced her to a friend of his, a duchess, who flirted with him brazenly; Ignazia was terribly jealous. By now she was desperately in love with Casanova, but her sense of duty and religion forbade such thoughts.

Finally, after days of torment, Ignazia sought out Casanova and took his hand: "My confessor tried to make me promise to never be alone with you again," she said, "and as I could not, he refused to give me absolution. It is the first time in my life such a thing has happened to me. I have put myself in God's hands. I have made up my mind, so long as you are here, to do all you wish. When to my sorrow you leave Spain, I shall find another confessor. My fancy for you is, after all, only a passing madness."

Casanova was perhaps the most successful seducer in history; few women could resist him. His method was simple: on meeting a woman, he would study her, go along with her moods, find out what was missing in her life, and provide it. He made himself the Ideal Lover. The bored burgomaster's wife needed adventure and romance; she wanted someone who would sacrifice time and comfort to have her. For Miss Pauline what was missing was friendship, lofty ideals, serious conversation; she wanted a man of breeding and generosity who would treat her like a lady. For Ignazia, what was missing was suffering and torment. Her life was too easy; to feel truly alive, and to have something real to confess, she needed to sin. In each case Casanova adapted himself to the woman's ideals, brought her fantasy to life. Once she had fallen under his spell, a little ruse or calculation would seal the romance (a day among rats, a contrived fall from a horse, an encounter with another woman to make Ignazia jealous).

The Ideal Lover is rare in the modern world, for the role takes effort. You will have to focus intensely on the other person, fathom what she is missing, what he is disappointed by. People will often reveal this in subtle ways: through gesture, tone of voice, a look in the eye. By seeming to be what they lack, you will fit their ideal.

To create this effect requires patience and attention to detail. Most people are so wrapped up in their own desires, so impatient, they are incapable of the Ideal Lover role. Let that be a source of infinite opportunity. Be an oasis in the desert of the self-absorbed; few can resist the temptation of following a person who seems so attuned to their desires, to bringing to life their fantasies. And as with Casanova, your reputation as one who gives such pleasure will precede you and make your seductions that much easier.

> *The cultivation of the pleasures of the senses was ever my principal aim in life. Knowing that I was personally calculated to please the fair sex, I always strove to make myself agreeable to it.*
>
> —CASANOVA

During the early 1970s, against a turbulent political backdrop that included the fiasco of American involvement in the Vietnam War and the downfall of President Richard Nixon's presidency in the Watergate scandal, a "me generation" sprang to prominence—and [Andy] Warhol was there to hold up its mirror. Unlike the radicalized protesters of the 1960s who wanted to change all the ills of society, the self-absorbed "me" people sought to improve their bodies and to "get in touch" with their own feelings. They cared passionately about their appearance, health, life-style, and bank accounts. Andy catered to their self-centeredness and inflated pride by offering his services as a portraitist. By the end of the decade, he would be internationally recognized as one of the leading portraitists of his era. . . . • Warhol offered his clients an irresistible product: a stylish and flattering portrait by a famous artist who was himself a certified celebrity. Conferring an alluring star presence upon even the most celebrated of faces, he transformed his subjects into glamorous apparitions, presenting their faces as he thought they wanted to be seen and remembered. By filtering his sitters' good features through his silkscreens and exaggerating their vivacity, he enabled them to gain entrée to a more mythic and rarefied level of existence. The possession of great wealth and power might do for everyday life, but the commissioning of a portrait by Warhol was a

The Beauty Ideal

In 1730, when Jeanne Poisson was a mere nine years old, a fortune-teller predicted that one day she would be the mistress of Louis XV. The prediction was quite ridiculous, since Jeanne came from the middle class, and it was a tradition stretching back for centuries that the king's mistress be chosen from among the nobility. To make matters worse, Jeanne's father was a notorious rake, and her mother had been a courtesan.

Fortunately for Jeanne, one of her mother's lovers was a man of great wealth who took a liking to the pretty girl and paid for her education. Jeanne learned to sing, to play the clavichord, to ride with uncommon skill, to act and dance; she was schooled in literature and history as if she were a boy. The playwright Crébillon instructed her in the art of conversation.

sure indication that the sitter intended to secure a posthumous fame as well. Warhol's portraits were not so much realistic documents of contemporary faces as they were designer icons awaiting future devotions.

—David Bourdon, *Warhol*

Women have served all these centuries as looking glasses possessing the magic and delicious power of reflecting the figure of a man at twice its natural size.

—Virginia Woolf, *A Room of One's Own*

On top of it all, Jeanne was beautiful, and had a charm and grace that set her apart early on. In 1741, she married a man of the lower nobility. Now known as Madame d'Etioles, she could realize a great ambition: she opened a literary salon. All of the great writers and philosophers of the time frequented the salon, many because they were enamored of the hostess. One of these was Voltaire, who became a lifelong friend.

Through all Jeanne's success, she never forgot the fortune-teller's prediction, and still believed that she would one day conquer the king's heart. It happened that one of her husband's country estates bordered on King Louis's favorite hunting grounds. She would spy on him through the fence, or find ways to cross his path, always while she happened to be wearing an elegant, yet fetching outfit. Soon the king was sending her gifts of game. When his official mistress died, in 1744, all of the court beauties vied to take her place; but he began to spend more and more time with Madame d'Etioles, dazzled by her beauty and charm. To the astonishment of the court, that same year he made this middle-class woman his official mistress, ennobling her with the title of the Marquise de Pompadour.

The king's need for novelty was notorious: a mistress would beguile him with her looks, but he would soon grow bored with her and find someone else. After the shock of his choice of Jeanne Poisson wore off, the courtiers reassured themselves that it could not last—that he had only chosen her for the novelty of having a middle-class mistress. Little did they know that Jeanne's first seduction of the king was not the last seduction she had in mind.

As time went by, the king found himself visiting his mistress more and more often. As he ascended the hidden stair that led from his quarters to hers in the palace of Versailles, anticipation of the delights that awaited him at the top would begin to turn his head. First, the room was always warm, and was filled with delightful scents. Then there were the visual delights: Madame de Pompadour always wore a different costume, each one elegant and surprising in its own way. She loved beautiful objects—fine porcelain, Chinese fans, golden flowerpots—and every time he visited, there would be something new and enchanting to see. Her manner was always lighthearted; she was never defensive or resentful. Everything for pleasure. Then there was their conversation: he had never been really able to talk with a woman before, or to laugh, but the marquise could discourse skillfully on any subject, and her voice was a pleasure to hear. And if the conversation waned, she would move to the piano, play a tune, and sing wonderfully.

If ever the king seemed bored or sad, Madame de Pompadour would propose some project—perhaps the building of a new country house. He would have to advise in the design, the layout of the gardens, the decor. Back at Versailles, Madame de Pompadour put herself in charge of the palace amusements, building a private theater for weekly performances under her direction. Actors were chosen from among the courtiers, but the female lead was always played by Madame de Pompadour, who was one of the finest amateur actresses in France. The king became obsessed with this theater; he could barely wait for its performances. Along with this interest came an increasing expenditure of money on the arts, and an involvement in philosophy and literature. A man who had cared only for hunting and gambling was spending less and less time with his male companions and becoming a great patron of the arts. Indeed he stamped a whole era with an aesthetic style, which became known as "Louis Quinze," rivaling the style associated with his illustrious predecessor, Louis XIV.

Lo and behold, year after year went by without Louis tiring of his mistress. In fact he made her a duchess, and her power and influence extended well beyond culture into politics. For twenty years, Madame de Pompadour ruled both the court and the king's heart, until her untimely death, in 1764, at the age of forty-three.

Louis XV had a powerful inferiority complex. The successor to Louis XIV, the most powerful king in French history, he had been educated and trained for the throne—yet who could follow his predecessor's act? Eventually he gave up trying, devoting himself instead to physical pleasures, which came to define how he was seen; the people around him knew they could sway him by appealing to the basest parts of his character.

Madame de Pompadour, genius of seduction, understood that inside Louis XV was a great man yearning to come out, and that his obsession with pretty young women indicated a hunger for a more lasting kind of beauty. Her first step was to cure his incessant bouts of boredom. It is easy for kings to be bored—everything they want is given to them, and they seldom learn to be satisfied with what they have. The Marquise de Pompadour dealt with this by bringing all sorts of fantasies to life, and creating constant suspense. She had many skills and talents, and just as important, she deployed them so artfully that he never discovered their limits. Once she had accustomed him to more refined pleasures, she appealed to the crushed ideals within him; in the mirror she held up to him, he saw his aspiration to be great, a desire that, in France, inevitably included leadership in culture. His previous series of mistresses had tickled only his sensual desires. In Madame de Pompadour he found a woman who made him feel greatness in himself. The other mistresses could easily be replaced, but he could never find another Madame de Pompadour.

Most people believe themselves to be inwardly greater than they outwardly appear to the world. They are full of unrealized ideals: they could be artists, thinkers, leaders, spiritual figures, but the world has crushed them, denied them the chance to let their abilities flourish. This is the key to their seduction—and to keeping them seduced over time. The Ideal Lover knows how to conjure up this kind of magic. Appeal only to people's physical side, as many amateur seducers do, and they will resent you for playing upon their basest instincts. But appeal to their better selves, to a higher standard of beauty, and they will hardly notice that they have been seduced. Make them feel elevated, lofty, spiritual, and your power over them will be limitless.

Love brings to light a lover's noble and hidden qualities—his rare and exceptional traits: it is thus liable to be deceptive as to his normal character.

—Friedrich Nietzsche

Keys to the Character

Each of us carries inside us an ideal, either of what we would like to become, or of what we want another person to be for us. This ideal goes back to our earliest years—to what we once felt was missing in our lives, what others did not give to us, what we could not give to ourselves. Maybe we were smothered in comfort, and we long for danger and rebellion. If we want danger but it frightens us, perhaps we look for someone who seems at home with it. Or perhaps our ideal is more elevated—we want to be more creative, nobler, and kinder than we ever manage to be. Our ideal is something we feel is missing inside us.

Our ideal may be buried in disappointment, but it lurks underneath, waiting to be sparked. If another person seems to have that ideal quality, or to have the ability to bring it out in us, we fall in love. That is the response to Ideal Lovers. Attuned to what is missing inside you, to the fantasy that will stir you, they reflect your ideal—and you do the rest, projecting on to them your deepest desires and yearnings. Casanova and Madame de Pompadour did not merely seduce their targets into a sexual affair, they made them fall in love.

The key to following the path of the Ideal Lover is the ability to observe. Ignore your targets' words and conscious behavior; focus on the tone of their voice, a blush here, a look there—those signs that betray what their words won't say. Often the ideal is expressed in contradiction. King Louis XV seemed to care only about chasing deer and young girls, but that in fact covered up his disappointment in himself; he yearned to have his nobler qualities flattered.

Never has there been a better moment than now to play the Ideal Lover. That is because we live in a world in which everything must seem elevated and well-intentioned. Power is the most taboo topic of all: although it is the reality we deal with every day in our struggles with people, there is nothing noble, self-sacrificing, or spiritual about it. Ideal Lovers make you feel nobler, make the sensual and sexual seem spiritual and aesthetic. Like all seducers, they play with power, but they disguise their manipulations behind the facade of an ideal. Few people see through them and their seductions last longer.

Some ideals resemble Jungian archetypes—they go back a long way in our culture, and their hold is almost unconscious. One such dream is that of the chivalrous knight. In the courtly love tradition of the Middle Ages, a troubadour/knight would find a lady, almost always a married one, and would serve as her vassal. He would go through terrible trials on her behalf, undertake dangerous pilgrimages in her name, suffer awful tortures to prove his love. (This could include bodily mutilation, such as tearing off of fingernails, the cutting of an ear, etc.) He would also write poems and sing beautiful songs to her, for no troubadour could succeed without some kind of aesthetic or spiritual quality to impress his lady. The key to the archetype is a sense of absolute devotion. A man who will not let matters of warfare, glory, or money intrude into the fantasy of courtship has limitless power. The troubadour role is an ideal because people who do not put themselves and their own interests first are truly rare. For a woman to attract the intense attention of such a man is immensely appealing to her vanity.

In eighteenth-century Osaka, a man named Nisan took the courtesan Dewa out walking, first taking care to sprinkle the clover bushes along the path with water, which looked like morning dew. Dewa was greatly moved by this beautiful sight. "I have heard," she said, "that loving couples of deer are wont to lie behind clover bushes. How I should like to see this in real life!" Nisan had heard enough. That very day he had a section of her house torn down and ordered the planting of dozens of clover bushes in what had once been a part of her bedroom. That night, he arranged for peasants to round up wild deer from the mountains and bring them to the house. The next day Dewa awoke to precisely the scene she had described. Once she appeared overwhelmed and moved, he had the clover and deer taken away and the house rebuilt.

One of history's most gallant lovers, Sergei Saltykov, had the misfortune to fall in love with one of history's least available women: the Grand Duchess Catherine, future empress of Russia. Catherine's every move was watched over by her husband, Peter, who suspected her of trying to cheat on him and appointed servants to keep an eye on her. She was isolated, unloved, and unable to do anything about it. Saltykov, a handsome young army officer, was determined to be her rescuer. In 1752 he befriended Peter, and also the couple in charge of watching over Catherine. In this way he was able to see her and occasionally exchange a word or two with her that revealed his intentions. He performed the most foolhardy and dangerous maneuvers to be able to see her alone, including diverting her horse during a royal hunt and riding off into the forest with her. He told her how much he sympathized with her plight, and that he would do anything to help her.

To be caught courting Catherine would have meant death, and eventually Peter came to suspect that something was up between his wife and Saltykov, though he was never sure. His enmity did not discourage the dashing officer, who just put still more energy and ingenuity into finding ways to arrange secret trysts. The couple were lovers for two years, and Saltykov was undoubtedly the father of Catherine's son Paul, later the emperor of Russia. When Peter finally got rid of him by sending him off to Sweden, news of his gallantry traveled ahead of him, and women swooned to be his next conquest. You may not have to go to as much trouble or risk, but you will always be rewarded for actions that reveal a sense of self-sacrifice or devotion.

The embodiment of the Ideal Lover for the 1920s was Rudolph Valentino, or at least the image created of him in film. Everything he did—the gifts, the flowers, the dancing, the way he took a woman's hand—showed a scrupulous attention to the details that would signify how much he was thinking of her. The image was of a man who made courtship take time, transforming it into an aesthetic experience. Men hated Valentino, because women now expected them to match the ideal of patience and attentiveness that he represented. Yet nothing is more seductive than patient attentiveness. It makes the affair seem lofty, aesthetic, not really about sex. The power of a Valentino, particularly nowadays, is that people like this are so rare. The art of playing to a woman's ideal has almost disappeared—which only makes it that much more alluring.

If the chivalrous lover remains the ideal for women, men often idealize the Madonna/whore, a woman who combines sensuality with an air of spirituality or innocence. Think of the great courtesans of the Italian Renaissance, such as Tullia d'Aragona—essentially a prostitute, like all courtesans, but able to disguise her social role by establishing a reputation as a poet and philosopher. Tullia was what was then known as an "honest courtesan." Honest courtesans would go to church, but they had an ulterior motive: for men, their presence at Mass was exciting. Their houses were pleasure palaces, but what made these homes so visually delightful was their artworks and shelves full of books, volumes of Petrarch and Dante. For the man, the thrill, the fantasy, was to sleep with a woman who was sexual yet had the ideal qualities of a mother and the spirit and intellect of an artist. Where the pure prostitute excited desire but also disgust, the honest courtesan made sex seem elevated and innocent, as if it were happening in the Garden of Eden. Such women held immense power over men. To this day they remain an ideal, if for no other reason than that they offer such a range of pleasures. The key is ambiguity—to combine the appearance of sensitivity to the pleasures of the flesh with an air of innocence, spirituality, a poetic sensibility. This mix of the high and the low is immensely seductive.

The dynamics of the Ideal Lover have limitless possibilities, not all of them erotic. In politics, Talleyrand essentially played the role of the Ideal Lover with Napoleon, whose ideal in both a cabinet minister and a friend was a man who was aristocratic, smooth with the ladies—all the things that Napoleon himself was not. In 1798, when Talleyrand was the French foreign minister, he hosted a party in Napoleon's honor after the great general's dazzling military victories in Italy. To the day Napoleon died, he remembered this party as the best he had ever attended. It was a lavish affair, and Talleyrand wove a subtle message into it by placing Roman busts around the house, and by talking to Napoleon of reviving the imperial glories of ancient Rome. This sparked a glint in the leader's eye, and indeed, a few years later, Napoleon gave himself the title of emperor—a move that only made Talleyrand more powerful. The key to Talleyrand's power was his ability to fathom Napoleon's secret ideal: his desire to be an emperor, a dictator. Talleyrand simply held up a mirror to Napoleon and let him glimpse that possibility. People are always vulnerable to insinuations like this, which stroke their vanity, almost everyone's weak spot. Hint at something for them to aspire to, reveal your faith in some untapped potential you see in them, and you will soon have them eating out of your hand.

If Ideal Lovers are masters at seducing people by appealing to their higher selves, to something lost from their childhood, politicians can benefit by applying this skill on a mass scale, to an entire electorate. This was what John F. Kennedy quite deliberately did with the American public, most obviously in creating the "Camelot" aura around himself. The word "Camelot" was applied to his presidency only after his death, but the romance he consciously projected through his youth and good looks was fully functioning during his lifetime. More subtly, he also played with America's images of its own greatness and lost ideals. Many Americans felt that with the wealth and comfort of the late 1950s had come great losses; ease and conformity had buried the country's pioneer spirit. Kennedy appealed to those lost ideals through the imagery of the New Frontier, which was exemplified by the space race. The American instinct for adventure could find outlets here, even if most of them were symbolic. And there were other calls for public service, such as the creation of the Peace Corps. Through appeals like these, Kennedy resparked the uniting sense of mission that had gone missing in America during the years since World War II. He also attracted to himself a more emotional response than presidents commonly got. People literally fell in love with him and the image.

Politicians can gain seductive power by digging into a country's past, bringing images and ideals that have been abandoned or repressed back to the surface. They only need the symbol; they do not really have to worry about re-creating the reality behind it. The good feelings they stir up are enough to ensure a positive response.

Symbol: *The Portrait Painter. Under his eye, all of your physical imperfections disappear. He brings out noble qualities in you, frames you in a myth, makes you godlike, immortalizes you. For his ability to create such fantasies, he is rewarded with great power.*

Dangers

The main dangers in the role of the Ideal Lover are the consequences that arise if you let reality creep in. You are creating a fantasy that involves an idealization of your own character. And this is a precarious task, for you are human, and imperfect. If your faults are ugly enough, or intrusive enough, they will burst the bubble you have blown, and your target will revile you. Whenever Tullia d'Aragona was caught acting like a common prostitute (when, for instance, she was caught having an affair just for money), she would have to leave town and establish herself elsewhere. The fantasy of her as a spiritual figure was broken. Casanova too faced this danger, but was usually able to surmount it by finding a clever way to break off the relationship before the woman realized that he was not what she had imagined: he would find some excuse to leave town, or, better still, he would choose a victim who was herself leaving town soon, and whose awareness that the affair would be short-lived would make her idealizing of him all the more intense. Reality and long intimate exposure have a way of dulling a person's perfection. The nineteenth-century poet Alfred de Musset was seduced by the writer George Sand, whose larger-than-life character appealed to his romantic nature. But when the couple visited Venice together, and Sand came down with dysentery, she was suddenly no longer an idealized figure but a woman with an unappealing physical problem. De Musset himself showed a whiny, babyish side on this trip, and the lovers separated. Once apart, however, they were able to idealize each other again, and reunited a few months later. When reality intrudes, distance is often a solution.

In politics the dangers are similar. Years after Kennedy's death, a string of revelations (his incessant sexual affairs, his excessively dangerous brinkmanship style of diplomacy, etc.) belied the myth he had created. His image has survived this tarnishing; poll after poll shows that he is still revered. Kennedy is a special case, perhaps, in that his assassination made him a martyr, reinforcing the process of idealization that he had already set in motion. But he is not the only example of an Ideal Lover whose attraction survives unpleasant revelations; these figures unleash such powerful fantasies, and there is such a hunger for the myths and ideals they have to sell, that they are often quickly forgiven. Still, it is always wise to be prudent, and to keep people from glimpsing the less-than-ideal side of your character.

the andy

Most of us feel trapped within the limited roles that the world expects us to play. We are instantly attracted to those who are more fluid, more ambiguous, than we are—those who create their own persona. Dandies excite us because they cannot be categorized, and hint at a freedom we want for ourselves. They play with masculinity and femininity; they fashion their own physical image, which is always startling; they are mysterious and elusive. They also appeal to the narcissism of each sex: to a woman they are psychologically female, to a man they are male. Dandies fascinate and seduce in large numbers. Use the power of the Dandy to create an ambiguous, alluring presence that stirs repressed desires.

The Feminine Dandy

When the eighteen-year-old Rodolpho Guglielmi emigrated from Italy to the United States in 1913, he came with no particular skills apart from his good looks and his dancing prowess. To put these qualities to advantage, he found work in the thés dansants, the Manhattan dance halls where young girls would go alone or with friends and hire a taxi dancer for a brief thrill. The taxi dancer would expertly twirl them around the dance floor, flirting and chatting, all for a small fee. Guglielmi soon made a name as one of the best—so graceful, poised, and pretty.

In working as a taxi dancer, Guglielmi spent a great deal of time around women. He quickly learned what pleased them—how to mirror them in subtle ways, how to put them at ease (but not too much). He began to pay attention to his clothes, creating his own dapper look: he danced with a corset under his shirt to give himself a trim figure, sported a wristwatch (considered effeminate in those days), and claimed to be a marquis. In 1915, he landed a job demonstrating the tango in fancy restaurants, and changed his name to the more evocative Rodolpho di Valentina. A year later he moved to Los Angeles: he wanted to try to make it in Hollywood.

Now known as Rudolph Valentino, Guglielmi appeared as an extra in several low-budget pictures. He eventually landed a somewhat larger role in the 1919 film *Eyes of Youth*, in which he played a seducer, and caught women's attention by how different a seducer he was: his movements were graceful and delicate, his skin so smooth and his face so pretty that when he swooped down on his victim and drowned her protests with a kiss, he seemed more thrilling than sinister. Next came *The Four Horsemen of the Apocalypse*, in which Valentino played the male lead, Julio the playboy, and became an overnight sex symbol through a tango sequence in which he seduced a young woman by leading her through the dance. The scene encapsulated the essence of his appeal: his feet smooth and fluid, his poise almost feminine, combined with an air of control. Female members of the audience literally swooned as he raised a married woman's hands to his lips, or shared the fragrance of a rose with his lover. He seemed so much more attentive to women than other men did; but mixed in with this delicacy was a hint of cruelty and menace that drove women wild.

In his most famous film, *The Sheik*, Valentino played an Arab prince (later revealed to be a Scottish lord abandoned in the Sahara as a baby) who rescues a proud English lady in the desert, then conquers her in a manner

Once a son was born to Mercury and the goddess Venus, and he was brought up by the naiads in Ida's caves. In his features, it was easy to trace resemblance to his father and to his mother. He was called after them, too, for his name was Hermaphroditus. As soon as he was fifteen, he left his native hills, and Ida where he had been brought up, and for the sheer joy of travelling visited remote places. . . .He went as far as the cities of Lycia, and on to the Carians, who dwell nearby. In this region he spied a pool of water, so clear that he could see right to the bottom. . . .The water was like crystal, and the edges of the pool were ringed with fresh turf, and grass that was always green. A nymph [Salmacis] dwelt there. . . .Often she would gather flowers, and it so happened that she was engaged in this pastime when she caught sight of the boy, Hermaphroditus. As soon as she had seen him, she longed to possess him. . . .She addressed him: "Fair boy, you surely deserve to be thought a god. If you are, perhaps you may be Cupid? . . . If there is such a girl [engaged to you], let me enjoy your love in secret: but if there is not, then I pray that I may be your bride, and that we may enter upon marriage together." The naiad said no more; but a blush stained the boy's cheeks, for he did not know what love was. Even blushing became him: his cheeks were the colour of ripe apples, hanging in a sunny orchard, like painted ivory or like the moon when, in eclipse, she shows a reddish hue beneath her brightness. . . . Incessantly the nymph demanded at least sisterly kisses, and tried to put her arms round his ivory neck. "Will you stop!" he cried, "or I shall run away and leave this place and you!" Salmacis was afraid: "I yield the spot to you, stranger, I shall not intrude," she said; and, turning from him, pretended to go away. . . . The boy, meanwhile, thinking himself unobserved and alone, strolled this way and that on the grassy sward, and dipped his toes in the lapping water—then his feet, up to the ankles. Then, tempted by the enticing coolness of the waters, he quickly stripped his young body of its soft garments. At the sight, Salmacis was spell-bound. She was on fire with passion to possess his naked beauty, and her very eyes flamed with a brilliance like that of the dazzling sun, when his bright disc is reflected in a mirror. . . . She longed to embrace him then, and with difficulty restrained her frenzy. Hermaphroditus, clapping his hollow palms against

that borders on rape. When she asks, "Why have you brought me here?," he replies, "Are you not woman enough to know?" Yet she ends up falling in love with him, as indeed women did in movie audiences all over the world, thrilling at his strange blend of the feminine and the masculine. In one scene in *The Sheik*, the English lady points a gun at Valentino; his response is to point a delicate cigarette holder back at her. She wears pants; he wears long flowing robes and abundant eye makeup. Later films would include scenes of Valentino dressing and undressing, a kind of striptease showing glimpses of his trim body. In almost all of his films he played some exotic period character—a Spanish bullfighter, an Indian rajah, an Arab sheik, a French nobleman—and he seemed to delight in dressing up in jewels and tight uniforms.

In the 1920s, women were beginning to play with a new sexual freedom. Instead of waiting for a man to be interested in them, they wanted to be able to initiate the affair, but they still wanted the man to end up sweeping them off their feet. Valentino understood this perfectly. His off-screen life corresponded to his movie image: he wore bracelets on his arm, dressed impeccably, and reportedly was cruel to his wife, and hit her. (His adoring public carefully ignored his two failed marriages and his apparently nonexistent sex life.) When he suddenly died—in New York in August 1926, at the age of thirty-one, from complications after surgery for an ulcer—the response was unprecedented: more than 100,000 people filed by his coffin, many female mourners became hysterical, and the whole nation was spellbound. Nothing like this had happened before for a mere actor.

There is a film of Valentino's, *Monsieur Beaucaire*, in which he plays a total fop, a much more effeminate role than he normally played, and without his usual hint of dangerousness. The film was a flop. Women did not respond to Valentino as a swish. They were thrilled by the ambiguity of a man who shared many of their own feminine traits, yet remained a man. Valentino dressed and played with his physicality like a woman, but his image was masculine. He wooed as a woman would woo if she were a man—slowly, attentively, paying attention to details, setting a rhythm instead of hurrying to a conclusion. Yet when the time came for boldness and conquest, his timing was impeccable, overwhelming his victim and giving her no chance to protest. In his movies, Valentino practiced the same gigolo's art of leading a woman on that he had mastered as a teenager on the dance floor—chatting, flirting, pleasing, but always in control.

Valentino remains an enigma to this day. His private life and his character are wrapped in mystery; his image continues to seduce as it did during his lifetime. He served as the model for Elvis Presley, who was obsessed with this star of the silents, and also for the modern male dandy who plays with gender but retains an edge of danger and cruelty.

Seduction was and will always remain the female form of power and warfare. It was originally the antidote to rape and violence. The man who uses this form of power on a woman is in essence turning the game around, employing feminine weapons against her; without losing his masculine identity, the more subtly feminine he becomes the more effective the seduction. Do not be one of those who believe that what is most seductive is being devastatingly masculine. The Feminine Dandy has a much more sinister effect. He lures the woman in with exactly what she wants—a familiar, pleasing, graceful presence. Mirroring feminine psychology, he displays attention to his appearance, sensitivity to detail, a slight coquettishness—but also a hint of male cruelty. Women are narcissists, in love with the charms of their own sex. By showing them feminine charm, a man can mesmerize and disarm them, leaving them vulnerable to a bold, masculine move.

The Feminine Dandy can seduce on a mass scale. No single woman really possesses him—he is too elusive—but all can fantasize about doing so. The key is ambiguity: your sexuality is decidedly heterosexual, but your body and psychology float delightfully back and forth between the two poles.

> *I am a woman. Every artist is a woman and should have a taste for other women. Artists who are homosexual cannot be true artists because they like men, and since they themselves are women they are reverting to normality.*
>
> —Pablo Picasso

The Masculine Dandy

In the 1870s, Pastor Henrik Gillot was the darling of the St. Petersburg intelligentsia. He was young, handsome, well-read in philosophy and literature, and he preached a kind of enlightened Christianity. Dozens of young girls had crushes on him and would flock to his sermons just to look at him. In 1878, however, he met a girl who changed his life. Her name was Lou von Salomé (later known as Lou Andreas-Salomé), and she was seventeen; he was forty-two.

Salomé was pretty, with radiant blue eyes. She had read a lot, particularly for a girl her age, and was interested in the gravest philosophical and religious issues. Her intensity, her intelligence, her responsiveness to ideas cast a spell over Gillot. When she entered his office for her increasingly frequent discussions with him, the place seemed brighter and more alive. Perhaps she was flirting with him, in the unconscious manner of a young girl—yet when Gillot admitted to himself that he was in love with her, and proposed marriage, Salomé was horrified. The confused pastor never quite got over Lou von Salomé, becoming the first of a long string of famous men to be the victim of a lifelong unfulfilled infatuation with her.

In 1882, the German philosopher Friedrich Nietzsche was wandering around Italy alone. In Genoa he received a letter from his friend Paul Rée, a Prussian philosopher whom he admired, recounting his discussions with a remarkable young Russian woman, Lou von Salomé, in Rome. Salomé was

his body, dived quickly into the stream. As he raised first one arm and then the other, his body gleamed in the clear water, as if someone had encased anivory statue or white lilies in transparent glass. "I have won! He is mine!" cried the nymph, and flinging aside her garments, plunged into the heart of the pool. The boy fought against her, but she held him, and snatched kisses as he struggled, placing her hands beneath him, stroking his unwilling breast, and clinging to him, now on this side, and now on that. • Finally, in spite of all his efforts to slip from her grasp, she twined around him, like a serpent when it is being carried off into the air by the king of birds: for, as it hangs from the eagle's beak, the snake coils round his head and talons and with its tail hampers his beating wings. . . . "You may fight, you rogue, but you will not escape. May the gods grant me this, may no time to come ever separate him from me, or me from him!" Her prayers found favour with the gods: for, as they lay together, their bodies were united and from being two persons they became one. As when a gardener grafts a branch on to a tree, and sees the two unite as they grow, and come to maturity together, so when their limbs met in that clinging embrace the nymph and the boy were no longer two, but a single form, possessed of a dual nature, which could not be called male or female, but seemed to be at once both and neither.

—Ovid, *Metamorphoses*, translated by Mary M. Innes

there on holiday with her mother; Rée had managed to accompany her on long walks through the city, unchaperoned, and they had had many conversations. Her ideas on God and Christianity were quite similar to Nietzsche's, and when Rée had told her that the famous philosopher was a friend of his, she had insisted that he invite Nietzsche to join them. In subsequent letters Rée described how mysteriously captivating Salomé was, and how anxious she was to meet Nietzsche. The philosopher soon went to Rome.

When Nietzsche finally met Salomé, he was overwhelmed. She had the most beautiful eyes he had ever seen, and during their first long talk those eyes lit up so intensely that he could not help feeling there was something erotic about her excitement. Yet he was also confused: Salomé kept her distance, and did not respond to his compliments. What a devilish young woman. A few days later she read him a poem of hers, and he cried; her ideas about life were so like his own. Deciding to seize the moment, Nietzsche proposed marriage. (He did not know that Rée had done so as well.) Salomé declined. She was interested in philosophy, life, adventure, not marriage. Undaunted, Nietzsche continued to court her. On an excursion to Lake Orta with Rée, Salomé, and her mother, he managed to get the girl alone, accompanying her on a walk up Monte Sacro while the others stayed behind. Apparently the views and Nietzsche's words had the proper passionate effect; in a later letter to her, he described this walk as "the most beautiful dream of my life." Now he was a man possessed: all he could think about was marrying Salomé and having her all to himself.

Dandyism is not even, as many unthinking people seem to suppose, an immoderate interest in personal appearance and material elegance. For the true dandy these things are only a symbol of the aristocratic superiority of his personality. . . . • What, then, is this ruling passion that has turned into a creed and created its own skilled tyrants? What is this unwritten constitution that has created so haughty a caste? It is, above all, a burning need to acquire originality, within the apparent bounds of convention. It is a sort of cult of oneself, which can dispense even with what are commonly called illusions. It is the delight in causing astonishment, and the proud satisfaction of never oneself being astonished. . . .

—Charles Baudelaire, *The Dandy*, quoted in *Vice: An Anthology*, edited by Richard Davenport-Hines

A few months later Salomé visited Nietzsche in Germany. They took long walks together, and stayed up all night discussing philosophy. She mirrored his deepest thoughts, anticipated his ideas about religion. Yet when he again proposed marriage, she scolded him as conventional: it was Nietzsche, after all, who had developed a philosophical defense of the superman, the man above everyday morality, yet Salomé was by nature far less conventional than he was. Her firm, uncompromising manner only deepened the spell she cast over him, as did her hint of cruelty. When she finally left him, making it clear that she had no intention of marrying him, Nietzsche was devastated. As an antidote to his pain, he wrote *Thus Spake Zarathustra,* a book full of sublimated eroticism and deeply inspired by his talks with her. From then on Salomé was known throughout Europe as the woman who had broken Nietzsche's heart.

Salomé moved to Berlin. Soon the city's greatest intellectuals were falling under the spell of her independence and free spirit. The playwrights Gerhart Hauptmann and Franz Wedekind became infatuated with her; in 1897, the great Austrian poet Rainer Maria Rilke fell in love with her. By that time her reputation was widely known, and she was a published novelist. This certainly played a part in seducing Rilke, but he was also attracted by a kind of masculine energy he found in her that he had never seen in a woman. Rilke was then twenty-two, Salomé thirty-six. He wrote her love letters and poems, followed her everywhere, and began an affair with her that was to last several years. She corrected his poetry, imposed discipline

In the midst of this display of statesmanship, eloquence, cleverness, and exalted ambition, Alcibiades lived a life of prodigious luxury, drunkenness, debauchery, and insolence. He was effeminate in his dress and would walk through the market-place trailing his long purple robes, and he spent extravagantly. He had the decks of his triremes cut away to allow him to sleep more comfortably, and his bedding was slung on cords, rather than spread on the hard planks. He had a golden shield made for him, which was emblazoned not with any

on his overly romantic verse, inspired ideas for new poems. But she was put off by his childish dependence on her, his weakness. Unable to stand weakness of any kind, she eventually left him. Consumed by her memory, Rilke long continued to pursue her. In 1926, lying on his deathbed, he begged his doctors, "Ask Lou what is wrong with me. She is the only one who knows."

One man wrote of Salomé, "There was something terrifying about her embrace. Looking at you with her radiant blue eyes, she would say, 'The reception of the semen is for me the height of ecstasy.' And she had an insatiable appetite for it. She was completely amoral . . . a vampire." The Swedish psychotherapist Poul Bjerre, one of her later conquests, wrote, "I think Nietzsche was right when he said that Lou was a thoroughly evil woman. Evil however in the Goethean sense: evil that produces good. . . . She may have destroyed lives and marriages but her presence was exciting."

ancestral device, but with the figure of Eros armed with a thunderbolt. The leading men of Athens watched all this with disgust and indignation and they were deeply disturbed by his contemptuous and lawless behaviour, which seemed to them monstrous and suggested the habits of a tyrant. The people's feelings towards him have been very aptly expressed by Aristophanes in the line: "They long for him, they hate him, they cannot do without him. . . ." • The fact was that his voluntary donations, the public shows he supported, his unrivalled munificence to the state, the fame of his ancestry, the power of his oratory and his physical strength and beauty . . . all combined to make the Athenians forgive him everything else, and they were constantly finding euphemisms for his lapses and putting them down to youthful high spirits andhonourable ambition.

—Plutarch, "The Life of Alcibiades," *The Rise and Fall of Athens: Nine Greek Lives*, translated by Ian Scott-Kilvert

The two emotions that almost every male felt in the presence of Lou Andreas-Salomé were confusion and excitement—the two prerequisite feelings for any successful seduction. People were intoxicated by her strange mix of the masculine and the feminine; she was beautiful, with a radiant smile and a graceful, flirtatious manner, but her independence and her intensely analytical nature made her seem oddly male. This ambiguity was expressed in her eyes, which were both coquettish and probing. It was confusion that kept men interested and curious: no other woman was like this. They wanted to know more. The excitement stemmed from her ability to stir up repressed desires. She was a complete nonconformist, and to be involved with her was to break all kinds of taboos. Her masculinity made the relationship seem vaguely homosexual; her slightly cruel, slightly domineering streak could stir up masochistic yearnings, as it did in Nietzsche. Salomé radiated a forbidden sexuality. Her powerful effect on men—the lifelong infatuations, the suicides (there were several), the periods of intense creativity, the descriptions of her as a vampire or a devil—attest to the obscure depths of the psyche that she was able to reach and disturb.

The Masculine Dandy succeeds by reversing the normal pattern of male superiority in matters of love and seduction. A man's apparent independence, his capacity for detachment, often seems to give him the upper hand in the dynamic between men and women. A purely feminine woman will arouse desire, but is always vulnerable to the man's capricious loss of interest; a purely masculine woman, on the other hand, will not arouse that interest at all. Follow the path of the Masculine Dandy, however, and you neutralize all a man's powers. Never give completely of yourself; while you are passionate and sexual, always retain an air of independence and self-possession. You might move on to the next man, or so he will think. You have other, more important matters to concern yourself with, such as your work. Men do not know how to fight women who use their own weapons against them; they are intrigued, aroused, and disarmed. Few men can resist the taboo pleasures offered up to them by the Masculine Dandy.

Further light—a whole flood of it—is thrown upon this attraction of the male in petticoats for the female, in the diary of the Abbé de Choisy, one of the most brilliant men-women of history, of whom we shall hear a great deal more later. The abbé, a churchman of Paris, was a constant masquerader in female attire. He lived in the days of Louis XIV, and was a great friend of Louis' brother, also addicted to women's clothes. A young girl, Mademoiselle Charlotte, thrown much into his company, fell desperately in love with the abbé, and when the affair had progressed to a liaison, the abbé asked her how she came to be won . . . • "I stood in no need of caution as I should have with a man. I saw nothing but a beautiful woman, and why should I be forbidden to love you? What advantages a woman's dress gives you! The heart of a man is there, and that makes a great impression upon us, and on the other hand, all the charms of the fair sex fascinate us, and prevent us from taking precautions."

—C. J. Bulliet, *Venus Castina*

The seduction emanating from a person of uncertain or dissimulated sex is powerful.

—Colette

Keys to the Character

Many of us today imagine that sexual freedom has progressed in recent years—that everything has changed, for better or worse. This is mostly an illusion; a reading of history reveals periods of licentiousness (imperial Rome, late-seventeenth-century England, the "floating world" of eighteenth-century Japan) far in excess of what we are currently experiencing. Gender roles are certainly changing, but they have changed before. Society is in a state of constant flux, but there is something that does not change: the vast majority of people conform to whatever is normal for the time. They play the role allotted to them. Conformity is a constant because humans are social creatures who are always imitating one another. At certain points in history it may be fashionable to be different and rebellious, but if a lot of people are playing that role, there is nothing different or rebellious about it.

We should never complain about most people's slavish conformity, however, for it offers untold possibilities of power and seduction to those who are up for a few risks. Dandies have existed in all ages and cultures (Alcibiades in ancient Greece, Korechika in late-tenth-century Japan), and wherever they have gone they have thrived on the conformist role playing of others. The Dandy displays a true and radical difference from other people, a difference of appearance and manner. Since most of us are secretly oppressed by our lack of freedom, we are drawn to those who are more fluid and flaunt their difference.

Beau Brummell was regarded as unbalanced in his passion for daily ablutions. His ritualistic morning toilet took upward of five hours, one hour spent inching himself into his skin-tight buckskin breeches, an hour with the hairdresser and another two hours tying and "creasing down" a series of starched cravats until perfection was achieved. But first of all two hours were spent scrubbing himself with fetish zeal from head to toe in milk, water and eau de Cologne. . . . Beau Brummell said he used only the froth of champagne to polish his Hessian boots. He had 365 snuff boxes, those suitable for summer wear being quite unthinkable in winter, and the fit of his gloves was achieved by entrusting their cut to two firms—one for the fingers, the other for the thumbs.

Dandies seduce socially as well as sexually; groups form around them, their style is wildly imitated, an entire court or crowd will fall in love with them. In adapting the Dandy character for your own purposes, remember that the Dandy is by nature a rare and beautiful flower. Be different in ways that are both striking and aesthetic, never vulgar; poke fun at current trends and styles, go in a novel direction, and be supremely uninterested in what anyone else is doing. Most people are insecure; they will wonder what you are up to, and slowly they will come to admire and imitate you, because you express yourself with total confidence.

The Dandy has traditionally been defined by clothing, and certainly most Dandies create a unique visual style. Beau Brummel, the most famous Dandy of all, would spend hours on his toilette, particularly the inimitably styled knot in his necktie, for which he was famous throughout early-nineteenth-century England. But a Dandy's style cannot be obvious, for Dandies are subtle, and never try hard for attention—attention comes to them. The person whose clothes are flagrantly different has little imagination or taste. Dandies show their difference in the little touches that mark their disdain for convention: Théophile Gautier's red vest, Oscar Wilde's green velvet suit, Andy Warhol's silver wigs. The great English Prime Minister Benjamin Disraeli had two magnificent canes, one for morning, one for evening; at noon he would change canes, no matter where he was. The female Dandy works similarly. She may adopt male clothing, say, but if she does, a touch here or there will set her truly apart: no man ever dressed quite like George Sand. The overtall hat, the riding boots worn on the streets of Paris, made her a sight to behold.

Sometimes, however, the tyranny of elegance became altogether insupportable. A Mr. Boothby committed suicide and left a note saying he could no longer endure the ennui of buttoning and unbuttoning.

—*The Game of Hearts: Harriette Wilson's Memoirs*, edited by Lesley Blanch

Remember, there must be a reference point. If your visual style is totally unfamiliar, people will think you at best an obvious attention-getter, at worst crazy. Instead, create your own fashion sense by adapting and altering prevailing styles to make yourself an object of fascination. Do this right and you will be wildly imitated. The Count d'Orsay, a great London dandy of the 1830s and 1840s, was closely watched by fashionable people; one day, caught in a sudden London rainstorm, he bought a *paltrok,* a kind of heavy, hooded duffle coat, off the back of a Dutch sailor. The *paltrok* immediately became *the* coat to wear. Having people imitate you, of course, is a sign of your powers of seduction.

The nonconformity of Dandies, however, goes far beyond appearances. It is an attitude toward life that sets them apart; adopt that attitude and a circle of followers will form around you.

This royal manner which [the dandy] raises to the height of true royalty, the dandy has taken this from women, who alone seem naturally made for such a role. It is a somewhat by using the manner and the method of women that the dandy dominates. And this usurpation of femininity, he makes women themselves approve of this. . . . The dandy has something antinatural and androgynous about him, which is precisely how he is able to endlessly seduce.

—Jules Lemaître, *Les Contemporains*

Dandies are supremely impudent. They don't give a damn about other people, and never try to please. In the court of Louis XIV, the writer La Bruyère noticed that courtiers who tried hard to please were invariably on the way down; nothing was more anti-seductive. As Barbey d'Aurevilly wrote, "Dandies please women by displeasing them."

Impudence was fundamental to the appeal of Oscar Wilde. In a London theater one night, after the first performance of one of Wilde's plays, the ecstatic audience yelled for the author to appear onstage. Wilde made them wait and wait, then finally emerged, smoking a cigarette and wearing an expression of total disdain. "It may be bad manners to appear here smoking, but it is far worse to disturb me when I am smoking," he scolded his fans. The Count d'Orsay was equally impudent. At a London club one night, a Rothschild who was notoriously cheap accidentally dropped a gold coin on the floor, then bent down to look for it. The count immediately whipped out a thousand-franc note (worth much more than the coin), rolled it up, lit it like a candle, and got down on all fours, as if to help light the way in the search. Only a Dandy could get away with such audacity. The insolence of the Rake is tied up with his desire to conquer a woman; he cares for nothing else. The insolence of the Dandy, on the other hand, is aimed at society and its conventions. It is not a woman he cares to conquer but a whole group, an entire social world. And since people are generally oppressed by the obligation of always being polite and self-sacrificing, they are delighted to spend time around a person who disdains such niceties.

Dandies are masters of the art of living. They live for pleasure, not for work; they surround themselves with beautiful objects and eat and drink with the same relish they show for their clothes. This was how the great Roman writer Petronius, author of the *Satyricon*, was able to seduce the emperor Nero. Unlike the dull Seneca, the great Stoic thinker and Nero's tutor, Petronius knew how to make every detail of life a grand aesthetic adventure, from a feast to a simple conversation. This is not an attitude you should impose on those around you—you can't make yourself a nuisance—but if you simply seem socially confident and sure of your taste, people will be drawn to you. The key is to make everything an aesthetic choice. Your ability to alleviate boredom by making life an art will make your company highly prized.

The opposite sex is a strange country we can never know, and this excites us, creates the proper sexual tension. But it is also a source of annoyance and frustration. Men do not understand how women think, and vice versa; each tries to make the other act more like a member of their own sex. Dandies may never try to please, but in this one area they have a pleasing effect: by adopting psychological traits of the opposite sex, they appeal to our inherent narcissism. Women identified with Rudolph Valentino's delicacy and attention to detail in courtship; men identified with Lou Andreas-Salomé's lack of interest in commitment. In the Heian court of eleventh-century Japan, Sei Shonagon, the writer of *The Pillow Book*, was powerfully seductive for men, especially literary types. She was fiercely independent, wrote poetry with the best, and had a certain emotional distance. Men wanted more from her than just to be her friend or companion, as if she were another man; charmed by her empathy for male psychology, they fell in love with her. This kind of mental transvestism—the ability to enter the spirit of the opposite sex, adapt to their way of thinking, mirror their tastes and attitudes—can be a key element in seduction. It is a way of mesmerizing your victim.

According to Freud, the human libido is essentially bisexual; most people are in some way attracted to people of their own sex, but social constraints (varying with culture and historical period) repress these impulses. The Dandy represents a release from such constraints. In several of Shakespeare's plays, a young girl (back then, the female roles in the theater were actually played by male actors) has to go into disguise and dresses up as a boy, eliciting all kinds of sexual interest from men, who later are delighted to find out that the boy is actually a girl. (Think, for example, of Rosalind in *As You Like It*.) Entertainers such as Josephine Baker (known as the Chocolate Dandy) and Marlene Dietrich would dress up as men in their acts, making themselves wildly popular—among men. Meanwhile the slightly feminized male, the pretty boy, has always been seductive to women. Valentino embodied this quality. Elvis Presley had feminine features (the face, the hips), wore frilly pink shirts and eye makeup, and attracted the attention of women early on. The filmmaker Kenneth Anger said of Mick Jagger that it was "a bisexual charm which constituted an important part of the attraction he had over young girls . . . and which acted upon their unconscious." In Western culture for centuries, in fact, feminine beauty has been far more fetishized than male beauty, so it is understandable that a feminine-looking face like that of Montgomery Clift would have more seductive power than that of John Wayne.

The Dandy figure has a place in politics as well. John F. Kennedy was a strange mix of the masculine and feminine, virile in his toughness with the Russians, and in his White House lawn football games, yet feminine in his graceful and dapper appearance. This ambiguity was a large part of his appeal. Disraeli was an incorrigible Dandy in dress and manner; some were suspicious of him as a result, but his courage in not caring what people thought of him also won him respect. And women of course adored him, for women always adore a Dandy. They appreciated the gentleness of his manner, his aesthetic sense, his love of clothes—in other words, his feminine qualities. The mainstay of Disraeli's power was in fact a female fan: Queen Victoria.

Do not be misled by the surface disapproval your Dandy pose may elicit. Society may publicize its distrust of androgyny (in Christian theology, Satan is often represented as androgynous), but this conceals its fascination; what is most seductive is often what is most repressed. Learn a playful dandyism and you will become the magnet for people's dark, unrealized yearnings.

The key to such power is ambiguity. In a society where the roles everyone plays are obvious, the refusal to conform to any standard will excite interest. Be both masculine and feminine, impudent and charming, subtle and outrageous. Let other people worry about being socially acceptable; those types are a dime a dozen, and you are after a power greater than they can imagine.

Symbol: *The Orchid. Its shape and color oddly suggest both sexes, its odor is sweet and decadent —it is a tropical flower of evil. Delicate and highly cultivated, it is prized for its rarity; it is unlike any other flower.*

Dangers

The Dandy's strength, but also the Dandy's problem, is that he or she often works through transgressive feelings relating to sex roles. Although this activity is highly charged and seductive, it is also dangerous, since it touches on a source of great anxiety and insecurity. The greater dangers will often come from your own sex. Valentino had immense appeal for women, but men hated him. He was constantly dogged with accusations of being perversely unmasculine, and this caused him great pain. Salomé was equally disliked by women; Nietzsche's sister, and perhaps his closest friend, considered her an evil witch, and led a virulent campaign against her in the press long after the philosopher's death. There is little to be done in the face of resentment like this. Some Dandies try to fight the image they themselves have created, but this is unwise: to prove his masculinity, Valentino would engage in a boxing match, anything to prove his masculinity. He wound up looking only desperate. Better to accept society's occasional gibes with grace and insolence. After all, the Dandies' charm is that they don't really care what people think of them. That is how Andy Warhol played the game: when people tired of his antics or some scandal erupted, instead of trying to defend himself he would simply move on to some new image—decadent bohemian, high-society portraitist, etc.—as if to say, with a hint of disdain, that the problem lay not with him but with other people's attention span.

Another danger for the Dandy is the fact that insolence has its limits. Beau Brummel prided himself on two things: his trimness of figure and his acerbic wit. His main social patron was the Prince of Wales, who, in later years, grew plump. One night at dinner, the prince rang for the butler, and Brummel snidely remarked, "Do ring, Big Ben." The prince did not appreciate the joke, had Brummel shown out, and never spoke to him again. Without royal patronage, Brummel fell into poverty and madness.

Even a Dandy, then, must measure out his impudence. A true Dandy knows the difference between a theatrically staged teasing of the powerful and a remark that will truly hurt, offend, or insult. It is particularly important to avoid insulting those in a position to injure you. In fact the pose may work best for those who can afford to offend—artists, bohemians, etc. In the work world, you will probably have to modify and tone down your Dandy image. Be pleasantly different, an amusement, rather than a person who challenges the group's conventions and makes others feel insecure.

the Natural

Childhood is the golden paradise we are always consciously or unconsciously trying to re-create. The Natural embodies the longed-for qualities of childhood—spontaneity, sincerity, unpretentiousness. In the presence of Naturals, we feel at ease, caught up in their playful spirit, transported back to that golden age. Naturals also make a virtue out of weakness, eliciting our sympathy for their trials, making us want to protect them and help them. As with a child, much of this is natural, but some of it is exaggerated, a conscious seductive maneuver. Adopt the pose of the Natural to neutralize people's natural defensiveness and infect them with helpless delight.

Psychological Traits of the Natural

Children are not as guileless as we like to imagine. They suffer from feelings of helplessness, and sense early on the power of their natural charm to remedy their weakness in the adult world. They learn to play a game: if their natural innocence can persuade a parent to yield to their desires in one instance, then it is something they can use strategically in another instance, laying it on thick at the right moment to get their way. If their vulnerability and weakness is so attractive, then it is something they can use for effect.

Long-past ages have a great and often puzzling attraction for men's imagination. Whenever they are dissatisfied with their present surroundings—and this happens often enough—they turn back to the past and hope that they will now be able to prove the truth of the inextinguishable dream of a golden age. They are probably still under the spell of their childhood, which is presented to them by their not impartial memory as a time of uninterrupted bliss.

—SIGMUND FREUD, *THE STANDARD EDITION OF THE COMPLETE PSYCHOLOGICAL WORKS OF SIGMUND FREUD*, VOLUME 23

Why are we seduced by children's naturalness? First, because anything natural has an uncanny effect on us. Since the beginning of time, natural phenomena—such as lightning storms or eclipses—have instilled in human beings an awe tinged with fear. The more civilized we become, the greater the effect such natural events have on us; the modern world surrounds us with so much that is manufactured and artificial that something sudden and inexplicable fascinates us. Children also have this natural power, but because they are unthreatening and human, they are not so much awe inspiring as charming. Most people try to please, but the pleasantness of the child comes effortlessly, defying logical explanation—and what is irrational is often dangerously seductive.

More important, a child represents a world from which we have been forever exiled. Because adult life is full of boredom and compromise, we harbor an illusion of childhood as a kind of golden age, even though it can often be a period of great confusion and pain. It cannot be denied, however, that childhood had certain privileges, and as children we had a pleasurable attitude to life. Confronted with a particularly charming child, we often feel wistful: we remember our own golden past, the qualities we have lost and wish we had again. And in the presence of the child, we get a little of that goldenness back.

Natural seducers are people who somehow avoided getting certain childish traits drummed out of them by adult experience. Such people can be as powerfully seductive as any child, because it seems uncanny and marvelous that they have preserved such qualities. They are not literally like children, of course; that would make them obnoxious or pitiful. Rather it is the spirit that they have retained. Do not imagine that this childishness is something beyond their control. Natural seducers learn early on the value of retaining a particular quality, and the seductive power it contains; they

When Hermes was born on Mount Cyllene his mother Maia laid him in swaddling bands on a winnowing fan, but he grew with astonishing quickness into a little boy, and as soon as her back was turned, slipped off and went looking for adventure. Arrived at Pieria, where Apollo was tending a fine herd of cows, he decided to

adapt and build upon those childlike traits that they managed to preserve, exactly as the child learns to play with its natural charm. This is the key. It is within your power to do the same, since there is lurking within all of us a devilish child straining to be let loose. To do this successfully, you have to be able to let go to a degree, since there is nothing less natural than seeming hesitant. Remember the spirit you once had; let it return, without self-consciousness. People are much more forgiving of those who go all the way, who seem uncontrollably foolish, than the halfhearted adult with a childish streak. Remember who you were before you became so polite and self-effacing. To assume the role of the Natural, mentally position yourself in any relationship as the child, the younger one.

The following are the main types of the adult Natural. Keep in mind that the greatest natural seducers are often a blend of more than one of these qualities.

The innocent. The primary qualities of innocence are weakness and misunderstanding of the world. Innocence is weak because it is doomed to vanish in a harsh, cruel world; the child cannot protect or hold on to its innocence. The misunderstandings come from the child's not knowing about good and evil, and seeing everything through uncorrupted eyes. The weakness of children elicits sympathy, their misunderstandings make us laugh, and nothing is more seductive than a mixture of laughter and sympathy.

The adult Natural is not truly innocent—it is impossible to grow up in this world and retain total innocence. Yet Naturals yearn so deeply to hold on to their innocent outlook that they manage to preserve the illusion of innocence. They exaggerate their weakness to elicit the proper sympathy. They act like they still see the world through innocent eyes, which in an adult proves doubly humorous. Much of this is conscious, but to be effective, adult Naturals must make it seem subtle and effortless—if they are seen as *trying* to act innocent, it will come across as pathetic. It is better for them to communicate weakness indirectly, through looks and glances, or through the situations they get themselves into, rather than anything obvious. Since this type of innocence is mostly an act, it is easily adaptable for your own purposes. Learn to play up any natural weaknesses or flaws.

The imp. Impish children have a fearlessness that we adults have lost. That is because they do not see the possible consequences of their actions—how some people might be offended, how they might physically hurt themselves in the process. Imps are brazen, blissfully uncaring. They infect you with their lighthearted spirit. Such children have not yet had their natural energy and spirit scolded out of them by the need to be polite and civil. Secretly, we envy them; we want to be naughty too.

Adult imps are seductive because of how different they are from the rest of us. Breaths of fresh air in a cautious world, they go full throttle, as if

steal them. But, fearing to be betrayed by their tracks, he quickly made a number of shoes from the bark of a fallen oak and tied them with plaited grass to the feet of the cows, which he then drove off by night along the road. Apollo discovered the loss, but Hermes's trick deceived him, and though he went as far as Pylus in his westward search, and to Onchestus in his eastern, he was forced, in the end, to offer a reward for the apprehension of the thief. Silenus and his satyrs, greedy of reward, spread out in different directions to track him down but, for a long while, without success. At last, as a party of them passed through Arcadia, they heard the muffled sound of music such as they had never heard before, and the nymph Cyllene, from the mouth of a cave, told them that a most gifted child had recently been born there, to whom she was acting as nurse: he had constructed an ingenious musical toy from the shell of a tortoise and some cow-gut, with which he had lulled his mother to sleep. • "And from whom did he get the cow-gut?" asked the alert satyrs, noticing two hides stretched outside the cave. "Do you charge the poor child with theft?" asked Cyllene. Harsh words were exchanged. • At that moment Apollo came up, having discovered the thief's identity by observing the suspicious behaviour of a long-winged bird. Entering the cave, he awakened Maia and told her severely that Hermes must restore the stolen cows. Maia pointed to the child, still wrapped in his

their impishness were uncontrollable, and thus natural. If you play the part, do not worry about offending people now and then—you are too lovable and inevitably they will forgive you. Just don't apologize or look contrite, for that would break the spell. Whatever you say or do, keep a glint in your eye to show that you do not take anything seriously.

The wonder. A wonder child has a special, inexplicable talent: a gift for music, for mathematics, for chess, for sport. At work in the field in which they have such prodigal skill, these children seem possessed, and their actions effortless. If they are artists or musicians, Mozart types, their work seems to spring from some inborn impulse, requiring remarkably little thought. If it is a physical talent that they have, they are blessed with unusual energy, dexterity, and spontaneity. In both cases they seem talented beyond their years. This fascinates us.

Adult wonders are often former wonder children who have managed, remarkably, to retain their youthful impulsiveness and improvisational skills. True spontaneity is a delightful rarity, for everything in life conspires to rob us of it—we have to learn to act carefully and deliberately, to think about how we look in other people's eyes. To play the wonder you need some skill that seems easy and natural, along with the ability to improvise. If in fact your skill takes practice, you must hide this and learn to make your work appear effortless. The more you hide the sweat behind what you do, the more natural and seductive it will appear.

The undefensive lover. As people get older, they protect themselves against painful experiences by closing themselves off. The price for this is that they grow rigid, physically and mentally. But children are by nature unprotected and open to experience, and this receptiveness is extremely attractive. In the presence of children we become less rigid, infected with their openness. That is why we want to be around them.

Undefensive lovers have somehow circumvented the self-protective process, retaining the playful, receptive spirit of the child. They often manifest this spirit physically: they are graceful, and seem to age less rapidly than other people. Of all the Natural's character qualities, this one is the most useful. Defensiveness is deadly in seduction; act defensive and you'll bring out defensiveness in other people. The undefensive lover, on the other hand, lowers the inhibitions of his or her target, a critical part of seduction. It is important to learn to not react defensively: bend instead of resist, be open to influence from others, and they will more easily fall under your spell.

swaddling bands and feigning sleep. "What an absurd charge!" she cried. But Apollo had already recognized the hides. He picked up Hermes, carried him to Olympus, and there formally accused him of theft, offering the hides as evidence. Zeus, loth to believe that his own new-born son was a thief, encouraged him to plead not guilty, but Apollo would not be put off and Hermes, at last, weakened and confessed. • "Very well, come with me," he said, "and you may have your herd. I slaughtered only two, and those I cut up into twelve equal portions as a sacrifice to the twelve gods" • "Twelve gods?" asked Apollo. "Who is the twelfth?" • "Your servant, sir," replied Hermes modestly. "I ate no more than my share, though I was very hungry, and duly burned the rest." • The two gods [Hermes and Apollo] returned to Mount Cyllene, where Hermes greeted his mother and retrieved something that he had hidden underneath a sheepskin. • "What have you there?" asked Apollo. • In answer, Hermes showed his newly-invented tortoise-shell lyre, and played such a ravishing tune on it with the plectrum he had also invented, at the same time singing in praise of Apollo's nobility, intelligence, and generosity, that he was forgiven at once. He led the surprised and delighted Apollo to Pylus, playing all the way, and there gave him the remainder of the cattle, which he had hidden in a cave. • "A bargain!" cried Apollo. "You keep the cows, and I take the lyre."

Examples of Natural Seducers

1. As a child growing up in England, Charlie Chaplin spent years in dire poverty, particularly after his mother was committed to an asylum. In his early teens, forced to work to live, he landed a job in vaudeville, eventually gaining some success as a comedian. But Chaplin was wildly ambitious, and so, in 1910, when he was only nineteen, he emigrated to the United States, hoping to break into the film business. Making his way to Hollywood, he found occasional bit parts, but success seemed elusive: the competition was fierce, and although Chaplin had a repertoire of gags that he had learned in vaudeville, he did not particularly excel at physical humor, a critical part of silent comedy. He was not a gymnast like Buster Keaton.

In 1914, Chaplin managed to get the lead in a film short called *Making a Living*. His role was that of a con artist. In playing around with the costume for the part, he put on a pair of pants several sizes too large, then added a derby hat, enormous boots that he wore on the wrong feet, a walking cane, and a pasted-on mustache. With the clothes, a whole new character seemed to come to life—first the silly walk, then the twirling of the cane, then all sorts of gags. Mack Sennett, the head of the studio, did not find *Making a Living* very funny, and doubted whether Chaplin had a future in the movies, but a few critics felt otherwise. A review in a trade magazine read, "The clever player who takes the role of a nervy and very nifty sharper in this picture is a comedian of the first water, who acts like one of Nature's own naturals." And audiences also responded—the film made money.

What seemed to touch a nerve in *Making a Living*, setting Chaplin apart from the horde of other comedians working in silent film, was the almost pathetic naïveté of the character he played. Sensing he was onto something, Chaplin shaped the role further in subsequent movies, rendering him more and more naive. The key was to make the character seem to see the world through the eyes of a child. In *The Bank*, he is the bank janitor who daydreams of great deeds while robbers are at work in the building; in *The Pawnbroker*, he is an unprepared shop assistant who wreaks havoc on a grandfather clock; in *Shoulder Arms*, he is a soldier in the bloody trenches of World War I, reacting to the horrors of war like an innocent child. Chaplin made sure to cast actors in his films who were physically larger than he was, subliminally positioning them as adult bullies and himself as the helpless infant. And as he went deeper into his character, something strange happened: the character and the real-life man began to merge. Although he had had a troubled childhood, he was obsessed with it. (For his film *Easy Street* he built a set in Hollywood that duplicated the London streets he had known as a boy.) He mistrusted the adult world, preferring the company of the young, or the young at heart: three of his four wives were teenagers when he married them.

More than any other comedian, Chaplin aroused a mix of laughter and sentiment. He made you empathize with him as the victim, feel sorry for

• "Agreed," said Hermes, and they shook hands on it. • . . . Apollo, taking the child back to Olympus, told Zeus all that had happened. Zeus warned Hermes that henceforth he must respect the rights of property and refrain from telling downright lies; but he could not help being amused. "You seem to be a very ingenious, eloquent, and persuasive godling," he said. • "Then make me your herald, Father," Hermes answered, "and I will be responsible for the safety of all divine property, and never tell lies, though I cannot promise always to tell the whole truth." • "That would not be expected of you," said Zeus with a smile. . . . Zeus gave him a herald's staff with white ribbons, which everyone was ordered to respect; a round hat against the rain, and winged golden sandals which carried him about with the swiftness of the wind.

—Robert Graves, *The Greek Myths*, volume I

A man may meet a woman and be shocked by her ugliness. Soon, if she is natural and unaffected, her expression makes him overlook the fault of her features. He begins to find her charming, it enters his head that she might be loved, and a week later he is living in hope. The following week he has been snubbed into despair, and the week afterwards he has gone mad.

—Stendhal, *Love*, translated by Gilbert and Suzanne Sale

him the way you would for a lost dog. You both laughed and cried. And audiences sensed that the role Chaplin played came from somewhere deep inside—that he was sincere, that he was actually playing himself. Within a few years after *Making a Living*, Chaplin was the most famous actor in the world. There were Chaplin dolls, comic books, toys; popular songs and short stories were written about him; he became a universal icon. In 1921, when he returned to London for the first time since he had left it, he was greeted by enormous crowds, as if at the triumphant return of a great general.

The greatest seducers, those who seduce mass audiences, nations, the world, have a way of playing on people's unconscious, making them react in a way they can neither understand nor control. Chaplin inadvertently hit on this power when he discovered the effect he could have on audiences by playing up his weakness, by suggesting that he had a child's mind in an adult body. In the early twentieth century, the world was radically and rapidly changing. People were working longer and longer hours at increasingly mechanical jobs; life was becoming steadily more inhuman and heartless, as the ravages of World War I made clear. Caught in the midst of revolutionary change, people yearned for a lost childhood that they imagined as a golden paradise.

An adult child like Chaplin has immense seductive power, for he offers the illusion that life was once simpler and easier, and that for a moment, or for as long as the movie lasts, you can win that life back. In a cruel, amoral world, naïveté has enormous appeal. The key is to bring it off with an air of total seriousness, as the straight man does in stand-up comedy. More important, however, is the creation of sympathy. Overt strength and power is rarely seductive—it makes us afraid, or envious. The royal road to seduction is to play up your vulnerability and helplessness. You cannot make this obvious; to seem to be begging for sympathy is to seem needy, which is entirely anti-seductive. Do not proclaim yourself a victim or underdog, but reveal it in your manner, in your confusion. A display of "natural" weakness will make you instantly lovable, both lowering people's defenses and making them feel delightfully superior to you. Put yourself in situations that make you seem weak, in which someone else has the advantage; they are the bully, you are the innocent lamb. Without any effort on your part, people will feel sympathy for you. Once people's eyes cloud over with sentimental mist, they will not see how you are manipulating them.

"Geographical" escapism has been rendered ineffective by the spread of air routes. What remains is "evolutionary" escapism—a downward course in one's development, back to the ideas and emotions of "golden childhood," which may well be defined as "regress towards infantilism," escape to a personal world of childish ideas. • In a strictly-regulated society, where life follows strictly-defined canons, the urge to escape from the chain of things "established once and for all" must be felt particularly strongly. . . . • And the most perfect of them [comedians] does this with utmost perfection, for he [Chaplin] serves this principle . . . through the subtlety of his method which, offering the spectator an infantile pattern to be imitated, pscyhologically infects him with infantilism and draws him into the "golden age" of the infantile paradise of childhood.

—Sergei Eisenstein, "Charlie the Kid," from *Notes of a Film Director*

2. Emma Crouch, born in 1842 in Plymouth, England, came from a respectable middle-class family. Her father was a composer and music professor who dreamed of success in the world of light opera. Among his many children, Emma was his favorite: she was a delightful child, lively and flirtatious, with red hair and a freckled face. Her father doted on her, and promised her a brilliant future in the theater. Unfortunately Mr. Crouch had a

Prince Gortschakoff used to say that she [Cora Pearl] was the last word in luxury, and that he would have tried to steal the sun to satisfy one of her whims.

—GUSTAVE CLAUDIN, CORA PEARL CONTEMPORARY

Apparently the possession of humor implies the possession of a number of typical habit-systems. The first is an emotional one: the habit of playfulness. Why should one be proud of being playful? For a double reason. First, playfulness connotes childhood and youth. If one can be playful, one still possesses something of the vigor and the joy of young life . . . • But there is a deeper implication. To be playful is, in a sense, to be free. When a person is playful, he momentarily disregards the binding necessities which compel him, in business and morals, in domestic and community life. . . . • What galls us is that the binding necessities do not permit us to shape our world as we please. . . . What we most deeply desire, however, is to create our world for ourselves. Whenever we can do that, even in the slightest degree, we are happy. Now in play we create our own world. . . .

—PROFESSOR H. A. OVERSTREET, *INFLUENCING HUMAN BEHAVIOR*

dark side: he was an adventurer, a gambler, and a rake, and in 1849 he abandoned his family and left for America. The Crouches were now in dire straits. Emma was told that her father had died in an accident and she was sent off to a convent. The loss of her father affected her deeply, and as the years went by she seemed lost in the past, acting as if he still doted on her.

One day in 1856, when Emma was walking home from church, a well-dressed gentleman invited her home for some cakes. She followed him to his house, where he proceeded to take advantage of her. The next morning this man, a diamond merchant, promised to set her up in a house of her own, treat her well, and give her plenty of money. She took the money but left him, determined to do what she had always wanted: never see her family again, never depend on anyone, and lead the grand life that her father had promised her.

With the money the diamond merchant had given her, Emma bought nice clothes and rented a cheap flat. Adopting the flamboyant name of Cora Pearl, she began to frequent London's Argyll Rooms, a fancy gin palace where harlots and gentlemen rubbed elbows. The proprietor of the Argyll, a Mr. Bignell, took note of this newcomer to his establishment—she was so brazen for a young girl. At forty-five, he was much older than she was, but he decided to be her lover and protector, lavishing her with money and attention. The following year he took her to Paris, which was at the height of its Second Empire prosperity. Cora was enthralled by Paris, and of all its sights, but what impressed her the most was the parade of rich coaches in the Bois de Boulogne. Here the fashionable came to take the air—the empress, the princesses, and, not least the grand courtesans, who had the most opulent carriages of all. This was the way to lead the kind of life Cora's father had wanted for her. She promptly told Bignell that when he went back to London, she would stay on alone.

Frequenting all the right places, Cora soon came to the attention of wealthy French gentlemen. They would see her walking the streets in a bright pink dress, to complement her flaming red hair, pale face, and freckles. They would glimpse her riding wildly through the Bois de Boulogne, cracking her whip left and right. They would see her in cafés surrounded by men, her witty insults making them laugh. They also heard of her exploits—of her delight in showing her body to one and all. The elite of Paris society began to court her, particularly the older men who had grown tired of the cold and calculating courtesans, and who admired her girlish spirit. As money began to pour in from her various conquests (the Duc de Mornay, heir to the Dutch throne; Prince Napoleon, cousin to the Emperor), Cora spent it on the most outrageous things—a multicolored carriage pulled by a team of cream-colored horses, a rose-marble bathtub with her initials inlaid in gold. Gentlemen vied to be the one who would spoil her the most. An Irish lover wasted his entire fortune on her, in only eight weeks. But money could not buy Cora's loyalty; she would leave a man on the slightest whim.

Cora Pearl's wild behavior and disdain for etiquette had all of Paris on edge. In 1864, she was to appear as Cupid in the Offenbach operetta *Orpheus in the Underworld.* Society was dying to see what she would do to cause a sensation, and soon found out: she came on stage practically naked, except for expensive diamonds here and there, barely covering her. As she pranced on stage, the diamonds fell off, each one worth a fortune; she did not stoop to pick them up, but let them roll off into the footlights. The gentlemen in the audience, some of whom had given her those diamonds, applauded her wildly. Antics like this made Cora the toast of Paris, and she reigned as the city's supreme courtesan for over a decade, until the Franco-Prussian War of 1870 put an end to the Second Empire.

People often mistakenly believe that what makes a person desirable and seductive is physical beauty, elegance, or overt sexuality. Yet Cora Pearl was not dramatically beautiful; her body was boyish, and her style was garish and tasteless. Even so, the most dashing men of Europe vied for her favors, often ruining themselves in the process. It was Cora's spirit and attitude that enthralled them. Spoiled by her father, she imagined that spoiling her was natural—that all men should do the same. The consequence was that, like a child, she never felt she had to try to please. It was Cora's powerful air of independence that made men want to possess her, tame her. She never pretended to be anything more than a courtesan, so the brazenness that in a lady would have been uncivil in her seemed natural and fun. And as with a spoiled child, a man's relationship with her was on her terms. The moment he tried to change that, she lost interest. This was the secret of her astounding success.

Spoiled children have an undeservedly bad reputation: while those who are spoiled with material things are indeed often insufferable, those who are spoiled with affection know themselves to be deeply seductive. This becomes a distinct advantage when they grow up. According to Freud (who was speaking from experience, since he was his mother's darling), spoiled children have a confidence that stays with them all their lives. This quality radiates outward, drawing others to them, and, in a circular process, making people spoil them still more. Since their spirit and natural energy were never tamed by a disciplining parent, as adults they are adventurous and bold, and often impish or brazen.

The lesson is simple: it may be too late to be spoiled by a parent, but it is never too late to make other people spoil you. It is all in your attitude. People are drawn to those who expect a lot out of life, whereas they tend to disrespect those who are fearful and undemanding. Wild independence has a provocative effect on us: it appeals to us, while also presenting us with a challenge—we want to be the one to tame it, to make the spirited person dependent on us. Half of seduction is stirring such competitive desires.

3. In October of 1925, Paris society was all excited about the opening of the Revue Nègre. Jazz, or in fact anything that came from black America,

All was quiet again. Genji slipped the latch open and tried the doors. They had not been bolted. A curtain had been set up just inside, and in the dim light he could make out Chinese chests and other furniture scattered in some disorder. He made his way through to her side. She lay by herself, a slight little figure. Though vaguely annoyed at being disturbed, she evidently took him for the woman Chujo until he pulled back the covers. • . . . His manner was so gently persuasive that devils and demons could not have gainsaid him. • . . . She was so small that he lifted her easily. As he passed through the doors to his own room, he came upon Chujo who had been summoned earlier. He called out in surprise. Surprised in turn, Chujo peered into the darkness. The perfume that came from his robes like a cloud of smoke told her who he was. . . . [Chujo] followed after, but Genji was quite unmoved by her pleas. • "Come for her in the morning," he said, sliding the doors closed. • The lady was bathed in perspiration and quite beside herself at the thought of what Chujo, and the others too, would be thinking. Genji had to feel sorry for her. Yet the sweet words poured forth, the whole gamut of pretty devices for making a woman surrender. . . . • One may imagine that he found many kind promises with which to comfort her. . . .

—Murasaki Shikibu, *The Tale of Genji*, translated by Edward G. Seidensticker

was the latest fashion, and the Broadway dancers and performers who made up the Revue Nègre were African-American. On opening night, artists and high society packed the hall. The show was spectacular, as they expected, but nothing prepared them for the last number, performed by a somewhat gawky long-legged woman with the prettiest face: Josephine Baker, a twenty-year-old chorus girl from East St. Louis. She came onstage bare-breasted, wearing a skirt of feathers over a satin bikini bottom, with feathers around her neck and ankles. Although she performed her number, called "*Danse Sauvage*," with another dancer, also clad in feathers, all eyes were riveted on her: her whole body seemed to come alive in a way the audience had never seen before, her legs moving with the litheness of a cat, her rear end gyrating in patterns that one critic likened to a hummingbird's. As the dance went on, she seemed possessed, feeding off the crowd's ecstatic reaction. And then there was the look on her face: she was having such fun. She radiated a joy that made her erotic dance oddly innocent, even slightly comic.

By the following day, word had spread: a star was born. Josephine became the heart of the Revue Nègre, and Paris was at her feet. Within a year, her face was on posters everywhere; there were Josephine Baker perfumes, dolls, clothes; fashionable Frenchwomen were slicking their hair back à la Baker, using a product called Bakerfix. They were even trying to darken their skin.

Such sudden fame represented quite a change, for just a few years earlier, Josephine had been a young girl growing up in East St. Louis, one of America's worst slums. She had gone to work at the age of eight, cleaning houses for a white woman who beat her. She had sometimes slept in a rat-infested basement; there had never been heat in the winter. (She had taught herself to dance in her wild fashion to help keep herself warm.) In 1919, Josephine had run away and become a part-time vaudeville performer, landing in New York two years later without money or connections. She had had some success as a clowning chorus girl, providing comic relief with her crossed eyes and screwed-up face, but she hadn't stood out. Then she was invited to Paris. Some other black performers had declined, fearing things might be still worse for them in France than in America, but Josephine jumped at the chance.

Despite her success with the Revue Nègre, Josephine did not delude herself: Parisians were notoriously fickle. She decided to turn the relationship around. First, she refused to be aligned with any club, and developed a reputation for breaking contracts at will, making it clear that she was ready to leave in an instant. Since childhood she had been afraid of dependence on anyone; now no one could take her for granted. This only made impresarios chase her and the public appreciate her the more. Second, she was aware that although black culture had become the vogue, what the French had fallen in love with was a kind of caricature. If that was what it took to be successful, so be it, but Josephine made it clear that she did not take the caricature seriously; instead she reversed it, becoming the ultimate

Frenchwoman of fashion, a caricature not of blackness but of whiteness. Everything was a role to play—the comedienne, the primitive dancer, the ultrastylish Parisian. And everything Josephine did, she did with such a light spirit, such a lack of pretension, that she continued to seduce the jaded French for years. Her funeral, in 1975, was nationally televised, a huge cultural event. She was buried with the kind of pomp normally reserved only for heads of state.

From very early on, Josephine Baker could not stand the feeling of having no control over the world. Yet what could she do in the face of her unpromising circumstances? Some young girls put all their hopes on a husband, but Josephine's father had left her mother soon after she was born, and she saw marriage as something that would only make her more miserable. Her solution was something children often do: confronted with a hopeless environment, she closed herself off in a world of her own making, oblivious to the ugliness around her. This world was filled with dancing, clowning, dreams of great things. Let other people wail and moan; Josephine would smile, remain confident and self-reliant. Almost everyone who met her, from her earliest years to her last, commented on how seductive this quality was. Her refusal to compromise, or to be what she was expected to be, made everything she did seem authentic and natural.

A child loves to play, and to create a little self-contained world. When children are absorbed in make believe, they are hopelessly charming. They infuse their imaginings with such seriousness and feeling. Adult Naturals do something similar, particularly if they are artists: they create their own fantasy world, and live in it as if it were the real one. Fantasy is so much more pleasant than reality, and since most people do not have the power or courage to create such a world, they enjoy being around those who do. Remember: the role you were given in life is not the role you have to accept. You can always live out a role of your own creation, a role that fits your fantasy. Learn to play with your image, never taking it too seriously. The key is to infuse your play with the conviction and feeling of a child, making it seem natural. The more absorbed you seem in your own joy-filled world, the more seductive you become. Do not go halfway: make the fantasy you inhabit as radical and exotic as possible, and you will attract attention like a magnet.

4. It was the Festival of the Cherry Blossom at the Heian court, in late-tenth-century Japan. In the emperor's palace, many of the courtiers were drunk, and others were fast asleep, but the young princess Oborozukiyo, the emperor's sister-in-law, was awake and reciting a poem: "What can compare with a misty moon of spring?" Her voice was smooth and delicate. She moved to the door of her apartment to look at the moon. Then, suddenly, she smelled something sweet, and a hand clutched the sleeve of her robe. "Who are you?" she said, frightened. "There is nothing to be afraid of," came a man's voice, and continued with a poem of his own: "Late in the night we enjoy a misty moon. There is nothing misty about the bond between us." Without another word, the man pulled the princess to him and picked her up, carrying her into a gallery outside her room, sliding the door closed behind him. She was terrified, and tried to call for help. In the darkness she heard him say, a little louder now, "It will do you no good. I am always allowed my way. Just be quiet, if you will, please."

Now the princess recognized the voice, and the scent: it was Genji, the young son of the late emperor's concubine, whose robes bore a distinctive perfume. This calmed her somewhat, since the man was someone she knew, but on the other hand she also knew of his reputation: Genji was the court's most incorrigible seducer, a man who stopped at nothing. He was drunk, it was near dawn, and the watchmen would soon be on their rounds; she did not want to be discovered with him. But then she began to make out the outlines of his face—so pretty, his look so sincere, without a trace of malice. Then came more poems, recited in that charming voice, the words so insinuating. The images he conjured filled her mind, and distracted her from his hands. She could not resist him.

As the light began to rise, Genji got to his feet. He said a few tender words, they exchanged fans, and then he quickly left. The serving women were coming through the emperor's rooms by now, and when they saw Genji scurrying away, the perfume of his robes lingering after him, they smiled, knowing he was up to his usual tricks; but they never imagined he would dare approach the sister of the emperor's wife.

In the days that followed, Oborozukiyo could only think of Genji. She knew he had other mistresses, but when she tried to put him out of her mind, a letter from him would arrive, and she would be back to square one. In truth, she had started the correspondence, haunted by his midnight visit. She had to see him again. Despite the risk of discovery, and the fact that her sister Kokiden, the emperor's wife, hated Genji, she arranged for further trysts in her apartment. But one night an envious courtier found them together. Word reached Kokiden, who naturally was furious. She demanded that Genji be banished from court and the emperor had no choice but to agree.

Genji went far away, and things settled down. Then the emperor died and his son took over. A kind of emptiness had come to the court: the dozens of women whom Genji had seduced could not endure his absence, and flooded him with letters. Even women who had never known him intimately would weep over any relic he had left behind—a robe, for instance, in which his scent still lingered. And the young emperor missed his jocular presence. And the princesses missed the music he had played on the koto. And Oborozukiyo pined for his midnight visits. Finally even Kokiden broke down, realizing that she could not resist him. So Genji was summoned back to the court. And not only was he forgiven, he was given a hero's welcome; the young emperor himself greeted the scoundrel with tears in his eyes.

* * *

The story of Genji's life is told in the eleventh-century novel *The Tale of Genji*, written by Murasaki Shikibu, a woman of the Heian court. The character was most likely based on a real-life man, Fujiwara no Korechika. Indeed another book of the period, *The Pillow Book* of Sei Shonagon, describes an encounter between the female author and Korechika, and reveals his incredible charm and his almost hypnotic effect on women. Genji is a Natural, an undefensive lover, a man who has a lifelong obsession with women but whose appreciation of and affection for them makes him irresistible. As he says to Oborozukiyo in the novel, "I am always allowed my way." This self-belief is half of Genji's charm. Resistance does not make him defensive; he retreats gracefully, reciting a little poetry, and as he leaves, the perfume of his robes trailing behind him, his victim wonders why she has been so afraid, and what she is missing by spurning him, and she finds a way to let him know that the next time things will be different. Genji takes nothing seriously or personally, and at the age of forty, an age at which most men of the eleventh century were already looking old and worn, he still seems like a boy. His seductive powers never leave him.

Human beings are immensely suggestible; their moods will easily spread to the people around them. In fact seduction depends on mimesis, on the conscious creation of a mood or feeling that is then reproduced by the other person. But hesitation and awkwardness are also contagious, and are deadly to seduction. If in a key moment you seem indecisive or self-conscious, the other person will sense that you are thinking of yourself, instead of being overwhelmed by his or her charms. The spell will be broken. As an undefensive lover, though, you produce the opposite effect: your victim might be hesitant or worried, but confronted with someone so sure and natural, he or she will be caught up in the mood. Like dancing with someone you lead effortlessly across the dance floor, it is a skill you can learn. It is a matter of rooting out the fear and awkwardness that have built up in you over the years, of becoming more graceful with your approach, less defensive when others seem to resist. Often people's resistance is a way of testing you, and if you show any awkwardness or hesitation, you not only will fail the test, but you will risk infecting them with your doubts.

Symbol: *The Lamb. So soft and endearing. At two days old the lamb can gambol gracefully; within a week it is playing "Follow the Leader." Its weakness is part of its charm. The Lamb is pure innocence, so innocent we want to possess it, even devour it.*

Dangers

A childish quality can be charming but it can also be irritating; the innocent have no experience of the world, and their sweetness can prove cloying. In Milan Kundera's novel *The Book of Laughter and Forgetting,* the hero dreams that he is trapped on an island with a group of children. Soon their wonderful qualities become intensely annoying to him; after a few days of exposure to them he cannot relate to them at all. The dream turns into a nightmare, and he longs to be back among adults, with real things to do and talk about. Because total childishness can quickly grate, the most seductive Naturals are those who, like Josephine Baker, combine adult experience and wisdom with a childlike manner. It is this mixture of qualities that is most alluring.

Society cannot tolerate too many Naturals. Given a crowd of Cora Pearls or Charlie Chaplins, their charm would quickly wear off. In any case it is usually only artists, or people with abundant leisure time, who can afford to go all the way. The best way to use the Natural character type is in specific situations when a touch of innocence or impishness will help lower your target's defenses. A con man plays dumb to make the other person trust him and feel superior. This kind of feigned naturalness has countless applications in daily life, where nothing is more dangerous than looking smarter than the next person; the Natural pose is the perfect way to disguise your cleverness. But if you are uncontrollably childish and cannot turn it off, you run the risk of seeming pathetic, earning not sympathy but pity and disgust.

Similarly, the seductive traits of the Natural work best in one who is still young enough for them to *seem* natural. They are much harder for an older person to pull off. Cora Pearl did not seem so charming when she was still wearing her pink flouncy dresses in her fifties. The Duke of Buckingham, who seduced everyone in the English court in the 1620s (including the homosexual King James I himself), was wondrously childish in looks and manner; but this became obnoxious and off-putting as he grew older, and he eventually made enough enemies that he ended up being murdered. As you age, then, your natural qualities should suggest more the child's open spirit, less an innocence that will no longer convince anyone.

the Coquette

The ability to delay satisfaction is the ultimate art of seduction—while waiting, the victim is held in thrall. Coquettes are the grand masters of this game, orchestrating a back-and-forth movement between hope and frustration. They bait with the promise of reward—the hope of physical pleasure, happiness, fame by association, power—all of which, however, proves elusive; yet this only makes their targets pursue them the more. Coquettes seem totally self-sufficient: they do not need you, they seem to say, and their narcissism proves devilishly attractive. You want to conquer them but they hold the cards. The strategy of the Coquette is never to offer total satisfaction. Imitate the alternating heat and coolness of the Coquette and you will keep the seduced at your heels.

The Hot and Cold Coquette

In the autumn of 1795, Paris was caught up in a strange giddiness. The Reign of Terror that had followed the French Revolution had ended; the sound of the guillotine was gone. The city breathed a collective sigh of relief, and gave way to wild parties and endless festivals.

The young Napoleon Bonaparte, twenty-six at the time, had no interest in such revelries. He had made a name for himself as a bright, audacious general who had helped quell rebellion in the provinces, but his ambition was boundless and he burned with desire for new conquests. So when, in October of that year, the infamous thirty-three-year-old widow Josephine de Beauharnais visited his offices, he couldn't help but be confused. Josephine was so exotic, and everything about her was languorous and sensual. (She capitalized on her foreignness—she came from the island of Martinique.) On the other hand she had a reputation as a loose woman, and the shy Napoleon believed in marriage. Even so, when Josephine invited him to one of her weekly soirees, he found himself accepting.

There are indeed men who are attached more by resistance than by yielding and who unwittingly prefer a variable sky, now splendid, now black and vexed by lightnings, to love's unclouded blue. Let us not forget that Josephine had to deal with a conqueror and that love resembles war. She did not surrender, she let herself be conquered. Had she been more tender, more attentive, more loving, perhaps Bonaparte would have loved her less.

—Imbert de Saint-Amand, quoted in *The Empress Josephine: Napoleon's Enchantress*, Philip W. Sergeant

At the soiree he felt totally out of his element. All of the city's great writers and wits were there, as well as the few of the nobility who had survived—Josephine herself was a vicomtesse, and had narrowly escaped the guillotine. The women were dazzling, some of them more beautiful than the hostess, but all the men congregated around Josephine, drawn by her graceful presence and queenly manner. Several times she left the men behind and went to Napoleon's side; nothing could have flattered his insecure ego more than such attention.

He began to pay her visits. Sometimes she would ignore him, and he would leave in a fit of anger. Yet the next day a passionate letter would arrive from Josephine, and he would rush to see her. Soon he was spending most of his time with her. Her occasional shows of sadness, her bouts of anger or of tears, only deepened his attachment. In March of 1796, Napoleon married Josephine.

Coquettes know how to please; not how to love, which is why men love them so much.

—Pierre Marivaux

Two days after his wedding, Napoleon left to lead a campaign in northern Italy against the Austrians. "You are the constant object of my thoughts," he wrote to his wife from abroad. "My imagination exhausts itself in guessing what you are doing." His generals saw him distracted: he would leave meetings early, spend hours writing letters, or stare at the miniature of Josephine he wore around his neck. He had been driven to this state by the unbearable distance between them and by a slight coldness he now detected in her—she wrote infrequently, and her letters lacked passion; nor did she join him in Italy. He had to finish his war fast, so that he could return to her side. Engaging the enemy with unusual zeal, he began to make mistakes. "To live for Josephine!" he wrote to her. "I work to get near you; I kill myself to reach you." His letters became more passionate and erotic; a friend of Josephine's who saw them wrote, "The handwriting [was] almost indecipherable, the spelling shaky, the style bizarre and confused . . . . What a position for a woman to find herself in—being the motivating force behind the triumphal march of an entire army."

An absence, the declining of an invitation to dinner, an unintentional, unconscious harshness are of more service than all the cosmetics and fine clothes in the world.

—Marcel Proust

Months went by in which Napoleon begged Josephine to come to Italy and she made endless excuses. But finally she agreed to come, and left Paris for Brescia, where he was headquartered. A near encounter with the enemy along the way, however, forced her to detour to Milan. Napoleon was away from Brescia, in battle; when he returned to find her still absent, he blamed his foe General Würmser and swore revenge. For the next few months he seemed to pursue two targets with equal energy: Würmser and Josephine. His wife was never where she was supposed to be: "I reach Milan, rush to your house, having thrown aside everything in order to clasp you in my arms. You are not there!" Napoleon would turn angry and jealous, but when he finally caught up with Josephine, the slightest of her favors melted his heart. He took long rides with her in a darkened carriage, while his generals fumed—meetings were missed, orders and strategies improvised. "Never," he later wrote to her, "has a woman been in such complete mastery of another's heart." And yet their time together was so short. During a campaign that lasted almost a year, Napoleon spent a mere fifteen nights with his new bride.

*There's also nightly, to the unintiated, \ A peril—not indeed like love or marriage, \ But not the less for this to be depreciated: \ It is—I meant and mean not to disparage \ The show of virtue even in the vitiated— \ It adds an outward grace unto their carriage— \ But to denounce the amphibious sort of harlot, * Couleur de rose, *who's neither white nor scarlet. \ Such is your cold coquette, who can't say say "no," \ And won't say "yes," and keeps you on- and off-ing \ On a lee shore, till it begins to blow— \ Then sees your heart wreck'd with an inward scoffing. \ This works a world of sentimental woe, \ And sends new Werters yearly to the coffin; \ But yet is merely innocent flirtation, \ Not quite adultery, but adulteration.*

—Lord Byron, *The Cold Coquette*

Napoleon later heard rumors that Josephine had taken a lover while he was in Italy. His feelings toward her cooled, and he himself took an endless series of mistresses. Yet Josephine was never really concerned about this threat to her power over her husband; a few tears, some theatrics, a little coldness on her part, and he remained her slave. In 1804, he had her crowned empress, and had she born him a son, she would have remained empress to the end. When Napoleon lay on his deathbed, the last word he uttered was "Josephine."

During the French Revolution, Josephine had come within minutes of losing her head on the guillotine. The experience left her without illusions, and with two goals in mind: to live a life of pleasure, and to find the man who could best supply it. She set her sights on Napoleon early on. He was young, and had a brilliant future. Beneath his calm exterior, Josephine sensed, he was highly emotional and aggressive, but this did not intimidate her—it only revealed his insecurity and weakness. He would be easy to enslave. First, Josephine adapted to his moods, charmed him with her feminine grace, warmed him with her looks and manner. He wanted to possess her. And once she had aroused this desire, her power lay in postponing its satisfaction, withdrawing from him, frustrating him. In fact the torture of

There is a way to represent one's cause and in doing so to treat the audience in such a cool and condescending manner that they are bound to notice one is not doing it to please them. The principle should always be not to make concessions to those who don't have anything to give but who have everything to gain from us. We can wait

the chase gave Napoleon a masochistic pleasure. He yearned to subdue her independent spirit, as if she were an enemy in battle.

People are inherently perverse. An easy conquest has a lower value than a difficult one; we are only really excited by what is denied us, by what we cannot possess in full. Your greatest power in seduction is your ability to turn away, to make others come after you, delaying their satisfaction. Most people miscalculate and surrender too soon, worried that the other person will lose interest, or that giving the other what he or she wants will grant the giver a kind of power. The truth is the opposite: once you satisfy someone, you no longer have the initiative, and you open yourself to the possibility that he or she will lose interest at the slightest whim. Remember: vanity is critical in love. Make your targets afraid that you may be withdrawing, that you may not really be interested, and you arouse their innate insecurity, their fear that as you have gotten to know them they have become less exciting to you. These insecurities are devastating. Then, once you have made them uncertain of you and of themselves, reignite their hope, making them feel desired again. Hot and cold, hot and cold—such coquetry is perversely pleasurable, heightening interest and keeping the initiative on your side. Never be put off by your target's anger; it is a sure sign of enslavement.

She who would long retain her power must use her lover ill.

—Ovid

until they are begging on their knees even if it takes a very long time.

—Sigmund Freud, in a letter to a pupil, quoted in Paul Roazen, *Freud and His Followers*

The Cold Coquette

In 1952, the writer Truman Capote, a recent success in literary and social circles, began to receive an almost daily barrage of fan mail from a young man named Andy Warhol. An illustrator for shoe designers, fashion magazines, and the like, Warhol made pretty, stylized drawings, some of which he sent to Capote, hoping the author would include them in one of his books. Capote did not respond. One day he came home to find Warhol talking to his mother, with whom Capote lived. And Warhol began to telephone almost daily. Finally Capote put an end to all this: "He seemed one of those hopeless people that you just know nothing's ever going to happen to. Just a hopeless, born loser," the writer later said.

Ten years later, Andy Warhol, aspiring artist, had his first one-man show at the Stable Gallery in Manhattan. On the walls were a series of silkscreened paintings based on the Campbell's soup can and the Coca-Cola bottle. At the opening and at the party afterward, Warhol stood to the side, staring blankly, talking little. What a contrast he was to the older generation of artists, the abstract expressionists—mostly hard-drinking womanizers full of bluster and aggression, big talkers who had dominated the art scene for the previous fifteen years. And what a change from the Warhol who had badgered Capote, and art dealers and patrons as well. The critics were both

When her time was come, that nymph most fair brought forth a child with whom one could have fallen in love even in his cradle, and she called him Narcissus. . . . Cephisus's child had reached his sixteenth year, and could be counted as at once boy and man. Many lads and many girls fell in love with him, but his soft young body housed a pride so unyielding that none of those boys or girls dared to touch him. One day, as he was driving timid deer into his nets, he was seen by that talkative nymph who cannot stay silent when another speaks, but yet has not learned to speak first herself. Her name is Echo, and she always answers back. . . . • So when she saw Narcissus wandering through the lonely countryside, Echo fell in love with him and followed secretly in his steps. The more closely she followed, the nearer was the fire which scorched her: just as sulphur, smeared round the tops of torches, is quickly kindled when a flame is brought near it. How often she wished to make flattering overtures to him, to approach him with tender pleas! • The boy, by chance, had wandered away from his faithful band of comrades, and he called out: "Is there anybody here?" Echo answered: "Here!" Narcissus stood still in astonishment, looking round in every direction. . . . He looked behind him, and when no one appeared, cried again: "Why are you avoiding me?" But all he heard were his own words echoed back. Still he persisted, deceived by what he took to be another's voice, and said, "Come here, and let us meet!" Echo answered: "Let us meet!" Never again would she reply more willingly to any sound. To make good her words she came out of the wood and made to throw her arms round the neck she loved: but he fled from her, crying as he did so, "Away with these embraces! I would die before I would have you touch me!" . . . Thus scorned, she concealed herself in the woods, hiding her shamed face in the shelter of the leaves, and ever since that day she dwells in lonely caves. Yet still her love remained firmly rooted in her heart, and was increased by the pain of having been rejected. . . . • Narcissus had played with her affections, treating her as he had previously treated other spirits of the waters and the woods, and his male admirers too. Then one of those he had scorned raised up his hands to heaven and prayed: "May he himself fall in love with another, as we have done with him! May he too be unable to gain his loved one!" Nemesis heard and granted his righteous prayer. . . . • Narcissus, wearied with hunting in the heat of the day, lay down here [by a clear pool]: for he was attracted by the beauty of the place, and by the spring. While he sought to quench his thirst, another thirst grew

baffled and intrigued by the coldness of Warhol's work; they could not figure out how the artist felt about his subjects. What was his position? What was he trying to say? When they asked, he would simply reply, "I just do it because I like it," or, "I love soup." The critics went wild with their interpretations: "An art like Warhol's is necessarily parasitic upon the myths of its time," one wrote; another, "The decision not to decide is a paradox that is equal to an idea which expresses nothing but then gives it dimension." The show was a huge success, establishing Warhol as a leading figure in a new movement, pop art.

In 1963, Warhol rented a large Manhattan loft space that he called the Factory, and that soon became the hub of a large entourage—hangers-on, actors, aspiring artists. Here, particularly at night, Warhol would simply wander about, or stand in a corner. People would gather around him, fight for his attention, throw questions at him, and he would answer, in his noncommittal way. But no one could get close to him, physically or mentally; he would not allow it. At the same time, if he walked by you without giving you his usual "Oh, hi," you were devastated. He hadn't noticed you; perhaps you were on the way out.

Increasingly interested in filmmaking, Warhol cast his friends in his movies. In effect he was offering them a kind of instant celebrity (their "fifteen minutes of fame"—the phrase is Warhol's). Soon people were competing for roles. He groomed women in particular for stardom: Edie Sedgwick, Viva, Nico. Just being around him offered a kind of celebrity by association. The Factory became *the* place to be seen, and stars like Judy Garland and Tennessee Williams would go to parties there, rubbing elbows with Sedgwick, Viva, and the bohemian lower echelons whom Warhol had befriended. People began sending limos to bring him to parties of their own; his presence alone was enough to turn a social evening into a scene—even though he would pass through in near silence, keeping to himself and leaving early.

In 1967, Warhol was asked to lecture at various colleges. He hated to talk, particularly about his own art; "The less something has to say," he felt, "the more perfect it is." But the money was good and Warhol always found it hard to say no. His solution was simple: he asked an actor, Allen Midgette, to impersonate him. Midgette was dark-haired, tan, part Cherokee Indian. He did not resemble Warhol in the least. But Warhol and friends covered his face with powder, sprayed his brown hair silver, gave him dark glasses, and dressed him in Warhol's clothes. Since Midgette knew nothing about art, his answers to students' questions tended to be as short and enigmatic as Warhol's own. The impersonation worked. Warhol may have been an icon, but no one really knew him, and since he often wore dark glasses, even his face was unfamiliar in any detail. The lecture audiences were far enough away to be teased by the thought of his presence, and no one got close enough to catch the deception. He remained elusive.

★ ★ ★

Early on in life, Andy Warhol was plagued by conflicting emotions: he desperately wanted fame, but he was naturally passive and shy. "I've always had a conflict," he later said, "because I'm shy and yet I like to take up a lot of personal space. Mom always said, 'Don't be pushy, but let everyone know you're around.' " At first Warhol tried to make himself more aggressive, straining to please and court. It didn't work. After ten futile years he stopped trying and gave in to his own passivity—only to discover the power that withdrawal commands.

Warhol began this process in his artwork, which changed dramatically in the early 1960s. His new paintings of soup cans, green stamps, and other widely known images did not assault you with meaning; in fact their meaning was totally elusive, which only heightened their fascination. They drew you in by their immediacy, their visual power, their coldness. Having transformed his art, Warhol also transformed himself: like his paintings, he became pure surface. He trained himself to hold himself back, to stop talking.

The world is full of people who try, people who impose themselves aggressively. They may gain temporary victories, but the longer they are around, the more people want to confound them. They leave no space around themselves, and without space there can be no seduction. Cold Coquettes create space by remaining elusive and making others pursue them. Their coolness suggests a comfortable confidence that is exciting to be around, even though it may not actually exist; their silence makes you want to talk. Their self-containment, their appearance of having no need for other people, only makes us want to do things for them, hungry for the slightest sign of recognition and favor. Cold Coquettes may be maddening to deal with—never committing but never saying no, never allowing closeness—but more often than not we find ourselves coming back to them, addicted to the coldness they project. Remember: seduction is a process of drawing people in, making them want to pursue and possess you. Seem distant and people will go mad to win your favor. Humans, like nature, hate a vacuum, and emotional distance and silence make them strain to fill up the empty space with words and heat of their own. Like Warhol, stand back and let them fight over you.

> *[Narcissistic] women have the greatest fascination for men. . . . The charm of a child lies to a great extent in his narcissism, his self-sufficiency and inaccessibility, just as does the charm of certain animals which seem not to concern themselves about us, such as cats. . . . It is as if we envied them their power of retaining a blissful state of mind—an unassailable libido-position which we ourselves have since abandoned.*
>
> —Sigmund Freud

in him, and as he drank, he was enchanted by the beautiful reflection that he saw. He fell in love with an insubstantial hope, mistaking a mere shadow for a real body. Spellbound by his own self, he remained there motionless, with fixed gaze, like a statue carved from Parian marble. . . . Unwittingly, he desired himself, and was himself the object of his own approval, at once seeking and sought, himself kindling the flame with which he burned. How often did he vainly kiss the treacherous pool, how often plunge his arms deep in the waters, as he tried to clasp the neck he saw! But he could not lay hold upon himself. He did not know what he was looking at, but was fired by the sight, and excited by the very illusion that deceived his eyes. Poor foolish boy, why vainly grasp at the fleeting image that eludes you? The thing you are seeking does not exist: only turn aside and you will lose what you love. What you see is but the shadow cast by your reflection; in itself it is nothing. It comes with you, and lasts while you are there; it will go when you go, if go you can. . . . • He laid down his weary head on the green grass, and death closed the eyes which so admired their owner's beauty. Even then, when he was received into the abode of the dead, he kept looking at himself in the waters of the Styx. His sisters, the nymphs of the spring, mourned for him, and cut off their hair in tribute to their brother. The wood nymphs mourned him too, and Echo sang her refrain to their lament. • The pyre, the tossing torches, and the bier, were now being prepared, but his body was nowhere to be found. Instead of his corpse, they discovered a flower with a circle of white petals round a yellow centre.

—OVID, *METAMORPHOSES*, TRANSLATED BY MARY M. INNES

Selfishness is one of the qualities apt to inspire love.

—NATHANIEL HAWTHORNE

The Socrates whom you see has a tendency to fall in love with good-looking young men, and is always in their society and in an ecstasy about them...but once you see beneath the surface you will discover a degree of self-control of which you can hardly form a notion, gentlemen. . . . He spends his whole life pretending and playing with people, and I doubt whether anyone has ever seen the treasures which are revealed when he grows serious and exposes what he keeps inside. • . . . Believing that he was serious in his admiration of my charms, I supposed that a wonderful piece of good luck had befallen me; I should now be able, in return for my favours, to find out all that Socrates knew; for you must know that there was no limit to the pride that I felt in my good looks. With this end in view I sent away my attendant, whom hitherto I had always kept with me in my encounters with Socrates, and left myself alone with him. I must tell you the whole truth; attend carefully, and do you,

Keys to the Character

According to the popular concept, Coquettes are consummate teases, experts at arousing desire through a provocative appearance or an alluring attitude. But the real essence of Coquettes is in fact their ability to trap people emotionally, and to keep their victims in their clutches long after that first titillation of desire. This is the skill that puts them in the ranks of the most effective seducers. Their success may seem somewhat odd, since they are essentially cold and distant creatures; should you ever get to know one well, you will sense his or her inner core of detachment and self-love. It may seem logical that once you become aware of this quality you will see through the Coquette's manipulations and lose interest, but more often we see the opposite. After years of Josephine's coquettish games, Napoleon was well aware of how manipulative she was. Yet this conqueror of kingdoms, this skeptic and cynic, could not leave her.

To understand the peculiar power of the Coquette, you must first understand a critical property of love and desire: the more obviously you pursue a person, the more likely you are to chase them away. Too much attention can be interesting for a while, but it soon grows cloying and finally becomes claustrophobic and frightening. It signals weakness and neediness, an unseductive combination. How often we make this mistake, thinking our persistent presence will reassure. But Coquettes have an inherent understanding of this particular dynamic. Masters of selective withdrawal, they hint at coldness, absenting themselves at times to keep their victim off balance, surprised, intrigued. Their withdrawals make them mysterious, and we build them up in our imaginations. (Familiarity, on the other hand, undermines what we have built.) A bout of distance engages the emotions further; instead of making us angry, it makes us insecure. Perhaps they don't really like us, perhaps we have lost their interest. Once our vanity is at stake, we succumb to the Coquette just to prove we are still desirable. Remember: the essence of the Coquette lies not in the tease and temptation but in the subsequent step back, the emotional withdrawal. That is the key to enslaving desire.

To adopt the power of the Coquette, you must understand one other quality: narcissism. Sigmund Freud characterized the "narcissistic woman" (most often obsessed with her appearance) as the type with the greatest effect on men. As children, he explains, we pass through a narcissistic phase that is immensely pleasurable. Happily self-contained and self-involved, we have little psychic need of other people. Then, slowly, we are socialized and taught to pay attention to others—but we secretly yearn for those blissful early days. The narcissistic woman reminds a man of that period, and makes him envious. Perhaps contact with her will restore that feeling of self-involvement.

A man is also challenged by the female Coquette's independence—he wants to be the one to make her dependent, to burst her bubble. It is far more likely, though, that he will end up becoming her slave, giving her incessant attention to gain her love, and failing. For the narcissistic woman is not emotionally needy; she is self-sufficient. And this is surprisingly seductive. Self-esteem is critical in seduction. (Your attitude toward yourself is read by the other person in subtle and unconscious ways.) Low self-esteem repels, confidence and self-sufficiency attract. The less you seem to need other people, the more likely others will be drawn to you. Understand the importance of this in all relationships and you will find your neediness easier to suppress. But do not confuse self-absorption with seductive narcissism. Talking endlessly about yourself is eminently anti-seductive, revealing not self-sufficiency but insecurity.

The Coquette is traditionally thought of as female, and certainly the strategy was for centuries one of the few weapons women had to engage and enslave a man's desire. One ploy of the Coquette is the withdrawal of sexual favors, and we see women using this trick throughout history: the great seventeenth-century French courtesan Ninon de l'Enclos was desired by all the preeminent men of France, but only attained real power when she made it clear that she would no longer sleep with a man as part of her duty. This drove her admirers to despair, which she knew how to make worse by favoring a man temporarily, granting him access to her body for a few months, then returning him to the pack of the unsatisfied. Queen Elizabeth I of England took coquettishness to the extreme, deliberately arousing the desires of her courtiers but sleeping with none of them.

Long a tool of social power for women, coquettishness was slowly adapted by men, particularly the great seducers of the seventeenth and eighteenth centuries who envied the power of such women. One seventeenth-century seducer, the Duc de Lauzun, was a master at exciting a woman, then suddenly acting aloof. Women went wild over him. Today, coquetry is genderless. In a world that discourages direct confrontation, teasing, coldness, and selective aloofness are a form of indirect power that brilliantly disguises its own aggression.

The Coquette must first and foremost be able to excite the target of his or her attention. The attraction can be sexual, the lure of celebrity, whatever it takes. At the same time, the Coquette sends contrary signals that stimulate contrary responses, plunging the victim into confusion. The eponymous heroine of Marivaux's eighteenth-century French novel *Marianne* is the consummate Coquette. Going to church, she dresses tastefully, but leaves her hair slightly uncombed. In the middle of the service she seems to notice this error and starts to fix it, revealing her bare arm as she does so; such things were not to be seen in an eighteenth-century church, and all male eyes fix on her for that moment. The tension is much more powerful than if she were outside, or were tartily dressed. Remember: obvious flirting will reveal your intentions too clearly. Better to be ambiguous and even contradictory, frustrating at the same time that you stimulate.

The great spiritual leader Jiddu Krishnamurti was an unconscious coquette. Revered by theosophists as their "World Teacher," Krishnamurti was also a dandy. He loved elegant clothing and was devilishly handsome. At the

Socrates, pull me up if anything I say is false. I allowed myself to be alone with him, I say, gentlemen, and I naturally supposed that he would embark on conversation of the type that a lover usually addresses to his darling when they are tête-à-tête, *and I was glad. Nothing of the kind; he spent the day with me in the sort of talk which is habitual with him, and then left me and went away. Next I invited him to train with me in the gymnasium, and I accompanied him there, believing that I should succeed with him now. He took exercise and wrestled with me frequently, with no one else present, but I need hardly say that I was no nearer my goal. Finding that this was no good either, I resolved to make a direct assault on him, and not to give up what I had once undertaken; I felt that I must get to the bottom of the matter. So I invited him to dine with me, behaving just like a lover who has designs upon his favourite. He was in no hurry to accept this invitation, but at last he agreed to come. The first time he came he rose to go away immediately after dinner, and on that occasion I was ashamed and let him go. But I returned to the attack, and this time I kept him in conversation after dinner far into the night, and then, when he wanted to be going, I compelled him to stay, on the plea that it was too late for him to go.* • *So he betook himself to rest, using as a bed the couch on which he had reclined at dinner, next to mine, and there was nobody sleeping in the room but ourselves. • . . . I swear by all the gods in heaven that for anything that had happened between us when I got up after sleeping with Socrates, I might have been sleeping with my father or elder brother. • What do you suppose to have been my state of mind after that? On the one hand I realized that I had been slighted, but on the other I felt a reverence for Socrates' character, his self-control and courage . . . The result was that I could neither bring myself to be angry with him and tear myself away from his society, nor find a way of subduing him to my will. . . . I was utterly disconcerted, and wandered about in a state of enslavement to the man the like of which has never been known.*

—ALCIBIADES, QUOTED IN PLATO, *THE SYMPOSIUM*

same time, he practiced celibacy, and had a horror of being touched. In 1929 he shocked theosophists around the world by proclaiming that he was not a god or even a guru, and did not want any followers. This only heightened his appeal: women fell in love with him in great numbers, and his advisers grew even more devoted. Physically and psychologically, Krishnamurti was sending contrary signals. While preaching a generalized love and acceptance, in his personal life he pushed people away. His attractiveness and his obsession with his appearance might have gained him attention but by themselves would not have made women fall in love with him; his lessons of celibacy and spiritual virtue would have created disciples but not physical love. The combination of these traits, however, both drew people in and frustrated them, a coquettish dynamic that created an emotional and physical attachment to a man who shunned such things. His withdrawal from the world had the effect of only heightening the devotion of his followers.

Coquetry depends on developing a pattern to keep the other person off balance. The strategy is extremely effective. Experiencing a pleasure once, we yearn to repeat it; so the Coquette gives us pleasure, then withdraws it. The alternation of heat and cold is the most common pattern, and has several variations. The eighth-century Chinese Coquette Yang Kuei-Fei totally enslaved the Emperor Ming Huang through a pattern of kindness and bitterness: having charmed him with kindness, she would suddenly get angry, blaming him harshly for the slightest mistake. Unable to live without the pleasure she gave him, the emperor would turn the court upside down to please her when she was angry or upset. Her tears had a similar effect: what had he done, why was she so sad? He eventually ruined himself and his kingdom trying to keep her happy. Tears, anger, and the production of guilt are all the tools of the Coquette. A similar dynamic appears in a lover's quarrel: when a couple fights, then reconciles, the joys of reconciliation only make the attachment stronger. Sadness of any sort is also seductive, particularly if it seems deep-rooted, even spiritual, rather than needy or pathetic—it makes people come to you.

Coquettes are never jealous—that would undermine their image of fundamental self-sufficiency. But they are masters at inciting jealousy: by paying attention to a third party, creating a triangle of desire, they signal to their victims that they may not be that interested. This triangulation is extremely seductive, in social contexts as well as erotic ones. Interested in narcissistic women, Freud was a narcissist himself, and his aloofness drove his disciples crazy. (They even had a name for it—his "god complex.") Behaving like a kind of messiah, too lofty for petty emotions, Freud always maintained a distance between himself and his students, hardly ever inviting them over for dinner, say, and keeping his private life shrouded in mystery. Yet he would occasionally choose an acolyte to confide in—Carl Jung, Otto Rank, Lou Andreas-Salomé. The result was that his disciples went berserk trying to win his favor, to be the one he chose. Their jealousy when he suddenly favored one of them only increased his power over them. People's natural insecurities are heightened in group settings; by maintaining aloofness, Coquettes start a competition to win their favor. If the ability to use third parties to make targets jealous is a critical seductive skill, Sigmund Freud was a grand Coquette.

All of the tactics of the Coquette have been adapted by political leaders to make the public fall in love. While exciting the masses, these leaders remain inwardly detached, which keeps them in control. The political scientist Roberto Michels has even referred to such politicians as Cold Coquettes. Napoleon played the Coquette with the French: after the grand successes of the Italian campaign had made him a beloved hero, he left France to conquer Egypt, knowing that in his absence the government would fall apart, the people would hunger for his return, and their love would serve as the base for an expansion of his power. After exciting the masses with a rousing speech, Mao Zedong would disappear from sight for days on end, making himself an object of cultish worship. And no one was more of a Coquette than Yugoslav leader Josef Tito, who alternated between distance from and emotional identification with his people. All of these political leaders were confirmed narcissists. In times of trouble, when people feel insecure, the effect of such political coquetry is even more powerful. It is important to realize that coquetry is extremely effective on a group, stimulating jealousy, love, and intense devotion. If you play such a role with a group, remember to keep an emotional and physical distance. This will allow you to cry and laugh on command, project self-sufficiency, and with such detachment you will be able play people's emotions like a piano.

Symbol: *The Shadow. It cannot be grasped. Chase your shadow and it will flee; turn your back on it and it will follow you. It is also a person's dark side, the thing that makes them mysterious. After they have given us pleasure, the shadow of their withdrawal makes us yearn for their return, much as clouds make us yearn for the sun.*

Dangers

Coquettes face an obvious danger: they play with volatile emotions. Every time the pendulum swings, love shifts to hate. So they must orchestrate everything carefully. Their absences cannot be too long, their bouts of anger must be quickly followed by smiles. Coquettes can keep their victims emotionally entrapped for a long time, but over months or years the dynamic can begin to prove tiresome. Jiang Qing, later known as Madame Mao, used coquettish skills to capture the heart of Mao Tse-tung, but after ten years the quarreling, the tears and the coolness became intensely irritating, and once irritation proved stronger than love, Mao was able to detach. Josephine, a more brilliant Coquette, was able to adapt, by spending a whole year without playing coy or withdrawing from Napoleon. Timing is everything. On the other hand, though, the Coquette stirs up powerful emotions, and breakups often prove temporary. The Coquette is addictive: after the failure of the social plan Mao called the Great Leap Forward, Madame Mao was able to reestablish her power over her devastated husband.

The Cold Coquette can stimulate a particularly deep hatred. Valerie Solanas was a young woman who fell under Andy Warhol's spell. She had written a play that amused him, and she was given the impression he might turn it into a film. She imagined becoming a celebrity. She also got involved in the feminist movement, and when, in June 1968, it dawned on her that Warhol was toying with her, she directed her growing rage at men on him and shot him three times, nearly killing him. Cold Coquettes may stimulate feelings that are not so much erotic as intellectual, less passion and more fascination. The hatred they can stir up is all the more insidious and dangerous, for it may not be counterbalanced by a deep love. They must realize the limits of the game, and the disturbing effects they can have on less stable people.

the Charmer

Charm is seduction without sex. Charmers are consummate manipulators, masking their cleverness by creating a mood of pleasure and comfort. Their method is simple: they deflect attention from themselves and focus it on their target. They understand your spirit, feel your pain, adapt to your moods. In the presence of a Charmer you feel better about yourself. Charmers do not argue or fight, complain, or pester—what could be more seductive? By drawing you in with their indulgence they make you dependent on them, and their power grows. Learn to cast the Charmer's spell by aiming at people's primary weaknesses: vanity and self-esteem.

The Art of Charm

Sexuality is extremely disruptive. The insecurities and emotions it stirs up can often cut short a relationship that would otherwise be deeper and longer lasting. The Charmer's solution is to fulfill the aspects of sexuality that are so alluring and addictive—the focused attention, the boosted self-esteem, the pleasurable wooing, the understanding (real or illusory)—but subtract the sex itself. It's not that the Charmer represses or discourages sexuality; lurking beneath the surface of any attempt at charm is a sexual tease, a possibility. Charm cannot exist without a hint of sexual tension. It cannot be maintained, however, unless sex is kept at bay or in the background.

Birds are taken with pipes that imitate their own voices, and men with those sayings that are most agreeable to their own opinions.

—Samuel Butler

The word "charm" comes from the Latin *carmen,* a song, but also an incantation tied to the casting of a magical spell. The Charmer implicitly grasps this history, casting a spell by giving people something that holds their attention, that fascinates them. And the secret to capturing people's attention, while lowering their powers of reason, is to strike at the things they have the least control over: their ego, their vanity, and their self-esteem. As Benjamin Disraeli said, "Talk to a man about himself and he will listen for hours." The strategy can never be obvious; subtlety is the Charmer's great skill. If the target is to be kept from seeing through the Charmer's efforts, and from growing suspicious, maybe even tiring of the attention, a light touch is essential. The Charmer is like a beam of light that doesn't play directly on a target but throws a pleasantly diffused glow over it.

Charm can be applied to a group as well as to an individual: a leader can charm the public. The dynamic is similar. The following are the laws of charm, culled from the stories of the most successful charmers in history.

Go with the bough, you'll bend it; \ Use brute force, it'll snap. \ Go with the current: that's how to swim across rivers— \ Fighting upstream's no good. \ Go easy with lions or tigers if you aim to tame them; \ The bull gets inured to the plough by slow degrees. . . . \ So, yield if she shows resistance: \ That way you'll win in the end. Just be sure to play \ The part she allots you. Censure the things she censures, \ Endorse her endorsements, echo her every word, \ Pro or con, and laugh whenever she laughs; remember, \ If she weeps, to weep too: take your cue \ From her every expression. Suppose she's playing a board game, \ Then throw the dice carelessly, move \ Your pieces all wrong. . . . \ Don't jib at a slavish task like holding \ Her mirror:

Make your target the center of attention. Charmers fade into the background; their targets become the subject of their interest. To be a Charmer you have to learn to listen and observe. Let your targets talk, revealing themselves in the process. As you find out more about them—their strengths, and more important their weaknesses—you can individualize your attention, appealing to their specific desires and needs, tailoring your flatteries to their insecurities. By adapting to their spirit and empathizing with their woes, you can make them feel bigger and better, validating their sense of self-worth. Make them the star of the show and they will become addicted to you and grow dependent on you. On a mass level, make gestures of self-sacrifice (no matter how fake) to show the public that you share their pain and are working in their interest, self-interest being the public form of egotism.

slavish or not, such attentions please. . . .

—OVID, *THE ART OF LOVE*, TRANSLATED BY PETER GREEN

Be a source of pleasure. No one wants to hear about your problems and troubles. Listen to your targets' complaints, but more important, distract them from their problems by giving them pleasure. (Do this often enough and they will fall under your spell.) Being lighthearted and fun is always more charming than being serious and critical. An energetic presence is likewise more charming than lethargy, which hints at boredom, an enormous social taboo; and elegance and style will usually win out over vulgarity, since most people like to associate themselves with whatever they think elevated and cultured. In politics, provide illusion and myth rather than reality. Instead of asking people to sacrifice for the greater good, talk of grand moral issues. An appeal that makes people feel good will translate into votes and power.

Bring antagonism into harmony. The court is a cauldron of resentment and envy, where the sourness of a single brooding Cassius can quickly turn into a conspiracy. The Charmer knows how to smooth out conflict. Never stir up antagonisms that will prove immune to your charm; in the face of those who are aggressive, retreat, let them have their little victories. Yielding and indulgence will charm the fight out of any potential enemies. Never criticize people overtly—that will make them insecure, and resistant to change. Plant ideas, insinuate suggestions. Charmed by your diplomatic skills, people will not notice your growing power.

Lull your victims into ease and comfort. Charm is like the hypnotist's trick with the swinging watch: the more relaxed the target, the easier it is to bend him or her to your will. The key to making your victims feel comfortable is to mirror them, adapt to their moods. People are narcissists—they are drawn to those most similar to themselves. Seem to share their values and tastes, to understand their spirit, and they will fall under your spell. This works particularly well if you are an outsider: showing that you share the values of your adopted group or country (you have learned their language, you prefer their customs, etc.) is immensely charming, since for you this preference is a choice, not a question of birth. Never pester or be overly persistent—these uncharming qualities will disrupt the relaxation you need to cast your spell.

Disraeli was asked to dinner, and came in green velvet trousers, with a canary waistcoat, buckle shoes, and lace cuffs. His appearance at first proved disquieting, but on leaving the table the guests remarked to each other that the wittiest talker at the luncheon-party was the man in the yellow waistcoat. Benjamin had made great advances in social conversation since the days of Murray's dinners. Faithful to his method, he noted the stages: "Do not talk too much at present; do not try to talk. But whenever you speak, speak with self-possession. Speak in a subdued tone, and always look at the person whom you are addressing. Before one can engage in general conversation with any effect, there is a certain acquaintance with trifling but amusing subjects which must be first attained. You will soon pick up sufficient by listening and observing. Never argue. In society nothing must be discussed; give only results. If any person differ from you, bow and turn the conversation. In society never think; always be on the watch, or you will miss many opportunities and say many disagreeable things. Talk to women, talk to women as much as you can. This is the best school. This is the way to gain fluency, because you need not care what you say, and had better not be sensible. They, too, will rally you on many points,

Show calm and self-possession in the face of adversity. Adversity and setbacks actually provide the perfect setting for charm. Showing a calm, unruffled exterior in the face of unpleasantness puts people at ease. You seem patient, as if waiting for destiny to deal you a better card—or as if you were confident you could charm the Fates themselves. Never show anger, ill temper, or vengefulness, all disruptive emotions that will make people defensive. In the politics of large groups, welcome adversity as a chance to show the charming qualities of magnanimity and poise. Let others get flustered and upset—the contrast will redound to your favor. Never whine, never complain, never try to justify yourself.

and as they are women you will not be offended. Nothing is of so much importance and of so much use to a young man entering life as to be well criticised by women."

—André Maurois, *Disraeli*, translated by Hamish Miles

You know what charm is: a way of getting the answer yes without having asked any clear question.

—Albert Camus

Make yourself useful. If done subtly, your ability to enhance the lives of others will be devilishly seductive. Your social skills will prove important here: creating a wide network of allies will give you the power to link people up with each other, which will make them feel that by knowing you they can make their lives easier. This is something no one can resist. Follow-through is key: so many people will charm by promising a person great things—a better job, a new contact, a big favor—but if they do not follow through they make enemies instead of friends. Anyone can make a promise; what sets you apart, and makes you charming, is your ability to come through in the end, following up your promise with a definite action. Conversely, if someone does you a favor, show your gratitude concretely. In a world of bluff and smoke, real action and true helpfulness are perhaps the ultimate charm.

A speech that carries its audience along with it and is applauded is often less suggestive simply because it is clear that it sets out to be persuasive. People talking together influence each other in close proximity by means of the tone of voice they adopt and the way they look at each other and not only by the kind of language they use. We are right to call a good conversationalist a charmer in the magical sense of the word.

—Gustave Tarde, *L'Opinion et la Foule*, quoted in Serge Moscovici, *The Age of the Crowd*

Examples of Charmers

1. In the early 1870s, Queen Victoria of England had reached a low point in her life. Her beloved husband, Prince Albert, had died in 1861, leaving her more than grief stricken. In all of her decisions she had relied on his advice; she was too uneducated and inexperienced to do otherwise, or so everyone made her feel. In fact, with Albert's death, political discussions and policy issues had come to bore her to tears. Now Victoria gradually withdrew from the public eye. As a result, the monarchy became less popular and therefore less powerful.

In 1874, the Conservative Party came to power, and its leader, the seventy-year-old Benjamin Disraeli, became prime minister. The protocol of his accession to his seat demanded that he come to the palace for a private meeting with the queen, who was fifty-five at the time. Two more unlikely associates could not be imagined: Disraeli, who was Jewish by birth, had dark skin and exotic features by English standards; as a young man he had been a dandy, his dress bordering on the flamboyant, and he had written popular novels that were romantic or even Gothic in style. The queen, on the other hand, was dour and stubborn, formal in manner and simple in

Wax, a substance naturally hard and brittle, can be made soft by the application of a little warmth, so that it will take any shape you please. In the same way, by being polite and friendly, you can make people pliable and obliging, even though they are apt to be crabbed and malevolent. Hence politeness is to human nature what warmth is to wax.

—Arthur Schopenhauer, *Counsels and Maxims*, translated by T. Bailey Saunders

Never explain. Never complain.

—Benjamin Disraeli

taste. To please her, Disraeli was advised, he should curb his natural elegance; but he disregarded what everyone had told him and appeared before her as a gallant prince, falling to one knee, taking her hand, and kissing it, saying, "I plight my troth to the kindest of mistresses." Disraeli pledged that his work now was to realize Victoria's dreams. He praised her qualities so fulsomely that she blushed; yet strangely enough, she did not find him comical or offensive, but came out of the encounter smiling. Perhaps she should give this strange man a chance, she thought, and she waited to see what he would do next.

Victoria soon began receiving reports from Disraeli—on parliamentary debates, policy issues, and so forth—that were unlike anything other ministers had written. Addressing her as the "Faery Queen," and giving the monarchy's various enemies all kinds of villainous code names, he filled his notes with gossip. In a note about a new cabinet member, Disraeli wrote, "He is more than six feet four inches in stature; like St. Peter's at Rome no one is at first aware of his dimensions. But he has the sagacity of the elephant as well as its form." The minister's blithe, informal spirit bordered on disrespect, but the queen was enchanted. She read his reports voraciously, and almost without her realizing it, her interest in politics was rekindled.

At the start of their relationship, Disraeli sent the queen all of his novels as a gift. She in return presented him with the one book she had written, *Journal of Our Life in the Highlands*. From then on he would toss out in his letters and conversations with her the phrase, "We authors." The queen would beam with pride. She would overhear him praising her to others—her ideas, common sense, and feminine instincts, he said, made her the equal of Elizabeth I. He rarely disagreed with her. At meetings with other ministers, he would suddenly turn and ask her for advice. In 1875, when Disraeli managed to finagle the purchase of the Suez Canal from the debt-ridden khedive of Egypt, he presented his accomplishment to the queen as if it were a realization of her own ideas about expanding the British Empire. She did not realize the cause, but her confidence was growing by leaps and bounds.

Victoria once sent flowers to her prime minister. He later returned the favor, sending primroses, a flower so ordinary that some recipients might have been insulted; but his gift came with a note: "Of all the flowers, the one that retains its beauty longest, is sweet primrose." Disraeli was enveloping Victoria in a fantasy atmosphere in which everything was a metaphor, and the simplicity of the flower of course symbolized the queen—and also the relationship between the two leaders. Victoria fell for the bait; primroses were soon her favorite flower. In fact everything Disraeli did now met with her approval. She allowed him to sit in her presence, an unheard-of privilege. The two began to exchange valentines every February. The queen would ask people what Disraeli had said at a party; when he paid a little too much attention to Empress Augusta of Germany, she grew jealous. The courtiers wondered what had happened to the stubborn, formal woman they had known—she was acting like an infatuated girl.

In 1876, Disraeli steered through Parliament a bill declaring Queen Victoria a "Queen-Empress." The queen was beside herself with joy. Out of gratitude and certainly love, she elevated this Jewish dandy and novelist to the peerage, making him Earl of Beaconsfield, the realization of a lifelong dream.

Disraeli knew how deceptive appearances can be: people were always judging him by his face and by his clothes, and he had learned never to do the same to them. So he was not deceived by Queen Victoria's dour, sober exterior. Beneath it, he sensed, was a woman who yearned for a man to appeal to her feminine side, a woman who was affectionate, warm, even sexual. The extent to which this side of Victoria had been repressed merely revealed the strength of the feelings he would stir once he melted her reserve.

Disraeli's approach was to appeal to two aspects of Victoria's personality that other people had squashed: her confidence and her sexuality. He was a master at flattering a person's ego. As one English princess remarked, "When I left the dining room after sitting next to Mr. Gladstone, I thought he was the cleverest man in England. But after sitting next to Mr. Disraeli, I thought I was the cleverest woman in England." Disraeli worked his magic with a delicate touch, insinuating an atmosphere of amusement and relaxation, particularly in relation to politics. Once the queen's guard was down, he made that mood a little warmer, a little more suggestive, subtly sexual—though of course without overt flirtation. Disraeli made Victoria feel desirable as a woman and gifted as a monarch. How could she resist? How could she deny him anything?

Our personalities are often molded by how we are treated: if a parent or spouse is defensive or argumentative in dealing with us, we tend to respond the same way. Never mistake people's exterior characteristics for reality, for the character they show on the surface may be merely a reflection of the people with whom they have been most in contact, or a front disguising its own opposite. A gruff exterior may hide a person dying for warmth; a repressed, sober-looking type may actually be struggling to conceal uncontrollable emotions. That is the key to charm—feeding what has been repressed or denied.

By indulging the queen, by making himself a source of pleasure, Disraeli was able to soften a woman who had grown hard and cantankerous. Indulgence is a powerful tool of seduction: it is hard to be angry or defensive with someone who seems to agree with your opinions and tastes. Charmers may appear to be weaker than their targets but in the end they are the more powerful side because they have stolen the ability to resist.

2. In 1971, the American financier and Democratic Party power-player Averell Harriman saw his life drawing to a close. He was seventy-nine, his wife of many years, Marie, had just died, and with the Democrats out of office his political career seemed over. Feeling old and depressed, he resigned himself to spending his last years with his grandchildren in quiet retirement.

A few months after Marie's death, Harriman was talked into attending a Washington party. There he met an old friend, Pamela Churchill, whom he had known during World War II, in London, where he had been sent as a personal envoy of President Franklin D. Roosevelt. She was twenty-one at the time, and was the wife of Winston Churchill's son Randolph. There had certainly been more beautiful women in the city, but none had been more pleasant to be around: she was so attentive, listening to his problems, befriending his daughter (they were the same age), and calming him whenever he saw her. Marie had remained in the States, and Randolph was in the army, so while bombs rained on London Averell and Pamela had begun an affair. And in the many years since the war, she had kept in touch with him: he knew about the breakup of her marriage, and about her endless series of affairs with Europe's wealthiest playboys. Yet he had not seen her since his return to America, and to his wife. What a strange coincidence to run into her at this particular moment in his life.

At the party Pamela pulled Harriman out of his shell, laughing at his jokes and getting him to talk about London in the glory days of the war. He felt his old power returning—it was as if *he* were charming *her*. A few days later she dropped in on him at one of his weekend homes. Harriman was one of the wealthiest men in the world, but was no lavish spender; he and Marie had lived a Spartan life. Pamela made no comment, but when she invited him to her own home, he could not help but notice the brightness and vibrancy of her life—flowers everywhere, beautiful linens on the bed, wonderful meals (she seemed to know all of his favorite foods). He had heard of her reputation as a courtesan and understood the lure of his wealth, yet being around her was invigorating, and eight weeks after that party, he married her.

Pamela did not stop there. She persuaded her husband to donate the art that Marie had collected to the National Gallery. She got him to part with some of his money—a trust fund for her son Winston, new houses, constant redecorations. Her approach was subtle and patient; she made him somehow feel good about giving her what she wanted. Within a few years, hardly any traces of Marie remained in their life. Harriman spent less time with his children and grandchildren. He seemed to be going through a second youth.

In Washington, politicians and their wives viewed Pamela with suspicion. They saw through her, and were immune to her charm, or so they thought. Yet they always came to the frequent parties she hosted, justifying themselves with the thought that powerful people would be there. Everything at these parties was calibrated to create a relaxed, intimate atmosphere. No one felt ignored: the least important people would find themselves talking to Pamela, opening up to that attentive look of hers. She made them feel powerful and respected. Afterward she would send them a personal note or gift, often referring to something they had mentioned in conversation. The wives who had called her a courtesan and worse slowly changed their minds. The men found her not only beguiling but useful—her worldwide contacts were invaluable. She could put them in touch with exactly the right person without them even having to ask. The Harrimans' parties soon evolved into fundraising events for the Democratic Party. Put at their ease, feeling elevated by the aristocratic atmosphere Pamela created and the sense of importance she gave them, visitors would empty their wallets without realizing quite why. This, of course, was exactly what all the men in her life had done.

In 1986, Averell Harriman died. By then Pamela was powerful and wealthy enough that she no longer needed a man. In 1993, she was named the U.S. ambassador to France, and easily transferred her personal and social charm into the world of political diplomacy. She was still working when she died, in 1997.

We often recognize Charmers as such; we sense their cleverness. (Surely Harriman must have realized that his meeting with Pamela Churchill in 1971 was no coincidence.) Nevertheless, we fall under their spell. The reason is simple: the feeling that Charmers provide is so rare as to be worth the price we pay.

The world is full of self-absorbed people. In their presence, we know that everything in our relationship with them is directed toward themselves—their insecurities, their neediness, their hunger for attention. That reinforces our own egocentric tendencies; we protectively close ourselves up. It is a syndrome that only makes us the more helpless with Charmers. First, they don't talk much about themselves, which heightens their mystery and disguises their limitations. Second, they seem to be interested in us, and their interest is so delightfully focused that we relax and open up to them. Finally, Charmers are pleasant to be around. They have none of most people's ugly qualities—nagging, complaining, self-assertion. They seem to know what pleases. Theirs is a diffused warmth; union without sex. (You may think a geisha is sexual as well as charming; her power, however, lies not in the sexual favors she provides but in her rare self-effacing attentiveness.) Inevitably, we become addicted, and dependent. And dependence is the source of the Charmer's power.

People who are physically beautiful, and who play on their beauty to create a sexually charged presence, have little power in the end; the bloom of youth fades, there is always someone younger and more beautiful, and in any case people tire of beauty without social grace. But they never tire of feeling their self-worth validated. Learn the power you can wield by making the other person feel like the star. The key is to diffuse your sexual presence: create a vaguer, more beguiling sense of excitement through a generalized flirtation, a socialized sexuality that is constant, addictive, and never totally satisfied.

3. In December of 1936, Chiang Kai-shek, leader of the Chinese Nationalists, was captured by a group of his own soldiers who were angry with his policies: instead of fighting the Japanese, who had just invaded China, he was continuing his civil war against the Communist armies of Mao Zedong. The soldiers saw no threat in Mao—Chiang had almost annhilated the Communists. In fact, they believed he should join forces with Mao against the common enemy—it was the only patriotic thing to do. The soldiers thought by capturing him they could compel Chiang to change his mind, but he was a stubborn man. Since Chiang was the main impediment to a unified war against the Japanese, the soldiers contemplated having him executed, or turned over to the Communists.

As Chiang lay in prison, he could only imagine the worst. Several days later he received a visit from Zhou Enlai—a former friend and now a leading Communist. Politely and respectfully, Zhou argued for a united front: Communists and Nationalists against the Japanese. Chiang could not begin to hear such talk; he hated the Communists with a passion, and became hopelessly emotional. To sign an agreement with the Communists in these circumstances, he yelled, would be humiliating, and would lose me all honor among my own army. It's out of the question. Kill me if you must.

Zhou listened, smiled, said barely a word. As Chiang's rant ended he told the Nationalist general that a concern for honor was something he understood, but that the honorable thing for them to do was actually to forget their differences and fight the invader. Chiang could lead both armies. Finally, Zhou said that under no circumstances would he allow his fellow Communists, or anyone for that matter, to execute such a great man as Chiang Kai-shek. The Nationalist leader was stunned and moved.

The next day, Chiang was escorted out of prison by Communist guards, transferred to one of his own army's planes, and sent back to his own headquarters. Apparently Zhou had executed this policy on his own, for when word of it reached the other Communist leaders, they were outraged: Zhou should have forced Chiang to fight the Japanese, or else should have ordered his execution—to release him without concessions was the height of pusillanimity, and Zhou would pay. Zhou said nothing and waited. A few months later, Chiang signed an agreement to halt the civil war and join with the Communists against the Japanese. He seemed to have come to his decision on his own, and his army respected it—they could not doubt his motives.

Working together, the Nationalists and the Communists expelled the Japanese from China. But the Communists, whom Chiang had previously almost destroyed, took advantage of this period of collaboration to regain strength. Once the Japanese had left, they turned on the Nationalists, who, in 1949, were forced to evacuate mainland China for the island of Formosa, now Taiwan.

Now Mao paid a visit to the Soviet Union. China was in terrible shape and in desperate need of assistance, but Stalin was wary of the Chinese, and lectured Mao about the many mistakes he had made. Mao argued back.

Stalin decided to teach the young upstart a lesson; he would give China nothing. Tempers rose. Mao sent urgently for Zhou Enlai who arrived the next day and went right to work.

In the long negotiating sessions, Zhou made a show of enjoying his hosts' vodka. He never argued, and in fact agreed that the Chinese had made many mistakes, had much to learn from the more experienced Soviets: "Comrade Stalin," he said, "we are the first large Asian country to join the socialist camp under *your* guidance." Zhou had come prepared with all kinds of neatly drawn diagrams and charts, knowing the Russians loved such things. Stalin warmed up to him. The negotiations proceeded, and a few days after Zhou's arrival, the two parties signed a treaty of mutual aid—a treaty far more useful to the Chinese than to the Soviets.

In 1959, China was again in deep trouble. Mao's Great Leap Forward, an attempt to spark an overnight industrial revolution in China, had been a devastating failure. The people were angry: they were starving while Beijing bureaucrats lived well. Many Beijing officials, Zhou among them, returned to their native towns to try to bring order. Most of them managed by bribes—by promising all kinds of favors—but Zhou proceeded differently: he visited his ancestral graveyard, where generations of his family were buried, and ordered that the tombstones be removed and the coffins buried deeper. Now the land could be farmed for food. In Confucian terms (and Zhou was an obedient Confucian), this was sacrilege, but everyone knew what it meant: Zhou was willing to suffer personally. Everyone had to sacrifice, even the leaders. His gesture had immense symbolic impact.

When Zhou died, in 1976, an unofficial and unorganized outpouring of public grief caught the government by surprise. They could not understand how a man who had worked behind the scenes, and had shunned the adoration of the masses, could have won such affection.

The capture of Chiang Kai-shek was a turning point in the civil war. To execute him might have been disastrous: it had been Chiang who had held the Nationalist army together, and without him it could have broken up into factions, allowing the Japanese to overrun the country. To force him to sign an agreement would have not helped either: he would have lost face before his army, would never have honored the agreement, and would have done everything he could to avenge his humiliation. Zhou knew that to execute or compel a captive will only embolden your enemy, and will have repercussions you cannot control. Charm, on the other hand, is a manipulative weapon that disguises its own manipulativeness, letting you gain a victory without stirring the desire for revenge.

Zhou worked on Chiang perfectly, paying him respect, playing the inferior, letting him pass from the fear of execution to the relief of unexpected release. The general was allowed to leave with his dignity intact. Zhou knew all this would soften him up, planting the seed of the idea that perhaps the Communists were not so bad after all, and that he could change his mind about them without looking weak, particularly if he did so independently rather than while he was in prison. Zhou applied the same philosophy to every situation: play the inferior, unthreatening and humble. What will this matter if in the end you get what you want: time to recover from a civil war, a treaty, the good will of the masses.

Time is the greatest weapon you have. Patiently keep in mind a long-term goal and neither person nor army can resist you. And charm is the best way of playing for time, of widening your options in any situation. Through charm you can seduce your enemy into backing off, giving you the psychological space to plot an effective counterstrategy. The key is to make other people emotional while you remain detached. They may feel grateful, happy, moved, arrogant—it doesn't matter, as long as they feel. An emotional person is a distracted person. Give them what they want, appeal to their self-interest, make them feel superior to you. When a baby has grabbed a sharp knife, do not try to grab it back; instead, stay calm, offer candy, and the baby will drop the knife to pick up the tempting morsel you offer.

4. In 1761, Empress Elizabeth of Russia died, and her nephew ascended to the throne as Czar Peter III. Peter had always been a little boy at heart—he played with toy soldiers long past the appropriate age—and now, as czar, he could finally do whatever he pleased and the world be damned. Peter concluded a treaty with Frederick the Great that was highly favorable to the foreign ruler (Peter adored Frederick, and particularly the disciplined way his Prussian soldiers marched). This was a practical debacle, but in matters of emotion and etiquette, Peter was even more offensive: he refused to properly mourn his aunt the empress, resuming his war games and parties a few days after the funeral. What a contrast he was to his wife, Catherine. She was respectful during the funeral, was still wearing black months later, and could be seen at all hours beside Elizabeth's tomb, praying and crying. She was not even Russian, but a German princess who had come east to marry Peter in 1745 without speaking a word of the language. Even the lowest peasant knew that Catherine had converted to the Russian Orthodox Church, and had learned to speak Russian with incredible speed, and beautifully. At heart, they thought, she was more Russian than all of those fops in the court.

During these difficult months, while Peter offended almost everyone in the country, Catherine discreetly kept a lover, Gregory Orlov, a lieutenant in the guards. It was through Orlov that word spread of her piety, her patriotism, her worthiness for rule; how much better to follow such a woman than to serve Peter. Late into the night, Catherine and Orlov would talk, and he would tell her the army was behind her and would urge her to stage a coup. She would listen attentively, but would always reply that this was not the time for such things. Orlov wondered to himself: perhaps she was too gentle and passive for such a great step.

Peter's regime was repressive, and the arrests and executions piled up. He also grew more abusive toward his wife, threatening to divorce her and marry his mistress. One drunken evening, driven to distraction by Catherine's silence and his inability to provoke her, he ordered her arrest. The news spread fast, and Orlov hurried to warn Catherine that she would be imprisoned or executed unless she acted fast. This time Catherine did not argue; she put on her simplest mourning gown, left her hair half undone, followed Orlov to a waiting carriage, and rushed to the army barracks. Here the soldiers fell to the ground, kissing the hem of her dress—they had heard so much about her but had never seen her in person, and she seemed to them like a statue of the Madonna come to life. They gave her an army uniform, marveling at how beautiful she looked in men's clothes, and set off under Orlov's command for the Winter Palace. The procession grew as it passed through the streets of St. Petersburg. Everyone applauded Catherine, everyone felt that Peter should be dethroned. Soon priests arrived to give Catherine their blessing, making the people even more excited. And through it all, she was silent and dignified, as if all were in the hands of fate.

When news reached Peter of this peaceful rebellion, he grew hysterical, and agreed to abdicate that very night. Catherine became empress without a single battle or even a single gunshot.

As a child, Catherine was intelligent and spirited. Since her mother had wanted a daughter who was obedient rather than dazzling, and who would therefore make a better match, the child was subjected to a constant barrage of criticism, against which she developed a defense: she learned to seem to defer to other people totally as a way to neutralize their aggression. If she was patient and did not force the issue, instead of attacking her they would fall under her spell.

When Catherine came to Russia—at the age of sixteen, without a friend or ally in the country—she applied the skills she had learned in dealing with her difficult mother. In the face of all the court monsters—the imposing Empress Elizabeth, her own infantile husband, the endless schemers and betrayers—she curtseyed, deferred, waited, and charmed. She had long wanted to rule as empress, and knew how hopeless her husband was. But what good would it do to seize power violently, laying a claim that some would certainly see as illegitimate, and then have to worry endlessly that she would be dethroned in turn? No, the moment had to be ripe, and she had to make the people carry her into power. It was a feminine style of revolution: by being passive and patient, Catherine suggested that she had no interest in power. The effect was soothing—charming.

There will always be difficult people for us to face—the chronically insecure, the hopelessly stubborn, the hysterical complainers. Your ability to disarm these people will prove an invaluable skill. You do have to be careful, though: if you are passive they will run all over you; if assertive you will make their monstrous qualities worse. Seduction and charm are the most effective counterweapons. Outwardly, be gracious. Adapt to their every mood. Enter their spirit. Inwardly, calculate and wait: your surrender is a strategy, not a way of life. When the time comes, and it inevitably will, the tables will turn. Their aggression will land them in trouble, and that will put you in a position to rescue them, regaining superiority. (You could also decide that you had had enough, and consign them to oblivion.) Your charm has prevented them from foreseeing this or growing suspicious. A whole revolution can be enacted without a single act of violence, simply by waiting for the apple to ripen and fall.

Symbol: *The Mirror. Your spirit holds a mirror up to others. When they see you they see themselves: their values, their tastes, even their flaws. Their lifelong love affair with their own image is comfortable and hypnotic; so feed it. No one ever sees what is behind the mirror.*

Dangers

There are those who are immune to a Charmer; particularly cynics, and confident types who do not need validation. These people tend to view Charmers as slippery and deceitful, and they can make problems for you. The solution is to do what most Charmers do by nature: befriend and charm as many people as possible. Secure your power through numbers and you will not have to worry about the few you cannot seduce. Catherine the Great's kindness to everyone she met created a vast amount of good will that paid off later. Also, it is sometimes charming to reveal a strategic flaw. There is one person you dislike? Confess it openly, do not try to charm such an enemy, and people will think you more human, less slippery. Disraeli had such a scapegoat with his great nemesis, William Gladstone.

The dangers of political charm are harder to handle: your conciliatory, shifting, flexible approach to politics will make enemies out of everyone who is a rigid believer in a cause. Social seducers such as Bill Clinton and Henry Kissinger could often win over the most hardened opponent with their personal charm, but they could not be everywhere at once. Many members of the English Parliament thought Disraeli a shifty conniver; in person his engaging manner could dispel such feelings, but he could not address the entire Parliament one-on-one. In difficult times, when people yearn for something substantial and firm, the political charmer may be in danger.

As Catherine the Great proved, timing is everything. Charmers must know when to hibernate and when the times are ripe for their persuasive powers. Known for their flexibility, they should sometimes be flexible enough to act inflexibly. Zhou Enlai, the consummate chameleon, could play the hard-core Communist when it suited him. Never become the slave to your own powers of charm; keep it under control, something you can turn off and on at will.

the Charismatic

Charisma is a presence that excites us. It comes from an inner quality—self-confidence, sexual energy, sense of purpose, contentment—that most people lack and want. This quality radiates outward, permeating the gestures of Charismatics, making them seem extraordinary and superior, and making us imagine there is more to them than meets the eye: they are gods, saints, stars. Charismatics can learn to heighten their charisma with a piercing gaze, fiery oratory, an air of mystery. They can seduce on a grand scale. Learn to create the charismatic illusion by radiating intensity while remaining detached.

Charisma and Seduction

Charisma is seduction on a mass level. Charismatics make crowds of people fall in love with them, then lead them along. The process of making them fall in love is simple and follows a path similar to that of a one-on-one seduction. Charismatics have certain qualities that are powerfully attractive and that make them stand out. This could be their self-belief, their boldness, their serenity. They keep the source of these qualities mysterious. They do not explain where their confidence or contentment comes from, but it can be felt by everyone; it radiates outward, without the appearance of conscious effort. The face of the Charismatic is usually animated, full of energy, desire, alertness—the look of a lover, one that is instantly appealing, even vaguely sexual. We happily follow Charismatics because we like to be led, particularly by people who promise adventure or prosperity. We lose ourselves in their cause, become emotionally attached to them, feel more alive by believing in them—we fall in love. Charisma plays on repressed sexuality, creates an erotic charge. Yet the origins of the word lie not in sexuality but in religion, and religion remains deeply embedded in modern charisma.

"Charisma" shall be understood to refer to an extraordinary quality of a person, regardless of whether this quality is actual, alleged or presumed. "Charismatic authority," hence, shall refer to a rule over men, whether predominately external or predominately internal, to which the governed submit because of their belief in the extraordinary quality of the specific person.

—Max Weber, from *Max Weber: Essays in Sociology*, edited by Hans Gerth and C.Wright Mills

Thousands of years ago, people believed in gods and spirits, but few could ever say that they had witnessed a miracle, a physical demonstration of divine power. A man, however, who seemed possessed by a divine spirit—speaking in tongues, ecstatic raptures, the expression of intense visions—would stand out as one whom the gods had singled out. And this man, a priest or a prophet, gained great power over others. What made the Hebrews believe in Moses, follow him out of Egypt, and remain loyal to him despite their endless wandering in the desert? The look in his eye, his inspired and inspiring words, the face that literally glowed when he came down from Mount Sinai—all these things gave him the appearance of having direct communication with God, and were the source of his authority. And these were what was meant by "charisma," a Greek word referring to prophets and to Christ himself. In early Christianity, charisma was a gift or talent vouchsafed by God's grace and revealing His presence. Most of the great religions were founded by a Charismatic, a person who physically displayed the signs of God's favor.

Over the years, the world became more rational. Eventually people came to hold power not by divine right but because they won votes, or proved their competence. The great early-twentieth-century German sociologist Max Weber, however, noticed that despite our supposed progress, there were more Charismatics than ever. What characterized a modern Charismatic, according to Weber, was the appearance of an extraordinary quality in their character, the equivalent of a sign of God's favor. How else to explain the power of a Robespierre or a Lenin? More than anything it was the force of their magnetic personalities that made these men stand out and was the source of their power. They did not speak of God but of a great cause, visions of a future society. Their appeal was emotional; they seemed possessed. And their audiences reacted as euphorically as earlier audiences had to a prophet. When Lenin died, in 1924, a cult formed around his memory, transforming the communist leader into a deity.

Today, anyone who has presence, who attracts attention when he or she enters a room, is said to possess charisma. But even these less-exalted types reveal a trace of the quality suggested by the word's original meaning. Their charisma is mysterious and inexplicable, never obvious. They have an unusual confidence. They have a gift—often a smoothness with language—that makes them stand out from the crowd. They express a vision. We may not realize it, but in their presence we have a kind of religious experience: we believe in these people, without having any rational evidence for doing so. When trying to concoct an effect of charisma, never forget the religious source of its power. You must radiate an inward quality that has a saintly or spiritual edge to it. Your eyes must glow with the fire of a prophet. Your charisma must seem natural, as if it came from something mysteriously beyond your control, a gift of the gods. In our rational, disenchanted world, people crave a religious experience, particularly on a group level. Any sign of charisma plays to this desire to believe in something. And there is nothing more seductive than giving people something to believe in and follow.

Charisma must seem mystical, but that does not mean you cannot learn certain tricks that will enhance the charisma you already possess, or will give you the outward appearance of it. The following are basic qualities that will help create the illusion of charisma:

And the Lord said to Moses, "Write these words; in accordance with these words I have made a covenant with you and with Israel." And he was there with the Lord forty days and forty nights; he neither ate bread nor drank water. And he wrote upon the tables the words of the covenant, the ten commandments. When Moses came down from Mount Sinai, with the two tables of the testimony in his hand as he came down from the mountain, Moses did not know that the skin of his face shone because he had been talking with God. And when Aaron and all the people of Israel saw Moses, behold, the skin of his face shone, and they were afraid to come near him. But Moses called to them; and Aaron and all the leaders of the congregation returned to him, and Moses talked with them. And afterward all the people of Israel came near, and he gave them in commandment all that the Lord had spoken with him in Mount Sinai. And when Moses had finished speaking with them, he put a veil on his face; but whenever Moses went in before the Lord to speak with him, he took the veil off, until he came out; and when he came out, and told the people of Israel what he was commanded, the people of Israel saw the face of Moses, that the skin of Moses's face shone; and Moses would put the veil upon his face again, until he went in to speak with him.

—EXODUS 34:27 OLD TESTAMENT

Purpose. If people believe you have a plan, that you know where you are going, they will follow you instinctively. The direction does not matter: pick a cause, an ideal, a vision and show that you will not sway from your goal. People will imagine that your confidence comes from something real—just as the ancient Hebrews believed Moses was in communion with God, simply because he showed the outward signs.

Purposefulness is doubly charismatic in times of trouble. Since most people hesitate before taking bold action (even when action is what is required), single-minded self-assurance will make you the focus of attention. People will believe in you through the simple force of your character. When Franklin Delano Roosevelt came to power amidst the Depression, much of the public had little faith he could turn things around. But in his first few months in office he displayed such confidence, such decisiveness and clarity in dealing with the country's many problems, that the public began to see him as their savior, someone with intense charisma.

That devil of a man exercises a fascination on me that I cannot explain even to myself, and in such a degree that, though I fear neither God nor devil, when I am in his presence I am ready to tremble like a child, and he could make me go through the eye of a needle to throw myself into the fire.

—General Vandamme, on Napoleon Bonaparte

Mystery. Mystery lies at charisma's heart, but it is a particular kind of mystery—a mystery expressed by contradiction. The Charismatic may be both proletarian and aristocratic (Mao Zedong), both cruel and kind (Peter the Great), both excitable and icily detached (Charles de Gaulle), both intimate and distant (Sigmund Freud). Since most people are predictable, the effect of these contradictions is devastatingly charismatic. They make you hard to fathom, add richness to your character, make people talk about you. It is often better to reveal your contradictions slowly and subtly—if you throw them out one on top of the other, people may think you have an erratic personality. Show your mysteriousness gradually and word will spread. You must also keep people at arm's length, to keep them from figuring you out.

Another aspect of mystery is a hint of the uncanny. The appearance of prophetic or psychic gifts will add to your aura. Predict things authoritatively and people will often imagine that what you have said has come true.

[The masses] have never thirsted after truth. They demand illusions, and cannot do without them. They constantly give what is unreal precedence over what is real; they are almost as strongly influenced by what is untrue as by what is true. They have an evident tendency not to distinguish between the two.

—Sigmund Freud, *The Standard Edition of the Complete Psychological Works of Sigmund Freud*, volume 18

Saintliness. Most of us must compromise constantly to survive; saints do not. They must live out their ideals without caring about the consequences. The saintly effect bestows charisma.

Saintliness goes far beyond religion: politicians as disparate as George Washington and Lenin won saintly reputations by living simply, despite their power—by matching their political values to their personal lives. Both men were virtually deified after they died. Albert Einstein too had a saintly aura—childlike, unwilling to compromise, lost in his own world. The key is that you must already have some deeply held values; that part cannot be faked, at least not without risking accusations of charlatanry that will destroy your charisma in the long run. The next step is to show, as simply and subtly as possible, that you live what you believe. Finally, the appearance of being mild and unassuming can eventually turn into charisma, as long as you seem completely comfortable with it. The source of Harry Truman's charisma, and even of Abraham Lincoln's, was to appear to be an Everyman.

Eloquence. A Charismatic relies on the power of words. The reason is simple: words are the quickest way to create emotional disturbance. They can uplift, elevate, stir anger, without referring to anything real. During the Spanish Civil War, Dolores Gómez Ibarruri, known as La Pasionaria, gave pro-Communist speeches that were so emotionally powerful as to determine several key moments in the war. To bring off this kind of eloquence, it helps if the speaker is as emotional, as caught up in words, as the audience is. Yet eloquence can be learned: the devices La Pasionaria used—

catchwords, slogans, rhythmic repetitions, phrases for the audience to repeat—can easily be acquired. Roosevelt, a calm, patrician type, was able to make himself a dynamic speaker, both through his style of delivery, which was slow and hypnotic, and through his brilliant use of imagery, alliteration, and biblical rhetoric. The crowds at his rallies were often moved to tears. The slow, authoritative style is often more effective than passion in the long run, for it is more subtly spellbinding, and less tiring.

Theatricality. A Charismatic is larger than life, has extra presence. Actors have studied this kind of presence for centuries; they know how to stand on a crowded stage and command attention. Surprisingly, it is not the actor who screams the loudest or gestures the most wildly who works this magic best, but the actor who stays calm, radiating self-assurance. The effect is ruined by trying too hard. It is essential to be self-aware, to have the ability to see yourself as others see you. De Gaulle understood that self-awareness was key to his charisma; in the most turbulent circumstances—the Nazi occupation of France, the national reconstruction after World War II, an army rebellion in Algeria—he retained an Olympian composure that played beautifully against the hysteria of his colleagues. When he spoke, no one could take their eyes off him. Once you know how to command attention this way, heighten the effect by appearing in ceremonial and ritual events that are full of exciting imagery, making you look regal and godlike. Flamboyancy has nothing to do with charisma—it attracts the wrong kind of attention.

Uninhibitedness. Most people are repressed, and have little access to their unconscious—a problem that creates opportunities for the Charismatic, who can become a kind of screen on which others project their secret fantasies and longings. You will first have to show that you are less inhibited than your audience—that you radiate a dangerous sexuality, have no fear of death, are delightfully spontaneous. Even a hint of these qualities will make people think you more powerful than you are. In the 1850s a bohemian American actress, Adah Isaacs Menken, took the world by storm through her unbridled sexual energy, and her fearlessness. She would appear on stage half-naked, performing death-defying acts; few women could dare such things in the Victorian period, and a rather mediocre actress became a figure of cultlike adoration.

An extension of your being uninhibited is a dreamlike quality in your work and character that reveals your openness to your unconscious. It was the possession of this quality that transformed artists like Wagner and Picasso into charismatic idols. Its cousin is a fluidity of body and spirit; while the repressed are rigid, Charismatics have an ease and an adaptability that show their openness to experience.

Fervency. You need to believe in something, and to believe in it strongly enough for it to animate all your gestures and make your eyes light up. This cannot be faked. Politicians inevitably lie to the public; what distinguishes Charismatics is that they believe their own lies, which makes them that much more believable. A prerequisite for fiery belief is some great cause to rally around—a crusade. Become the rallying point for people's discontent, and show that you share none of the doubts that plague normal humans. In 1490, the Florentine Girolamo Savonarola railed at the immorality of the pope and the Catholic Church. Claiming to be divinely inspired, he became so animated during his sermons that hysteria would sweep the crowd. Savonarola developed such a following that he briefly took over the city, until the pope had him captured and burned at the stake. People believed in him because of the depth of his conviction. His example has more relevance today than ever: people are more and more isolated, and long for communal experience. Let your own fervent and contagious faith, in virtually anything, give them something to believe in.

Vulnerability. Charismatics display a need for love and affection. They are open to their audience, and in fact feed off its energy; the audience in turn is electrified by the Charismatic, the current increasing as it passes back and forth. This vulnerable side to charisma softens the self-confident side, which can seem fanatical and frightening.

Since charisma involves feelings akin to love, you in turn must reveal your love for your followers. This was a key component to the charisma that Marilyn Monroe radiated on camera. "I knew I belonged to the Public," she wrote in her diary, "and to the world, not because I was talented or even beautiful but because I had never belonged to anything or anyone else. The Public was the only family, the only Prince Charming and the only home I had ever dreamed of." In front of a camera, Monroe suddenly came to life, flirting with and exciting her unseen public. If the audience does not sense this quality in you they will turn away from you. On the other hand, you must never seem manipulative or needy. Imagine your public as a single person whom you are trying to seduce—nothing is more seductive to people than the feeling that they are desired.

Adventurousness. Charismatics are unconventional. They have an air of adventure and risk that attracts the bored. Be brazen and courageous in your actions—be seen taking risks for the good of others. Napoleon made sure his soldiers saw him at the cannons in battle. Lenin walked openly on the streets, despite the death threats he had received. Charismatics thrive in troubled waters; a crisis situation allows them to flaunt their daring, which enhances their aura. John F. Kennedy came to life in dealing with the Cuban missile crisis, Charles de Gaulle when he confronted rebellion in

In such conditions, where half the battle was hand-to-hand, concentrated into a small space, the spirit and example of the leader counted for much. When we remember this, it becomes easier to understand the astonishing effect of Joan's presence upon the French troops. Her position as a leader was a unique one. She was not a professional soldier; she was not really a soldier at all; she was not even a man. She was ignorant of war. She was a girl dressed up. But she believed, and had made others willing to believe, that she was the mouthpiece of God. • On Friday, April 29th, 1429, the news spread in Orléans that a force, led by the Pucelle of Domrémy, was on its way to the relief of the city, a piece of news which, as the chronicler remarks, comforted them greatly.

—Vita Sackville-West, *Saint Joan of Arc*

Algeria. They needed these problems to seem charismatic, and in fact some have even accused them of stirring up situations (Kennedy through his brinkmanship style of diplomacy, for instance) that played to their love of adventure. Show heroism to give yourself a charisma that will last you a lifetime. Conversely, the slightest sign of cowardice or timidity will ruin whatever charisma you had.

Magnetism. If any physical attribute is crucial in seduction, it is the eyes. They reveal excitement, tension, detachment, without a word being spoken. Indirect communication is critical in seduction, and also in charisma. The demeanor of Charismatics may be poised and calm, but their eyes are magnetic; they have a piercing gaze that disturbs their targets' emotions, exerting force without words or action. Fidel Castro's aggressive gaze can reduce his opponents to silence. When Benito Mussolini was challenged, he would roll his eyes, showing the whites in a way that frightened people. President Kusnasosro Sukarno of Indonesia had a gaze that seemed as if it could have read thoughts. Roosevelt could dilate his pupils at will, making his stare both hypnotizing and intimidating. The eyes of the Charismatic never show fear or nerves.

All of these skills are acquirable. Napoleon spent hours in front of a mirror, modeling his gaze on that of the great contemporary actor Talma. The key is self-control. The look does not necessarily have to be aggressive; it can also show contentment. Remember: your eyes can emanate charisma, but they can also give you away as a faker. Do not leave such an important attribute to chance. Practice the effect you desire.

Genuine charisma thus means the ability to internally generate and externally express extreme excitement, an ability which makes one the object of intense attention and unreflective imitation by others.

—Liah Greenfield

Charismatic Types—Historical Examples

The miraculous prophet. In the year 1425, Joan of Arc, a peasant girl from the French village of Domrémy, had her first vision: "I was in my thirteenth year when God sent a voice to guide me." The voice was that of Saint Michael and he came with a message from God: Joan had been chosen to rid France of the English invaders who now ruled most of the country, and of the resulting chaos and war. She was also to restore the French crown to the prince—the Dauphin, later Charles VII—who was its rightful heir. Saint Catherine and Saint Margaret also spoke to Joan. Her visions were extraordinarily vivid: she saw Saint Michael, touched him, smelled him.

At first Joan told no one what she had seen; for all anyone knew, she was a quiet farm girl. But the visions became even more intense, and so in 1429 she left Domrémy, determined to realize the mission for which God had chosen her. Her goal was to meet Charles in the town of Chinon, where he had established his court in exile. The obstacles were enormous: Chinon was far, the journey was dangerous, and Charles, even if she reached him, was a lazy and cowardly young man who was unlikely to crusade against the English. Undaunted, she moved from village to village, explaining her mission to soldiers and asking them to escort her to Chinon. Young girls with religious visions were a dime a dozen at the time, and there was nothing in Joan's appearance to inspire confidence; one soldier, however, Jean de Metz, was intrigued with her. What fascinated him was the detail of her visions: she would liberate the besieged town of Orléans, have the king crowned at the cathedral in Reims, lead the army to Paris; she knew how she would be wounded, and where; the words she attributed to Saint Michael were quite unlike the language of a farm girl; and she was so calmly confident, she glowed with conviction. De Metz fell under her spell. He swore allegiance and set out with her for Chinon. Soon others offered assistance, too, and word reached Charles of the strange young girl on her way to meet him.

On the 350-mile road to Chinon, accompanied only by a handful of soldiers, through a land infested with warring bands, Joan showed neither fear nor hesitation. The journey took several months. When she finally arrived, the Dauphin decided to meet the girl who had promised to restore him to his throne, despite the advice of his counselors; but he was bored, and wanted amusement, and decided to play a trick on her. She was to meet him in a hall packed with courtiers; to test her prophetic powers, he disguised himself as one of these men, and dressed another man as the prince. Yet when Joan arrived, to the amazement of the crowd, she walked straight up to Charles and curtseyed: "The King of Heaven sends me to you with the message that you shall be the lieutenant of the King of Heaven, who is the king of France." In the talk that followed, Joan seemed to echo Charles's most private thoughts, while once again recounting in extraordinary detail the feats she would accomplish. Days later, this indecisive, flighty man declared himself convinced and gave her his blessing to lead a French army against the English.

Amongst the surplus population living on the margin of society [in the Middle Ages] there was always a strong tendency to take as leader a layman, or maybe an apostate friar or monk, who imposed himself not simply as a holy man but as a prophet or even as a living god. On the strength of inspirations or revelations for which he claimed divine origin this leader would decree for his followers a communal mission of vast dimensions and world-shaking importance. The conviction of having such a mission, of being divinely appointed to carry out a prodigious task, provided the disoriented and the frustrated with new bearings and new hope. It gave them not simply a place in the world but a unique and resplendent place. A fraternity of this kind felt itself an elite, set infinitely apart from and above ordinary mortals, sharing also in his miraculous powers.

—Norman Cohn, *The Pursuit of the Millennium*

Miracles and saintliness aside, Joan of Arc had certain basic qualities that made her exceptional. Her visions were intense; she could describe them in such detail that they had to be real. Details have that effect: they lend a sense of reality to even the most preposterous statements. Furthermore, in a time of great disorder, she was supremely focused, as if her strength came from somewhere unworldly. She spoke with authority, and she predicted things people wanted: the English would be defeated, prosperity would return. She also had a peasant's earthy common sense. She had surely heard descriptions of Charles on the road to Chinon; once at court, she could have sensed the trick he was playing on her, and could have confidently picked out his pampered face in the crowd. The following year, her visions abandoned her, and her confidence as well—she made many mistakes, leading to her capture by the English. She was indeed human.

We may no longer believe in miracles, but anything that hints at strange, unworldly, even supernatural powers will create charisma. The psychology is the same: you have visions of the future, and of the wondrous things you can accomplish. Describe these things in great detail, with an air of authority, and suddenly you stand out. And if your prophecy—of prosperity, say—is just what people want to hear, they are likely to fall under your spell and to see later events as a confirmation of your predictions. Exhibit remarkable confidence and people will think your confidence comes from real knowledge. You will create a self-fulfilling prophecy: people's belief in you will translate into actions that help realize your visions. Any hint of success will make them see miracles, uncanny powers, the glow of charisma.

The authentic animal. One day in 1905, the St. Petersburg salon of Countess Ignatiev was unusually full. Politicians, society ladies, and courtiers had all arrived early to await the remarkable guest of honor: Grigori Efimovich Rasputin, a forty-year-old Siberian monk who had made a name for himself throughout Russia as a healer, perhaps a saint. When Rasputin arrived, few could disguise their disappointment: his face was ugly, his hair was stringy, he was gangly and awkward. They wondered why they had come. But then Rasputin approached them one by one, wrapping his big hands around their fingers and gazing deep into their eyes. At first his gaze was unsettling: as he looked them up and down, he seemed to be probing and judging them. Yet suddenly his expression would change, and kindness, joy, and understanding would radiate from his face. Several of the ladies he actually hugged, in a most effusive manner. This startling contrast had profound effects.

The mood in the salon soon changed from disappointment to excitement. Rasputin's voice was so calm and deep; his language was coarse, yet the ideas it expressed were delightfully simple, and had the ring of great spiritual truth. Then, just as the guests were beginning to relax with this dirty-looking peasant, his mood suddenly changed to anger: "I know you, I can read your souls. You are all too pampered. . . . These fine clothes and arts of yours are useless and pernicious. Men must learn to humble themselves! You must be simpler, far, far simpler. Only then will God come nearer to you." The monk's face grew animated, his pupils expanded, he looked completely different. How impressive that angry look was, recalling Jesus throwing the moneylenders from the temple. Now Rasputin calmed down, returned to being gracious, but the guests already saw him as someone strange and remarkable. Next, in a performance he would soon repeat

"How peculiar [Rasputin's] eyes are," confesses a woman who had made efforts to resist his influence. She goes on to say that every time she met him she was always amazed afresh at the power of his glance, which it was impossible to withstand for any considerable time. There was something oppressive in this kind and gentle, but at the same time sly and cunning, glance; people were helpless under the spell of the powerful will which could be felt in his whole being. However tired you might be of this charm, and however much you wanted to escape it, somehow or other you always found yourself attracted back and held. • A young girl who had heard of the strange new saint came from her province to the capital, and visited him in search of edification and spiritual instruction. She had never seen either him or a portrait of him before, and met him for the first time in his house. When he came up to her and spoke to her, she thought him like one of the peasant preachers she had often seen in her own country home. His gentle, monastic gaze and the plainly parted light brown hair around the worthy simple face, all at first inspired her confidence. But when he came nearer to her, she felt immediately that another quite different man, mysterious, crafty, and corrupting, looked out from behind the eyes that radiated goodness and gentleness. • He sat down opposite her, edged quite close up to her, and his light blue eyes changed color, and became deep and

in salons throughout the city, he led the guests in a folk song, and as they sang, he began to dance, a strange uninhibited dance of his own design, and as he danced, he circled the most attractive women there, and with his eyes invited them to join him. The dance turned vaguely sexual; as his partners fell under his spell, he whispered suggestive comments in their ears. Yet none of them seemed to be offended.

Over the next few months, women from every level of St. Petersburg society visited Rasputin in his apartment. He would talk to them of spiritual matters, but then without warning he would turn sexual, murmuring the crassest come-ons. He would justify himself through spiritual dogma: how can you repent if you have not sinned? Salvation only comes to those who go astray. One of the few who rejected his advances was asked by a friend, "How can one refuse anything to a saint?" "Does a saint need sinful love?" she replied. Her friend said, "He makes everything that comes near him holy. I have already belonged to him, and I am proud and happy to have done so." "But you are married! What does your husband say?" "He considers it a very great honor. If Rasputin desires a woman we all think it a blessing and a distinction, our husbands as well as ourselves."

Rasputin's spell soon extended over Czar Nicholas and more particularly over his wife, the Czarina Alexandra, after he apparently healed their son from a life-threatening injury. Within a few years, he had become the most powerful man in Russia, with total sway over the royal couple.

dark. A keen glance reached her from the corner of his eyes, bored into her, and held her fascinated. A leaden heaviness overpowered her limbs as his great wrinkled face, distorted with desire, came closer to hers. She felt his hot breath on her cheeks, and saw how his eyes, burning from the depths of their sockets, furtively roved over her helpless body, until he dropped his lids with a sensuous expression. His voice had fallen to a passionate whisper, and he murmured strange, voluptuous words in her ear. • Just as she was on the point of abandoning herself to her seducer, a memory stirred in her dimly and as if from some far distance; she recalled that she had come to ask him about God.

—René Fülöp-Miller, *Rasputin: The Holy Devil*

People are more complicated than the masks they wear in society. The man who seems so noble and gentle is probably disguising a dark side, which will often come out in strange ways; if his nobility and refinement are in fact a put-on, sooner or later the truth will out, and his hypocrisy will disappoint and alienate. On the other hand, we are drawn to people who seem more comfortably human, who do not bother to disguise their contradictions. This was the source of Rasputin's charisma. A man so authentically himself, so devoid of self-consciousness or hypocrisy, was immensely appealing. His wickedness and saintliness were so extreme that it made him seem larger than life. The result was a charismatic aura that was immediate and preverbal; it radiated from his eyes, and from the touch of his hands.

Most of us are a mix of the devil and the saint, the noble and the ignoble, and we spend our lives trying to repress the dark side. Few of us can give free rein to both sides, as Rasputin did, but we can create charisma to a smaller degree by ridding ourselves of self-consciousness, and of the discomfort most of us feel about our complicated natures. You cannot help being the way you are, so be genuine. That is what attracts us to animals: beautiful and cruel, they have no self-doubt. That quality is doubly fascinating in humans. Outwardly people may condemn your dark side, but it is not virtue alone that creates charisma; anything extraordinary will do. Do not apologize or go halfway. The more unbridled you seem, the more magnetic the effect.

By its very nature, the existence of charismatic authority is specifically unstable. The holder may forego his charisma; he may feel "forsaken by his God," as Jesus did on the cross; he may prove to his followers that "virtue is gone out of him." It is then that his mission is extinguished, and hope waits and searches for a new holder of charisma.

—MAX WEBER, FROM *MAX WEBER: ESSAYS IN SOCIOLOGY*, EDITED BY HANS GERTH AND C. WRIGHT MILLS

The demonic performer. Throughout his childhood Elvis Presley was thought a strange boy who kept pretty much to himself. In high school in Memphis, Tennessee, he attracted attention with his pompadoured hair and sideburns, his pink and black clothing, but people who tried to talk to him found nothing there—he was either terribly bland or hopelessly shy. At the high school prom, he was the only boy who didn't dance. He seemed lost in a private world, in love with the guitar he took everywhere. At the Ellis Auditorium, at the end of an evening of gospel music or wrestling, the concessions manager would often find Elvis onstage, miming a performance and taking bows before an imaginary audience. Asked to leave, he would quietly walk away. He was a very polite young man.

In 1953, just out of high school, Elvis recorded his first song, in a local studio. The record was a test, a chance for him to hear his own voice. A year later the owner of the studio, Sam Phillips, called him in to record two blues songs with a couple of professional musicians. They worked for hours, but nothing seemed to click; Elvis was nervous and inhibited. Then, near the end of the evening, giddy with exhaustion, he suddenly let loose and started to jump around like a child, in a moment of complete self-abandon. The other musicians joined in, the song getting wilder and wilder. Phillips's eyes lit up—he had something here.

A month later Elvis gave his first public performance, outdoors in a Memphis park. He was as nervous as he had been at the recording session, and could only stutter when he had to speak; but once he broke into song, the words came out. The crowd responded excitedly, rising to peaks at certain moments. Elvis couldn't figure out why. "I went over to the manager after the song," he later said, "and I asked him what was making the crowd go nuts. He told me, 'I'm not really sure, but I think that every time you wiggle your left leg, they start to scream. Whatever it is, just don't stop.' "

A single Elvis recorded in 1954 became a hit. Soon he was in demand. Going onstage filled him with anxiety and emotion, so much so that he became a different person, as if possessed. "I've talked to some singers and they get a little nervous, but they say their nerves kind of settle down after they get into it. Mine never do. It's sort of this energy . . . something maybe like sex." Over the next few months he discovered more gestures and sounds—twitching dance movements, a more tremulous voice—that made the crowds go crazy, particularly teenage girls. Within a year he had become the hottest musician in America. His concerts were exercises in mass hysteria.

Elvis Presley had a dark side, a secret life. (Some have attributed it to the death, at birth, of his twin brother.) This dark side he deeply repressed as a young man; it included all kinds of fantasies which he could only give in to when he was alone, although his unconventional clothing may also have been a symptom of it. When he performed, though, he was able to let these demons loose. They came out as a dangerous sexual power. Twitching, androgynous, uninhibited, he was a man enacting strange fantasies before the public. The audience sensed this and was excited by it. It wasn't a flamboyant style and appearance that gave Elvis charisma, but rather the electrifying expression of his inner turmoil.

A crowd or group of any sort has a unique energy. Just below the surface is desire, a constant sexual excitement that has to be repressed because it is socially unacceptable. If you have the ability to rouse those desires, the crowd will see you as having charisma. The key is learning to access your own unconscious, as Elvis did when he let go. You are full of an excitement that seems to come from some mysterious inner source. Your uninhibitedness will invite other people to open up, sparking a chain reaction: their excitement in turn will animate you still more. The fantasies you bring to the surface do not have to be sexual—any social taboo, anything repressed and yearning for an outlet, will suffice. Make this felt in your recordings, your artwork, your books. Social pressure keeps people so repressed that they will be attracted to your charisma before they have even met you in person.

He is their god. He leads them like a thing \ Made by some other deity than nature, \ That shapes man better; and they follow him \ Against us brats with no less confidence \ Than boys pursuing summer butterflies \ Or butchers killing flies. . . .

—William Shakespeare, *Coriolanus*

The Savior. In March of 1917, the Russian parliament forced the country's ruler, Czar Nicholas, to abdicate and established a provisional government. Russia was in ruins. Its participation in World War I had been a disaster; famine was spreading widely, the vast countryside was riven by looting and lynch law, and soldiers were deserting from the army en masse. Politically the country was bitterly divided; the main factions were the right, the social democrats, and the left-wing revolutionaries, and each of these groups was itself afflicted by dissension.

Into this chaos came the forty-seven-year-old Vladimir Ilyich Lenin. A Marxist revolutionary, the leader of the Bolshevik Communist party, he had suffered a twelve-year exile in Europe until, recognizing the chaos overcoming Russia as the chance he had long been waiting for, he had hurried back home. Now he called for the country to end its participation in the war and for an immediate socialist revolution. In the first weeks after his arrival, nothing could have seemed more ridiculous. As a man, Lenin looked unimpressive; he was short and plain-featured. He had also spent years away in Europe, isolated from his people and immersed in reading and intellectual argument. Most important, his party was small, representing only a splinter group within the loosely organized left coalition. Few took him seriously as a national leader.

Undaunted, Lenin went to work. Wherever he went, he repeated the same simple message: end the war, establish the rule of the proletariat, abolish private property, redistribute wealth. Exhausted with the nation's endless political infighting and the complexity of its problems, people began to listen. Lenin was so determined, so confident. He never lost his cool. In the midst of a raucous debate, he would simply and logically debunk each one of his adversaries' points. Workers and soldiers were im-

The roof did lift as Presley came onstage. He sang for twenty-five minutes while the audience erupted like Mount Vesuvius. "I never saw such excitement and screaming in my entire life, ever before or since," said [film director Hal] Kanter. As an observer, he describ-ed being stunned by "an exhibition of public mass hysteria . . . a tidal wave of adoration surging up from 9,000 people, over the wall of police flanking the stage, up over the flood-lights, to the performer and beyond him, lifting him to frenzied heights of response."

—A description of Elvis Presley's concert at the Hayride Theater, Shreveport, Louisiana, December 17, 1956, in Peter Whitmer, *The Inner Elvis: A Psychological Biography of Elvis Aaron Presley*

pressed by his firmness. Once, in the midst of a brewing riot, Lenin amazed his chauffeur by jumping onto the running board of his car and directing the way through the crowd, at considerable personal risk. Told that his ideas had nothing to do with reality, he would answer, "So much the worse for reality!"

Allied to Lenin's messianic confidence in his cause was his ability to organize. Exiled in Europe, his party had been scattered and diminished; in keeping them together he had developed immense practical skills. In front of a large crowd, he was a also powerful orator. His speech at the First All-Russian Soviet Congress made a sensation; either revolution or a bourgeois government, he cried, but nothing in between—enough of this compromise in which the left was sharing. At a time when other politicians were scrambling desperately to adapt to the national crisis, and seemed weak in the process, Lenin was rock stable. His prestige soared, as did the membership of the Bolshevik party.

Most astounding of all was Lenin's effect on workers, soldiers, and peasants. He would address these common people wherever he found them—in the street, standing on a chair, his thumbs in his lapel, his speech an odd mix of ideology, peasant aphorisms, and revolutionary slogans. They would listen, enraptured. When Lenin died, in 1924—seven years after single-handedly opening the way to the October Revolution of 1917, which had swept him and the Bolsheviks into power—these same ordinary Russians went into mourning. They worshiped at his tomb, where his body was preserved on view; they told stories about him, developing a body of Lenin folklore; thousands of newborn girls were christened "Ninel," Lenin spelled backwards. This cult of Lenin assumed religious proportions.

No one could so fire others with their plans, no one could so impose his will and conquer by force of his personality as this seemingly so ordinary and somewhat coarse man who lacked any obvious sources of charm. . . . Neither Plekhanov nor Martov nor anyone else possessed the secret radiating from Lenin of positively hypnotic effect upon people—I would even say, domination of them. Plekhanov was treated with deference, Martov was loved, but Lenin alone was followed unhesitatingly as the only indisputable leader. For only Lenin represented that rare phenomenon, especially rare in Russia, of a man of iron will and indomitable energy who combines fanatical faith in the movement, the cause, with no less faith in himself.

—A. N. POTRESOV, QUOTED IN DANKWART A. RUSTOW, ED., *PHILOSOPHERS AND KINGS: STUDIES IN LEADERSHIP*

There all kinds of misconceptions about charisma, which, paradoxically, only add to its mystique. Charisma has little to do with an exciting physical appearance or a colorful personality, qualities that elicit short-term interest. Particularly in times of trouble, people are not looking for entertainment—they want security, a better quality of life, social cohesion. Believe it or not, a plain-looking man or woman with a clear vision, a quality of single-mindedness, and practical skills can be devastatingly charismatic, provided it is matched with some success. Never underestimate the power of success in enhancing one's aura. But in a world teeming with compromisers and fudgers whose indecisiveness only creates more disorder, one clear-minded soul will be a magnet of attention—will have charisma.

One on one, or in a Zurich café before the revolution, Lenin had little or no charisma. (His confidence was attractive, but many found his strident manner irritating.) He won charisma when he was seen as the man who could save the country. Charisma is not a mysterious quality that inhabits you outside your control; it is an illusion in the eyes of those who see you as having what they lack. Particularly in times of trouble, you can enhance that illusion through calmness resolution, and clear-minded practicality. It also helps to have a seductively simple message. Call it the Savior Syn-

"I had hoped to see the mountain eagle of our party, the great man, great physically as well as politically. I had fancied Lenin as a giant, stately and imposing. How great was my disappointment to see a most ordinary-looking man, below average height, in no way, literally in no way distinguishable from ordinary mortals."

—JOSEPH STALIN, ON MEETING LENIN FOR THE FIRST TIME IN 1905, QUOTED IN RONALD W. CLARK, *LENIN: THE MAN BEHIND THE MASK*

drome: once people imagine you can save them from chaos, they will fall in love with you, like a person who melts in the arms of his or her rescuer. And mass love equals charisma. How else to explain the love ordinary Russians felt for a man as emotionless and unexciting as Vladimir Lenin.

First and foremost there can be no prestige without mystery, for familiarity breeds contempt. . . . In the design, the demeanor and the mental operations of a leader there must always be a "something" which others cannot altogether fathom, which puzzles them, stirs them, and rivets their attention . . . to hold in reserve some piece of secret knowledge which may any moment intervene, and the more effectively from being in the nature of a surprise. The latent faith of the masses will do the rest. Once the leader has been judged capable of adding the weight of his personality to the known factors of any situation, the ensuing hope and confidence will add immensely to the faith reposed in him.

—CHARLES DE GAULLE, *THE EDGE OF THE SWORD*, IN DAVID SCHOENBRUN, *THE THREE LIVES OF CHARLES DE GAULLE*

The guru. According to the beliefs of the Theosophical Society, every two thousand years or so the spirit of the World Teacher, Lord Maitreya, inhabits the body of a human. First there was Sri Krishna, born two thousand years before Christ; then there was Jesus himself; and at the start of the twentieth century another incarnation was due. One day in 1909, the theosophist Charles Leadbeater saw a boy on an Indian beach and had an epiphany: this fourteen-year-old lad, Jiddu Krishnamurti, would be the World Teacher's next vehicle. Leadbeater was struck by the simplicity of the boy, who seemed to lack the slightest trace of selfishness. The members of the Theosophical Society agreed with his assessment and adopted this scraggly underfed youth, whose teachers had repeatedly beaten him for stupidity. They fed and clothed him and began his spiritual instruction. The scruffy urchin turned into a devilishly handsome young man.

In 1911, the theosophists formed the Order of the Star in the East, a group intended to prepare the way for the coming of the World Teacher. Krishnamurti was made head of the order. He was taken to England, where his education continued, and everywhere he went he was pampered and revered. His air of simplicity and contentment could not help but impress.

Soon Krishnamurti began to have visions. In 1922 he declared, "I have drunk at the fountain of Joy and eternal Beauty. I am God-intoxicated." Over the next few years he had psychic experiences that the theosophists interpreted as visits from the World Teacher. But Krishnamurti had actually had a different kind of revelation: the truth of the universe came from within. No god, no guru, no dogma could ever make one realize it. He himself was no god or messiah, but just another man. The reverence that he was treated with disgusted him. In 1929, much to his followers' shock, he disbanded the Order of the Star and resigned from the Theosophical Society.

And so Krishnamurti became a philosopher, determined to spread the truth he had discovered: you must be simple, removing the screen of language and past experience. Through these means anyone could attain contentment of the kind that radiated from Krishnamurti. The theosophists abandoned him but his following grew larger than ever. In California, where he spent much of his time, the interest in him verged on cultic adoration. The poet Robinson Jeffers said that whenever Krishnamurti entered a room you could feel a brightness filling the space. The writer Aldous Huxley met him in Los Angeles and fell under his spell. Hearing him speak, he wrote: "It was like listening to the discourse of the Buddha—such power, such intrinsic authority." The man radiated enlightenment. The actor John Barrymore asked him to play the role of Buddha in a film.

Only a month after Evita's death, the newspaper vendors' union put forward her name for canonization, and although this gesture was an isolated one and was never taken seriously by the Vatican, the idea of Evita's holiness remained with many people and was reinforced by the publication of devotional literature subsidized by the government; by the renaming of cities, schools, and subway stations; and by the stamping of medallions, the casting of busts, and the issuing of ceremonial stamps. The time of the evening news broadcast was changed from 8:30 P.M. to 8:25 P.M., the time when Evita had "passed into immortality," and each month there were torch-lit processions on the twenty-sixth of the month, the day of her death. On the first anniversary of her death, La Prensa *printed a story about one of its readers seeing Evita's face in the face of the moon, and after this there were many more such sightings reported in the newspapers. For the most part, official publications stopped short of claiming sainthood for her, but their restraint was not always convincing. . . . In the calendar for 1953 of the Buenos Aires newspaper vendors, as in other unofficial images, she was depicted in the traditional blue robes of the Virgin, her hands crossed, her sad head to one side and surrounded by a halo.*

—NICHOLAS FRASER AND MARYSA NAVARRO, *EVITA*

(Krishnamurti politely declined.) When he visited India, hands would reach out from the crowd to try to touch him through the open car window. People prostrated themselves before him.

Repulsed by all this adoration, Krishnamurti grew more and more detached. He even talked about himself in the third person. In fact, the ability to disengage from one's past and view the world anew was part of his philosophy, yet once again the effect was the opposite of what he expected: the affection and reverence people felt for him only grew. His followers fought jealously for signs of his favor. Women in particular fell deeply in love with him, although he was a lifelong celibate.

Krishnamurti had no desire to be a guru or a Charismatic, but he inadvertently discovered a law of human psychology that disturbed him. People do not want to hear that your power comes from years of effort or discipline. They prefer to think that it comes from your personality, your character, something you were born with. They also hope that proximity to the guru or Charismatic will make some of that power rub off on them. They did not want to have to read Krishnamurti's books, or to spend years practicing his lessons—they simply wanted to be near him, soak up his aura, hear him speak, feel the light that entered the room with him. Krishnamurti advocated simplicity as a way of opening up to the truth, but his own simplicity just allowed people to see what they wanted in him, attributing powers to him that he not only denied but ridiculed.

This is the guru effect, and it is surprisingly simple to create. The aura you are after is not the fiery one of most Charismatics, but one of incandescence, enlightenment. An enlightened person has understood something that makes him or her content, and this contentment radiates outward. That is the appearance you want: you do not need anything or anyone, you are fulfilled. People are naturally drawn to those who emit happiness; maybe they can catch it from you. The less obvious you are, the better: let people conclude that you are happy, rather than hearing it from you. Let them see it in your unhurried manner, your gentle smile, your ease and comfort. Keep your words vague, letting people imagine what they will. Remember: being aloof and distant only stimulates the effect. People will fight for the slightest sign of your interest. A guru is content and detached—a deadly Charismatic combination.

The drama saint. It began on the radio. Throughout the late 1930s and early 1940s, Argentine women would hear the plaintive, musical voice of Eva Duarte in one of the lavishly produced soap operas that were so popular at the time. She never made you laugh, but how often she could make you cry—with the complaints of a betrayed lover, or the last words of Marie Antoinette. The very thought of her voice made you shiver with emotion. And she was pretty, with her flowing blond hair and her serious face, which was often on the covers of the gossip magazines.

In 1943, those magazines published a most exciting story: Eva had begun an affair with one of the most dashing men in the new military government, Colonel Juan Perón. Now Argentines heard her doing propaganda spots for the government, lauding the "New Argentina" that glistened in the future. And finally, this fairy tale story reached its perfect conclusion: in 1945 Juan and Eva married, and the following year, the handsome colonel, after many trials and tribulations (including a spell in prison, from which he was freed by the efforts of his devoted wife) was elected president. He was a champion of the *descamisados*—the "shirtless ones," the workers and the poor, just as his wife was. Only twenty-six at the time, she had grown up in poverty herself.

As for me, I have the gift of electrifying men.

—Napoleon Bonaparte, in Pieter Geyl, *Napoleon: For and Against*

Now that this star was the first lady of the republic, she seemed to change. She lost weight, most definitely; her outfits became less flamboyant, even downright austere; and that beautiful flowing hair was now pulled back, rather severely. It was a shame—the young star had grown up. But as Argentines saw more of the new Evita, as she was now known, her new look affected them more strongly. It was the look of a saintly, serious woman, one who was indeed what her husband called the "Bridge of Love" between himself and his people. She was now on the radio all the time, and listening to her was as emotional as ever, but she also spoke magnificently in public. Her voice was lower and her delivery slower; she stabbed the air with her fingers, reached out as if to touch the audience. And her words pierced you to the core: "I left my dreams by the wayside in order to watch over the dreams of others. . . . I now place my soul at the side of the soul of my people. I offer them all my energies so that my body may be a bridge erected toward the happiness of all. Pass over it . . . toward the supreme destiny of the new fatherland."

I do not pretend to be a divine man, but I do believe in divine guidance, divine power, and divine prophecy. I am not educated, nor am I an expert in any particular field—but I am sincere and my sincerity is my credentials.

—Malcolm X, quoted in Eugene Victor Wolfenstein, *The Victims of Democracy: Malcolm X and the Black Revolution*

It was no longer only through magazines and the radio that Evita made herself felt. Almost everyone was personally touched by her in some way. Everyone seemed to know someone who had met her, or who had visited her in her office, where a line of supplicants wound its way through the hallways to her door. Behind her desk she sat, so calm and full of love. Film crews recorded her acts of charity: to a woman who had lost everything, Evita would give a house; to one with a sick child, free care in the finest hospital. She worked so hard, no wonder rumor had it that she was ill. And everyone heard of her visits to the shanty towns and to hospitals for the poor, where, against the wishes of her staff, she would kiss people with all kinds of maladies (lepers, syphilitic men, etc.) on the cheek. Once an assistant appalled by this habit tried to dab Evita's lips with alcohol, to sterilize them. This saint of a woman grabbed the bottle and smashed it against the wall.

Yes, Evita was a saint, a living madonna. Her appearance alone could heal the sick. And when she died of cancer, in 1952, no outsider to Argentina could possibly understand the sense of grief and loss she left behind. For some, the country never recovered.

* * *

Most of us live in a semi-somnambulistic state: we do our daily tasks and the days fly by. The two exceptions to this are childhood and those moments when we are in love. In both cases, our emotions are more engaged, more open and active. And we equate feeling emotional with feeling more alive. A public figure who can affect people's emotions, who can make them feel communal sadness, joy, or hope, has a similar effect. An appeal to the emotions is far more powerful than an appeal to reason.

Eva Perón knew this power early on, as a radio actress. Her tremulous voice could make audiences weep; because of this, people saw in her great charisma. She never forgot the experience. Her every public act was framed in dramatic and religious motifs. Drama is condensed emotion, and the Catholic religion is a force that reaches into your childhood, hits you where you cannot help yourself. Evita's uplifted arms, her staged acts of charity, her sacrifices for the common folk—all this went straight to the heart. It was not her goodness alone that was charismatic, although the appearance of goodness is alluring enough. It was her ability to dramatize her goodness.

You must learn to exploit the two great purveyors of emotion: drama and religion. Drama cuts out the useless and banal in life, focusing on moments of pity and terror; religion deals with matters of life and death. Make your charitable actions dramatic, give your loving words religious import, bathe everything in rituals and myths going back to childhood. Caught up in the emotions you stir, people will see over your head the halo of charisma.

The deliverer. In Harlem in the early 1950s, few African-Americans knew much about the Nation of Islam, or ever stepped into its temple. The Nation preached that white people were descended from the devil and that someday Allah would liberate the black race. This doctrine had little meaning for Harlemites, who went to church for spiritual solace and turned in practical matters to their local politicians. But in 1954, a new minister for the Nation of Islam arrived in Harlem.

The minister's name was Malcolm X, and he was well-read and eloquent, yet his gestures and words were angry. Word spread: whites had lynched Malcolm's father. He had grown up in a juvenile facility, then had survived as a small-time hustler before being arrested for burglary and spending six years in prison. His short life (he was only twenty-nine at the time) had been one long run-in with the law, yet look at him now—so confident and educated. No one had helped him; he had done it all on his own. Harlemites began to see Malcolm X everywhere, handing out fliers, addressing the young. He would stand outside their churches, and as the congregation dispersed, he would point to the preacher and say, "He represents the white man's god; I represent the black man's god." The curious began to come to hear him preach at a Nation of Islam temple. He would ask them to look at the actual conditions of their lives: "When you get through looking at where you live, then . . . take a walk across Central Park," he would tell them. "Look at the white man's apartments. Look at his Wall Street!" His words were powerful, particularly coming from a minister.

In 1957, a young Muslim in Harlem witnessed the beating of a drunken black man by several policemen. When the Muslim protested, the police pummeled him senseless and carted him off to jail. An angry crowd gathered outside the police station, ready to riot. Told that only Malcolm X could forestall violence, the police commissioner brought him in and told him to break up the mob. Malcolm refused. Speaking more temperately, the commissioner begged him to reconsider. Malcolm calmly set conditions for his cooperation: medical care for the beaten Muslim, and proper punishment for the police officers. The commissioner reluctantly agreed. Outside the station, Malcolm explained the agreement and the crowd dispersed. In Harlem and around the country, he was an overnight hero—finally a man who took action. Membership in his temple soared.

Malcolm began to speak all over the United States. He never read from a text; looking out at the audience, he made eye contact, pointed his finger. His anger was obvious, not so much in his tone—he was always controlled and articulate—as in his fierce energy, the veins popping out on his neck. Many earlier black leaders had used cautious words, and had asked their followers to deal patiently and politely with their social lot, no matter how unfair. What a relief Malcolm was. He ridiculed the racists, he ridiculed the liberals, he ridiculed the president; no white person escaped his scorn. If whites were violent, Malcolm said, the language of violence should be spoken back to them, for it was the only language they understood. "Hostility is good!" he cried out. "It's been bottled up too long." In response to the growing popularity of the nonviolent leader Martin Luther King, Jr., Malcolm said, "Anybody can sit. An old woman can sit. A coward can sit. . . . It takes a man to stand."

Malcolm X had a bracing effect on many who felt the same anger he did but were frightened to express it. At his funeral—he was assassinated in 1965, at one of his speeches—the actor Ossie Davis delivered the eulogy before a large and emotional crowd: "Malcolm," he said, "was our own black shining prince."

Malcolm X was a Charismatic of Moses' kind: he was a deliverer. The power of this sort of Charismatic comes from his or her expression of dark emotions that have built up over years of oppression. In doing so, the deliverer provides an opportunity for the release of bottled-up emotions by other people—of the hostility masked by forced politeness and smiles. Deliverers have to be one of the suffering crowd, only more so: their pain must be exemplary. Malcolm's personal history was an integral part of his charisma. His lesson—that blacks should help themselves, not wait for whites to lift them up—meant a great deal more because of his own years in prison, and because he had followed his own doctrine by educating himself, lifting himself up from the bottom. The deliverer must be a living example of personal redemption.

The essence of charisma is an overpowering emotion that communicates itself in your gestures, in your tone of voice, in subtle signs that are the more powerful for being unspoken. You feel something more deeply than others, and no emotion is more powerful and more capable of creating a charismatic reaction than hatred, particularly if it comes from deep-rooted feelings of oppression. Express what others are afraid to express and they will see great power in you. Say what they want to say but cannot. Never be afraid of going too far. If you represent a release from oppression, you have the leeway to go still farther. Moses spoke of violence, of destroying every last one of his enemies. Language like this brings the oppressed together and makes them feel more alive. This is not, however, something that is uncontrollable on your part. Malcolm X felt rage from early on, but only in prison did he teach himself the art of oratory, and how to channel his emotions. Nothing is more charismatic than the sense that someone is struggling with great emotion rather than simply giving in to it.

The Olympian actor. On January 24, 1960 an insurrection broke out in Algeria, then still a French colony. Led by right-wing French soldiers, its purpose was to forestall the proposal of President Charles de Gaulle to grant Algeria the right of self-determination. If necessary, the insurrectionists would take over Algeria in the name of France.

For several tense days, the seventy-year-old de Gaulle maintained a strange silence. Then on January 29, at eight in the evening, he appeared on French national television. Before he had uttered a word, the audience was astonished, for he wore his old uniform from World War II, a uniform that everyone recognized and that created a strong emotional response. De Gaulle had been the hero of the resistance, the savior of the country at its darkest moment. But that uniform had not been seen for quite some time. Then de Gaulle spoke, reminding his public, in his cool and confident manner, of all they had accomplished together in liberating France from the Germans. Slowly he moved from these charged patriotic issues to the rebellion in Algeria, and the affront it presented to the spirit of the liberation. He finished his address by repeating his famous words of June 18, 1940: "Once again I call all Frenchmen, wherever they are, whatever they are, to reunite with France. *Vive la République! Vive la France!*"

The speech had two purposes. It showed that de Gaulle was determined not to give an inch to the rebels, and it reached for the heart of all patriotic Frenchmen, particularly in the army. The insurrection quickly died, and no one doubted the connection between its failure and de Gaulle's performance on television.

The following year, the French voted overwhelmingly in favor of Algerian self-determination. On April 11, 1961, de Gaulle gave a press conference in which he made it clear that France would soon grant the country full independence. Eleven days later, French generals in Algeria issued a communiqué stating that they had taken over the country and declaring a state of siege. This was the most dangerous moment of all: faced with Algeria's imminent independence, these right-wing generals would go all the way. A civil war could break out, toppling de Gaulle's government.

The following night, de Gaulle appeared once again on television, once again wearing his old uniform. He mocked the generals, comparing them to a South American junta. He talked calmly and sternly. Then, suddenly, at the very end of the address, his voice rose and even trembled as he called out to the audience: *"Françaises, Français, aidez-moi!"* ("Frenchwomen, Frenchmen, help me!") It was the most stirring moment of all his television appearances. French soldiers in Algeria, listening on transistor radios, were overwhelmed. The next day they held a mass demonstration in favor of de Gaulle. Two days later the generals surrendered. On July 1, 1962, de Gaulle proclaimed Algeria's independence.

In 1940, after the German invasion of France, de Gaulle escaped to England to recruit an army that would eventually return to France for the liberation. At the beginning, he was alone, and his mission seemed hopeless. But he had the support of Winston Churchill, and with Churchill's blessing he gave a series of radio talks that the BBC broadcast to France. His strange, hypnotic voice, with its dramatic tremolos, would enter French living rooms in the evenings. Few of his listeners even knew what he looked like, but his tone was so confident, so stirring, that he recruited a silent army of believers. In person, de Gaulle was a strange, brooding man whose confident manner could just as easily irritate as win over. But over the radio that voice had intense charisma. De Gaulle was the first great master of modern media, for he easily transferred his dramatic skills to television, where his iciness, his calmness, his total self-possession, made audiences feel both comforted and inspired.

The world has grown more fractured. A nation no longer comes together on the streets or in the squares; it is brought together in living rooms, where people watching television all over the country can simultaneously be alone and with others. Charisma must now be communicable over the airwaves or it has no power. But it is in some ways easier to project on television, both because television makes a direct one-on-one appeal (the Charismatic seems to address *you*) and because charisma is fairly easy to fake for the few moments you spend in front of the camera. As de Gaulle understood, when appearing on television it is best to radiate calmness and control, to use dramatic effects sparingly. De Gaulle's overall iciness made doubly effective the brief moments in which he raised his voice, or let loose a biting joke. By remaining calm and underplaying it, he hypnotized his audience. (Your face can express much more if your voice is less strident.) He conveyed emotion visually—the uniform, the setting—and through the use of certain charged words: the liberation, Joan of Arc. The less he strained for effect, the more sincere he appeared.

All this must be carefully orchestrated. Punctuate your calmness with surprises; rise to a climax; keep things short and terse. The only thing that cannot be faked is self-confidence, the key component to charisma since the days of Moses. Should the camera lights betray your insecurity, all the tricks in the world will not put your charisma back together again.

Symbol: *The Lamp. Invisible to the eye, a current flowing through a wire in a glass vessel generates a heat that turns into candescence. All we see is the glow. In the prevailing darkness, the Lamp lights the way.*

Dangers

On a pleasant May day in 1794, the citizens of Paris gathered in a park for the Festival of the Supreme Being. The focus of their attention was Maximilien de Robespierre, head of the Committee of Public Safety, and the man who had thought up the festival in the first place. The idea was simple: to combat atheism, "to recognize the existence of a Supreme Being and the Immortality of the Soul as the guiding forces of the universe."

It was Robespierre's day of triumph. Standing before the masses in his sky-blue suit and white stockings, he initiated the festivities. The crowd adored him; after all, he had safeguarded the purposes of the French Revolution through the intense politicking that had followed it. The year before, he had initiated the Reign of Terror, which cleansed the revolution of its enemies by sending them to the guillotine. He had also helped guide the country through a war against the Austrians and the Prussians. What made crowds, and particularly women, love him was his incorruptible virtue (he lived very modestly), his refusal to compromise, the passion for the revolution that was evident in everything he did, and the romantic language of his speeches, which could not fail to inspire. He was a god. The day was beautiful and augured a great future for the revolution.

Two months later, on July 26, Robespierre delivered a speech that he thought would ensure his place in history, for he intended to hint at the end of the Terror and a new era for France. Rumor also had it that he was to call for a last handful of people to be sent to the guillotine, a final group that threatened the safety of the revolution. Mounting the rostrum to address the country's governing convention, Robespierre wore the same clothes he had worn on the day of the festival. The speech was long, almost three hours, and included an impassioned description of the values and virtues he had helped protect. There was also talk of conspiracies, treachery, unnamed enemies.

The response was enthusiastic, but a little less so than usual. The speech had tired many representatives. Then a lone voice was heard, that of a man named Bourdon, who spoke against printing Robespierre's speech, a veiled sign of disapproval. Suddenly others stood up on all sides, and accused him of vagueness: he had talked of conspiracies and threats without naming the guilty. Asked to be specific, he refused, preferring to name names later on. The next day Robespierre stood to defend his speech, and the representatives shouted him down. A few hours later, he was the one sent to the guillotine. On July 28, amid a gathering of citizens who seemed to be in an even more festive mood than at the Festival of the Supreme Being, Robespierre's head fell into the basket, to resounding cheers. The Reign of Terror was over.

Many of those who seemed to admire Robespierre actually harbored a gnawing resentment of him—he was *so* virtuous, *so* superior, it was oppressive. Some of these men had plotted against him, and were waiting for the slightest sign of weakness—which appeared on that fateful day when he gave his last speech. In refusing to name his enemies, he had shown either a desire to end the bloodshed or a fear that they would strike at him before he could have them killed. Fed by the conspirators, this one spark turned into fire. Within two days, first a governing body and then a nation turned against a Charismatic who two months before had been revered.

Charisma is as volatile as the emotions it stirs. Most often it stirs sentiments of love. But such feelings are hard to maintain. Psychologists talk of "erotic fatigue"—the moments after love in which you feel tired of it, resentful. Reality creeps in, love turns to hate. Erotic fatigue is a threat to all Charismatics. The Charismatic often wins love by acting the savior, rescuing people from some difficult circumstance, but once they feel secure, charisma is less seductive to them. Charismatics need danger and risk. They are not plodding bureaucrats; some of them deliberately keep danger going, as de Gaulle and Kennedy were wont to do, or as Robespierre did through the Reign of Terror. But people tire of this, and at your first sign of weakness they turn on you. The love they showed before will be matched by their hatred now.

The only defense is to master your charisma. Your passion, your anger, your confidence make you charismatic, but too much charisma for too long creates fatigue, and a desire for calmness and order. The better kind of charisma is created consciously and is kept under control. When you need to you can glow with confidence and fervor, inspiring the masses. But when the adventure is over, you can settle into a routine, turning the heat, not out, but down. (Robespierre may have been planning that move, but it came a day too late.) People will admire your self-control and adaptability. Their love affair with you will move closer to the habitual affection of a man and wife. You will even have the leeway to look a little boring, a little simple—a role that can also seem charismatic, if played correctly. Remember: charisma depends on success, and the best way to maintain success, after the initial charismatic rush, is to be practical and even cautious. Mao Zedong was a distant, enigmatic man who for many had an awe-inspiring charisma. He suffered many setbacks that would have spelled the end of a less clever man, but after each reversal he retreated, becoming practical, tolerant, flexible; at least for a while. This protected him from the dangers of a counterreaction.

There is another alternative: to play the armed prophet. According to Machiavelli, although a prophet may acquire power through his charismatic personality, he cannot long survive without the strength to back it up. He needs an army. The masses will tire of him; they will need to be forced. Being an armed prophet may not literally involve arms, but it demands a forceful side to your character, which you can back up with action. Unfortunately this means being merciless with your enemies for as long as you retain power. And no one creates more bitter enemies than the Charismatic.

Finally, there is nothing more dangerous than succeeding a Charismatic. These characters are unconventional, and their rule is personal in style, being stamped with the wildness of their personalities. They often leave chaos in their wake. The one who follows after a Charismatic is left with a mess, which the people, however, do not see. They miss their inspirer and blame the successor. Avoid this situation at all costs. If it is unavoidable, do not try to continue what the Charismatic started; go in a new direction. By being practical, trustworthy, and plain-speaking, you can often generate a strange kind of charisma through contrast. That was how Harry Truman not only survived the legacy of Roosevelt but established his own type of charisma.

the Star

Daily life is harsh, and most of us constantly seek escape from it in fantasies and dreams. Stars feed on this weakness; standing out from others through a distinctive and appealing style, they make us want to watch them. At the same time, they are vague and ethereal, keeping their distance, and letting us imagine more than is there. Their dreamlike quality works on our unconscious; we are not even aware how much we imitate them. Learn to become an object of fascination by projecting the glittering but elusive presence of the Star.

The Fetishistic Star

One day in 1922, in Berlin, Germany, a casting call went out for the part of a voluptuous young woman in a film called *Tragedy of Love*. Of the hundreds of struggling young actresses who showed up, most would do anything to get the casting director's attention, including exposing themselves. There was one young woman in the line, however, who was simply dressed, and performed none of the other girls' desperate antics. Yet she stood out anyway.

The girl carried a puppy on a leash, and had draped an elegant necklace around the puppy's neck. The casting director noticed her immediately. He watched her as she stood in line, calmly holding the dog in her arms and keeping to herself. When she smoked a cigarette, her gestures were slow and suggestive. He was fascinated by her legs and face, the sinuous way she moved, the hint of coldness in her eyes. By the time she had come to the front, he had already cast her. Her name was Marlene Dietrich.

The cool, bright face which didn't ask for anything, which simply existed, waiting—it was an empty face, he thought; a face that could change with any wind of expression. One could dream into it anything. It was like a beautiful empty house waiting for carpets and pictures. It had all possibilities—it could become a palace or a brothel. It depended on the one who filled it. How limited by comparison was all that was already completed and labeled.

—Erich Maria Remarque, on Marlene Dietrich, *Arch of Triumph*

By 1929, when the Austrian-American director Josef von Sternberg arrived in Berlin to begin work on the film *The Blue Angel*, the twenty-seven-year-old Dietrich was well known in the Berlin film and theater world. *The Blue Angel* was to be about a woman called Lola-Lola who preys sadistically on men, and all of Berlin's best actresses wanted the part—except, apparently, Dietrich, who made it known that she thought the role demeaning; von Sternberg should choose from the other actresses he had in mind. Shortly after arriving in Berlin, however, von Sternberg attended a performance of a musical to watch a male actor he was considering for *The Blue Angel*. The star of the musical was Dietrich, and as soon as she came onstage, von Sternberg found that he could not take his eyes off her. She stared at him directly, insolently, like a man; and then there were those legs, and the way she leaned provocatively against the wall. Von Sternberg forgot about the actor he had come to see. He had found his Lola-Lola.

Marlene Dietrich is not an actress, like Sarah Bernhardt; she is a myth, like Phryne.

—André Malraux, quoted in Edgar Morin, *The Stars*, translated by Richard Howard

Von Sternberg managed to convince Dietrich to take the part, and immediately he went to work, molding her into the Lola of his imagination. He changed her hair, drew a silver line down her nose to make it seem thinner, taught her to look at the camera with the insolence he had seen onstage. When filming began, he created a lighting system just for her—a light that tracked her wherever she went, and was strategically heightened by gauze and smoke. Obsessed with his "creation," he followed her everywhere. No one else could go near her.

When Pygmalion saw these women, living such wicked lives, he was

revolted by the many faults which nature has implanted in the female sex, and long lived a bachelor existence, without any wife to share his home. But meanwhile, with marvelous artistry, he skillfully carved a snowy ivory statue. He made it lovelier than any woman born, and fell in love with his own creation. The statue had all the appearance of a real girl, so that it seemed to be alive, to want to move, did not modesty forbid. So cleverly did his art conceal its art. Pygmalion gazed in wonder, and in his heart there rose a passionate love for this image of a human form. Often he ran his hands over the work, feeling it to see whether it was flesh or ivory, and would not yet admit that ivory was all it was. He kissed the statue, and imagined that it kissed him back, spoke to it and embraced it, and thought he felt his fingers sink into the limbs he touched, so that he was afraid lest a bruise appear where he had pressed the flesh. Sometimes he addressed it in flattering speeches, sometimes brought the kind of presents that girls enjoy. . . . He dressed the limbs of his statue in woman's robes, and put rings on its fingers, long necklaces round its neck. . . . All this finery became the image well, but it was no less lovely unadorned. Pygmalion then placed the statue on a couch that was covered with cloths of Tyrian purple, laid its head to rest on soft down pillows, as if it could appreciate them, and called it his bedfellow. • The festival of Venus, which is celebrated with the greatest

The Blue Angel was a huge success in Germany. Audiences were fascinated with Dietrich: that cold, brutal stare as she spread her legs over a stool, baring her underwear; her effortless way of commanding attention on screen. Others besides von Sternberg became obsessed with her. A man dying of cancer, Count Sascha Kolowrat, had one last wish: to see Marlene's legs in person. Dietrich obliged, visiting him in the hospital and lifting up her skirt; he sighed and said "Thank you. Now I can die happy." Soon Paramount Studios brought Dietrich to Hollywood, where everyone was quickly talking about her. At a party, all eyes would turn toward her when she came into the room. She would be escorted by the most handsome men in Hollywood, and would be wearing an outfit both beautiful and unusual—gold-lamé pajamas, a sailor suit with a yachting cap. The next day the look would be copied by women all over town; next it would spread to magazines, and a whole new trend would start.

The real object of fascination, however, was unquestionably Dietrich's face. What had enthralled von Sternberg was her blankness—with a simple lighting trick he could make that face do whatever he wanted. Dietrich eventually stopped working with von Sternberg, but never forgot what he had taught her. One night in 1951, the director Fritz Lang, who was about to direct her in the film *Rancho Notorious*, was driving past his office when he saw a light flash in the window. Fearing a burglary, he got out of his car, crept up the stairs, and peeked through the crack in the door: it was Dietrich taking pictures of herself in the mirror, studying her face from every angle.

Marlene Dietrich had a distance from her own self: she could study her face, her legs, her body, as if she were someone else. This gave her the ability to mold her look, transforming her appearance for effect. She could pose in just the way that would most excite a man, her blankness letting him see her according to his fantasy, whether of sadism, voluptuousness, or danger. And every man who met her, or who watched her on screen, fantasized endlessly about her. The effect worked on women as well; in the words of one writer, she projected "sex without gender." But this self-distance gave her a certain coldness, whether on film or in person. She was like a beautiful object, something to fetishize and admire the way we admire a work of art.

The fetish is an object that commands an emotional response and that makes us breathe life into it. Because it is an object we can imagine whatever we want to about it. Most people are too moody, complex, and reactive to let us see them as objects that we can fetishize. The power of the Fetishistic Star comes from an ability to become an object, and not just any object but an object we fetishize, one that stimulates a variety of fantasies. Fetishistic Stars are perfect, like the statue of a Greek god or goddess. The effect is startling, and seductive. Its principal requirement is self-distance. If you see yourself as an object, then others will too. An ethereal, dreamlike air will heighten the effect.

You are a blank screen. Float through life noncommittally and people will want to seize you and consume you. Of all the parts of your body that draw this fetishistic attention, the strongest is the face; so learn to tune your face like an instrument, making it radiate a fascinating vagueness for effect. And since you will have to stand out from other Stars in the sky, you will need to develop an attention-getting style. Dietrich was the great practitioner of this art; her style was chic enough to dazzle, weird enough to enthrall. Remember, your own image and presence are materials you can control. The sense that you are engaged in this kind of play will make people see you as superior and worthy of imitation.

She had such natural poise . . . such an economy of gesture, that she became as absorbing as a Modigliani. . . . She had the one essential star quality: she could be magnificent doing nothing.

—Berlin actress Lili Darvas on Marlene Dietrich

pomp all through Cyprus, was now in progress, and heifers, their crooked horns gilded for the occasion, had fallen at the altar as the axe struck their snowy necks. Smoke was rising from the incense, when Pygmalion, having made his offering, stood by the altar and timidly prayed, saying: "If you gods can give all things, may I have as my wife, I pray—" he did not dare to say: "the ivory maiden," but finished: "one like the ivory maid." However, golden Venus, present at her festival in person, understood what his prayers meant, and as a sign that the gods were kindly disposed, the flames burned up three times, shooting a tongue of fire into the air. When Pygmalion returned home, he made straight for the statue of the girl he loved, leaned over the couch, and kissed her. She seemed warm: he laid his lips on hers again, and touched her breast with his hands—at his touch the ivory lost its hardness, and grew soft.

—Ovid, *Metamorphoses*, translated by Mary M. Innes

The Mythic Star

On July 2, 1960, a few weeks before that year's Democratic National Convention, former President Harry Truman publicly stated that John F. Kennedy—who had won enough delegates to be chosen his party's candidate for the presidency—was too young and inexperienced for the job. Kennedy's response was startling: he called a press conference, to be televised live, and nationwide, on July 4. The conference's drama was heightened by the fact that he was away on vacation, so that no one saw or heard from him until the event itself. Then, at the appointed hour, Kennedy strode into the conference room like a sheriff entering Dodge City. He began by stating that he had run in all of the state primaries, at considerable expense of money and effort, and had beaten his opponents fairly and squarely. Who was Truman to circumvent the democratic process? "This is a young country," Kennedy went on, his voice getting louder, "founded by young men . . . and still young in heart. . . . The world is changing, the old ways will not do. . . . It is time for a new generation of leadership to cope with new problems and new opportunities." Even Kennedy's enemies agreed that his speech that day was stirring. He turned Truman's challenge around: the issue was not his inexperience but the older generation's monopoly on power. His style was as eloquent as his words, for his performance evoked films of the time—Alan Ladd in *Shane* confronting the corrupt older ranchers, or James Dean in *Rebel Without a Cause*. Kennedy even resembled Dean, particularly in his air of cool detachment.

[John F.] Kennedy brought to television news and photojournalism the components most prevalent in the world of film: star quality and mythic story. With his telegenic looks, skills at self-presentation, heroic fantasies, and creative intelligence, Kennedy was brilliantly prepared to project a major screen persona. He appropriated the discourses of mass culture, especially of Hollywood, and transferred them to the

A few months later, now approved as the Democrats' presidential candidate, Kennedy squared off against his Republican opponent, Richard Nixon, in their first nationally televised debate. Nixon was sharp; he knew

news. By this strategy he made the news like dreams and like the movies—a realm in which images played out scenarios that accorded with the viewer's deepest yearnings. . . . Never appearing in an actual film, but rather turning the television apparatus into his screen, he became the greatest movie star of the twentieth century.

—John Hellmann, *The Kennedy Obsession: The American Myth of JFK*

But we have seen that, considered as a total phenomenon, the history of the stars repeats, in its own proportions, the history of the gods. Before the gods (before the stars) the mythical universe (the screen) was peopled with specters or phantoms endowed with the glamour and magic of the double. • Several of these presences have progressively assumed body and substance, have taken form, amplified, and flowered into gods and goddesses. And even as certain major gods of the ancient pantheons metamorphose themselves into hero-gods of salvation, the star-goddesses humanize themselves and become new mediators between the fantastic world of dreams and man's daily life on earth. . . . • The heroes of the movies . . . are, in an obviously attenuated way, mythological heroes in this sense of becoming divine. The star is the actor or actress who absorbs some of the heroic—i.e., divinized and mythic—substance of the hero or heroine of the movies, and who in turn enriches this substance by

the answers to the questions and debated with aplomb, quoting statistics on the accomplishments of the Eisenhower administration, in which he had served as vice-president. But beneath the glare of the cameras, on black and white television, he was a ghastly figure—his five o'clock shadow covered up with powder, streaks of sweat on his brow and cheeks, his face drooping with fatigue, his eyes shifting and blinking, his body rigid. What was he so worried about? The contrast with Kennedy was startling. If Nixon looked only at his opponent, Kennedy looked out at the audience, making eye contact with his viewers, addressing them in their living rooms as no politician had ever done before. If Nixon talked data and niggling points of debate, Kennedy spoke of freedom, of building a new society, of recapturing America's pioneer spirit. His manner was sincere and emphatic. His words were not specific, but he made his listeners imagine a wonderful future.

The day after the debate, Kennedy's poll numbers soared miraculously, and wherever he went he was greeted by crowds of young girls, screaming and jumping. His beautiful wife Jackie by his side, he was a kind of democratic prince. Now his television appearances were events. He was in due course elected president, and his inaugural address, also broadcast on television, was stirring. It was a cold and wintry day. In the background, Eisenhower sat huddled in coat and scarf, looking old and beaten. But Kennedy stood hatless and coatless to address the nation: "I do not believe that any of us would exchange places with any other people or any other generation. The energy, the faith, the devotion which we bring to this endeavor will light our country and all who serve it—and the glow from that fire can truly light the world."

Over the months to come Kennedy gave innumerable live press conferences before the TV cameras, something no previous president had dared. Facing the firing squad of lenses and questions, he was unafraid, speaking coolly and slightly ironically. What was going on behind those eyes, that smile? People wanted to know more about him. The magazines teased its readers with information—photographs of Kennedy with his wife and children, or playing football on the White House lawn, interviews creating a sense of him as a devoted family man, yet one who mingled as an equal with glamorous stars. The images all melted together—the space race, the Peace Corps, Kennedy facing up to the Soviets during the Cuban missile crisis just as he had faced up to Truman.

After Kennedy was assassinated, Jackie said in an interview that before he went to bed, he would often play the soundtracks to Broadway musicals, and his favorite of these was *Camelot,* with its lines, "Don't let it be forgot / that once there was a spot / For one brief shining moment / That was known as Camelot." There would be great presidents again, Jackie said, but never "another Camelot." The name "Camelot" seemed to stick, making Kennedy's thousand days in office resonate as myth.

Kennedy's seduction of the American public was conscious and calculated. It was also more Hollywood than Washington, which was not surprising:

Kennedy's father, Joseph, had once been a movie producer, and Kennedy himself had spent time in Hollywood, hobnobbing with actors and trying to figure out what made them stars. He was particularly fascinated with Gary Cooper, Montgomery Clift, and Cary Grant; he often called Grant for advice.

Hollywood had found ways to unite the entire country around certain themes, or myths—often the great American myth of the West. The great stars embodied mythic types: John Wayne the patriarch, Clift the Promethean rebel, Jimmy Stewart the noble hero, Marilyn Monroe the siren. These were not mere mortals but gods and goddesses to be dreamed and fantasized about. All of Kennedy's actions were framed in the conventions of Hollywood. He did not argue with his opponents, he confronted them dramatically. He posed, and in visually fascinating ways—whether with his wife, with his children, or alone onstage. He copied the facial expressions, the presence, of a Dean or a Cooper. He did not discuss policy details but waxed eloquent about grand mythic themes, the kind that could unite a divided nation. And all this was calculated for television, for Kennedy mostly existed as a televised image. That image haunted our dreams. Well before his assassination, Kennedy attracted fantasies of America's lost innocence with his call for a renaissance of the pioneer spirit, a New Frontier.

Of all the character types, the Mythic Star is perhaps the most powerful of all. People are divided by all kinds of consciously recognized categories—race, gender, class, religion, politics. It is impossible, then, to gain power on a grand scale, or to win an election, by drawing on conscious awareness; an appeal to any one group will only alienate another. Unconsciously, however, there is much we share. All of us are mortal, all of us know fear, all of us have been stamped with the imprint of parent figures; and nothing conjures up this shared experience more than myth. The patterns of myth, born out of warring feelings of helplessness on the one hand and thirst for immortality on the other, are deeply engraved in us all.

Mythic Stars are figures of myth come to life. To appropriate their power, you must first study their physical presence—how they adopt a distinctive style, are cool and visually arresting. Then you must assume the pose of a mythic figure: the rebel, the wise patriarch, the adventurer. (The pose of a Star who has struck one of these mythic poses might do the trick.) Make these connections vague; they should never be obvious to the conscious mind. Your words and actions should invite interpretation beyond their surface appearance; you should seem to be dealing not with specific, nitty-gritty issues and details but with matters of life and death, love and hate, authority and chaos. Your opponent, similarly, should be framed not merely as an enemy for reasons of ideology or competition but as a villain, a demon. People are hopelessly susceptible to myth, so make yourself the hero of a great drama. And keep your distance—let people identify with you without being able to touch you. They can only watch and dream.

his or her own contribution. When we speak of the myth of the star, we mean first of all the process of divinization which the movie actor undergoes, a process that makes him the idol of crowds.

—Edgar Morin, *The Stars*, translated by Richard Howard

Age: 22, Sex: female, Nationality: British, Profession: medical student "[Deanna Durbin] became my first and only screen idol. I wanted to be as much like her as possible, both in my manners and clothes. Whenever I was to get a new dress, I would find from my collection a particularly nice picture of Deanna and ask for a dress like she was wearing. I did my hair as much like hers as I could manage. If I found myself in any annoying or aggravating situation . . . I found myself wondering what Deanna would do and modified my own reactions accordingly. . . ." • Age: 26, Sex: female, Nationality: British "I only fell in love once with a movie actor. It was Conrad Veidt. His magnetism and his personality got me. His voice and gestures fascinated me. I hated him, feared him, loved him. When he died it seemed to me that a vital part of my imagination died too, and my world of dreams was bare."

—J. P. Mayer, *British Cinemas and Their Audiences*

The savage worships idols of wood and stone; the civilized man, idols of flesh and blood.

—George Bernard Shaw

Jack's life had more to do with myth, magic, legend, saga, and story than with political theory or political science.

—Jacqueline Kennedy, a week after John Kennedy's death

Keys to the Character

When the eye's rays encounter some clear, well-polished object—be it burnished steel or glass or water, a brilliant stone, or any other polished and gleaming substance having luster, glitter, and sparkle . . . those rays of the eye are reflected back, and the observer then beholds himself and obtains an ocular vision of his own person. This is what you see when you look into a mirror; in that situation you are as it were looking at yourself through the eyes of another.

—Ibn Hazm, *The Ring of the Dove: A Treatise on the Art and Practice of Arab Love*, translated by A. J. Arberry

Seduction is a form of persuasion that seeks to bypass consciousness, stirring the unconscious mind instead. The reason for this is simple: we are so surrounded by stimuli that compete for our attention, bombarding us with obvious messages, and by people who are overtly political and manipulative, that we are rarely charmed or deceived by them. We have grown increasingly cynical. Try to persuade a person by appealing to their consciousness, by saying outright what you want, by showing all your cards, and what hope do you have? You are just one more irritation to be tuned out.

To avoid this fate you must learn the art of insinuation, of reaching the unconscious. The most eloquent expression of the unconscious is the dream, which is intricately connected to myth; waking from a dream, we are often haunted by its images and ambiguous messages. Dreams obsess us because they mix the real and the unreal. They are filled with real characters, and often deal with real situations, yet they are delightfully irrational, pushing realities to the extremes of delirium. If everything in a dream were realistic, it would have no power over us; if everything were unreal, we would feel less involved in its pleasures and fears. Its fusion of the two is what makes it haunting. This is what Freud called the "uncanny": something that seems simultaneously strange and familiar.

The only important constellation of collective seduction produced by modern times [is] that of film stars or cinema idols. . . . They were our only myth in an age incapable of generating great myths or figures of seduction comparable to those of mythology or art. • The cinema's power lives in its myth. Its stories, its psychological portraits, its imagination or realism, the meaningful impressions it leaves—these are all secondary. Only the myth is powerful, and at the heart of the cinematographic myth lies seduction—that of the renowned seductive figure, a man or woman (but

We sometimes experience the uncanny in waking life—in a déjà vu, a miraculous coincidence, a weird event that recalls a childhood experience. People can have a similar effect. The gestures, the words, the very being of men like Kennedy or Andy Warhol, for example, evoke both the real and the unreal: we may not realize it (and how could we, really), but they are like dream figures to us. They have qualities that anchor them in reality—sincerity, playfulness, sensuality—but at the same time their aloofness, their superiority, their almost surreal quality makes them seem like something out of a movie.

These types have a haunting, obsessive effect on people. Whether in public or in private, they seduce us, making us want to possess them both physically and psychologically. But how can we possess a person from a dream, or a movie star or political star, or even one of those real-life fascinators, like a Warhol, who may cross our path? Unable to have them, we become obsessed with them—they haunt our thoughts, our dreams, our fantasies. We imitate them unconsciously. The psychologist Sandor Ferenczi calls this "introjection": another person becomes part of our ego, we internalize their character. That is the insidious seductive power of a Star, a power you can appropriate by making yourself into a cipher, a mix of the real and the unreal. Most people are hopelessly banal; that is, far too real.

What you need to do is etherealize yourself. Your words and actions seem to come from your unconscious—have a certain looseness to them. You hold yourself back, occasionally revealing a trait that makes people wonder whether they really know you.

The Star is a creation of modern cinema. That is no surprise: film recreates the dream world. We watch a movie in the dark, in a semisomnolent state. The images are real enough, and to varying degrees depict realistic situations, but they are projections, flickering lights, images—we know they are not real. It as if we were watching someone else's dream. It was the cinema, not the theater, that created the Star.

On a theater stage, actors are far away, lost in the crowd, too real in their bodily presence. What enabled film to manufacture the Star was the close-up, which suddenly separates actors from their contexts, filling your mind with their image. The close-up seems to reveal something not so much about the character they are playing but about themselves. We glimpse something of Greta Garbo herself when we look so closely into her face. Never forget this while fashioning yourself as a Star. First, you must have such a large presence that you can fill your target's mind the way a close-up fills the screen. You must have a style or presence that makes you stand out from everyone else. Be vague and dreamlike, yet not distant or absent—you don't want people to be unable to focus on or remember you. They have to be seeing you in their minds when you're not there.

Second, cultivate a blank, mysterious face, the center that radiates Starness. This allows people to read into you whatever they want to, imagining they can see your character, even your soul. Instead of signaling moods and emotions, instead of emoting or overemoting, the Star draws in interpretations. That is the obsessive power in the face of Garbo or Dietrich, or even of Kennedy, who molded his expressions on James Dean's.

A living thing is dynamic and changing while an object or image is passive, but in its passivity it stimulates our fantasies. A person can gain that power by becoming a kind of object. The great eighteenth-century charlatan Count Saint-Germain was in many ways a precursor of the Star. He would suddenly appear in town, no one knew from where; he spoke many languages, but his accent belonged to no single country. Nor was it clear how old he was—not young, clearly, but his face had a healthy glow. The count only went out at night. He always wore black, and also spectacular jewels. Arriving at the court of Louis XV, he was an instant sensation; he reeked wealth, but no one knew its source. He made the king and Madame de Pompadour believe he had fantastic powers, including even the ability to turn base matter into gold (the gift of the Philosopher's Stone), but he never made any great claims for himself; it was all insinuation. He never said yes or no, only perhaps. He would sit down for dinner but was never seen eating. He once gave Madame de Pompadour a gift of candies in a box that changed color and aspect depending on how she held it; this entrancing object, she said, reminded her of the count himself. Saint-Germain painted the strangest paintings anyone had ever seen—the colors

above all a woman) linked to the ravishing but specious power of the cinematographic image itself. . . . • The star is by no means an ideal or sublime being: she is artificial. . . . Her presence serves to submerge all sensibility and expression beneath a ritual fascination with the void, beneath ecstasy of her gaze and the nullity of her smile. This is how she achieves mythical status and becomes subject to collective rites of sacrificial adulation. • The ascension of the cinema idols, the masses' divinities, was and remains a central story of modern times. . . . There is no point in dismissing it as merely the dreams of mystified masses. It is a seductive occurrence. . . . • To be sure, seduction in the age of the masses is no longer like that of . . . Les Liaisons Dangereuses *or* The Seducer's Diary, *nor for that matter, like that found in ancient mythology, which undoubtedly contains the stories richest in seduction. In these seduction is hot, while that of our modern idols is cold, being at the intersection of two cold mediums, that of the image and that of the masses. . . .• The great stars or seductresses never dazzle because of their talent or intelligence, but because of their absence. They are dazzling in their nullity, and in their coldness—the coldness of makeup and ritual hieraticism. . . . • These great seductive effigies are our masks, our Eastern Island statues.*

—JEAN BAUDRILLARD, *SEDUCTION*, TRANSLATED BY BRIAN SINGER

If you want to know all about Andy Warhol, just look at the surface of my paintings and films and me, and there I am. There's nothing behind it.

—Andy Warhol, quoted in Stephen Koch, *Stargazer: The Life, World & Films of Andy Warhol*

were so vibrant that when he painted jewels, people thought they were real. Painters were desperate to know his secrets but he never revealed them. He would leave town as he had entered, suddenly and quietly. His greatest admirer was Casanova, who met him and never forgot him. When he died, no one believed it; years, decades, a century later, people were certain he was hiding somewhere. A person with powers like his never dies.

The count had all the Star qualities. Everything about him was ambiguous and open to interpretation. Colorful and vibrant, he stood out from the crowd. People thought he was immortal, just as a star seems neither to age nor to disappear. His words were like his presence—fascinating, diverse, strange, their meaning unclear. Such is the power you can command by transforming yourself into a glittering object.

Andy Warhol too obsessed everyone who knew him. He had a distinctive style—those silver wigs—and his face was blank and mysterious. People never knew what he was thinking; like his paintings, he was pure surface. In the quality of their presence Warhol and Saint-Germain recall the great trompe l'oeil paintings of the seventeenth century, or the prints of M. C. Escher—fascinating mixtures of realism and impossibility, which make people wonder if they are real or imaginary.

A Star must stand out, and this may involve a certain dramatic flair, of the kind that Dietrich revealed in her appearances at parties. Sometimes, though, a more haunting, dreamlike effect can be created by subtle touches: the way you smoke a cigarette, a vocal inflection, a way of walking. It is often the little things that get under people's skin, and make them imitate you—the lock of hair over Veronica Lake's right eye, Cary Grant's voice, Kennedy's ironic smile. Although these nuances may barely register to the conscious mind, subliminally they can be as attractive as an object with a striking shape or odd color. Unconsciously we are strangely drawn to things that have no meaning beyond their fascinating appearance.

Stars make us want to know more about them. You must learn to stir people's curiosity by letting them glimpse something in your private life, something that seems to reveal an element of your personality. Let them fantasize and imagine. A trait that often triggers this reaction is a hint of spirituality, which can be devilishly seductive, like James Dean's interest in Eastern philosophy and the occult. Hints of goodness and big-heartedness can have a similar effect. Stars are like the gods on Mount Olympus, who live for love and play. The things you love—people, hobbies, animals—reveal the kind of moral beauty that people like to see in a Star. Exploit this desire by showing people peeks of your private life, the causes you fight for, the person you are in love with (for the moment).

Another way Stars seduce is by making us identify with them, giving us a vicarious thrill. This was what Kennedy did in his press conference about Truman: in positioning himself as a young man wronged by an older man, evoking an archetypal generational conflict, he made young people identify with him. (The popularity in Hollywood movies of the figure of the disaffected, wronged adolescent helped him here.) The key is to represent a type, as Jimmy Stewart represented the quintessential middle-American, Cary Grant the smooth aristocrat. People of your type will gravitate to you, identify with you, share your joy or pain. The attraction must be unconscious, conveyed not in your words but in your pose, your attitude. Now more than ever, people are insecure, and their identities are in flux. Help them fix on a role to play in life and they will flock to identify with you. Simply make your type dramatic, noticeable, and easy to imitate. The power you have in influencing people's sense of self in this manner is insidious and profound.

Remember: everyone is a public performer. People never know exactly what you think or feel; they judge you on your appearance. You are an actor. And the most effective actors have an inner distance: like Dietrich, they can mold their physical presence as if they perceived it from the outside. This inner distance fascinates us. Stars are playful about themselves, always adjusting their image, adapting it to the times. Nothing is more laughable than an image that was fashionable ten years ago but isn't any more. Stars must always renew their luster or face the worst possible fate: oblivion.

Symbol: *The Idol. A piece of stone carved into the shape of a god, perhaps glittering with gold and jewels. The eyes of the worshippers fill the stone with life, imagining it to have real powers. Its shape allows them to see what they want to see—a god—but it is actually just a piece of stone. The god lives in their imaginations.*

Dangers

Stars create illusions that are pleasurable to see. The danger is that people tire of them—the illusion no longer fascinates—and turn to another Star. Let this happen and you will find it very difficult to regain your place in the galaxy. You must keep all eyes on you at any cost.

Do not worry about notoriety, or about slurs on your image; we are remarkably forgiving of our Stars. After the death of President Kennedy, all kinds of unpleasant truths came to light about him—the endless affairs, the addiction to risk and danger. None of this diminished his appeal, and in fact the public still considers him one of America's greatest presidents. Errol Flynn faced many scandals, including a notorious rape case; they only enhanced his rakish image. Once people have recognized a Star, any kind of publicity, even bad, simply feeds the obsession. Of course you can go too far: people like a Star to have a transcendent beauty, and too much human frailty will eventually disillusion them. But bad publicity is less of a danger than disappearing for too long, or growing too distant. You cannot haunt people's dreams if they never see you. At the same time, you cannot let the public get too familiar with you, or let your image become predictable. People will turn against you in an instant if you begin to bore them, for boredom is the ultimate social evil.

Perhaps the greatest danger Stars face is the endless attention they elicit. Obsessive attention can become disconcerting and worse. As any attractive woman can attest, it is tiring to be gazed at all the time, and the effect can be destructive, as is shown by the story of Marilyn Monroe. The solution is to develop the kind of distance from yourself that Dietrich had—take the attention and idolatry with a grain of salt, and maintain a certain detachment from them. Approach your own image playfully. Most important, never become obsessed with the obsessive quality of people's interest in you.

the anti-Seducer

Seducers draw you in by the focused, individualized attention they pay to you. Anti-Seducers are the opposite: insecure, self-absorbed, and unable to grasp the psychology of another person, they literally repel. Anti-Seducers have no self-awareness, and never realize when they are pestering, imposing, talking too much. They lack the subtlety to create the promise of pleasure that seduction requires. Root out anti-seductive qualities in yourself, and recognize them in others—there is no pleasure or profit in dealing with the Anti-Seducer.

Typology of the Anti-Seducers

Anti-Seducers come in many shapes and kinds, but almost all of them share a single attribute, the source of their repellence: insecurity. We are all insecure, and we suffer for it. Yet we are able to surmount these feelings at times; a seductive engagement can bring us out of our usual self-absorption, and to the degree that we seduce or are seduced, we feel charged and confident. Anti-Seducers, however, are insecure to such a degree that they cannot be drawn into the seductive process. Their needs, their anxieties, their self-consciousness close them off. They interpret the slightest ambiguity on your part as a slight to their ego; they see the merest hint of withdrawal as a betrayal, and are likely to complain bitterly about it.

It seems easy: Anti-Seducers repel, so be repelled—avoid them. Unfortunately, however, many Anti-Seducers cannot be detected as such at first glance. They are more subtle, and unless you are careful they will ensnare you in a most unsatisfying relationship. You must look for clues to their self-involvement and insecurity: perhaps they are ungenerous, or they argue with unusual tenacity, or are excessively judgmental. Perhaps they lavish you with undeserved praise, declaring their love before knowing anything about you. Or, most important, they pay no attention to details. Since they cannot see what makes you different, they cannot surprise you with nuanced attention.

It is critical to recognize anti-seductive qualities not only in others but also in ourselves. Almost all of us have one or two of the Anti-Seducer's qualities latent in our character, and to the extent that we can consciously root them out, we become more seductive. A lack of generosity, for instance, need not signal an Anti-Seducer if it is a person's only fault, but an ungenerous person is seldom truly attractive. Seduction implies opening yourself up, even if only for the purposes of deception; being unable to give by spending money usually means being unable to give in general. Stamp ungenerosity out. It is an impediment to power and a gross sin in seduction.

It is best to disengage from Anti-Seducers early on, before they sink their needy tentacles into you, so learn to read the signs. These are the main types.

Count Lodovico then remarked with a smile: "I promise you that our sensible courtier will never act so stupidly to gain a woman's favor." • Cesare Gonzaga replied: "Nor so stupidly as a gentleman I remember, of some repute, whom to spare men's blushes I don't wish to mention by name." • "Well, at least tell us what he did," said the Duchess. • Then Cesare continued: "He was loved by a very great lady, and at her request he came secretly to the town where she was. After he had seen her and enjoyed her company for as long as she would let him in the time, he sighed and wept bitterly, to show the anguish he was suffering at having to leave her, and he begged her never to forget him; and then he added that she should pay for his lodging at the inn, since it was she who had sent for him and he thought it only right, therefore, that he shouldn't be involved in any expense over the journey." • At this, all the ladies began to laugh and to say that the man concerned hardly deserved the name of gentleman; and many of the men felt as ashamed as he should have been, had he ever had the sense to recognize such disgraceful behavior for what it was.

—Baldassare Castiglione, *The Book of the Courtier*, translated by George Bull

The Brute. If seduction is a kind of ceremony or ritual, part of the pleasure is its duration—the time it takes, the waiting that increases anticipation. Brutes have no patience for such things; they are concerned only with their own pleasure, never with yours. To be patient is to show that you are thinking of the other person, which never fails to impress. Impatience has the opposite effect: assuming you are so interested in them you have no reason to wait, Brutes offend you with their egotism. Underneath that egotism, too, there is often a gnawing sense of inferiority, and if you spurn them or make them wait, they overreact. If you suspect you are dealing with a Brute, do a test—make that person wait. His or her response will tell you everything you need to know.

Let us see now how love is diminished. This happens through the easy accessibility of its consolations, through one's being able to see and converse lengthily with a lover, through a lover's unsuitable garb and gait, and by the sudden onset of poverty. . . . • Another cause of diminution of love is the realization of the notoriety of one's lover, and accounts of his miserliness, bad character, and general wickedness; also any affair with another woman, even if it involves no feelings of love. Love is also diminished if a woman realizes that her lover is foolish and undiscerning, or if she sees him going too far in demands of love, giving no thought to his partner's modesty nor wishing to pardon her blushes. A faithful lover ought to choose the harshest pains of love rather than by his demands cause his partner embarrassment, or take pleasure in spurning her modesty; for one who thinks only of the outcome of his own pleasure, and ignores the welfare of his partner, should be called a traitor rather than a lover. • Love also suffers decrease if the woman realizes that her lover is fearful in war,

The Suffocator. Suffocators fall in love with you before you are even half-aware of their existence. The trait is deceptive—you might think they have found you overwhelming—but the fact is they suffer from an inner void, a deep well of need that cannot be filled. Never get involved with Suffocators; they are almost impossible to free yourself from without trauma. They cling to you until you are forced to pull back, whereupon they smother you with guilt. We tend to idealize a loved one, but love takes time to develop. Recognize Suffocators by how quickly they adore you. To be so admired may give a momentary boost to your ego, but deep inside you sense that their intense emotions are not related to anything you have done. Trust these instincts.

A subvariant of the Suffocator is the Doormat, a person who slavishly imitates you. Spot these types early on by seeing whether they are capable of having an idea of their own. An inability to disagree with you is a bad sign.

The Moralizer. Seduction is a game, and should be undertaken with a light heart. All is fair in love and seduction; morality never enters the picture. The character of the Moralizer, however, is rigid. These are people who follow fixed ideas and try to make you bend to their standards. They want to change you, to make you a better person, so they endlessly criticize and judge—that is their pleasure in life. In truth, their moral ideas stem from their own unhappiness, and mask their desire to dominate those around them. Their inability to adapt and to enjoy makes them easy to recognize; their mental rigidity may also be accompanied by a physical stiffness. It is hard not to take their criticisms personally so it is better to avoid their presence and their poisoned comments.

The Tightwad. Cheapness signals more than a problem with money. It is a sign of something constricted in a person's character—something that keeps them from letting go or taking a risk. It is the most anti-seductive trait of all, and you cannot allow yourself to give in to it. Most tightwads do not realize they have a problem; they actually imagine that when they give someone some paltry crumb, they are being generous. Take a hard look at yourself—you are probably cheaper than you think. Try giving more freely of both your money and yourself and you will see the seductive potential in selective generosity. Of course you must keep your generosity under control. Giving too much can be a sign of desperation, as if you were trying to buy someone.

or sees that he has no patience, or is stained with the vice of pride. There is nothing which appears more appropriate to the character of any lover than to be clad in the adornment of humility, utterly untouched by the nakedness of pride. • Then too the prolixity of a fool or a madman often diminishes love. There are many keen to prolong their crazy words in the presence of a woman, thinking that they please her if they employ foolish, ill-judged language, but in fact they are strangely deceived. Indeed, he who thinks that his foolish behavior pleases a wise woman suffers from the greatest poverty of sense.

—Andreas Capellanus, "How Love Is Diminished," translated by P. G. Walsh

The Bumbler. Bumblers are self-conscious, and their self-consciousness heightens your own. At first you may think they are thinking about you, and so much so that it makes them awkward. In fact they are only thinking of themselves—worrying about how they look, or about the consequences for them of their attempt to seduce you. Their worry is usually contagious: soon you are worrying too, about yourself. Bumblers rarely reach the final stages of a seduction, but if they get that far, they bungle that too. In seduction, the key weapon is boldness, refusing the target the time to stop and think. Bumblers have no sense of timing. You might find it amusing to try to train or educate them, but if they are still Bumblers past a certain age, the case is probably hopeless—they are incapable of getting outside themselves.

The Windbag. The most effective seductions are driven by looks, indirect actions, physical lures. Words have a place, but too much talk will generally break the spell, heightening surface differences and weighing things down. People who talk a lot most often talk about themselves. They have never acquired that inner voice that wonders, Am I boring you? To be a Windbag is to have a deep-rooted selfishness. Never interrupt or argue with these types—that only fuels their windbaggery. At all costs learn to control your own tongue.

*Real men \ Shouldn't primp their good looks. . . . \ Keep pleasantly clean, take exercise, work up an outdoor \ Tan; make quite sure that your toga fits \ And doesn't show spots; don't lace your shoes too tightly \ Or ignore any rusty buckles, or slop \ Around in too large a fitting. Don't let some incompetent barber \ Ruin your looks: both hair and beard demand \ Expert attention. Keep your nails pared, and dirt-free; \ Don't let those long hairs sprout \ In your nostrils, make sure your breath is never offensive, \ Avoid the rank male stench \ That wrinkles noses. . . . \ I was about to warn you [women] against rank goatish armpits \ And bristling hair on your legs, *

The Reactor. Reactors are far too sensitive, not to you but to their own egos. They comb your every word and action for signs of a slight to their vanity. If you strategically back off, as you sometimes must in seduction, they will brood and lash out at you. They are prone to whining and complaining, two very anti-seductive traits. Test them by telling a gentle joke or story at their expense: we should all be able to laugh at ourselves a little, but the Reactor cannot. You can read the resentment in their eyes. Erase any reactive qualities in your own character—they unconsciously repel people.

The Vulgarian. Vulgarians are inattentive to the details that are so important in seduction. You can see this in their personal appearance—their clothes are tasteless by any standard—and in their actions: they do not know that it is sometimes better to control oneself and refuse to give in to one's impulses. Vulgarians will blab, saying anything in public. They have no sense of timing and are rarely in harmony with your tastes. Indiscretion is a sure sign of the Vulgarian (talking to others of your affair, for example); it may seem impulsive, but its real source is their radical selfishness, their inability to see themselves as others see them. More than just avoiding Vulgarians, you must make yourself their opposite—tact, style, and attention to detail are all basic requirements of a seducer.

But I'm not instructing hillbilly girls from the Caucasus, \ Or Mysian river-hoydens—so what need \ To remind you not to let your teeth get all discolored \ Through neglect, or forget to wash \ Your hands every morning? You know how to brighten your complexion \ With powder, add rouge to a bloodless face, \ Skillfully block in the crude outline of an eyebrow, \ Stick a patch on one flawless cheek. \ You don't shrink from lining your eyes with dark mascara \ Or a touch of Cilician saffron. . . . \ But don't let your lover find all those jars and bottles \ On your dressing-table: the best \ Makeup remains unobtrusive. A face so thickly plastered \ With pancake it runs down your sweaty neck \ Is bound to create repulsion. And that goo from unwashed fleeces— \ Athenian maybe, but my dear, the smell!— \ That's used for face-cream: avoid it. When you have company \ Don't dab stuff on your pimples, don't start cleaning your teeth: \ The result may be attractive, but the process is sickening. . . .

—OVID, *THE ART OF LOVE*, TRANSLATED BY PETER GREEN

Examples of the Anti-Seducer

1. Claudius, the step-grandson of the great Roman emperor Augustus, was considered something of an imbecile as a young man, and was treated badly by almost everyone in his family. His nephew Caligula, who became emperor in A.D. 37, made it a sport to torture him, making him run around the palace at top speed as penance for his stupidity, having soiled sandals tied to his hands at supper, and so on. As Claudius grew older, he seemed to become even more slow-witted, and while all of his relatives lived under the constant threat of assassination, he was left alone. So it came as a great surprise to everyone, including Claudius himself, that when, in A.D. 41, a cabal of soldiers assassinated Caligula, they also proclaimed Claudius emperor. Having no desire to rule, he delegated most of the governing to confidantes (a group of freed slaves) and spent his time doing what he loved best: eating, drinking, gambling, and whoring.

Claudius's wife, Valeria Messalina, was one of the most beautiful women in Rome. Although he seemed fond of her, Claudius paid her no attention, and she started to have affairs. At first she was discreet, but over the years, provoked by her husband's neglect, she became more and more debauched. She had a room built for her in the palace where she entertained scores of men, doing her best to imitate the most notorious prostitute in Rome, whose name was written on the door. Any man who refused her advances was put to death. Almost everyone in Rome knew about these frolics, but Claudius said nothing; he seemed oblivious.

So great was Messalina's passion for her favorite lover, Gaius Silius, that she decided to marry him, although both of them were married already. While Claudius was away, they held a wedding ceremony, authorized by a marriage contract that Claudius himself had been tricked into signing. After the ceremony, Gaius moved into the palace. Now the shock and disgust of the whole city finally forced Claudius into action, and he ordered the execution of Gaius and of Messalina's other lovers—but not of Messalina herself. Nevertheless, a gang of soldiers, inflamed by the scandal, hunted her down and stabbed her to death. When this was reported to the emperor, he merely ordered more wine and continued his meal. Several nights later, to the amazement of his slaves, he asked why the empress was not joining him for dinner.

Nothing is more infuriating than being paid no attention. In the process of seduction, you may have to pull back at times, subjecting your target to moments of doubt. But prolonged inattention will not only break the seductive spell, it can create hatred. Claudius was an extreme of this behavior. His insensitivity was created by necessity: in acting like an imbecile, he hid his ambition and protected himself among dangerous competitors. But the insensitivity became second nature. Claudius grew slovenly, and no longer noticed what was going on around him. His inattentiveness had a profound effect on his wife: How, she wondered, can a man, especially a physically unappealing man like Claudius, not notice me, or care about my affairs with other men? But nothing she did seemed to matter to him.

Claudius marks the extreme, but the spectrum of inattention is wide. A lot of people pay too little attention to the details, the signals another person gives. Their senses are dulled by work, by hardship, by self-absorption. We often see this turning off the seductive charge between two people, notably between couples who have been together for years. Carried further, it will stir angry, bitter feelings. Often, the one who has been cheated on by a partner started the dynamic by patterns of inattention.

2. In 1639, a French army besieged and took possession of the Italian city of Turin. Two French officers, the Chevalier (later Count) de Grammont and his friend Matta, decided to turn their attention to the city's beautiful women. The wives of some of Turin's most illustrious men were more than susceptible—their husbands were busy, and kept mistresses of their own. The wives' only requirement was that the suitor play by the rules of gallantry.

The chevalier and Matta were quick to find partners, the chevalier choosing the beautiful Mademoiselle de Saint-Germain, who was soon to be betrothed, and Matta offering his services to an older and more experienced woman, Madame de Senantes. The chevalier took to wearing green, Matta blue, these being their ladies' favorite colors. On the second day of their courtships the couples visited a palace outside the city. The chevalier was all charm, making Mademoiselle de Saint-Germain laugh uproariously at his witticisms, but Matta did not fare so well; he had no patience for this gallantry business, and when he and Madame de Senantes took a stroll, he squeezed her hand and boldly declared his affections. The lady of course was aghast, and when they got back to Turin she left without looking at him. Unaware that he had offended her, Matta imagined that she was overcome with emotion, and felt rather pleased with himself. But the Chevalier de Grammont, wondering why the pair had parted, visited Madame de Senantes and asked her how it went. She told him the truth—Matta had dispensed with the formalities and was ready to bed her. The chevalier

But if, like the winter cat upon the hearth, the lover clings when he is dismissed, and cannot bear to go, certain means must be taken to make him understand; and these should be progressively ruder and ruder, until they touch him to the quick of his flesh. • She should refuse him the bed, and jeer at him, and make him angry; she should stir up her mother's enmity against him; she should treat him with an obvious lack of candor, and spread herself in long considerations about his ruin; his departure should be openly anticipated, his tastes and desires should be thwarted, his poverty outraged; she should let him see that she is in sympathy with another man, she should blame him with harsh words on every occasion; she should tell lies about him to her parasites, she should interrupt his sentences, and send him on frequent errands away from the house. She should seek occasions of quarrel, and make him the victim of a thousand domestic perfidies; she should rack her brains to vex him; she should play with the glances of another in his presence, and give herself up to reprehensible profligacy before his face; she should leave the house as often as possible, and let it be seen that she has no real need to do so. All these means are good for showing a man the door.

—EASTERN LOVE, VOLUME II: *THE HARLOT'S BREVIARY OF KSHEMENDRA*, TRANSLATED BY E. POWYS MATHERS

laughed and thought to himself how differently he would manage affairs if he were the one wooing the lovely Madame.

Over the next few days Matta continued to misread the signs. He did not pay a visit to Madame de Senantes's husband, as custom required. He did not wear her colors. When the two went riding together, he went chasing after hares, as if they were the more interesting prey, and when he took snuff he failed to offer her some. Meanwhile he continued to make his overforward advances. Finally Madame had had enough, and complained to him directly. Matta apologized; he had not realized his errors. Moved by his apology, the lady was more than ready to resume the courtship—but a few days later, after a few trifling stabs at wooing, Matta once again assumed that she was ready for bed. To his dismay, she refused him as before. "I do not think that [women] can be mightily offended," Matta told the chevalier, "if one sometimes leaves off trifling, to come to the point." But Madame de Senantes would have nothing more to do with him, and the Chevalier de Grammont, seeing an opportunity he could not pass by, took advantage of her displeasure by secretly courting her properly, and eventually winning the favors that Matta had tried to force.

There is nothing more anti-seductive than feeling that someone has assumed that you are theirs, that you cannot possibly resist them. The slightest appearance of this kind of conceit is deadly to seduction; you must prove yourself, take your time, win your target's heart. Perhaps you fear that he or she will be offended by a slower pace, or will lose interest. It is more likely, however, that your fear reflects your own insecurity, and insecurity is always anti-seductive. In truth, the longer you take, the more you show the depth of your interest, and the deeper the spell you create.

In a world of few formalities and ceremony, seduction is one of the few remnants from the past that retains the ancient patterns. It is a ritual, and its rites must be observed. Haste reveals not the depth of your feelings but the degree of your self-absorption. It may be possible sometimes to hurry someone into love, but you will only be repaid by the lack of pleasure this kind of love affords. If you are naturally impetuous, do what you can to disguise it. Strangely enough, the effort you spend on holding yourself back may be read by your target as deeply seductive.

3. In Paris in the 1730s lived a young man named Meilcour, who was just of an age to have his first affair. His mother's friend Madame de Lursay, a widow of around forty, was beautiful and charming, but had a reputation for being untouchable; as a boy, Meilcour had been infatuated with her, but never expected his love would be returned. So it was with great surprise and excitement that he realized that now that he was old enough, Madame de Lursay's tender looks seemed to indicate a more than motherly interest in him.

Just as ladies do love men which be valiant and bold under arms, so likewise do they love such as be of like sort in love; and the man which is cowardly and over and above respectful toward them, will never win their good favor. Not that they would have them so overweening, bold, and presumptuous, as that they should by main force lay them on the floor; but rather they desire in them a certain hardy modesty, or perhaps better a certain modest hardihood. For while themselves are not exactly wantons, and will neither solicit a man nor yet actually offer their favors, yet do they know well how to rouse the appetites and passions, and prettily allure to the skirmish in such wise that he which doth not take occasion by the forelock and join encounter, and that without the least awe of rank and greatness, without a scruple of conscience or a fear or any sort of hesitation, he verily is a fool and a spiritless poltroon, and one which doth merit to be forever abandoned of kind fortune. • I have heard of two honorable gentlemen and comrades, for the which two very honorable ladies, and of by no means humble quality, made tryst one day at Paris to go walking in a garden. Being come thither, each lady did separate apart one from the other, each alone with her own cavalier, each in a several alley of the garden, that was so close covered in with a fair trellis of boughs as that daylight could really scarce penetrate there at all, and the coolness of the place was very grateful.

For two months Meilcour trembled in de Lursay's presence. He was afraid of her, and did not know what to do. One evening they were discussing a recent play. How well one character had declared his love to a woman, Madame remarked. Noting Meilcour's obvious discomfort, she went on, "If I am not mistaken, a declaration can only seem such an embarrassing matter because you yourself have one to make." Madame de Lursay knew full well that she was the source of the young man's awkwardness, but she was a tease; you must tell me, she said, with whom you are in love. Finally Meilcour confessed: it was indeed Madame whom he desired. His mother's friend advised him to not think of her that way, but she also sighed, and gave him a long and languid look. Her words said one thing, her eyes another—perhaps she was not as untouchable as he had thought. As the evening ended, though, Madame de Lursay said she doubted his feelings would last, and she left young Meilcour troubled that she had said nothing about reciprocating his love.

Over the next few days, Meilcour repeatedly asked de Lursay to declare her love for him, and she repeatedly refused. Eventually the young man decided his cause was hopeless, and gave up; but a few nights later, at a soirée at her house, her dress seemed more enticing than usual, and her looks at him stirred his blood. He returned them, and followed her around, while she took care to keep a bit of distance, lest others sense what was happening. Yet she also managed to arrange that he could stay without arousing suspicion when the other visitors left.

When they were finally alone, she made him sit beside her on the sofa. He could barely speak; the silence was uncomfortable. To get him talking she raised the same old subject: his youth would make his love for her a passing fancy. Instead of denying it he looked dejected, and continued to keep a polite distance, so that she finally exclaimed, with obvious irony, "If it were known that you were here with my consent, that I had voluntarily arranged it with you . . . what might not people say? And yet how wrong they would be, for no one could be more respectful than you are." Goaded into action, Meilcour grabbed her hand and looked her in the eye. She blushed and told him he should go, but the way she arranged herself on the sofa and looked back at him suggested he should do the opposite. Yet Meilcour still hesitated: she had told him to go, and if he disobeyed she might cause a scene, and might never forgive him; he would have made a fool of himself, and everyone, including his mother, would hear of it. He soon got up, apologizing for his momentary boldness. Her astonished and somewhat cold look meant he had indeed gone too far, he imagined, and he said goodbye and left.

Meilcour and Madame de Lursay appear in the novel *The Wayward Head and Heart*, written in 1738 by Crébillon fils, who based his characters on libertines he knew in the France of the time. For Crébillon fils, seduction is all about signs—about being able to send them and read them. This is not

Now one of the twain was a bold man, and well knowing how the party had been made for something else than merely to walk and take the air, and judging by his lady's face, which he saw to be all a-fire, that she had longings to taste other fare than the muscatels that hung on the trellis, as also by her hot, wanton, and wild speech, he did promptly seize on so fair an opportunity. So catching hold of her without the least ceremony, he did lay her on a little couch that was there made of turf and clods of earth, and did very pleasantly work his will of her, without her ever uttering a word but only: "Heavens! Sir, what are you at? Surely you be the maddest and strangest fellow ever was! If anyone comes, whatever will they say? Great heavens! get out!" But the gentleman, without disturbing himself, did so well continue what he had begun that he did finish, and she to boot, with such content as that after taking three or four turns up and down the alley, they did presently start afresh. Anon, coming forth into another, open, alley, they did see in another part of the garden the other pair, who were walking about together just as they had left them at first. Whereupon the lady, well content, did say to the gentleman in the like condition, "I verily believe so and so hath played the silly prude, and hath given his lady no other entertainment but only words, fine speeches, and promenading." • *Afterward when all four were come together, the two ladies did fall to asking one another*

because sexuality is repressed and requires speaking in code. It is rather because wordless communication (through clothes, gestures, actions) is the most pleasurable, exciting, and seductive form of language.

In Crébillon fils's novel, Madame de Lursay is an ingenious seductress who finds it exciting to initiate young men. But even she cannot overcome the youthful stupidity of Meilcour, who is incapable of reading her signs because he is absorbed in his own thoughts. Later in the story, she does manage to educate him, but in real life there are many who cannot be educated. They are too literal and insensitive to the details that contain seductive power. They do not so much repel as irritate and infuriate you by their constant misinterpretations, always viewing life from behind the screen of their ego and unable to see things as they really are. Meilcour is so caught up in himself he cannot see that Madame is expecting him to make the bold move to which she will have to succumb. His hesitation shows that he is thinking of himself, not of her; that he is worrying about how he will look, not feeling overwhelmed by her charms. Nothing could be more anti-seductive. Recognize such types, and if they are past the young age that would give them an excuse, do not entangle yourself in their awkwardness—they will infect you with doubt.

how it had fared with each. Then the one which was well content did reply she was exceeding well, indeed she was; indeed for the nonce she could scarce be better. The other, which was ill content, did declare for her part she had had to do with the biggest fool and most coward lover she had ever seen; and all the time the two gentlemen could see them laughing together as they walked and crying out: "Oh! the silly fool! the shamefaced poltroon and coward!" At this the successful gallant said to his companion: "Hark to our ladies, which do cry out at you, and mock you sore. You will find you have overplayed the prude and coxcomb this bout." So much he did allow; but there was no more time to remedy his error, for opportunity gave him no other handle to seize her by.

—SEIGNEUR DE BRANTÔME, *LIVES OF FAIR & GALLANT LADIES*, TRANSLATED BY A. R. ALLINSON

4. In the Heian court of late-tenth-century Japan, the young nobleman Kaoru, purported son of the great seducer Genji himself, had had nothing but misfortune in love. He had become infatuated with a young princess, Oigimi, who lived in a dilapidated home in the countryside, her father having fallen on hard times. Then one day he had an encounter with Oigimi's sister, Nakanokimi, that convinced him she was the one he actually loved. Confused, he returned to court, and did not visit the sisters for some time. Then their father died, followed shortly thereafter by Oigimi herself.

Now Kaoru realized his mistake: he had loved Oigimi all along, and she had died out of despair that he did not care for her. He would never meet her like again; she was all he could think about. When Nakanokimi, her father and sister dead, came to live at court, Kaoru had the house where Oigimi and her family had lived turned into a shrine.

One day, Nakanokimi, seeing the melancholy into which Kaoru had fallen, told him that there was a third sister, Ukifune, who resembled his beloved Oigimi and lived hidden away in the countryside. Kaoru came to life—perhaps he had a chance to redeem himself, to change the past. But how could he meet this woman? There came a time when he visited the shrine to pay his respects to the departed Oigimi, and heard that the mysterious Ukifune was there as well. Agitated and excited, he managed to catch a glimpse of her through the crack in a door. The sight of her took his breath away: although she was a plain-looking country girl, in Kaoru's eyes she was the living incarnation of Oigimi. Her voice, meanwhile, was like the voice of Nakanokimi, whom he had loved as well. Tears welled up in his eyes.

A few months later Kaoru managed to find the house in the mountains where Ukifune lived. He visited her there, and she did not disappoint. "I once had a glimpse of you through a crack in a door," he told her, and "you have been very much on my mind ever since." Then he picked her up in his arms and carried her to a waiting carriage. He was taking her back to the shrine, and the journey there brought back to him the image of Oigimi; again his eyes clouded with tears. Looking at Ukifune, he silently compared her to Oigimi—her clothes were less nice but she had beautiful hair.

When Oigimi was alive, she and Kaoru had played the koto together, so once at the shrine he had kotos brought out. Ukifune did not play as well as Oigimi had, and her manners were less refined. Not to worry—he would give her lessons, change her into a lady. But then, as he had done with Oigimi, Kaoru returned to court, leaving Ukifune languishing at the shrine. Some time passed before he visited her again; she had improved, was more beautiful than before, but he could not stop thinking of Oigimi. Once again he left her, promising to bring her to court, but more weeks passed, and finally he received the news that Ukifune had disappeared, last seen heading toward a river. She had most likely committed suicide.

At the funeral ceremony for Ukifune, Kaoru was wracked with guilt: why had he not come for her earlier? She deserved a better fate.

Kaoru and the others appear in the eleventh-century Japanese novel *The Tale of Genji*, by the noblewoman Murasaki Shikibu. The characters are based on people the author knew, but Kaoru's type appears in every culture and period: these are men and women who seem to be searching for an ideal partner. The one they have is never quite right; at first glance a person excites them, but they soon see faults, and when a new person crosses their path, he or she looks better and the first person is forgotten. These types often try to work on the imperfect mortal who has excited them, to improve them culturally and morally. But this proves extremely unsatisfactory for both parties.

The truth about this type is not that they are searching for an ideal but that they are hopelessly unhappy with themselves. You may mistake their dissatisfaction for a perfectionist's high standards, but in point of fact nothing will really satisfy them, for their unhappiness is deep-rooted. You can recognize them by their past, which will be littered with short-lived, stormy romances. Also, they will tend to compare you to others, and to try to remake you. You may not realize at first what you have gotten into, but people like this will eventually prove hopelessly anti-seductive because they cannot see your individual qualities. Cut the romance off before it happens. These types are closet sadists and will torture you with their unreachable goals.

5. In 1762, in the city of Turin, Italy, Giovanni Giacomo Casanova made the acquaintance of one Count A.B., a Milanese gentleman who seemed to like him enormously. The count had fallen on hard times and Casanova lent him some money. In gratitude, the count invited Casanova to stay with him and his wife in Milan. His wife, he said, was from Barcelona, and was admired far and wide for her beauty. He showed Casanova her letters, which had an intriguing wit; Casanova imagined her as a prize worth seducing. He went to Milan.

Arriving at the house of Count A.B., Casanova found that the Spanish lady was certainly beautiful, but that she was also quiet and serious. Something about her bothered him. As he was unpacking his clothes, the countess saw a stunning red dress, trimmed with sable, among his belongings. It was a gift, Casanova explained, for any Milanese lady who won his heart.

The following evening at dinner, the countess was suddenly more friendly, teasing and bantering with Casanova. She described the dress as a bribe—he would use it to persuade a woman to give in to him. On the contrary, said Casanova, he only gave gifts afterward, as tokens of his appreciation. That evening, in a carriage on the way back from the opera, she asked him if a wealthy friend of hers could buy the dress, and when he said no, she was clearly vexed. Sensing her game, Casanova offered to give her the sable dress if she was kind to him. This only made her angry, and they quarreled.

Finally Casanova had had enough of the countess's moods: he sold the dress for 15,000 francs to her wealthy friend, who in turn gave it to her, as she had planned all along. But to prove his lack of interest in money, Casanova told the countess he would give her the 15,000 francs, no strings attached. "You are a very bad man," she said, "but you can stay, you amuse me." She resumed her coquettish manner, but Casanova was not fooled. "It is not my fault, madame, if your charms have so little power over me," he told her. "Here are 15,000 francs to console you." He laid the money on a table and walked out, leaving the countess fuming and vowing revenge.

When Casanova first met the Spanish lady, two things about her repelled him. First, her pride: rather than engaging in the give-and-take of seduction, she demanded a man's subjugation. Pride can reflect self-assurance, signaling that you will not abase yourself before others. Just as often, though, it stems from an inferiority complex, which demands that others abase themselves before you. Seduction requires an openness to the other person, a willingness to bend and adapt. Excessive pride, without anything to justify it, is highly anti-seductive.

The second quality that disgusted Casanova was the countess's greed: her coquettish little games were designed only to get the dress—she had no interest in romance. For Casanova, seduction was a lighthearted game that people played for their mutual amusement. In his scheme of things, it was fine if a woman wanted money and gifts as well; he could understand that desire, and he was a generous man. But he also felt that this was a desire a woman should disguise—she should create the impression that what she was after was pleasure. The person who is obviously angling for money or other material reward can only repel. If that is your intention, if you are looking for something other than pleasure—for money, for power—never show it. The suspicion of an ulterior motive is anti-seductive. Never let anything break the illusion.

6. In 1868, Queen Victoria of England hosted her first private meeting with the country's new prime minister, William Gladstone. She had met him before, and knew his reputation as a moral absolutist, but this was to be a ceremony, an exchange of pleasantries. Gladstone, however, had no patience for such things. At that first meeting he explained to the queen his theory of royalty: the queen, he believed, had to play an exemplary role in England—a role she had lately failed to live up to, for she was overly private.

This lecture set a bad tone for the future, and things only got worse: soon Victoria was receiving letters from Gladstone, addressing the subject in even greater depth. Half of them she never bothered to read, and soon she was doing everything she could to avoid contact with the leader of her government; if she had to see him, she made the meeting as brief as possible. To that end, she never allowed him to sit down in her presence, hoping that a man his age would soon tire and leave. For once he got going on a subject dear to his heart, he did not notice your look of disinterest or the tears in your eyes from yawning. His memoranda on even the simplest of issues would have to be translated into plain English for her by a member of her staff. Worst of all, Gladstone argued with her, and his arguments had a way of making her feel stupid. She soon learned to nod her head and appear to agree with whatever abstract point he was trying to make. In a letter to her secretary, referring to herself in the third person, she wrote, "She always felt in [Gladstone's] manner an overbearing obstinacy and imperiousness . . . which she never experienced from *anyone* else, and which she found most disagreeable." Over the years, these feelings hardened into an unwaning hatred.

As the head of the Liberal Party, Gladstone had a nemesis, Benjamin Disraeli, the head of the Conservative Party. He considered Disraeli amoral, a devilish Jew. At one session of Parliament, Gladstone tore into his rival, scoring point after point as he described where his opponent's policies would lead. Growing angry as he spoke (as usually happened when he talked of Disraeli), he pounded the speaker's table with such force that pens and papers went flying. Through all of this Disraeli seemed half-asleep. When Gladstone had finished, he opened his eyes, rose to his feet, and calmly walked up to the table. "The right honorable gentleman," he said, "has spoken with much passion, much eloquence, and much—*ahem*—violence." Then, after a drawn-out pause, he continued, "But the damage can be repaired"—and he proceeded to gather up everything that had fallen from the table and put them back in place. The speech that followed was all the more masterful for its calm and ironic contrast to Gladstone's. The members of Parliament were spellbound, and all of them agreed he had won the day.

If Disraeli was the consummate social seducer and charmer, Gladstone was the Anti-Seducer. Of course he had supporters, mostly among the more puritanical elements of society—he twice defeated Disraeli in a general election. But he found it hard to broaden his appeal beyond the circle of believers. Women in particular found him insufferable. Of course they had no vote at the time, so they were little political liability; but Gladstone had no patience for a feminine point of view. A woman, he felt, had to learn to see things as a man did, and it was his purpose in life to educate those he felt were irrational or abandoned by God.

It did not take long for Gladstone to wear on anyone's nerves. That is the nature of people who are convinced of some truth, but have no patience for a different perspective or for dealing with someone else's psychology. These types are bullies, and in the short term they often get their way, particularly among the less aggressive. But they stir up a lot of resentment and unspoken antipathy, which eventually trips them up. People see through their righteous moral stance, which is most often a cover for a power play—morality is a form of power. A seducer never seeks to persuade directly, never parades his or her morality, never lectures or imposes. Everything is subtle, psychological, and indirect.

Symbol: *The Crab. In a harsh world, the crab survives by its hardened shell, by the threat of its pincers, and by burrowing into the sand. No one dares get too close. But the Crab cannot surprise its enemy and has little mobility. Its defensive strength is its supreme limitation.*

Uses of Anti-Seduction

The best way to avoid entanglements with Anti-Seducers is to recognize them right away and give them a wide berth, but they often deceive us. Involvements with these types are painful, and are hard to disengage from, because the more emotional response you show, the more engaged you seem to be. Do not get angry—that may only encourage them or exacerbate their anti-seductive tendencies. Instead, act distant and indifferent, pay no attention to them, make them feel how little they matter to you. The best antidote to an Anti-Seducer is often to be anti-seductive yourself.

Cleopatra had a devastating effect on every man who crossed her path. Octavius—the future Emperor Augustus, and the man who would defeat and destroy Cleopatra's lover Mark Antony—was well aware of her power, and defended himself against it by being always extremely amiable with her, courteous to the extreme, but never showing the slightest emotion, whether of interest or dislike. In other words, he treated her as if she were any other woman. Facing this front, she could not sink her hooks into him. Octavius made anti-seduction his defense against the most irresistible woman in history. Remember: seduction is a game of attention, of slowly filling the other person's mind with your presence. Distance and inattention will create the opposite effect, and can be used as a tactic when the need arises.

Finally, if you really want to "anti-seduce," simply feign the qualities listed at the beginning of the chapter. Nag; talk a lot, particularly about yourself; dress against the other person's tastes; pay no attention to detail; suffocate, and so on. A word of warning: with the arguing type, the Windbag, never talk back too much. Words will only fan the flames. Adopt the Queen Victoria strategy: nod, seem to agree, then find an excuse to cut the conversation short. This is the only defense.

the seducer's Victims—The Eighteen Types

The people around you are all potential victims of a seduction, but first you must know what type of victim you are dealing with. Victims are categorized by what they feel they are missing in life—adventure, attention, romance, a naughty experience, mental or physical stimulation, etc. Once you identify their type, you have the necessary ingredients for a seduction: you will be the one to give them what they lack and cannot get on their own. In studying potential victims, learn to see the reality behind the appearance. A timid person may yearn to play the star; a prude may long for a transgressive thrill. Never try to seduce your own type.

○ ○ ○

○ ○

○

Victim Theory

Nobody in this world feels whole and complete. We all sense some gap in our character, something we need or want but cannot get on our own. When we fall in love, it is often with someone who seems to fill that gap. The process is usually unconscious and depends on luck: we wait for the right person to cross our path, and when we fall for them we hope they return our love. But the seducer does not leave such things to chance.

Look at the people around you. Forget their social exterior, their obvious character traits; look behind all of that, focusing on the gaps, the missing pieces in their psyche. That is the raw material of any seduction. Pay close attention to their clothes, their gestures, their offhand comments, the things in their house, certain looks in their eyes; get them to talk about their past, particularly past romances. And slowly the outline of those missing pieces will come into view. Understand: people are constantly giving out signals as to what they lack. They long for completeness, whether the illusion of it or the reality, and if it has to come from another person, that person has tremendous power over them. We may call them victims of a seduction, but they are almost always willing victims.

This chapter outlines the eighteen types of victims, each one of which has a dominant lack. Although your target may well reveal the qualities of more than one type, there is usually a common need that ties them together. Perhaps you see someone as both a New Prude and a Crushed Star, but what is common to both is a feeling of repression, and therefore a desire to be naughty, along with a fear of not being able or daring enough. In identifying your victim's type, be careful to not be taken in by outward appearances. Both deliberately and unconsciously, we often develop a social exterior designed specifically to disguise our weaknesses and lacks. For instance, you may think you are dealing with someone who is tough and cynical, without realizing that deep inside they have a soft sentimental core. They secretly pine for romance. And unless you identify their type and the emotions beneath their toughness, you lose the chance to truly seduce them. Most important: expunge the nasty habit of thinking that other people have the same lacks you do. You may crave comfort and security, but in giving comfort and security to someone else, on the assumption they must want them as well, you are more likely smothering and pushing them away.

Never try to seduce someone who is of your own type. You will be like two puzzles missing the same parts.

The Eighteen Types

The Reformed Rake or Siren. People of this type were once happy-go-lucky seducers who had their way with the opposite sex. But the day came when they were forced to give this up—someone corraled them into a relationship, they were encountering too much social hostility, they were getting older and decided to settle down. Whatever the reason, you can be sure they feel some resentment and a sense of loss, as if a limb were missing. We are always trying to recapture pleasures we experienced in the past, but the temptation is particularly great for the Reformed Rake or Siren because the pleasures they found in seduction were intense. These types are ripe for the picking: all that is required is that you cross their path and offer them the opportunity to resume their rakish or siren ways. Their blood will stir and the call of their youth will overwhelm them.

It is critical, though, to give these types the illusion that they are the ones doing the seducing. With the Reformed Rake, you must spark his interest indirectly, then let him burn and glow with desire. With the Reformed Siren, you want to give her the impression that she still has the irresistible power to draw a man in and make him give up everything for her. Remember that what you are offering these types is not another relationship, another constriction, but rather the chance to escape the corral and have some fun. Do not be put off if they are in a relationship; a preexisting commitment is often the perfect foil. If hooking them into a relationship is what you want, hide it as best you can and realize it may not be possible. The Rake or Siren is unfaithful by nature; your ability to spark the old feeling gives you power, but then you will have to live with the consequences of their feckless ways.

The Disappointed Dreamer. As children, these types probably spent a lot of time alone. To entertain themselves they developed a powerful fantasy life, fed by books and films and other kinds of popular culture. And as they get older, it becomes increasingly difficult to reconcile their fantasy life with reality, and so they are often disappointed by what they get. This is particularly true in relationships. They have been dreaming of romantic heroes, of danger and excitement, but what they have is lovers with human frailties, the petty weaknesses of everyday life. As the years pass, they may force themselves to compromise, because otherwise they would have to spend their lives alone; but beneath the surface they are bitter and still hungering for something grand and romantic.

You can recognize this type by the books they read and films they go to, the way their ears prick up when told of the real-life adventures some people manage to live out. In their clothes and home furnishings, a taste for exuberant romance or drama will peek through. They are often trapped in drab relationships, and little comments here and there will reveal their disappointment and inner tension.

These types make for excellent and satisfying victims. First, they usually have a great deal of pent-up passion and energy, which you can release and focus on yourself. They also have great imaginations and will respond to anything vaguely mysterious or romantic that you offer them. All you need do is disguise some of your less than exalted qualities and give them a part of their dream. This could be the chance to live out their adventures or be courted by a chivalrous soul. If you give them a part of what they want they will imagine the rest. At all cost, do not let reality break the illusion you are creating. One moment of pettiness and they will be gone, more bitterly disappointed than ever.

The Pampered Royal. These people were the classic spoiled children. All of their wants and desires were met by an adoring parent—endless entertainments, a parade of toys, whatever kept them happy for a day or two. Where many children learn to entertain themselves, inventing games and finding friends, Pampered Royals are taught that others will do the entertaining for them. Being spoiled, they get lazy, and as they get older and the parent is no longer there to pamper them, they tend to feel quite bored and restless. Their solution is to find pleasure in variety, to move quickly from person to person, job to job, or place to place before boredom sets in. They do not settle into relationships well because habit and routine of some kind are inevitable in such affairs. But their ceaseless search for variety is tiring for them and comes with a price: work problems, strings of unsatisfying romances, friends scattered across the globe. Do not mistake their restlessness and infidelity for reality—what the Pampered Prince or Princess is really looking for is one person, that parental figure, who will give them the spoiling they crave.

To seduce this type, be ready to provide a lot of distraction—new places to visit, novel experiences, color, spectacle. You will have to maintain an air of mystery, continually surprising your target with a new side to your character. Variety is the key. Once Pampered Royals are hooked, things get easier for they will quickly grow dependent on you and you can put out less effort. Unless their childhood pampering has made them too difficult and lazy, these types make excellent victims—they will be as loyal to you as they once were to mommy or daddy. But you will have to do much of the work. If you are after a long relationship, disguise it. Offer long-term security to a Pampered Royal and you will induce a panicked flight. Recognize these types by the turmoil in their past—job changes, travel, short-term relationships—and by the air of aristocracy, no matter their social class, that comes from once being treated like royalty.

The New Prude. Sexual prudery still exists, but it is less common than it was. Prudery, however, is never just about sex; a prude is someone who is excessively concerned with appearances, with what society considers appropriate and acceptable behavior. Prudes rigorously stay within the boundaries of correctness because more than anything they fear society's judgment. Seen in this light, prudery is just as prevalent as it always was.

The New Prude is excessively concerned with standards of goodness, fairness, political sensitivity, tastefulness, etc. What marks the New Prude, though, as well as the old one, is that deep down they are actually excited and intrigued by guilty, transgressive pleasures. Frightened by this attraction, they run in the opposite direction and become the most correct of all. They tend to wear drab colors; they certainly never take fashion risks. They can be very judgmental and critical of people who do take risks and are less correct. They are also addicted to routine, which gives them a way to tamp down their inner turmoil.

New Prudes are secretly oppressed by their correctness and long to transgress. Just as sexual prudes make prime targets for a Rake or Siren, the New Prude will often be most tempted by someone with a dangerous or naughty side. If you desire a New Prude, do not be taken in by their judgments of you or their criticisms. That is only a sign of how deeply you fascinate them; you are on their mind. You can often draw a New Prude into a seduction, in fact, by giving them the chance to criticize you or even try to reform you. Take nothing of what they say to heart, of course, but now you have the perfect excuse to spend time with them—and New Prudes can be seduced simply through being in contact with you. These types actually make excellent and rewarding victims. Once you open them up and get them to let go of their correctness, they are flooded with feelings and energies. They may even overwhelm you. Perhaps they are in a relationship with someone as drab as they themselves seem to be—do not be put off. They are simply asleep, waiting to be awakened.

The Crushed Star. We all want attention, we all want to shine, but with most of us these desires are fleeting and easily quieted. The problem with Crushed Stars is that at one point in their lives they did find themselves the center of attention—perhaps they were beautiful, charming and effervescent, perhaps they were athletes, or had some other talent—but those days are gone. They may seem to have accepted this, but the memory of having once shone is hard to get over. In general, the appearance of wanting attention, of trying to stand out, is not seen too kindly in polite society or in the workplace. So to get along, Crushed Stars learn to tamp down their desires; but failing to get the attention they feel they deserve, they also become resentful. You can recognize Crushed Stars by certain unguarded moments: they suddenly receive some attention in a social setting, and it makes them glow; they mention their glory days, and there is a little glint in the eye; a little wine in the system, and they become effervescent.

Seducing this type is simple: just make them the center of attention. When you are with them, act as if they were stars and you were basking in their glow. Get them to talk, particularly about themselves. In social situations, mute your own colors and let them look funny and radiant by comparison. In general, play the Charmer. The reward of seducing Crushed Stars is that you stir up powerful emotions. They will feel intensely grateful to you for letting them shine. To whatever extent they had felt crushed and bottled up, the easing of that pain releases intensity and passion, all directed at you. They will fall madly in love. If you yourself have any star or dandy tendencies it is wise to avoid such victims. Sooner or later those tendencies will come out, and the competition between you will be ugly.

The Novice. What separates Novices from ordinary innocent young people is that they are fatally curious. They have little or no experience of the world, but have been exposed to it secondhand—in newspapers, films, books. Finding their innocence a burden, they long to be initiated into the ways of the world. Everyone sees them as so sweet and innocent, but they know this isn't so—they cannot be as angelic as people think them.

Seducing a Novice is easy. To do it well, however, requires a bit of art. Novices are interested in people with experience, particularly people with a touch of corruption and evil. Make that touch too strong, though, and it will intimidate and frighten them. What works best with a Novice is a mix of qualities. You are somewhat childlike yourself, with a playful spirit. At the same time, it is clear that you have hidden depths, even sinister ones. (This was the secret of Lord Byron's success with so many innocent women.) You are initiating your Novices not just sexually but experientially, exposing them to new ideas, taking them to new places, new worlds both literal and metaphoric. Do not make your seduction ugly or seedy—everything must be romantic, even including the evil and dark side of life. Young people have their ideals; it is best to initiate them with an aesthetic touch. Seductive language works wonders on Novices, as does attention to detail. Spectacles and colorful events appeal to their sensitive senses. They are easily misled by these tactics, because they lack the experience to see through them.

Sometimes Novices are a little older and have been at least somewhat educated in the ways of the world. Yet they put on a show of innocence, for they see the power it has over older people. These are coy Novices, aware of the game they are playing—but Novices they remain. They may be less easily misled than purer Novices, but the way to seduce them is pretty much the same—mix innocence and corruption and you will fascinate them.

The Conqueror. These types have an unusual amount of energy, which they find difficult to control. They are always on the prowl for people to conquer, obstacles to surmount. You will not always recognize Conquerors by their exterior—they can seem a little shy in social situations and can have a degree of reserve. Look not at their words or appearance but at their actions, in work and in relationships. They love power, and by hook or by crook they get it.

Conquerors tend to be emotional, but their emotion only comes out in outbursts, when pushed. In matters of romance, the worst thing you can do with them is lie down and make yourself easy prey; they may take advantage of your weakness, but they will quickly discard you and leave you the worse for wear. You want to give Conquerors a chance to be aggressive, to overcome some resistance or obstacle, before letting them think they have overwhelmed you. You want to give them a good chase. Being a little difficult or moody, using coquetry, will often do the trick. Do not be intimidated by their aggressiveness and energy—that is precisely what you can turn to your advantage. To break them in, keep them charging back and forth like a bull. Eventually they will grow weak and dependent, as Napoleon became the slave of Josephine.

The Conqueror is generally male but there are plenty of female Conquerors out there—Lou Andreas-Salomé and Natalie Barney are famous ones. Female Conquerors will succumb to coquetry, though, just as the male ones will.

The Exotic Fetishist. Most of us are excited and intrigued by the exotic. What separates Exotic Fetishists from the rest of us is the degree of this interest, which seems to govern all their choices in life. In truth they feel empty inside and have a strong dose of self-loathing. They do not like wherever it is they come from, their social class (usually middle or upper), and their culture because they do not like themselves.

These types are easy to recognize. They like to travel; their houses are filled with *objets* from faraway places; they fetishize the music or art of this or that foreign culture. They often have a strong rebellious streak. Clearly the way to seduce them is to position yourself as exotic—if you do not at least appear to come from a different background or race, or to have some alien aura, you should not even bother. But it is always possible to play up what makes you exotic, to make it a kind of theater for their amusement. Your clothes, the things you talk about, the places you take them, make a show of your difference. Exaggerate a little and they will imagine the rest, because such types tend to be self-deluders. Exotic Fetishists, however, do not make particularly good victims. Whatever exoticism you have will soon seem banal to them, and they will want something else. It will be a struggle to hold their interest. Their underlying insecurity will also keep you on edge.

One variation on this type is the man or woman who is trapped in a stultifying relationship, a banal occupation, a dead-end town. It is circumstance, as opposed to personal neurosis, that makes such people fetishize the exotic; and these Exotic Fetishists are better victims than the self-loathing kind, because you can offer them a temporary escape from whatever oppresses them. Nothing, however, will offer true Exotic Fetishists escape from themselves.

The Drama Queen. There are people who cannot do without some constant drama in their lives—it is their way of deflecting boredom. The greatest mistake you can make in seducing these Drama Queens is to come offering stability and security. That will only make them run for the hills. Most often, Drama Queens (and there are plenty of men in this category) enjoy playing the victim. They want something to complain about, they want pain. Pain is a source of pleasure for them. With this type, you have to be willing and able to give them the mental rough treatment they desire. That is the only way to seduce them in a deep manner. The moment you turn too nice, they will find some reason to quarrel or get rid of you.

You will recognize Drama Queens by the number of people who have hurt them, the tragedies and traumas that have befallen them. At the extreme, they can be hopelessly selfish and anti-seductive, but most of them are relatively harmless and will make fine victims if you can live with the sturm und drang. If for some reason you want something long term with this type, you will constantly have to inject drama into your relationship. For some this can be an exciting challenge and a source for constantly renewing the relationship. Generally, however, you should see an involvement with a Drama Queen as something fleeting and a way to bring a little drama into your own life.

The Professor. These types cannot get out of the trap of analyzing and criticizing everything that crosses their path. Their minds are overdeveloped and overstimulated. Even when they talk about love or sex, it is with great thought and analysis. Having developed their minds at the expense of their bodies, many of them feel physically inferior and compensate by lording their mental superiority over others. Their conversation is often wry or ironic—you never quite know what they are saying, but you sense them looking down on you. They would like to escape their mental prisons, they would like pure physicality, without any analysis, but they cannot get there on their own. Professor types sometimes engage in relationships with other professor types, or with people they can treat as inferiors. But deep down they long to be overwhelmed by someone with physical presence—a Rake or a Siren, for instance.

Professors can make excellent victims, for underneath their intellectual strength lie gnawing insecurities. Make them feel like Don Juans or Sirens, to even the slightest degree, and they are your slaves. Many of them have a masochistic streak that will come out once you stir their dormant senses. You are offering an escape from the mind, so make it as complete as possible: if you have intellectual tendencies yourself, hide them. They will only stir your target's competitive juices and get their minds turning. Let your Professors keep their sense of mental superiority; let them judge you. You will know what they will try to hide: that you are the one in control, for you are giving them what no one else can give them—physical stimulation.

The Beauty. From early on in life, the Beauty is gazed at by others. Their desire to look at her is the source of her power, but also the source of much unhappiness: she constantly worries that her powers are waning, that she is no longer attracting attention. If she is honest with herself, she also senses that being worshiped only for one's appearance is monotonous and unsatisfying—and lonely. Many men are intimidated by beauty and prefer to worship it from afar; others are drawn in, but not for the purpose of conversation. The Beauty suffers from isolation.

Because she has so many lacks, the Beauty is relatively easy to seduce, and if done right, you will have won not only a much prized catch but someone who will grow dependent on what you provide. Most important in this seduction is to validate those parts of the Beauty that no one else appreciates—her intelligence (generally higher than people imagine), her skills, her character. Of course you must worship her body—you cannot stir up any insecurities in the one area in which she knows her strength, and the strength on which she most depends—but you also must worship her mind and soul. Intellectual stimulation will work well on the Beauty, distracting her from her doubts and insecurities, and making it seem that you value that side of her personality.

Because the Beauty is always being looked at, she tends to be passive. Beneath her passivity, though, there often lies frustration: the Beauty would love to be more active and to actually do some chasing of her own. A little coquettishness can work well here: at some point in all your worshiping, you might go a little cold, inviting her to come after you. Train her to be more active and you will have an excellent victim. The only downside is that her many insecurities require constant attention and care.

The Aging Baby. Some people refuse to grow up. Perhaps they are afraid of death or of growing old; perhaps they are passionately attached to the life they led as children. Disliking responsibility, they struggle to turn everything into play and recreation. In their twenties they can be charming, in their thirties interesting, but by the time they reach their forties they are beginning to wear thin.

Contrary to what you might imagine, one Aging Baby does not want to be involved with another Aging Baby, even though the combination might seem to increase the chances for play and frivolity. The Aging Baby does not want competition, but an adult figure. If you desire to seduce this type, you must be prepared to be the responsible, staid one. That may be a strange way of seducing, but in this case it works. You should appear to like the Aging Baby's youthful spirit (it helps if you actually do), can engage with it, but you remain the indulgent adult. By being responsible you free the Baby to play. Act the loving adult to the hilt, never judging or criticizing their behavior, and a strong attachment will form. Aging Babies can be amusing for a while, but, like all children, they are often potently narcissistic. This limits the pleasure you can have with them. You should see them as short-term amusements or temporary outlets for your frustrated parental instincts.

The Rescuer. We are often drawn to people who seem vulnerable or weak—their sadness or depression can actually be quite seductive. There are people, however, who take this much further, who seem to be attracted only to people with problems. This may seem noble, but Rescuers usually have complicated motives: they often have sensitive natures and truly want to help. At the same time, solving people's problems gives them a kind of power they relish—it makes them feel superior and in control. It is also the perfect way to distract them from their own problems. You will recognize these types by their empathy—they listen well and try to get you to open up and talk. You will also notice they have histories of relationships with dependent and troubled people.

Rescuers can make excellent victims, particularly if you enjoy chivalrous or maternal attention. If you are a woman, play the damsel in distress, giving a man the chance so many men long for—to act the knight. If you are a man, play the boy who cannot deal with this harsh world; a female Rescuer will envelop you in maternal attention, gaining for herself the added satisfaction of feeling more powerful and in control than a man. An air of sadness will draw either gender in. Exaggerate your weaknesses, but not through overt words or gestures—let them *sense* that you have had too little love, that you have had a string of bad relationships, that you have gotten a raw deal in life. Having lured your Rescuer in with the chance to help you, you can then stoke the relationship's fires with a steady supply of needs and vulnerabilities. You can also invite moral rescue: you are bad. You have done bad things. You need a stern yet loving hand. In this case the Rescuer gets to feel morally superior, but also the vicarious thrill of involvement with someone naughty.

The Roué. These types have lived the good life and experienced many pleasures. They probably have, or once had, a good deal of money to finance their hedonistic lives. On the outside they tend to seem cynical and jaded, but their worldliness often hides a sentimentality that they have struggled to repress. Roués are consummate seducers, but there is one type that can easily seduce them—the young and the innocent. As they get older, they hanker after their lost youth; missing their long-lost innocence, they begin to covet it in others.

If you should want to seduce them, you will probably have to be somewhat young and to have retained at least the appearance of innocence. It is easy to play this up—make a show of how little experience you have in the world, how you still see things as a child. It is also good to seem to resist their advances: Roués will think it lively and exciting to chase you. You can even seem to dislike or distrust them—that will really spur them on. By being the one who resists, you control the dynamic. And since you have the youth that they are missing, you can maintain the upper hand and make them fall deeply in love. They will often be susceptible to such a fall, because they have tamped down their own romantic tendencies for so long that when it bursts forth, they lose control. Never give in too early, and never let your guard down—such types can be dangerous.

The Idol Worshiper. Everyone feels an inner lack, but Idol Worshipers have a bigger emptiness than most people. They cannot be satisfied with themselves, so they search the world for something to worship, something to fill their inner void. This often assumes the form of a great interest in spiritual matters or in some worthwhile cause; by focusing on something supposedly elevated, they distract themselves from their own void, from what they dislike about themselves. Idol Worshipers are easy to spot—they are the ones pouring their energies into some cause or religion. They often move around over the years, leaving one cult for another.

The way to seduce these types is to simply become their object of worship, to take the place of the cause or religion to which they are so dedicated. At first you may have to seem to share their spiritual interest, joining them in their worship, or perhaps exposing them to a new cause; eventually you will displace it. With this type you have to hide your flaws, or at least to give them a saintly sheen. Be banal and Idol Worshipers will pass you by. But mirror the qualities they aspire to have for themselves and they will slowly transfer their adoration to you. Keep everything on an elevated plane—let romance and religion flow into one.

Keep two things in mind when seducing this type. First, they tend to have overactive minds, which can make them quite suspicious. Because they often lack physical stimulation, and because physical stimulation will distract them, give them some: a mountain trek, a boat trip, or sex will do the trick. But this takes a lot of work, for their minds are always ticking. Second, they often suffer from low self-esteem. Do not try to raise it; they will see through you, and your efforts at praising them will clash with their own self-image. They are to worship you; you are not to worship them. Idol Worshipers make perfectly adequate victims in the short term, but their endless need to search will eventually lead them to look for something new to adore.

The Sensualist. What marks these types is not their love of pleasure but their overactive senses. Sometimes they show this quality in their appearance—their interest in fashion, color, style. But sometimes it is more subtle: because they are so sensitive, they are often quite shy, and they will shrink from standing out or being flamboyant. You will recognize them by how responsive they are to their environment, how they cannot stand a room without sunlight, are depressed by certain colors, or excited by certain smells. They happen to live in a culture that deemphasizes sensual experience (except perhaps for the sense of sight). And so what the Sensualist lacks is precisely enough sensual experiences to appreciate and relish.

The key to seducing them is to aim for their senses, to take them to beautiful places, pay attention to detail, envelop them in spectacle, and of course use plenty of physical lures. Sensualists, like animals, can be baited with colors and smells. Appeal to as many senses as possible, keeping your targets distracted and weak. Seductions of Sensualists are often easy and quick, and you can use the same tactics again and again to keep them interested, although it is wise to vary your sensual appeals somewhat, in kind if not in quality. That is how Cleopatra worked on Mark Antony, an inveterate Sensualist. These types make superb victims because they are relatively docile if you give them what they want.

The Lonely Leader. Powerful people are not necessarily different from everyone else, but they are treated differently, and this has a big effect on their personalities. Everyone around them tends to be fawning and courtierlike, to have an angle, to want something from them. This makes them suspicious and distrustful, and a little hard around the edges, but do not mistake the appearance for the reality: Lonely Leaders long to be seduced, to have someone break through their isolation and overwhelm them. The problem is that most people are too intimidated to try, or use the kind of tactics—flattery, charm—that they see through and despise. To seduce such types, it is better to act like their equal or even their superior—the kind of treatment they never get. If you are blunt with them you will seem genuine, and they will be touched—you care enough to be honest, even perhaps at some risk. (Being blunt with the powerful can be dangerous.) Lonely Leaders can be made emotional by inflicting some pain, followed by tenderness.

This is one of the hardest types to seduce, not only because they are suspicious but because their minds are burdened with cares and responsibilities. They have less mental space for a seduction. You will have to be patient and clever, slowly filling their minds with thoughts of you. Succeed, though, and you can gain great power in turn, for in their loneliness they will come to depend on you.

The Floating Gender. All of us have a mix of the masculine and the feminine in our characters, but most of us learn to develop and exhibit the socially acceptable side while repressing the other. People of the Floating Gender type feel that the separation of the sexes into such distinct genders is a burden. They are sometimes thought to be repressed or latent homosexuals, but this is a misunderstanding: they may well be heterosexual but their masculine and feminine sides are in flux, and because this may discomfit others if they show it, they learn to repress it, perhaps by going to one extreme. They would actually love to be able to play with their gender, to give full expression to both sides. Many people fall into this type without its being obvious: a woman may have a masculine energy, a man a developed aesthetic side. Do not look for obvious signs, because these types often go underground, keeping it under wraps. This makes them vulnerable to a powerful seduction.

What Floating Gender types are really looking for is another person of uncertain gender, their counterpart from the opposite sex. Show them that in your presence and they can relax, express the repressed side of their character. If you have such proclivities, this is the one instance where it would be best to seduce the same type of the opposite sex. Each person will stir up repressed desires in the other and will suddenly have license to explore all kinds of gender combinations, without fear of judgment. If you are not of the Floating Gender, leave this type alone. You will only inhibit them and create more discomfort.

Part Two

the Seductive process

Most of us understand that certain actions on our part will have a pleasing and seductive effect on the person we would like to seduce. The problem is that we are generally too self-absorbed: We think more about what we want from others than what they could want from us. We may occasionally do something that is seductive, but often we follow this up a with a selfish or aggressive action (we are in a hurry to get what we want); or, unaware of what we are doing, we show a side of ourselves that is petty and banal, deflating any illusions or fantasies a person might have about us. Our attempts at seduction usually do not last long enough to create much of an effect.

You will not seduce anyone by simply depending on your engaging personality, or by occasionally doing something noble or alluring. Seduction is a process that occurs over time—the longer you take and the slower you go, the deeper you will penetrate into the mind of your victim. It is an art that requires patience, focus, and strategic thinking. You need to always be one step ahead of your victim, throwing dust in their eyes, casting a spell, keeping them off balance.

The twenty-four chapters in this section will arm you with a series of tactics that will help you get out of yourself and into the mind of your victim, so that you can play it like an instrument. The chapters are placed in a loose order, going from the initial contact with your victim to the successful conclusion. This order is based on certain timeless laws of human psychology. Because people's thoughts tend to revolve around their daily concerns and insecurities, you cannot proceed with a seduction until you slowly put their anxieties to sleep and fill their distracted minds with thoughts of you. The opening chapters will help you accomplish this. There is a natural tendency in relationships for people to become so familiar with one another that boredom and stagnation set in. Mystery is the lifeblood of seduction and to maintain it you have to constantly surprise your victims, stir things up, even shock them. A seduction should never settle into a comfortable routine. The middle and later chapters will instruct you in the art of alternating hope and despair, pleasure and pain, until your victims weaken and succumb. In each instance, one tactic is setting up the next one, allowing you to push it further with something bolder and more violent. A seducer cannot be timid or merciful.

To help you move the seduction along, the chapters are arranged in four phases, each phase with a particular goal to aim for: getting the victim to think of you; gaining access to their emotions by creating moments of pleasure and confusion; going deeper by working on their unconscious, stirring up repressed desires; and finally, inducing physical surrender. (The phases are clearly marked and explained with a short introduction.) By following these phases you will work more effectively on your victim's mind and create the slow and hypnotic pace of a ritual. In fact, the seductive process may be thought of as a kind of initiation ritual, in which you are uprooting people from their habits, giving them novel experiences, putting them through tests, before initiating them into a new life.

It is best to read all of the chapters and gain as much knowledge as possible. When it comes time to apply these tactics, you will want to pick and choose which ones are appropriate for your particular victim; sometimes only a few are sufficient, depending on the level of resistance you meet and the complexity of your victim's problems. These tactics are equally applicable to social and political seductions, minus the sexual component in Phase Four.

At all cost, resist the temptation to hurry to the climax of your seduction, or to improvise. You are not being seductive but selfish. Everything in daily life is hurried and improvised, and you need to offer something different. By taking your time and respecting the seductive process you will not only break down your victim's resistance, you will make them fall in love.

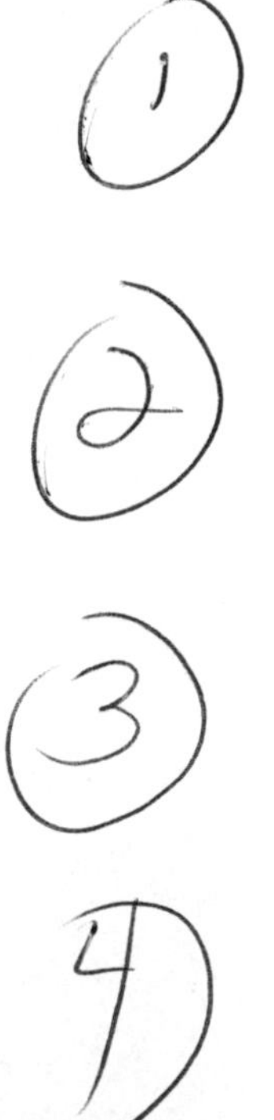

Phase One

Separation—
Stirring Interest and Desire

Your victims live in their own worlds, their minds occupied with anxieties and daily concerns. Your goal in this initial phase is to slowly separate them from that closed world and fill their minds with thoughts of you. Once you have decided whom to seduce (1: Choose the right victim), your first task is to get your victims' attention, to stir interest in you. For those who might be more resistant or difficult, you should try a slower and more insidious approach, first winning their friendship (2: Create a false sense of security—approach indirectly); for those who are bored and less difficult to reach, a more dramatic approach will work, either fascinating them with a mysterious presence (3: Send mixed signals) or seeming to be someone who is coveted and fought over by others (4: Appear to be an object of desire).

Once the victim is properly intrigued, you need to transform their interest into something stronger—desire. Desire is generally preceded by feelings of emptiness, of something missing inside that needs fulfillment. You must deliberately instill such feelings, make your victims aware of the adventure and romance that are lacking in their lives (5: Create a need—stir anxiety and discontent). If they see you as the one to fill their emptiness, interest will blossom into desire. The desire should be stoked by subtly planting ideas in their minds, hints of the seductive pleasures that await them (6: Master the art of insinuation). Mirroring your victims' values, indulging them in their wants and moods will charm and delight them (7: Enter their spirit). Without realizing how it has happened, more and more of their thoughts now revolve around you. The time has come for something stronger. Lure them with an irresistible pleasure or adventure (8: Create temptation) and they will follow your lead.

1
Choose the Right Victim

Everything depends on the target of your seduction. Study your prey thoroughly, and choose only those who will prove susceptible to your charms. The right victims are those for whom you can fill a void, who see in you something exotic. They are often isolated or at least somewhat unhappy (perhaps because of recent adverse circumstances), or can easily be made so—for the completely contented person is almost impossible to seduce. The perfect victim has some natural quality that attracts you. The strong emotions this quality inspires will help make your seductive maneuvers seem more natural and dynamic. The perfect victim allows for the perfect chase.

Preparing for the Hunt

The young Vicomte de Valmont was a notorious libertine in the Paris of the 1770s, the ruin of many a young girl and the ingenious seducer of the wives of illustrious aristocrats. But after a while the repetitiveness of it all began to bore him; his successes came too easily. So one year, during the sweltering, slow month of August, he decided to take a break from Paris and visit his aunt at her château in the provinces. Life there was not what he was used to—there were country walks, chats with the local vicar, card games. His city friends, particularly his fellow libertine and confidante the Marquise de Merteuil, expected him to hurry back.

There were other guests at the château, however, including the Présidente de Tourvel, a twenty-two-year-old woman whose husband was temporarily absent, having work to do elsewhere. The Présidente had been languishing at the château, waiting for him to join her. Valmont had met her before; she was certainly beautiful, but had a reputation as a prude who was extremely devoted to her husband. She was not a court lady; her taste in clothing was atrocious (she always covered her neck with ghastly frills) and her conversation lacked wit. For some reason, however, far from Paris, Valmont began to see these traits in a new light. He followed her to the chapel where she went every morning to pray. He caught glimpses of her at dinner, or playing cards. Unlike the ladies of Paris, she seemed unaware of her charms; this excited him. Because of the heat, she wore a simple linen dress, which revealed her figure. A piece of muslin covered her breasts, letting him more than imagine them. Her hair, unfashionable in its slight disorder, conjured the bedroom. And her face—he had never noticed how expressive it was. Her features lit up when she gave alms to a beggar; she blushed at the slightest praise. She was so natural and unself-conscious. And when she talked of her husband, or religious matters, he could sense the depth of her feelings. If such a passionate nature were ever detoured into a love affair. . . .

Valmont extended his stay at the château, much to the delight of his aunt, who could not have guessed at the reason. And he wrote to the Marquise de Merteuil, explaining his new ambition: to seduce Madame de Tourvel. The Marquise was incredulous. He wanted to seduce this prude? If he succeeded, how little pleasure she would give him, and if he failed, what a disgrace—the great libertine unable to seduce a wife whose husband was far away! She wrote a sarcastic letter, which only inflamed Valmont fur-

The ninth • Have I become blind? Has the inner eye of the soul lost its power? I have seen her, but it is as if I had seen a heavenly revelation—so completely has her image vanished again for me. In vain do I summon all the powers of my soul in order to conjure up this image. If I ever see her again, I shall be able to recognize her instantly, even though she stands among a hundred others. Now she has fled, and the eye of my soul tries in vain to overtake her with its longing. I was walking along Langelinie, seemingly nonchalantly and without paying attention to my surroundings, although my reconnoitering glance left nothing unobserved—and then my eyes fell upon her. My eyes fixed unswervingly upon her. They no longer obeyed their master's will; it was impossible for me to shift my gaze and thus overlook the object I wanted to see—I did not look, I stared. As a fencer freezes in his lunge, so my eyes were fixed, petrified in the direction initially taken. It was impossible to look

ther. The conquest of this notoriously virtuous woman would prove his greatest seduction. His reputation would only be enhanced.

There was an obstacle, though, that seemed to make success almost impossible: everyone knew Valmont's reputation, including the Présidente. She knew how dangerous it was to ever be alone with him, how people would talk about the least association with him. Valmont did everything to belie his reputation, even going so far as to attend church services and seem repentant of his ways. The Présidente noticed, but still kept her distance. The challenge she presented to Valmont was irresistible, but could he meet it?

Valmont decided to test the waters. One day he arranged a little walk with the Présidente and his aunt. He chose a delightful path that they had never taken before, but at a certain point they reached a little ditch, unsuitable for a lady to cross on her own. And yet, Valmont said, the rest of the walk was too nice for them to turn back, and he gallantly picked up his aunt in his arms and carried her across the ditch, making the Présidente laugh uproariously. But then it was her turn, and Valmont purposefully picked her up a little awkwardly, so that she caught at his arms, and while he was holding her against him he could feel her heart beating faster, and saw her blush. His aunt saw this too, and cried out, "The child is afraid!" But Valmont sensed otherwise. Now he knew that the challenge could be met, that the Présidente could be won. The seduction could proceed.

down, impossible to withdraw my glance, impossible to see, because I saw far too much. The only thing I have retained is that she had on a green cloak, that is all—one could call it capturing the cloud instead of Juno; she has escaped me . . . and left only her cloak behind. . . . The girl made an impression on me. • The sixteenth • . . . I feel no impatience, for she must live here in the city, and at this moment that is enough for me. This possibility is the condition for the proper appearance of her image—everything will be enjoyed in slow drafts. . . . • The nineteenth • Cordelia, then, is her name! Cordelia! It is a beautiful name, and that, too, is important, since it can often be very disturbing to have to name an ugly name together with the most tender adjectives.

—Søren Kierkegaard, *The Seducer's Diary*, translated by Howard V. Hong and Edna H. Hong

Interpretation. Valmont, the Présidente de Tourvel, and the Marquise de Merteuil are all characters in the eighteenth-century French novel *Dangerous Liaisons,* by Choderlos de Laclos. (The character of Valmont was inspired by several real-life libertines of the time, most prominent of all the Duke de Richelieu.) In the story, Valmont worries that his seductions have become mechanical; he makes a move, and the woman almost always responds the same way. But no two seductions should be the same—a different target should change the whole dynamic. Valmont's problem is that he is always seducing the same type—the *wrong* type. He realizes this when he meets Madame de Tourvel.

Love as understood by Don Juan is a feeling akin to a taste for hunting. It is a craving for an activity which needs an incessant diversity of stimuli to challenge skill.

—Stendhal, *Love*, translated by Gilbert and Suzanne Sale

It is not because her husband is a count that he decides to seduce her, or because she is stylishly dressed, or is desired by other men—the usual reasons. He chooses her because, in her unconscious way, she has already seduced him. A bare arm, an unrehearsed laugh, a playful manner—all these have captured his attention, because none of them is contrived. Once he falls under her spell, the strength of his desire will make his subsequent maneuvers seem less calculated; he is apparently unable to help himself. And his strong emotions will slowly infect her.

It is not the quality of the desired object that gives us pleasure, but rather the energy of our appetites.

—Charles Baudelaire, *The End of Don Juan*

Beyond the effect the Présidente has on Valmont, she has other traits that make her the perfect victim. She is bored, which draws her toward adventure. She is naive, and unable to see through his tricks. Finally, the Achilles' heel: she believes herself immune to seduction. Almost all of us are vulnerable to the attractions of other people, and we take precautions against unwanted lapses. Madame de Tourvel takes none. Once Valmont has tested her at the ditch, and has seen she is physically vulnerable, he knows that eventually she will fall.

Life is short, and should not be wasted pursuing and seducing the wrong people. The choice of target is critical; it is the set up of the seduction and it will determine everything else that follows. The perfect victim does not have certain facial features, or the same taste in music, or similar goals in life. That is how a banal seducer chooses his or her targets. The perfect victim is the person who stirs you in a way that cannot be explained in words, whose effect on you has nothing to do with superficialities. He or she often has a quality that you yourself lack, and may even secretly envy—the Présidente, for example, has an innocence that Valmont long ago lost or never had. There should be a little bit of tension—the victim may fear you a little, even slightly dislike you. Such tension is full of erotic potential and will make the seduction much livelier. Be more creative in choosing your prey and you will be rewarded with a more exciting seduction. Of course, it means nothing if the potential victim is not open to your influence. Test the person first. Once you feel that he or she is also vulnerable to you then the hunting can begin.

> *It is a stroke of good fortune to find one who is worth seducing. . . . Most people rush ahead, become engaged or do other stupid things, and in a turn of the hand everything is over, and they know neither what they have won nor what they have lost.*
>
> —Søren Kierkegaard

The daughter of desire should strive to have the following lovers in their turn, as being mutually restful to her: a boy who has been loosed too soon from the authority and counsel of his father, an author enjoying office with a rather simple-minded prince, a merchant's son whose pride is in rivaling other lovers, an ascetic who is the slave of love in secret, a king's son whose follies are boundless and who has a taste for rascals, the countrified son of some village Brahman, a married woman's lover, a singer who has just pocketed a very large sum of money, the master of a caravan but recently come in. . . . These brief instructions admit of infinitely varied interpretation, dear child, according to the circumstance; and it requires intelligence, insight and reflection to make the best of each particular case.

—*Eastern Love*, volume II: *The Harlot's Breviary of Kshemendra*, translated by E. Powys Mathers

Keys to Seduction

Throughout life we find ourselves having to persuade people—to seduce them. Some will be relatively open to our influence, if only in subtle ways, while others seem impervious to our charms. Perhaps we find this a mystery beyond our control, but that is an ineffective way of dealing with life. Seducers, whether sexual or social, prefer to pick the odds. As often as possible they go toward people who betray some vulnerability to them, and avoid the ones who cannot be moved. To leave people who are inaccessible to you alone is a wise path; you cannot seduce everyone. On the other hand, you must actively hunt out the prey that responds the right way. This will make your seductions that much more pleasurable and satisfying.

How do you recognize your victims? By the way they respond to you. You should not pay so much attention to their conscious responses—a person who is obviously trying to please or charm you is probably playing to your vanity, and wants something from you. Instead, pay greater attention to those responses outside conscious control—a blush, an involuntary mir-

The women who can be easily won over to congress: . . . a woman who looks sideways at you; . . . a woman who hates her husband, or who is hated by him; . . . a woman who has not had any children; . . . a woman who is very fond of society; a woman who is apparently very affectionate toward her husband; the wife of an actor; a widow; . . . a woman fond of enjoyments; . . . a vain woman; a woman whose husband is inferior to her in rank or ability; a woman who is proud of her skill in the arts; . . . a woman who is slighted by her husband without any cause; . . . a woman whose husband is devoted to travelling; the wife of a jeweler; a jealous woman; a covetous woman.

—The Hindu Art of Love, edited by Edward Windsor

roring of some gesture of yours, an unusual shyness, even perhaps a flash of anger or resentment. All of these show that you are having an effect on a person who is open to your influence.

Like Valmont, you can also recognize the right targets by the effect they are having on you. Perhaps they make you uneasy—perhaps they correspond to a deep-rooted childhood ideal, or represent some kind of personal taboo that excites you, or suggest the person you imagine you would be if you were the opposite sex. When a person has such a deep effect on you, it transforms all of your subsequent maneuvers. Your face and gestures become more animated. You have more energy; when victims resist you (as a good victim should) you in turn will be more creative, more motivated to overcome their resistance. The seduction will move forward like a good play. Your strong desire will infect the target and give them the dangerous sensation that they have a power over you. Of course, you are the one ultimately in control since you are making your victims emotional at the right moments, leading them back and forth. Good seducers choose targets that inspire them but they know how and when to restrain themselves.

Leisure stimulates love, leisure watches the lovelorn, \ Leisure's the cause and sustenance of this sweet \ Evil. Eliminate leisure, and Cupid's bow is broken, \ His torches lie lightless, scorned. \ As a plane-tree rejoices in wine, as a poplar in water, \ As a marsh-reed in swampy ground, so Venus loves \ Leisure. . . . \ Why do you think Aegisthus \ Became an adulterer? Easy: he was idle—and bored. \ Everyone else was away at Troy on a lengthy \ Campaign: all Greece had shipped \ Its contingent across. Suppose he hankered for warfare? Argos \ Had no wars to offer. Suppose he fancied the courts? \ Argos lacked litigation. Love was better than doing nothing. \ That's how Cupid slips in; that's how he stays.

—Ovid, *Cures for Love*, translated by Peter Green

Never rush into the waiting arms of the first person who seems to like you. That is not seduction but insecurity. The need that draws you will make for a low-level attachment, and interest on both sides will sag. Look at the types you have not considered before—that is where you will find challenge and adventure. Experienced hunters do not choose their prey by how easily it is caught; they want the thrill of the chase, a life-and-death struggle—the fiercer the better.

Although the victim who is perfect for you depends on you, certain types lend themselves to a more satisfying seduction. Casanova liked young women who were unhappy, or had suffered a recent misfortune. Such women appealed to his desire to play the savior, but it also responded to necessity: happy people are much harder to seduce. Their contentment makes them inaccessible. It is always easier to fish in troubled waters. Also, an air of sadness is itself quite seductive—Genji, the hero of the Japanese novel *The Tale of Genji*, could not resist a woman with a melancholic air. In Kierkegaard's book *The Seducer's Diary*, the narrator, Johannes, has one main requirement in his victim: she must have imagination. That is why he chooses a woman who lives in a fantasy world, a woman who will envelop his every gesture in poetry, imagining far more than is there. Just as it is hard to seduce a person who is happy, it is hard to seduce a person who has no imagination.

The Chinese have a proverb: "When Yang is in the ascendant, Yin is born," which means, translated into our language, that when a man has devoted the better of his life to the ordinary business of living, the Yin,

For women, the manly man is often the perfect victim. Mark Antony was of this type—he loved pleasure, was quite emotional, and when it came to women, found it hard to think straight. He was easy for Cleopatra to manipulate. Once she gained a hold on his emotions, she kept him permanently on a string. A woman should never be put off by a man who seems overly aggressive. He is often the perfect victim. It is easy, with a few coquettish tricks, to turn that aggression around and make him your slave. Such men actually enjoy being made to chase after a woman.

Be careful with appearances. The person who seems volcanically passionate is often hiding insecurity and self-involvement. This was what most men failed to perceive in the nineteenth-century courtesan Lola Montez. She seemed so dramatic, so exciting. In fact, she was a troubled, self-obsessed woman, but by the time men discovered this it was too late—they had become involved with her and could not extricate themselves without months of drama and torture. People who are outwardly distant or shy are often better targets than extroverts. They are dying to be drawn out, and still waters run deep.

People with a lot of time on their hands are extremely susceptible to seduction. They have mental space for you to fill. Tullia d'Aragona, the infamous sixteenth-century Italian courtesan, preferred young men as her victims; besides the physical reason for such a preference, they were more idle than working men with careers, and therefore more defenseless against an ingenious seductress. On the other hand, you should generally avoid people who are preoccupied with business or work—seduction demands attention, and busy people have too little space in their minds for you to occupy.

According to Freud, seduction begins early in life, in our relationship with our parents. They seduce us physically, both with bodily contact and by satisfying desires such as hunger, and we in turn try to seduce them into paying us attention. We are creatures by nature vulnerable to seduction throughout our lives. We all want to be seduced; we yearn to be drawn out of ourselves, out of our routines and into the drama of eros. And what draws us more than anything is the feeling that someone has something we don't, a quality we desire. Your perfect victims are often people who think you have something they don't, and who will be enchanted to have it provided for them. Such victims may have a temperament quite the opposite of yours, and this difference will create an exciting tension.

When Jiang Qing, later known as Madame Mao, first met Mao Tse-tung in 1937 in his mountain retreat in western China, she could sense how desperate he was for a bit of color and spice in his life: all the camp's women dressed like the men, and abjured any feminine finery. Jiang had been an actress in Shanghai, and was anything but austere. She supplied what he lacked, and she also gave him the added thrill of being able to educate her in communism, appealing to his Pygmalion complex—the desire to dominate, control, and remake a person. In fact it was Jiang Qing who controlled her future husband.

The greatest lack of all is excitement and adventure, which is precisely what seduction offers. In 1964, the Chinese actor Shi Pei Pu, a man who had gained fame as a female impersonator, met Bernard Bouriscout, a young diplomat assigned to the French embassy in China. Bouriscout had come to China looking for adventure, and was disappointed to have little contact with Chinese people. Pretending to be a woman who, when still a child, had been forced to live as a boy—supposedly the family already had too many daughters—Shi Pei Pu used the young Frenchman's boredom and

or emotional side of his nature, rises to the surface and demands its rights. When such a period occurs, all that which has formerly seemed important loses its significance. The will-of-the-wisp of illusion leads the man hither and thither, taking him on strange and complicated deviations from his former path in life. Ming Huang, the "Bright Emperor" of the T'ang dynasty, was an example of the profound truth of this theory. From the moment he saw Yang Kuei-fei bathing in the lake near his palace in the Li mountains, he was destined to sit at her feet, learning from her the emotional mysteries of what the Chinese call Yin.

—Eloise Talcott Hibbert, *Embroidered Gauze: Portraits of Famous Chinese Ladies*

discontent to manipulate him. Inventing a story of the deceptions he had had to go through, he slowly drew Bouriscout into an affair that would last many years. (Bouriscout had had previous homosexual encounters, but considered himself heterosexual.) Eventually the diplomat was led into spying for the Chinese. All the while, he believed Shi Pei Pu was a woman—his yearning for adventure had made him that vulnerable. Repressed types are perfect victims for a deep seduction.

People who repress the appetite for pleasure make ripe victims, particularly later in their lives. The eighth-century Chinese Emperor Ming Huang spent much of his reign trying to rid his court of its costly addiction to luxuries, and was himself a model of austerity and virtue. But the moment he saw the concubine Yang Kuei-fei bathing in a palace lake, everything changed. The most charming woman in the realm, she was the mistress of his son. Exerting his power, the emperor won her away—only to become her abject slave.

The choice of the right victim is equally important in politics. Mass seducers such as Napoleon or John F. Kennedy offer their public just what it lacks. When Napoleon came to power, the French people's sense of pride was beaten down by the bloody aftermath of the French Revolution. He offered them glory and conquest. Kennedy recognized that Americans were bored with the stultifying comfort of the Eisenhower years; he gave them adventure and risk. More important, he tailored his appeal to the group most vulnerable to it: the younger generation. Successful politicians know that not everyone will be susceptible to their charm, but if they can find a group of believers with a need to be filled, they have supporters who will stand by them no matter what.

Symbol:

Big Game. Lions are dangerous—to hunt them is to know the thrill of risk. Leopards are clever and swift, offering the excitement of a difficult chase. Never rush into the hunt. Know your prey and choose it carefully. Do not waste time with small game—the rabbits that back into snares, the mink that walk into a scented trap. Challenge is pleasure.

Reversal

There is no possible reversal. There is nothing to be gained from trying to seduce the person who is closed to you, or who cannot provide the pleasure and chase that you need.

2

Create a False Sense of Security—Approach Indirectly

If you are too direct early on, you risk stirring up a resistance that will never be lowered. At first there must be nothing of the seducer in your manner. The seduction should begin at an angle, indirectly, so that the target only gradually becomes aware of you. Haunt the periphery of your target's life—approach through a third party, or seem to cultivate a relatively neutral relationship, moving gradually from friend to lover. Arrange an occasional "chance" encounter, as if you and your target were destined to become acquainted—nothing is more seductive than a sense of destiny. Lull the target into feeling secure, then strike.

Friend to Lover

Anne Marie Louis d'Orléans, the Duchess de Montpensier, known in seventeenth-century France as *La Grande Mademoiselle,* had never known love in her life. Her mother had died when she was young; her father remarried and ignored her. She came from one of Europe's most illustrious families: her grandfather had been King Henry IV; the future King Louis XIV was her cousin. When she was young, matches had been proposed between her and the widowed king of Spain, the son of the Holy Roman emperor, and even cousin Louis himself, among many others. But all of these matches were designed for political purposes, or because of her family's enormous wealth. No one bothered to woo her; she rarely even met her suitors. To make matters worse, the Grande Mademoiselle was an idealist who believed in the old-fashioned values of chivalry: courage, honesty, virtue. She loathed the schemers whose motives in courting her were dubious at best. Whom could she trust? One by one she found a reason to spurn them. Spinsterhood seemed to be her fate.

Many women adore the elusive, \ Hate overeagerness. So, play hard to get, \ Stop boredom developing. And don't let your entreaties \ Sound too confident of possession. Insinuate sex \ Camouflaged as friendship. I've seen ultrastubborn creatures \ Fooled by this gambit, the switch from companion to stud.

—Ovid, *The Art of Love*, translated by Peter Green

In April of 1669, the Grande Mademoiselle, then forty-two, met one of the strangest men in the court: the Marquis Antonin Péguilin, later known as the Duke de Lauzun. A favorite of Louis XIV's, the thirty-six-year-old Marquis was a brave soldier with an acid wit. He was also an incurable Don Juan. Although he was short, and certainly not handsome, his impudent manners and his military exploits made him irresistible to women. The Grande Mademoiselle had noticed him some years before, admiring his elegance and boldness. But it was only this time, in 1669, that she had a real conversation with him, if a short one, and although she knew of his lady-killer reputation, she found him charming. A few days later they ran into each other again; this time the conversation was longer, and Lauzun proved more intelligent than she had imagined—they talked of the playwright Corneille (her favorite), of heroism, and of other elevated topics. Now their encounters became more frequent. They had become friends. Anne Marie noted in her diary that her conversations with Lauzun, when they occurred, were the highlight of her day; when he was not at court, she felt his absence. Surely her encounters with him came frequently enough that they could not be accidental on his part, but he always seemed surprised to see her. At the same time, she recorded feeling uneasy—strange emotions were stealing up on her, she did not know why.

On the street, I do not stop her, or I exchange a greeting with her but never come close, but always strive for distance. Presumably our repeated encounters are clearly noticeable to her; presumably she does perceive that on her horizon a new planet has loomed, which in its course has encroached disturbingly upon hers in a curiously undisturbing way, but she has no inkling of the law underlying this movement. . . . Before I begin my attack, I must first become acquainted with her and her whole mental state.

—Søren Kierkegaard, *The Seducer's Diary*, translated by Howard V. Hong and Edna H. Hong

Time passed, and the Grande Mademoiselle was to leave Paris for a week or two. Now Lauzun approached her without warning and made an emotional plea to be considered her confidante, the great friend who would execute any commission she needed done while she was away. He was poetic and chivalrous, but what did he really mean? In her diary, Anne Marie finally confronted the emotions that had been stirring in her since their first conversation: "I told myself, these are not vague musings; there must be an object to all of these feelings, and I could not imagine who it was. . . . Finally, after troubling myself with this for several days, I realized that it was M. de Lauzun whom I loved, it was he who had somehow slipped into my heart and captured it."

No sooner had he spoken than the bullocks, driven from their mountain pastures, were on their way to the beach, as Jove had directed; they were making for the sands where the daughter [Europa] of the great king used to play with the young girls of Tyre, who were her companions. • . . . Abandoning the dignity of his scepter, the father and ruler of the gods, whose hand wields the flaming three-forked bolt, whose nod shakes the universe, adopted the guise of a bull; and, mingling with the other bullocks, joined in the lowing and ambled in the tender grass, a fair sight to see. His hide was white as untrodden snow, snow not yet melted by the rainy South wind. The muscles stood out on his neck, and deep folds of skin hung along his flanks. His horns were small, it is true, but so beautifully made that you would swear they were the work of an artist, more polished and shining than any jewel. There was no menace in the set of his head or in his eyes; he looked completely placid. • Agenor's daughter [Europa] was filled with admiration for one so handsome and so friendly. But, gentle though he seemed, she was afraid at first to touch him; then she went closer, and held out flowers to his shining lips. The lover was delighted

Made aware of the source of her feelings, the Grande Mademoiselle became more direct. If Lauzun was to be her confidante, she could talk to him of marriage, of the matches that were still being offered to her. The topic might give him a chance to express his feelings; perhaps he might show jealousy. Unfortunately Lauzun did not seem to take the hint. Instead, he asked her why she was thinking of marriage at all—she seemed so happy. Besides, who could possibly be worthy of her? This went on for weeks. She could pry nothing personal out of him. In a way, she understood—there were the differences in rank (she was far above him) and age (she was six years older). Then, a few months later, the wife of the king's brother died, and King Louis suggested to the Grande Mademoiselle that she replace his late sister-in-law—that is, that she marry his brother. Anne Marie was disgusted; clearly the brother was trying to get his hands on her fortune. She asked Lauzun his opinion. As the king's loyal servants, he replied, they must obey the royal wish. His answer did not please her, and to make things worse, he stopped visiting her, as if it were no longer proper for them to be friends. This was the last straw. The Grande Mademoiselle told the king she would not marry his brother, and that was that.

Now Anne Marie met with Lauzun, and told him she would write on a piece of paper the name of the man she had wanted to marry all along. He was to put the paper under his pillow and read it the next morning. When he did, he found the words *"C'est vous"*—It is you. Seeing the Grande Mademoiselle the following evening, Lauzun said she must have been joking; she would make him the laughing stock of the court. She insisted that she was serious. He seemed shocked, surprised—but not as surprised as the rest of the court was a few weeks later, when an engagement was announced between this relatively low-ranking Don Juan and the second-highest-ranking lady in France, a woman known for both her virtue and her skill at defending it.

Interpretation. The Duke de Lauzun was one of the greatest seducers in history, and his slow and steady seduction of the Grande Mademoiselle was his masterpiece. His method was simple: indirection. Sensing her interest in him in that first conversation, he decided to beguile her with friendship.

He would become her most devoted friend. At first this was charming; a man was taking the time to talk to her, of poetry, history, the deeds of war—her favorite subjects. She slowly began to confide in him. Then, almost without her realizing it, her feelings shifted: the consummate ladies' man was only interested in friendship? He was not attracted to her as a woman? Such thoughts made her aware that she had fallen in love with him. This, in part, was what eventually made her turn down the match with the king's brother—a decision cleverly and indirectly provoked by Lauzun himself, when he stopped visiting her. And how could he be after money or position, or sex, when he had never made any kind of move? No, the brilliance of Lauzun's seduction was that the Grande Mademoiselle believed it was she who was making all the moves.

Once you have chosen the right victim, you must get his or her attention and stir desire. To move from friendship to love can win success without calling attention to itself as a maneuver. First, your friendly conversations with your targets will bring you valuable information about their characters, their tastes, their weaknesses, the childhood yearnings that govern their adult behavior. (Lauzun, for example, could adapt cleverly to Anne Marie's tastes once he had studied her close up.) Second, by spending time with your targets you can make them comfortable with you. Believing you are interested only in their thoughts, in their company, they will lower their resistance, dissipating the usual tension between the sexes. Now they are vulnerable, for your friendship with them has opened the golden gate to their body: their mind. At this point any offhand comment, any slight physical contact, will spark a different thought, which will catch them off-guard: perhaps there could be something else between you. Once that feeling has stirred, they will wonder why you haven't made a move, and will take the initiative themselves, enjoying the illusion that they are in control. There is nothing more effective in seduction than making the seduced think that they are the ones doing the seducing.

and, until he could achieve his hoped-for pleasure, kissed her hands. He could scarcely wait for the rest, only with great difficulty did he restrain himself. • Now he frolicked and played on the green turf, now lay down, all snowy white on the yellow sand. Gradually the princess lost her fear, and with her innocent hands she stroked his breast when he offered it for her caress, and hung fresh garlands on his horns: till finally she even ventured to mount the bull, little knowing on whose back she was resting. Then the god drew away from the shore by easy stages, first planting the hooves that were part of his disguise in the surf at the water's edge, and then proceeding farther out to sea, till he bore his booty away over the wide stretches of mid ocean.

—OVID, *METAMORPHOSES*, TRANSLATED BY MARY M. INNES

> *I do not approach her, I merely skirt the periphery of her existence. . . . This is the first web into which she must be spun.*
>
> —SØREN KIERKEGAARD

Key to Seduction

What you are after as a seducer is the ability to move people in the direction you want them to go. But the game is perilous; the moment they suspect they are acting under your influence, they will become resentful. We are creatures who cannot stand feeling that we are obeying someone else's will. Should your targets catch on, sooner or later they will turn against you. But what if you can make them do what you want them to without their realizing it? What if they think *they* are in control? That is

These few reflections lead us to the understanding that, since in attempting a seduction it is up to the man to make the first steps, for the seducer, to seduce is nothing more than reducing the distance, in this case that of the difference between the sexes and that, in order to accomplish this, it is necessary to feminize himself or at least identify himself with the object of his seduction. . . . As Alain Roger writes: "If there is a seduction, it is the seducer who is first lead astray, in the sense that he abdicates his own sex. . . . Seduction undoubtedly aims at sexual consummation, but it only gets there in creating a kind

Don't crowd her

of simulacra of Gomorra. The seducer is nothing more than a lesbian."

—Frédéric Monneyron, *Séduire: L'Imaginaire de la Séduction de don Giovanni à Mick Jagger*

the power of indirection and no seducer can work his or her magic without it.

The first move to master is simple: once you have chosen the right person, you must make the target come to you. If, in the opening stages, you can make your targets think that they are the ones making the first approach, you have won the game. There will be no resentment, no perverse counterreaction, no paranoia.

As he [Jupiter] was hurrying busily to and fro, he stopped short at the sight of an Arcadian maiden. The fire of passion kindled the very marrow of his bones. This girl was not one who spent her time in spinning soft fibers of wool, or in arranging her hair in different styles. She was one of Diana's warriors, wearing her tunic pinned together with a brooch, her tresses carelessly caught back by a white ribbon, and carrying in her hand a light javelin or her bow. . . . • The sun on high had passed its zenith, when she entered a grove whose trees had never felt the axe. Here she took her quiver from her shoulders, unstrung her pliant bow, and lay down on the turf, resting her head on her painted quiver. When Jupiter saw her thus, tired and unprotected, he said: "Here is a secret of which my wife will know nothing; or if she does get to know of it, it will be worth her reproaches!" • Without wasting time he assumed the appearance and the dress of Diana, and spoke to the girl. "Dearest of all my companions," he said, "where have you been hunting? On what mountain ridges?" She raised herself from the grass: "Greeting, divine mistress," she cried, "greater in my sight than

To make them come to you requires giving them space. This can be accomplished in several ways. You can haunt the periphery of their existence, letting them notice you in different places but never approaching them. You will get their attention this way, and if they want to bridge the gap, they will have to come to you. You can befriend them, as Lauzun did the Grande Mademoiselle, moving steadily closer while always maintaining the distance appropriate for friends of the opposite sex. You can also play cat and mouse with them, first seeming interested, then stepping back—actively luring them to follow you into your web. Whatever you do, and whatever kind of seduction you are practicing, you must at all cost avoid the natural tendency to crowd your targets. Do not make the mistake of thinking they will lose interest unless you apply pressure, or that they will enjoy a flood of attention. Too much attention early on will actually just suggest insecurity, and raise doubts as to your motives. Worst of all, it gives your targets no room for imagination. Take a step back; let the thoughts you are provoking come to them as if they were their own. This is doubly important if you are dealing with someone who has a deep effect on you.

We can never really understand the opposite sex. They are always mysterious to us, and it is this mystery that provides the tension so delightful in seduction; but it is also a source of unease. Freud famously wondered what women really wanted; even to this most insightful of psychological thinkers, the opposite sex was a foreign land. For both men and women, there are deep-rooted feelings of fear and anxiety in relation to the opposite sex. In the initial stages of a seduction, then, you must find ways to calm any sense of mistrust that the other person may experience. (A sense of danger and fear can heighten the seduction later on, but if you stir such emotions in the first stages, you will more likely scare the target away.) Establish a neutral distance, seem harmless, and you give yourself room to move. Casanova cultivated a slight femininity in his character—an interest in clothes, theater, domestic matters—that young girls found comforting. The Renaissance courtesan Tullia d'Aragona, developing friendships with the great thinkers and poets of her time, talked of literature and philosophy—anything but the boudoir (and anything but the money that was also her goal). Johannes, the narrator of Søren Kierkegaard's *The Seducer's Diary*, follows his target, Cordelia, from a distance; when their paths cross, he is polite and apparently shy. As Cordelia gets to know him, he doesn't frighten her. In fact he is so innocuous she begins to wish he were less so.

Duke Ellington, the great jazz artist and a consummate seducer, would initially dazzle the ladies with his good looks, stylish clothing, and charisma. But once he was alone with a woman, he would take a slight step back, becoming excessively polite, making only small talk. Banal conversation can be a brilliant tactic; it hypnotizes the target. The dullness of your front gives the subtlest suggestive word, the slightest look, an amplified power. Never mention love and you make its absence speak volumes—your victims will wonder why you never discuss your emotions, and as they have such thoughts, they will go further, imagining what else is going on in your mind. They will be the ones to bring up the topic of love or affection. Deliberate dullness has many applications. In psychotherapy, the doctor makes monosyllabic responses to draw patients in, making them relax and open up. In international negotiations, Henry Kissinger would lull diplomats with boring details, then strike with bold demands. Early in a seduction, less-colorful words are often more effective than vivid ones—the target tunes them out, looks at your face, begins to imagine, fantasize, fall under your spell.

Jove himself—I care not if he hears me!" Jove laughed to hear her words. Delighted to be preferred to himself, he kissed her—not with the restraint becoming to a maiden's kisses: and as she began to tell of her hunting exploits in the forest, he prevented her by his embrace, and betrayed his real self by a shameful action. So far from complying, she resisted him as far as a woman could . . . but how could a girl overcome a man, and who could defeat Jupiter? He had his way, and returned to the upper air.

—OVID, *METAMORPHOSES*, TRANSLATED BY MARY M. INNES

Getting to your targets through other people is extremely effective; infiltrate their circle and you are no longer a stranger. Before the seventeenth-century seducer Count de Grammont made a move, he would befriend his target's chambermaid, her valet, a friend, even a lover. In this way he could gather information, finding a way to approach her in an unthreatening manner. He could also plant ideas, saying things the third party was likely to repeat, things that would intrigue the lady, particularly when they came from someone she knew.

I had rather hear my dog bark at a crow than a man swear he loves me.

—BEATRICE, IN WILLIAM SHAKESPEARE, *MUCH ADO ABOUT NOTHING*

Ninon de l'Enclos, the seventeenth-century courtesan and strategist of seduction, believed that disguising one's intentions was not only a necessity, it added to the pleasure of the game. A man should never declare his feelings, she felt, particularly early on. It is irritating and provokes mistrust. "A woman is much better persuaded that she is loved by what she guesses than by what she is told," Ninon once remarked. Often a person's haste in declaring his or her feelings comes from a false desire to please, thinking this will flatter the other. But the desire to please can annoy and offend. Children, cats, and coquettes draw us to them by apparently not trying, even by seeming uninterested. Learn to disguise your feelings and let people figure out what is happening for themselves.

In all arenas of life, you should never give the impression that you are angling for something—that will raise a resistance that you will never lower. Learn to approach people from the side. Mute your colors, blend in, seem unthreatening, and you will have more room to maneuver later on. The same holds true in politics, where overt ambition often frightens people. Vladimir Ilyich Lenin at first glance looked like an everyday Russian; he dressed like a worker, spoke with a peasant accent, had no air of greatness. This made the public feel comfortable and identify with him. Yet beneath this apparently bland appearance, of course, was a deeply clever man who was always maneuvering. By the time people realized this it was too late.

I know of a man whose beloved was completely friendly and at ease with him; but if he had disclosed by the least gesture that he was in love, the beloved would have become as remote from him as the Pleiades, whose stars hang so high in heaven. It is a sort of statesmanship that is required in such cases; the party concerned was enjoying the pleasure of his loved one's company intensely and to the last degree, but if he had so much as hinted at his inner feelings he would have attained but a miserable fraction of the beloved's favor, and endured into the bargain all the arrogance and caprice of which love is capable.

—Ibn Hazm, *The Ring of the Dove: A Treatise on the Art and Practice of Arab Love*, translated by A. J. Arberry

Symbol: *The Spider's Web. The spider finds an innocuous corner in which to spin its web. The longer the web takes, the more fabulous its construction, yet few really notice it—its gossamer threads are nearly invisible. The spider has no need to chase for food, or even to move. It quietly sits in the corner, waiting for its victims to come to it on their own, and ensnare themselves in the web.*

Reversal

In warfare, you need space to align your troops, room to maneuver. The more space you have, the more intricate your strategy can be. But sometimes it is better to overwhelm the enemy, giving them no time to think or react. Although Casanova adapted his strategies to the woman in question, he would often try to make an immediate impression, stirring her desire at the first encounter. Perhaps he would perform some gallantry, rescuing a woman in danger; perhaps he would dress so that his target would notice him in a crowd. In either case, once he had the woman's attention he would move with lightning speed. A Siren like Cleopatra tries to have an immediate physical effect on men, giving her victims no time or space to retreat. She uses the element of surprise. The first period of your contact with someone can involve a level of desire that will never be repeated; boldness will carry the day.

But these are short seductions. The Sirens and the Casanovas only get pleasure from the number of their victims, moving quickly from conquest to conquest, and this can be tiring. Casanova burned himself out; Sirens, insatiable, are never satisfied. The indirect, carefully constructed seduction may reduce the number of your conquests, but more than compensate by their quality.

3

Send Mixed Signals

Once people are aware of your presence, and perhaps vaguely intrigued, you need to stir their interest before it settles on someone else. What is obvious and striking may attract their attention at first, but that attention is often short-lived; in the long run, ambiguity is much more potent. Most of us are much too obvious—instead, be hard to figure out. Send mixed signals: both tough and tender, both spiritual and earthy, both innocent and cunning. A mix of qualities suggests depth, which fascinates even as it confuses. An elusive, enigmatic aura will make people want to know more, drawing them into your circle. Create such a power by hinting at something contradictory within you.

Good and Bad

In 1806, when Prussia and France were at war, Auguste, the handsome twenty-four-year-old prince of Prussia and nephew of Frederick the Great, was captured by Napoleon. Instead of locking him up, Napoleon allowed him to wander around French territory, keeping a close watch on him through spies. The prince was devoted to pleasure, and spent his time moving from town to town, seducing young girls. In 1807 he decided to visit the Château de Coppet, in Switzerland, where lived the great French writer Madame de Staël.

Auguste was greeted by his hostess with as much ceremony as she could muster. After she had introduced him to her other guests, they all retired to a drawing room, where they talked of Napoleon's war in Spain, the current Paris fashions, and so on. Suddenly the door opened and another guest entered, a woman who had somehow stayed in her room during the hubbub of the prince's entrance. It was the thirty-year-old Madame Récamier, Madame de Staël's closest friend. She introduced herself to the prince, then quickly retired to her bedroom.

Auguste had known that Madame Récamier was at the château. In fact he had heard many stories about this infamous woman, who, in the years after the French Revolution, was considered the most beautiful in France. Men had gone wild over her, particularly at balls when she would take off her evening wrap, revealing the diaphanous white dresses that she had made famous, and dance with such abandon. The painters Gérard and David had immortalized her face and fashions, and even her feet, considered the most beautiful anyone had ever seen; and she had broken the heart of Lucien Bonaparte, the Emperor Napoleon's brother. Auguste liked his girls younger than Madame Récamier, and he had come to the château to rest. But those few moments in which she had stolen the scene with her sudden entrance caught him off guard: she was as beautiful as people had said, but more striking than her beauty was that look of hers that seemed so sweet, indeed heavenly, with a hint of sadness in the eyes. The other guests continued their conversations, but Auguste could only think of Madame Récamier.

Over dinner that evening, he watched her. She did not talk much, and kept her eyes downward, but once or twice she looked up—directly at the prince. After dinner the guests assembled in the gallery, and a harp was brought in. To the prince's delight, Madame Récamier began to play,

Reichardt had seen Juliette at another ball, protesting coyly that she would not dance, and then, after a while, throwing off her heavy evening gown, to reveal a light dress underneath. On all sides, there were murmurs and whisperings about her coquetry and affectation. As ever, she wore white satin, cut very low in the back, revealing her charming shoulders. The men implored her to dance for them. . . . To soft music she floated into the room in her diaphanous Greek robe. Her head was bound with a muslin fichu. She bowed timidly to the audience, and then, spinning round lightly, she shook a transparent scarf with her fingertips, so that in turns it billowed into the semblance of a drapery, a veil, a cloud. All this with a strange blend of precision and languor. She used her eyes in a subtle fascinating way—"she danced with her eyes." The women thought that all that serpentine undulating of the body, all that nonchalant rhythmic nodding of the head, were sensuous; the men were wafted into a realm of unearthly bliss. Juliette was an ange fatal, and much more dangerous for looking like an angel! The music grew fainter. Suddenly, by a deft trick, Juliette's chestnut hair was loosened and fell in clouds around her. A little out of breath, she disappeared into her dimly lit boudoir. And there the crowd followed her and beheld her reclining on her daybed in a loose tea-gown, looking fashionably pale, like Gérard's Psyche, while her maids cooled her brow with toilet water.

—Margaret Trouncer, *Madame Récamier*

singing a love song. And now, suddenly, she changed: there was a roguish look in her eye as she glanced at him. The angelic voice, the glances, the energy animating her face, sent his mind reeling. He was confused. When the same thing happened the next night, the prince decided to extend his stay at the château.

In the days that followed, the prince and Madame Récamier took walks together, rowed out on the lake, and attended dances, where he finally held her in his arms. They would talk late into the night. But nothing grew clear to him: she would seem so spiritual, so noble, and then there would be a touch of the hand, a sudden flirtatious remark. After two weeks at the château, the most eligible bachelor in Europe forgot all his libertine habits and proposed marriage to Madame Récamier. He would convert to Catholicism, her religion, and she would divorce her much older husband. (She had told him her marriage had never been consummated and so the Catholic church could annul it.) She would then come to live with him in Prussia. Madame promised to do as he wished. The prince hurried off to Prussia to seek the approval of his family, and Madame returned to Paris to secure the required annulment. Auguste flooded her with love letters, and waited. Time passed; he felt he was going mad. Then, finally, a letter: she had changed her mind.

Some months later, Madame Récamier sent Auguste a gift: Gérard's famous painting of her reclining on a sofa. The prince spent hours in front of it, trying to pierce the mystery behind her gaze. He had joined the company of her conquests—of men like the writer Benjamin Constant, who said of her, "She was my last love. For the rest of my life I was like a tree struck by lightning."

The idea that two distinct elements are combined in Mona Lisa's smile is one that has struck several critics. They accordingly find in the beautiful Florentine's expression the most perfect representation of the contrasts that dominate the erotic life of women; the contrast between reserve and seduction, and between the most devoted tenderness and a sensuality that is ruthlessly demanding—consuming men as if they were alien beings.

—Sigmund Freud, *Leonardo da Vinci and a Memory of His Childhood*, translated by Alan Tyson

Interpretation. Madame Récamier's list of conquests became only more impressive as she grew older: there was Prince Metternich, the Duke of Wellington, the writers Constant and Chateaubriand. For all of these men she was an obsession, which only increased in intensity when they were away from her. The source of her power was twofold. First, she had an angelic face, which drew men to her. It appealed to paternal instincts, charming with its innocence. But then there was a second quality peeking through, in the flirtatious looks, the wild dancing, the sudden gaiety—all these caught men off guard. Clearly there was more to her than they had thought, an intriguing complexity. When alone, they would find themselves pondering these contradictions, as if a poison were coursing through their blood. Madame Récamier was an enigma, a problem that had to be solved. Whatever it was that you wanted, whether a coquettish she-devil or an unattainable goddess, she could seem to be. She surely encouraged this illusion by keeping her men at a certain distance, so they could never figure her out. And she was the queen of the calculated effect, like her surprise entrance at the Château de Coppet, which made her the center of attention, if only for a few seconds.

[Oscar Wilde's] hands were fat and flabby; his handshake lacked grip, and at a first encounter one recoiled from its plushy limpness, but this aversion was soon overcome when he began to talk, for his genuine kindliness and desire to please made one forget what was unpleasant

The seductive process involves filling someone's mind with your image. Your innocence, or your beauty, or your flirtatiousness can attract their attention but not their obsession; they will soon move on to the next striking image. To deepen their interest, you must hint at a complexity that cannot be grasped in a week or two. You are an elusive mystery, an irresistible lure, promising great pleasure if only it can be possessed. Once they begin to fantasize about you, they are on the brink of the slippery slope of seduction, and will not be able to stop themselves from sliding down.

Artificial and Natural

The big Broadway hit of 1881 was Gilbert and Sullivan's operetta *Patience*, a satire on the bohemian world of aesthetes and dandies that had become so fashionable in London. To cash in on this vogue, the operetta's promoters decided to invite one of England's most infamous aesthetes to America for a lecture tour: Oscar Wilde. Only twenty-seven at the time, Wilde was more famous for his public persona than for his small body of work. The American promoters were confident that their public would be fascinated by this man, whom they imagined as always walking around with a flower in his hand, but they did not expect it to last; he would do a few lectures, then the novelty would wear off, and they would ship him home. The money was good and Wilde accepted. On his arrival in New York, a customs man asked him whether he had anything to declare: "I have nothing to declare," he replied, "except my genius."

The invitations poured in—New York society was curious to meet this oddity. Women found Wilde enchanting, but the newspapers were less kind; *The New York Times* called him an "aesthetic sham." Then, a week after his arrival, he gave his first lecture. The hall was packed; more than a thousand people came, many of them just to see what he looked like. They were not disappointed. Wilde did not carry a flower, and was taller than they had expected, but he had long flowing hair and wore a green velvet suit and cravat, as well as knee breeches and silk stockings. Many in the audience were put off; as they looked up at him from their seats, the combination of his large size and pretty attire were rather repulsive. Some people openly laughed, others could not hide their unease. They expected to hate the man. Then he began to speak.

The subject was the "English Renaissance," the "art for art's sake" movement in late-nineteenth-century England. Wilde's voice proved hypnotic; he spoke in a kind of meter, mannered and artificial, and few really understood what he was saying, but the speech was so witty, and it flowed. His appearance was certainly strange, but overall, no New Yorker had ever seen or heard such an intriguing man, and the lecture was a huge success. Even the newspapers warmed up to it. In Boston a few weeks later, some sixty Harvard boys had prepared an ambush: they would make fun of this effeminate poet by dressing in knee breeches, carrying flowers, and ap-

in his physical appearance and contact, gave charm to his manners, and grace to his precision of speech. The first sight of him affected people in various ways. Some could hardly restrain their laughter, others felt hostile, a few were afflicted with the "creeps," many were conscious of being uneasy, but except for a small minority who could never recover from the first sensation of distaste and so kept out of his way, both sexes found him irresistible, and to the young men of his time, says W. B. Yeats, he was like a triumphant and audacious figure from another age.

—Hesketh Pearson, *Oscar Wilde: His Life and Wit*

Once upon a time there was a magnet, and in its close neighborhood lived some steel filings. One day two or three little filings felt a sudden desire to go and visit the magnet, and they began to talk of what a pleasant thing it would be to do. Other filings nearby overheard their conversation, and they, too, became infected with the same desire. Still others joined them, till at last all the filings began to discuss the matter, and more and more their vague desire grew into an impulse. "Why not go today?" said one of them; but others were of opinion that it would be better to wait until tomorrow. Meanwhile, without their having noticed it, they had been involuntarily moving nearer to the magnet, which lay there quite still, apparently taking no heed of them. And so they went on discussing, all the time

plauding far too loudly at his entrance. Wilde was not the least bit flustered. The audience laughed hysterically at his improvised comments, and when the boys heckled him he kept his dignity, betraying no anger at all. Once again, the contrast between his manner and his physical appearance made him seem rather extraordinary. Many were deeply impressed, and Wilde was well on his way to becoming a sensation.

The short lecture tour turned into a cross-country affair. In San Francisco, this visiting lecturer on art and aesthetics proved able to drink everyone under the table and play poker, which made him the hit of the season. On his way back from the West Coast, Wilde was to make stops in Colorado, and was warned that if the pretty-boy poet dared to show up in the mining town of Leadville, he would be hung from the highest tree. It was an invitation Wilde could not refuse. Arriving in Leadville, he ignored the hecklers and nasty looks; he toured the mines, drank and played cards, then lectured on Botticelli and Cellini in the saloons. Like everyone else, the miners fell under his spell, even naming a mine after him. One cowboy was heard to say, "That fellow is some art guy, but he can drink any of us under the table and afterwards carry us home two at a time."

insensibly drawing nearer to their neighbor; and the more they talked, the more they felt the impulse growing stronger, till the more impatient ones declared that they would go that day, whatever the rest did. Some were heard to say that it was their duty to visit the magnet, and they ought to have gone long ago. And, while they talked, they moved always nearer and nearer, without realizing that they had moved. Then, at last, the impatient ones prevailed, and, with one irresistible impulse, the whole body cried out, "There is no use waiting. We will go today. We will go now. We will go at once." And then in one unanimous mass they swept along, and in another moment were clinging fast to the magnet on every side. Then the magnet smiled—for the steel filings had no doubt at all but that they were paying that visit of their own free will.

—Oscar Wilde, as quoted by Richard Le Gallienne in Hesketh Pearson, *Oscar Wilde: His Life and Wit*

Interpretation. In a fable he improvised at dinner once, Oscar Wilde talked about some steel filings that had a sudden desire to visit a nearby magnet. As they talked to each other about this, they found themselves moving closer to the magnet without realizing how or why. Finally they were swept in one mass to the magnet's side. "Then the magnet smiled—for the steel filings had no doubt at all but that they were paying that visit of their own free will." Such was the effect that Wilde himself had on everyone around him.

Wilde's attractiveness was more than just a by-product of his character, it was quite calculated. An adorer of paradox, he consciously played up his own weirdness and ambiguity, the contrast between his mannered appearance and his witty, effortless performance. Naturally warm and spontaneous, he constructed an image that ran counter to his nature. People were repelled, confused, intrigued, and finally drawn to this man who seemed impossible to figure out.

Paradox is seductive because it plays with meaning. We are secretly oppressed by the rationality in our lives, where everything is meant to mean something; seduction, by contrast, thrives on ambiguity, on mixed signals, on anything that eludes interpretation. Most people are painfully obvious. If their character is showy, we may be momentarily attracted, but the attraction wears off; there is no depth, no contrary motion, to pull us in. The key to both attracting and holding attention is to radiate mystery. And no one is naturally mysterious, at least not for long; mystery is something you have to work at, a ploy on your part, and something that must be used early on in the seduction. Let one part of your character show, so everyone notices it. (In the example of Wilde, this was the mannered affectation con-

Now that the bohort [impromptu joust] was over and the knights were dispersing and each making his way to where his thoughts inclined him, it chanced that Rivalin was heading for where lovely Blancheflor was sitting. Seeing this, he galloped up to her and looking her in the eyes saluted her most pleasantly. • "God save you, lovely woman!" • "Thank you," said the girl, and continued very bashfully, "may God Almighty, who makes all hearts glad, gladden your heart and mind! And my

veyed by his clothes and poses.) But also send out a mixed signal—some sign that you are not what you seem, a paradox. Do not worry if this underquality is a negative one, like danger, cruelty, or amorality; people will be drawn to the enigma anyway, and pure goodness is rarely seductive.

> *Paradox with him was only truth standing on its head to attract attention.*
>
> —Richard Le Gallienne, on his friend Oscar Wilde

Keys to Seduction

Nothing can proceed in seduction unless you can attract and hold your victim's attention, your physical presence becoming a haunting mental presence. It is actually quite easy to create that first stir—an alluring style of dress, a suggestive glance, something extreme about you. But what happens next? Our minds are barraged with images—not just from media but from the disorder of daily life. And many of these images are quite striking. You become just one more thing screaming for attention; your attractiveness will pass unless you spark the more enduring kind of spell that makes people think of you in your absence. That means engaging their imaginations, making them think there is more to you than what they see. Once they start embellishing your image with their fantasies, they are hooked.

This must, however, be done early on, before your targets know too much and their impressions of you are set. It should occur the moment they lay eyes on you. By sending mixed signals in that first encounter, you create a little surprise, a little tension: you seem to be one thing (innocent, brash, intellectual, witty), but you also throw them a glimpse of something else (devilish, shy, spontaneous, sad). Keep things subtle: if the second quality is too strong, you will seem schizophrenic. But make them wonder why you might be shy or sad underneath your brash intellectual wit, and you will have their attention. Give them an ambiguity that lets them see what they want to see, capture their imagination with little voyeuristic glimpses into your dark soul.

The Greek philosopher Socrates was one of history's greatest seducers; the young men who followed him as students were not just fascinated by his ideas, they fell in love with him. One such youth was Alcibiades, the notorious playboy who became a powerful political figure near the end of the fifth century B.C. In Plato's *Symposium*, Alcibiades describes Socrates's seductive powers by comparing him to the little figures of Silenus that were made back then. In Greek myth, Silenus was quite ugly, but also a wise prophet. Accordingly the statues of Silenus were hollow, and when you took them apart, you would find little figures of gods inside them—the inner truth and beauty under the unappealing exterior. And so, for Alcibiades, it was the same with Socrates, who was so ugly as to be repellent but whose face radiated inner beauty and contentment. The effect was confus-

grateful thanks to you!—yet not forgetting a bone I have to pick with you." • *"Ah, sweet woman, what have I done?" was courteous Rivalin's reply.* • *"You have annoyed me through a friend of mine, the best I ever had."* • *"Good heavens," thought he, "what does this mean? What have I done to displease her? What does she say I have done?" and he imagined that unwittingly he must have injured a kinsman of hers some time at their knightly sports and that was why she was vexed with him. But no, the friend she referred to was her heart, in which he made her suffer: that was the friend she spoke of. But he knew nothing of that.* • *"Lovely woman," he said with all his accustomed charm, "I do not want you to be angry with me or bear me any ill will. So, if what you tell me is true, pronounce sentence on me yourself: I will do whatever you command."* • *"I do not hate you overmuch for what has happened," was the sweet girl's answer, "nor do I love you for it. But to see what amends you will make for the wrong you have done me, I shall test you another time."* • *And so he bowed as if to go, and she, lovely girl, sighed at him most secretly and said with tender feeling:* • *"Ah, dear friend, God bless you!" From this time on the thoughts of each ran on the other.* • *Rivalin turned away, pondering many things. He pondered from many sides why Blancheflor should be vexed, and what lay behind it all. He considered her greeting, her*

ing and attractive. Antiquity's other great seducer, Cleopatra, also sent out mixed signals: by all accounts physically alluring, in voice, face, body, and manner, she also had a brilliantly active mind, which for many writers of the time made her seem somewhat masculine in spirit. These contrary qualities gave her complexity, and complexity gave her power.

To capture and hold attention, you need to show attributes that go against your physical appearance, creating depth and mystery. If you have a sweet face and an innocent air, let out hints of something dark, even vaguely cruel in your character. It is not advertised in your words, but in your manner. The actor Errol Flynn had a boyishly angelic face and a slight air of sadness. Beneath this outward appearance, however, women could sense an underlying cruelty, a criminal streak, an exciting kind of dangerousness. This play of contrary qualities attracted obsessive interest. The female equivalent is the type epitomized by Marilyn Monroe; she had the face and voice of a little girl, but something sexual and naughty emanated powerfully from her as well. Madame Récamier did it all with her eyes—the gaze of an angel, suddenly interrupted by something sensual and flirtatious.

Playing with gender roles is a kind of intriguing paradox that has a long history in seduction. The greatest Don Juans have had a touch of prettiness and femininity, and the most attractive courtesans have had a masculine streak. The strategy, though, is only powerful when the underquality is merely hinted at; if the mix is too obvious or striking it will seem bizarre or even threatening. The great seventeenth-century French courtesan Ninon de l'Enclos was decidedly feminine in appearance, yet everyone who met her was struck by a touch of aggressiveness and independence in her—but just a touch. The late nineteenth-century Italian novelist Gabriele d'Annunzio was certainly masculine in his approaches, but there was a gentleness, a consideration, mixed in, and an interest in feminine finery. The combinations can be juggled every which way: Oscar Wilde was quite feminine in appearance and manner, but the underlying suggestion that he was actually quite masculine drew both men and women to him.

A potent variation on this theme is the blending of physical heat and emotional coldness. Dandies like Beau Brummel and Andy Warhol combine striking physical appearances with a kind of coldness of manner, a distance from everything and everyone. They are both enticing and elusive, and people spend lifetimes chasing after such men, trying to shatter their unattainability. (The power of apparently unattainable people is devilishly seductive; we want to be the one to break them down.) They also wrap themselves in ambiguity and mystery, either talking very little or talking only of surface matters, hinting at a depth of character you can never reach. When Marlene Dietrich entered a room, or arrived at a party, all eyes inevitably turned to her. First there were her startling clothes, chosen to make heads turn. Then there was her air of nonchalant indifference. Men, and women too, became obsessed with her, thinking of her long after other memories of the evening had faded. Remember: that first impression, that

words; he examined her sigh minutely, her farewell, he whole behavior . . . But since he was uncertain of her motive—whether she had acted from enmity or love—he wavered in perplexity. He wavered in his thoughts now here, now there. At one moment he was off in one direction, then suddenly in another, till he had so ensnared himself in the toils of his own desire that he was powerless to escape . . . • His entanglement had placed him in a quandary, for he did not know whether she wished him well or ill; he could not make out whether she loved or hated him. No hope or despair did he consider which did not forbid him either to advance or retreat—hope and despair led him to and fro in unresolved dissension. Hope spoke to him of love, despair of hatred. Because of this discord he could yield his firm belief neither to hatred nor yet to love. Thus his feelings drifted in an unsure haven—hope bore him on, despair away. He found no constancy in either; they agreed neither one way or another. When despair came and told him that his Blancheflor was his enemy he faltered and sought to escape: but at once came hope, bringing him her love, and a fond aspiration, and so perforce he remained. In the face of such discord he did not know where to turn: nowhere could he go forward. The more he strove to flee, the more firmly love forced him back. The harder he struggled to escape, love drew him back more firmly.

—GOTTFRIED VON STRASSBURG, *TRISTAN*, TRANSLATED BY A.T. HATTO

entrance, is critical. To show too much desire for attention is to signal insecurity, and will often drive people away; play it too cold and disinterested, on the other hand, and no one will bother coming near. The trick is to combine the two attitudes at the same moment. It is the essence of coquetry.

Perhaps you have a reputation for a particular quality, which immediately comes to mind when people see you. You will better hold their attention by suggesting that behind this reputation some other quality lies lurking. No one had a darker, more sinful reputation than Lord Byron. What drove women wild was that behind his somewhat cold and disdainful exterior, they could sense that he was actually quite romantic, even spiritual. Byron played this up with his melancholic airs and occasional kind deed. Transfixed and confused, many women thought that they could be the one to lead him back to goodness, to make him a faithful lover. Once a woman entertained such a thought, she was completely under his spell. It is not difficult to create such a seductive effect. Should you be known as eminently rational, say, hint at something irrational. Johannes, the narrator in Kierkegaard's *The Seducer's Diary*, first treats the young Cordelia with businesslike politeness, as his reputation would lead her to expect. Yet she very soon overhears him making remarks that hint at a wild, poetic streak in his character; and she is excited and intrigued.

These principles have applications far beyond sexual seduction. To hold the attention of a broad public, to seduce them into thinking about you, you need to mix your signals. Display too much of one quality—even if it is a noble one, like knowledge or efficiency—and people will feel that you lack humanity. We are all complex and ambiguous, full of contradictory impulses; if you show only one side, even if it is your good side, you will wear on people's nerves. They will suspect you are a hypocrite. Mahatma Gandhi, a saintly figure, openly confessed to feelings of anger and vengefulness. John F. Kennedy, the most seductive American public figure of modern times, was a walking paradox: an East Coast aristocrat with a love of the common man, an obviously masculine man—a war hero—with a vulnerability you could sense underneath, an intellectual who loved popular culture. People were drawn to Kennedy like the steel filings in Wilde's fable. A bright surface may have a decorative charm, but what draws your eye into a painting is a depth of field, an inexpressible ambiguity, a surreal complexity.

***Symbol**: The Theater Curtain. Onstage, the curtain's heavy deep-red folds attract your eye with their hypnotic surface. But what really fascinates and draws you in is what you think might be happening behind the curtain—the light peeking through, the suggestion of a secret, something about to happen. You feel the thrill of a voyeur about to watch a performance.*

Reversal

The complexity you signal to other people will only affect them properly if they have the capacity to enjoy a mystery. Some people like things simple, and lack the patience to pursue a person who confuses them. They prefer to be dazzled and overwhelmed. The great Belle Epoque courtesan known as La Belle Otero would work a complex magic on artists and political figures who fell for her, but in dealing with the more uncomplicated, sensual male she would astound them with spectacle and beauty. When meeting a woman for the first time, Casanova might dress in the most fantastic outfit, with jewels and brilliant colors to dazzle the eye; he would use the target's reaction to gauge whether or not she would demand a more complicated seduction. Some of his victims, particularly young girls, needed no more than the glittering and spellbinding appearance, which was really what they wanted, and the seduction would stay on that level.

Everything depends on your target: do not bother creating depth for people who are insensitive to it, or who may even be put off or disturbed by it. You can recognize such types by their preference for the simpler pleasures in life, their lack of patience for a more nuanced story. With them, keep it simple.

4

Appear to Be an Object of Desire —Create Triangles

Few are drawn to the person whom others avoid or neglect; people gather around those who have already attracted interest. We want what other people want. To draw your victims closer and make them hungry to possess you, you must create an aura of desirability—of being wanted and courted by many. It will become a point of vanity for them to be the preferred object of your attention, to win you away from a crowd of admirers. Manufacture the illusion of popularity by surrounding yourself with members of the opposite sex—friends, former lovers, present suitors. Create triangles that stimulate rivalry and raise your value. Build a reputation that precedes you: if many have succumbed to your charms, there must be a reason.

Ask questions

Creating Triangles

One evening in 1882, the thirty-two-year-old Prussian philosopher Paul Rée, living in Rome at the time, visited the house of an older woman who ran a salon for writers and artists. Rée noticed a newcomer there, a twenty-one-year-old Russian girl named Lou von Salomé, who had come to Rome on holiday with her mother. Rée introduced himself and they began a conversation that lasted well into the night. Her ideas about God and morality were like his own; she talked with such intensity, yet at the same time her eyes seemed to flirt with him. Over the next few days Rée and Salomé took long walks through the city. Intrigued by her mind yet confused by the emotions she aroused, he wanted to spend more time with her. Then, one day, she startled him with a proposition: she knew he was a close friend of the philosopher Friedrich Nietzsche, then also visiting Italy. The three of them, she said, should travel together—no, actually live together, in a kind of philosophers' ménage à trois. A fierce critic of Christian morals, Rée found this idea delightful. He wrote to his friend about Salomé, describing how desperate she was to meet him. After a few such letters, Nietzsche hurried to Rome.

Rée had made this invitation to please Salomé, and to impress her; he also wanted to see if Nietzsche shared his enthusiasm for the young girl's ideas. But as soon as Nietzsche arrived, something unpleasant happened: the great philosopher, who had always been a loner, was obviously smitten with Salomé. Instead of the three of them sharing intellectual conversations together, Nietzsche seemed to be conspiring to get the girl alone. When Rée caught glimpses of Nietzsche and Salomé talking without including him, he felt shivers of jealousy. Forget about some philosophers' ménage à trois: Salomé was his, he had discovered her, and he would not share her, even with his good friend. Somehow he had to get her alone. Only then could he woo and win her.

Madame Salomé had planned to escort her daughter back to Russia, but Salomé wanted to stay in Europe. Rée intervened, offering to travel with the Salomés to Germany and introduce them to his own mother, who, he promised, would look after the girl and act as a chaperone. (Rée knew that his mother would be a lax guardian at best.) Madame Salomé agreed to this proposal, but Nietzsche was harder to shake: he decided to join them on their northward journey to Rée's home in Prussia. At one point in the trip, Nietzsche and Salomé took a walk by themselves, and

Let me tell you about a gentleman I once knew who, although he was of pleasing appearance and modest behavior, and also a very capable warrior, was not so outstanding as regards any of these qualities that there were not to be found many who were his equal and even better. However, as luck would have it, a certain lady fell very deeply in love with him. She saw that he felt the same way, and as her love grew day by day, there not being any way for them to speak to each other, she revealed her sentiments to another lady, who she hoped would be of service to her in this affair. Now this lady neither in rank nor beauty was a whit inferior to the first; and it came about that when she heard the young man (whom she had never seen) spoken of so affectionately, and came to realize that the other woman, whom she knew was extremely discreet and intelligent, loved him beyond words, she straight away began to imagine that he must be the most handsome, the wisest, the most discreet of men, and, in short, the

when they came back, Rée had the feeling that something physical had happened between them. His blood boiled; Salomé was slipping from his grasp.

Finally the group split up, the mother returning to Russia, Nietzsche to his summer place in Tautenburg, Rée and Salomé staying behind at Rée's home. But Salomé did not stay long: she accepted an invitation of Nietzsche's to visit him, unchaperoned, in Tautenburg. In her absence Rée was consumed with doubts and anger. He wanted her more than ever, and was prepared to redouble his efforts. When she finally came back, Rée vented his bitterness, railing against Nietzsche, criticizing his philosophy, and questioning his motives toward the girl. But Salomé took Nietzsche's side. Rée was in despair; he felt he had lost her for good. Yet a few days later she surprised him again: she had decided she wanted to live with him, and with him alone.

At last Rée had what he had wanted, or so he thought. The couple settled in Berlin, where they rented an apartment together. But now, to Rée's dismay, the old pattern repeated. They lived together but Salomé was courted on all sides by young men. The darling of Berlin's intellectuals, who admired her independent spirit, her refusal to compromise, she was constantly surrounded by a harem of men, who referred to her as "Her Excellency." Once again Rée found himself competing for her attention. Driven to despair, he left her a few years later, and eventually committed suicide.

In 1911, Sigmund Freud met Salomé (now known as Lou Andreas-Salomé) at a conference in Germany. She wanted to devote herself to the psychoanalytical movement, she said, and Freud found her enchanting, although, like everyone else, he knew the story of her infamous affair with Nietzsche (see page 46, "The Dandy"). Salomé had no background in psychoanalysis or in therapy of any kind, but Freud admitted her into the inner circle of followers who attended his private lectures. Soon after she joined the circle, one of Freud's most promising and brilliant students, Dr. Victor Tausk, sixteen years younger than Salomé, fell in love with her. Salomé's relationship with Freud had been platonic, but he had grown extremely fond of her. He was depressed when she missed a lecture, and would send her notes and flowers. Her involvement in a love affair with Tausk made him intensely jealous, and he began to compete for her attention. Tausk had been like a son to him, but the son was threatening to steal the father's platonic lover. Soon, however, Salomé left Tausk. Now her friendship with Freud was stronger than ever, and so it lasted until her death, in 1937.

Interpretation. Men did not just fall in love with Lou Andreas-Salomé; they were overwhelmed with the desire to possess her, to wrest her away from others, to be the proud owner of her body and spirit. They rarely saw her alone; she always in some way surrounded herself with other men.

man most worthy of her love in all the world. So, never having set eyes on him, she fell in love with him so passionately that she set out to win him not for her friend but for herself. And in this she succeeded with little effort, for indeed she was a woman more to be wooed than to do the wooing. And now listen to the splendid sequel: not long afterward it happened that a letter which she had written to her lover fell into the hands of another woman of comparable rank, charm, and beauty; and since she, like most women, was curious and eager to learn secrets, she opened the letter and read it. Realizing that it was written from the depths of passion, in the most loving and ardent terms, she was at first moved with compassion, for she knew very well from whom the letter came and to whom it was addressed; then, however, such was the power of the words she read, turning them over in her mind and considering what kind of man it must be who had been able to arouse such great love, she at once began to fall in love with him herself; and the letter was without doubt far more effective than if the young man had himself written it to her. And just as it sometimes happens that the poison prepared for a prince kills the one who tastes his food, so that poor woman, in her greediness, drank the love potion prepared for another. What more is there to say? The affair was no secret, and things so developed that many other women besides, partly to spite the others and partly to follow their

When she saw that Rée was interested in her, she mentioned her desire to meet Nietzsche. This inflamed Rée, and made him want to marry her and to keep him for himself, but she insisted on meeting his friend. His letters to Nietzsche betrayed his desire for this woman, and this in turn kindled Nietzsche's own desire for her, even before he had met her. Every time one of the two men was alone with her, the other was in the background. Then, later on, most of the men who met her knew of the infamous Nietzsche affair, and this only increased their desire to possess her, to compete with Nietzsche's memory. Freud's affection for her, similarly, turned into potent desire when he had to vie with Tausk for her attention. Salomé was intelligent and attractive enough on her own account; but her constant strategy of imposing a triangle of relationships on her suitors made her desirability intense. And while they fought over her, she had the power, being desired by all and subject to none.

example, put every care and effort into winning this man's love, squabbling over it for a while as boys do for cherries.

—Baldassare Castiglione, *The Book of the Courtier*, translated by George Bull

Our desire for another person almost always involves social considerations: we are attracted to those who are attractive to other people. We want to possess them and steal them away. You can believe all the sentimental nonsense you want to about desire, but in the end, much of it has to do with vanity and greed. Do not whine and moralize about people's selfishness, but simply use it to your advantage. The illusion that you are desired by others will make you more attractive to your victims than your beautiful face or your perfect body. And the most effective way to create that illusion is to create a triangle: impose another person between you and your victim, and subtly make your victim aware of how much this other person wants you. The third point on the triangle does not have to be just one person: surround yourself with admirers, reveal your past conquests—in other words, envelop yourself in an aura of desirability. Make your targets compete with your past and your present. They will long to possess you all to themselves, giving you great power for as long as you elude their grasp. Fail to make yourself an object of desire right from the start, and you will end up the sorry slave to the whims of your lovers—they will abandon you the moment they lose interest.

Most of the time we prefer one thing to another because that is what our friends already prefer or because that object has marked social significance. Adults, when they are hungry, are just like children in that they seek out the foods that others take. In their love affairs, they seek out the man or woman whom others find attractive and abandon those who are not sought after. When we say of a man or woman that he or she is desirable, what we really mean is that others desire them. It is not that they have some particular quality, but because they conform to some currently modish model.

—Serge Moscovici, *The Age of the Crowd: A Historical Treatise on Mass Psychology*, translated by J. C. Whitehouse

> *[A person] will desire any object so long as he is convinced that it is desired by another person whom he admires.*
>
> —René Girard

Keys to Seduction

We are social creatures, and are immensely influenced by the tastes and desires of other people. Imagine a large social gathering. You see a man alone, whom nobody talks to for any length of time, and who is wandering around without company; isn't there a kind of self-fulfilling isolation about him? Why is he alone, why is he avoided? There has to be a reason. Until someone takes pity on this man and starts up a conversation

It will be greatly to your advantage to entertain the lady you would win with an account of the number of women who are in love with you, and of the decided advances which they have made to you; for this will not only prove that you are a great favorite with the ladies, and a man of true honor, but it will convince her that she may have the honor of being enrolled in the same list, and of being praised in the

with him, he will look unwanted and unwantable. But over there, in another corner, is a woman surrounded by people. They laugh at her remarks, and as they laugh, others join the group, attracted by its gaiety. When she moves around, people follow. Her face is glowing with attention. There has to be a reason.

same way, in the presence of your other female friends. This will greatly delight her, and you need not be surprised if she testifies her admiration of your character by throwing her arms around your neck on the spot.

—Lola Montez, *The Arts and Secrets of Beauty, with Hints to Gentlemen on the Art of Fascinating*

In both cases, of course, there doesn't actually have to be a reason at all. The neglected man may have quite charming qualities, supposing you ever talk to him; but most likely you won't. Desirability is a social illusion. Its source is less what you say or do, or any kind of boasting or self-advertisement, than the sense that other people desire you. To turn your targets' interest into something deeper, into desire, you must make them see you as a person whom others cherish and covet. Desire is both imitative (we like what others like) and competitive (we want to take away from others what they have). As children, we wanted to monopolize the attention of a parent, to draw it away from other siblings. This sense of rivalry pervades human desire, repeating throughout our lives. Make people compete for your attention, make them see you as sought after by everyone else. The aura of desirability will envelop you.

[René] Girard's mimetic desire occurs when an individual subject desires an object because it is desired by another subject, here designated as the rival: desire is modeled on the wishes or actions of another. Philippe Lacoue-Labarthe says that "the basic hypothesis upon which rests Girard's famous analysis [is that] every desire is the desire of the other (and not immediately desire of an object), every structure of desire is triangular (including the other—mediator or model—whose desire desire imitates), every desire is thus from its inception tapped by hatred and rivalry; in short, the origin of desire is mimesis—mimeticism—and no desire is ever forged which does not desire forthwith the death or disappearance of the model or exemplary character which gave rise to it.

—James Mandrell, *Don Juan and the Point of Honor*

Your admirers can be friends or even suitors. Call it the harem effect. Pauline Bonaparte, sister of Napoleon, raised her value in men's eyes by always having a group of worshipful men around her at balls and parties. If she went for a walk, it was never with one man, always with two or three. Perhaps these men were simply friends, or even just props and hangers-on; the sight of them was enough to suggest that she was prized and desired, a woman worth fighting over. Andy Warhol, too, surrounded himself with the most glamorous, interesting people he could find. To be part of his inner circle meant that you were desirable as well. By placing himself in the middle but keeping himself aloof from it all, he made everyone compete for his attention. He stirred people's desire to possess him by holding back.

Practices like these not only stimulate competitive desires, they take aim at people's prime weakness: their vanity and self-esteem. We can endure feeling that another person has more talent, or more money, but the sense that a rival is more desirable than we are—that is unbearable. In the early eighteenth century, the Duke de Richelieu, a great rake, managed to seduce a young woman who was rather religious but whose husband, a dolt, was often away. He then proceeded to seduce her upstairs neighbor, a young widow. When the two women discovered that he was going from one to the other in the same night, they confronted him. A lesser man would have fled, but not the duke; he understood the dynamic of vanity and desire. Neither woman wanted to feel that he preferred the other. And so he managed to arrange a little ménage à trois, knowing that now they would struggle between themselves to be the favorite. When people's vanity is at risk, you can make them do whatever you want. According to Stendhal, if there is a woman you are interested in, pay attention to her sister. That will stir a triangular desire.

Your reputation—your illustrious past as a seducer—is an effective way of creating an aura of desirability. Women threw themselves at Errol Flynn's feet, not because of his handsome face, and certainly not because of his acting skills, but because of his reputation. They knew that other women had found him irresistible. Once he had established that reputation, he did not have to chase women anymore; they came to him. Men who believe that a rakish reputation will make women fear or distrust them, and should be played down, are quite wrong. On the contrary, it makes them more attractive. The virtuous Duchess de Montpensier, the *Grande Mademoiselle* of seventeenth-century France, began by enjoying a friendship with the rake Lauzun, but a troubling thought soon occurred to her: if a man with Lauzun's past did not see her as a possible lover, something had to be wrong with her. This anxiety eventually pushed her into his arms. To be part of a great seducer's club of conquests can be a matter of vanity and pride. We are happy to be in such company, to have our name broadcast as this man or woman's lover. Your own reputation may not be so alluring, but you must find a way to suggest to your victim that others, many others, have found you desirable. It is reassuring. There is nothing like a restaurant full of empty tables to persuade you not to go in.

It's annoying that our new acquaintance likes the boy. But aren't the best things in life free to all? The sun shines on everyone. The moon, accompanied by countless stars, leads even the beasts to pasture. What can you think of lovelier than water? But it flows for the whole world. Is love alone then something furtive rather than something to be gloried in? Exactly, that's just it—I don't want any of the good things of life unless people are envious of them.

—Petronius, *The Satyricon*, translated by J. P. Sullivan

A variation on the triangle strategy is the use of contrasts: careful exploitation of people who are dull or unattractive may enhance your desirability by comparison. At a social affair, for instance, make sure that your target has to chat with the most boring person available. Come to the rescue and your target will be delighted to see you. In *The Seducer's Diary*, by Søren Kierkegaard, Johannes has designs on the innocent young Cordelia. Knowing that his friend Edward is hopelessly shy and dull, he encourages this man to court her; a few weeks of Edward's attentions will make her eyes wander in search of someone else, *anyone* else, and Johannes will make sure that they settle on him. Johannes chose to strategize and maneuver, but almost any social environment will contain contrasts you can make use of almost naturally. The seventeenth-century English actress Nell Gwyn became the main mistress of King Charles II because her humor and unaffectedness made her that much more desirable among the many stiff and pretentious ladies of Charles's court. When the Shanghai actress Jiang Qing met Mao Zedong, in 1937, she did not have to do much to seduce him; the other women in his mountain camp in Yenan dressed like men, and were decidedly unfeminine. The sight alone of Jiang was enough to seduce Mao, who soon left his wife for her. To make use of contrasts, either develop and display those attractive attributes (humor, vivacity, and so on) that are the scarcest in your own social group, or choose a group in which your natural qualities are rare, and will shine.

The use of contrasts has vast political ramifications, for a political figure must also seduce and seem desirable. Learn to play up the qualities that your rivals lack. Peter II, czar in eighteenth-century Russia, was arrogant and irresponsible, so his wife, Catherine the Great, did all she could to seem modest and dependable. When Vladimir Lenin returned to Russia in 1917 after Czar Nicholas II had been deposed, he made a show of decisiveness and discipline—precisely what no other leader had at the time. In the American presidential race of 1980, the irresoluteness of Jimmy Carter made the single-mindedness of Ronald Reagan look desirable. Contrasts are eminently seductive because they do not depend on your own words or self-advertisements. The public reads them unconsciously, and sees what it wants to see.

Finally, appearing to be desired by others will raise your value, but often how you carry yourself can influence this as well. Do not let your targets see you so often; keep your distance, seem unattainable, out of their reach. An object that is rare and hard to obtain is generally more prized.

***Symbol**: The Trophy.*
What makes you want to win the trophy, and to see it as something worth having, is the sight of the other competitors. Some, out of a spirit of kindness, may want to reward everyone for trying, but the Trophy then loses its value. It must represent not only your victory but everyone else's defeat.

Reversal

There is no reversal. It is essential to appear desirable in the eyes of others.

5
Create a Need—
Stir Anxiety and Discontent

A perfectly satisfied person cannot be seduced. Tension and disharmony must be instilled in your targets' minds. Stir within them feelings of discontent, an unhappiness with their circumstances and with themselves: their life lacks adventure, they have strayed from the ideals of their youth, they have become boring. The feelings of inadequacy that you create will give you space to insinuate yourself, to make them see you as the answer to their problems. Pain and anxiety are the proper precursors to pleasure. Learn to manufacture the need that you can fill.

Opening a Wound

In the coal-mining town of Eastwood, in central England, David Herbert Lawrence was considered something of a strange lad. Pale and delicate, he had no time for games or boyish pursuits, but was interested in literature; and he preferred the company of girls, who made up most of his friends. Lawrence often visited the Chambers family, who had been his neighbors until they moved out of Eastwood to a farm not far away. He liked to study with the Chambers sisters, particularly Jessie; she was shy and serious, and getting her to open up and confide in him was a pleasurable challenge. Jessie grew quite attached to Lawrence over the years, and they became good friends.

One day in 1906, Lawrence, twenty-one at the time, did not show up at the usual hour for his study session with Jessie. He finally arrived much later, in a mood she had never seen before—preoccupied and quiet. Now it was her turn to make him open up. Finally he talked: he felt she was getting too close to him. What about her future? Whom would she marry? Certainly not him, he said, for they were just friends. But it was unfair of him to keep her from seeing others. They should of course remain friends and have their talks, but maybe less often. When he finished and left, she felt a strange emptiness. She had yet to think much about love or marriage. Suddenly she had doubts. What would her future be? Why wasn't she thinking about it? She felt anxious and upset, without understanding why.

Lawrence continued to visit, but everything had changed. He criticized her for this and that. She wasn't very physical. What kind of wife would she make anyway? A man needed more from a woman than just talk. He likened her to a nun. They began to see each other less often. When, some time later, Lawrence accepted a teaching position at a school outside London, she felt part relieved to be rid of him for a while. But when he said goodbye to her, and intimated that it might be for the last time, she broke down and cried. Then he started sending her weekly letters. He would write about girls he was seeing; maybe one of them would be his wife. Finally, at his behest, she visited him in London. They got along well, as in the old times, but he continued to badger her about her future, picking at that old wound. At Christmas he was back in Eastwood, and when he visited her he seemed exultant. He had decided that it was Jessie he should marry, that he had in fact been attracted to her all along. They should keep it quiet for a while; although his writing career was taking off (his first

No one can fall in love if he is even partially satisfied with what he has or who he is. The experience of falling in love originates in an extreme depression, an inability to find something that has value in everyday life. The "symptom" of the predisposition to fall in love is not the conscious desire to do so, the intense desire to enrich our lives; it is the profound sense of being worthless and of having nothing that is valuable and the shame of not having it. . . . For this reason, falling in love occurs more frequently among young people, since they are profoundly uncertain, unsure of their worth, and often ashamed of themselves. The same thing applies to people of other ages when they lose something in their lives—when their youth ends or when they start to grow old.

—Francesco Alberoni, *Falling in Love*, translated by Lawrence Venuti

novel was about to be published), he needed to make more money. Caught off guard by this sudden announcement, and overwhelmed with happiness, Jessie agreed to everything, and they became lovers.

Soon, however, the familiar pattern repeated: criticisms, breakups, announcements that he was engaged to another girl. This only deepened his hold on her. It was not until 1912 that she finally decided never to see him again, disturbed by his portrayal of her in the autobiographical novel *Sons and Lovers*. But Lawrence remained a lifelong obsession for her.

In 1913, a young English woman named Ivy Low, who had read Lawrence's novels, began to correspond with him, her letters gushing with admiration. By now Lawrence was married, to a German woman, the Baroness Frieda von Richthofen. To Low's surprise, though, he invited her to visit him and his wife in Italy. She knew he was probably something of a Don Juan, but was eager to meet him, and accepted his invitation. Lawrence was not what she had expected: his voice was high-pitched, his eyes were piercing, and there was something vaguely feminine about him. Soon they were taking walks together, with Lawrence confiding in Low. She felt that they were becoming friends, which delighted her. Then suddenly, just before she was to leave, he launched into a series of criticisms of her—she was so unspontaneous, so predictable, less human being than robot. Devastated by this unexpected attack, she nevertheless had to agree—what he had said was true. What could he have seen in her in the first place? Who was she anyway? Low left Italy feeling empty—but then Lawrence continued to write to her, as if nothing had happened. She soon realized that she had fallen hopelessly in love with him, despite everything he had said to her. Or was it not despite what he had said, but because of it?

In 1914, the writer John Middleton-Murry received a letter from Lawrence, a good friend of his. In the letter, out of nowhere, Lawrence criticized Middleton-Murry for being passionless and not gallant enough with his wife, the novelist Katherine Mansfield. Middleton-Murry later wrote, "I had never felt for a man before what his letter made me feel for him. It was a new thing, a unique thing, in my experience; and it was to remain unique." He felt that beneath Lawrence's criticisms lay some weird kind of affection. Whenever he saw Lawrence from then on, he felt a strange physical attraction that he could not explain.

Interpretation. The number of women, and of men, who fell under Lawrence's spell is astonishing given how unpleasant he could be. In almost every case the relationship began in friendship—with frank talks, exchanges of confidences, a spiritual bond. Then, invariably, he would suddenly turn against them, voicing harsh personal criticisms. He would know them well by that time, and the criticisms were often quite accurate, and hit a nerve. This would inevitably trigger confusion in his victims, and a sense of anxiety, a feeling that something was wrong with them. Jolted out of their usual sense of normality, they would feel divided inside. With half of their minds

"What can Love be then?" I said. "A mortal?" "Far from it." "Well, what?" "As in my previous examples, he is half-way between mortal and immortal." What sort of being is he then, Diotima?" "He is a great spirit, Socrates; everything that is of the nature of a spirit is half-god and half-man." . . . "Who are his parents?" I asked. "That is rather a long story," she answered, "but I will tell you. On the day that Aphrodite was born the gods were feasting, among them Contrivance the son of Invention; and after dinner, seeing that a party was in progress, Poverty came to beg and stood at the door. Now Contrivance was drunk with nectar—wine, I may say, had not yet been discovered—and went out into the garden of Zeus, and was overcome by sleep. So Poverty, thinking to alleviate her wretched condition by bearing a child to Contrivance, lay with him and conceived Love. Since Love was begotten on Aphrodite's birthday, and since he has also an innate passion for the beautiful, and so for the beauty of Aphrodite herself, he became her follower and servant. Again, having Contrivance for his father and Poverty for his mother, he bears the following character. He is always poor, and, far from being sensitive and beautiful, as most people imagine, he is hard and weather-beaten, shoeless and homeless, always sleeping out for want of a bed, on the ground, on doorsteps, and in the street. So far he takes after his mother and lives in want. But, being also his father's

they wondered why he was doing this, and felt he was unfair; with the other half, they believed it was all true. Then, in those moments of self-doubt, they would get a letter or a visit from him in which he was his old charming self.

Now they saw him differently. Now they were weak and vulnerable, in need of something; and he would seem so strong. Now he drew them to him, feelings of friendship turning into affection and desire. Once they felt uncertain about themselves, they were susceptible to falling in love.

Most of us protect ourselves from the harshness of life by succumbing to routines and patterns, by closing ourselves off from others. But underlying these habits is a tremendous sense of insecurity and defensiveness. We feel we are not really living. The seducer must pick at this wound and bring these semiconscious thoughts into full awareness. This was what Lawrence did: his sudden, brutally unexpected jabs would hit people at their weak spot.

Although Lawrence had great success with his frontal approach, it is often better to stir thoughts of inadequacy and uncertainty indirectly, by hinting at comparisons to yourself or to others, and by insinuating somehow that your victims' lives are less grand than they had imagined. You want them to feel at war with themselves, torn in two directions, and anxious about it. Anxiety, a feeling of lack and need, is the precursor of all desire. These jolts in the victim's mind create space for you to insinuate your poison, the siren call of adventure or fulfillment that will make them follow you into your web. Without anxiety and a sense of lack there can be no seduction.

son, he schemes to get for himself whatever is beautiful and good; he is bold and forward and strenuous, always devising tricks like a cunning huntsman."

—Plato, *Symposium*, translated by Walter Hamilton

We are all like pieces of the coins that children break in half for keepsakes—making two out of one, like the flatfish—and each of us is forever seeking the half that will tally with himself. . . . And so all this to-do is a relic of that original state of ours when we were whole, and now, when we are longing for and following after that primeval wholeness, we say we are in love.

—Aristophanes's speech in Plato's *Symposium*, quoted in James Mandrell, *Don Juan and the Point of Honor*

> *Desire and love have for their object things or qualities which a man does not at present possess but which he lacks.*
>
> —Socrates

Keys to Seduction

Everyone wears a mask in society; we pretend to be more sure of ourselves than we are. We do not want other people to glimpse that doubting self within us. In truth, our egos and personalities are much more fragile than they appear to be; they cover up feelings of confusion and emptiness. As a seducer, you must never mistake a person's appearance for the reality. People are always susceptible to being seduced, because in fact everyone lacks a sense of completeness, feels something missing deep inside. Bring their doubts and anxieties to the surface and they can be led and lured to follow you.

No one can see you as someone to follow or fall in love with unless they first reflect on themselves somehow, and on what they are missing. Before the seduction proceeds, you must place a mirror in front of them in

Don John: Well met, pretty lass! What! Are there such handsome Creatures as you amongst these Fields, these Trees, and Rocks? • Charlotta: I am as you see, Sir. • Don John: Are you of this Village? • Charlotta: Yes, Sir. • Don John: What's your name? • Charlotta: Charlotta, Sir, at your Service. • Don John: Ah what a fine Person 'tis! What piercing Eyes! • Charlotta: Sir, you make me ashamed. . . . • Don John: Pretty Charlotta, you are not marry'd, are you? • Charlotta: No, Sir, but I am soon to be, with Pierrot, son to Goody Simonetta. • Don John: What! Shou'd such a one as you be Wife to a

which they glimpse that inner emptiness. Made aware of a lack, they now can focus on you as the person who can fill that empty space. Remember: most of us are lazy. To relieve our feelings of boredom or inadequacy on our own takes too much effort; letting someone else do the job is both easier and more exciting. The desire to have someone fill up our emptiness is the weakness on which all seducers prey. Make people anxious about the future, make them depressed, make them question their identity, make them sense the boredom that gnaws at their life. The ground is prepared. The seeds of seduction can be sown.

Peasant! No, no; that's a profanation of so much Beauty. You was not born to live in a Village. You certainly deserve a better Fortune, and Heaven, which knows it well, brought me hither on purpose to hinder this Marriage and do justice to your Charms; for in short, fair Charlotta, I love you with all my Heart, and if you'll consent I'll deliver you from this miserable Place, and put you in the Condition you deserve. This Love is doubtless sudden, but 'tis an Effect of your great Beauty. I love you as much in a quarter of an Hour as I shou'd another in six Months.

—Molière, *Don John; or, The Libertine*, translated by John Ozell, in Oscar Mandel, ed., *The Theatre of Don Juan*

In Plato's dialogue *Symposium*—the West's oldest treatise on love, and a text that has had a determining influence on our ideas of desire—the courtesan Diotima explains to Socrates the parentage of Eros, the god of love. Eros's father was Contrivance, or Cunning, and his mother was Poverty, or Need. Eros takes after his parents: he is constantly in need, which he is constantly contriving to fill. As the god of love, he knows that love cannot be induced in another person unless they too feel need. And that is what his arrows do: piercing people's flesh, they make them feel a lack, an ache, a hunger. This is the essence of your task as a seducer. Like Eros, you must create a wound in your victim, aiming at their soft spot, the chink in their self-esteem. If they are stuck in a rut, make them feel it more deeply, "innocently" bringing it up and talking about it. What you want is a wound, an insecurity you can expand a little, an anxiety that can best be relieved by involvement with another person, namely you. They must feel the wound before they fall in love. Notice how Lawrence stirred anxiety, always hitting at his victims' weak spot: for Jessie Chambers, her physical coldness; for Ivy Low, her lack of spontaneity; for Middleton-Murry, his lack of gallantry.

Cleopatra got Julius Caesar to sleep with her the first night he met her, but the real seduction, the one that made him her slave, began later. In their ensuing conversations she talked repeatedly of Alexander the Great, the hero from whom she was supposedly descended. No one could compare to him. By implication, Caesar was made to feel inferior. Understanding that beneath his bravado Caesar was insecure, Cleopatra awakened in him an anxiety, a hunger to prove his greatness. Once he felt this way he was easily further seduced. Doubts about his masculinity was his tender spot.

When Caesar was assassinated, Cleopatra turned her sights on Mark Antony, one of Caesar's successors in the leadership of Rome. Antony loved pleasure and spectacle, and his tastes were crude. She appeared to him first on her royal barge, then wined and dined and banqueted him. Everything was geared to suggest to him the superiority of the Egyptian way of life over the Roman, at least when it came to pleasure. The Romans were boring and unsophisticated by comparison. And once Antony was made to feel how much he was missing in spending his time with his dull soldiers and his matronly Roman wife, he could be made to see Cleopatra as the incarnation of all that was exciting. He became her slave.

For I stand tonight facing west on what was once the last frontier. From the lands that stretch three thousand miles behind me, the pioneers of old gave up their safety, their comfort, and sometimes their lives to build a new world here in the West. They were not the captives of their own doubts, the prisoners of their own price tags. Their motto was not "every man for himself"—but "all for the common cause." They were determined to make that new world strong and free, to overcome its hazards and its hardships, to conquer the enemies that threatened from without and within. . . . • Today some would say that those struggles are all over—that all the horizons have been explored, that all the battles have been won, that there is no longer an

This is the lure of the exotic. In your role of seducer, try to position yourself as coming from outside, as a stranger of sorts. You represent change, difference, a breakup of routines. Make your victims feel that by comparison their lives are boring and their friends less interesting than they had thought. Lawrence made his targets feel personally inadequate; if you find it hard to be so brutal, concentrate on their friends, their circumstances, the externals of their lives. There are many legends of Don Juan, but they often describe him seducing a village girl by making her feel that her life is horribly provincial. He, meanwhile, wears glittering clothes and has a noble bearing. Strange and exotic, he is always from somewhere else. First she feels the boredom of her life, then she sees him as her salvation. Remember: people prefer to feel that if their life is uninteresting, it not because of themselves but because of their circumstances, the dull people they know, the town into which they were born. Once you make them feel the lure of the exotic, seduction is easy.

Another devilishly seductive area to aim at is the victim's past. To grow old is to renounce or compromise youthful ideals, to become less spontaneous, less alive in a way. This knowledge lies dormant in all of us. As a seducer you must bring it to the surface, make it clear how far people have strayed from their past goals and ideals. You, in turn, present yourself as representing that ideal, as offering a chance to recapture lost youth through adventure—through seduction. In her later years, Queen Elizabeth I of England was known as a rather stern and demanding ruler. She made it a point not to let her courtiers see anything soft or weak in her. But then Robert Devereux, the second Earl of Essex, came to court. Much younger than the queen, the dashing Essex would often chastize her for her sourness. The queen would forgive him—he was so exuberant and spontaneous, he could not control himself. But his comments got under her skin; in the presence of Essex she came to remember all the youthful ideals—spiritedness, feminine charm—that had since vanished from her life. She also felt a little of that girlish spirit return when she was around him. He quickly became her favorite, and soon she was in love with him. Old age is constantly seduced by youth, but first the young people must make it clear what the older ones are missing, how they have lost their ideals. Only then will they feel that the presence of the young will let them recapture that spark, the rebellious spirit that age and society have conspired to repress.

This concept has infinite applications. Corporations and politicians know that they cannot seduce their public into buying what they want them to buy, or doing what they want them to do, unless they first awaken a sense of need and discontent. Make the masses uncertain about their identity and you can help define it for them. It is as true of groups or nations as it is of individuals: they cannot be seduced without being made to feel some lack. Part of John F. Kennedy's election strategy in 1960 was to make Americans unhappy about the 1950s, and how far the country had strayed from its ideals. In talking about the 1950s, he did not mention the nation's economic stability or its emergence as a superpower. Instead, he implied that the period was marked by conformity, a lack of risk and adventure, a loss of our frontier values. To vote for Kennedy was to embark

American frontier. • But I trust that no one in this vast assemblage will agree with those sentiments. . . . • . . . I tell you the New Frontier is here, whether we seek it or not. . . . It would be easier to shrink back from that frontier, to look to the safe mediocrity of the past, to be lulled by good intentions and high rhetoric—and those who prefer that course should not cast their votes for me, regardless of party. • But I believe that the times demand invention, innovation, imagination, decision. I am asking each of you to be new pioneers on that New Frontier. My call is to the young in heart, regardless of age.

—JOHN F. KENNEDY, ACCEPTANCE SPEECH AS THE PRESIDENTIAL NOMINEE OF THE DEMOCRATIC PARTY, QUOTED IN JOHN HELLMANN, *THE KENNEDY OBSESSION: THE AMERICAN MYTH OF JFK*

The normal rhythm of life oscillates in general between a mild satisfaction with oneself and a slight discomfort, originating in the knowledge of one's personal shortcomings. We should like to be as handsome, young, strong or clever as other people of our acquaintance. We wish we could achieve as much as they do, long for similar advantages, positions, the same or greater success. To be delighted with oneself is the exception and, often enough, a smoke screen which we produce for ourselves and of course for others. Somewhere in it is a lingering feeling of discomfort with ourselves and a slight self-dislike. I assert that an increase of

on a collective adventure, to go back to ideals we had given up. But before anyone joined his crusade they had to be made aware of how much they had lost, what was missing. A group, like an individual, can get mired in routine, losing track of its original goals. Too much prosperity saps it of strength. You can seduce an entire nation by aiming at its collective insecurity, that latent sense that not everything is what it seems. Stirring dissatisfaction with the present and reminding people about the glorious past can unsettle their sense of identity. Then you can be the one to redefine it—a grand seduction.

this spirit of discontent renders a person especially susceptible to "falling in love." . . . In most cases this attitude of disquiet is unconscious, but in some it reaches the threshold of awareness in the form of a slight uneasiness, or a stagnant dissatisfaction, or a realization of being upset without knowing why.

—Theodor Reik, *Of Love and Lust*

***Symbol**: Cupid's Arrow. What awakens desire in the seduced is not a soft touch or a pleasant sensation; it is a wound. The arrow creates a pain, an ache, a need for relief. Before desire there must be pain. Aim the arrow at the victim's weakest spot, creating a wound that you can open and reopen.*

Reversal

If you go too far in lowering the targets' self-esteem they may feel too insecure to enter into your seduction. Do not be heavy-handed; like Lawrence, always follow up the wounding attack with a soothing gesture. Otherwise you will simply alienate them.

Charm is often a subtler and more effective route to seduction. The Victorian Prime Minister Benjamin Disraeli always made people feel *better* about themselves. He deferred to them, made them the center of attention, made them feel witty and vibrant. He was a boon to their vanity, and they grew addicted to him. This is a kind of diffused seduction, lacking in tension and in the deep emotions that the sexual variety stirs; it bypasses people's hunger, their need for some kind of fulfillment. But if you are subtle and clever, it can be a way of lowering their defenses, creating an unthreatening friendship. Once they are under your spell in this way, you can then open the wound. Indeed, after Disraeli had charmed Queen Victoria and established a friendship with her, he made her feel vaguely inadequate in the establishment of an empire and the realization of her ideals. Everything depends on the target. People who are riddled with insecurities may require the gentler variety. Once they feel comfortable with you, aim your arrows.

6

Master the Art of Insinuation

Making your targets feel dissatisfied and in need of your attention is essential, but if you are too obvious, they will see through you and grow defensive. There is no known defense, however, against insinuation—the art of planting ideas in people's minds by dropping elusive hints that take root days later, even appearing to them as their own idea. Insinuation is the supreme means of influencing people. Create a sublanguage—bold statements followed by retraction and apology, ambiguous comments, banal talk combined with alluring glances—that enters the target's unconscious to convey your real meaning. Make everything suggestive.

Insinuating Desire

One evening in the 1770s, a young man went to the Paris Opera to meet his lover, the Countess de___. The couple had been fighting, and he was anxious to see her again. The countess had not arrived yet at her box, but from an adjacent one a friend of hers, Madame de T___, called out to the young man to join her, remarking that it was an excellent stroke of luck that they had met that evening—he must keep her company on a trip she had to take. The young man wanted urgently to see the countess, but Madame was charming and insistent and he agreed to go with her. Before he could ask why or where, she quickly escorted him to her carriage outside, which then sped off.

Now the young man enjoined his hostess to tell him where she was taking him. At first she just laughed, but finally she told him: to her husband's château. The couple had been estranged, but had decided to reconcile; her husband was a bore, however, and she felt a charming young man like himself would liven things up. The young man was intrigued: Madame was an older woman, with a reputation for being rather formal, though he also knew she had a lover, a marquis. Why had she chosen him for this excursion? Her story was not quite credible. Then, as they traveled, she suggested he look out the window at the passing landscape, as she was doing. He had to lean over toward her to do so, and just as he did, the carriage jolted. She grabbed his hand and fell into his arms. She stayed there for a moment, then pulled away from him rather abruptly. After an awkward silence, she said, "Do you intend to convince me of my imprudence in your regard?" He protested that the incident had been an accident and reassured her he would behave himself. In truth, however, having her in his arms had made him think otherwise.

They arrived at the château. The husband came to meet them, and the young man expressed his admiration of the building: "What you see is nothing," Madame interrupted, "I must take you to Monsieur's apartment." Before he could ask what she meant, the subject was quickly changed. The husband was indeed a bore, but he excused himself after supper. Now Madame and the young man were alone. She invited him to walk with her in the gardens; it was a splendid evening, and as they walked, she slipped her arm in his. She was not worried that he would take advantage of her, she said, because she knew how attached he was to her good friend the countess. They talked of other things, and then she returned to the topic of

As we were about to enter the chamber, she stopped me. "Remember," she said gravely, "you are supposed never to have seen, never even suspected, the sanctuary you're about to enter. . . ." • . . . All this was like an initiation rite. She led me by the hand across a small, dark corridor. My heart was pounding as though I were a young proselyte being put to the test before the celebration of the great mysteries. . . . • "But your Countess . . ." she said, stopping. I was about to reply when the doors opened; my answer was interrupted by admiration. I was astonished, delighted, I no longer know what became of me, and I began in good faith to believe in magic. . . . In truth, I found myself in a vast cage of mirrors on which images were so artistically painted that they produced the illusion of all the objects they represented.

—Vivant Denon, "No Tomorrow," in Michel Feher, ed., *The Libertine Reader*

A few short years ago, in our native city, where fraud and cunning prosper more than love or loyalty, there was a noblewoman of striking beauty and impeccable breeding, who was endowed by Nature with as lofty a temperament and shrewd an intellect as could be found in any other woman of her time. . . . • This lady, being of gentle birth and finding herself married off to a master woollen-draper because he happened to be very rich, was unable to stifle her heartfelt contempt, for she was firmly of the opinion that no man of low condition, however wealthy, was deserving of a noble wife. And on discovering that all he was capable of, despite his massive wealth, was distinguishing wool from cotton, supervising the setting up of a loom, or debating the virtues of a particular yarn with a spinner-woman, she resolved that as far as it lay within her power she would have nothing whatsoever to do with his beastly caresses. Moreover she was determined to seek her pleasure elsewhere, in the company of one who seemed more worthy of her affection, and so it was that she fell deeply in love with an extremely eligible man in his middle thirties. And whenever a day passed without her having set eyes upon him, she was restless for the whole of the following night. • However, the gentleman suspected nothing of all this, and took no notice of her; and for her part, being very cautious, she would not venture to declare her love by dispatching a maidservant or writing him

his lover: "Is she making you quite happy? Oh, I fear the contrary, and this distresses me. . . . Are you not often the victim of her strange whims?" To the young man's surprise, Madame began to talk of the countess in a way that made it seem that she had been unfaithful to him (which was something he had suspected). Madame sighed—she regretted saying such things about her friend, and asked him to forgive her; then, as if a new thought had occurred to her, she mentioned a nearby pavilion, a delightful place, full of pleasant memories. But the shame of it was, it was locked and she had no key. And yet they found their way to the pavilion, and lo and behold, the door had been left open. It was dark inside, but the young man could sense that it was a place for trysts. They entered and sank onto a sofa, and before he knew what had come over him, he took her in his arms. Madame seemed to push him away, but then gave in. Finally she came to her senses: they must return to the house. Had he gone too far? He must try to control himself.

As they strolled back to the house, Madame remarked, "What a delicious night we've just spent." Was she referring to what had happened in the pavilion? "There is an even more charming room in the château," she went on, "but I can't show you anything," implying he had been too forward. She had mentioned this room ("Monsieur's apartment") several times before; he could not imagine what could be so interesting about it, but by now he was dying to see it and insisted she show it to him. "If you promise to be good," she replied, her eyes widening. Through the darkness of the house she led him into the room, which, to his delight, was a kind of temple of pleasure: there were mirrors on the walls, trompe l'oeil paintings evoking a forest scene, even a dark grotto, and a garlanded statue of Eros. Overwhelmed by the mood of the place, the young man quickly resumed what he had started in the pavilion, and would have lost all track of time if a servant had not rushed in and warned them that it was getting light outside—Monsieur would soon be up.

They quickly separated. Later that day, as the young man prepared to leave, his hostess said, "Goodbye, Monsieur; I owe you so many pleasures; but I have paid you with a beautiful dream. Now your love summons you to return. . . . Don't give the Countess cause to quarrel with me." Reflecting on his experience on the way back, he could not figure out what it meant. He had the vague sensation of having been used, but the pleasures he remembered outweighed his doubts.

Interpretation. Madame de T___ is a character in the eighteenth-century libertine short story "No Tomorrow," by Vivant Denon. The young man is the story's narrator. Although fictional, Madame's techniques were clearly based on those of several well-known libertines of the time, masters of the game of seduction. And the most dangerous of their weapons was insinuation—the means by which Madame cast her spell on the young man, making him seem the aggressor, giving her the night of pleasure she desired, and safeguarding her guiltless reputation, all in one stroke. After all, he was the one who initiated physical contact, or so it seemed. In truth, she was the one in control, planting precisely the ideas in his mind that she wanted. That first physical encounter in the carriage, for instance, that she had set up by inviting him closer: she later rebuked him for being forward, but what lingered in his mind was the excitement of the moment. Her talk of the countess made him confused and guilty; but then she hinted that his lover was unfaithful, planting a different seed in his mind: anger, and the desire for revenge. Then she asked him to forget what she had said and forgive her for saying it, a key insinuating tactic: "I am asking you to forget what I have said, but I know you cannot; the thought will remain in your mind." Provoked this way, it was inevitable he would grab her in the pavilion. She several times mentioned the room in the château—of course he insisted on going there. She enveloped the evening in an air of ambiguity. Even her words "If you promise to be good" could be read several ways. The young man's head and heart were inflamed with all of the feelings—discontent, confusion, desire—that she had indirectly instilled in him.

Particularly in the early phases of a seduction, learn to make everything you say and do a kind of insinuation. Insinuate doubt with a comment here and there about other people in the victim's life, making the victim feel vulnerable. Slight physical contact insinuates desire, as does a fleeting but memorable look, or an unusually warm tone of voice, both for the briefest of moments. A passing comment suggests that something about the victim interests you; but keep it subtle, your words revealing a possibility, creating a doubt. You are planting seeds that will take root in the weeks to come. When you are not there, your targets will fantasize about the ideas you have stirred up, and brood upon the doubts. They are slowly being led into your web, unaware that you are in control. How can they resist or become defensive if they cannot even see what is happening?

> *What distinguishes a suggestion from other kinds of psychical influence, such as a command or the giving of a piece of information or instruction, is that in the case of a suggestion an idea is aroused in another person's brain which is not examined in regard to its origin but is accepted just as though it had arisen spontaneously in that brain.*
>
> —Sigmund Freud

Keys to Seduction

You cannot pass through life without in one way or another trying to persuade people of something. Take the direct route, saying exactly what you want, and your honesty may make you feel good but you are probably not getting anywhere. People have their own sets of ideas, which are hardened into stone by habit; your words, entering their minds, com-

a letter, for fear of the dangers that this might entail. But having perceived that he was on very friendly terms with a certain priest, a rotund, uncouth, individual who was nevertheless regarded as an outstandingly able friar on account of his very saintly way of life, she calculated that this fellow would serve as an ideal go-between for her and the man she loved. And so, after reflecting on the strategy she would adopt, she paid a visit, at an appropriate hour of the day, to the church where he was to be found, and having sought him out, she asked him whether he would agree to confess her. • Since he could tell at a glance that she was a lady of quality, the friar gladly heard her confession, and when she had got to the end of it, she continued as follows: • "Father, as I shall explain to you presently, there is a certain matter about which I am compelled to seek your advice and assistance. Having already told you my name, I feel sure you will know my family and my husband. He loves me more dearly than life itself, and since he is enormously rich, he never has the slightest difficulty or hesitation in supplying me with every single object for which I display a yearning. Consequently, my love for him is quite unbounded, and if my mere thoughts, to say nothing of my actual behavior, were to run contrary to his wishes and his honor, I would be more deserving of hellfire than the wickedest woman who ever lived. • "Now, there is a certain person, of respectable outward appearance, who unless I am mistaken is a close acquaintance of yours. I really couldn't say what his name is, but he is tall and handsome, his clothes are brown and elegantly cut, and, possibly because he is unaware of my resolute nature, he appears to have laid siege to me. He turns up infallibly whenever I either look out of my window or stand at the front door or leave the house, and I am surprised, in fact, that he is not here now. Needless to say, I am very upset about all this, because his sort of conduct frequently gives an honest woman a bad name, even though she is quite innocent. • ". . . For the love of God, therefore, I implore you to speak to him severely and persuade him to refrain from his importunities. There are plenty of other women who doubtless find this sort of thing amusing, and who will enjoy being ogled and spied upon by him, but I personally have no inclination for it whatsoever, and I find his behavior exceedingly disagreeable." • And having reached the end of her speech, the lady bowed her head as though she were going to burst into tears. • The reverend friar realized immediately who it was to whom she was referring, and having warmly commended her purity of mind . . . he promised to take all necessary steps to ensure that the fellow ceased to annoy her. . . . • Shortly afterward, the gentleman in question paid one of his regular visits to the reverend friar, and after they had conversed together for a while on general

pete with the thousands of preconceived notions that are already there, and get nowhere. Besides, people resent your attempt to persuade them, as if they were incapable of deciding by themselves—as if you knew better. Consider instead the power of insinuation and suggestion. It requires some patience and art, but the results are more than worth it.

The way insinuation works is simple: disguised in a banal remark or encounter, a hint is dropped. It is about some emotional issue—a possible pleasure not yet attained, a lack of excitement in a person's life. The hint registers in the back of the target's mind, a subtle stab at his or her insecurities; its source is quickly forgotten. It is too subtle to be memorable at the time, and later, when it takes root and grows, it seems to have emerged naturally from the target's own mind, as if it was there all along. Insinuation lets you bypass people's natural resistance, for they seem to be listening only to what has originated in themselves. It is a language on its own, communicating directly with the unconscious. No seducer, no persuader, can hope to succeed without mastering the language and art of insinuation.

A strange man once arrived at the court of Louis XV. No one knew anything about him, and his accent and age were unplaceable. He called himself Count Saint-Germain. He was obviously wealthy; all kinds of gems and diamonds glittered on his jacket, his sleeves, his shoes, his fingers. He could play the violin to perfection, paint magnificently. But the most intoxicating thing about him was his conversation.

In truth, the count was the greatest charlatan of the eighteenth century—a man who had mastered the art of insinuation. As he spoke, a word here and there would slip out—a vague allusion to the philosopher's stone, which turned base metal into gold, or to the elixir of life. He did not say he possessed these things, but he made you associate him with their powers. Had he simply claimed to have them, no one would have believed him and people would have turned away. The count might refer to a man who had died forty years earlier as if he had known him personally; had this been so, the count would have had to be in his eighties, although he looked to be in his forties. He mentioned the elixir of life. . . . he seems so young. . . .

The key to the count's words was vagueness. He always dropped his hints into a lively conversation, grace notes in an ongoing melody. Only later would people reflect on what he had said. After a while, people started to come to him, inquiring about the philosopher's stone and the elixir of life, not realizing that it was he who had planted these ideas in their minds. Remember: to sow a seductive idea you must engage people's imaginations, their fantasies, their deepest yearnings. What sets the wheels spinning is suggesting things that people already want to hear—the possibility of pleasure, wealth, health, adventure. In the end, these good things turn out to be precisely what you seem to offer them. They will come to you as if on their own, unaware that you insinuated the idea in their heads.

In 1807, Napoleon Bonaparte decided it was critical for him to win the Russian Czar Alexander I to his side. He wanted two things out of the czar: a peace treaty in which they agreed to carve up Europe and the Middle East; and a marriage alliance, in which he would divorce his wife Josephine and marry into the czar's family. Instead of proposing these things directly, Napoleon decided to seduce the czar. Using polite social encounters and friendly conversations as his battlefields, he went to work. An apparent slip of the tongue revealed that Josephine could not bear children; Napoleon quickly changed the subject. A comment here and there seemed to suggest a linking of the destinies of France and Russia. Just before they were to part one evening, he talked of his desire for children, sighed sadly, then excused himself for bed, leaving the czar to sleep on this. He escorted the czar to a play on the themes of glory, honor, and empire; now, in later conversations, he could disguise his insinuations under the cover of discussing the play. Within a few weeks, the czar was speaking to his ministers of a marriage alliance and a treaty with France as if they were his own ideas.

Slips of the tongue, apparently inadvertent "sleep on it" comments, alluring references, statements for which you quickly apologize—all of these have immense insinuating power. They get under people's skin like a poison, and take on a life of their own. The key to succeeding with your insinuations is to make them when your targets are at their most relaxed or distracted, so that they are not aware of what is happening. Polite banter is often the perfect front for this; people are thinking about what they will say next, or are absorbed in their own thoughts. Your insinuations will barely register, which is how you want it.

In one of his early campaigns, John F. Kennedy addressed a group of veterans. Kennedy's brave exploits during World War II—the PT-109 incident had made him a war hero—were known to all; but in the speech, he talked of the other men on the boat, never mentioning himself. He knew, however, that what he had done was on everyone's mind, because in fact he had put it there. Not only did his silence on the subject make them think of it on their own, it made Kennedy seem humble and modest, qualities that go well with heroism. In seduction, as the French courtesan Ninon de l'Enclos advised, it is better not to talk about your love for a person. Let your target read it in your manner. Your silence on the subject will have more insinuating power than if you had addressed it directly.

Not only words insinuate; pay attention to gestures and looks. Madame Récamier's favorite technique was to keep her words banal and the look in her eyes enticing. The flow of conversation would keep men from thinking too deeply about these occasional looks, but they would be haunted by them. Lord Byron had his famous "underlook": while everyone was discussing some uninteresting subject, he would seem to hang his head, but then a young woman (the target) would see him glancing upward at her, his head still tilted. It was a look that seemed dangerous, challenging, but also ambiguous; many women were hooked by it. The face speaks its own language. We are used to trying to read people's faces, which are often better indicators of their feelings than what they say, which is so easy to control.

topics, the friar drew him to one side and reproached him in a very kindly sort of way for the amorous glances which, as the lady had given him to understand, he believed him to be casting in her direction. • Not unnaturally, the gentleman was amazed, for he had never so much as looked at the lady and it was very seldom that he passed by her house. . . . • The gentleman, being rather more perceptive than the reverend friar, was not exactly slow to appreciate the lady's cleverness, and putting on a somewhat sheepish expression, he promised not to bother her any more. But after leaving the friar, he made his way toward the house of the lady, who was keeping continuous vigil at a tiny little window so that she would see him if he happened to pass by. . . . And from that day forward, proceeding with the maximum prudence and conveying the impression that he was engaged in some other business entirely, he became a regular visitor to the neighborhood.

—Giovanni Boccaccio, *The Decameron*, translated by G. H. McWilliam

Glances are the heavy artillery of the flirt: everything can be conveyed in a look, yet that look can always be denied, for it cannot be quoted word for word.

—Stendhal, quoted in Richard Davenport-Hines, ed., *Vice: An Anthology*

Since people are always reading your looks, use them to transmit the insinuating signals you choose.

Finally, the reason insinuation works so well is not just that it bypasses people's natural resistance. It is also the language of pleasure. There is too little mystery in the world; too many people say exactly what they feel or want. We yearn for something enigmatic, for something to feed our fantasies. Because of the lack of suggestion and ambiguity in daily life, the person who uses them suddenly seems to have something alluring and full of promise. It is a kind of titillating game—what is this person up to? What does he or she mean? Hints, suggestions, and insinuations create a seductive atmosphere, signaling that their victim is no longer involved in the routines of daily life but has entered another realm.

Symbol: *The Seed. The soil is carefully prepared. The seeds are planted months in advance. Once they are in the ground, no one knows what hand threw them there. They are part of the earth. Disguise your manipulations by planting seeds that take root on their own.*

Reversal

The danger in insinuation is that when you leave things ambiguous your target may misread them. There are moments, particularly later on in a seduction, when it is best to communicate your idea directly, particularly once you know the target will welcome it. Casanova often played things that way. When he could sense that a woman desired him, and needed little preparation, he would use a direct, sincere, gushing comment to go straight to her head like a drug and make her fall under his spell. When the rake and writer Gabriele D'Annunzio met a woman he desired, he rarely delayed. Flattery flowed from his mouth and pen. He would charm with his "sincerity" (sincerity can be feigned, and is just one stratagem among others). This only works, however, when you sense that the target is easily yours. If not, the defenses and suspicions you raise by direct attack will make your seduction impossible. When in doubt, indirection is the better route.

7
Enter Their Spirit

Most people are locked in their own worlds, making them stubborn and hard to persuade. The way to lure them out of their shell and set up your seduction is to enter their spirit. Play by their rules, enjoy what they enjoy, adapt yourself to their moods. In doing so you will stroke their deep-rooted narcissism and lower their defenses. Hypnotized by the mirror image you present, they will open up, becoming vulnerable to your subtle influence. Soon you can shift the dynamic: once you have entered their spirit you can make them enter yours, at a point when it is too late to turn back. Indulge your targets' every mood and whim, giving them nothing to react against or resist.

The Indulgent Strategy

In October of 1961, the American journalist Cindy Adams was granted an exclusive interview with President Sukarno of Indonesia. It was a remarkable coup, for Adams was a little-known journalist at the time, while Sukarno was a world figure in the midst of a crisis. A leader of the fight for Indonesia's independence, he had been the country's president since 1949, when the Dutch finally gave up the colony. By the early 1960s, his daring foreign policy had made him hated in the United States, some calling him the Hitler of Asia.

Adams decided that in the interests of a lively interview, she would not be cowed or overawed by Sukarno, and she began the conversation by joking with him. To her pleasant surprise, her ice-breaking tactic seemed to work: Sukarno warmed up to her. He let the interview run well over an hour, and when it was over he loaded her with gifts. Her success was remarkable enough, but even more so were the friendly letters she began to receive from Sukarno after she and her husband had returned to New York. A few years later, he proposed that she collaborate with him on his autobiography.

Adams, who was used to doing puff pieces on third-rate celebrities, was confused. She knew Sukarno had a reputation as a devilish Don Juan—*le grand séducteur,* the French called him. He had had four wives and hundreds of conquests. He was handsome, and obviously he was attracted to her, but why choose her for this prestigious task? Perhaps his libido was too powerful for him to care about such things. Nevertheless, it was an offer she could not refuse.

In January of 1964, Adams returned to Indonesia. Her strategy, she had decided, would stay the same: she would be the brassy, straight-talking lady who had seemed to charm Sukarno three years earlier. During her first interview with him for the book, she complained in rather strong terms about the rooms she had been given as lodgings. As if he were her secretary, she dictated a letter to him, which he was to sign, detailing the special treatment she was to be given by one and all. To her amazement, he dutifully copied out the letter, and signed it.

Next on Adams's schedule was a tour of Indonesia to interview people who had known Sukarno in his youth. So she complained to him about the plane she had to fly on, which she said was unsafe. "I tell you what, honey," she told him, "I think you should give me my own plane." "Okay," he an-

You're anxious to keep your mistress? \ Convince her she's knocked you all of a heap \ With her stunning looks. If it's purple she's wearing, praise purple; \ When she's in a silk dress, say silk \ Suits her best of all. . . Admire \ Her singing voice, her gestures as she dances, \ Cry "Encore!" when she stops. You can even praise \ Her performance in bed, her talent for love-making— \ Spell out what turned you on. \ Though she may show fiercer in action than any Medusa, \ Her lover will always describe her as kind \ And gentle. But take care not to give yourself away while \ Making such tongue-in-cheek compliments, don't allow \ Your expression to ruin the message. Art's most effective \ When concealed. Detection discredits you for good.

—Ovid, *The Art of Love,* translated by Peter Green

The little boy (or girl) seeks to fascinate his or her parents. In Oriental literature, imitation is

swered, apparently somewhat abashed. One, however, was not enough, she went on; she required several planes, and a helicopter, and her own personal pilot, a good one. He agreed to everything. The leader of Indonesia seemed to be not just intimidated by Adams but totally under her spell. He praised her intelligence and wit. At one point he confided, "Do you know why I'm doing this biography? . . . Only because of you, that's why." He paid attention to her clothes, complimenting her outfits, noticing any change in them. He was more like a fawning suitor than the "Hitler of Asia."

reckoned to be one of the ways of attracting. The Sanskrit texts, for example, give an important part to the trick of the woman copying the dress, expressions, and speech of her beloved. This kind of mimetic drama is urged on the woman who, "being unable to unite with her beloved, imitates him to distract his thoughts." • The child too, using the devices of imitating attitudes, dress, and so on, seeks to fascinate, with a magical intention, the father or mother and thus to "distract its thoughts." Identification means that one is abandoning and not abandoning amorous desires. It is a lure which the child uses to capture his parents and which, it must be admitted, they fall for. The same is true for the masses, who imitate their leader, bear his name and repeat his gestures. They bow to him, but at the same time they are unconsciously baiting a trap to hold him. Great ceremonies and demonstrations are just as much occasions when the multitudes charm the leader as vice versa.

—Serge Moscovici, *The Age of the Crowd*, translated by J. C. Whitehouse

Inevitably, of course, he made passes at her. She was an attractive woman. First there was the hand on top of her hand, then a stolen kiss. She spurned him every time, making it clear she was happily married, but she was worried: if all he had wanted was an affair, the whole book deal could fall apart. Once again, though, her straightforward strategy seemed the right one. Surprisingly, he backed down without anger or resentment. He promised that his affection for her would remain platonic. She had to admit that he was not at all what she had expected, or what had been described to her. Perhaps he liked being dominated by a woman.

The interviews continued for several months, and she noticed slight changes in him. She still addressed him familiarly, spicing the conversation with brazen comments, but now he returned them, delighting in this kind of saucy banter. He assumed the same lively mood that she strategically forced on herself. At first he had dressed in military uniform, or in his Italian suits. Now he dressed casually, even going barefoot, conforming to the casual style of their relationship. One night he remarked that he liked the color of her hair. It was Clairol, blue-black, she explained. He wanted to have the same color; she had to bring him a bottle. She did as he asked, imagining he was joking, but a few days later he requested her presence at the palace to dye his hair for him. She did so, and now they had the exact same hair color.

The book, *Sukarno: An Autobiography as Told to Cindy Adams*, was published in 1965. To American readers' surprise, Sukarno came across as remarkably charming and lovable, which was indeed how Adams described him to one and all. If anyone argued, she would say that they did not know him the way she did. Sukarno was well pleased, and had the book distributed far and wide. It helped gain sympathy for him in Indonesia, where he was now being threatened with a military coup. And Sukarno was not surprised—he had known all along that Adams would do a far better job with his memoirs than any "serious" journalist.

My sixth brother, he who had both his lips cut off, Prince of the Faithful, is called Shakashik. • In his youth he was very poor. One day, as he was begging in the streets of Baghdad, he passed by a splendid mansion, at the gates of which stood an impressive array of attendants. Upon inquiry my brother was informed

Interpretation. Who was seducing whom? It was Sukarno who was doing the seducing, and his seduction of Adams followed a classical sequence. First, he chose the right victim. An experienced journalist would have resisted the lure of a personal relationship with the subject, and a man would have been less susceptible to his charm. And so he picked a woman, and one whose journalistic experience lay elsewhere. At his first meeting with Adams, he sent mixed signals: he was friendly to her, but hinted at another kind of interest as well. Then, having insinuated a doubt in her mind (Perhaps he just wants an affair?), he proceeded to mirror her. He indulged her every mood, retreating every time she complained. Indulging a person is a form of entering their spirit, letting them dominate for the time being.

Perhaps Sukarno's passes at Adams showed his uncontrollable libido at work, or perhaps they were more cunning. He had a reputation as a Don Juan; failing to make a pass at her would have hurt her feelings. (Women are often less offended at being found attractive than one imagines, and Sukarno was clever enough to have given each of his four wives the impression that she was his favorite.) The pass out of the way, he moved further into her spirit, taking on her casual air, even slightly feminizing himself by adopting her hair color. The result was that she decided he was not what she had expected or feared him to be. He was not in the least threatening, and after all, she was the one in control. What Adams failed to realize was that once her defenses were lowered, she was oblivious to how deeply he had engaged her emotions. She had not charmed him, he had charmed her. What he wanted all along was what he got: a personal memoir written by a sympathetic foreigner, who gave the world a rather engaging portrait of a man of whom many were suspicious.

Of all the seductive tactics, entering someone's spirit is perhaps the most devilish of all. It gives your victims the feeling that they are seducing you. The fact that you are indulging them, imitating them, entering their spirit, suggests that you are under their spell. You are not a dangerous seducer to be wary of, but someone compliant and unthreatening. The attention you pay to them is intoxicating—since you are mirroring them, everything they see and hear from you reflects their own ego and tastes. What a boost to their vanity. All this sets up the seduction, the series of maneuvers that will turn the dynamic around. Once their defenses are down, they are open to your subtle influence. Soon you will begin to take over the dance, and without even noticing the shift, they will find themselves entering *your* spirit. This is the endgame.

> *Women are not at their ease except with those who take chances with them, and enter into their spirit.*
>
> —Ninon de l'Enclos

Keys to Seduction

One of the great sources of frustration in our lives is other people's stubbornness. How hard it is to reach them, to make them see things our way. We often have the impression that when they seem to be listening to us, and apparently agreeing with us, it is all superficial—the moment we are gone, they revert to their own ideas. We spend our lives butting up

that the house belonged to a member of the wealthy and powerful Barmecide family. Shakashik approached the door-keepers and solicited alms. • "Go in," they said, "and our master will give you all that you desire." • My brother entered the lofty vestibule and proceeded to a spacious, marble-paved hall, hung with tapestry and overlooking a beautiful garden. He stood bewildered for a moment, not knowing where to turn his steps, and then advanced to the far end of the hall. There, among the cushions, reclined a handsome old man with a long beard, whom my brother recognized at once as the master of the house. • "What can I do for you, my friend?" asked the old man, as he rose to welcome my brother. • When Shakashik replied that he was a hungry beggar, the old man expressed the deepest compassion and rent his fine robes, crying: "Is it possible that there should be a man as hungry as yourself in a city where I am living? It is, indeed, a disgrace that I cannot endure!" Then he comforted my brother, adding: "I insist that you stay with me and partake of my dinner." • With this the master of the house clapped his hands and called out to one of the slaves: "Bring in the basin and ewer." Then he said to my brother: "Come forward, my friend, and wash your hands." • Shakashik rose to do so, but saw neither ewer nor basin. He was bewildered to see his host make gestures as though he were pouring water on his hands from an invisible vessel and then drying them with an invisible towel. When he finished, the host called out to his attendants: "Bring in the table!" • Numerous servants hurried in and out of the hall, as though they were preparing for a meal. My brother could still see nothing. Yet his host invited him to sit at the imaginary table, saying, "Honor me by eating of this meat." • The old man moved his hands about as though he were touching invisible dishes, and also moved his jaws and lips as though he were chewing. Then said he to Shakashik: "Eat your fill, my friend, for you must be famished." • My brother began to move his jaws, to chew and swallow, as though he were eating, while the old man still coaxed him, saying: "Eat, my friend, and note the excellence of this bread and its whiteness." • "This man," thought Shakashik, "must be fond of practical jokes." So he said, "It is, sir, the whitest bread I have ever seen, and I have never tasted the like in all my life." • "This bread," said the host, "was baked by a slave girl whom I bought for five hundred dinars." Then he called out to one of his slaves: "Bring in the meat pudding, and let there be plenty of fat in it!" • . . . Thereupon the host moved his fingers as though to pick up a morsel from an imaginary dish, and popped the invisible delicacy into my brother's mouth. • The old man continued to enlarge upon the excellences of the various dishes, while my brother became so ravenously hungry that he would have willingly died

against people, as if they were stone walls. But instead of complaining about how misunderstood or ignored you are, why not try something different: instead of seeing other people as spiteful or indifferent, instead of trying to figure out why they act the way they do, look at them through the eyes of the seducer. The way to lure people out of their natural intractability and self-obsession is to enter their spirit.

All of us are narcissists. When we were children our narcissism was physical: we were interested in our own image, our own body, as if it were a separate being. As we grow older, our narcissism grows more psychological: we become absorbed in our own tastes, opinions, experiences. A hard shell forms around us. Paradoxically, the way to entice people out of this shell is to become more like them, in fact a kind of mirror image of them. You do not have to spend days studying their minds; simply conform to their moods, adapt to their tastes, play along with whatever they send your way. In doing so you will lower their natural defensiveness. Their sense of self-esteem does not feel threatened by your strangeness or different habits. People truly love themselves, but what they love most of all is to see their ideas and tastes reflected in another person. This validates them. Their habitual insecurity vanishes. Hypnotized by their mirror image, they relax. Now that their inner wall has crumbled, you can slowly draw them out, and eventually turn the dynamic around. Once they are open to you, it becomes easy to infect them with your own moods and heat. Entering the other person's spirit is a kind of hypnosis; it is the most insidious and effective form of persuasion known to man.

In the eighteenth-century Chinese novel *The Dream of the Red Chamber*, all the young girls in the prosperous house of Chia are in love with the rakish Pao Yu. He is certainly handsome, but what makes him irresistible is his uncanny ability to enter a young girl's spirit. Pao Yu has spent his youth around girls, whose company he has always preferred. As a result, he never comes over as threatening and aggressive. He is granted entry to girls' rooms, they see him everywhere, and the more they see him the more they fall under his spell. It is not that Pao Yu is feminine; he remains a man, but one who can be more or less masculine as the situation requires. His familiarity with young girls allows him the flexibility to enter their spirit.

This is a great advantage. The difference between the sexes is what makes love and seduction possible, but it also involves an element of fear and distrust. A woman may fear male aggression and violence; a man is often unable to enter a woman's spirit, and so he remains strange and threatening. The greatest seducers in history, from Casanova to John F. Kennedy, grew up surrounded by women and had a touch of femininity themselves. The philosopher Søren Kierkegaard, in his novel *The Seducer's Diary*, recommends spending more time with the opposite sex, getting to know the "enemy" and its weaknesses, so that you can turn this knowledge to your advantage.

Ninon de l'Enclos, one of the greatest seductresses who ever lived, had definite masculine qualities. She could impress a man with her intense philosophical keenness, and charm him by seeming to share his interest in politics and warfare. Many men first formed deep friendships with her, only to later fall madly in love. The masculine in a woman is as soothing to men as the feminine in a man is to women. To a man, a woman's strangeness can create frustration and even hostility. He may be lured into a sexual encounter, but a longer-lasting spell cannot be created without an accompanying mental seduction. The key is to enter his spirit. Men are often seduced by the masculine element in a woman's behavior or character.

In the novel *Clarissa* (1748) by Samuel Richardson, the young and devout Clarissa Harlowe is being courted by the notorious rake Lovelace. Clarissa knows Lovelace's reputation, but for the most part he has not acted as she would expect: he is polite, seems a little sad and confused. At one point she finds out that he has done a most noble and charitable deed to a family in distress, giving the father money, helping the man's daughter get married, giving them wholesome advice. At last Lovelace confesses to Clarissa what she has suspected: he wants to repent, to change his ways. His letters to her are emotional, almost religious in their passion. Perhaps she will be the one to lead him to righteousness? But of course Lovelace has trapped her: he is using the seducer's tactic of mirroring her tastes, in this case her spirituality. Once she lets her guard down, once she believes she can reform him, she is doomed: now he can slowly insinuate his own spirit into his letters and encounters with her. Remember: the operative word is "spirit," and that is often exactly where to take aim. By seeming to mirror someone's spiritual values you can seem to establish a deep-rooted harmony between the two of you, which can then be transferred to the physical plane.

When Josephine Baker moved to Paris, in 1925, as part of an all-black revue, her exoticism made her an overnight sensation. But the French are notoriously fickle, and Baker sensed that their interest in her would quickly pass to someone else. To seduce them for good, she entered their spirit. She learned French and began to sing in it. She started dressing and acting as a stylish French lady, as if to say that she preferred the French way of life to the American. Countries are like people: they have vast insecurities, and they feel threatened by other customs. It is often quite seductive to a people to see an outsider adopting their ways. Benjamin Disraeli was born and lived all his life in England, but he was Jewish by birth, and had exotic features; the provincial English considered him an outsider. Yet he was more English in his manners and tastes than many an Englishman, and this was part of his charm, which he proved by becoming the leader of the Conservative Party. Should you be an outsider (as most of us ultimately are), turn it to advantage: play on your alien nature in such a way as to show the group how deeply you prefer their tastes and customs to your own.

In 1752, the notorious rake Saltykov determined to be the first man in the Russian court to seduce the twenty-three-year-old grand duchess, the future Empress Catherine the Great. He knew that she was lonely; her husband Peter ignored her, as did many of the other courtiers. And yet the ob-

for a crust of barley bread. • "Have you ever tasted anything more delicious," went on the old man, "than the spices in these dishes?" • "Never, indeed," replied Shakashik. • "Eat heartily, then," said his host, "and do not be ashamed!" • "I thank you, sir," answered Shakashik, "but I have already eaten my fill." • Presently, however, the old man clapped his hands again and cried: "Bring in the wine!" • . . . "Sir," said Shakashik, "your generosity overwhelms me!" He lifted the invisible cup to his lips, and made as if to drain it at one gulp. • "Health and joy to you!" exclaimed the old man, as he pretended to pour himself some wine and drink it off. He handed another cup to his guest, and they both continued to act in this fashion until Shakashik, feigning himself drunk, began to roll his head from side to side. Then, taking his bounteous host unawares, he suddenly raised his arm so high that the white of his armpit could be seen, and dealt him a blow on the neck which made the hall echo with the sound. And this he followed by a second blow. • The old man rose in anger and cried: "What are you doing, vile creature?" • "Sir," replied my brother, "you have received your humble slave into your house and loaded him with your generosity; you have fed him with the choicest food and quenched his thirst with the most potent wines. Alas, he became drunk, and forgot his manners! But you are so noble, sir, that you will surely pardon his offence." • When he heard these words, the old man burst out laughing and said: "For a long time I have jested with all types of men, but no one has ever had the patience or the wit to enter into my humors as you have done. Now, therefore, I pardon you, and ask you in truth to eat and drink with me, and to be my companion as long as I live." • Then the old man ordered his attendants to serve all the dishes which they had consumed in fancy, and when he and my brother had eaten their fill they repaired to the drinking chamber, where beautiful young women sang and made music. The old Barmecide gave Shakashik a robe of honor and made him his constant companion.

—"The Tale of Shakashik, the Barber's Sixth Brother," *Tales from the Thousand and One Nights*, translated by N. J. Dawood

stacles were immense: she was spied on day and night. Still, Saltykov managed to befriend the young woman, and to enter her all-too-small circle. He finally got her alone, and made it clear to her how well he understood her loneliness, how deeply he disliked her husband, and how much he shared her interest in the new ideas that were sweeping Europe. Soon he found himself able to arrange further meetings, where he gave her the impression that when he was with her, nothing else in the world mattered. Catherine fell deeply in love with him, and he did in fact become her first lover. Saltykov had entered her spirit.

When you mirror people, you focus intense attention on them. They will sense the effort you are making, and will find it flattering. Obviously you have chosen them, separating them out from the rest. There seems to be nothing else in your life but them—their moods, their tastes, their spirit. The more you focus on them, the deeper the spell you produce, and the intoxicating effect you have on their vanity.

Many of us have difficulty reconciling the person we are right now with the person we want to be. We are disappointed that we have compromised our youthful ideals, and we still imagine ourselves as that person who had so much promise, but whom circumstances prevented from realizing it. When you are mirroring someone, do not stop at the person they have become; enter the spirit of that ideal person they wanted to be. This is how the French writer Chateaubriand managed to become a great seducer, despite his physical ugliness. When he was growing up, in the latter eighteenth century, romanticism was coming into fashion, and many young women felt deeply oppressed by the lack of romance in their lives. Chateaubriand would reawaken the fantasy they had had as young girls of being swept off their feet, of fulfilling romantic ideals. This form of entering another's spirit is perhaps the most effective kind, because it makes people feel better about themselves. In your presence, they live the life of the person they had wanted to be—a great lover, a romantic hero, whatever it is. Discover those crushed ideals and mirror them, bringing them back to life by reflecting them back to your target. Few can resist such a lure.

***Symbol**: The Hunter's Mirror. The lark is a savory bird, but difficult to catch. In the field, the hunter places a mirror on a stand. The lark lands in front of the glass, steps back and forth, entranced by its own moving image and by the imitative mating dance it sees performed before its eyes. Hypnotized, the bird loses all sense of its surroundings, until the hunter's net traps it against the mirror.*

Reversal

In 1897 in Berlin, the poet Rainer Maria Rilke, whose reputation would later circle the world, met Lou Andreas-Salomé, the Russian-born writer and beauty who was notorious for having broken Nietzsche's heart. She was the darling of Berlin intellectuals, and although Rilke was twenty-two and she was thirty-six, he fell head over heels in love with her. He flooded her with love letters, which showed that he had read all her books and knew her tastes intimately. The two became friends. Soon she was editing his poetry, and he hung on her every word.

Salomé was flattered by Rilke's mirroring of her spirit, enchanted by the intense attention he paid her and the spiritual communion they began to develop. She became his lover. But she was worried about his future; it was difficult to make a living as a poet, and she encouraged him to learn her native language, Russian, and become a translator. He followed her advice so avidly that within months he could speak Russian. They visited Russia together, and Rilke was overwhelmed by what he saw—the peasants, the folk customs, the art, the architecture. Back in Berlin, he turned his rooms into a kind of shrine to Russia, and started wearing Russian peasant blouses and peppering his conversation with Russian phrases. Now the charm of his mirroring soon wore off. At first Salomé had been flattered that he shared her interests so intensely, but now she saw this as something else: he seemed to have no real identity. He had become dependent on her for his own self-esteem. It was all so slavish. In 1899, much to his horror, she broke off the relationship.

The lesson is simple: your entry into a person's spirit must be a tactic, a way to bring him or her under your spell. You cannot be simply a sponge, soaking up the other person's moods. Mirror them for too long and they will see through you and be repelled by you. Beneath the similarity to them that you make them see, you must have a strong underlying sense of your own identity. When the time comes, you will want to lead them into your spirit; you cannot live on their turf. Never take mirroring too far, then. It is only useful in the first phase of a seduction; at some point the dynamic must be reversed.

This desire for a double of the other sex that resembles us absolutely while still being other, for a magical creature who is ourself while possessing the advantage, over all our imaginings, of an autonomous existence. . . . We find traces of it in even the most banal circumstances of love: in the attraction linked to any change, any disguise, as in the importance of unison and the repetition of self in the other. . . . The great, the implacable amorous passions are all linked to the fact that a being imagines he sees his most secret self spying upon him behind the curtain of another's eyes.

—Robert Musil, quoted in Denis de Rougemont, *Love Declared*, translated by Richard Howard

8
Create Temptation

Lure the target deep into your seduction by creating the proper temptation: a glimpse of the pleasures to come. As the serpent tempted Eve with the promise of forbidden knowledge, you must awaken a desire in your targets that they cannot control. Find that weakness of theirs, that fantasy that has yet to be realized, and hint that you can lead them toward it. It could be wealth, it could be adventure, it could be forbidden and guilty pleasures; the key is to keep it vague. Dangle the prize before their eyes, postponing satisfaction, and let their minds do the rest. The future seems ripe with possibility. Stimulate a curiosity stronger than the doubts and anxieties that go with it, and they will follow you.

The Tantalizing Object

Some time in the 1880s, a gentleman named Don Juan de Todellas was wandering through a park in Madrid when he saw a woman in her early twenties getting out of a coach, followed by a two-year-old child and a nursemaid. The young woman was elegantly dressed, but what took Don Juan's breath away was her resemblance to a woman he had known nearly three years before. Surely she could not be the same person. The woman he had known, Cristeta Moreruela, was a showgirl in a second-rate theater. She had been an orphan and was quite poor—her circumstances could not have changed that much. He moved closer: the same beautiful face. And then he heard her voice. He was so shocked that he had to sit down: it was indeed the same woman.

Don Juan was an incorrigible seducer, whose conquests were innumerable and of every variety. But he remembered his affair with Cristeta quite clearly, because she had been so young—the most charming girl he had ever met. He had seen her in the theater, had courted her assiduously, and had managed to persuade her to take a trip with him to a seaside town. Although they had separate rooms, nothing could stop Don Juan: he made up a story about business troubles, gained her sympathy, and in a tender moment took advantage of her weakness. A few days later he left her, on the pretext that he had to attend to business. He believed he would never see her again. Feeling a little guilty—a rare occurrence with him—he sent her 5,000 pesetas, pretending he would eventually rejoin her. Instead he went to Paris. He had only recently returned to Madrid.

As he sat and remembered all this, an idea troubled him: the child. Could the boy possibly be his? If not, she must have married almost immediately after their affair. How could she do such a thing? She was obviously wealthy now. Who could her husband be? Did he know her past? Mixed with his confusion was intense desire. She was so young and beautiful. Why had he given her up so easily? Somehow, even if she was married, he had to get her back.

Don Juan began to frequent the park every day. He saw her a few more times; their eyes met, but she pretended not to notice him. Tracing the nursemaid during one of her errands, he struck up a conversation with her, and asked her about her mistress's husband. She told him the man's name was Señor Martínez, and that he was away on an extended business trip; she also told him where Cristeta now lived. Don Juan gave her a note to give to

For these two crimes Tantalus was punished with the ruin of his kingdom and, after his death by Zeus's own hand, with eternal torment in the company of Ixion, Sisyphus, Tityus, the Danaids, and others. Now he hangs, perennially consumed by thirst and hunger, from the bough of a fruit tree which leans over a marshy lake. Its waves lap against his waist, and sometimes reach his chin, yet whenever he bends down to drink, they slip away, and nothing remains but the black mud at his feet; or, if he ever succeeds in scooping up a handful of water, it slips through his fingers before he can do more than wet his cracked lips, leaving him thirstier than ever. The tree is laden with pears, shining apples, sweet figs, ripe olives and pomegranates, which dangle against his shoulders; but whenever he reaches for the luscious fruit, a gust of wind whirls them out of his reach.

—Robert Graves, *The Greek Myths*, volume 2

her mistress. Then he strolled by Cristeta's house—a beautiful palace. His worst suspicions were confirmed: she had married for money.

Cristeta refused to see him. He persisted, sending more notes. Finally, to avoid a scene, she agreed to meet him, just once, in the park. He prepared for the meeting carefully: seducing her again would be a delicate operation. But when he saw her coming toward him, in her beautiful clothes, his emotions, and his lust, got the better of him. She could only belong to him, never to another man, he told her. Cristeta took offense at this; obviously her present circumstances prevented even one more meeting. Still, beneath her coolness he could sense strong emotions. He begged to see her again, but she left without promising anything. He sent her more letters, meanwhile wracking his brains trying to piece it all together: Who was this Señor Martínez? Why would he marry a showgirl? How could Cristeta be wrested away from him?

Finally Cristeta agreed to meet Don Juan one more time, in the theater, where he dared not risk a scandal. They took a box, where they could talk. She reassured him the child was not his. She said he only wanted her now because she belonged to another, because he could not have her. No, he said, he had changed; he would do anything to get her back. Disconcertingly, at moments her eyes seemed to be flirting with him. But then she seemed to be about to cry, and rested her head on his shoulder—only to get up immediately, as if realizing this was a mistake. This was their last meeting, she said, and quickly fled. Don Juan was beside himself. She was playing with him; she was a coquette. He had only been claiming to have changed, but perhaps it was true: no woman had ever treated him this way before. He would never have allowed it.

For the next few nights Don Juan slept poorly. All he could think about was Cristeta. He had nightmares about killing her husband, about growing old and being alone. It was all too much. He had to leave town. He sent her a goodbye note, and to his amazement, she replied: she wanted to see him, she had something to tell him. By now he was too weak to resist. As she had requested, he met her on a bridge, at night. This time she made no effort to control herself: yes, she still loved Don Juan, and was ready to run away with him. But he should come to her house tomorrow, in broad daylight, and take her away. There could be no secrecy.

Beside himself with joy, Don Juan agreed to her demands. The next day he showed up at her palace at the appointed hour, and asked for Señora Martínez. There was no one there by that name, said the woman at the door. Don Juan insisted: her name is Cristeta. Ah, Cristeta, the woman said: she lives in the back, with the other tenants. Confused, Don Juan went to the back of the palace. There he thought he saw her son, playing in the street in dirty clothes. But no, he said to himself, it must be some other child. He came to Cristeta's door, and instead of her servant, Cristeta herself opened it. He entered. It was the room of a poor person. Hanging on improvised racks, however, were Cristeta's elegant clothes. As if in a dream, he sat down, dumbfounded, and listened as Cristeta revealed the truth.

Don Juan: Arminta, listen to the truth—for are not women friends of truth? I am a nobleman, heir to the ancient family of the Tenorios, the conquerors of Seville. After the king, my father is the most powerful and considered man at court. . . . By chance I happened on this road and saw you. Love sometimes behaves in a manner that surprises even himself. . . . • Arminta: I don't know if what you're saying is truth or lying rhetoric. I am married to Batricio, everybody knows it. How can the marriage be annulled, even if he abandons me? • Don Juan: When the marriage is not consummated, whether by malice or deceit, it can be annulled. . . . • Arminta: You are right. But, God help me, won't you desert me the moment you have separated me from my husband? . . . • Don Juan: Arminta, light of my eyes, tomorrow your beautiful feet will slip into polished silver slippers with buttons of the purest gold. And your alabaster throat will be imprisoned in beautiful necklaces; on your fingers, rings set with amethysts will shine like stars, and from your ears will dangle oriental pearls. • Arminta: I am yours.

—Tirso de Molina, *The Playboy of Seville*, translated by Adrienne M. Schizzano and Oscar Mandel, in Mandel, ed., *The Theatre of Don Juan*

Now the serpent was more subtle than any other wild creature that the LORD GOD had made. He said to the woman, "Did God say, 'You shall not eat of

She was not married, she had no child. Months after he had left her, she had realized that she had been the victim of a consummate seducer. She still loved Don Juan, but she was determined to turn the tables. Finding out through a mutual friend that he had returned to Madrid, she took the five thousand pesetas he had sent her and bought expensive clothes. She borrowed a neighbor's child, asked the neighbor's cousin to play the child's nursemaid, and rented a coach—all to create an elaborate fantasy that existed only in his mind. Cristeta did not even have to lie: she never actually said she was married or had a child. She knew that being unable to have her would make him want her more than ever. It was the only way to seduce a man like him.

Overwhelmed by the lengths she had gone to, and by the emotions she had so skillfully stirred in him, Don Juan forgave Cristeta and offered to marry her. To his surprise, and perhaps to his relief, she politely declined. The moment they married, she said, his eyes would wander elsewhere. Only if they stayed as they were could she maintain the upper hand. Don Juan had no choice but to agree.

any tree of the garden'?" And the woman said to the serpent, "We may eat of the fruit of the trees of the garden; but God said, 'You shall not eat of the fruit of the tree which is in the midst of the garden, neither shall you touch it, lest you die.' " But the serpent said to the woman, "You will not die. For God knows that when you eat of it your eyes will be opened, and you will be like God, knowing good and evil." So when the woman saw that the tree was good for food, and that it was a delight to the eyes, and that the tree was to be desired to make one wise, she took of its fruit and ate; and she also gave some to her husband, and he ate.

—Genesis 3:1, Old Testament

Interpretation. Cristeta and Don Juan are characters in the novel *Dulce y Sabrosa* (*Sweet and Savory*, 1891), by the Spanish writer Jacinto Octavio Picón. Most of Picón's work deals with male seducers and their feminine victims, a subject he studied and knew much about. Abandoned by Don Juan, and reflecting on his nature, Cristeta decided to kill two birds with one stone: she would get revenge and get him back. But how could she lure such a man? The fruit once tasted, he no longer wanted it. What came easily to him, or fell into his arms, held no allure for him. What would tempt Don Juan into desiring Cristeta again, into pursuing her, was the sense that she was already taken, that she was forbidden fruit. That was his weakness—that was why he pursued virgins and married women, women he was not supposed to have. To a man, she reasoned, the grass always seems greener somewhere else. She would make herself that distant, alluring object, just out of reach, tantalizing him, stirring up emotions he could not control. He knew how charming and desirable she had once been to him. The idea of possessing her again, and the pleasure he imagined it would bring, were too much for him: he swallowed the bait.

Thou strong seducer, Opportunity.

—John Dryden

Temptation is a twofold process. First you are coquettish, flirtatious; you stimulate a desire by promising pleasure and distraction from daily life. At the same time, you make it clear to your targets that they cannot have you, at least not right away. You are establishing a barrier, some kind of tension.

In days gone by such barriers were easy to create, by taking advantage of preexisting social obstacles—of class, race, marriage, religion. Today the barriers have to be more psychological: your heart is taken by someone else; you are really not interested in the target; some secret holds you back; the timing is bad; you are not good enough for the other person; the other

As he listened, Masetto experienced such a longing to go and stay with these nuns that his whole body tingled with excitement, for it was clear from what he had heard that he should be able to achieve what he had in mind. Realizing, however, that he would get nowhere by revealing his intentions to Nuto, he replied: • "How right you were to come away from the [nunnery]! What sort of a life can any man lead when he's surrounded by a lot of women? He might as well be living with a pack of devils. Why, six times out of seven they don't even know their own minds." • But when they had finished talking, Masetto began to consider what steps he ought to take so that he could go and stay with them. Knowing himself to be perfectly capable of carrying out the duties mentioned by Nuto, he had no worries about losing the job on that particular score, but he was afraid lest he should be turned down because of his youth and his unusually attractive appearance. And so, having rejected a number of other possible expedients, he eventually thought to himself: "The convent is a long way off, and there's nobody there who knows me. If I can pretend to be dumb, they'll take me on for sure." Clinging firmly to this conjecture, he therefore dressed himself in pauper's rags and slung an ax over his shoulder, and without telling anyone where he was going, he set out for the convent. On his arrival, he wandered into the courtyard, where as luck would have it he came across the steward, and with the aid of gestures such as dumb people use, he conveyed the impression that he was begging for something to eat, in return for which he would attend to any wood-chopping that needed to be done. • The steward gladly provided him with something to eat, after which he presented him with a pile of logs that Nuto had been unable to chop. . . . Now, when the steward had discovered what an excellent gardener he was, he gestured to Masetto, asking him whether he would like to stay there, and the latter made signs to indicate that he was willing to do whatever the steward

person is not good enough for you; and so on. Conversely, you can choose someone who has a built-in barrier: they are taken, they are not meant to want you. These barriers are more subtle than the social or religious variety, but they are barriers nevertheless, and the psychology remains the same. People are perversely excited by what they cannot or should not have. Create this inner conflict—there is excitement and interest, but you are unavailable—and you will have them grasping like Tantalus for water. And as with Don Juan and Cristeta, the more you make your targets pursue you, the more they imagine that it is they who are the aggressors. Your seduction is perfectly disguised.

The only way to get rid of temptation is to yield to it.

—Oscar Wilde

Keys to Seduction

Most of the time, people struggle to maintain security and a sense of balance in their lives. If they were always uprooting themselves in pursuit of every new person or fantasy that passed them by, they could not survive the daily grind. They usually win the struggle, but it does not come easy. The world is full of temptation. They read about people who have more than they do, about adventures others are having, about people who have found wealth and happiness. The security that they strive for, and that they seem to have in their lives, is actually an illusion. It covers up a constant tension.

As a seducer, you can never mistake people's appearance for reality. You know that their fight to keep order in their lives is exhausting, and that they are gnawed by doubts and regrets. It is hard to be good and virtuous, always having to repress the strongest desires. With that knowledge in mind, seduction is easier. What people want is not temptation; temptation happens every day. What people want is to give into temptation, to yield. That is the only way to get rid of the tension in their lives. It costs much more to resist temptation than to surrender.

Your task, then, is to create a temptation that is stronger than the daily variety. It has to be focused on them, aimed at them as individuals—at their weakness. Understand: everyone has a principal weakness, from which others stem. Find that childhood insecurity, that lack in their life, and you hold the key to tempting them. Their weakness may be greed, vanity, boredom, some deeply repressed desire, a hunger for forbidden fruit. They signal it in little details that elude their conscious control: their style of clothing, an offhand comment. Their past, and particularly their past romances, will be littered with clues. Give them a potent temptation, tailored to their weakness, and you can make the hope of pleasure that you stir in them figure more prominently than the doubts and anxieties that accompany it.

In 1621, King Philip III of Spain desperately wanted to forge an alliance with England by marrying his daughter to the son of the English king, James I. James seemed open to the idea, but he stalled for time. Spain's ambassador to the English court, a man called Gondomar, was given the task of advancing Philip's plan. He set his sights on the king's favorite, the Duke (former Earl) of Buckingham.

Gondomar knew the duke's main weakness: vanity. Buckingham hungered for the glory and adventure that would add to his fame; he was bored with his limited tasks, and he pouted and whined about this. The ambassador first flattered him profusely—the duke was the ablest man in the country and it was a shame he was given so little to do. Then, he began to whisper to him of a great adventure. The duke, as Gondomar knew, was in favor of the match with the Spanish princess, but these damned marriage negotiations with King James were taking so long, and getting nowhere. What if the duke were to accompany the king's son, his good friend Prince Charles, to Spain? Of course, this would have to be done in secret, without guards or escorts, for the English government and its ministers would never sanction such a trip. But that would make it all the more dangerous and romantic. Once in Madrid, the prince could throw himself at Princess Maria's feet, declare his undying love, and carry her back to England in triumph. What a chivalrous deed it would be and all for love. The duke would get all the credit and it would make his name famous for centuries.

The duke fell for the idea, and convinced Charles to go along; after much arguing, they also convinced a reluctant King James. The trip was a near disaster (Charles would have had to convert to Catholicism to win Maria), and the marriage never happened, but Gondomar had done his job. He did not bribe the duke with offers of money or power—he aimed at the childlike part of him that never grew up. A child has little power to resist. It wants everything, now, and rarely thinks of the consequences. A child lies lurking in everyone—a pleasure that was denied them, a desire that was repressed. Hit at that point, tempt them with the proper toy (adventure, money, fun), and they will slough off their normal adult reasonableness. Recognize their weakness by whatever childlike behavior they reveal in daily life—it is the tip of the iceberg.

Napoleon Bonaparte was appointed the supreme general of the French army in 1796. His commission was to defeat the Austrian forces that had taken over northern Italy. The obstacles were immense: Napoleon was only twenty-six at the time; the generals below him were envious of his position and doubtful of his abilities. His soldiers were tired, underfed, underpaid, and grumpy. How could he motivate this group to fight the highly experienced Austrian army? As he prepared to cross the Alps into Italy, Napoleon gave a speech to his troops that may have been the turning point in his career, and in his life: "Soldiers, you are half starved and half naked. The government owes you much, but can do nothing for you. Your patience, your courage, do you honor, but give you no glory. . . . I will lead you into the most fertile plains of the world. There you will find flourishing cities, teeming provinces. There you will reap honor, glory, and wealth." The

wanted. . . . • Now, one day, when Masetto happened to be taking a rest after a spell of strenuous work, he was approached by two very young nuns who were out walking in the garden. Since he gave them the impression that he was asleep, they began to stare at him, and the bolder of the two said to her companion: • "If I could be sure that you would keep it a secret, I would tell you about an idea that has often crossed my mind, and one that might well work out to our mutual benefit." • "Do tell me," replied the other. "You can be quite certain that I shan't talk about it to anyone." • The bold one began to speak more plainly. • "I wonder," she said, "whether you have ever considered what a strict life we have to lead, and how the only men who ever dare set foot in this place are the steward, who is elderly, and this dumb gardener of ours. Yet I have often heard it said, by several of the ladies who have come to visit us, that all other pleasures in the world are mere trifles by comparison with the one experienced by a woman when she goes with a man. I have thus been thinking, since I have nobody else to hand, that I would like to discover with the aid of this dumb fellow whether they are telling the truth. As it happens, there couldn't be a better man for the purpose, because even if he wanted to let the cat out of the bag, he wouldn't be able to. He wouldn't even know how to explain, for you can see for yourself what a mentally retarded, dim-witted hulk of a youth the fellow is. I would be glad to know what you think of the idea." • "Dear me!" said the other. "Don't you realize that we have promised God to preserve our virginity?" • "Pah!" she said. "We are constantly making Him promises that we never keep! What does it matter if we fail to keep this one? He can always find other girls to preserve their virginity for Him." • . . . Before the time came for them to leave, they had each made repeated trials of the dumb fellow's riding ability, and later on, when they were busily swapping tales about it all, they agreed that it was every bit as pleasant an experience as they had been led to believe, indeed more so. And from then on, whenever the opportunity arose, they whiled away many a pleasant hour in the dumb fellow's arms. • One day, however, a companion of theirs happened to look out from the window of her cell, saw the goings-on, and drew the attention of two others to what was afoot. Having talked the matter over between themselves, they at first decided to report the pair to the abbess. But then they changed their minds, and by common agreement with the other two, they took up shares in Masetto's holding. And because of various indiscretions, these five were subsequently joined by the remaining three, one after the other. • Finally, the abbess, who was still unaware of all this, was taking a stroll one very hot day in the garden, all by herself, when she came across Masetto stretched out fast asleep in the shade of an almond

speech had a powerful effect. Days later these same soldiers, after a rough climb over the mountains, gazed down on the Piedmont valley. Napoleon's words echoed in their ears, and a ragged, grumbling gang became an inspired army that would sweep across northern Italy in pursuit of the Austrians.

Napoleon's use of temptation had two elements: behind you is a grim past; ahead of you is a future of wealth and glory, *if* you follow me. Integral to the temptation strategy is a clear demonstration that the target has nothing to lose and everything to gain. The present offers little hope, the future can be full of pleasure and excitement. Remember to keep the future gains vague, though, and somewhat out of reach. Be too specific and you will disappoint; make the promise too close at hand, and you will not be able to postpone satisfaction long enough to get what you want.

The barriers and tensions in temptation are there to stop people from giving in too easily and too superficially. You *want* them to struggle, to resist, to be anxious. Queen Victoria surely fell in love with her prime minister, Benjamin Disraeli, but there were barriers of religion (he was a dark-skinned Jew), class (she, of course, was a queen), social taste (she was a paragon of virtue, he a notorious dandy). The relationship was never consummated, but what deliciousness those barriers gave to their daily encounters, which were full of constant flirtation.

Many such social barriers are gone today, so they have to be manufactured—it is the only way to put spice into seduction. Taboos of any kind are a source of tension, and they are psychological now, not religious. You are looking for some repression, some secret desire that will make your victim squirm uncomfortably if you hit upon it, but will tempt them all the more. Search in their past; whatever they seem to fear or flee from might hold the key. It could be a yearning for a mother or father figure, or a latent homosexual desire. Perhaps you can satisfy that desire by presenting yourself as a masculine woman or a feminine man. For others you play the Lolita, or the daddy—someone they are not supposed to have, the dark side of their personality. Keep the connection vague—you want them to reach for something elusive, something that comes out of their own mind.

In London in 1769, Casanova met a young woman named Charpillon. She was much younger than he, as beautiful a woman as he had ever known, and with a reputation for destroying men. In one of their first encounters she told him straight out that he would fall for her and she would ruin him. To everyone's disbelief, Casanova pursued her. In each encounter she hinted she might give in—perhaps the next time, if he was nice to her. She inflamed his curiosity—what pleasure she would yield; he would be the first, he would tame her. "The venom of desire penetrated my whole being so completely," he later wrote, "that had she so wished it, she could have despoiled me of everything I possessed. I would have beggared myself for one little kiss." This "affair" indeed proved his ruin; she humiliated him. Charpillon had rightly gauged that Casanova's primary weakness was his need for conquest, to overcome challenge, to taste what no other man had tasted. Beneath this was a kind of masochism, a pleasure in the pain a woman could give him. Playing the impossible woman, enticing and then frustrating him, she offered the ultimate temptation. What will often do the trick is to give the target the sense that you are a challenge, a prize to be won. In possessing you they will get what no other has had. They may even get pain; but pain is close to pleasure, and offers its own temptations.

In the Old Testament we read that "David arose from his couch and was walking upon the roof of the king's house . . . [and] he saw from the roof a woman bathing; and the woman was very beautiful." The woman was Bathsheba. David summoned her, seduced her (supposedly), then proceeded to get rid of her husband, Uriah, in battle. In fact, however, it was Bathsheba who had seduced David. She bathed on her roof at an hour when she knew he would be standing on his balcony. After tempting a man she knew had a weakness for women, she played the coquette, forcing him to come after her. This is the opportunity strategy: give someone weak the chance to have what they lust after by merely placing yourself within their reach, as if by accident. Temptation is often a matter of timing, of crossing the path of the weak at the right moment, giving them the opportunity to surrender.

Bathsheba used her entire body as a lure, but it is often more effective to use only a part of the body, creating a fetishlike effect. Madame Récamier would let you glimpse her body beneath the sheer dresses she wore, but only briefly, when she took off her overgarment to dance. Men would leave that evening dreaming of what little they had seen. Empress Josephine made a point of baring her beautiful arms in public. Give the target only a part of you to fantasize about, thereby creating a constant temptation in their mind.

tree. Too much riding by night had left him with very little strength for the day's labors, and so there he lay, with his clothes ruffled up in front by the wind, leaving him all exposed. Finding herself alone, the lady stood with her eyes riveted to this spectacle, and she was seized by the same craving to which her young charges had already succumbed. So, having roused Masetto, she led him away to her room, where she kept him for several days, thus provoking bitter complaints from the nuns over the fact that the handyman had suspended work in the garden. Before sending him back to his own quarters, she repeatedly savored the one pleasure for which she had always reserved her most fierce disapproval, and from then on she demanded regular supplementary allocations, amounting to considerably more than her fair share.

—GIOVANNI BOCCACCIO, *THE DECAMERON*, TRANSLATED BY G. H. MCWILLIAM

Symbol:

The Apple in the Garden of Eden. The fruit looks deeply inviting, and you are not supposed to eat of it; it is forbidden. But that is precisely why you think of it day and night. You see it but cannot have it. And the only way to get rid of this temptation is to yield and taste the fruit.

Reversal

The reverse of temptation is security or satisfaction, and both are fatal to seduction. If you cannot tempt someone out of their habitual comfort, you cannot seduce them. If you satisfy the desire you have awakened, the seduction is over. There is no reversal to temptation. Although some stages can be passed over, no seduction can proceed without some form of temptation, so it is always better to plan it carefully, tailoring it to the weakness and childishness in your particular target.

Phase Two

Lead Astray—
Creating Pleasure and Confusion

Your victims are sufficiently intrigued and their desire for you is growing, but their attachment is weak and at any moment they could decide to turn back. The goal in this phase is to lead your victims so far astray—keeping them emotional and confused, giving them pleasure but making them want more—that retreat is no longer possible. Springing on them a pleasant surprise will make them see you as delightfully unpredictable, but will also keep them off balance (9: Keep them in suspense—what comes next?). The artful use of soft and pleasant words will intoxicate them and stimulate fantasies (10: Use the demonic power of words to sow confusion). Aesthetic touches and pleasant little rituals will titillate their senses, distract their minds (11: Pay attention to detail).

Your greatest danger in this phase is the mere hint of routine or familiarity. You need to maintain some mystery, to keep a little distance so that in your absence your victims become obsessed with you (12: Poeticize your presence). They may realize they are falling for you, but they must never suspect how much of this has come from your manipulations. A well-timed display of your weakness, of how emotional you *have become under their influence will help cover your tracks (13: Disarm through strategic weakness and vulnerability). To excite your victims and make them highly emotional, you must give them the feeling that they are actually living some of the fantasies you have stirred in their imagination (14: Confuse desire and reality). By giving them only a part of the fantasy, you will keep them coming back for more. Focusing your attention on them so that the rest of the world fades away, even taking them on a trip, will lead them far astray (15: Isolate your victim). There is no turning back.*

9

Keep Them in Suspense—What Comes Next?

The moment people feel they know what to expect from you, your spell on them is broken. More: you have ceded them power. The only way to lead the seduced along and keep the upper hand is to create suspense, a calculated surprise. People love a mystery, and this is the key to luring them further into your web. Behave in a way that leaves them wondering, What are you up to? Doing something they do not expect from you will give them a delightful sense of spontaneity—they will not be able to foresee what comes next. You are always one step ahead and in control. Give the victim a thrill with a sudden change of direction.

The Calculated Surprise

In 1753, the twenty-eight-old Giovanni Casanova met a young girl named Caterina with whom he fell in love. Her father knew what kind of man Casanova was, and to prevent some mishap before he could marry her off, he sent her away to a convent on the Venetian island of Murano, where she was to remain for four years.

Casanova, however, was not one to be daunted. He smuggled letters to Caterina. He began to attend Mass at the convent several times a week, catching glimpses of her. The nuns began to talk among themselves: who was this handsome young man who appeared so often? One morning, as Casanova, leaving Mass, was about to board a gondola, a servant girl from the convent passed by and dropped a letter at his feet. Thinking it might be from Caterina, he picked it up. It was indeed intended for him, but it was not from Caterina; its author was a nun at the convent, who had noticed him on his many visits and wanted to make his acquaintance. Was he interested? If so, he should come to the convent's parlor at a particular time, when the nun would be receiving a visitor from the outside world, a friend of hers who was a countess. He could stand at a distance, observe her, and decide whether she was to his liking.

I count upon taking [the French people] by surprise. A bold deed upsets people's equanimity, and they are dumbfounded by a great novelty.

—Napoleon Bonaparte, quoted in Emil Ludwig, *Napoleon*, translated by Eden and Cedar Paul

Casanova was most intrigued by the letter: its style was dignified, but there was something naughty about it as well—particularly from a nun. He had to find out more. At the appointed day and time, he stood to the side in the convent parlor and saw an elegantly dressed woman talking with a nun seated behind a grating. He heard the nun's name mentioned, and was astonished: it was Mathilde M., a well-known Venetian in her early twenties, whose decision to enter a convent had surprised the whole city. But what astonished him most was that beneath her nun's habit, he could see that she was a beautiful young woman, particularly in her eyes, which were a brilliant blue. Perhaps she needed a favor done, and intended that he would serve as her cat's-paw.

His curiosity got the better of him. A few days later he returned to the convent and asked to see her. As he waited for her, his heart was beating a mile a minute—he did not know what to expect. She finally appeared and sat down behind the grating. They were alone in the room, and she said that she could arrange for them to have supper together at a little villa nearby. Casanova was delighted, but wondered what kind of nun he was dealing with. "And—have you no lover but me?" he asked. "I have a

The first care of any dandy is to never do what one expects them to do, to always go beyond. . . . The unexpected can be nothing more than a gesture, but a gesture that is totally uncommon. Alcibiades cut off the tail of his dog in order to surprise people. When he saw the looks on his friends as they gazed upon the mutilated animal, he said: "Ah, that is precisely what I wanted to happen: as long as the Athenians gossip about this, they will not say anything worse about me." • Attracting attention is not the only goal of a dandy, he wants to hold it by unexpected, even ridiculous means. After Alcibiades, how many apprentice dandies cut off the tails of their dogs! The baron of Saint-Cricq, for example, with his ice cream boots: one very hot day, he ordered at Tortonis two ice creams, the vanilla served in his right boot, the strawberry in his left boot. . . . The Count Saint-Germain loved to bring his friends to the theater, in his voluptuous carriage lined in pink satin and drawn by two black horses with enormous tails; he asked his friends in that inimitable tone of his: "Which piece of entertainment did you wish to see? Vaudeville, the Variety show, the Palais-Royal theater? I took the liberty of purchasing a box for all three of them." Once the choice was made, with a look of great disdain, he would take the unused tickets, roll them up, and use them to light his cigar.

—MAUD DE BELLEROCHE, *DU DANDY AU PLAY-BOY*

friend, who is also absolutely my master," she replied. "It is to him I owe my wealth." She asked if he had a lover. Yes, he replied. She then said, in a mysterious tone, "I warn you that if you once allow me to take her place in your heart, no power on earth can tear me from it." She then gave him the key to the villa and told him to meet her there in two nights. He kissed her through the grating and left in a daze. "I passed the next two days in a state of feverish impatience," he wrote, "which prevented me from sleeping or eating. Over and above birth, beauty, and wit, my new conquest possessed an additional charm: she was forbidden fruit. I was about to become a rival of the Church." He imagined her in her habit, and with her shaven head.

He arrived at the villa at the appointed hour. Mathilde was waiting for him. To his surprise, she wore an elegant dress, and somehow she had avoided having her head shaved, for her hair was in a magnificent chignon. Casanova began to kiss her. She resisted, but only slightly, and then pulled back, saying a meal was ready for them. Over dinner she filled in a few more of the gaps: her money allowed her to bribe certain people, so that she could escape from the convent every so often. She had mentioned Casanova to her friend and master, and he had approved their liaison. He must be old? Casanova asked. No, she replied, a glint in her eye, he is in his forties, and quite handsome. After supper, a bell rang—her signal to hurry back to the convent, or she would be caught. She changed back into her habit and left.

A beautiful vista now seemed to stretch before Casanova, of months spent in the villa with this delightful creature, all of it courtesy of the mysterious master who paid for it all. He soon returned to the convent to arrange the next meeting. They would rendezvous in a square in Venice, then retire to the villa. At the appointed time and place, Casanova saw a man approach him. Fearing it was her mysterious friend, or some other man sent to kill him, he recoiled. The man circled behind him, then came up close: it was Mathilde, wearing a mask and men's clothes. She laughed at the fright she had given him. What a devilish nun. He had to admit that dressed as a man she excited him even more.

Casanova began to suspect that all was not as it seemed. For one, he found a collection of libertine novels and pamphlets in Mathilde's house. Then she made blasphemous comments, for example about the joy they would have together during Lent, "mortifying their flesh." Now she referred to her mysterious friend as her lover. A plan evolved in his mind to take her away from this man and from the convent, eloping with her and possessing her himself.

A few days later he received a letter from her, in which she made a confession: during one of their more passionate trysts at the villa, her lover had hidden in a closet, watching the whole thing. The lover, she told him, was the French ambassador to Venice, and Casanova had impressed him. Casanova was not one to be fooled with like this, yet the next day he was back at the convent, submissively arranging for another tryst. This time she showed up at the hour they had named, and he embraced her—only to

While Shahzaman sat at one of the windows overlooking the king's garden, he saw a door open in the palace, through which came twenty slave girls and twenty negroes. In their midst was his brother's [King Shahriyar's] queen, a woman of surpassing beauty. They made their way to the fountain, where they all undressed and sat on the grass. The king's wife then called out: "Come Mass'ood!" and there promptly came to her a black slave, who mounted her after smothering her with embraces and kisses. So also did the negroes with the slave girls, reveling together till the approach of night. . . . • . . . And so find that he was embracing Caterina, dressed up in Mathilde's clothes. Mathilde had befriended Caterina and learned her story. Apparently taking pity on her, she had arranged it so that Caterina could leave the convent for the evening, and meet up with Casanova. Only a few months before Casanova had been in love with this girl, but he had forgotten about her. Compared to the ingenious Mathilde, Caterina was a simpering bore. He could not conceal his disappointment. He burned to see Mathilde.

Casanova was angry at the trick Mathilde had played. But a few days later, when he saw her again, all was forgiven. As she had predicted during their first interview, her power over him was complete. He had become her slave, addicted to her whims, and to the dangerous pleasures she offered. Who knows what rash act he might have committed on her behalf had their affair not been cut short by circumstance.

Interpretation. Casanova was almost always in control in his seductions. He was the one who led, taking his victim on a trip to an unknown destination, luring her into his web. In all of his memoirs the story of Mathilde is the only seduction in which the tables are happily turned: he is the seduced, the bewildered victim.

What made Casanova Mathilde's slave was the same tactic he had used on countless girls: the irresistible lure of being led by another person, the thrill of being surprised, the power of mystery. Each time he left Mathilde his head was spinning with questions. Her ability to go on surprising him kept her always in his mind, deepening her spell and blotting Caterina out. Each surprise was carefully calculated for the effect it would produce. The first unexpected letter piqued his curiosity, as did that first sight of her in the waiting room; suddenly seeing her dressed as an elegant woman stirred intense desire; then seeing her dressed as a man intensified the excitingly transgressive nature of their liaison. The surprises put him off balance, yet left him quivering with anticipation of the next one. Even an unpleasant surprise, such as the encounter with Caterina that Mathilde had set up, kept him emotional and weak. Meeting the somewhat bland Caterina at that moment only made him long that much more for Mathilde.

In seduction, you need to create constant tension and suspense, a feeling that with you nothing is predictable. Do not think of this as a painful challenge. You are creating drama in real life, so pour your creative energies into it, have some fun. There are all kinds of calculated surprises you can spring on your victims—sending a letter from out of the blue, showing up unexpectedly, taking them to a place they have never been. But best of all are surprises that reveal something new about your character. This needs to be set up. In those first few weeks, your targets will tend to make certain snap judgments about you, based on appearances. Perhaps they see you as a bit shy, practical, puritanical. You know that this is not the real you, but it is how you act in social situations. Let them, however, have these impressions, and in fact accentuate them a little, without overacting: for instance,

Shahzaman related to [his brother King Shahriyar] all that he had seen in the king's garden that day. . . . • Upon this Shahriyar announced his intention to set forth on another expedition. The troops went out of the city with the tents, and King Shahriyar followed them. And after he had stayed a while in the camp, he gave orders to his slaves that no one was to be admitted to the king's tent. He then disguised himself and returned unnoticed to the palace, where his brother was waiting for him. They both sat at one of the windows overlooking the garden; and when they had been there a short time, the queen and her women appeared with the black slaves, and behaved as Shahzaman had described. . . . • As soon as they entered the palace, King Shahriyar put his wife to death, together with her women and the black slaves. Thenceforth he made it his custom to take a virgin in marriage to his bed each night, and kill her the next morning. This he continued to do for three years, until a clamor rose among the people, some of whom fled the country with their daughters. • Now the vizier had two daughters. The elder was called Shahrazad, and the younger Dunyazad. Shahrazad possessed many accomplishments and was versed in the wisdom of the poets and the legends of ancient kings. • That day Shahrazad noticed her father's anxiety and asked him what it was that troubled him. When the vizier told her of his predicament, she said: "Give me in marriage to this king; either I shall die and be a ransom for the daughters of Moslems, or live and be the cause of their deliverance." He earnestly pleaded with her against such a hazard; but Shahrazad was resolved, and would not yield to her father's entreaties. . . . • So the vizier arrayed his daughter in bridal garments and decked her with jewels and made ready to announce Shahrazad's wedding to the king. • Before saying farewell to her sister, Shahrazad gave her these instructions: "When I am received by the king, I shall send for you. Then when the king has finished his act with me, you must say: 'Tell me, my sister, some tale of marvel to beguile the night.' Then I will tell you a tale which, if Allah wills, shall be the means of our deliverance." • The vizier went with his daughter to the king. And when the king had taken the maiden Shahrazad to his chamber and had lain with her, she wept and said: "I have a young sister to whom I wish to bid farewell." • The king sent for Dunyazad. When she arrived, she threw her arms around her sister's neck, and seated herself by her side. • Then Dunyazad said to Shahrazad: "Tell us, my sister, a tale of marvel, so that the night may pass pleasantly." • "Gladly," she answered, "if the king permits." • And the king, who was troubled with sleeplessness, eagerly listened to the tale of Shahrazad: Once upon the time, in the city of Basrah, there lived a prosperous tailor who was fond of sport and merriment. . . . • [Nearly

seem a little more reserved than usual. Now you have room to suddenly surprise them with some bold or poetic or naughty action. Once they have changed their minds about you, surprise them again, as Mathilde did with Casanova—first a nun who wants an affair, then a libertine, then a seductress with a sadistic streak. As they strain to figure you out, they will be thinking about you all of the time, and will want to know more about you. Their curiosity will lead them further into your web, until it is too late for them to turn back.

> *This is always the law for the interesting. . . . If one just knows how to surprise, one always wins the game. The energy of the person involved is temporarily suspended; one makes it impossible for her to act.*
>
> —Søren Kierkegaard

Keys to Seduction

A child is usually a willful, stubborn creature who will deliberately do the opposite of what we ask. But there is one scenario in which children will happily give up their usual willfulness: when they are promised a surprise. Perhaps it is a present hidden in a box, a game with an unforeseeable ending, a journey with an unknown destination, a suspenseful story with a surprise finish. In those moments when children are waiting for a surprise, their willpower is suspended. They are in your thrall for as long as you dangle possibility before them. This childish habit is buried deep within us, and is the source of an elemental human pleasure: being led by a person who knows where they are going, and who takes us on a journey. (Maybe our joy in being carried along involves a buried memory of being literally carried, by a parent, when we are small.)

We get a similar thrill when we watch a movie or read a thriller: we are in the hands of a director or author who is leading us along, taking us through twists and turns. We stay in our seats, we turn the pages, happily enslaved by the suspense. It is the pleasure a woman has in being led by a confident dancer, letting go of any defensiveness she may feel and letting another person do the work. Falling in love involves anticipation; we are about to head off in a new direction, enter a new life, where everything will be strange. The seduced wants to be led, to be carried along like a child. If you are predictable, the charm wears off; everyday life is predictable. In the Arabian *Tales from the Thousand and One Nights,* each night King Shahriyar takes a virgin as his wife, then kills her the following morning. One such virgin, Shahrazad, manages to escape this fate by telling the king a story that can only be completed the following day. She does this night after night, keeping the king in constant suspense. When one story finishes, she quickly starts up another. She does this for nearly three years, until the king finally decides to spare her life. You are like Shahrazad: without new stories, without a feeling of anticipation, your seduction will die. Keep stoking the fires night after night. Your targets must never know what's coming next—what surprises you have in store for them. As with King Shahriyar, they will be under your control for as long as you can keep them guessing.

In 1765, Casanova met a young Italian countess named Clementina who lived with her two sisters in a château. Clementina loved to read, and had little interest in the men who swarmed around her. Casanova added himself to their number, buying her books, engaging her in literary discussions, but she was no less indifferent to him than she had been to them. Then one day he invited the entire family on a little trip. He would not tell them where they were going. They piled into the carriage, all the way trying to guess their destination. A few hours later they entered Milan—what joy, the sisters had never been there. Casanova led them to his apartment, where three dresses had been laid out—the most magnificent dresses the girls had ever seen. There was one for each of the sisters, he told them, and the green one was for Clementina. Stunned, she put it on, and her face lit up. The surprises did not stop—there was a delicious meal, champagne, games. By the time they returned to the château, late in the evening, Clementina had fallen hopelessly in love with Casanova.

The reason was simple: surprise creates a moment when people's defenses come down and new emotions can rush in. If the surprise is pleasurable, the seductive poison enters their veins without their realizing it. Any sudden event has a similar effect, striking directly at our emotions before we get defensive. Rakes know this power well.

A young married woman in the court of Louis XV, in eighteenth-century France, noticed a handsome young courtier watching her, first at the opera, then in church. Making inquiries, she found it was the Duc de Richelieu, the most notorious rake in France. No woman was safe from this man, she was warned; he was impossible to resist, and she should avoid him at all costs. Nonsense, she replied, she was happily married. He could not possibly seduce her. Seeing him again, she laughed at his persistence. He would disguise himself as a beggar and approach her in the park, or his coach would suddenly come alongside hers. He was never aggressive, and seemed harmless enough. She let him talk to her at court; he was charming and witty, and even asked to meet her husband.

The weeks passed, and the woman realized she had made a mistake: she looked forward to seeing the marquis. She had let down her guard. This had to stop. Now she started avoiding him, and he seemed to respect her feelings: he stopped bothering her. Then one day, weeks later, she was at the country manor of a friend when the marquis suddenly appeared. She blushed, trembled, walked away, but his unexpected appearance had caught her unawares—it had pushed her over the edge. A few days later she became another of Richelieu's victims. Of course he had set the whole thing up, including the supposed surprise encounter.

Not only does suddenness create a seductive jolt, it conceals manipula-

three years pass.] Now during this time Shahrazad had borne King Shahriyar three sons. On the thousand and first night, when she had ended the tale of Ma'aruf, she rose and kissed the ground before him, saying: "Great King, for a thousand and one nights I have been recounting to you the fables of past ages and the legends of ancient kings. May I be so bold as to crave a favor of your majesty?" • The king replied: "Ask, and it shall be granted." • Shahrazad called out to the nurses, saying: "Bring me my children." • . . . "Behold these three [little boys] whom Allah has granted to us. For their sake I implore you to spare my life. For if you destroy the mother of these infants, they will find none among women to love them as I would." • The king embraced his three sons, and his eyes filled with tears as he answered: "I swear by Allah, Shahrazad, that you were already pardoned before the coming of these children. I loved you because I found you chaste and tender, wise and eloquent. May Allah bless you, and bless your father and mother, your ancestors, and all your descendants. O, Shahrazad, this thousand and first night is brighter for us than the day!"

—*Tales from the Thousand and One Nights*, translated by N. J. Dawood

tions. Appear somewhere unexpectedly, say or do something sudden, and people will not have time to figure out that your move was calculated. Take them to some new place as if it only just occurred to you, suddenly reveal some secret. Made emotionally vulnerable, they will be too bewildered to see through you. Anything that happens suddenly seems natural, and anything that seems natural has a seductive charm.

Only months after arriving in Paris in 1926, Josephine Baker had completely charmed and seduced the French public with her wild dancing. But less than a year later she could feel their interest wane. Since childhood she had hated feeling out of control of her life. Why be at the mercy of the fickle public? She left Paris and returned a year later, her manner completely altered—now she played the part of an elegant Frenchwoman, who happened to be an ingenious dancer and performer. The French fell in love again; the power was back on her side. If you are in the public eye, you must learn from this trick of surprise. People are bored, not only with their own lives but with people who are meant to keep them from being bored. The minute they feel they can predict your next step, they will eat you alive. The artist Andy Warhol kept moving from incarnation to incarnation, and no one could predict the next one—artist, filmmaker, society man. Always keep a surprise up your sleeve. To keep the public's attention, keep them guessing. Let the moralists accuse you of insincerity, of having no core or center. They are actually jealous of the freedom and playfulness you reveal in your public persona.

Finally, you might think it wiser to present yourself as someone reliable, not given to caprice. If so, you are in fact merely timid. It takes courage and effort to mount a seduction. Reliability is fine for drawing people in, but stay reliable and you stay a bore. Dogs are reliable, a seducer is not. If, on the other hand, you prefer to improvise, imagining that any kind of planning or calculation is antithetical to the spirit of surprise, you are making a grave mistake. Constant improvisation simply means you are lazy, and thinking only about yourself. What often seduces a person is the feeling that you have expended effort on their behalf. You do not need to trumpet this too loudly, but make it clear in the gifts you make, the little journeys you plan, the little teases you lure people with. Little efforts like these will be more than amply rewarded by the conquest of the heart and willpower of the seduced.

Symbol: *The Roller Coaster.*

The car rises slowly to the top, then suddenly hurtles you into space, whips you to the side, throws you upside down, in every possible direction. The riders laugh and scream. What thrills them is to let go, to grant control to someone else, who propels them in unexpected directions. What new thrill awaits them around the next corner?

Reversal

Surprise can be unsurprising if you keep doing the same thing again and again. Jiang Qing would try to surprise her husband Mao Zedong with sudden changes of mood, from harshness to kindness and back. At first he was captivated; he loved the feeling of never knowing what was coming. But it went on for years, and was always the same. Soon, Madame Mao's supposedly unpredictable mood swings just annoyed him. You need to vary the method of your surprises. When Madame de Pompadour was the lover of the inveterately bored King Louis XV, she made each surprise different—a new amusement, a new game, a new fashion, a new mood. He could never predict what would come next, and while he waited for the next surprise, his willpower was temporarily suspended. No man was ever more of a slave to a woman than was Louis to Madame de Pompadour. When you change direction, make the new direction truly new.

10

Use the Demonic Power of Words to Sow Confusion

It is hard to make people listen; they are consumed with their own thoughts and desires, and have little time for yours. The trick to making them listen is to say what they want to hear, to fill their ears with whatever is pleasant to them. This is the essence of seductive language. Inflame people's emotions with loaded phrases, flatter them, comfort their insecurities, envelop them in fantasies, sweet words, and promises, and not only will they listen to you, they will lose their will to resist you. Keep your language vague, letting them read into it what they want. Use writing to stir up fantasies and to create an idealized portrait of yourself.

Seductive Oratory

On May 13, 1958, right-wing Frenchmen and their sympathizers in the army seized control of Algeria, which was then a French colony. They had been afraid that France's socialist government would grant Algeria its independence. Now, with Algeria under their control, they threatened to take over all of France. Civil war seemed imminent.

At this dire moment all eyes turned to General Charles de Gaulle, the World War II hero who had played a crucial role in liberating France from the Nazis. For the last ten years de Gaulle had stayed away from politics, disgusted with the infighting among the various parties. He remained very popular, and was generally seen as the one man who could unite the country, but he was also a conservative, and the right-wingers felt certain that if he came to power he would support their cause. Days after the May 13 coup, the French government—the Fourth Republic—collapsed, and the parliament called on de Gaulle to help form a new government, the Fifth Republic. He asked for and was granted full powers for four months. On June 4, days after becoming the head of government, de Gaulle flew to Algeria.

After Operation Sedition, we are being treated to Operation Seduction.

—Maurice Kriegel-Valrimont on Charles de Gaulle, shortly after the general assumed power

The French colonials were ecstatic. It was their coup that had indirectly brought de Gaulle to power; surely, they imagined, he was coming to thank them, and to reassure them that Algeria would remain French. When he arrived in Algiers, thousands of people filled the city's main plaza. The mood was extremely festive—there were banners, music, and endless chants of *"Algérie française,"* the French-colonial slogan. Suddenly de Gaulle appeared on a balcony overlooking the plaza. The crowd went wild. The general, an extremely tall man, raised his arms above his head, and the chanting doubled in volume. The crowd was begging him to join in. Instead he lowered his arms until silence fell, then opened them wide, and slowly intoned, in his deep voice, *"Je vous ai compris"*—I have understood you. There was a moment of quiet, and then, as his words sank in, a deafening roar: he understood them. That was all they needed to hear.

My mistress staged a lock-out. . . . \ I went back to verses and compliments, \ My natural weapons. Soft words \ Remove harsh door-chains. There's magic in poetry, its power \ Can pull down the bloody moon, \ Turn back the sun, make serpents burst asunder \ Or rivers flow upstream. \ Doors are no match for such spellbinding, the toughest \ Locks can be open-sesamed by its charms. \ But epic's a dead loss for me. I'll get nowhere with swift-footed \ Achilles, or with either of Atreus' sons. \ Old what's-his-name wasting twenty years on war and travel, \ Poor Hector dragged in the dust— \ No good. But lavish fine words on some young girl's profile \ And sooner or later she'll tender herself as the fee, \ An ample reward for your

De Gaulle proceeded to talk of the greatness of France. More cheers. He promised there would be new elections, and "with those elected representatives we will see how to do the rest." Yes, a new government, just what the crowd wanted—more cheers. He would "find the place for Algeria" in the French "ensemble." There must be "total discipline, without qualification and without conditions"—who could argue with that? He closed with a loud call: *"Vive la République! Vive la France!,"* the emotional slogan that

labors. So farewell, heroic \ Figures of legend—the quid \ Pro quo you offer won't tempt me. A bevy of beauties \ All swooning over my love-songs—that's what I want.

—Ovid, *The Amores*, translated by Peter Green

had been the rallying cry in the fight against the Nazis. Everyone shouted it back. In the next few days de Gaulle made similar speeches around Algeria, to equally delirious crowds.

Only after de Gaulle had returned to France did the words of his speeches sink in: not once had he promised to keep Algeria French. In fact he had hinted that he might give the Arabs the vote, and might grant an amnesty to the Algerian rebels who had been fighting to force the French from the country. Somehow, in the excitement his words had created, the colonists had failed to focus on what they had actually meant. De Gaulle had duped them. And indeed, in the months to come, he worked to grant Algeria its independence—a task he finally accomplished in 1962.

When she has received a letter, when its sweet poison has entered her blood, then a word is sufficient to make her love burst forth. . . . My personal presence will prevent ecstasy. If I am present only in a letter, then she can easily cope with me; to some extent, she mistakes me for a more universal creature who dwells in her love. Then, too, in a letter one can more readily have free rein; in a letter I can throw myself at her feet in superb fashion, etc.—something that would easily seem like nonsense if I did it in person, and the illusion would be lost. . . . • On the whole, letters are and will continue to be a priceless means of making an impression on a young girl; the dead letter of writing often has much more influence than the living word. A letter is a secretive communication; one is master of the situation, feels no pressure from anyone's actual presence, and I do believe a young girl would prefer to be alone with her ideal.

—Søren Kierkegaard, *The Seducer's Diary*, translated by Howard V. Hong and Edna H. Hong

Interpretation. De Gaulle cared little about an old French colony, and about what it symbolized to some French people. Nor did he have any sympathy for anyone who fomented civil war. His one concern was to make France a modern power. And so, when he went to Algiers, he had a long-term plan: weaken the right-wingers by getting them to fight among themselves, and work toward Algerian independence. His short-term goal had to be to defuse the tension and buy himself some time. He would not lie to the colonials by saying he supported their cause—that would cause trouble back home. Instead he would beguile them with seductive oratory, intoxicate them with words. His famous "I have understood you" could easily have meant, "I understand what a danger you represent." But a jubilant crowd expecting his support read it the way they wanted. To keep them at a fever pitch, de Gaulle made emotional references—to the French Resistance during World War II, for example, and to the need for "discipline," a word with great appeal to right-wingers. He filled their ears with promises—a new government, a glorious future. He got them to chant, creating an emotional bond. He spoke with dramatic pitch and quivering emotion. His words created a kind of delirium.

De Gaulle was not trying to express his feelings or speak the truth; he was trying to produce an effect. This is the key to seductive oratory. Whether you are talking to a single individual or to a crowd, try a little experiment: rein in your desire to speak your mind. Before you open your mouth, ask yourself a question: what can I say that will have the most pleasant effect on my listeners? Often this entails flattering their egos, assuaging their insecurities, giving them vague hopes for the future, sympathizing with their travails ("I have understood you"). Start off with something pleasant and everything to come will be easy: people's defenses will go down. They will grow amenable, open to suggestion. Think of your words as an intoxicating drug that will make people emotional and confused. Keep your language vague and ambiguous, letting your listeners fill in the gaps with their fantasies and imaginings. Instead of tuning you out, getting irritated or defensive, being impatient for you to shut up, they will be pliant, happy with your sweet-sounding words.

Seductive Writing

One spring afternoon in the late 1830s, in a street in Copenhagen, a man named Johannes caught a glimpse of a beautiful young girl. Self-absorbed yet delightfully innocent, she fascinated him, and he followed her, from a distance, and found out where she lived. Over the next few weeks he made inquiries and found out more about her. Her name was Cordelia Wahl, and she lived with her aunt. The two led a quiet existence; Cordelia liked to read, and to be alone. Seducing young girls was Johannes's specialty, but Cordelia would be a catch: she had already turned down several eligible suitors.

Johannes imagined that Cordelia might hunger for something more out of life, something grand, something resembling the books she had read and the daydreams that presumably filled her solitude. He arranged an introduction and began to frequent her house, accompanied by a friend of his named Edward. This young man had his own thoughts of courting Cordelia, but he was awkward, and strained to please her. Johannes, on the other hand, virtually ignored her, instead befriending her aunt. They would talk about the most banal things—farm life, whatever was in the news. Occasionally Johannes would veer off into a more philosophical discussion, for he had noticed, out of the corner of his eye, that on these occasions Cordelia would listen to him closely, while still pretending to listen to Edward.

This went on for several weeks. Johannes and Cordelia barely spoke, but he could tell that he intrigued her, and that Edward irritated her to no end. One morning, knowing her aunt was out, he visited their house. It was the first time he and Cordelia had been alone together. As dryly and politely as possible, he proceeded to propose to her. Needless to say she was shocked and flustered. A man who had shown not the slightest interest in her suddenly wanted to marry her? She was so surprised that she referred the matter to her aunt, who, as Johannes had expected, gave her approval. Had Cordelia resisted, her aunt would have respected her wishes; but she did not.

On the outside, everything had changed. The couple were engaged. Johannes now came to the house alone, sat with Cordelia, held her hand, talked with her. But inwardly he made sure things were the same. He remained distant and polite. He would sometimes warm up, particularly when talking about literature (Cordelia's favorite subject), but at a certain point he always went back to more mundane matters. He knew this frustrated Cordelia, who had expected that now he would be different. Yet even when they went out together, he took her to formal socials arranged for engaged couples. How conventional! Was this what love and marriage were supposed to be about, these prematurely aged people talking about houses and their own drab futures? Cordelia, who was shy at the best of times, asked Johannes to stop dragging her to these affairs.

The battlefield was prepared. Cordelia was confused and anxious.

Let wax pave the way for you, spread out on smooth tablets, \ Let wax go before as witness to your mind— \ Bring her your flattering words, words that ape the lover: \ And remember, whoever you are, to throw in some good \ Entreaties. Entreaties are what made Achilles give back \ Hector's Body to Priam; even an angry god \ Is moved by the voice of prayer. Make promises, what's the harm in \ Promising? Here's where anyone can play rich. . . . \ A persuasive letter's \ The thing to lead off with, explore her mind, \ Reconnoiter the landscape. A message scratched on an apple \ Betrayed Cydippe: she was snared by her own words. \ My advice, then, young men of Rome, is to learn the noble \ Advocate's arts—not only to let you defend \ Some trembling client: a woman, no less than the populace, \ Elite senator, or grave judge, \ Will surrender to eloquence. Nevertheless, dissemble \ Your powers, avoid long words, \ Don't look too highbrow. Who but a mindless ninny \ Declaims to his mistress? An overlettered style \ Repels girls as often as not. Use ordinary language, \ Familiar yet coaxing words—as though \ You were there, in her presence. If she refuses your letter, \ Sends it back unread, persist.

—OVID, *THE ART OF LOVE*, TRANSLATED BY PETER GREEN

Therefore, the person who is unable to write letters and notes never becomes a dangerous seducer.

—Søren Kierkegaard, *Either/Or*, translated by Howard V. Hong and Edna H. Hong

Then, a few weeks after their engagement, Johannes sent her a letter. Here he described the state of his soul, and his certainty that he loved her. He spoke in metaphor, suggesting that he had been waiting for years, lantern in hand, for Cordelia's appearance; metaphor melted into reality, back and forth. The style was poetic, the words glowed with desire, but the whole was delightfully ambiguous—Cordelia could reread the letter ten times without being sure what it said. The next day Johannes received a response. The writing was simple and straightforward, but full of sentiment: his letter had made her so happy, Cordelia wrote, and she had not imagined this side to his character. He replied by writing that *he had changed*. He did not say how or why, but the implication was that it was because of her.

Standing on a crag of Olympus \ Gold-throned Hera saw her brother, \ Who was her husband's brother too, \ Busy on the fields of human glory, \ And her heart sang. Then she saw Zeus \ Sitting on the topmost peak of Ida \ And was filled with resentment. Cow-eyed Hera \ Mused for a while on how to trick \ The mind of Zeus Aegis-holder, \ And the plan that seemed best to her \ Was to make herself up and go to Ida, \ Seduce him, and then shed on his eyelids \ And cunning mind a sleep gentle and warm. . . . \ When everything was perfect, she stepped \ Out of her room and called Aphrodite \ And had a word with her in private: \ "My dear child, will you do something for me, \ I wonder, or will you refuse, angry because \ I favor the Greeks and you the Trojans?" \ And Zeus' daughter Aphrodite replied: \ "Goddess revered as Cronus's daughter, \ Speak your mind. Tell me what you want \ And I'll oblige you if I possibly can." \ And Hera, with every intention to deceive: \ "Give me now the Sex and Desire \ You use to subdue immortals and humans. . . . " \ And Aphrodite, who loved to smile: \ "How could I, or would I, refuse someone \ Who sleeps in the arms of

Now his letters came almost daily. They were mostly of the same length, in a poetic style that had a touch of madness to it, as if he were intoxicated with love. He talked of Greek myth, comparing Cordelia to a nymph and himself to a river that fell in love with a maiden. His soul, he said, merely reflected back her image; she was all he could see or think of. Meanwhile he detected changes in Cordelia: her letters became more poetic, less restrained. Without realizing it she repeated his ideas, imitating his style and his imagery as if they were her own. Also, when they saw each other in person, she was nervous. He made a point of remaining the same, aloof and regal, but he could tell that she saw him differently, sensing depths in him that she could not fathom. In public she hung on his every word. She must have memorized his letters, for she referred to them constantly in their talks. It was a secret life they shared. When she held his hand, she did so more tightly than before. Her eyes expressed an impatience, as if she were hoping that at any moment he would do something bold.

Johannes made his letters shorter but more numerous, sometimes sending several in one day. The imagery became more physical and more suggestive, the style more disjointed, as if he could barely organize his thoughts. Sometimes he sent a note of just a sentence or two. Once, at a party at Cordelia's house, he dropped such a note into her knitting basket and watched as she ran away to read it, her face flushed. In her letters he saw signs of emotion and turmoil. Echoing a sentiment he had hinted at in an earlier letter, she wrote that she hated the whole engagement business—it was so beneath their love.

Everything was ready. Soon she would be his, the way he wanted it. She would break off the engagement. A rendezvous in the country would be simple to arrange—in fact she would be the one to propose it. This would be his most skillful seduction.

Interpretation. Johannes and Cordelia are characters in the loosely autobiographical novel *The Seducer's Diary* (1843), by the Danish philosopher Søren Kierkegaard. Johannes is a most experienced seducer, who specializes in working on his victim's mind. This is precisely where Cordelia's previous suitors have failed: they have begun by imposing themselves, a common mistake. We think that by being persistent, by overwhelming our targets with romantic attention, we are convincing them of our affection. Instead we are convincing them of our impatience and insecurity. Aggressive attention is not flattering because it is not personalized. It is unbridled libido at work; the target sees through it. Johannes is too clever to begin so obviously. Instead, he takes a step back, intriguing Cordelia by acting a little cold, and carefully creating the impression of a formal, somewhat secretive man. Only then does he surprise her with his first letter. Obviously there is more to him than she has thought, and once she has come to believe this, her imagination runs rampant. Now he can intoxicate her with his letters, creating a presence that haunts her like a ghost. His words, with their images and poetic references, are constantly in her mind. And this is the ultimate seduction: to possess her mind before moving to conquer her body.

The story of Johannes shows what a weapon in a seducer's armory a letter can be. But it is important to learn how to incorporate letters in seduction. It is best not to begin your correspondence until at least several weeks after your initial contact. Let your victims get an impression of you: you seem intriguing, yet you show no particular interest in them. When you sense that they are thinking about you, that is the time to hit them with your first letter. Any desire you express for them will come as a surprise; their vanity will be tickled and they will want more. Now make your letters frequent, in fact more frequent than your personal appearances. This will give them the time and space to idealize you, which would be more difficult if you were always in their face. After they have fallen under your spell, you can always take a step back, making the letters fewer—let them think you are losing interest and they will be hungry for more.

Design your letters as homages to your targets. Make everything you write come back to them, as if they were all you could think about—a delirious effect. If you tell an anecdote, make it somehow relate to them. Your correspondence is a kind of mirror you are holding up to them—they get to see themselves reflected through your desire. If for some reason they do not like you, write to them as if they did. Remember: the tone of your letters is what will get under their skin. If your language is elevated, poetic, creative in its praise, it will infect them despite themselves. Never argue, never defend yourself, never accuse them of being heartless. That would ruin the spell.

A letter can suggest emotion by seeming disordered, rambling from one subject to another. Clearly it is hard for you to think; your love has unhinged you. Disordered thoughts are exciting thoughts. Do not waste time on real information; focus on feelings and sensations, using expressions that are ripe with connotation. Plant ideas by dropping hints, writing suggestively without explaining yourself. Never lecture, never seem intellectual or superior—you will only make yourself pompous, which is deadly. Far better to speak colloquially, though with a poetic edge to lift the language above the commonplace. Do not become sentimental—it is tiring, and too

*almighty Zeus?" \ And with that she unbound from her breast \ An ornate sash inlaid with magical charms. \ Sex is in it, and Desire, and seductive \ Sweet Talk, that fools even the wise. . . . \ Hera was fast approaching Gargarus, \ Ida's highest peak, when Zeus saw her. \ And when he saw her, lust enveloped him, \ Just as it had the first time they made love, \ Slipping off to bed behind their parents' backs. \ He stood close to her and said: \ "Hera, why have you left Olympus? \ And where are your horses and chariot?" \ And Hera, with every intention to deceive: \ "I'm off to visit the ends of the earth \ And Father Ocean and Mother Tethys \ Who nursed and doted on me in their house. . . ." \ And Zeus, clouds scudding about him: \ "You can go there later just as well. \ Let's get in bed now and make love. \ No goddess or woman has ever \ Made me feel so overwhelmed with lust. . . . \ I've never loved anyone as I love you now, \ Never been in the grip of desire so sweet." \ And Hera, with every intention to deceive: \ "What a thing to say, my awesome lord. \ The thought of us lying down here on Ida \ And making love outdoors in broad daylight! \ What if one of the Immortals saw us \ Asleep, and went to all the other gods \ And told them? I could never get up \ And go back home. It would be shameful. \ But if you really do want to do this, \ There is the bedroom your dear son Hephaestus \ Built for you, with good solid doors. Let's go \ There and lie down, since you're in the mood." *

And Zeus, who masses the clouds, replied: \ "Hera, don't worry about any god or man \ Seeing us. I'll enfold you in a cloud so dense \ And golden not even Helios could spy on us, \ And his light is the sharpest vision there is."

—Homer, *The Iliad*, translated by Stanley Lombardo

ANTONY: Friends, Romans, countrymen, lend me your ears; \ I come to bury Caesar, not to praise him. \ The evil that men do lives after them; \ The good is oft interred with their bones. \ So let it be with Caesar. . . . \ I speak not to disprove what Brutus spoke, \ But here I am to speak what I do know. \ You all did love him once, not without cause. \ What cause withholds you then to mourn for him? \ O judgment, thou art fled to brutish beasts, \ And men have lost their reason! Bear with me. \ My heart is in the coffin there with Caesar, \ And I must pause till it come back to me. . . . \ PLEBEIAN: Poor soul! his eyes are red as fire with weeping. \ PLEBEIAN: There's not a nobler man in Rome than Antony. \ PLEBEIAN: Now mark him. He begins again to speak. \ ANTONY: But yesterday the word of Caesar might \ Have stood against the world. Now lies he there, \ And none so poor to do him reverence. \ O masters! If I were disposed to stir \ Your hearts and minds to mutiny and rage, \ I should do Brutus wrong, and Cassius wrong, \ Who, you all know, are

direct. Better to suggest the effect your target has on you than to gush about how you feel. Stay vague and ambiguous, allowing the reader the space to imagine and fantasize. The goal of your writing is not to express yourself but to create emotion in the reader, spreading confusion and desire.

You will know that your letters are having the proper effect when your targets come to mirror your thoughts, repeating words you wrote, whether in their own letters or in person. This is the time to move to the more physical and erotic. Use language that quivers with sexual connotation, or, better still, suggest sexuality by making your letters shorter, more frequent, and even more disordered than before. There is nothing more erotic than the short abrupt note. Your thoughts are unfinished; they can only be completed by the other person.

> *Sganarelle to Don Juan: Well, what I have to say is . . . I don't know what to say; for you turn things in such a manner with your words, that it seems that you are right; and yet, the truth of it is, you are not. I had the finest thoughts in the world, and your words have totally scrambled them up.*
>
> —Molière

Keys to Seduction

We rarely think before we talk. It is human nature to say the first thing that comes into our head—and usually what comes first is something about ourselves. We primarily use words to express our own feelings, ideas, and opinions. (Also to complain and to argue.) This is because we are generally self-absorbed—the person who interests us most is our own self. To a certain extent this is inevitable, and through much of our lives there is nothing much wrong with it; we can function quite well this way. In seduction, however, it limits our potential.

You cannot seduce without an ability to get outside your own skin and inside another person's, piercing their psychology. The key to seductive language is not the words you utter, or your seductive tone of voice; it is a radical shift in perspective and habit. You have to stop saying the first thing that comes to your mind—you have to control the urge to prattle and vent your opinions. The key is to see words as a tool not for communicating true thoughts and feelings but for confusing, delighting, and intoxicating.

The difference between normal language and seductive language is like the difference between noise and music. Noise is a constant in modern life, something irritating we tune out if we can. Our normal language is like noise—people may half-listen to us as we go on about ourselves, but just as often their thoughts are a million miles away. Every now and then their ears prick up when something we say touches on them, but this lasts only until we return to yet another story about ourselves. As early as childhood we learn to tune out this kind of noise (particularly when it comes from our parents).

Music, on the other hand, is seductive, and gets under our skin. It is intended for pleasure. A melody or rhythm stays in our blood for days after we have heard it, altering our moods and emotions, relaxing or exciting us. To make music instead of noise, you must say things that please—things that relate to people's lives, that touch their vanity. If they have many problems, you can produce the same effect by distracting them, focusing their attention away from themselves by saying things that are witty and entertaining, or that make the future seem bright and hopeful. Promises and flattery are music to anyone's ears. This is language designed to move people and lower their resistance. It is language designed for them, not directed at them.

The Italian writer Gabriele D'Annunzio was physically unattractive, yet women could not resist him. Even those who knew of his Don Juan reputation and disliked him for it (the actress Eleanora Duse and the dancer Isadora Duncan, for instance) fell under his spell. The secret was the flow of words in which he enveloped a woman. His voice was musical, his language poetic, and most devastating of all, he knew how to flatter. His flattery was aimed precisely at a woman's weaknesses, the areas where she needed validation. A woman was beautiful, yet lacked confidence in her own wit and intelligence? He made sure to say that he was bewitched not by her beauty but by her mind. He might compare her to a heroine of literature, or to a carefully chosen mythological figure. Talking to him, her ego would double in size.

Flattery is seductive language in its purest form. Its purpose is not to express a truth or a real feeling, but only to create an effect on the recipient. Like D'Annunzio, learn to aim your flattery directly at a person's insecurities. For instance, if a man is a fine actor and feels confident about his professional skills, to flatter him about his acting will have little effect, and may even accomplish the opposite—he could feel that he is above the need to have his ego stroked, and your flattery will seem to say otherwise. But let us say that this actor is an amateur musician or painter. He does this work on his own, without professional support or publicity, and he is well aware that others make their living at it. Flattery of his artistic pretensions will go straight to his head and earn you double points. Learn to sniff out the parts of a person's ego that need validation. Make it a surprise, something no one else has thought to flatter before—something you can describe as a talent or positive quality that others have not noticed. Speak with a little tremor, as if your target's charms had overwhelmed you and made you emotional.

Flattery can be a kind of verbal foreplay. Aphrodite's powers of seduction, which were said to come from the magnificent girdle she wore, involved a sweetness of language—a skill with the soft, flattering words that prepare the way for erotic thoughts. Insecurities and nagging self-doubts have a dampening effect on the libido. Make your targets feel secure and alluring through your flattering words and their resistance will melt away.

honorable men. \ I will not do them wrong. . . . \ But here's a parchment with the seal of Caesar. \ I found it in his closet; 'tis his will. \ Let but the commons hear this testament, \ Which (pardon me) I do not mean to read, \ And they would go and kiss dead Caesar's wounds \ And dip their napkins in his sacred blood. . . . \ PLEBEIAN: We'll hear the will! Read it, Mark Antony. \ ALL: The will, the will! We will hear Caesar's will! \ ANTONY: Have patience, gentle friends; I must not read it. \ It is not meet you know how Caesar loved you. \ You are not wood, you are not stones, but men; \ And being men, hearing the will of Caesar, \ It will inflame you, it will make you mad. \ 'Tis good you know not that you are his heirs; \ For if you should, O, what would come of it? . . . \ If you have tears, prepare to shed them now. \ You all do know this mantle. I remember \ The first time ever Caesar put it on. . . . \ Look, in this place ran Cassius' dagger through. \ See what a rent the envious Casca made. \ Through this the well-beloved Brutus stabbed; \ And as he plucked his cursed steel away, \ Mark how the blood of Caesar followed it. . . . \ For Brutus, as you know, was Caesar's angel. \ Judge, O you gods, how dearly Caesar loved him! \ This was the most unkindest cut of all; \ For when the noble Caesar saw him stab, \ Ingratitude, more strong than traitors' arms, \ Quite vanquished him. . . . \ O, now you weep, and I perceive you feel \ The dint of pity. These are gracious *drops. \ Kind souls, what weep you when you but behold \ Our Caesar's vesture wounded? Look you here! \ Here is himself, marred as you see with traitors.*

—William Shakespeare, *Julius Caesar*

Sometimes the most pleasant thing to hear is the promise of something wonderful, a vague but rosy future that is just around the corner. President Franklin Delano Roosevelt, in his public speeches, talked little about specific programs for dealing with the Depression; instead he used rousing rhetoric to paint a picture of America's glorious future. In the various legends of Don Juan, the great seducer would immediately focus women's attention on the future, a fantastic world to which he promised to whisk them off. Tailor your sweet words to your targets' particular problems and fantasies. Promise something realizable, something possible, but do not make it too specific; you are inviting them to dream. If they are mired in dull routine, talk of adventure, preferably with you. Do not discuss how it will be accomplished; speak as if it magically already existed, somewhere in the future. Lift people's thoughts into the clouds and they will relax, their defenses will come down, and it will be that much easier to maneuver and lead them astray. Your words become a kind of elevating drug.

The most anti-seductive form of language is argument. How many silent enemies do we create by arguing? There is a superior way to get people to listen and be persuaded: humor and a light touch. The nineteenth-century English politician Benjamin Disraeli was a master at this game. In Parliament, to fail to reply to an accusation or slanderous comment was a deadly mistake: silence meant the accuser was right. Yet to respond angrily, to get into an argument, was to look ugly and defensive. Disraeli used a different tactic: he stayed calm. When the time came to reply to an attack, he would slowly make his way to the speaker's table, pause, then utter a humorous or sarcastic retort. Everyone would laugh. Now that he had warmed people up, he would proceed to refute his enemy, still mixing in amusing comments; or perhaps he would simply move on to another subject, as if he were above it all. His humor took out the sting of any attack on him. Laughter and applause have a domino effect: once your listeners have laughed, they are more likely to laugh again. In this lighthearted mood they are also more apt to listen. A subtle touch and a bit of irony give you room to persuade them, move them to your side, mock your enemies. That is the seductive form of argument.

Shortly after the murder of Julius Caesar, the head of the band of conspirators who had killed him, Brutus, addressed an angry mob. He tried to reason with the crowd, explaining that he had wanted to save the Roman Republic from dictatorship. The people were momentarily convinced—yes, Brutus seemed a decent man. Then Mark Antony took the stage, and he in turn delivered a eulogy for Caesar. He seemed overwhelmed with emotion. He talked of his love for Caesar, and of Caesar's love for the Roman people. He mentioned Caesar's will; the crowd clamored to hear it, but Antony said no, for if he read it they would know how deeply Caesar had loved them, and how dastardly this murder was. The crowd again insisted he read the will; instead he held up Caesar's bloodstained cloak, noting its rents and tears. This was where Brutus had stabbed the great general, he said; Cassius had stabbed him here. Then finally he read the will, which told how much wealth Caesar had left to the Roman people. This was the coup de grâce—the crowd turned against the conspirators and went off to lynch them.

Antony was a clever man, who knew how to stir a crowd. According to the Greek historian Plutarch, "When he saw that his oratory had cast a spell over the people and that they were deeply stirred by his words, he began to introduce into his praises [of Caesar] a note of pity and of indignation at Caesar's fate." Seductive language aims at people's emotions, for emotional people are easier to deceive. Antony used various devices to stir the crowd: a tremor in his voice, a distraught and then an angry tone. An emotional voice has an immediate, contagious effect on the listener. Antony also teased the crowd with the will, holding off the reading of it to the end, knowing it would push people over the edge. Holding up the cloak, he made his imagery visceral.

Perhaps you are not trying to whip a crowd into a frenzy; you just want to bring people over to your side. Choose your strategy and words carefully. You might think it is better to reason with people, explain your ideas. But it is hard for an audience to decide whether an argument is reasonable as they listen to you talk. They have to concentrate and listen closely, which requires great effort. People are easily distracted by other stimuli, and if they miss a part of your argument, they will feel confused, intellectually inferior, and vaguely insecure. It is more persuasive to appeal to people's hearts than their heads. Everyone shares emotions, and no one feels inferior to a speaker who stirs up their feelings. The crowd bonds together, everyone contagiously experiencing the same emotions. Antony talked of Caesar as if he and the listeners were experiencing the murder from Caesar's point of view. What could be more provocative? Use such changes of perspective to make your listeners feel what you are saying. Orchestrate your effects. It is more effective to move from one emotion to another than to just hit one note. The contrast between Antony's affection for Caesar and his indignation at the murderers was much more powerful than if he had stayed with one feeling or the other.

The emotions you are trying to arouse should be strong ones. Do not speak of friendship and disagreement; speak of love and hate. And it is crucial to try to feel something of the emotions you are trying to elicit. You will be more believable that way. This should not be difficult: imagine the reasons for loving or hating before you speak. If necessary, think of something from your past that fills you with rage. Emotions are contagious; it is easier to make someone cry if you are crying yourself. Make your voice an instrument, and train it to communicate emotion. Learn to seem sincere. Napoleon studied the greatest actors of his time, and when he was alone he would practice putting emotion into his voice.

The goal of seductive speech is often to create a kind of hypnosis: you are distracting people, lowering their defenses, making them more vulnerable to suggestion. Learn the hypnotist's lessons of repetition and affirmation, key elements in putting a subject to sleep. Repetition involves using the same words over and over, preferably a word with emotional content: "taxes," "liberals," "bigots." The effect is mesmerizing—ideas can be permanently implanted in people's unconscious simply by being repeated often enough. Affirmation is simply the making of strong positive statements, like the hypnotist's commands. Seductive language should have a kind of boldness, which will cover up a multitude of sins. Your audience will be so caught up in your bold language that they won't have time to reflect on whether or not it is true. Never say "I don't think the other side made a wise decision"; say "We deserve better," or "They have made a mess of things." Affirmative language is active language, full of verbs, imperatives, and short sentences. Cut out "I believe," "Perhaps," "In my opinion." Head straight for the heart.

You are learning to speak a different kind of language. Most people employ symbolic language—their words stand for something real, the feelings, ideas, and beliefs they really have. Or they stand for concrete things in the real world. (The origin of the word "symbolic" lies in a Greek word meaning "to bring things together"—in this case, a word and something real.) As a seducer you are using the opposite: *diabolic* language. Your words do not stand for anything real; their sound, and the feelings they evoke, are more important than what they are supposed to stand for. (The word "diabolic" ultimately means to separate, to throw things apart—here, words and reality.) The more you make people focus on your sweet-sounding language, and on the illusions and fantasies it conjures, the more you diminish their contact with reality. You lead them into the clouds, where it is hard to distinguish truth from untruth, real from unreal. Keep your words vague and ambiguous, so people are never quite sure what you mean. Envelop them in demonic, diabolical language and they will not be able to focus on your maneuvers, on the possible consequences of your seduction. And the more they lose themselves in illusion, the easier it will be to lead them astray and seduce them.

Symbol: *The Clouds. In the clouds it is hard to see the exact forms of things. Everything seems vague; the imagination runs wild, seeing things that are not there. Your words must lift people into the clouds, where it is easy for them to lose their way.*

Reversal

Do not confuse flowery language with seduction: in using flowery language you run the risk of wearing on people's nerves, of seeming pretentious. Excess verbiage is a sign of selfishness, of your inability to rein in your natural tendencies. Often with language, less is more; the elusive, vague, ambiguous phrase leaves the listener more room for imagination than does a sentence full of bombast and self-indulgence.

You must always think first of your targets, and of what will be pleasant to their ears. There will be many times when silence is best. What you do not say can be suggestive and eloquent, making you seem mysterious. In the eleventh-century Japanese court diary *The Pillow Book of Sei Shonagon*, the counselor Yoshichika is intrigued by a lady he sees in a carriage, silent and beautiful. He sends her a note, and she sends one back; he is the only one to read it, but by his reaction everyone can tell it is in bad taste, or badly written. It spoils the effect of her beauty. Shonagon writes, "I have heard people suggest that no reply at all is better than a bad one." If you are not eloquent, if you cannot master seductive language, at least learn to curb your tongue—use silence to cultivate an enigmatic presence.

Finally, seduction has a pace and rhythm. In phase one, you are cautious and indirect. It is often best to disguise your intentions, to put your target at ease with deliberately neutral words. Your conversation should be harmless, even a bit bland. In this second phase, you turn more to the attack; this is the time for seductive language. Now when you envelop them in your seductive words and letters, it comes as a pleasant surprise. It gives them the immensely pleasing feeling that they are the ones to suddenly inspire you with such poetry and intoxicating words.

11
Pay Attention to Detail

Lofty words and grand gestures can be suspicious: why are you trying so hard to please? The details of a seduction—the subtle gestures, the offhand things you do—are often more charming and revealing. You must learn to distract your victims with a myriad of pleasant little rituals—thoughtful gifts tailored just for them, clothes and adornments designed to please them, gestures that show the time and attention you are paying them. All of their senses are engaged in the details you orchestrate. Create spectacles to dazzle their eyes; mesmerized by what they see, they will not notice what you are really up to. Learn to suggest the proper feelings and moods through details.

The Mesmerizing Effect

In December 1898, the wives of the seven major Western ambassadors to China received a strange invitation: the sixty-three-year-old Empress Dowager Tzu Hsi was hosting a banquet in their honor in the Forbidden City in Beijing. The ambassadors themselves had been quite displeased with the empress dowager, for several reasons. She was a Manchu, a race of northerners who had conquered China in the early seventeenth century, establishing the Ching Dynasty and ruling the country for nearly three hundred years. By the 1890s, the Western powers had begun to carve up parts of China, a country they considered backward. They wanted China to modernize, but the Manchus were conservative, and resisted all reform. Earlier in 1898, the Chinese Emperor Kuang Hsu, the empress dowager's twenty-seven-year-old nephew, had actually begun a series of reforms, with the blessings of the West. Then, one hundred days into this period of reform, word reached the Western diplomats from the Forbidden City that the emperor was quite ill, and that the empress dowager had taken power. They suspected foul play; the empress had probably acted to stop the reforms. The emperor was being mistreated, probably poisoned—perhaps he was already dead. When the seven ambassadors' wives were preparing for their unusual visit, their husbands warned them: Do not trust the empress dowager. A wily woman with a cruel streak, she had risen from obscurity to become the concubine of a previous emperor and had managed over the years to accumulate great power. Far more than the emperor, she was the most feared person in China.

On the appointed day, the women were borne into the Forbidden City in a procession of sedan chairs carried by court eunuchs in dazzling uniforms. The women themselves, not to be outdone, wore the latest Western fashions—tight corsets, long velvet dresses with leg-of-mutton sleeves, billowing petticoats, tall plumed hats. The residents of the Forbidden City looked at their clothes in amazement, and particularly at the way their dresses displayed their prominent bosoms. The wives felt sure they had impressed their hosts. At the Audience Hall they were greeted by princes and princesses, as well as lower royalty. The Chinese women were wearing magnificent Manchu costumes with the traditional high, jewel-encrusted black headdresses; they were arranged in a hierarchical order reflected in the color of their dresses, an astounding rainbow of color.

The wives were served tea in the most delicate porcelain cups, then

The barge she sat in, like a burnish'd throne, \ Burn'd on the water: the poop was beaten gold; \ Purple the sails, and so perfumed that \ The winds were love-sick with them; the oars were silver, \ Which to the tune of flutes kept stroke, and made \ The water which they beat to follow faster, \ As amorous of their strokes. For her own person, \ It beggar'd all description: she did lie \ In her pavilion—cloth-of-gold of tissue— \ O'er picturing that Venus where we see \ The fancy outwork nature: on each side her \ Stood pretty dimpled boys, like smiling Cupids, \ With divers-colour'd fans, whose wind did seem \ To glow the delicate cheeks which they did cool, \ And what they undid did. . . . \ Her gentlewomen, like the Nereids, \ So many mermaids, tended her i' the eyes, \ And made their bends adornings: at the helm \ A seeming mermaid steers: the silken tackle \ Swell with the touches of those flower-soft hands \ That yarely frame the office. From the barge \ A strange invisible perfume hits the sense \ Of the *adjacent wharfs. The city cast \ Her people out upon her; and Antony, \ Enthron'd i' the market-place, did sit alone, \ Whistling to the air; which, but for vacancy, \ Had gone to gaze on Cleopatra too \ And made a gap in nature.*

—William Shakespeare, *Antony and Cleopatra*

were escorted into the presence of the empress dowager. The sight took their breath away. The empress was seated on the Dragon Throne, which was studded with jewels. She wore heavily brocaded robes, a magnificent headdress bearing diamonds, pearls, and jade, and an enormous necklace of perfectly matched pearls. She was a tiny woman, but on the throne, in that dress, she seemed a giant. She smiled at the ladies with much warmth and sincerity. To their relief, seated below her on a smaller throne was her nephew the emperor. He looked pale, but he greeted them enthusiastically and seemed in good spirits. Maybe he was indeed simply ill.

The empress shook the hand of each of the women. As she did so, an attendant eunuch handed her a large gold ring set with a large pearl, which she slipped onto each woman's hand. After this introduction, the wives were escorted into another room, where they again took tea, and then were led into a banqueting hall, where the empress now sat on a chair of yellow satin—yellow being the imperial color. She spoke to them for a while; she had a beautiful voice. (It was said that her voice could literally charm birds out of trees.) At the end of the conversation, she took the hand of each woman again, and with much emotion, told them, "One family—all one family." The women then saw a performance in the imperial theater. Finally the empress received them one last time. She apologized for the performance they had just seen, which was certainly inferior to what they were used to in the West. There was one more round of tea, and this time, as the wife of the American ambassador reported it, the empress "stepped forward and tipped each cup of tea to her own lips and took a sip, then lifted the cup on the other side, to our lips, and said again, 'One family—all one family.' " The women were given more gifts, then were escorted back to their sedan chairs and borne out of the Forbidden City.

In the palmy days of the gay quarters at Edo there was a connoisseur of fashion named Sakakura who grew intimate with the great courtesan Chitosé. This woman was much given to drinking sake; as a side dish she relished the so-called flower crabs, to be found in the Mogami River in the East, and these she had pickled in salt for her enjoyment. Knowing this, Sakakura commissioned a painter of the Kano School to execute her bamboo crest in powdered gold on the tiny shells of these crabs; he fixed the price of each painted shell at one rectangular piece of gold, and presented them to Chitosé throughout the year, so that she never lacked for them.

—Ihara Saikaku, *The Life of an Amorous Woman, and Other Writings*, translated by Ivan Morris

The women relayed to their husbands their earnest belief that they had all been wrong about the empress. The American ambassador's wife reported, "She was bright and happy and her face glowed with good will. There was no trace of cruelty to be seen. . . . Her actions were full of freedom and warmth. . . . [We left] full of admiration for her majesty and hopes for China." The husbands reported back to their governments: the emperor was fine, and the empress could be trusted.

Interpretation. The foreign contingent in China had no idea what was really happening in the Forbidden City. In truth, the emperor had conspired to arrest and possibly murder his aunt. Discovering the plot, a terrible crime in Confucian terms, she forced him to sign his own abdication, had him confined, and told the outside world that he was ill. As part of his punishment, he was to appear at state functions and act as if nothing had happened.

For such men as have practised love, have ever held this a sound maxim that there is naught to be compared with a woman in her clothes. Again when you reflect how a man doth brave, rumple, squeeze and make light of his lady's finery, and how he doth

The empress dowager loathed Westerners, whom she considered barbarians. She disliked the ambassadors' wives, with their ugly fashions and simpering ways. The banquet was a show, a seduction, to appease the Western powers, which had been threatening invasion if the emperor had been killed. The goal of the seduction was simple: dazzle the wives with color, spectacle, theater. The empress applied all her expertise to the task, and she was a genius for detail. She had designed the spectacles in a rising order—the uniformed eunuchs first, then the Manchu ladies in their headdresses, and finally the empress herself. It was pure theater, and it was overwhelming. Then the empress brought the spectacle down a notch, humanizing it with gifts, warm greetings, the reassuring presence of the emperor, teas, and entertainments, which were in no way inferior to anything in the West. She ended the banquet on another high note—the little drama with the sharing of the teacups, followed by even more magnificent gifts. The women's heads were spinning when they left. In truth they had never seen such exotic splendor—and they never understood how carefully its details had been orchestrated by the empress. Charmed by the spectacle, they transferred their happy feelings to the empress and gave her their approval—all that she required.

The key to distracting people (seduction is distraction) is to fill their eyes and ears with details, little rituals, colorful objects. Detail is what makes things seem real and substantial. A thoughtful gift won't seem to have an ulterior motive. A ritual full of charming little actions is so enjoyable to watch. Jewelry, handsome furnishings, touches of color in clothing, dazzle the eye. It is a childish weakness of ours: we prefer to focus on the pleasant little details rather than on the larger picture. The more senses you appeal to, the more mesmerizing the effect. The objects you use in your seduction (gifts, clothes, etc.) speak their own language, and it is a powerful one. Never ignore a detail or leave one to chance. Orchestrate them into a spectacle and no one will notice how manipulative you are being.

The Sensuous Effect

One day a messenger told Prince Genji—the aging but still consummate seducer in the Heian court of late-tenth-century Japan—that one of his youthful conquests had suddenly died, leaving behind an orphan, a young woman named Tamakazura. Genji was not Tamakazura's father, but he decided to bring her to court and be her protector anyway. Soon after her arrival, men of the highest rank began to woo her. Genji had told everyone she was a lost daughter of his; as a result, they assumed that she was beautiful, for Genji was the handsomest man in the court. (At the time, men rarely saw a young girl's face before marriage; in theory, they were allowed to talk to her only if she was on the other side of a screen.) Genji showered her with attention, helping her sort through all the love letters she was receiving and advising her on the right match.

As Tamakazura's protector, Genji was able to see her face, and she was indeed beautiful. He fell in love with her. What a shame, he thought, to give this lovely creature away to another man. One night, overwhelmed by

work ruin and loss to the grand cloth of gold and web of silver, to tinsel and silken stuffs, pearls and precious stones, 'tis plain how his ardour and satisfaction be increased manifold—far more than with some simple shepherdess or other woman of like quality, be she as fair as she may. • And why of yore was Venus found so fair and so desirable, if not that with all her beauty she was always gracefully attired likewise, and generally scented, that she did ever smell sweet an hundred paces away? For it hath ever been held of all how that perfumes be a great incitement to love. • This is the reason why the Empresses and great dames of Rome did make much usage of these perfumes, as do likewise our great ladies of France—and above all those of Spain and Italy, which from the oldest times have been more curious and more exquisite in luxury than Frenchwomen, as well in perfumes as in costumes and magnificent attire, whereof the fair ones of France have since borrowed the patterns and copied the dainty workmanship. Moreover the others, Italian and Spanish, had learned the same from old models and ancient statues of Roman ladies, the which are to be seen among sundry other antiquities yet extant in Spain and Italy; the which, if any man will regard them carefully, will be found very perfect in mode of hair-dressing and fashion of robes, and very meet to incite love.

—Seigneur De Brantôme, *Lives of Fair & Gallant Ladies*, translated by A. R. Allinson

her charms, he held her hand and told her how much she resembled her mother, whom he once had loved. She trembled—not with excitement, however, but with fear, for although he was not her father, he was supposed to be her protector, not a suitor. Her attendants were away and it was a beautiful night. Genji silently threw off his perfumed robe and pulled her down beside him. She began to cry, and to resist. Always a gentleman, Genji told her that he would respect her wishes, he would always care for her, and she had nothing to fear. He then politely excused himself.

Several days later Genji was helping Tamakazura with her correspondence when he read a love letter from his younger brother, Prince Hotaru, who numbered among her suitors. In the letter, Hotaru berated Tamakazura for not letting him get physically close enough to talk to her and tell her his feelings. Tamakazura had not replied; unused to the manners of the court, she had felt shy and intimidated. As if to help her, Genji got one of his servants to write to Hotaru in her name. The letter, written on beautiful perfumed paper, warmly invited the prince to visit her.

Hotaru appeared at the appointed hour. He smelled a beguiling incense, mysterious and seductive. (Mixed into this scent was Genji's own perfume.) The prince felt a wave of excitement. Approaching the screen behind which Tamakazura sat, he confessed his love for her. Without making a sound, she retreated to another screen, farther away. Suddenly there was a flash of light, as if a torch had flared up, and Hotaru saw her profile behind the screen: she was more beautiful than he had imagined. Two things delighted the prince: the sudden, mysterious flash of light, and the brief glimpse of his beloved. Now he was truly in love.

Hotaru began to court her assiduously. Meanwhile, feeling reassured that Genji was no longer chasing her, Tamakazura saw her protector more often. And now she could not help noticing little details: Genji's robes seemed to glow, in pleasing and vibrant colors, as if dyed by unworldly hands. Hotaru's robes seemed drab by comparison. And the perfumes burned into Genji's garments, how intoxicating they were. No one else bore such a scent. Hotaru's letters were polite and well written, but the letters Genji sent her were on magnificent paper, perfumed and dyed, and they quoted lines of poetry, always surprising yet always appropriate for the occasion. Genji also grew and gathered flowers—wild carnations, for instance—that he gave as gifts and that seemed to symbolize his unique charm.

One evening Genji proposed to teach Tamakazura how to play the koto. She was delighted. She loved to read romance novels, and whenever Genji played the koto, she felt as if she were transported into one of her books. No one played the instrument better than Genji; she would be honored to learn from him. Now he saw her often, and the method of his lessons was simple: she would choose a song for him to play, and then would try to imitate him. After they played, they would lie down side by side, their heads resting on the koto, staring up at the moon. Genji would have torches set up in the garden, giving the view the softest glow.

The more Tamakazura saw of the court—of Prince Hotaru, the other

For years after her entry into the palace, a large number of court-maidens were especially set aside for preparing Kuei-fei's dresses, which were chosen and fashioned according to the flowers of the season. For instance, for New Year (spring) she had blossoms of apricot, plum and narcissus; for summer, she adopted the lotus; for autumn, she patterned them after the peony; for winter, she employed the chrysanthemum. Of jewelry she was fondest of pearls, and the finest products of the world found their way into her boudoir and were frequently embroidered on her numerous dresses. • Kuei-fei was the embodiment of all that was lovely and extravagant. No wonder that no king, prince, courtier or humble attendant who ever met her could resist the allurement of her charms. Besides, she was the most artful of women and knew how to use her natural gifts to the best purpose. . . . The Emperor Ming Huang, supreme in the land and with thousands of the most handsome maidens to choose from, became a complete slave to her magnetic powers . . . spending day and night in her company and giving up his whole kingdom for her sake.

—Shu-Chiung, *Yang Kuei-fei: The Most Famous Beauty of China*

Then [Pao-yu] called Bright Design to him and said to her, "Go and see what [Black Jade] is doing. If she asks about me, just say that I am quite all

suitors, the emperor himself—the more she realized that none could compare to Genji. He was supposed to be her protector, yes, that was still true, but was it such a sin to fall in love with him? Confused, she found herself giving in to the caresses and kisses that he began to surprise her with, now that she was too weak to resist.

Interpretation. Genji is the protagonist in the eleventh-century novel *The Tale of Genji*, written by Murasaki Shikibu, a woman of the Heian court. The character was most likely inspired by the real-life seducer Fujiwara no Korechika.

In his seduction of Tamakazura, Genji's strategy was simple: he would make her realize indirectly how charming and irresistible he was by surrounding her with unspoken details. He also brought her in contact with his brother; comparison with this drab, stiff figure would make Genji's superiority clear. The night Hotaru first visited her, Genji set everything up, as if to support Hotaru's seducing—the mysterious scent, then the flash of light by the screen. (The light came from a novel effect: earlier in the evening, Genji had collected hundreds of fireflies in a cloth bag. At the proper moment he let them all go at once.) But when Tamakazura saw Genji encouraging Hotaru's pursuit of her, her defenses against her protector relaxed, allowing her senses to be filled by this master of seductive effects. Genji orchestrated every possible detail—the scented paper, the colored robes, the lights in the garden, the wild carnations, the apt poetry, the koto lessons which induced an irresistible feeling of harmony. Tamakazura found herself dragged into a sensual whirlpool. Bypassing the shyness and mistrust that words or actions would only have worsened, Genji surrounded his ward with objects, sights, sounds, and scents that symbolized the pleasure of his company far more than his actual physical presence would have—in fact his presence could only have been threatening. He knew that a young girl's senses are her most vulnerable point.

The key to Genji's masterful orchestration of detail was his attention to the target of his seduction. Like Genji, you must attune your own senses to your targets, watching them carefully, adapting to their moods. You sense when they are defensive and retreat. You also sense when they are giving in, and move forward. In between, the details you set up—gifts, entertainments, the clothes you wear, the flowers you choose—are aimed precisely at their tastes and predilections. Genji knew he was dealing with a young girl who loved romantic novels; his wild flowers, koto playing, and poetry brought their world to life for her. Attend to your targets' every move and desire, and reveal your attentiveness in the details and objects you surround them with, filling their senses with the mood you need to inspire. They can argue with your words, but not with the effect you have on their senses.

right now." • "You'll have to think of a better excuse than that," Bright Design said. "Isn't there anything that you can send or want to borrow? I don't want to go there and feel like a fool without anything to say." • Pao-yu thought for a moment and then took two handkerchiefs from under his pillow and gave them to the maid, saying, "Well then, tell her that I sent you with these." • "What a strange present to send," the maid smiled. "What does she want two old handkerchiefs for? She will be angry again and say that you are trying to make fun of her." • "Don't worry," Pao-yu assured her. "She will understand." • Black Jade had already retired when Bright Design arrived at the Bamboo Retreat. "What brought you at this hour?" Black Jade asked. • "[Pao-yu] asked me to bring these handkerchiefs for [Black Jade]." • For a moment Black Jade was at a loss to see why Pao-yu should send her such a present at that particular moment. She said, "I suppose they must be something unusual that somebody gave him. Tell him to keep them himself or give them to someone who will appreciate them. I have no need of them." • "They are nothing unusual," Bright Design said. "Just two ordinary handkerchiefs that he happened to have around." Black Jade was even more puzzled, and then it suddenly dawned upon her: Pao-yu knew that she would weep for him and so sent two handkerchiefs of his own. • "You can leave them, then," she said to Bright Design, who in turn was surprised that Black Jade did not take offense at what seemed to her a crude joke. • As Black Jade thought over the significance of the handkerchiefs she was happy and sad by turns: happy because Pao-yu read her innermost thoughts and sad because she wondered if what was uppermost in her thoughts would ever be fulfilled. Thinking thus to herself of the future and of the past, she could not fall asleep. Despite Purple Cuckoo's remonstrances, she had her lamp relit and began to compose a series of quatrains, writing them directly on the handkerchiefs which Pao-yu had sent.

—Tsao Hsueh Chin, *Dream of the Red Chamber*, translated by Chi-Chen Wang

Therefore in my view when the courtier wishes to declare his love he should do so by his actions rather than by speech, for a man's feelings are sometimes more clearly revealed by . . . a gesture of respect or a certain shyness than by volumes of words.

—Baldassare Castiglione

Keys to Seduction

When we were children, our senses were much more active. The colors of a new toy, or a spectacle such as a circus, held us in thrall; a smell or a sound could fascinate us. In the games we created, many of them reproducing something in the adult world on a smaller scale, what pleasure we took in orchestrating every detail. We noticed everything.

As we grow older our senses get dulled. We no longer notice as much, for we are constantly hurrying to get things done, to move on to the next task. In seduction, you are always trying to bring the target back to the golden moments of childhood. A child is less rational, more easily deceived. A child is also more attuned to the pleasures of the senses. So when your targets are with you, you must never give them the feeling they normally get in the real world, where we are all rushed, ruthless, out for ourselves. You need to deliberately slow things down, and return them to the simpler times of their youth. The details that you orchestrate—colors, gifts, little ceremonies—are aimed at their senses, at the childish delight we take in the immediate charms of the natural world. Their senses filled with delightful things, they grow less capable of reason and rationality. Pay attention to detail and you will find yourself assuming a slower pace; your targets will not focus on what you might be after (sexual favors, power, etc.) because you seem so considerate, so attentive. In the childish realm of the senses in which you envelop them, they get a clear sense that you are involving them in something distinct from the real world—an essential ingredient of seduction. Remember: the more you get people to focus on the little things, the less they will notice your larger direction. The seduction will assume the slow, hypnotic pace of a ritual, in which the details have a heightened importance and the moments are full of ceremony.

In eighth-century China, Emperor Ming Huang caught a glimpse of a beautiful young woman, combing her hair beside an imperial pool. Her name was Yang Kuei-fei, and even though she was the concubine of the emperor's son, he had to have her for himself. Since he was emperor, nobody could stop him. The emperor was a practical man—he had many concubines, and they all had their charms, but he had never lost his head over a woman. Yang Kuei-fei, though, was different. Her body exuded the most wonderful fragrance. She wore gowns made of the sheerest silk gauze, each embroidered with different flowers, depending on the season. In walking she seemed to float, her tiny steps invisible beneath her gown. She danced to perfection, wrote songs in his honor that she sang magnificently, had a way of looking at him that made his blood boil with desire. She quickly became his favorite.

Yang Kuei-fei drove the emperor to distraction. He built palaces for her, spent all his time with her, satisfied her every whim. Before long his kingdom was bankrupt and ruined. Yang Kuei-fei was an artful seductress who had a devastating effect on all of the men who crossed her path. There were so many ways her presence charmed—the scents, the voice, the movements, the witty conversation, the artful glances, the embroidered gowns. These pleasurable details turned a mighty king into a distracted baby.

Since time immemorial, women have known that within the most apparently self-possessed man is an animal whom they can lead by filling his senses with the proper physical lures. The key is to attack on as many fronts as possible. Do not ignore your voice, your gestures, your walk, your clothes, your glances. Some of the most alluring women in history have so distracted their victims with sensual detail that the men fail to notice it is all an illusion.

From the 1940s on into the early 1960s, Pamela Churchill Harriman had a series of affairs with some of the most prominent and wealthy men in the world—Averill Harriman (whom years later she married), Gianni Agnelli (heir to the Fiat fortune), Baron Elie de Rothschild. What attracted these men, and kept them in thrall, was not her beauty or her lineage or her vivacious personality, but her extraordinary attention to detail. It began with her attentive look as she listened to your every word, soaking up your tastes. Once she found her way into your home, she would fill it with your favorite flowers, get your chef to cook that dish you had tasted only in the finest restaurants. You mentioned an artist you liked? A few days later that artist would be attending one of your parties. She found the perfect antiques for you, dressed in the way that most pleased or excited you, and she did this without your saying a word—she spied, gathered information from third parties, overheard you talking to someone else. Harriman's attention to detail had an intoxicating effect on all the men in her life. It had something in common with the pampering of a mother, there to bring order and comfort into their lives, attending to their needs. Life is harsh and competitive. Attending to detail in a way that is soothing to the other person makes them dependent upon you. The key is probing their needs in a way that is not too obvious, so that when you make precisely the right gesture, it seems uncanny, as if you had read their mind. This is another way of returning your targets to childhood, when all of their needs were met.

In the eyes of women all over the world, Rudolph Valentino reigned as the Great Lover through much of the 1920s. The qualities behind his appeal certainly included his handsome, almost pretty face, his dancing skills, the strangely exciting streak of cruelty in his manner. But his perhaps most endearing trait was his time-consuming approach to courtship. His films would show him seducing a woman *slowly,* with careful details—sending her flowers (choosing the variety to match the mood he wanted to induce), taking her hand, lighting her cigarette, escorting her to romantic places, leading her on the dance floor. These were silent movies, and his audiences never got to hear him speak—it was all in his gestures. Men came to hate him, for their wives and girlfriends now expected the slow, careful Valentino treatment.

Valentino had a feminine streak; it was said that he wooed a woman the way another woman would. But femininity need not figure in this approach to seduction. In the early 1770s, Prince Gregory Potemkin began an affair with Empress Catherine the Great of Russia that was to last many years. Potemkin was a manly man, and not at all handsome. But he managed to win the empress's heart by the many little things he did, and continued to do long after the affair had begun. He spoiled her with wonderful gifts, never tired of writing her long letters, arranged for all kinds of entertainments for her, composed songs to her beauty. Yet he would appear before her barefoot, hair uncombed, clothes wrinkled. There was no kind of fussiness in his attention, which, however, did make it clear he would go to the ends of the earth for her. A woman's senses are more refined than a man's; to a woman, Yang Kuei-fei's overt sensual appeal would seem too hurried and direct. What that means, though, is that all the man really has to do is take it slowly, making seduction a ritual full of all kinds of little things he has to do for his target. If he takes his time, he will have her eating out of his hand.

Everything in seduction is a sign, and nothing more so than clothes. It is not that you have to dress interestingly, elegantly, or provocatively, but that you have to dress for your target—have to appeal to your target's tastes. When Cleopatra was seducing Mark Antony, her dress was not brazenly sexual; she dressed as a Greek goddess, knowing his weakness for such fantasy figures. Madame de Pompadour, the mistress of King Louis XV, knew the king's weakness, his chronic boredom; she constantly wore different clothes, changing not only their color but their style, supplying the king with a constant feast for his eyes. Pamela Harriman was subdued in the fashions she wore, befitting her role as a high-society geisha and reflecting the sober tastes of the men she seduced. Contrast works well here: at work or at home, you might dress nonchalantly—Marilyn Monroe, for example, wore jeans and a T-shirt at home—but when you are with the target you wear something elaborate, as if you were putting on a costume. Your Cinderella transformation will stir excitement, and the feeling that you have done something just for the person you are with. Whenever your attention is individualized (you would not dress like that for anyone else), it is infinitely more seductive.

In the 1870s, Queen Victoria found herself wooed by Benjamin Disraeli, her own prime minister. Disraeli's words were flattering and his manner insinuating; he also sent her flowers, valentines, gifts—but not just any flowers or gifts, the kind that most men would send. The flowers were primroses, symbols of their simple yet beautiful friendship. From then on, whenever Victoria saw a primrose she thought of Disraeli. Or he would write on a valentine that he, "no longer in the sunset, but the twilight of his existence, must encounter a life of anxiety and toil; but this, too, has its romance, when he remembers that he labors for the most gracious of beings!" Or he might send her a little box, with no inscription, but with a heart transfixed by an arrow on one side and the word "Fideliter," or "Faithfully," on the other. Victoria fell in love with Disraeli.

A gift has immense seductive power, but the object itself is less important than the gesture, and the subtle thought or emotion that it communicates. Perhaps the choice relates to something from the target's past, or symbolizes something between you, or merely represents the lengths you will go to to please. It was not the money Disraeli spent that impressed Victoria, but the time he took to find the appropriate thing or make the appropriate gesture. Expensive gifts have no sentiment attached; they may temporarily excite their recipient but they are quickly forgotten, as a child forgets a new toy. The object that reflects its giver's attentiveness has a lingering sentimental power, which resurfaces every time its owner sees it.

In 1919, the Italian writer and war hero Gabriele D'Annunzio managed to put together a band of followers and take over the town of Fiume, on the Adriatic coast (now part of Slovenia). They established their own government there, which lasted for over a year. D'Annunzio initiated a series of public spectacles that were to be immensely influential on politicians elsewhere. He would address the public from a balcony overlooking the town's main square, which would be full of colorful banners, flags, pagan religious symbols, and, at night, torches. The speeches would be followed by processions. Although D'Annunzio was not at all a Fascist, what he did in Fiume crucially affected Benito Mussolini, who borrowed his Roman salutes, his use of symbols, his mode of public address. Spectacles like these have been used since then by governments everywhere, even democratic ones. Their overall impression may be grand, but it is the orchestrated details that make them work—the number of senses they appeal to, the variety of emotions they stir. You are aiming to distract people, and nothing is more distracting than a wealth of detail—fireworks, flags, music, uniforms, marching soldiers, the feel of the crowd packed together. It becomes difficult to think straight, particularly if the symbols and details stir up patriotic emotions.

Finally, words are important in seduction, and have a great deal of power to confuse, distract, and boost the vanity of the target. But what is most seductive in the long run is what you do not say, what you communicate indirectly. Words come easily, and people distrust them. Anyone can say the right words; and once they are said, nothing is binding, and they may even be forgotten altogether. The gesture, the thoughtful gift, the little details seem much more real and substantial. They are also much more charming than lofty words about love, precisely because they speak for themselves and let the seduced read into them more than is there. Never tell someone what you are feeling; let them guess it in your looks and gestures. That is the more convincing language.

Symbol: *The Banquet. A feast has been prepared in your honor. Everything has been elaborately coordinated—the flowers, the decorations, the selection of guests, the dancers, the music, the five-course meal, the endlessly flowing wine. The Banquet loosens your tongue, and also your inhibitions.*

Reversal

There is no reversal. Details are essential to any successful seduction, and cannot be ignored.

12

Poeticize Your Presence

Important things happen when your targets are alone: the slightest feeling of relief that you are not there, and it is all over. Familiarity and overexposure will cause this reaction. Remain elusive, then, so that when you are away, they will yearn to see you again, and will associate you only with pleasant thoughts. Occupy their minds by alternating an exciting presence with a cool distance, exuberant moments followed by calculated absences. Associate yourself with poetic images and objects, so that when they think of you, they begin to see you through an idealized halo. The more you figure in their minds, the more they will envelop you in seductive fantasies. Feed these fantasies by subtle inconsistencies and changes in your behavior.

Poetic Presence/Absence

In 1943, the Argentine military overthrew the government. A popular forty-eight-year old colonel, Juan Perón, was named secretary of labor and social affairs. Perón was a widow who had a fondness for young girls; at the time of his appointment he was involved with a teenager whom he introduced to one and all as his daughter.

One evening in January of 1944, Perón was seated among the other military leaders in a Buenos Aires stadium, attending an artists' festival. It was late and there were some empty seats around him; out of nowhere two beautiful young actresses asked his permission to sit down. Were they joking? He would be delighted. He recognized one of the actresses—it was Eva Duarte, a star of radio soap operas whose photograph was often on the covers of the tabloids. The other actress was younger and prettier, but Perón could not take his eyes off Eva, who was talking to another colonel. She was really not his type at all. She was twenty-four, far too old for his taste; she was dressed rather garishly; and there was something a little icy in her manner. But she looked at him occasionally, and her glance excited him. He looked away for a moment, and the next thing he knew she had changed seats and was sitting next to him. They started to talk. She hung on his every word. Yes, everything he said was precisely how she felt—the poor, the workers, they were the future of Argentina. She had known poverty herself. There were almost tears in her eyes when she said, at the end of the conversation, "Thank you for existing."

He who does not know how to encircle a girl so that she loses sight of everything he does not want her to see, he who does not know how to poetize himself into a girl so that it is from her that everything proceeds as he wants it—he is and remains a bungler. . . . To poetize oneself into a girl is an art.

—Søren Kierkegaard, *The Seducer's Diary*, translated by Howard V. Hong and Edna H. Hong

In the next few days, Eva managed to get rid of Perón's "daughter" and establish herself in his apartment. Everywhere he turned, there she was, fixing him meals, caring for him when he was ill, advising him on politics. Why did he let her stay? Usually he would have a fling with a superficial young girl, then get rid of her when she seemed to be sticking around too much. But there was nothing superficial about Eva. As time went by he found himself getting addicted to the feeling she gave him. She was intensely loyal, mirroring his every idea, puffing him up endlessly. He felt more masculine in her presence, that was it, and more powerful—she believed he would make the country's ideal leader, and her belief affected him. She was like the women in the tango ballads he loved so much—the suffering women of the streets who became saintly mother figures and looked after their men. Perón saw her every day, but he never felt he fully knew her; one day her comments were a little obscene, the next she was

*What else? If she's out, reclining in her litter, \ Make your approach discreet, \ And—just to fox the sharp ears of those around you— \ Cleverly riddle each phrase \ With ambiguous subtleties. If she's taking a leisurely \ Stroll down the colonnade, then you stroll there too— \ Vary your pace to hers, march ahead, drop behind her, \ Dawdling and brisk by turns. Be bold, \ Dodge in round the columns between you, brush your person \ Lingeringly past hers. You must never fail *

the perfect lady. He had one worry: she was angling to get married, and he could never marry her—she was an actress with a dubious past. The other colonels were already scandalized by his involvement with her. Nevertheless, the affair went on.

In 1945, Perón was dismissed from his post and jailed. The colonels feared his growing popularity and distrusted the power of his mistress, who seemed to have total influence over him. It was the first time in almost two years that he was truly alone, and truly separated from Eva. Suddenly he felt new emotions sweeping over him: he pinned her photographs all over the wall. Outside, massive strikes were being organized to protest his imprisonment, but all he could think about was Eva. She was a saint, a woman of destiny, a heroine. He wrote to her, "It is only being apart from loved ones that we can measure our affection. From the day I left you . . . I have not been able to calm my sad heart. . . . My immense solitude is full of your memory." Now he promised to marry her.

The strikes grew in intensity. After eight days, Perón was released from prison; he promptly married Eva. A few months later he was elected president. As first lady, Eva attended state functions in her somewhat gaudy dresses and jewelry; she was seen as a former actress with a large wardrobe. Then, in 1947, she left for a tour of Europe, and Argentines followed her every move—the ecstatic crowds that greeted her in Spain, her audience with the pope—and in her absence their opinion of her changed. How well she represented the Argentine spirit, its noble simplicity, its flair for drama. When she returned a few weeks later, they overwhelmed her with attention.

Eva too had changed during her trip to Europe: now her dyed blond hair was pulled into a severe chignon, and she wore tailored suits. It was a serious look, befitting a woman who was to become the savior of the poor. Soon her image could be seen everywhere—her initials on the walls, the sheets, the towels of the hospitals for the poor; her profile on the jerseys of a soccer team from the poorest part of Argentina, whose club she sponsored; her giant smiling face covering the sides of buildings. Since finding out anything personal about her had become impossible, all kinds of elaborate fantasies began to spring up about her. And when cancer cut her life short, in 1952, at the age of thirty-three (the age of Christ when he died), the country went into mourning. Millions filed past her embalmed body. She was no longer a radio actress, a wife, a first lady, but Evita, a saint.

To attend the theater when she does, gaze at her beauty— \ From the shoulders up she's time \ Most delectably spent, a feast for adoring glances, \ For the eloquence of eyebrows, the speaking sign. \ Applaud when some male dancer struts on as the heroine, \ Cheer for each lover's role. \ When she leaves, leave too—but sit there as long as she does: \ Waste time at your mistress's whim. . . . \ Get her accustomed to you; \ Habit's the key, spare no pains till that's achieved. \ Let her always see you around, always hear you talking, \ Show her your face night and day. \ When you're confident you'll be missed, when your absence \ Seems sure to cause her regret, \ Then give her some respite: a field improves when fallow, \ Parched soil soaks up the rain. \ Demophoön's presence gave Phyllis no more than mild excitement; \ It was his sailing caused arson in her heart. \ Penelope was racked by crafty Ulysses's absence, \ Protesilaus, abroad, made Laodameia burn. \ Short partings do best, though: time wears out affections, \ The absent love fades, a new one takes its place. \ With Menelaus away, Helen's disinclination for sleeping \ Alone led her into her guest's \ Warm bed at night. Were you crazy, Menelaus?

—OVID, *THE ART OF LOVE*, TRANSLATED BY PETER GREEN

Interpretation. Eva Duarte was an illegitimate child who had grown up in poverty, escaped to Buenos Aires to become an actress, and been forced to do many tawdry things to survive and get ahead in the theater world. Her dream was to escape all of the constraints on her future, for she was intensely ambitious. Perón was the perfect victim. He imagined himself a great leader, but the reality was that he was fast becoming a lecherous old man who was too weak to raise himself up. Eva injected poetry into his

Concerning the Birth of Love • Here is what happens in the soul: • 1. Admiration. • 2. You think, "How delightful it

life. Her language was florid and theatrical; she surrounded him with attention, indeed to the point of suffocation, but a woman's dutiful service to a great man was a classic image, and was celebrated in innumerable tango ballads. Yet she managed to remain elusive, mysterious, like a movie star you see all the time on the screen but never really know. And when Perón was finally alone, in prison, these poetic images and associations burst forth in his mind. He idealized her madly; as far as he was concerned, she was no longer an actress with a tawdry past. She seduced an entire nation the same way. The secret was her dramatic poetic presence, combined with a touch of elusive distance; over time, you would see whatever you wanted to in her. To this day people fantasize about what Eva was really like.

Familiarity destroys seduction. This rarely happens early on; there is so much to learn about a new person. But a midpoint may arrive when the target has begun to idealize and fantasize about you, only to discover that you are not what he or she thought. It is not a question of being seen too often, of being too available, as some imagine. In fact, if your targets see you too rarely, you give them nothing to feed on, and their attention may be caught by someone else; you have to occupy their mind. It is more a matter of being too consistent, too obvious, too human and real. Your targets cannot idealize you if they know too much about you, if they start to see you as all too human. Not only must you maintain a degree of distance, but there must be something fantastical and bewitching about you, sparking all kinds of delightful possibilities in their mind. The possibility Eva held out was the possibility that she was what in Argentine culture was considered the ideal woman—devoted, motherly, saintly—but there are any number of poetic ideals you can try to embody. Chivalry, adventure, romance, and so on, are just as potent, and if you have a whiff of them about you, you can breathe enough poetry into the air to fill people's minds with fantasies and dreams. At all costs, you must embody something, even if it is roguery and evil. Anything to avoid the taint of familiarity and commonness.

> *What I need is a woman who is something, anything; either very beautiful or very kind or in the last resort very wicked; very witty or very stupid, but something.*
>
> —Alfred de Musset

Keys to Seduction

We all have a self-image that is more flattering than the truth: we think of ourselves as more generous, selfless, honest, kindly, intelligent, or good-looking than in fact we are. It is extremely difficult for us to be honest with ourselves about our own limitations; we have a desperate need to idealize ourselves. As the writer Angela Carter remarks, we would rather align ourselves with angels than with the higher primates from which we are actually descended.

would be to kiss her, to be kissed by her," and so on. . . . • 3. Hope. You observe her perfections, and it is at this moment that a woman really ought to surrender, for the utmost physical pleasure. Even the most reserved women blush to the whites of their eyes at this moment of hope. The passion is so strong, and the pleasure so sharp, that they betray themselves unmistakably. • 4. Love is born. To love is to enjoy seeing, touching, and sensing with all the senses, as closely as possible, a lovable object which loves in return. • 5. The first crystallization begins. If you are sure that a woman loves you, it is a pleasure to endow her with a thousand perfections and to count your blessings with infinite satisfaction. In the end you overrate wildly, and regard her as something fallen from Heaven, unknown as yet, but certain to be yours. • Leave a lover with his thoughts for twenty-four hours, and this is what will happen: • At the salt mines of Salzburg, they throw a leafless wintry bough into one of the abandoned workings. Two or three months later they haul it out covered with a shining deposit of crystals. The smallest twig, no bigger than a tom-tit's claw, is studded with a galaxy of scintillating diamonds. The original branch is no longer recognizable. • What I have called crystallization is a mental process which draws from everything that happens new proofs of the perfection of the loved one. . . . • A man in love sees every perfection in the object of his love, but his attention is liable to wander after a time because one gets tired of anything uniform, even perfect happiness. • This is what happens next to fix the attention: • 6. Doubt creeps in. . . . He is met with indifference, coldness, or even anger if he appears too confident. . . . The lover begins to be less sure of the good fortune he was anticipating and subjects his grounds for hope to a critical examination. • He tries to recoup by indulging in other pleasures but finds them inane. He is seized by the dread of a frightful calamity and now concentrates fully. Thus begins: • 7. The second crystallization, which deposits diamond layers of proof that "she loves me." • Every few minutes throughout the night which follows the birth of doubt, the lover has a moment of dreadful misgiving, and then reassures himself, "she loves me"; and crystallization begins to reveal new charms. Then once again the haggard eye of doubt pierces him and he stops transfixed. He forgets to draw breath and mutters, "But does she love me?" Torn between doubt and delight, the poor lover convinces himself that she could give him such pleasure as he could find nowhere else on earth.

—STENDHAL, *LOVE*, TRANSLATED BY GILBERT AND SUZANNE SALE

This need to idealize extends to our romantic entanglements, because when we fall in love, or under the spell of another person, we see a reflection of ourselves. The choice we make in deciding to become involved with another person reveals something important and intimate about us: we resist seeing ourselves as having fallen for someone who is cheap or tacky or tasteless, because it reflects badly on who we are. Furthermore, we are often likely to fall for someone who resembles us in some way. Should that person be deficient, or worst of all ordinary, then there is something deficient and ordinary about us. No, at all costs the loved one must be overvalued and idealized, at least for the sake of our own self-esteem. Besides, in a world that is harsh and full of disappointment, it is a great pleasure to be able to fantasize about a person you are involved with.

This makes the seducer's task easy: people are dying to be given the chance to fantasize about *you*. Do not spoil this golden opportunity by overexposing yourself, or becoming so familiar and banal that the target sees you exactly as you are. You do not have to be an angel, or a paragon of virtue—that would be quite boring. You can be dangerous, naughty, even somewhat vulgar, depending on the tastes of your victim. But never be ordinary or limited. In poetry (as opposed to reality), anything is possible.

Soon after we fall under a person's spell, we form an image in our minds of who they are and what pleasures they might offer. Thinking of them when we are alone, we tend to make this image more and more idealized. The novelist Stendhal, in his book *On Love*, calls this phenomenon "crystallization," telling the story of how, in Salzburg, Austria, they used to throw a leafless branch into the abandoned depths of a salt mine in the middle of winter. When the branch was pulled out months later, it would be covered with spectacular crystals. That is what happens to a loved one in our minds.

According to Stendhal, though, there are two crystallizations. The first happens when we first meet the person. The second and more important one happens later, when a bit of doubt creeps in—you desire the other person, but they elude you, you are not sure they are yours. This bit of doubt is critical—it makes your imagination work double, deepens the poeticizing process. In the seventeenth century, the great rake the Duc de Lauzun pulled off one of the most spectacular seductions in history—that of the Grande Mademoiselle, the cousin of King Louis XIV, and the wealthiest and most powerful woman in France. He tickled her imagination with a few brief encounters at the court, letting her catch glimpses of his wit, his audacity, his cool manner. She would begin to think of him when she was alone. Next she started to bump into him more often at court, and they would have little conversations or walks. When these meetings were over, she would be left with a doubt: is he or is he not interested in me? This made her want to see him more, in order to allay her doubts. She began to idealize him all out of proportion to the reality, for the duke was an incorrigible scoundrel.

Falling in love automatically tends toward madness. Left to itself, it goes to utter extremes. This is well known by the "conquistadors" of both sexes. Once a woman's

Remember: if you are easily had, you cannot be worth that much. It is hard to wax poetic about a person who comes so cheaply. If, after the initial interest, you make it clear that you cannot be taken for granted, if you stir a bit of doubt, the target will imagine there is something special, lofty, and unattainable about you. Your image will *crystallize* in the other person's mind.

Cleopatra knew that she was really no different from any other woman, and in fact her face was not particularly beautiful. But she knew that men have a tendency to overvalue a woman. All that is required is to hint that there is something different about you, to make them associate you with something grand or poetic. She made Caesar aware of her connection to the great kings and queens of Egypt's past; with Antony, she created the fantasy that she was descended from Aphrodite herself. These men were cavorting not just with a strong-willed woman but a kind of goddess. Such associations might be difficult to pull off today, but people still get deep pleasure from associating others with some kind of childhood fantasy figure. John F. Kennedy presented himself as a figure of chivalry—noble, brave, charming. Pablo Picasso was not just a great painter with a thirst for young girls, he was the Minotaur of Greek legend, or the devilish trickster figure that is so seductive to women. These associations should not be made too early; they are only powerful once the target has begun to fall under your spell, and is vulnerable to suggestion. A man who had just met Cleopatra would have found the Aphrodite association ludicrous. But a person who is falling in love will believe almost anything. The trick is to associate your image with something mythic, through the clothes you wear, the things you say, the places you go.

In Marcel Proust's novel *Remembrance of Things Past*, the character Swann finds himself gradually seduced by a woman who is not really his type. He is an aesthete, and loves the finer things in life. She is of a lower class, less refined, even a little tasteless. What poeticizes her in his mind is a series of exuberant moments they share together, moments that from then on he associates with her. One of these is a concert in a salon that they attend, in which he is intoxicated by a little melody in a sonata. Whenever he thinks of her, he remembers this little phrase. Little gifts she has given him, objects she has touched or handled, begin to assume a life of their own. Any kind of heightened experience, artistic or spiritual, lingers in the mind much longer than normal experience. You must find a way to share such moments with your targets—a concert, a play, a spiritual encounter, whatever it takes—so that they associate something elevated with you. Shared moments of exuberance have immense seductive pull. Also, any kind of object can be imbued with poetic resonance and sentimental associations, as discussed in the last chapter. The gifts you give and other objects can become imbued with your presence; if they are associated with pleasant memories, the sight of them keeps you in mind and accelerates the poeticization process.

Although it is said that absence makes the heart grow fonder, an absence too early will prove deadly to the crystallization process. Like Eva

attention is fixed upon a man, it is very easy for him to dominate her thoughts completely. A simple game of blowing hot and cold, of solicitousness and disdain, of presence and absence is all that is required. The rhythm of that technique acts upon a woman's attention like a pneumatic machine and ends by emptying her of all the rest of the world. How well our people put it: "to suck one's senses"! In fact: one is absorbed—absorbed by an object! Most "love affairs" are reduced to this mechanical play of the beloved upon the lover's attention. • The only thing that can save a lover is a violent shock from the outside, a treatment which is forced upon him. Many think that absence and long trips are a good cure for lovers. Observe that these are cures for one's attention. Distance from the beloved starves our attention toward him; it prevents anything further from rekindling the attention. Journeys, by physically obliging us to come out of ourselves and resolve hundreds of little problems, by uprooting us from our habitual setting and forcing hundreds of unexpected objects upon us, succeed in breaking down the maniac's haven and opening channels in his sealed consciousness, through which fresh air and normal perspective enter.

—José Ortega y Gasset, *On Love: Aspects of a Single Theme*, translated by Toby Talbot

Excessive familiarity can destroy crystallization. *A charming girl of sixteen was becoming too fond of a handsome young man of the same age, who used to make a practice of passing beneath her window every evening at nightfall. Her mother invited him to spend a week with them in the country. It was a bold remedy, I admit, but the girl was of a romantic disposition, and the young man a trifle dull; within three days she despised him.*

—STENDHAL, *LOVE*, TRANSLATED BY GILBERT AND SUZANNE SALE

Perón, you must surround your targets with focused attention, so that in those critical moments when they are alone, their mind is spinning with a kind of afterglow. Do everything you can to keep the target thinking about you. Letters, mementos, gifts, unexpected meetings—all these give you an omnipresence. Everything must remind them of you.

Finally, if your targets should see you as elevated and poetic, there is much to be gained by making them feel elevated and poeticized in their turn. The French writer Chateaubriand would make a woman feel like a goddess, she had such a powerful effect on him. He would send her poems that she supposedly had inspired. To make Queen Victoria feel as if she were both a seductive woman and a great leader, Benjamin Disraeli would compare her to mythological figures and great predecessors, such as Queen Elizabeth I. By idealizing your targets this way, you will make them idealize you in return, since you must be equally great to be able to appreciate and see all of their fine qualities. They will also grow addicted to the elevated feeling you give them.

Symbol: *The Halo. Slowly, when the target is alone, he or she begins to imagine a kind of faint glow around your head, formed by all of the possible pleasures you might offer, the radiance of your charged presence, your noble qualities. The Halo separates you from other people. Do not make it disappear by becoming familiar and ordinary.*

Reversal

It might seem that the reverse tactic would be to reveal everything about yourself, to be completely honest about your faults and virtues. This kind of sincerity was a quality Lord Byron had—he almost got a thrill out of disclosing all of his nasty, ugly qualities, even going so far, later on in his life, as to tell people about his incestuous involvements with his half sister. This kind of dangerous intimacy can be immensely seductive. The target will poeticize your vices, and your honesty about them; they will start to see more than is there. In other words, the idealization process is unavoidable. The only thing that cannot be idealized is mediocrity, but there is nothing seductive about mediocrity. There is no possible way to seduce without creating some kind of fantasy and poeticization.

13

Disarm Through Strategic Weakness and Vulnerability

Too much maneuvering on your part may raise suspicion. The best way to cover your tracks is to make the other person feel superior and stronger. If you seem to be weak, vulnerable, enthralled by the other person, and unable to control yourself, you will make your actions look more natural, less calculated. Physical weakness—tears, bashfulness, paleness—will help create the effect. To further win trust, exchange honesty for virtue: establish your "sincerity" by confessing some sin on your part—it doesn't have to be real. Sincerity is more important than goodness. Play the victim, then transform your target's sympathy into love.

The Victim Strategy

That sweltering August in the 1770s when the Présidente de Tourvel was visiting the château of her old friend Madame de Rosemonde, leaving her husband at home, she was expecting to be enjoying the peace and quiet of country life more or less on her own. But she loved the simple pleasures, and soon her daily life at the château assumed a comfortable pattern—daily Mass, walks in the country, charitable work in the neighboring villages, card games in the evening. When Madame de Rosemonde's nephew arrived for a visit, then, the Présidente felt uncomfortable—but also curious.

The nephew, the Vicomte de Valmont, was the most notorious libertine in Paris. He was certainly handsome, but he was not what she had expected: he seemed sad, somewhat downtrodden, and strangest of all, he paid hardly any attention to her. The Présidente was no coquette; she dressed simply, ignored fashions, and loved her husband. Still, she was young and beautiful, and was used to fending off men's attentions. In the back of her mind, she was slightly perturbed that he took so little notice of her. Then, at Mass one day, she caught a glimpse of Valmont apparently lost in prayer. The idea dawned on her that he was in the midst of a period of soul-searching.

The weak ones do have a power over us. The clear, forceful ones I can do without. I am weak and indecisive by nature myself, and a woman who is quiet and withdrawn and follows the wishes of a man even to the point of letting herself be used has much the greater appeal. A man can shape and mold her as he wishes, and becomes fonder of her all the while.

—Murasaki Shikibu, *The Tale of Genji*, translated by Edward G. Seidensticker

As soon as word had leaked out that Valmont was at the château, the Présidente had received a letter from a friend warning her against this dangerous man. But she thought of herself as the last woman in the world to be vulnerable to him. Besides, he seemed on the verge of repenting his evil past; perhaps she could help move him in that direction. What a wonderful victory that would be for God. And so the Présidente took note of Valmont's comings and goings, trying to understand what was happening in his head. It was strange, for instance, that he would often leave in the morning to go hunting, yet would never return with any game. One day, she decided to have her servant do a little harmless spying, and she was amazed and delighted to learn that Valmont had not gone hunting at all; he had visited a local village, where he had doled out money to a poor family about to be evicted from their home. Yes, she was right, his passionate soul was moving from sensuality to virtue. How happy that made her feel.

That evening, Valmont and the Présidente found themselves alone for the first time, and Valmont suddenly burst out with a startling confession. He was head-over-heels in love with the Présidente, and with a love he had

Hera, daughter of Cronus and Rhea, having been born on the island of Samos or, some say, at Argos, was brought up in Arcadia by Temenus, son of Pelasgus. The Seasons were her nurses. After banishing their father Cronus, Hera's twin brother Zeus sought her out at Cnossus in Crete or, some say, on Mount Thornax (now called Cuckoo Mountain) in Argolis, where he courted her, at first unsuccessfully. She took pity on him only when he adopted the disguise of a bedraggled cuckoo and tenderly warmed him in her bosom. There he at once resumed his true shape and ravished her, so that she was shamed into marrying him.

—Robert Graves, *The Greek Myths*

In a strategy (?) of seduction one draws the other into one's area of weakness, which is also his or her area of weakness. A calculated weakness, an incalculable weakness: one challenges the other to be taken in. . . . • To seduce is to appear weak. To seduce is to render weak. We seduce with our weakness, never with strong signs or powers. In seduction we enact this weakness, and this is what gives seduction its strength. • We seduce with our death, our vulnerability, and with the void that haunts us. The secret is to know how to play with death in the absence of a gaze or gesture, in the absence of knowledge or meaning. • Psychoanalysis tells us to assume our fragility and passivity, but in almost religious terms, turns them into a form of resignation and acceptance in order to promote a well-tempered psychic equilibrium. Seduction, by contrast, plays triumphantly with weakness, making a game of it, with its own rules.

—Jean Baudrillard, *Seduction*, translated by Brian Singer

never experienced before: her virtue, her goodness, her beauty, her kind ways had completely overwhelmed him. His generosity to the poor that afternoon had been for her sake—perhaps inspired by her, perhaps something more sinister: it had been to impress her. He would never have confessed to this, but finding himself alone with her, he could not control his emotions. Then he got down on his knees and begged for her to help him, to guide him in his misery.

The Présidente was caught off guard, and began to cry. Intensely embarrassed, she ran from the room, and for the next few days pretended to be ill. She did not know how to react to the letters Valmont now began to send her, begging her to forgive him. He praised her beautiful face and her beautiful soul, and claimed she had made him rethink his whole life. These emotional letters produced disturbing emotions, and Tourvel prided herself on her calmness and prudence. She knew she should insist that he leave the château, and wrote him to that effect; he reluctantly agreed, but on one condition—that she allow him to write to her from Paris. She consented, as long as the letters were not offensive. When he told Madame de Rosemonde that he was leaving, the Présidente felt a pang of guilt: his hostess and aunt would miss him, and he looked so pale. He was obviously suffering.

Now the letters from Valmont began to arrive, and Tourvel soon regretted allowing him this liberty. He ignored her request that he avoid the subject of love—indeed he vowed to love her forever. He rebuked her for her coldness and insensitivity. He explained his bad path in life—it was not his fault, he had had no direction, had been led astray by others. Without her help he would fall back into that world. Do not be cruel, he said, *you* are the one who seduced *me*. I am your slave, the victim of your charms and goodness; since you are strong, and do not feel as I do, you have nothing to fear. Indeed the Présidente de Tourvel came to pity Valmont—he seemed so weak, so out of control. How could she help him? And why was she even thinking of him, which she now did more and more? She was a happily married woman. No, she must at least put an end to this tiresome correspondence. No more talk of love, she wrote, or she would not reply. His letters stopped coming. She felt relief. Finally some peace and quiet.

One evening, however, as she was seated at the dinner table, she suddenly heard Valmont's voice from behind her, addressing Madame de Rosemonde. On the spur of the moment, he said, he had decided to return for a short visit. She felt a shiver up and down her spine, her face flushed; he approached and sat down beside her. He looked at her, she looked away, and soon made an excuse to leave the table and go up to her room. But she could not completely avoid him over the next few days, and she saw that he seemed paler than ever. He was polite, and a whole day might pass without her seeing him, but these brief absences had a paradoxical effect: now Tourvel realized what had happened. She missed him, she wanted to see him. This paragon of virtue and goodness had somehow fallen in love with an incorrigible rake. Disgusted with herself and what she had allowed to happen, she left the château in the middle of the night, without telling anyone, and headed for Paris, where she planned somehow to repent this awful sin.

Interpretation. The character of Valmont in Choderlos de Laclos's epistolary novel *Dangerous Liaisons* is based on several of the great real-life libertines of eighteenth-century France. Everything Valmont does is calculated for effect—the ambiguous actions that make Tourvel curious about him, the act of charity in the village (he knows he is being followed), the return visit to the château, the paleness of his face (he is having an affair with a girl at the château, and their all-night carousals give him a wasted look). Most devastating of all is his positioning of himself as the weak one, the seduced, the victim. How can the Présidente imagine he is manipulating her when everything suggests he is simply overwhelmed by her beauty, whether physical or spiritual? He cannot be a deceiver when he repeatedly makes a point of confessing the "truth" about himself: he admits that his charity was questionably motivated, he explains why he has gone astray, he lets her in on his emotions. (All of this "honesty," of course, is calculated.) In essence he is like a woman, or at least like a woman of those times—emotional, unable to control himself, moody, insecure. She is the one who is cold and cruel, like a man. In positioning himself as Tourvel's victim, Valmont can not only disguise his manipulations but elicit pity and concern. Playing the victim, he can stir up the tender emotions produced by a sick child or a wounded animal. And these emotions are easily channeled into love—as the Présidente discovers to her dismay.

Seduction is a game of reducing suspicion and resistance. The cleverest way to do this is to make the other person feel stronger, more in control of things. Suspicion usually comes out of insecurity; if your targets feel superior and secure in your presence, they are unlikely to doubt your motives. You are too weak, too emotional, to be up to something. Take this game as far as it will go. Flaunt your emotions and how deeply they have affected you. Making people feel the power they have over you is immensely flattering to them. Confess to something bad, or even to something bad that you did, or contemplated doing, to them. Honesty is more important than virtue, and one honest gesture will blind them to many deceitful acts. Create an impression of weakness—physical, mental, emotional. Strength and confidence can be frightening. Make your weakness a comfort, and play the victim—of their power over you, of circumstances, of life in general. This is the best way to cover your tracks.

> *You know, a man ain't worth a damn if he can't cry at the right time.*
>
> —Lyndon Baines Johnson

The old American proverb says if you want to con someone, you must first get him to trust you, or at least feel superior to you (these two ideas are related), and get him to let down his guard. The proverb explains a great deal about television commercials. If we assume that people are not stupid, they must react to TV commercials with a feeling of superiority that permits them to believe they are in control. As long as this illusion of volition persists, they would consciously have nothing to fear from the commercials. People are prone to trust anything over which they believe they have control. . . . • TV commercials appear foolish, clumsy, and ineffectual on purpose. They are made to appear this way at the conscious level in order to be consciously ridiculed and rejected. . . . Most ad men will confirm that over the years the seemingly worst commercials have sold the best. An effective TV commercial is purposefully designed to insult the viewer's conscious intelligence, thereby penetrating his defenses.

—Wilson Bryan Key, *Subliminal Seduction*

It takes great art to use bashfulness, but one does achieve a great deal with it. How often I have used bashfulness to trick a little miss! Ordinarily, young girls speak very harshly about bashful men, but secretly they like them. A little bashfulness flatters a teenage girl's vanity, makes her feel superior; it is her earnest money. When they are lulled to sleep, then at the very time they believe you are about to perish from bashfulness, you show them that you are so far from it that you are quite self-reliant. Bashfulness makes a man lose his masculine significance, and therefore it is a relatively good means for neutralizing the sex relation.

—SØREN KIERKEGAARD, *THE SEDUCER'S DIARY*, TRANSLATED BY HOWARD V. HONG AND EDNA H. HONG

Keys to Seduction

We all have weaknesses, vulnerabilities, frailnesses in our mental makeup. Perhaps we are shy or oversensitive, or need attention—whatever the weakness is, it is something we cannot control. We may try to compensate for it, or to hide it, but this is often a mistake: people sense something inauthentic or unnatural. Remember: what is natural to your character is inherently seductive. A person's vulnerability, what they seem to be unable to control, is often what is most seductive about them. People who display no weaknesses, on the other hand, often elicit envy, fear, and anger—we want to sabotage them just to bring them down.

Do not struggle against your vulnerabilities, or try to repress them, but put them into play. Learn to transform them into power. The game is subtle: if you wallow in your weakness, overplay your hand, you will be seen as angling for sympathy, or, worse, as pathetic. No, what works best is to allow people an occasional glimpse into the soft, frail side of your character, and usually only after they have known you for a while. That glimpse will humanize you, lowering their suspicions, and preparing the ground for a deeper attachment. Normally strong and in control, at moments you let go, give in to your weakness, let them see it.

Yet another form of Charity is there, which is oft times practised towards poor prisoners who are shut up in dungeons and robbed of all enjoyments with women. On such do the gaolers' wives and women that have charge over them, or châtelaines who have prisoners of war in their Castle, take pity and give them share of their love out of very charity and mercifulness. . . . • Thus do these gaolers' wives, noble châtelaines and others, treat their prisoners, the which, captive and unhappy though they be, yet cease not for that to feel the prickings of the flesh, as much as ever they did in their best days. . . . • To confirm what I say, I will instance a tale that Captain Beaulieu, Captain of the King's Galleys, of whom I have before spoke once and again, did tell me. He was in the service of the late Grand Prior of France, a member of the house of Lorraine, who was much attached to him. Going one time to take his patron on board at Malta in a

Valmont used his weakness this way. He had lost his innocence long ago, and yet, somewhere inside, he regretted it. He was vulnerable to someone truly innocent. His seduction of the Présidente was successful because it was not totally an act; there was a genuine weakness on his part, which even allowed him to cry at times. He let the Présidente see this side to him at key moments, in order to disarm her. Like Valmont, you can be acting and sincere at the same time. Suppose you are genuinely shy—at certain moments, give your shyness a little weight, lay it on a little thick. It should be easy for you to embellish a quality you already have.

After Lord Byron published his first major poem, in 1812, he became an instant celebrity. Beyond being a talented writer, he was so handsome, even pretty, and he was as brooding and enigmatic as the characters he wrote about. Women went wild over Lord Byron. He had an infamous "underlook," slightly lowering his head and glancing upward at a woman, making her tremble. But Byron had other qualities: when you first met him, you could not help noticing his fidgety movements, his ill-fitting clothes, his strange shyness, and his noticeable limp. This infamous man, who scorned all conventions and seemed so dangerous, was personally insecure and vulnerable.

In Byron's poem *Don Juan*, the hero is less a seducer of women than a man constantly pursued by them. The poem was autobiographical; women wanted to take care of this somewhat fragile man, who seemed to have little control over his emotions. More than a century later, John F. Kennedy, as a boy, became obsessed with Byron, the man he most wanted to emulate. He even tried to borrow Byron's "underlook." Kennedy himself was a frail youth, with constant health problems. He was also a little pretty, and friends saw something slightly feminine in him. Kennedy's weaknesses—physical and mental, for he too was insecure, shy, and oversensitive—were exactly what drew women to him. If Byron and Kennedy had tried to cover up their vulnerabilities with a masculine swagger they would have had no seductive charm. Instead, they learned how to subtly display their weaknesses, letting women sense this soft side to them.

There are fears and insecurities peculiar to each sex; your use of strategic weakness must always take these differences into account. A woman, for instance, may be attracted by a man's strength and self-confidence, but too much of it can create fear, seeming unnatural, even ugly. Particularly intimidating is the sense that the man is cold and unfeeling. She may feel insecure that he is only after sex, and nothing else. Male seducers long ago learned to become more feminine—to show their emotions, and to seem interested in their targets' lives. The medieval troubadours were the first to master this strategy; they wrote poetry in honor of women, emoted endlessly about their feelings, and spent hours in their ladies' boudoirs, listening to the women's complaints and soaking up their spirit. In return for their willingness to play weak, the troubadours earned the right to love.

Little has changed since then. Some of the greatest seducers in recent history—Gabriele D' Annunzio, Duke Ellington, Errol Flynn—understood the value of acting slavishly to a woman, like a troubadour on bended knee. The key is to indulge your softer side while still remaining as masculine as possible. This may include an occasional show of bashfulness, which the philosopher Søren Kierkegaard thought an extremely seductive tactic for a man—it gives the woman a sense of comfort, and even of superiority. Remember, though, to keep everything in moderation. A glimpse of shyness is sufficient; too much of it and the target will despair, afraid that she will end up having to do all the work.

A man's fears and insecurities often concern his sense of masculinity; he usually will feel threatened by a woman who is too overtly manipulative, who is too much in control. The greatest seductresses in history knew how to cover up their manipulations by playing the little girl in need of masculine protection. A famous courtesan of ancient China, Su Shou, used to make up her face to look particularly pale and weak. She would also walk in a way that made her seem frail. The great nineteenth-century courtesan Cora Pearl would literally dress and act like a little girl. Marilyn Monroe knew how to give the impression that she depended on a man's strength to survive. In all of these instances, the women were the ones in control of the dynamic, boosting a man's sense of masculinity in order to ultimately enslave him. To make this most effective, a woman should seem both in need of protection and sexually excitable, giving the man his ultimate fantasy.

The Empress Josephine, wife of Napoleon Bonaparte, won dominance over her husband early on through a calculated coquetry. Later on, though, she held on to that power through her constant—and not so innocent—use of tears. Seeing someone cry usually has an immediate effect on our emo-

frigate, he was taken by the Sicilian galleys, and carried prisoner to the Castel-à-mare at Palermo, where he was shut up in an exceeding narrow, dark and wretched dungeon, and very ill entreated by the space of three months. By good hap the Governor of the Castle, who was a Spaniard, had two very fair daughters, who hearing him complaining and making moan, did one day ask leave of their father to visit him, for the honor of the good God; and this he did freely give them permission to do. And seeing the Captain was of a surety a right gallant gentleman, and as ready-tongued as most, he was able so to win them over at this, the very first visit, that they did gain their father's leave for him to quit his wretched dungeon and to be put in a seemly enough chamber and receive better treatment. Nor was this all, for they did crave and get permission to come and see him freely every day and converse with him. • *And this did fall out so well that presently both the twain of them were in love with him, albeit he was not handsome to look upon, and they very fair ladies. And so, without a thought of the chance of more rigorous imprisonment or even death, but rather tempted by such opportunities, he did set himself to the enjoyment of the two girls with good will and hearty appetite. And these pleasures did continue without any scandal, for so fortunate was he in this conquest of his for the space of eight whole months, that no scandal did ever hap all that time, and no ill,*

tions: we cannot remain neutral. We feel sympathy, and most often will do anything to stop the tears—including things that we normally would not do. Weeping is an incredibly potent tactic, but the weeper is not always so innocent. There is usually something real behind the tears, but there may also be an element of acting, of playing for effect. (And if the target senses this the tactic is doomed.) Beyond the emotional impact of tears, there is something seductive about sadness. We want to comfort the other person, and as Tourvel discovered, that desire quickly turns into love. Affecting sadness, even crying sometimes, has great strategic value, even for a man. It is a skill you can learn. The central character of the eighteenth-century French novel *Marianne*, by Marivaux, would think of something sad in her past to make herself cry or look sad in the present.

Use tears sparingly, and save them for the right moment. Perhaps this might be a time when the target seems suspicious of your motives, or when you are worrying about having no effect on him or her. Tears are a sure barometer of how deeply the other person is falling for you. If they seem annoyed, or resist the bait, your case is probably hopeless.

In social and political situations, seeming too ambitious, or too controlled, will make people fear you; it is crucial to show your soft side. The display of a single weakness will hide a multitude of manipulations. Emotion or even tears will work here too. Most seductive of all is playing the victim. For his first speech in Parliament, Benjamin Disraeli prepared an elaborate oration, but when he delivered it the opposition yelled and laughed so loudly that hardly any of it could be heard. He plowed ahead and gave the whole speech, but by the time he sat down he felt he had failed miserably. Much to his amazement, his colleagues told him the speech was a marvelous success. It would have been a failure if he had complained or given up; but by going ahead as he did, he positioned himself as the victim of a cruel and unreasonable faction. Almost everyone sympathized with him now, which would serve him well in the future. Attacking your mean-spirited opponents can make you seem ugly as well; instead, soak up their blows, and play the victim. The public will rally to your side, in an emotional response that will lay the groundwork for a grand political seduction.

inconvenience, nor any surprise or discovery at all. For indeed the two sisters had so good an understanding between them and did so generously lend a hand to each other and so obligingly play sentinel to one another, that no ill hap did ever occur. And he sware to me, being my very intimate friend as he was, that never in his days of greatest liberty had he enjoyed so excellent entertainment or felt keener ardor or better appetite for it than in the said prison—which truly was a right good prison for him, albeit folk say no prison can be good. And this happy time did continue for the space of eight months, till the truce was made betwixt the Emperor and Henri II., King of France, whereby all prisoners did leave their dungeons and were released. He sware that never was he more grieved than at quitting this good prison of his, but was exceeding sorry to leave these fair maids, with whom he was in such high favor, and who did express all possible regrets at his departing.

—Seigneur De Brantôme, *Lives of Fair & Gallant Ladies*, translated by A. R. Allinson

Symbol: *The Blemish. A beautiful face is a delight to look at, but if it is too perfect it leaves us cold, and even slightly intimidated. It is the little mole, the beauty mark, that makes the face human and lovable. So do not conceal all of your blemishes. You need them to soften your features and elicit tender feelings.*

Reversal

Timing is everything in seduction; you should always look for signs that the target is falling under your spell. A person falling in love tends to ignore the other person's weaknesses, or to see them as endearing. An unseduced, rational person, on the other hand, may find bashfulness or emotional outbursts pathetic. There are also certain weaknesses that have no seductive value, no matter how in love the target may be.

The great seventeenth-century courtesan Ninon de l'Enclos liked men with a soft side. But sometimes a man would go too far, complaining that she did not love him enough, that she was too fickle and independent, that he was being mistreated and wronged. For Ninon, such behavior would break the spell, and she would quickly end the relationship. Complaining, whining, neediness, and actively appealing for sympathy will appear to your targets not as charming weaknesses but as manipulative attempts at a kind of negative power. So when you play the victim, do it subtly, without overadvertising it. The only weaknesses worth playing up are the ones that will make you seem lovable. All others should be repressed and eradicated at all costs.

14

Confuse Desire and Reality—The Perfect Illusion

To compensate for the difficulties in their lives, people spend a lot of their time daydreaming, imagining a future full of adventure, success, and romance. If you can create the illusion that through you they can live out their dreams, you will have them at your mercy. It is important to start slowly, gaining their trust, and gradually constructing the fantasy that matches their desires. Aim at secret wishes that have been thwarted or repressed, stirring up uncontrollable emotions, clouding their powers of reason. The perfect illusion is one that does not depart too much from reality, but has a touch of the unreal to it, like a waking dream. Lead the seduced to a point of confusion in which they can no longer tell the difference between illusion and reality.

Fantasy in the Flesh

In 1964, a twenty-year-old Frenchman named Bernard Bouriscout arrived in Beijing, China, to work as an accountant in the French embassy. His first weeks there were not what he had expected. Bouriscout had grown up in the French provinces, dreaming of travel and adventure. When he had been assigned to come to China, images of the Forbidden City, and of the gambling dens of Macao, had danced in his mind. But this was Communist China, and contact between Westerners and Chinese was almost impossible at the time. Bouriscout had to socialize with the other Europeans stationed in the city, and what a boring and cliquish lot they were. He grew lonely, regretted taking the assignment, and began making plans to leave.

Lovers and madmen have such seething brains, \ Such shaping fantasies, that apprehend \ More than cool reason ever comprehends.

—William Shakespeare, *A Midsummer Night's Dream*

Then, at a Christmas party that year, Bouriscout's eyes were drawn to a young Chinese man in a corner of the room. He had never seen anyone Chinese at any of these affairs. The man was intriguing: he was slender and short, a bit reserved, but he had an attractive presence. Bouriscout went up and introduced himself. The man, Shi Pei Pu, proved to be a writer of Chinese-opera librettos who also taught Chinese to members of the French embassy. Aged twenty-six, he spoke perfect French. Everything about him fascinated Bouriscout; his voice was like music, soft and whispery, and he left you wanting to know more about him. Bouriscout, although usually shy, insisted on exchanging telephone numbers. Perhaps Pei Pu could be his Chinese tutor.

He was not a sex person. He was like . . . somebody who had come down from the clouds. He was not human. You could not say he was a man friend or a woman friend; he was somebody different anyway. . . . You feel he was only a friend who was coming from another planet and so nice also, so overwhelming and separated from the life of the ground.

—Bernard Bouriscout, in Joyce Wadler, *Liaison*

They met a few days later in a restaurant. Bouriscout was the only Westerner there—at last a taste of something real and exotic. Pei Pu, it turned out, had been a well-known actor in Chinese operas and came from a family with connections to the former ruling dynasty. Now he wrote operas about the workers, but he said this with a look of irony. They began to meet regularly, Pei Pu showing Bouriscout the sights of Beijing. Bouriscout loved his stories—Pei Pu talked slowly, and every historical detail seemed to come alive as he spoke, his hands moving to embellish his words. This, he might say, is where the last Ming emperor hung himself, pointing to the spot and telling the story at the same time. Or, the cook in the restaurant we just ate in once served in the palace of the last emperor, and then another magnificent tale would follow. Pei Pu also talked of life in the Beijing Opera, where men often played women's parts, and sometimes became famous for it.

Romance had again come her way personified by a handsome young German officer, Lieutenant Konrad Friedrich, who called upon her at Neuilly to ask her help. He wanted Pauline [Bonaparte] to use her

The two men became friends. Chinese contact with foreigners was restricted, but they managed to find ways to meet. One evening Bouriscout tagged along when Pei Pu visited the home of a French official to tutor the children. He listened as Pei Pu told them "The Story of the Butterfly," a tale from the Chinese opera: a young girl yearns to attend an imperial school, but girls are not accepted there. She disguises herself as a boy, passes the exams, and enters the school. A fellow student falls in love with her, and she is attracted to him, so she tells him that she is actually a girl. Like most of these tales, the story ends tragically. Pei Pu told it with unusual emotion; in fact he had played the role of the girl in the opera.

A few nights later, as they were walking before the gates of the Forbidden City, Pei Pu returned to "The Story of the Butterfly." "Look at my hands," he said, "Look at my face. That story of the butterfly, it is my story too." In his slow, dramatic delivery he explained that his mother's first two children had been girls. Sons were far more important in China; if the third child was a girl, the father would have to take a second wife. The third child came: another girl. But the mother was too frightened to reveal the truth, and made an agreement with the midwife: they would say that the child was a boy, and it would be raised as such. This third child was Pei Pu.

Over the years, Pei Pu had had to go to extreme lengths to disguise her sex. She never used public bathrooms, plucked her hairline to look as if she were balding, on and on. Bouriscout was enthralled by the story, and also relieved, for like the boy in the butterfly tale, deep down he felt attracted to Pei Pu. Now everything made sense—the small hands, the high-pitched voice, the delicate neck. He had fallen in love with her, and, it seemed, the feelings were reciprocated.

Pei Pu started visiting Bouriscout's apartment, and soon they were sleeping together. She continued to dress as a man, even in his apartment, but women in China wore men's clothes anyway, and Pei Pu acted more like a woman than any of the Chinese women he had seen. In bed, she had a shyness and a way of directing his hands that was both exciting and feminine. She made everything romantic and heightened. When he was away from her, her every word and gesture resonated in his mind. What made the affair all the more exciting was the fact that they had to keep it secret.

In December of 1965, Bouriscout left Beijing and returned to Paris. He traveled, had other affairs, but his thoughts kept returning to Pei Pu. The Cultural Revolution broke out in China, and he lost contact with her. Before he had left, she had told him she was pregnant with their child. He had no idea whether the baby had been born. His obsession with her grew too strong, and in 1969 he finagled another government job in Beijing.

Contact with foreigners was now even more discouraged than on his first visit, but he managed to track Pei Pu down. She told him she had borne a son, in 1966, but he had looked like Bouriscout, and given the growing hatred of foreigners in China, and the need to keep the secret of her sex, she had him sent him away to an isolated region near Russia. It was so cold there—perhaps he was dead. She showed Bouriscout photographs

influence with Napoleon in connection with providing for the needs of the French troops in the Papal States. He made an instantaneous impression on the princess, who escorted him around her garden until they arrived at the rockery. There she stopped and, looking into the young man's eyes mysteriously, commanded him to return to this same spot at the same hour next day when she might have some good news for him. The young officer bowed and took his leave. . . . In his memoirs he revealed in detail what took place after the first meeting with Pauline: • *"At the hour agreed on I again proceeded to Neuilly, made my way to the appointed spot in the garden and stood waiting at the rockery. I had not been there very long when a lady made her appearance, greeted me pleasantly and led me through a side door into the interior of the rockery where there were several rooms and galleries and in one splendid salon a luxurious-looking bath. The adventure was beginning to strike me as very romantic, almost like a fairy tale, and just as I was wondering what the outcome might be a woman in a robe of the sheerest cambric entered by a side door, came up to me, and smilingly asked how I liked being there. I at once recognized Napoleon's beautiful sister, whose perfect figure was clearly outlined by every movement of her robe. She held out her hand for me to kiss and told me to sit down on the couch beside her. On this occasion I certainly was not the*

of the boy, and he did see some resemblance. Over the next few weeks they managed to meet here and there, and then Bouriscout had an idea: he sympathized with the Cultural Revolution, and he wanted to get around the prohibitions that were preventing him from seeing Pei Pu, so he offered to do some spying. The offer was passed along to the right people, and soon Bouriscout was stealing documents for the Communists. The son, named Bertrand, was recalled to Beijing, and Bouriscout finally met him. Now a threefold adventure filled Bouriscout's life: the alluring Pei Pu, the thrill of being a spy, and the illicit child, whom he wanted to bring back to France.

In 1972, Bouriscout left Beijing. Over the next few years he tried repeatedly to get Pei Pu and his son to France, and a decade later he finally succeeded; the three became a family. In 1983, though, the French authorities grew suspicious of this relationship between a Foreign Office official and a Chinese man, and with a little investigating they uncovered Bouriscout's spying. He was arrested, and soon made a startling confession: the man he was living with was really a woman. Confused, the French ordered an examination of Pei Pu; as they had thought, he was very much a man. Bouriscout went to prison.

Even after Bouriscout had heard his former lover's own confession, he was still convinced that Pei Pu was a woman. Her soft body, their intimate relationship—how could he be wrong? Only when Pei Pu, imprisoned in the same jail, showed him the incontrovertible proof of his sex did Bouriscout finally accept it.

seducer. . . . After an interval Pauline pulled a bell rope and ordered the woman who answered to prepare a bath which she asked me to share. Wearing bathgowns of the finest linen we remained for nearly an hour in the crystal-clear bluish water. Then we had a grand dinner served in another room and lingered on together until dusk. When I left I had to promise to return again soon and I spent many afternoons with the princess in the same way."

—HARRISON BRENT, *PAULINE BONAPARTE: A WOMAN OF AFFAIRS*

Interpretation. The moment Pei Pu met Bouriscout, he realized he had found the perfect victim. Bouriscout was lonely, bored, desperate. The way he responded to Pei Pu suggested that he was probably also homosexual, or perhaps bisexual—at least confused. (Bouriscout in fact had had homosexual encounters as a boy; guilty about them, he had tried to repress this side of himself.) Pei Pu had played women's parts before, and was quite good at it; he was slight and effeminate; physically it was not a stretch. But who would believe such a story, or at least not be skeptical of it?

The critical component of Pei Pu's seduction, in which he brought the Frenchman's fantasy of adventure to life, was to start slowly and set up an idea in his victim's mind. In his perfect French (which, however, was full of interesting Chinese expressions), he got Bouriscout used to hearing stories and tales, some true, some not, but all delivered in that dramatic yet believable tone. Then he planted the idea of gender impersonation with his "Story of the Butterfly." By the time he confessed the "truth" of his gender, Bouriscout was already completely enchanted with him.

Bouriscout warded off all suspicious thoughts because he *wanted* to believe Pei Pu's story. From there it was easy. Pei Pu faked his periods; it didn't take much money to get hold of a child he could reasonably pass off as their son. More important, he played the fantasy role to the hilt, remaining elusive and mysterious (which was what a Westerner would expect from an

The courtesan is meant to be a half-defined, floating figure never fixing herself surely in the imagination. She is the memory of an experience, the point at which a dream is transformed into reality or reality into a dream. The bright colors fade, her name becomes a mere echo—echo of an echo, since she has probably adopted it from some ancient predecessor. The idea of the courtesan is a garden of delights in which the lover walks, smelling first this flower and then that but never understanding whence comes the fragrance that intoxicates him. Why should the courtesan not elude analysis? She does not want to be recognized for what she is, but rather to be allowed to be potent and effective. She offers the truth of herself—or, rather, of the passions that become directed toward her. And what she gives back is one's self and an hour of grace in her presence. Love revives when you look at her: is that not enough? She is the generative force of an illusion, the birth point of desire, the threshold of contemplation of bodily beauty.

—Lynne Lawner, *Lives of the Courtesans: Portraits of the Renaissance*

Asian woman) while enveloping his past and indeed their whole experience in titillating bits of history. As Bouriscout later explained, "Pei Pu screwed me in the head. . . . I was having relations and in my thoughts, my dreams, I was light-years away from what was true."

Bouriscout thought he was having an exotic adventure, an enduring fantasy of his. Less consciously, he had an outlet for his repressed homosexuality. Pei Pu embodied his fantasy, giving it flesh, by working first on his mind. The mind has two currents: it wants to believe in things that are pleasant to believe in, yet it has a self-protective need to be suspicious of people. If you start off too theatrical, trying too hard to create a fantasy, you will feed that suspicious side of the mind, and once fed, the doubts will not go away. Instead, you must start slowly, building trust, while perhaps letting people see a little touch of something strange or exciting about you to tease their interest. Then you build up your story, like any piece of fiction. You have established a foundation of trust—now the fantasies and dreams you envelop them in are suddenly believable.

Remember: people want to believe in the extraordinary; with a little groundwork, a little mental foreplay, they will fall for your illusion. If anything, err on the side of reality: use real props (like the child Pei Pu showed Bouriscout) and add the fantastical touches in your words, or an occasional gesture that gives you a slight unreality. Once you sense that they are hooked, you can deepen the spell, go further and further into the fantasy. At that point they will have gone so far into their own minds that you will no longer have to bother with verisimilitude.

It was on March 16, the same day the Duke of Gloucester wrote to Sir William, that Goethe recorded the first known performance of what were destined to be called Emma's Attitudes. Just what these were, we shall learn shortly. First, it must be emphasized that the Attitudes were a show for favored eyes only. • . . . Goethe, disciple of Winckelmann, was at this date thrilled by the human form, as a contemporary writes. Here was the ideal spectator for the classical drama Emma and Sir William had wrought in the long winter evenings. Let us take our seats beside Goethe and settle to watch the show as he describes it. • "Sir William Hamilton . . . has now, after many years of devotion to the arts and the study of nature, found the acme of these delights in the person of an English girl of twenty with a beautiful face and a perfect figure. He has had a Greek costume made for her which becomes her extremely. Dressed in this, she lets down her hair and, with a few shawls, gives so much variety to her poses, gestures, expressions, etc. that the spectator can hardly believe his eyes. He sees what thousands of artists would have liked to

Wish Fulfillment

In 1762, Catherine, wife of Czar Peter III, staged a coup against her ineffectual husband and proclaimed herself empress of Russia. Over the next few years Catherine ruled alone, but kept a series of lovers. The Russians called these men the *vremienchiki,* "the men of the moment," and in 1774 the man of the moment was Gregory Potemkin, a thirty-five-year-old lieutenant, ten years younger than Catherine, and a most unlikely candidate for the role. Potemkin was coarse and not at all handsome (he had lost an eye in an accident). But he knew how to make Catherine laugh, and he worshiped her so intensely that she eventually succumbed. He quickly became the love of her life.

Catherine promoted Potemkin higher and higher in the hierarchy, eventually making him the governor of White Russia, a large southwestern area including the Ukraine. As governor, Potemkin had to leave St. Petersburg and go to live in the south. He knew that Catherine could not do without male companionship, so he took it upon himself to name Catherine's subsequent *vremienchiki.* She not only approved of this arrangement, she made it clear that Potemkin would always remain her favorite.

Catherine's dream was to start a war with Turkey, recapture Constantinople for the Orthodox Church, and drive the Turks out of Europe. She offered to share this crusade with the young Hapsburg emperor, Joseph II, but Joseph never quite brought himself to sign the treaty that would unite them in war. Growing impatient, in 1783 Catherine annexed the Crimea, a southern peninsula that was mostly populated by Muslim Tartars. She asked Potemkin to do there what he had already managed to do in the Ukraine—rid the area of bandits, build roads, modernize the ports, bring prosperity to the poor. Once he had cleaned it up, the Crimea would make the perfect launching post for the war against Turkey.

The Crimea was a backward wasteland, but Potemkin loved the challenge. Getting to work on a hundred different projects, he grew intoxicated with visions of the miracles he would perform there. He would establish a capital on the Dnieper River, Ekaterinoslav ("To the glory of Catherine"), that would rival St. Petersburg and would house a university outshining anything in Europe. The countryside would hold endless fields of corn, orchards with rare fruits from the Orient, silkworm farms, new towns with bustling marketplaces. On a visit to the empress in 1785, Potemkin talked of these things as if they already existed, so vivid were his descriptions. The empress was delighted, but her ministers were skeptical—Potemkin loved to talk. Ignoring their warnings, in 1787 Catherine arranged for a tour of the area. She asked Joseph II to join her—he would be so impressed with the modernization of the Crimea that he would immediately sign on for the war against Turkey. Potemkin, naturally, was to organize the whole affair.

express realized before him in movements and surprising transformations—standing, kneeling, sitting, reclining, serious, sad, playful, ecstatic, contrite, alluring, threatening, anxious, one pose follows another without a break. She knows how to arrange the folds of her veil to match each mood, and has a hundred ways of turning it into a headdress. The old knight idolizes her and is quite enthusiastic about everything she does. In her he has found all the antiquities, all the profiles of Sicilian coins, even the Apollo Belvedere. This much is certain: as a performance it's like nothing you ever saw before in your life. We have already enjoyed it on two evenings."

—Flora Fraser, *Emma, Lady Hamilton*

And so, in May of that year, after the Dnieper had thawed, Catherine prepared for a journey from Kiev, in the Ukraine, to Sebastopol, in the Crimea. Potemkin arranged for seven floating palaces to carry Catherine and her retinue down the river. The journey began, and as Catherine, Joseph, and the courtiers looked at the shores to either side, they saw triumphal arches in front of clean-looking towns, their walls freshly painted; healthy-looking cattle grazing in the pastures; streams of marching troops on the roads; buildings going up everywhere. At dusk they were entertained by bright-costumed peasants, and smiling girls with flowers in their hair, dancing on the shore. Catherine had traveled through this area many years before, and the poverty of the peasantry there had saddened her—she had determined then that she would somehow change their lot. To see before her eyes the signs of such a transformation overwhelmed her, and she berated Potemkin's critics: Look at what my favorite has accomplished, look at these miracles!

They anchored at three towns along the way, staying in each place in a magnificent, newly built palace with artificial waterfalls in the English-style gardens. On land they moved through villages with vibrant marketplaces; the peasants were happily at work, building and repairing. Everywhere they spent the night, some spectacle filled their eyes—dances, parades, mythological tableaux vivants, artificial volcanoes illuminating Moorish gardens. Finally, at the end of the trip, in the palace at Sebastopol, Catherine and

For this uncanny is in reality nothing new or alien, but something which is familiar and old—established in the mind and which has become alienated from it only through the process of repression. This reference to the factor of repression enables us, furthermore, to understand Schelling's definition of the uncanny as something which ought to have remained hidden but has come to light. . . .
• . . . There is one more point of general application which I should like to add. . . . This is that an uncanny effect is often and easily produced when the distinction between imagination and reality is effaced, as when something that we have hitherto regarded as imaginary

appears before us in reality, or when a symbol takes over the full functions of the thing it symbolizes, and so on. It is this factor which contributes not a little to the uncanny effect attaching to magical practices. The infantile element in this, which also dominates the minds of neurotics, is the overaccentuation of psychical reality in comparison with material reality—a feature closely allied to the belief in the omnipotence of thoughts.

—SIGMUND FREUD, "THE UNCANNY," IN *PSYCHOLOGICAL WRITINGS AND LETTERS*

Joseph discussed the war with Turkey. Joseph reiterated his concerns. Suddenly Potemkin interrupted: "I have 100,000 troops waiting for me to say 'Go!' " At that moment the windows of the palace were flung open, and to the sounds of booming cannons they saw lines of troops as far as the eye could see, and a fleet of ships filling the harbor. Awed by the sight, images of Eastern European cities retaken from the Turks dancing in his mind, Joseph II finally signed the treaty. Catherine was ecstatic, and her love for Potemkin reached new heights. He had made her dreams come true.

Catherine never suspected that almost everything she had seen was pure fakery, perhaps the most elaborate illusion ever conjured up by one man.

Interpretation. In the four years that he had been governor of the Crimea, Potemkin had accomplished little, for this backwater would take decades to improve. But in the few months before Catherine's visit he had done the following: every building that faced the road or the shore was given a fresh coat of paint; artificial trees were set up to hide unseemly spots in the view; broken roofs were repaired with flimsy boards painted to look like tile; everyone the party would see was instructed to wear their best clothes and look happy; everyone old and infirm was to stay indoors. Floating in their palaces down the Dnieper, the imperial entourage saw brand-new villages, but most of the buildings were only facades. The herds of cattle were shipped from great distances, and were moved at night to fresh fields along the route. The dancing peasants were trained for the entertainments; after each one they were loaded into carts and hurriedly transported to a new downriver location, as were the marching soldiers who seemed to be everywhere. The gardens of the new palaces were filled with transplanted trees that died a few days later. The palaces themselves were quickly and badly built, but were so magnificently furnished that no one noticed. One fortress along the way had been built of sand, and was destroyed a little later by a thunderstorm.

The cost of this vast illusion had been enormous, and the war with Turkey would fail, but Potemkin had accomplished his goal. To the observant, of course, there were signs along the way that all was not as it seemed, but when the empress herself insisted that everything was real and glorious, the courtiers could only agree. This was the essence of the seduction: Catherine had wanted so desperately to be seen as a loving and progressive ruler, one who would defeat the Turks and liberate Europe, that when she saw signs of change in the Crimea, her mind filled in the picture.

When our emotions are engaged, we often have trouble seeing things as they are. Feelings of love cloud our vision, making us color events to coincide with our desires. To make people believe in the illusions you create, you need to feed the emotions over which they have least control. Often the best way to do this is to ascertain their unsatisfied desires, their wishes crying out for fulfillment. Perhaps they want to see themselves as noble or romantic, but life has thwarted them. Perhaps they want an adventure. If something seems to validate this wish, they become emotional and irrational, almost to the point of hallucination.

Remember to envelop them in your illusion *slowly.* Potemkin did not start with grand spectacles, but with simple sights along the way, such as grazing cattle. Then he brought them on land, heightening the drama, until the calculated climax when the windows were flung open to reveal a mighty war machine—actually a few thousand men and boats lined up in such a way as to suggest many more. Like Potemkin, involve the target in some kind of journey, physical or otherwise. The feeling of a shared adventure is rife with fantasy associations. Make people feel that they are getting to see and live out something that relates to their deepest yearnings and they will see happy, prosperous villages where there are only facades.

> *Here the real journey through Potemkin's fairyland began. It was like a dream—the waking dream of some magician who had discovered the secret of materializing his visions. . . . [Catherine] and her companions had left the world of reality behind. . . . Their talk was of Iphigenia and the ancient gods, and Catherine felt that she was both Alexander and Cleopatra.*
>
> —Gina Kaus

Keys to Seduction

The real world can be unforgiving: events occur over which we have little control, other people ignore our feelings in their quests to get what they need, time runs out before we accomplish what we had wanted. If we ever stopped to look at the present and future in a completely objective way, we would despair. Fortunately we develop the habit of dreaming early on. In this other, mental world that we inhabit, the future is full of rosy possibilities. Perhaps tomorrow we will sell that brilliant idea, or meet the person who will change our lives. Our culture stimulates these fantasies with constant images and stories of marvelous occurrences and happy romances.

The problem is, these images and fantasies exist only in our minds, or on-screen. They really aren't enough—we crave the real thing, not this endless daydreaming and titillation. Your task as a seducer is to bring some flesh and blood into someone's fantasy life by embodying a fantasy figure, or creating a scenario resembling that person's dreams. No one can resist the pull of a secret desire that has come to life before their eyes. You must first choose targets who have some repression or dream unrealized—always the most likely victims of a seduction. Slowly and gradually, you will build up the illusion that they are getting to see and feel and live those dreams of theirs. Once they have this sensation they will lose contact with reality, and begin to see your fantasy as more real than anything else. And once they lose touch with reality, they are (to quote Stendhal on Lord Byron's female victims) like roasted larks that fall into your mouth.

Most people have a misconception about illusion. As any magician knows, it need not be built out of anything grand or theatrical; the grand and theatrical can in fact be destructive, calling too much attention to you and your schemes. Instead create the appearance of normality. Once your targets feel secure—nothing is out of the ordinary—you have room to deceive them. Pei Pu did not spin the lie about his gender immediately; he took his time, made Bouriscout come to him. Once Bouriscout had fallen for it, Pei Pu continued to wear men's clothes. In animating a fantasy, the great mistake is imagining it must be larger than life. That would border on camp, which is entertaining but rarely seductive. Instead, what you aim for is what Freud called the "uncanny," something strange and familiar at the same time, like a déjà vu, or a childhood memory—anything slightly irrational and dreamlike. The uncanny, the mix of the real and the unreal, has immense power over our imaginations. The fantasies you bring to life for your targets should not be bizarre or exceptional; they should be rooted in reality, with a hint of the strange, the theatrical, the occult (in talk of destiny, for example). You vaguely remind people of something in their childhood, or a character in a film or book. Even before Bouriscout heard Pei Pu's story, he had the uncanny feeling of something remarkable and fantastical in this normal-looking man. The secret to creating an uncanny effect is to keep it subtle and suggestive.

Emma Hart came from a prosaic background, her father a country blacksmith in eighteenth-century England. Emma was beautiful, but had no other talents to her credit. Yet she rose to become one of the greatest seductresses in history, seducing first Sir William Hamilton, the English ambassador to the court of Naples, and then (as Lady Hamilton, Sir William's wife) Vice-Admiral Lord Nelson. What was strangest when you met her was an uncanny sense that she was a figure from the past, a woman out of Greek myth or ancient history. Sir William was a collector of Greek and Roman antiquities; to seduce him, Emma cleverly made herself resemble a Greek statue, and mythical figures in paintings of the time. It was not just the way she wore her hair, or dressed, but her poses, the way she carried herself. It was as if one of the paintings he collected had come to life. Soon Sir William began to host parties in his home in Naples at which Emma would wear costumes and pose, re-creating images from mythology and history. Dozens of men fell in love with her, for she embodied an image from their childhood, an image of beauty and perfection. The key to this fantasy creation was some shared cultural association—mythology, historical seductresses like Cleopatra. Every culture has a pool of such figures from the distant and not-so-distant past. You hint at a similarity, in spirit and in appearance—but you are flesh and blood. What could be more thrilling than the sense of being in the presence of some fantasy figure going back to your earliest memories?

One night Pauline Bonaparte, the sister of Napoleon, held a gala affair in her house. Afterward, a handsome German officer approached her in the garden and asked for her help in passing along a request to the emperor. Pauline said she would do her best, and then, with a rather mysterious look in her eye, asked him to come back to the same spot the next night. The officer returned, and was greeted by a young woman who led him to some rooms near the garden and then to a magnificent salon, complete with an extravagant bath. Moments later, another young woman entered through a side door, dressed in the sheerest garments. It was Pauline. Bells were rung, ropes were pulled, and maids appeared, preparing the bath, giving the officer a dressing gown, then disappearing. The officer later described the evening as something out of a fairy tale, and he had the feeling that Pauline was deliberately acting the part of some mythical seductress. Pauline was beautiful and powerful enough to get almost any man she wanted, and she wasn't interested simply in luring a man into bed; she wanted to envelop him in romantic adventure, seduce his mind. Part of the adventure was the feeling that she was playing a role, and was inviting her target along into this shared fantasy.

Role playing is immensely pleasurable. Its appeal goes back to childhood, where we first learn the thrill of trying on different parts, imitating adults or figures out of fiction. As we get older and society fixes a role on us, a part of us yearns for the playful approach we once had, the masks we were able to wear. We still want to play that game, to act a different role in life. Indulge your targets in this wish by first making it clear that you are playing a role, then inviting them to join you in a shared fantasy. The more you set things up like a play or a piece of fiction, the better. Notice how Pauline began the seduction with a mysterious request that the officer reappear the next night; then a second woman led him into a magical series of rooms. Pauline herself delayed her entrance, and when she appeared, she did not mention his business with Napoleon, or anything remotely banal. She had an ethereal air about her; he was being invited to enter a fairy tale. The evening was real, but had an uncanny resemblance to an erotic dream.

Casanova took role playing still further. He traveled with an enormous wardrobe and a trunk full of props, many of them gifts for his targets—fans, jewels, other accouterments. And some of the things he said and did were borrowed from novels he had read and stories he had heard. He enveloped women in a romantic atmosphere that was heightened yet quite real to their senses. Like Casanova, you must see the world as a kind of theater. Inject a certain lightness into the roles you are playing; try to create a sense of drama and illusion; confuse people with the slight unreality of words and gestures inspired by fiction; in daily life, be the consummate actor. Our culture reveres actors because of their freedom to play roles. It is something that all of us envy.

For years, the Cardinal de Rohan had been afraid that he had somehow offended his queen, Marie Antoinette. She would not so much as look at him. Then, in 1784, the Comtesse de Lamotte-Valois suggested to him that the queen was prepared not only to change this situation but actually to befriend him. The queen, said Lamotte-Valois, would indicate this in her next formal reception—she would nod to him in a particular way.

During the reception, Rohan indeed noticed a slight change in the queen's behavior toward him, and a barely perceptible glance at him. He was overjoyed. Now the countess suggested they exchange letters, and Rohan spent days writing and rewriting his first letter to the queen. To his delight he received one back. Next the queen requested a private interview with him in the gardens of Versailles. Rohan was beside himself with happiness and anxiety. At nightfall he met the queen in the gardens, fell to the ground, and kissed the hem of her dress. "You may hope that the past will be forgotten," she said. At this moment they heard voices approaching, and the queen, frightened that someone would see them together, quickly fled with her servants. But Rohan soon received a request from her, again through the countess: she desperately wanted to acquire the most beautiful diamond necklace ever created. She needed a go-between to purchase it for her, since the king thought it too expensive. She had chosen Rohan for the task. The cardinal was only too willing; in performing this task he would prove his loyalty, and the queen would be indebted to him forever. Rohan acquired the necklace. The countess was to deliver it to the queen. Now Rohan waited for the queen both to thank him and slowly to pay him back.

Yet this never happened. The countess was in fact a grand swindler; the queen had never nodded to him, he had only imagined it. The letters he had received from her were forgeries, and not even very good ones. The woman he had met in the park had been a prostitute paid to dress and act the part. The necklace was of course real, but once Rohan had paid for it, and handed it over to the countess, it disappeared. It was broken into parts, which were hawked all over Europe for enormous amounts. And when Rohan finally complained to the queen, news of the extravagant purchase spread rapidly. The public believed Rohan's story—that the queen had indeed bought the necklace, and was pretending otherwise. This fiction was the first step in the ruin of her reputation.

Everyone has lost something in life, has felt the pangs of disappointment. The idea that we can get something back, that a mistake can be righted, is immensely seductive. Under the impression that the queen was prepared to forgive some mistake he had made, Rohan hallucinated all kinds of things—nods that did not exist, letters that were the flimsiest of forgeries, a prostitute who became Marie Antoinette. The mind is infinitely vulnerable to suggestion, and even more so when strong desires are involved. And nothing is stronger than the desire to change the past, right a wrong, satisfy a disappointment. Find these desires in your victims and creating a believable fantasy will be simple for you: few have the power to see through an illusion they desperately want to believe in.

Symbol: *Shangri-La. Everyone has a vision in their mind of a perfect place where people are kind and noble, where their dreams can be realized and their wishes fulfilled, where life is full of adventure and romance. Lead the target on a journey there, give them a glimpse of Shangri-La through the mists on the mountain, and they will fall in love.*

Reversal

There is no reversal to this chapter. No seduction can proceed without creating illusion, the sense of a world that is real but separate from reality.

15

Isolate the Victim

An isolated person is weak. By slowly isolating your victims, you make them more vulnerable to your influence. Their isolation may be psychological: by filling their field of vision through the pleasurable attention you pay them, you crowd out everything else in their mind. They see and think only of you. The isolation may also be physical: you take them away from their normal milieu, friends, family, home. Give them the sense of being marginalized, in limbo—they are leaving one world behind and entering another. Once isolated like this, they have no outside support, and in their confusion they are easily led astray. Lure the seduced into your lair, where nothing is familiar.

Isolation—the Exotic Effect

In the early fifth century B.C., Fu Chai, the Chinese king of Wu, defeated his great enemy, Kou Chien, the king of Yueh, in a series of battles. Kou Chien was captured and forced to serve as a groom in Fu Chai's stables. He was finally allowed to return home, but every year he had to pay a large tribute of money and gifts to Fu Chai. Over the years, this tribute added up, so that the kingdom of Wu prospered and Fu Chai grew wealthy.

One year Kou Chien sent a delegation to Fu Chai: they wanted to know if he would accept a gift of two beautiful maidens as part of the tribute. Fu Chai was curious, and accepted the offer. The women arrived a few days later, amid much anticipation, and the king received them in his palace. The two approached the throne—their hair was magnificently coiffured, in what was called "the cloud-cluster" style, ornamented with pearl ornaments and kingfisher feathers. As they walked, jade pendants hanging from their girdles made the most delicate sound. The air was full of some delightful perfume. The king was extremely pleased. The beauty of one of the girls far surpassed that of the other; her name was Hsi Shih. She looked him in the eye without a hint of shyness; in fact she was confident and coquettish, something he was not used to seeing in such a young girl.

Fu Chai called for festivities to commemorate the occasion. The halls of the palace filled with revelers; inflamed with wine, Hsi Shih danced before the king. She sang, and her voice was beautiful. Reclining on a couch of white jade, she looked like a goddess. The king could not leave her side. The next day he followed her everywhere. To his astonishment, she was witty, sharp, and knowledgeable, and could quote the classics better than he could. When he had to leave her to deal with royal affairs, his mind was full of her image. Soon he brought her with him to his councils, asking her advice on important matters. She told him to listen less to his ministers; he was wiser than they were, his judgment superior.

Hsi Shih's power grew daily. Yet she was not easy to please; if the king failed to grant some wish of hers, tears would fill her eyes, his heart would melt, and he would yield. One day she begged him to build her a palace outside the capital. Of course, he obliged her. And when he visited the palace, he was astounded at its magnificence, even though he had paid the bills: Hsi Shih had filled it with the most extravagant furnishings. The grounds contained an artificial lake with marble bridges crossing over it. Fu Chai spent more and more time here, sitting by a pool and watching Hsi

In the state of Wu great preparations had been made for the reception of the two beauties. The king received them in audience surrounded by his ministers and all his court. As they approached him the jade pendants attached to their girdles made a musical sound and the air was fragrant with the scent of their gowns. Pearl ornaments and kingfisher feathers adorned their hair. • Fu Chai, the king of Wu, looked into the lovely eyes of Hsi Shih (495–472 B.C.) and forgot his people and his state. Now she did not turn away and blush as she had done three years previously beside the little brook. She was complete mistress of the art of seduction and she knew how to encourage the king to look again. Fu Chai hardly noticed the second girl, whose quiet charms did not attract him. He had eyes only for Hsi Shih, and before the audience was over those at court realized that the girl would be a force to be reckoned with and that she would be able to influence

Shih comb her hair, using the pool as a mirror. He would watch her playing with her birds, in their jeweled cages, or simply walking through the palace, for she moved like a willow in the breeze. The months went by; he stayed in the palace. He missed councils, ignored his family and friends, neglected his public functions. He lost track of time. When a delegation came to talk to him of urgent matters, he was too distracted to listen. If anything but Hsi Shih took up his time, he worried unbearably that she would be angry.

Finally word reached him of a growing crisis: the fortune he had spent on the palace had bankrupted the treasury, and the people were discontented. He returned to the capital, but it was too late: an army from the kingdom of Yueh had invaded Wu, and had reached the capital. All was lost. Fu Chai had no time to rejoin his beloved Hsi Shih. Instead of letting himself be captured by the king of Yueh, the man who had once served in his stables, he committed suicide.

Little did he know that Kou Chien had plotted this invasion for years, and that Hsi Shih's elaborate seduction was the main part of his plan.

Interpretation. Kou Chien wanted to make sure that his invasion of Wu would not fail. His enemy was not Fu Chai's armies, or his wealth and his resources, but his mind. If he could be deeply distracted, his mind filled with something other than affairs of state, he would fall like ripe fruit.

Kou Chien found the most beautiful maiden in his realm. For three years he had her trained in all of the arts—not just singing, dancing, and calligraphy, but how to dress, how to talk, how to play the coquette. And it worked: Hsi Shih did not allow Fu Chai a moment's rest. Everything about her was exotic and unfamiliar. The more attention he paid to her hair, her moods, her glances, the way she moved, the less he thought about diplomacy and war. He was driven to distraction.

All of us today are kings protecting the tiny realm of our own lives, weighed down by all kinds of responsibilities, surrounded by ministers and advisers. A wall forms around us—we are immune to the influence of other people, because we are so preoccupied. Like Hsi Shih, then, you must lure your targets away, gently, slowly, from the affairs that fill their mind. And what will best lure them from their castles is the whiff of the exotic. Offer something unfamiliar that will fascinate them and hold their attention. Be different in your manners and appearance, and slowly envelop them in this different world of yours. Keep your targets off balance with coquettish changes of mood. Do not worry that the disruption you represent is making them emotional—that is a sign of their growing weakness. Most people are ambivalent: on the one hand they feel comforted by their habits and duties, on the other they are bored, and ripe for anything that seems exotic, that seems to come from somewhere else. They may struggle or have doubts, but exotic pleasures are irresistible. The more you can get them

the king either for good or ill. . . . • Amidst the revelers in the halls of Wu, Hsi Shih wove her net of fascination about the heart of the susceptible monarch. . . . "Inflamed by wine, she now begins to sing / The songs of Wu to please the fatuous king; / And in the dance of Tsu she subtly blends / All rhythmic movements to her sensuous ends." . . . But she could do more than sing and dance to amuse the king. She had wit, and her grasp of politics astonished him. When there was anything she wanted she could shed tears which so moved her lover's heart that he could refuse her nothing. For she was, as Fan Li had said, the one and only, the incomparable Hsi Shih, whose magnetic personality attracted everyone, many even against their own will. . . . • Embroidered silk curtains encrusted with coral and gems, scented furniture and screens inlaid with jade and mother-of-pearl were among the luxuries which surrounded the favorite. . . . On one of the hills near the palace there was a celebrated pool of clear water which has been known ever since as the pool of the king of Wu. Here, to amuse her lover, Hsi Shih would make her toilet, using the pool as a mirror while the infatuated king combed her hair. . . .

—Eloise Talcott Hibbert, *Embroidered Gauze: Portraits of Famous Chinese Ladies*

into your world, the weaker they become. As with the king of Wu, by the time they realize what has happened, it is too late.

Isolation—The "Only You" Effect

In 1948, the twenty-nine-year-old actress Rita Hayworth, known as Hollywood's Love Goddess, was at a low point in her life. Her marriage to Orson Welles was breaking up, her mother had died, and her career seemed stalled. That summer she headed for Europe. Welles was in Italy at the time, and in the back of her mind she was dreaming of a reconciliation.

Rita stopped first at the French Riviera. Invitations poured in, particularly from wealthy men, for at the time she was considered the most beautiful woman in the world. Aristotle Onassis and the Shah of Iran telephoned her almost daily, begging for a date. She turned them all down. A few days after her arrival, though, she received an invitation from Elsa Maxwell, the society hostess, who was giving a little party in Cannes. Rita balked but Maxwell insisted, telling her to buy a new dress, show up a little late, and make a grand entrance.

Rita played along, and arrived at the party wearing a white Grecian gown, her red hair falling over her bare shoulders. She was greeted by a reaction she had grown used to: all conversation stopped as both men and women turned in their chairs, the men gazing in amazement, the women jealous. A man hurried to her side and escorted her to her table. It was thirty-seven-year-old Prince Aly Khan, the son of the Aga Khan III, who was the worldwide leader of the Islamic Ismaili sect and one of the richest men in the world. Rita had been warned about Aly Khan, a notorious rake. To her dismay, they were seated next to each other, and he never left her side. He asked her a million questions—about Hollywood, her interests, on and on. She began to relax a little and open up. There were other beautiful women there, princesses, actresses, but Aly Khan ignored them all, acting as if Rita were the only woman there. He led her onto the dance floor, and though he was an expert dancer, she felt uncomfortable—he held her a little too close. Still, when he offered to drive her back to her hotel, she agreed. They sped along the Grande Corniche; it was a beautiful night. For one evening she had managed to forget her many problems, and she was grateful, but she was still in love with Welles, and an affair with a rake like Aly Khan was not what she needed.

Aly Khan had to fly off on business for a few days; he begged her to stay at the Riviera until he got back. While he was away, he telephoned constantly. Every morning a giant bouquet of flowers arrived. On the telephone he seemed particularly annoyed that the Shah of Iran was trying hard to see her, and he made her promise to break the date to which she had finally agreed. During this time, a gypsy fortune-teller visited the hotel, and Rita agreed to have her fortune read. "You are about to embark on the

In Cairo Aly bumped into [the singer] Juliette Greco again. He asked her to dance. • "You have too bad a reputation," she replied. "We're going to sit very much apart." • "What are you doing tomorrow?" he insisted. • "Tomorrow I take a plane to Beirut." • When she boarded the plane, Aly was already on it, grinning at her surprise. . . . • Dressed in tight black leather slacks and a black sweater [Greco] stretched languorously in an armchair of her Paris house and observed: • "They say I am a dangerous woman. Well, Aly was a dangerous man. He was charming in a very special way. There is a kind of man who is very clever with women. He takes you out to a restaurant and if the most beautiful woman comes in, he doesn't look at her. He makes you feel you are a queen. Of course, I understood it. I didn't believe it. I would laugh and point out the beautiful woman. But that is me. . . . Most women are made very happy by that kind of attention. It's pure vanity. She thinks, 'I'll be the one and the others will leave.' • " . . . With Aly, how the woman felt was most important. . . . He was a great charmer, a great seducer. He made you feel fine and that everything was easy. No problems. Nothing to worry about. Or regret. It was always, 'What can I do for you? What do you need?' Airplane tickets, cars, boats; you felt you were on a pink cloud."

—Leonard Slater, *Aly: A Biography*

ANNE: Didst thou not kill this king [Henry VI]? \ RICHARD: I grant ye. . . . \ ANNE: And thou unfit for any place, but hell. \ RICHARD: Yes, one place else, if you will hear me name it. \ ANNE: Some dungeon. \ RICHARD: Your bedchamber. \ ANNE: Ill rest betide the chamber where thou liest! \ RICHARD: So will it, madam, till I lie with you. . . . But gentle Lady Anne . . . \ Is not the causer of the timeless deaths \ Of these Plantagenets, Henry and Edward, \ As blameful as the executioner? \ ANNE: Thou wast the cause and most accursed effect. \ RICHARD: Your beauty was the cause of that effect— \ Your beauty, that did haunt me in my sleep \ To undertake the death of all the world, \ So I might live one hour in your sweet bosom.

—WILLIAM SHAKESPEARE, *THE TRAGEDY OF KING RICHARD III*

greatest romance of your life," the gypsy told her. "He is somebody you already know. . . . You must relent and give in to him totally. Only if you do that will you find happiness at long last." Not knowing who this man could be, Rita, who had a weakness for the occult, decided to extend her stay. Aly Khan came back; he told her that his château overlooking the Mediterranean was the perfect place to escape from the press and forget her troubles, and that he would behave himself. She relented. Life in the château was like a fairy tale; wherever she turned, his Indian helpers were there to attend to her every wish. At night he would take her into his enormous ballroom, where they would dance all by themselves. Could this be the man the fortune-teller meant?

Aly Khan invited his friends over to meet her. Among this strange company she felt alone again, and depressed; she decided to leave the château. Just then, as if he had read her thoughts, Aly Khan whisked her off to Spain, the country that fascinated her most. The press caught on to the affair, and began to hound them in Spain: Rita had had a daughter with Welles—was this any way for a mother to act? Aly Khan's reputation did not help, but he stood by her, shielding her from the press as best he could. Now she was more alone than ever, and more dependent on him.

Near the end of the trip, Aly Khan proposed to Rita. She turned him down; she did not think he was the kind of man you married. He followed her to Hollywood, where her former friends were less friendly than before. Thank God she had Aly Khan to help her. A year later she finally succumbed, abandoning her career, moving to Aly Khan's château, and marrying him.

My child, my sister, dream \ How sweet all things would seem \ Were we in that kind land to live together, \ And there love slow and long, \ There love and die among \ Those scenes that image you, that sumptuous weather. \ Drowned suns that glimmer there \ Through cloud-dishevelled air \ Move me with such a mystery as appears \ Within those other skies \ Of your treacherous eyes \ When I behold them shining through their tears. \ There, there is nothing else but grace and measure, \ Richness, quietness, and pleasure. . . . \ See,

Interpretation. Aly Khan, like a lot of men, fell in love with Rita Hayworth the moment he saw the film *Gilda*, in 1948. He made up his mind that he would seduce her somehow. The moment he heard she was coming to the Riviera, he got his friend Elsa Maxwell to lure her to the party and seat her next to him. He knew about the breakup of her marriage, and how vulnerable she was. His strategy was to block out everything else in her world—problems, other men, suspicion of him and his motives, etc. His campaign began with the display of an intense interest in her life—constant phone calls, flowers, gifts, all to keep him in her mind. He set up the fortune-teller to plant the seed. When she began to fall for him, he introduced her to his friends, knowing she would feel alienated among them, and therefore dependent on him. Her dependence was heightened by the trip to Spain, where she was on unfamiliar territory, besieged by reporters, and forced to cling to him for help. He slowly came to dominate her thoughts. Everywhere she turned, there he was. Finally she succumbed, out of weakness and the boost to her vanity that his attention represented. Under his spell, she forgot about his horrid reputation, relinquishing the suspicions that were the only thing protecting her from him.

It was not Aly Khan's wealth or looks that made him a great seducer.

He was not in fact very handsome, and his wealth was more than offset by his bad reputation. His success was strategic: he isolated his victims, working so slowly and subtly that they did not notice it. The intensity of his attention made a woman feel that in his eyes, at that moment, she was the only woman in the world. This isolation was experienced as pleasure; the woman did not notice her growing dependence, how the way he filled up her mind with his attention slowly isolated her from her friends and her milieu. Her natural suspicions of the man were drowned out by his intoxicating effect on her ego. Aly Khan almost always capped off his seductions by taking the woman to some enchanted place on the globe—a place that he knew well, but where the woman felt lost.

Do not give your targets the time or space to worry about, suspect, or resist you. Flood them with the kind of attention that crowds out all other thoughts, concerns, and problems. Remember—people secretly yearn to be led astray by someone who knows where they are going. It can be a pleasure to let go, and even to feel isolated and weak, if the seduction is done slowly and gracefully.

Put them in a spot where they have no place to go, and they will die before fleeing.

—Sun-tzu

sheltered from the swells \ There in the still canals \ Those drowsy ships that dream of sailing forth; \ It is to satisfy \ Your least desire, they ply \ Hither through all the waters of the earth. \ The sun at close of day \ Clothes the fields of hay, \ Then the canals, at last the town entire \ In hyacinth and gold: \ Slowly the land is rolled \ Sleepward under a sea of gentle fire. \ There, there is nothing else but grace and measure, \ Richness, quietness, and pleasure.

—Charles Baudelaire, "Invitation to the Voyage," *The Flowers of Evil*, translated by Richard Wilbur

Keys to Seduction

The people around you may seem strong, and more or less in control of their lives, but that is merely a facade. Underneath, people are more brittle than they let on. What lets them seem strong is the series of nests and safety nets they envelop themselves in—their friends, their families, their daily routines, which give them a feeling of continuity, safety, and control. Suddenly pull the rug out from under them, drop them alone into some foreign place where the familiar signposts are gone or scrambled, and you will see a very different person.

A target who is strong and settled is hard to seduce. But even the strongest people can be made vulnerable if you can isolate them from their nests and safety nets. Block out their friends and family with your constant presence, alienate them from the world they are used to, and take them to places they do not know. Get them to spend time in *your* environment. Deliberately disturb their habits, get them to do things they have never done. They will grow emotional, making it easier to lead them astray. Disguise all this in the form of a pleasurable experience, and your targets will wake up one day distanced from everything that normally comforts them. Then they will turn to you for help, like a child crying out for its mother when the lights are turned out. In seduction, as in warfare, the isolated target is weak and vulnerable.

In Samuel Richardson's *Clarissa*, written in 1748, the rake Lovelace is attempting to seduce the novel's beautiful heroine. Clarissa is young, virtuous, and very much protected by her family. But Lovelace is a conniving seducer. First he courts Clarissa's sister, Arabella. A match between them seems likely. Then he suddenly switches attention to Clarissa, playing on sibling rivalry to make Arabella furious. Their brother, James, is angered by Lovelace's change in sentiments; he fights with Lovelace and is wounded. The whole family is in an uproar, united against Lovelace, who, however, manages to smuggle letters to Clarissa, and to visit her when she is at the house of a friend. The family finds out, and accuses her of disloyalty. Clarissa is innocent; she has not encouraged Lovelace's letters or visits. But now her parents are determined to marry her off, to a rich older man. Alone in the world, about to be married to a man she finds repulsive, she turns to Lovelace as the only one who can save her from this mess. Eventually he rescues her by getting her to London, where she can escape this dreaded marriage, but where she is also hopelessly isolated. In these circumstances her feelings toward him soften. All of this has been masterfully orchestrated by Lovelace himself—the turmoil within the family, Clarissa's eventual alienation from them, the whole scenario.

Your worst enemies in a seduction are often your targets' family and friends. They are outside your circle and immune to your charms; they may provide a voice of reason to the seduced. You must work silently and subtly to alienate the target from them. Insinuate that they are jealous of your target's good fortune in finding you, or that they are parental figures who have lost a taste for adventure. The latter argument is extremely effective with young people, whose identities are in flux and who are more than ready to rebel against any authority figure, particularly their parents. You represent excitement and life; the friends and parents represent habit and boredom.

In Shakespeare's *The Tragedy of King Richard III*, Richard, when still the Duke of Gloucester, has murdered King Henry VI and his son, Prince Edward. Shortly thereafter he accosts Lady Anne, Prince Edward's widow, who knows what he has done to the two men closest to her, and who hates him as much as a woman can hate. Yet Richard attempts to seduce her. His method is simple: he tells her that what he did, he did because of his love for her. He wanted there to be no one in her life but him. His feelings were so strong he was driven to murder. Of course Lady Anne not only resists this line of reasoning, she abhors him. But he persists. Anne is at a moment of extreme vulnerability—alone in the world, with no one to support her, at the height of grief. Incredibly, his words begin to have an effect.

Murder is not a seductive tactic, but the seducer does enact a kind of killing—a psychological one. Our past attachments are a barrier to the present. Even people we have left behind can continue to have a hold on us. As a seducer you will be held up to the past, compared to previous suitors, perhaps found inferior. *Do not let it get to that point.* Crowd out the past with your attentions in the present. If necessary, find ways to disparage their previous lovers—subtly or not so subtly, depending on the situation. Even go so far as to open old wounds, making them feel old pain and seeing by contrast how much better the present is. The more you can isolate them from their past, the deeper they will sink with you into the present.

The principle of isolation can be taken literally by whisking the target off to an exotic locale. This was Aly Khan's method; a secluded island worked best, and indeed islands, cut off from the rest of the world, have always been associated with the pursuit of sensual pleasures. The Roman Emperor Tiberius descended into debauchery once he made his home on the island of Capri. The danger of travel is that your targets are intimately exposed to you—it is hard to maintain an air of mystery. But if you take them to a place alluring enough to distract them, you will prevent them from focusing on anything banal in your character. Cleopatra lured Julius Caesar into taking a voyage down the Nile. Moving deeper into Egypt, he was further isolated from Rome, and Cleopatra was all the more seductive. The early-twentieth-century lesbian seductress Natalie Barney had an on-again-off-again affair with the poet Renée Vivien; to regain her affections, she took Renée on a trip to the island of Lesbos, a place Natalie had visited many times. In doing so she not only isolated Renée but disarmed and distracted her with the associations of the place, the home of the legendary lesbian poet Sappho. Vivien even began to imagine that Natalie was Sappho herself. Do not take the target just anywhere; pick the place that will have the most effective associations.

The seductive power of isolation goes beyond the sexual realm. When new adherents joined Mahatma Gandhi's circle of devoted followers, they were encouraged to cut off their ties with the past—with their family and friends. This kind of renunciation has been a requirement of many religious sects over the centuries. People who isolate themselves in this way are much more vulnerable to influence and persuasion. A charismatic politician feeds off and even encourages people's feelings of alienation. John F. Kennedy did this to great effect when he subtly disparaged the Eisenhower years; the comfort of the 1950s, he implied, compromised American ideals. He invited Americans to join him in a new life, on a "New Frontier," full of danger and excitement. It was an extremely seductive lure, particularly for the young, who were Kennedy's most enthusiastic supporters.

Finally, at some point in the seduction there must be a hint of danger in the mix. Your targets should feel that they are gaining a great adventure in following you, but are also losing something—a part of their past, their cherished comfort. Actively encourage these ambivalent feelings. An element of fear is the proper spice; although too much fear is debilitating, in small doses it makes us feel alive. Like diving out of an airplane, it is exciting, a thrill, at the same time that it is a little frightening. And the only person there to break the fall, or catch them, is you.

Symbol: *The Pied Piper. A jolly fellow in his red and yellow cloak, he lures the children from their homes with the delightful sounds of his flute. Enchanted, they do not notice how far they are walking, how they are leaving their families behind. They do not even notice the cave he eventually leads them into, and which closes upon them forever.*

Reversal

The risks of this strategy are simple: isolate someone too quickly and you will induce a sense of panic that may end up in the target's taking flight. The isolation you bring must be gradual, and disguised as pleasure—the pleasure of knowing you, leaving the world behind. In any case, some people are too fragile to be cut off from their base of support. The great modern courtesan Pamela Harriman had a solution to this problem: she isolated her victims from their families, their former or present wives, and in place of those old connections she quickly set up new comforts for her lovers. She overwhelmed them with attention, attending to their every need. In the case of Averill Harriman, the billionaire who eventually married her, she literally established a new home for him, one that had no associations with the past and was full of the pleasures of the present. It is unwise to keep the seduced dangling in midair for too long, with nothing familiar or comforting in sight. Instead, replace the familiar things you have cut them off from with a new home, a new series of comforts.

Phase Three

The Precipice—Deepening the Effect Through Extreme Measures

The goal in this phase is to make everything deeper—the effect you have on their mind, feelings of love and attachment, tension within your victims. With your hooks deep into them, you can then push them back and forth, between hope and despair, until they weaken and snap. Showing how far you are willing to go for your victims, doing some noble or chivalrous deed (16: Prove yourself) will create a powerful jolt, spark an intensely positive reaction. Everyone has scars, repressed desires, and unfinished business from childhood. Bring these desires and wounds to the surface, make your victims feel they are getting what they never got as a child and you will penetrate deep into their psyche, stir uncontrollable emotions (17: Effect a regression). Now you can take your victims past their limits, getting them to act out their dark sides, adding a sense of danger to your seduction (18: Stir up the transgressive and taboo).

You need to deepen the spell, and nothing will more confuse and enchant your victims than giving your seduction a spiritual veneer. It is not lust that motivates you, but destiny, divine thoughts and everything elevated (19: Use spiritual lures). The erotic lurks beneath the spiritual. Now your victims have been properly set up. By deliberately hurting them, instilling fears and anxieties, you will lead them to the edge of the precipice from which it will be easy to push and make them fall (20: Mix pleasure with pain). They feel great tension and are yearning for relief.

16

Prove Yourself

Most people want to be seduced. If they resist your efforts, it is probably because you have not gone far enough to allay their doubts—about your motives, the depth of your feelings, and so on. One well-timed action that shows how far you are willing to go to win them over will dispel their doubts. Do not worry about looking foolish or making a mistake—any kind of deed that is self-sacrificing and for your targets' sake will so overwhelm their emotions, they won't notice anything else. Never appear discouraged by people's resistance, or complain. Instead, meet the challenge by doing something extreme or chivalrous. Conversely, spur others to prove themselves by making yourself hard to reach, unattainable, worth fighting over.

Seductive Evidence

Anyone can talk big, say lofty things about their feelings, insist on how much they care for us, and also for all oppressed peoples in the far reaches of the planet. But if they never behave in a way that will back up their words, we begin to doubt their sincerity—perhaps we are dealing with a charlatan, or a hypocrite or a coward. Flattery and fine words can only go so far. A time will eventually arrive when you will have to show your victim some evidence, to match your words with deeds.

This kind of evidence has two functions. First, it allays any lingering doubts about you. Second, an action that reveals some positive quality in you is immensely seductive in and of itself. Brave or selfless deeds create a powerful and positive emotional reaction. Don't worry, your deeds do not have to be so brave and selfless that you lose everything in the process. The appearance alone of nobility will often suffice. In fact, in a world where people overanalyze and talk too much, any kind of action has a bracing, seductive effect.

It is normal in the course of a seduction to encounter resistance. The more obstacles you overcome, of course, the greater the pleasure that awaits you, but many a seduction fails because the seducer does not correctly read the resistances of the target. More often than not, you give up too easily. First, understand a primary law of seduction: resistance is a sign that the other person's emotions are engaged in the process. The only person you cannot seduce is somebody distant and cold. Resistance is emotional, and can be transformed into its opposite, much as, in jujitsu, the physical resistance of an opponent can be used to make him fall. If people resist you because they don't trust you, an apparently selfless deed, showing how far you are willing to go to prove yourself, is a powerful remedy. If they resist because they are virtuous, or because they are loyal to someone else, all the better—virtue and repressed desire are easily overcome by action. As the great seductress Natalie Barney once wrote, "Most virtue is a demand for greater seduction."

Love is a species of warfare. Slack troopers, go elsewhere! \ It takes more than cowards to guard \ These standards. Night-duty in winter, long-route marches, every \ Hardship, all forms of suffering: these await \ The recruit who expects a soft option. You'll often be out in \ Cloudbursts, and bivouac on the bare \ Ground. . . . Is lasting \ Love your ambition? Then put away all pride. \ The simple, straightforward way in may be denied you, \ Doors bolted, shut in your face — \ So be ready to slip down from the roof through a lightwell, \ Or sneak in by an upper-floor window. She'll be glad \ To know you're risking your neck, and for her sake: that will offer \ Any mistress sure proof of your love.

—OVID, *THE ART OF LOVE*, TRANSLATED BY PETER GREEN

There are two ways to prove yourself. First, the spontaneous action: a situation arises in which the target needs help, a problem needs solving, or, simply, he or she needs a favor. You cannot foresee these situations, but you must be ready for them, for they can spring up at any time. Impress the target by going further than really necessary—sacrificing more money, more time, more effort than they had expected. Your target will often use these

The man says: " . . . A fruit picked from one's own orchard ought to taste sweeter than one obtained from a stranger's tree, and what has been attained by

greater effort is cherished more dearly than what is gained with little trouble. As the proverb says: 'Prizes great cannot be won unless some heavy labor's done.'" • The woman says: "If no great prizes can be won unless some heavy labor's done, you must suffer the exhaustion of many toils to be able to attain the favors you seek, since what you ask for is a greater prize." • The man says: "I give you all the thanks that I can express for so sagely promising me your love when I have performed great toils. God forbid that I or any other could win the love of so worthy a woman without first attaining it by many labors."

—Andreas Capellanus, *On Love*, translated by P. G. Walsh

moments, or even manufacture them, as a kind of test: will you retreat? Or will you rise to the occasion? You cannot hesitate or flinch, even for a moment, or all is lost. If necessary, make the deed seem to have cost you more than it has, never with words, but indirectly—exhausted looks, reports spread through a third party, whatever it takes.

The second way to prove yourself is the brave deed that you plan and execute in advance, on your own and at the right moment—preferably some way into the seduction, when any doubts the victim still has about you are more dangerous than earlier on. Choose a dramatic, difficult action that reveals the painful time and effort involved. Danger can be extremely seductive. Cleverly lead your victim into a crisis, a moment of danger, or indirectly put them in an uncomfortable position, and you can play the rescuer, the gallant knight. The powerful feelings and emotions this elicits can easily be redirected into love.

Some Examples

1. In France in the 1640s, Marion de l'Orme was the courtesan men lusted after the most. Renowned for her beauty, she had been the mistress of Cardinal Richelieu, among other notable political and military figures. To win her bed was a sign of achievement.

For weeks the rake Count Grammont had wooed de l'Orme, and finally she had given him an appointment for a particular evening. The count prepared himself for a delightful encounter, but on the day of the appointment he received a letter from her in which she expressed, in polite and tender terms, her terrible regrets—she had the most awful headache, and would have to stay in bed that evening. Their appointment would have to be postponed. The count felt certain he was being pushed to the side for someone else, for de l'Orme was as capricious as she was beautiful.

One day, [Saint-Preuil] pleaded more than usual that [Madame de la Maisonfort] grant him the ultimate favors a woman could offer, and he went beyond just words in his pleading. Madame, saying he had gone way too far, ordered him to never ever appear before her again. He left her room. Only an hour later, the lady was taking her customary walk along one of those beautiful canals at Bagnolet, when Saint-Preuil leapt out from behind a hedge, totally naked, and standing before his mistress in this state, he cried out, "For the last time, Madame—Goodbye!" Thereupon, he threw himself into the canal, head first. The lady, terrified by such a sight,

Grammont did not hesitate. At nightfall he rode to the Marais, where de l'Orme lived, and scouted the area. In a square near her home he spotted a man approaching on foot. Recognizing the Duc de Brissac, he immediately knew that this man was to supplant him in the courtesan's bed. Brissac seemed unhappy to see the count, and so Grammont approached him hurriedly and said, "Brissac, my friend, you must do me a service of the greatest importance: I have an appointment, for the first time, with a girl who lives near this place; and as this visit is only to concert measures, I shall make but a very short stay. Be so kind as to lend me your cloak, and walk my horse a little, until I return; but above all, do not go far from this place." Without waiting for an answer, Grammont took the duke's cloak and handed him the bridle of his horse. Looking back, he saw that Brissac was watching him, so he pretended to enter a house, slipped out through the back, circled around, and reached de l'Orme's house without being seen.

Grammont knocked at the door, and a servant, mistaking him for the duke, let him in. He headed straight for the lady's chamber, where he found her lying on a couch, in a sheer gown. He threw off Brissac's cloak and she gasped in fright. "What is the matter, my fair one?" he asked. "Your headache, to all appearance, is gone?" She seemed put out, exclaimed she still had the headache, and insisted that he leave. It was up to her, she said, to make or break appointments. "Madam," Grammont said calmly, "I know what perplexes you: you are afraid lest Brissac should meet me here; but you may make yourself easy on that account." He then opened the window and revealed Brissac out in the square, dutifully walking back and forth with a horse, like a common stable boy. He looked ridiculous; de l'Orme burst out laughing, threw her arms around the count, and exclaimed, "My dear Chevalier, I can hold out no longer; you are too amiable and too eccentric not to be pardoned." He told her the whole story, and she promised that the duke could exercise horses all night, but she would not let him in. They made an appointment for the following evening. Outside, the count returned the cloak, apologized for taking so long, and thanked the duke. Brissac was most gracious, even holding Grammont's horse for him to mount, and waving goodbye as he rode off.

began to cry and to run in the direction of her house, where upon arriving, she fainted. As soon as she could speak, she ordered that someone go and see what had happened to Saint-Preuil, who in truth had not stayed very long in the canal, and having quickly put his clothes back on, hurried to Paris where he hid himself for several days. Meanwhile, the rumor spread that he had died. Madame de la Maisonfort was deeply moved by the extreme measures he had adopted to prove his sentiments. This act of his appeared to her to be a sign of an extraordinary love; and having perhaps noticed some charms in his naked presence that she had not seen fully clothed, she deeply regretted her cruelty, and publicly stated her feeling of loss. Word of this reached Saint-Preuil, and he immediately resurrected himself, and did not lose time in taking advantage of such a favorable feeling in his mistress.

—Count Bussy-Rabutin, *Histoires Amoureuses des Gaules*

Interpretation. Count Grammont knew that most would-be seducers give up too easily, mistaking capriciousness or apparent coolness as a sign of a genuine lack of interest. In fact it can mean many things: perhaps the person is testing you, wondering if you are really serious. Prickly behavior is exactly this kind of test—if you give up at the first sign of difficulty, you obviously do not want them that much. Or it could be that they themselves are uncertain about you, or are trying to choose between you and someone else. In any event, it is absurd to give up. One incontrovertible demonstration of how far you are willing to go will overwhelm all doubts. It will also defeat your rivals, since most people are timid, worried about making fools of themselves, and so rarely risk anything.

When dealing with difficult or resistant targets, it is usually best to improvise, the way Grammont did. If your action seems sudden and a surprise, it will make them more emotional, loosen them up. A little roundabout accumulation of information—a little spying—is always a good idea. Most important is the spirit in which you enact your proof. If you are lighthearted and playful, if you make the target laugh, proving yourself and amusing them at the same time, it won't matter if you mess up, or if they see you have employed a little trickery. They will give in to the pleasant mood you have created. Notice that the count never whined or grew angry or defensive. All he had to do was pull back the curtain and reveal the duke walking his horse, melting de l'Orme's resistance with laughter. In one well-executed act, he showed what he would do for a night of her favors.

To become a lady's vassal . . . the troubadour was expected to pass through four stages, i.e.: aspirant, supplicant, postulant, and lover. When he had attained the last stage of amorous initiation he made a vow of fidelity and this homage was sealed by a kiss. • In this idealistic form of courtly love reserved for the aristocratic elite of chivalry, the phenomenon of love was considered to be a state

2. Pauline Bonaparte, the sister of Napoleon, had so many affairs with different men over the years that doctors were afraid for her health. She could not stay with one man for more than a few weeks; novelty was her only pleasure. After Napoleon married her off to Prince Camillo Borghese, in 1803, her affairs only multiplied. And so, when she met the dashing Major Jules de Canouville, in 1810, everyone assumed the affair would last no longer than the others. Of course the major was a decorated soldier, well educated, an accomplished dancer, and one of the most handsome men in the army. But Pauline, thirty years old at the time, had had affairs with dozens of men who could have matched that résumé.

A few days after the affair began, the imperial dentist arrived chez Pauline. A toothache had been causing her sleepless nights, and the dentist saw he would have to pull out the bad tooth right then and there. No painkillers were used at the time, and as the man began to take out his various instruments, Pauline grew terrified. Despite the pain of the tooth, she changed her mind and refused to have it pulled.

Major Canouville was lounging on a couch in a silken robe. Taking all this in, he tried to encourage her to have it done: "A moment or two of pain and it's over forever. . . . A child could go through with it and not utter a sound." "I'd like to see you do it," she said. Canouville got up, went over to the dentist, chose a tooth in the back of his own mouth, and ordered that it be pulled. A perfectly good tooth was extracted, and Canouville barely batted an eyelash. After this, not only did Pauline let the dentist do his job, her opinion of Canouville changed: no man had ever done anything like this for her before.

The affair had been going to last but a few weeks; now it stretched on. Napoleon was not pleased. Pauline was a married woman; short affairs were allowed, but a deep attachment was embarrassing. He sent Canouville to Spain, to deliver a message to a general there. The mission would take weeks, and in the meantime Pauline would find someone else.

Canouville, though, was not your average lover. Riding day and night, without stopping to eat or sleep, he arrived in Salamanca within a few days. There he found that he could proceed no farther, since communications had been cut off, and so, without waiting for further orders, he rode back to Paris, without an escort, through enemy territory. He could meet with Pauline only briefly; Napoleon sent him right back to Spain. It was months before he was finally allowed to return, but when he did, Pauline immediately resumed her affair with him—an unheard-of act of loyalty on her part. This time Napoleon sent Canouville to Germany and finally to Russia, where he died bravely in battle in 1812. He was the only lover Pauline ever waited for, and the only one she ever mourned.

Interpretation. In seduction, the time often comes when the target has begun to fall for you, but suddenly pulls back. Your motives have begun to

of grace, while the initiation that followed, and the final sealing of the pact—or equivalent of the knightly accolade—were linked with the rest of a nobleman's training and valorous exploits. The hallmarks of a true lover and of a perfect knight were almost identical. The lover was bound to serve and obey his lady as a knight served his lord. In both cases the pledge was of a sacred nature.

—NINA EPTON, *LOVE AND THE FRENCH*

In one of the goodly towns of the kingdom of France there dwelt a nobleman of good birth, who attended the schools that he might learn how virtue and honor are to be acquired among virtuous men. But although he was so accomplished that at the age of seventeen or eighteen years he was, as it were, both precept and example to others, Love failed not to add his lesson to the rest; and, that he might be the better harkened to and received, concealed himself in the face and the eyes of the fairest lady in the whole country round, who had come to the city in order to advance a suit-at-law. But before Love sought to vanquish the gentleman by means of this lady's beauty, he had first won her heart by letting her see the perfections of this young lord; for in good looks, grace, sense and excellence of speech he was surpassed by none. • You, who know what speedy way is made by the fire of love when once it fastens on the heart and fancy, will

seem dubious—perhaps all you are after is sexual favors, or power, or money. Most people are insecure and doubts like these can ruin the seductive illusion. In the case of Pauline Bonaparte, she was quite accustomed to using men for pleasure, and she knew perfectly well that she was being used in turn. She was totally cynical. But people often use cynicism to cover up insecurity. Pauline's secret anxiety was that none of her lovers had ever really loved her—that all of them to a man had really just wanted sex or political favors from her. When Canouville showed, through concrete actions, the sacrifices he would make for her—his tooth, his career, his life—he transformed a deeply selfish woman into a devoted lover. Not that her response was completely unselfish: his deeds were a boost to her vanity. If she could inspire these actions from him, she must be worth it. But if he was going to appeal to the noble side of her nature, she had to rise to that level as well, and prove herself by remaining loyal to him.

Making your deed as dashing and chivalrous as possible will elevate the seduction to a new level, stir up deep emotions, and conceal any ulterior motives you may have. The sacrifices you are making must be visible; talking about them, or explaining what they have cost you, will seem like bragging. Lose sleep, fall ill, lose valuable time, put your career on the line, spend more money than you can afford. You can exaggerate all this for effect, but don't get caught boasting about it or feeling sorry for yourself: cause yourself pain and let them see it. Since almost everyone else in the world seems to have an angle, your noble and selfless deed will be irresistible.

3. Throughout the 1890s and into the early twentieth century, Gabriele D'Annunzio was considered one of Italy's premier novelists and playwrights. Yet many Italians could not stand the man. His writing was florid, and in person he seemed full of himself, overdramatic—riding horses naked on the beach, pretending to be a Renaissance man, and more of the kind. His novels were often about war, and about the glory of facing and defeating death—an entertaining subject for someone who had never actually done so. And so, at the start of World War I, no one was surprised that D'Annunzio led the call for Italy to side with the Allies and enter the fray. Everywhere you turned, there he was, giving a speech in favor of war—a campaign that succeeded in 1915, when Italy finally declared war on Germany and Austria. D'Annunzio's role so far had been completely predictable. But what did surprise the Italian public was what this fifty-two-year-old man did next: he joined the army. He had never served in the military, boats made him seasick, but he could not be dissuaded. Eventually the authorities gave him a post in a cavalry division, hoping to keep him out of combat.

Italy had little experience in war, and its military was somewhat chaotic. The generals somehow lost track of D'Annunzio—who, in any

readily imagine that between two subjects so perfect as these it knew little pause until it had them at its will, and had so filled them with its clear light, that thought, wish, and speech were all aflame with it. Youth, begetting fear in the young lord, led him to urge his suit with all the gentleness imaginable; but she, being conquered by love, had no need of force to win her. Nevertheless, shame, which tarries with ladies as long as it can, for some time restrained her from declaring her mind. But at last the heart's fortress, which is honor's abode, was shattered in such sort that the poor lady consented to that which she had never been minded to refuse. • In order, however, to make trial of her lover's patience, constancy, and love, she granted him what he sought on a very hard condition, assuring him that if he fulfilled it she would love him perfectly forever; whereas, if he failed in it, he would certainly never win her as long as he lived. And the condition was this: she would be willing to talk with him, both being in bed together, clad in their linen only, but he was to ask nothing more from her than words and kisses. • He, thinking there was no joy to be compared to that which she promised him, agreed to the proposal, and that evening the promise was kept; in such wise that, despite all the caresses she bestowed on him and the temptations that beset him, he would not break his oath. And albeit his torment seemed to him no less than that of Purgatory,

case, had decided to leave his cavalry division and form units of his own. (He was an artist, after all, and could not be subjected to army discipline.) Calling himself *Commandante*, he overcame his habitual seasickness and directed a series of daring raids, leading groups of motorboats in the middle of the night into Austrian harbors and firing torpedoes at anchored ships. He also learned how to fly, and began to lead dangerous sorties. In August of 1915, he flew over the city of Trieste, then in enemy hands, and dropped Italian flags and thousands of pamphlets containing a message of hope, written in his inimitable style: "The end of your martyrdom is at hand! The dawn of your joy is imminent. From the heights of heaven, on the wings of Italy, I throw you this pledge, this message from my heart." He flew at altitudes unheard of at the time, and through thick enemy fire. The Austrians put a price on his head.

On a mission in 1916, D'Annunzio fell against his machine gun, permanently injuring one eye and seriously damaging the other. Told his flying days were over, he convalesced in his home in Venice. At the time, the most beautiful and fashionable woman in Italy was generally considered to be the Countess Morosini, former mistress of the German Kaiser. Her palace was on the Grand Canal, opposite the home of D'Annunzio. Now she found herself besieged by letters and poems from the writer-soldier, mixing details of his flying exploits with declarations of his love. In the middle of air raids on Venice, he would cross the canal, barely able to see out of one eye, to deliver his latest poem. D'Annunzio was much beneath Morosini's station, a mere writer, but his willingness to brave anything on her behalf won her over. The fact that his reckless behavior could get him killed any day only hastened the seduction.

D'Annunzio ignored the doctors' advice and returned to flying, leading even more daring raids than before. By the end of the war, he was Italy's most decorated hero. Now, wherever in the nation he appeared, the public filled the piazzas to hear his speeches. After the war, he led a march on Fiume, on the Adriatic coast. In the negotiations to settle the war, Italians believed they should have been awarded this city, but the Allies had not agreed. D'Annunzio's forces took over the city and the poet became a leader, ruling Fiume for more than a year as an autonomous republic. By then, everyone had forgotten about his less-than-glorious past as a decadent writer. Now he could do no wrong.

Interpretation. The appeal of seduction is that of being separated from our normal routines, experiencing the thrill of the unknown. Death is the ultimate unknown. In periods of chaos, confusion, and death—the plagues that swept Europe in the Middle Ages, the Terror of the French Revolution, the air raids on London during World War II—people often let go of their usual caution and do things they never would otherwise. They experience a kind of delirium. There is something immensely seductive about

yet was his love so great and his hope so strong, sure as he felt of the ceaseless continuance of the love he had thus painfully won, that he preserved his patience and rose from beside her without having done anything contrary to her expressed wish. • The lady was, I think, more astonished than pleased by such virtue; and giving no heed to the honor, patience, and faithfulness her lover had shown in the keeping of his oath, she forthwith suspected that his love was not so great as she had thought, or else that he had found her less pleasing than he had expected. • She therefore resolved, before keeping her promise, to make a further trial of the love he bore her; and to this end she begged him to talk to a girl in her service, who was younger than herself and very beautiful, bidding him make love speeches to her, so that those who saw him come so often to the house might think that it was for the sake of this damsel and not of herself. • The young lord, feeling sure that his own love was returned in equal measure, was wholly obedient to her commands, and for love of her compelled himself to make love to the girl; and she, finding him so handsome and well-spoken, believed his lies more than other truth, and loved him as much as though she herself were greatly loved by him. • The mistress finding that matters were thus well advanced, albeit the young lord did not cease to claim her promise, granted him permission to come and see her at one hour after midnight, saying that after

danger, about heading into the unknown. Show that you have a reckless streak and a daring nature, that you lack the usual fear of death, and you are instantly fascinating to the bulk of humanity.

What you are proving in this instance is not how you feel toward another person but something about yourself: you are willing to go out on a limb. You are not just another talker and braggart. It is a recipe for instant charisma. Any political figure—Churchill, de Gaulle, Kennedy—who has proven himself on the battlefield has an unmatchable appeal. Many had thought of D'Annunzio as a foppish womanizer; his experience in the war gave him a heroic sheen, a Napoleonic aura. In fact he had always been an effective seducer, but now he was even more devilishly appealing. You do not necessarily have to risk death, but putting yourself in its vicinity will give you a seductive charge. (It is often best to do this some way into the seduction, making it come as a pleasant surprise.) You are willing to enter the unknown. No one is more seductive than the person who has had a brush with death. People will be drawn to you; perhaps they are hoping that some of your adventurous spirit will rub off on them.

4. According to one version of the Arthurian legend, the great knight Sir Lancelot once caught a glimpse of Queen Guinevere, King Arthur's wife, and that glimpse was enough—he fell madly in love. And so when word reached him that Queen Guinevere had been kidnapped by an evil knight, Lancelot did not hesitate—he forgot his other chivalrous tasks and hurried in pursuit. His horse collapsed from the chase, so he continued on foot. Finally it seemed that he was close, but he was exhausted and could go no farther. A horse-driven cart passed by; the cart was filled with loathsome-looking men shackled together. In those days it was the tradition to place criminals—murderers, traitors, cowards, thieves—in such a cart, which then passed through every street in town so that people could see it. Once you had ridden in the cart, you lost all feudal rights for the rest of your life. The cart was such a dreadful symbol that seeing an empty one made you shiver and give the sign of the cross. Even so, Sir Lancelot accosted the cart's driver, a dwarf: "In the name of God, tell me if you've seen my lady the queen pass by this way?" "If you want to get into this cart I'm driving," said the dwarf, "by tomorrow you'll know what has become of the queen." Then he drove the cart onward. Lancelot hesitated for but two of the horse's steps, then ran after it and climbed in.

Wherever the cart went, townspeople heckled it. They were most curious about the knight among the passengers. What was his crime? How will he be put to death—flayed? Drowned? Burned upon a fire of thorns? Finally the dwarf let him get out, without a word as to the whereabouts of the queen. To make matters worse, no one now would go near or talk to Lancelot, for he had been in the cart. He kept on chasing the queen, and all along the way he was cursed at, spat upon, challenged by other knights. He

having so fully tested the love and obedience he had shown towards her, it was but just that he should be rewarded for his long patience. Of the lover's joy on hearing this you need have no doubt, and he failed not to arrive at the appointed time. • But the lady, still wishing to try the strength of his love, had said to her beautiful damsel—"I am well aware of the love a certain nobleman bears to you, and I think you are no less in love with him; and I feel so much pity for you both, that I have resolved to afford you time and place that you may converse together at your ease." • The damsel was so enchanted that she could not conceal her longings, but answered that she would not fail to be present. • In obedience, therefore, to her mistress's counsel and command, she undressed herself and lay down on a handsome bed, in a room the door of which the lady left half open, whilst within she set a light so that the maiden's beauty might be clearly seen. Then she herself pretended to go away, but hid herself near to the bed so carefully that she could not be seen. • Her poor lover, thinking to find her according to her promise, failed not to enter the room as softly as he could, at the appointed hour; and after he had shut the door and put off his garments and fur shoes, he got into the bed, where he looked to find what he desired. But no sooner did he put out his arms to embrace her whom he believed to be his mistress, than the poor girl, believing him entirely her

had disgraced knighthood by riding in the cart. But no one could stop him or slow him down, and finally he discovered that the queen's kidnapper was the wicked Meleagant. He caught up with Meleagant and the two fought a duel. Still weak from the chase, Lancelot seemed to be near defeat, but when word reached him that the queen was watching the battle, he recovered his strength and was on the verge of killing Meleagant when a truce was called. Guinevere was handed over to him.

Lancelot could hardly contain his joy at the thought of finally being in his lady's presence. But to his shock, she seemed angry, and would not look at her rescuer. She told Meleagant's father, "Sire, in truth he has wasted his efforts. I shall always deny that I feel any gratitude toward him." Lancelot was mortified but he did not complain. Much later, after undergoing innumerable further trials, she finally relented and they became lovers. One day he asked her: when she had been abducted by Meleagant, had she heard the story of the cart, and how he had disgraced knighthood? Was that why she had treated him so coldly that day? The queen replied, "By delaying for two steps you showed your unwillingness to climb into it. That, to tell the truth, is why I didn't wish to see you or speak with you."

Interpretation. The opportunity to do your selfless deed often comes upon you suddenly. You have to show your worth in an instant, right there on the spot. It could be a rescue situation, a gift you could make or a favor you could do, a sudden request to drop everything and come to their aid. What matters most is not whether you act rashly, make a mistake, and do something foolish, but that you seem to act on their behalf without thought for yourself or the consequences.

At moments like these, hesitation, even for a few seconds, can ruin all the hard work of your seduction, revealing you as self-absorbed, unchivalrous, and cowardly. This, at any rate, is the moral of Chrétien de Troyes's twelfth-century version of the story of Lancelot. Remember: not only what you do matters, but how you do it. If you are naturally self-absorbed, learn to disguise it. React as spontaneously as possible, exaggerating the effect by seeming flustered, overexcited, even foolish—love has driven you to that point. If you have to jump into the cart for Guinevere's sake, make sure she sees that you do it without the slightest hesitation.

5. In Rome sometime around 1531, word spread of a sensational young woman named Tullia d'Aragona. By the standards of the period, Tullia was not a classic beauty; she was tall and thin, at a time when the plump and voluptuous woman was considered the ideal. And she lacked the cloying, giggling manner of most young girls who wanted masculine attention. No, her quality was nobler. Her Latin was perfect, she could discuss the latest literature, she played the lute and sang. In other words, she was a novelty, and since that was all most men were looking for, they began to visit her in

own, had her arms round his neck, speaking to him the while in such loving words and with so beautiful a countenance, that there is not a hermit so holy but he would have forgotten his beads for love of her. • But when the gentleman recognized her with both eye and ear, and found he was not with her for whose sake he had so greatly suffered, the love that had made him get so quickly into the bed, made him rise from it still more quickly. And in anger equally with mistress and damsel, he said—"Neither your folly nor the malice of her who put you there can make me other than I am. But do you try to be an honest woman, for you shall never lose that good name through me." • So saying he rushed out of the room in the greatest wrath imaginable, and it was long before he returned to see his mistress. However love, which is never without hope, assured him that the greater and more manifest his constancy was proved to be by all these trials, the longer and more delightful would be his bliss. • The lady, who had seen and heard all that passed, was so delighted and amazed at beholding the depth and constancy of his love, that she was impatient to see him again in order to ask his forgiveness for the sorrow that she had caused him to endure. And as soon as she could meet with him, she failed not to address him in such excellent and pleasant words, that he not only forgot all his troubles but even deemed them very fortunate, seeing that their issue was to the glory of his constancy and the perfect

great numbers. She had a lover, a diplomat, and the thought that one man had won her physical favors drove them all mad. Her male visitors began to compete for her attention, writing poems in her honor, vying to become her favorite. None of them succeeded, but they kept on trying.

assurance of his love, the fruit of which he enjoyed from that time as fully as he could desire.

—Queen Margaret of Navarre, *The Heptameron*, quoted in *The Vice Anthology*, edited by Richard Davenport-Hines

Of course there were some who were offended by her, stating publicly that she was no more than a high-class whore. They repeated the rumor (perhaps true) that she had made older men dance while she played the lute, and if their dancing pleased her, they could hold her in their arms. To Tullia's faithful followers, all of noble birth, this was slander. They wrote a document that was distributed far and wide: "Our honored mistress, the well-born and honorable lady Tullia d'Aragona, doth surpass all ladies of the past, present, or future by her dazzling qualities. . . . Anyone who refuses to conform to this statement is hereby charged to enter the lists with one of the undersigned knights, who will convince him in the customary manner."

Tullia left Rome in 1535, going first to Venice, where the poet Tasso became her lover, and eventually to Ferrara, which was then perhaps the most civilized court in Italy. And what a sensation she caused there. Her voice, her singing, even her poems were praised far and wide. She opened a literary academy devoted to ideas of freethinking. She called herself a muse and, as in Rome, a group of young men collected around her. They would follow her around the city, carving her name in trees, writing sonnets in her honor, and singing them to anyone who would listen.

One young nobleman was driven to distraction by this cult of adoration: it seemed that everyone loved Tullia but no one received her love in return. Determined to steal her away and marry her, this young man tricked her into allowing him to visit her at night. He proclaimed his undying devotion, showered her with jewels and presents, and asked for her hand. She refused. He pulled out a knife, she still refused, and so he stabbed himself. He lived, but now Tullia's reputation was even greater than before: not even money could buy her favors, or so it seemed. As the years went by and her beauty faded, some poet or intellectual would always come to her defense and protect her. Few of them ever pondered the reality: that Tullia was indeed a courtesan, one of the most popular and well paid in the profession.

A soldier lays siege to cities, a lover to girls' houses, \ The one assaults city gates, the other front doors. \ Love, like war, is a toss-up. The defeated can recover, \ While some you might think invincible collapse; \ So if you've got love written off as an easy option \ You'd better think twice. Love calls \ For guts and initiative. Great Achilles sulks for Briseis— \ Quick, Trojans, smash through the Argive wall! \ Hector went into battle from Andromache's embraces \ Helmeted by his wife. \ Agamemnon himself, the Supremo, was struck into raptures \ At the sight of Cassandra's tumbled hair; \ Even Mars was caught on the job, felt the blacksmith's meshes— \ Heaven's best scandal in years. Then take \ My own case. I was idle, born to leisure en deshabille, \ Mind softened by lazy scribbling in the shade. \ But love for a pretty girl soon drove the sluggard \ To action, made him join up. \ And just look at me now—fighting fit, dead keen on night exercises: \ If you want a cure for slackness, fall in love!

—Ovid, *The Amores*, translated by Peter Green

Interpretation. All of us have defects of some sort. Some of these we are born with, and cannot help. Tullia had many such defects. Physically she was not the Renaissance ideal. Also, her mother had been a courtesan, and she was illegitimate. Yet the men who fell under her spell did not care. They were too distracted by her image—the image of an elevated woman, a woman you would have to fight over to win. Her pose came straight out of the Middle Ages, the days of knights and troubadours. Then, a woman, most often married, was able to control the power dynamic between the sexes by withholding her favors until the knight somehow proved his worth and the sincerity of his sentiments. He could be sent on a quest, or made to live among lepers, or compete in a possibly fatal joust for her honor. And this he had to do without complaint. Although the days of the troubadour are long gone, the pattern remains: a man actually loves to be able to prove himself, to be challenged, to compete, to undergo tests and trials and emerge victorious. He has a masochistic streak; a part of him loves pain. And strangely enough, the more a woman asks for, the worthier she seems. A woman who is easy to get cannot be worth much.

Make people compete for your attention, make them prove themselves in some way, and you will find them rising to the challenge. The heat of seduction is raised by such challenges—show me that you *really* love me. When one person (of either sex) rises to the occasion, often the other person is now expected to do the same, and the seduction heightens. By making people prove themselves, too, you raise your value and cover up your defects. Your targets are too busy trying to prove themselves to notice your blemishes and faults.

Symbol: *The Tournament. On the field, with its bright pennants and caparisoned horses, the lady looks on as knights fight for her hand. She has heard them declare love on bended knee, their endless songs and pretty promises. They are all good at such things. But then the trumpet sounds and the combat begins. In the tournament there can be no faking or hesitation. The knight she chooses must have blood on his face, and a few broken limbs.*

Reversal

When trying to prove that you are worthy of your target, remember that every target sees things differently. A show of physical prowess will not impress someone who does not value physical prowess; it will just show that you are after attention, flaunting yourself. Seducers must adapt their way of proving themselves to the doubts and weaknesses of the seduced. For some, fine words are better proofs than daredevil deeds, particularly if they are written down. With these people show your sentiments in a letter—a different kind of physical proof, and one with more poetic appeal than some showy bit of action. Know your target well, and aim your seductive evidence at the source of their doubts or resistance.

17
Effect a Regression

People who have experienced a certain kind of pleasure in the past will try to repeat or relive it. The deepest-rooted and most pleasurable memories are usually those from earliest childhood, and are often unconsciously associated with a parental figure. Bring your targets back to that point by placing yourself in the oedipal triangle and positioning them as the needy child. Unaware of the cause of their emotional response, they will fall in love with you. Alternatively, you too can regress, letting them play the role of the protecting, nursing parent. In either case you are offering the ultimate fantasy: the chance to have an intimate relationship with mommy or daddy, son or daughter.

The Erotic Regression

As adults we tend to overvalue our childhood. In their dependency and powerlessness, children genuinely suffer, yet when we get older we conveniently forget about that and sentimentalize the supposed paradise we have left behind. We forget the pain and remember only the pleasure. Why? Because the responsibilities of adult life are a burden so oppressive at times that we secretly yearn for the dependency of childhood, for that person who looked after our every need, assumed our cares and worries. This daydream of ours has a strong erotic component, for the child's feeling of being dependent on the parent is charged with sexual undertones. Give people a sensation similar to that protected, dependent feeling of childhood and they will project all kinds of fantasies onto you, including feelings of love or sexual attraction that they will attribute to something else. We won't admit it, but we long to regress, to shed our adult exterior and vent the childish emotions that linger beneath the surface.

Early in his career, Sigmund Freud confronted a strange problem: many of his female patients were falling in love with him. He thought he knew what was happening: encouraged by Freud, the patient would delve into her childhood, which of course was the source of her illness or neurosis. She would talk about her relationship with her father, her earliest experiences of tenderness and love, and also of neglect and abandonment. The process would stir up powerful emotions and memories. In a way, she would be transported back into her childhood. Intensifying this effect was the fact that Freud himself said little and made himself a little cold and distant, although he seemed to be caring—in other words, quite like the traditional father figure. Meanwhile the patient was lying on a couch, in a helpless or passive position, so that the situation duplicated the roles of parent and child. Eventually she would begin to direct some of the confused emotions she was dealing with toward Freud himself. Unaware of what was happening, she would relate to him as to her father. She would regress and fall in love. Freud called this phenomenon "transference," and it would become an active part of his therapy. By getting patients to transfer some of their repressed feelings onto the therapist, he would bring their problems into the open, where they could be dealt with on a conscious level.

The transference effect was so potent, though, that Freud was often unable to move his patients past their infatuation. In fact transference is a powerful way of creating an emotional attachment—the goal of any seduc-

[In Japan,] much in the traditional way of child-rearing seems to foster passive dependence. The child is rarely left alone, day or night, for it usually sleeps with the mother. When it goes out the child is not pushed ahead in a pram, to face the world alone, but is tightly bound to the mother's back in a snug cocoon. When the mother bows, the child does too, so the social graces are acquired automatically while feeling the mother's heartbeat. Thus emotional security tends to depend almost entirely on the physical presence of the mother. • . . . Children learn that a show of passive dependence is the best way to get favors as well as affection. There is a verb for this in Japanese: amaeru, *translated in the dictionary as "to presume upon another's love; to play the baby." According to the psychiatrist Doi Takeo this is the main key to understanding the Japanese personality. It goes on in adult life too: juniors do it to seniors in companies, or any other group, women do it to men, men do it to their*

mothers, and sometimes wives. . . . • . . . A magazine called Young Lady *featured an article (January 1982) on "how to make ourselves beautiful." How, in other words, to attract men. An American or European magazine would then go on to tell the reader how to be sexually desirable, no doubt suggesting various puffs, creams, and sprays. Not so with* Young Lady. *"The most attractive women," it informs us, "are women full of maternal love. Women without maternal love are the types men never want to marry. . . . One has to look at men through the eyes of a mother."*

—IAN BURUMA, *BEHIND THE MASK: ON SEXUAL DEMONS, SACRED MOTHERS, TRANSVESTITES, GANGSTERS, DRIFTERS AND OTHER JAPANESE CULTURAL HEROES*

tion. The method has infinite applications outside psychoanalysis. To practice it in real life, you need to play the therapist, encouraging people to talk about their childhood. Most of us are only too happy to oblige; and our memories are so vivid and emotional that a part of us regresses just in talking about our early years. Also, in the course of talking, little secrets slip out: we reveal all kinds of valuable information about our weaknesses and our mental makeup, information you must attend to and remember. Do not take your targets' words at face value; they will often sugarcoat or overdramatize events in childhood. But pay attention to their tone of voice, to any nervous tics as they talk, and particularly to anything they do not want to talk about, anything they deny or that makes them emotional. Many statements actually mean their opposite: should they say they hated their father, for instance, you can be sure that they are hiding a lot of disappointment—that they actually loved their father only too much, and perhaps never quite got what they wanted from him. Listen closely for recurring themes and stories. Most important, learn to analyze emotional responses and see what lies behind them.

While they talk, maintain the therapist's pose—attentive but quiet, making occasional, nonjudgmental comments. Be caring yet distant—somewhat blank, in fact—and they will begin to transfer emotions and project fantasies onto you. With the information you have gathered about their childhood, and the trusting bond you have forged, you can now begin to effect the regression. Perhaps you have uncovered a powerful attachment to a parent, a sibling, a teacher, or any early infatuation, a person who casts a shadow over their present lives. Knowing what it was about this person that affected them so powerfully, you can now take over that role. Or perhaps you have learned of an immense gap in their childhood—a neglectful father, for instance. You act like that parent now, but you replace the original neglect with the attention and affection that the real parent never supplied. Everyone has unfinished business from childhood—disappointments, lacks, painful memories. Finish what is unfinished. Discover what your target never got and you have the ingredients for a deep-rooted seduction.

I have stressed the fact that the beloved person is a substitute for the ideal ego. Two people who love each other are interchanging their ego-ideals. That they love each other means they love the ideal of themselves in the other one. There would be no love on earth if this phantom were not there. We fall in love because we cannot attain the image that is our better self and the best of our self. From this concept it is obvious that love itself is only possible on a certain cultural level or after a certain phase in the development of the personality has been reached. The creation of an ego-ideal itself marks human progress. When people are entirely satisfied

The key is not just to talk about memories—that is weak. What you want is to get people to act out in their present old issues from their past, without their being aware of what is happening. The regressions you can effect fall into four main types.

The Infantile Regression. The first bond—the bond between a mother and her infant—is the most powerful one. Unlike other animals, human babies have a long period of helplessness during which they are dependent on their mother, creating an attachment that influences the rest of their lives. The key to effecting this regression is to reproduce the sense of unconditional love a mother has for her child. Never judge your targets—let them do whatever they want, including behaving badly; at the same time surround them with loving attention, smother them with comfort. A part of them will regress to those earliest years when their mother took care of everything and rarely left them alone. This works on almost everyone, for unconditional love is the rarest and most treasured form. You do not even have to tailor your behavior to anything specific in their childhood; most of us have experienced this kind of attention. Meanwhile, create atmospheres that reinforce the feeling you are generating—warm environments, playful activities, bright, happy colors.

with their actual selves, love is impossible. • The transfer of the ego-ideal to a person is the most characteristic trait of love.

—THEODOR REIK, *OF LOVE AND LUST*

The Oedipal Regression. After the bond between mother and child comes the oedipal triangle of mother, father, and child. This triangle forms during the period of the child's earliest erotic fantasies. A boy wants his mother to himself, a girl does the same with her father, but they never quite have it that way, for a parent will always have competing connections to a spouse or to other adults. Unconditional love has gone; now, inevitably, the parent must sometimes deny what the child desires. Transport your victims back to this period. Play a parental role, be loving, but also sometimes scold and instill some discipline. Children actually love a little discipline—it makes them feel that the adult cares about them. And adult children too will be thrilled if you mix your tenderness with a little toughness and punishment.

Unlike infantile regression, oedipal regression must be tailored to your target. It depends on the information you have gathered. Without knowing enough, you might treat a person like a child, scolding them now and then, only to discover that you are stirring up ugly memories—they had too much discipline as child. Or you might stir up memories of a parent they loathed, and they will transfer those feelings to you. Do not go ahead with the regression until you have learned everything you can about their childhood—what they had too much of, what they lacked, and so on. If the target was strongly attached to a parent, but that attachment was partially negative, the oedipal regression strategy can still be quite effective. We always feel ambivalent toward a parent; even as we love them, we resent having had to depend on them. Don't worry about stirring up these ambivalences, which don't keep us from being tied to our parents. Remember to include an erotic component in your parental behavior. Now your targets are not only getting their mother or father all to themselves, they are getting something more, something previously forbidden but now allowed.

I gave [Sylphide] the eyes of one girl in the village, the fresh complexion of another. The portraits of great ladies of the time of Francis I, Henry IV, and Louis XIV, hanging in our drawing room, lent me other features, and I even borrowed beauties from the pictures of the Madonna in the churches. This magic creature followed me invisibly everywhere, I conversed with her as if with a real person; she changed her appearance according to the degree of my madness; Aphrodite without a veil, Diana shrouded in azure and rose, Thalia in a laughing mask, Hebe with the goblet of youth—or she became a fairy, giving me dominion over nature. . . . The delusion lasted two whole years, in the course of which my soul attained the highest peak of exaltation.

—CHATEAUBRIAND, *MEMOIRS FROM BEYOND THE GRAVE*, QUOTED IN FRIEDRICH SIEBURG, *CHATEAUBRIAND*, TRANSLATED BY VIOLET M. MACDONALD

The Ego Ideal Regression. As children, we often form an ideal figure out of our dreams and ambitions. First, that ideal figure is the person we want to be. We imagine ourselves as brave adventurers, romantic figures. Then, in our adolescence, we turn our attention to others, often projecting our ideals onto them. The first boy or girl we fall in love with may seem to have the ideal qualities we wanted for ourselves, or else may make us feel that we can play that ideal role in relation to them. Most of us carry these ideals around with us, buried just below the surface. We are secretly disappointed in how much we have had to compromise, how far below the ideal we have fallen as we have gotten older. Make your targets feel they are living out this youthful ideal, and coming closer to being the person they wanted to be, and you will effect a different kind of regression, creating a feeling reminiscent of adolescence. The relationship between you and the seduced is in this instance more equal than in the previous kinds of regressions—more like the affection between siblings. In fact the ideal is often modeled on a brother or sister. To create this effect, strive to reproduce the intense, innocent mood of a youthful infatuation.

The Reverse Parental Regression. Here you are the one to regress: you deliberately play the role of the cute, adorable, yet also sexually charged child. Older people always find younger people incredibly seductive. In the presence of youth, they feel a little of their own youth return; but they are in fact older, and mixed into the invigoration they feel in young people's company is the pleasure of playing the mother or father to them. If a child has erotic feelings toward a parent, feelings that are quickly repressed, the parent must deal with the same problem in reverse. Assume the role of the child in relation to your targets, however, and they get to act out some of those repressed erotic sentiments. The strategy may seem to call for a difference in age, but this is actually not critical. Marilyn Monroe's exaggerated little-girl qualities worked just fine on men her age. Emphasizing a weakness or vulnerability on your part will give the target a chance to play the protector.

Some Examples

1. The parents of Victor Hugo separated shortly after the novelist was born, in 1802. Hugo's mother, Sophie, had been carrying on an affair with her husband's superior officer, a general. She took the three Hugo boys away from their father and went off to Paris to raise them on her own. Now the boys led a tumultuous life, featuring bouts of poverty, frequent moves, and their mother's continued affair with the general. Of all the boys, Victor was the most attached to his mother, adopting all her ideas and pet peeves, particularly her hatred of his father. But with all the turmoil in his childhood he never felt he got enough love and attention from the mother he adored. When she died, in 1821, poor and debt-ridden, he was devastated.

The following year Hugo married his childhood sweetheart, Adèle, who physically resembled his mother. It was a happy marriage for a while, but soon Adèle came to resemble his mother in more ways than one: in 1832, he discovered that she was having an affair with the French literary critic Sainte-Beuve, who also happened to be Hugo's best friend at the time. Hugo was a celebrated writer by now, but he was not the calculating type. He generally wore his heart on his sleeve. Yet he could not confide in anyone about Adèle's affair; it was too humiliating. His only solution was to have affairs of his own, with actresses, courtesans, married women. Hugo had a prodigious appetite, sometimes visiting three different women in the same day.

Near the end of 1832, production began on one of Hugo's plays, and he was to supervise the casting. A twenty-six-year-old actress named Juliette Drouet auditioned for one of the smaller roles. Normally quite adroit with the ladies, Hugo found himself stuttering in Juliette's presence. She was quite simply the most beautiful woman he had ever seen, and this and her composed manner intimidated him. Naturally, Juliette won the part. He found himself thinking about her all the time. She always seemed to be surrounded by a group of adoring men. Clearly she was not interested in him, or so he thought. One evening, though, after a performance of the play, he followed her home, to find that she was neither angry nor surprised—indeed she invited him up to her apartment. He spent the night, and soon he was spending almost every night there.

Hugo was happy again. To his delight, Juliette quit her career in the theater, dropped her former friends, and learned to cook. She had loved fancy clothes and social affairs; now she became Hugo's secretary, rarely leaving the apartment in which he had established her and seeming to live only for his visits. After a while, however, Hugo returned to his old ways and started to have little affairs on the side. She did not complain—as long as she remained the one woman he kept returning to. And Hugo had in fact grown quite dependent on her.

In 1843, Hugo's beloved daughter died in an accident and he sank into a depression. The only way he knew to get over his grief was to have an affair with someone new. And so, shortly thereafter, he fell in love with a young married aristocrat named Léonie d'Aunet. He began to see Juliette less and less. A few years later, Léonie, feeling certain she was the preferred one, gave him an ultimatum: stop seeing Juliette altogether, or it was over. Hugo refused. Instead he decided to stage a contest: he would continue to see both women, and in a few months his heart would tell him which one he preferred. Léonie was furious, but she had no choice. Her affair with Hugo had already ruined her marriage and her standing in society; she was dependent on him. Anyway, how could she lose—she was in the prime of life, whereas Juliette had gray hair by now. So she pretended to go along with this contest, but as time went on, she grew increasingly resentful about it, and complained. Juliette, on the other hand, behaved as if nothing had changed. Whenever he visited, she treated him as she always had, dropping everything to comfort and mother him.

The contest lasted several years. In 1851, Hugo was in trouble with Louis-Napoleon, the cousin of Napoleon Bonaparte and now the president of France. Hugo had attacked his dictatorial tendencies in the press, bitterly and perhaps recklessly, for Louis-Napoleon was a vengeful man. Fearing for the writer's life, Juliette managed to hide him in a friend's house and arranged for a false passport, a disguise, and safe passage to Brussels. Everything went according to plan; Juliette joined him a few days later, carrying his most valuable possessions. Clearly her heroic actions had won the contest for her.

And yet, after the novelty of Hugo's new life wore off, his affairs resumed. Finally, fearing for his health, and worried that she could no longer compete with yet another twenty-year-old coquette, Juliette made a calm but stern demand: no more women or she was leaving him. Taken completely by surprise, yet certain that she meant every word, Hugo broke down and sobbed. An old man by now, he got down on his knees and swore, on the Bible and then on a copy of his famous novel *Les Misérables,* that he would stray no more. Until Juliette's death, in 1883, her spell over him was complete.

Interpretation. Hugo's love life was determined by his relationship with his mother. He never felt she had loved him enough. Almost all the women he had affairs with bore a physical resemblance to her; somehow he would make up for her lack of love for him by sheer volume. When Juliette met him, she could not have known all this, but she must have sensed two things: he was extremely disappointed in his wife, and he had never really grown up. His emotional outbursts and his need for attention made him more a little boy than a man. She would gain ascendancy over him for the rest of his life by supplying the one thing he had never had: complete, unconditional mother-love.

Juliette never judged Hugo, or criticized him for his naughty ways. She lavished him with attention; visiting her was like returning to the womb. In her presence, in fact, he was more a little boy than ever. How could he refuse her a favor or ever leave her? And when she finally threatened to leave him, he was reduced to the state of a wailing infant crying for his mother. In the end she had total power over him.

Unconditional love is rare and hard to find, yet it is what we all crave, since we either experienced it once or wish we had. You do not have to go as far as Juliette Drouet; the mere hint of devoted attention, of accepting your lovers for who they are, of meeting their needs, will place them in an infantile position. A sense of dependency may frighten them a little, and they may feel an undercurrent of ambivalence, a need to assert themselves periodically, as Hugo did through his affairs. But their ties to you will be strong and they will keep coming back for more, bound by the illusion that they are recapturing the mother-love they had seemingly lost forever, or never had.

2. Around the turn of the twentieth century, Professor Mut, a schoolmaster at a college for young men in a small German town, began to develop a keen hatred of his students. Mut was in his late fifties, and had worked at the same school for many years. He taught Greek and Latin and was a distinguished classical scholar. He had always felt a need to impose discipline, but now it was getting ugly: the students were simply not interested in Homer anymore. They listened to bad music and only liked modern literature. Although they were rebellious, Mut considered them soft and undisciplined. He wanted to teach them a lesson and make their lives miserable; his usual way of dealing with their bouts of rowdiness was sheer bullying, and most often it worked.

One day a student Mut loathed—a haughty, well-dressed young man named Lohmann—stood up in class and said, "I can't go on working in this room, Professor. There is such a smell of mud." Mud was the boys' nickname for Professor Mut. The professor seized Lohmann by the arm, twisted it hard, then banished him from the room. He later noticed that Lohmann had left his exercise book behind, and thumbing through it he saw a paragraph about an actress named Rosa Fröhlich. A plot hatched in Mut's mind: he would catch Lohmann cavorting with this actress, no doubt a woman of ill repute, and would get the boy kicked out of school.

First he had to find out where she performed. He searched high and low, finally finding her name up outside a club called the Blue Angel. He went in. It was a smoke-filled place, full of the working-class types he looked down on. Rosa was onstage. She was singing a song; the way she looked everyone in the audience in the eye was rather brazen, but for some reason Mut found this disarming. He relaxed a little, had some wine. After her performance he made his way to her dressing room, determined to grill her about Lohmann. Once there he felt strangely uncomfortable, but he gathered up his courage, accused her of leading schoolboys astray, and threatened to get the police to close the place down. Rosa, however, was not intimidated. She turned all of Mut's sentences around: perhaps *he* was the one leading boys astray. Her tone was cajoling and teasing. Yes, Lohmann had bought her flowers and champagne—so what? No one had ever talked to Mut this way before; his authoritative tone usually made people give way. He should have felt offended: she was low class and a woman, and he was a schoolmaster, but she was talking to him as if they were equals. Instead, however, he neither got angry nor left—something compelled him to stay.

Now she was silent. She picked up a stocking and started to darn it, ignoring him; his eyes followed her every move, particularly the way she rubbed her bare knee. Finally he brought up Lohmann again, and the police. "You've no idea what this life's like," she said. "Everyone who comes here thinks he's the only pebble on the beach. If you don't give them what they want they threaten you with the police!" "I certainly regret having hurt a lady's feelings," he replied sheepishly. As she got up from her chair, their knees rubbed, and he felt a shiver up his spine. Now she was nice to him again, and poured him some more wine. She invited him to come back, then left abruptly to perform another number.

The next day he kept thinking about her words, her looks. Thinking about her while he was teaching gave him a kind of naughty thrill. That night he went back to the club, still determined to catch Lohmann in the act, and once again found himself in Rosa's dressing room, drinking wine and becoming strangely passive. She asked him to help her get dressed; that seemed quite an honor and he obliged her. Helping her with her corset and her makeup, he forgot about Lohmann. He felt he was being initiated into some new world. She pinched his cheeks and stroked his chin, and occasionally let him glimpse her bare leg as she rolled up a stocking.

Now Professor Mut showed up night after night, helping her dress, watching her perform, all with a strange kind of pride. He was there so often that Lohmann and his friends no longer showed up. He had taken their place—he was the one to bring her flowers, pay for her champagne, the one to serve her. Yes, an old man like himself had bested the youthful Lohmann, who thought himself so suave! He liked it when she stroked his chin, complimented him for doing things right, but he felt even more excited when she rebuked him, throwing a powder puff in his face or pushing him off a chair. It meant she liked him. And so, gradually, he began to pay for all her caprices. It cost him a pretty penny but kept her away from other men. Eventually he proposed to her. They married, and scandal ensued: he lost his job, and soon all his money; finally he landed in prison. To the very end, however, he could never get angry with Rosa. Instead he felt guilty: he had never done enough for her.

Interpretation. Professor Mut and Rosa Fröhlich are characters in the novel *The Blue Angel*, written by Heinrich Mann in 1905, and later made into a film starring Marlene Dietrich. Rosa's seduction of Mut follows the classic oedipal regression pattern. First, the woman treats the man the way a mother would treat a little boy. She scolds him, but the scolding is not threatening; it is tender, and has a teasing edge. Like a mother, she knows she is dealing with someone weak, who cannot help his naughty behavior. She mixes plenty of praise and approval in with her taunts. Once the man begins to regress, she adds physical excitement—some bodily contact to excite him, subtle sexual overtones. As a reward for his regression, the man may get the thrill of finally sleeping with his mother. But there is always an element of competition, which the mother figure must heighten. The man gets to possess her all on his own, something he could not do with father in the way, but he first has to win her away from others.

The key to this kind of regression is to see and treat your targets as children. Nothing about them intimidates you, no matter how much authority or social standing they have. Your manner makes it clear that you feel you are the stronger party. To accomplish this it may be helpful to imagine or visualize them as the children they once were; suddenly, powerful people do not seem so powerful and threatening when you regress them in your imagination. Keep in mind that certain types are more vulnerable to an oedipal regression. Look for those who, like Professor Mut, seem outwardly the most adult—straitlaced, serious, a little full of themselves. They are struggling to repress their regressive tendencies, overcompensating for their weaknesses. Often those who seem the most in command of themselves are the ripest for regression. In fact they are secretly longing for it, because their power, position, and responsibilities are more a burden than a pleasure.

3. Born in 1768, the French writer François René de Chateaubriand grew up in a medieval castle in Brittany. The castle was cold and gloomy, as if inhabited by the ghosts of its past. The family lived there in semiseclusion. Chateaubriand spent much of his time with his sister Lucile, and his attachment to her was strong enough that rumors of incest made the rounds. But when he was around fifteen, a new woman named Sylphide entered his life—a woman he created in his imagination, a composite of all the heroines, goddesses, and courtesans he had read about in books. He was constantly seeing her features in his mind, and hearing her voice. Soon she was taking walks with him, carrying on conversations. He imagined her innocent and exalted, yet they would sometimes do things that were not so innocent. He carried on this relationship for two whole years, until finally he left for Paris, and replaced Sylphide with women of flesh and blood.

The French public, weary after the terrors of the 1790s, greeted Chateaubriand's first books enthusiastically, sensing a new spirit in them. His novels were full of windswept castles, brooding heroes, and passionate heroines. Romanticism was in the air. Chateaubriand himself resembled the characters in his novels, and despite his rather unattractive appearance, women went wild over him—with him, they could escape their boring marriages and live out the kind of turbulent romance he wrote about. Chateaubriand's nickname was the Enchanter, and although he was married, and an ardent Catholic, the number of his affairs increased with the years. But he had a restless nature—he traveled to the Middle East, to the United States, all over Europe. He could not find what he was looking for anywhere, and not the right woman either: after the novelty of an affair wore off, he would leave. By 1807 he had had so many affairs, and still felt so unsatisfied, that he decided to retire to his country estate, called Vallée aux Loups. He filled the place with trees from all over the world, transforming the grounds into something out of one of his novels. There he began to write the memoirs that he envisioned would be his masterpiece.

By 1817, however, Chateaubriand's life had fallen apart. Money problems had forced him to sell Vallée aux Loups. Almost fifty, he suddenly felt old, his inspiration dried up. That year he visited the writer Madame de Staël, who had been ill and was now close to death. He spent several days at her bedside, along with her closest friend, Juliette Récamier. Madame Récamier's affairs were infamous. She was married to a much older man, but they had not lived together for some time; she had broken the hearts of the most illustrious men in Europe, including Prince Metternich, the Duke of

Wellington, and the writer Benjamin Constant. It had also been rumored that despite all her flirtations she was still a virgin. She was now almost forty, but she was the type of woman who seems youthful at any age. Drawn together by their grief over de Staël's death, she and Chateaubriand became friends. She listened so attentively to him, adopting his moods and echoing his sentiments, that he felt that he had at last met a woman who understood him. There was also something rather ethereal about Madame Récamier. Her walk, her voice, her eyes—more than one man had compared her to some unearthly angel. Chateaubriand soon burned with the desire to possess her physically.

The year after their friendship began, she had a surprise for him: she had convinced a friend to purchase Vallée aux Loups. The friend was away for a few weeks, and she invited Chateaubriand to spend some time with her at his former estate. He happily accepted. He showed her around, explaining what each little patch of ground had meant to him, the memories the place conjured up. He felt youthful feelings welling up inside him, feelings he had forgotten about. He delved further into the past, describing events in his childhood. At moments, walking with Madame Récamier and looking into those kind eyes, he felt a shiver of recognition, but he could not quite identify it. All he knew was that he had to go back to the memoirs that he had laid aside. "I intend to employ the little time that is left to me in describing my youth," he said, "so long as its essence remains palpable to me."

It seemed that Madame Récamier returned Chateaubriand's love, but as usual she struggled to keep it a spiritual affair. The Enchanter, however, deserved his nickname. His poetry, his air of melancholy, and his persistence finally won the day and she succumbed, perhaps for the first time in her life. Now, as lovers, they were inseparable. But as always with Chateaubriand, over time one woman was not enough. The restless spirit returned. He began to have affairs again. Soon he and Récamier stopped seeing each other.

In 1832, Chateaubriand was traveling through Switzerland. Once again his life had taken a downward turn; only this time he truly was old, in body and spirit. In the Alps, strange thoughts of his youth began to assail him, memories of the castle in Brittany. Word reached him that Madame Récamier was in the area. He had not seen her in years, and he hurried to the inn where she was staying. She was as kind to him as ever; during the day they took walks together, and at night they stayed up late, talking.

One day, Chateaubriand told Récamier he had finally decided to finish his memoirs. And he had a confession to make: he told her the story of Sylphide, his imaginary lover when he was growing up. He had once hoped to meet a Sylphide in real life, but the women he had known had paled in comparison. Over the years he had forgotten about his imaginary lover, but now he was an old man, and he not only thought of her again, he could see her face and hear her voice. And with those memories he realized that he had in fact met Sylphide in real life—it was Madame Récamier. The face and voice were close. More important, there was the calm spirit, the innocent, virginal quality. Reading to her the prayer to Sylphide he had just written, he told her he wanted to be young again, and seeing her had brought his youth back to him. Reconciled with Madame Récamier, he began to work again on the memoirs, which were eventually published under the title *Memoirs from Beyond the Grave.* Most critics agreed that the book was his masterpiece. The memoirs were dedicated to Madame Récamier, to whom he remained devoted until his death, in 1848.

Interpretation. All of us carry within us an image of an ideal type of person whom we yearn to meet and love. Most often the type is a composite made up of bits and pieces of different people from our youth, and even of characters in books and movies. People who influenced us inordinately—a teacher for instance—may also figure. The traits have nothing to do with superficial interests. Rather, they are unconscious, hard to verbalize.

We searched hardest for this ideal type in our adolescence, when we were more idealistic. Often our first loves have more of these traits than our subsequent affairs. For Chateaubriand, living with his family in their secluded castle, his first love was his sister Lucile, whom he adored and idealized. But since love with her was impossible, he created a figure out of his imagination who had all her positive attributes—nobility of spirit, innocence, courage.

Madame Récamier could not have known about Chateaubriand's ideal type, but she did know something about him, well before she ever met him. She had read all of his books, and his characters were highly autobiographical. She knew of his obsession with his lost youth; and everyone knew of his endless and unsatisfying affairs with women, his hyperrestless spirit. Madame Récamier knew how to mirror people, entering their spirit, and one of her first acts was to take Chateaubriand to Vallée aux Loups, where he felt he had left part of his youth. Alive with memories, he regressed further into his childhood, to the days in the castle. She actively encouraged this. Most important, she embodied a spirit that came naturally to her, but that matched his youthful ideal: innocent, noble, kind. (The fact that so many men fell in love with her suggests that many men had the same ideals.) Madame Récamier was Lucile/Sylphide. It took him years to realize it, but when he did, her spell over him was complete.

It is nearly impossible to embody someone's ideal completely. But if you come close enough, if you evoke some of that ideal spirit, you can lead that person into a deep seduction. To effect this regression you must play the role of the therapist. Get your targets to open up about their past, particularly their former loves and most particularly their first love. Pay attention to any expressions of disappointment, how this or that person did not give them what they wanted. Take them to places that evoke their youth. In this regression you are creating not so much a relationship of dependency and immaturity but rather the adolescent spirit of a first love. There is a touch of innocence to the relationship. So much of adult life involves compromise, conniving, and a certain toughness. Create the ideal atmosphere by keeping such things out, drawing the other person into a kind of mutual weakness, conjuring a second virginity. There should be a dreamlike quality to the affair, as if the target were reliving that first love but could not quite believe it. Let all of this unfold slowly, each encounter revealing more ideal qualities. The sense of reliving a past pleasure is simply impossible to resist.

4. Some time in the summer of 1614, several members of England's upper nobility, including the Archbishop of Canterbury, met to decide what to do about the Earl of Somerset, the favorite of King James I, who was forty-eight at the time. After eight years as the favorite, the young earl had accumulated such power and wealth, and so many titles, that nothing was left for anyone else. But how to get rid of this powerful man? For the time being the conspirators had no answer.

A few weeks later the king was inspecting the royal stables when he caught sight of a young man who was new to the court: the twenty-two-year-old George Villiers, a member of the lower nobility. The courtiers who accompanied the king that day watched the king's eyes following Villiers, and saw with what interest he asked about this young man. Indeed everyone had to agree that he was a most handsome youth, with the face of an angel and a charmingly childish manner. When news of the king's interest in Villiers reached the conspirators, they instantly knew they had found what they had been looking for: a young man who could seduce the king and supplant the dreaded favorite. Left to nature, though, the seduction would never happen. They had to help it along. So, without telling Villiers of their plan, they befriended him.

King James was the son of Mary Queen of Scots. His childhood had been a nightmare: his father, his mother's favorite, and his own regents had all been murdered; his mother had first been exiled, later executed. When James was young, to escape suspicion he played the part of a fool. He hated the sight of a sword and could not stand the slightest sign of argument. When his cousin Queen Elizabeth I died in 1603, leaving no heir, he became king of England.

James surrounded himself with bright, happy young men, and seemed to prefer the company of boys. In 1612, his son, Prince Henry, died. The king was inconsolable. He needed distraction and good cheer, and his favorite, the Earl of Somerset, was no longer so young and attractive. The timing for a seduction was perfect. And so the conspirators went to work on Villiers, under the guise of trying to help him advance within the court. They supplied him with a magnificent wardrobe, jewels, a glittering carriage, the kind of things the king noticed. They worked on his riding, fencing, tennis, dancing, his skills with birds and dogs. He was instructed in the art of conversation—how to flatter, tell a joke, sigh at the right moment. Fortunately Villiers was easy to work with; he had a naturally buoyant manner and nothing seemed to bother him. That same year the conspirators managed to get him appointed the royal cup-bearer: every night he poured out the king's wine, so that the king could see him up close. After a few weeks, the king was in love. The boy seemed to crave attention and tenderness, exactly what he yearned to offer. How wonderful it would be to mold and educate him. And what a perfect figure he had!

The conspirators convinced Villiers to break off his engagement to a young lady; the king was single-minded in his affections, and could not stand competition. Soon James wanted to be around Villiers all the time, for he had the qualities the king admired: innocence and a lighthearted spirit. The king appointed Villiers gentleman of the bedchamber, making it possible for them to be alone together. What particularly charmed James was that Villiers never asked for anything, which made it all the more delightful to spoil him.

By 1616, Villiers had completely supplanted the former favorite. He was now the Earl of Buckingham, and a member of the king's privy council. To the conspirators' dismay, however, he quickly accumulated even more privileges than the Earl of Somerset had done. The king would call him sweetheart in public, fix his doublets, comb his hair. James zealously protected his favorite, anxious to preserve the young man's innocence. He tended to the youth's every whim, in effect became his slave. In fact the king seemed to regress; whenever Steenie, his nickname for Villiers, entered the room, he started to act like a child. The two were inseparable until the king's death, in 1625.

Interpretation. We are most definitely stamped forever by our parents, in ways we can never fully understand. But the parents are equally influenced and seduced by the child. They may play the role of the protector, but in the process they absorb the child's spirit and energy, relive a part of their own childhood. And just as the child struggles against sexual feelings toward the parent, the parent must repress comparable erotic feelings that lie just beneath the tenderness they feel. The best and most insidious way to seduce people is often to position yourself as the child. Imagining themselves stronger, more in control, they will be lured into your web. They will feel they have nothing to fear. Emphasize your immaturity, your weakness, and you let them indulge in fantasies of protecting and parenting you—a strong desire as people get older. What they do not realize is that you are getting under their skin, insinuating yourself—it is the child who is controlling the adult. Your innocence makes them want to protect you, but it is also sexually charged. Innocence is highly seductive; some people even long to play the corrupter of innocence. Stir up their latent sexual feelings and you can lead them astray with the hope of fulfilling a strong yet repressed fantasy: sleeping with the child figure. In your presence, too, they will begin to regress as well, infected by your childish, playful spirit.

Most of this came naturally to Villiers, but you will probably have to use some calculation. Fortunately, all of us have strong childish tendencies within us that are easy to access and exaggerate. Make your gestures seem spontaneous and unplanned. Any sexual element of your behavior should seem innocent, unconscious. Like Villiers, don't push for favors. Parents prefer to spoil children who don't ask for things but invite them in their manner. Seeming nonjudgmental and uncritical of those around you will make everything you do seem more natural and naive. Have a happy, cheerful demeanor, but with a playful edge. Emphasize any weaknesses you might have, things you cannot control. Remember: most of us remember our early years fondly, but often, paradoxically, the people with the strongest attachment to those times are the ones who had the most difficult childhoods. Actually, circumstances kept them from getting to *be* children, so they never really grew up, and they long for the paradise they never got to experience. James I falls into this category. These types are ripe targets for a reverse regression.

Symbol: *The Bed. Lying alone in bed, the child feels unprotected, afraid, and needy. In a nearby room, there is the parent's bed. It is large and forbidding, site of things you are not supposed to know about. Give the seduced both feelings—helplessness and transgression—as you lay them into bed and put them to sleep.*

Reversal

To reverse the strategies of regression, the parties to a seduction would have to remain adults during the process. This is not only rare, it is not very pleasurable. Seduction means realizing certain fantasies. Being a mature and responsible adult is not a fantasy, it is a duty. Furthermore, a person who remains an adult in relation to you is harder to seduce. In all kinds of seduction—political, media, personal—the target must regress. The only danger is that the child, wearying of dependence, turns against the parent and rebels. You must be prepared for this, and unlike a parent, never take it personally.

18

Stir Up the Transgressive and Taboo

There are always social limits on what one can do. Some of these, the most elemental taboos, go back centuries; others are more superficial, simply defining polite and acceptable behavior. Making your targets feel that you are leading them past either kind of limit is immensely seductive. People yearn to explore their dark side. Not everything in romantic love is supposed to be tender and soft; hint that you have a cruel, even sadistic streak. You do not respect age differences, marriage vows, family ties. Once the desire to transgress draws your targets to you, it will be hard for them to stop. Take them further than they imagined—the shared feeling of guilt and complicity will create a powerful bond.

The Lost Self

In March of 1812, the twenty-four-year-old George Gordon Byron published the first cantos of his poem *Childe Harold.* The poem was filled with familiar gothic imagery—a dilapidated abbey, debauchery, travels to the mysterious East—but what made it different was that the hero of the poem was also its villain: Harold was a man who led a life of vice, disdaining society's conventions yet somehow going unpunished. Also, the poem was not set in some faraway land but in present-day England. *Childe Harold* created an instant stir, becoming the talk of London. The first printing quickly sold out. Within days a rumor made the rounds: the poem, about a debauched young nobleman, was in fact autobiographical.

It is a matter of a certain kind of feeling: that of being overwhelmed. There are many who have a great fear of being overwhelmed by someone; for example, someone who makes them laugh against their will, or tickles them to death, or, worse, tells them things that they sense to be accurate but which they do not quite understand, things that go beyond their prejudices and received wisdom. In other words, they do not want to be seduced, since seduction means confronting people with their limits, limits that are supposed to be set and stable but that the seducer suddenly causes to waver. Seduction is the desire of being overwhelmed, taken beyond.

—Daniel Sibony, *L'Amour Inconscient*

Now the cream of society clamored to meet Lord Byron, and many of them left their calling cards at his London residence. Soon he was showing up at their homes. Strangely enough, he exceeded their expectations. He was devilishly handsome, with curling hair and the face of an angel. His black attire set off his pale complexion. He did not talk much, which made an impression of itself, and when he did, his voice was low and hypnotic and his tone a little disdainful. He had a limp (he was born with a clubfoot), so when an orchestra struck up a waltz (the dance craze of 1812), he would stand to the side, a faraway look in his eye. The ladies went wild over Byron. Upon meeting him, Lady Roseberry felt her heart beating so violently (a mix of fear and excitement) that she had to walk away. Women fought to be seated next to him, to win his attention, to be seduced by him. Was it true that he was guilty of a secret sin, like the hero of his poem?

Lady Caroline Lamb—wife of William Lamb, son of Lord and Lady Melbourne—was a glittering young woman on the social scene, but deep inside she was unhappy. As a young girl she had dreamt of adventure, romance, travel. Now she was expected to play the role of the polite young wife, and it did not suit her. Lady Caroline was one of the first to read *Childe Harold*, and something more than its novelty stirred her. When she saw Lord Byron at a dinner party, surrounded by women, she looked at his face, then walked away; that night she wrote of him in her journal, "Mad, bad, and dangerous to know." She added, "That beautiful pale face is my fate."

Just lately I saw a tight-reined stallion \ Get the bit in his teeth and bolt \ Like lightning—yet the minute he felt the reins slacken, \ Drop loose on his flying mane, \ He stopped dead.

The next day, to Lady Caroline's surprise, Lord Byron called on her. Evidently he had seen her walking away from him, and her shyness had intrigued him—he disliked the aggressive women who were constantly at his heels, as it seemed he disdained everything, including his success. Soon he was visiting Lady Caroline daily. He lingered in her boudoir, played with her children, helped her choose her dress for the day. She pressed him to talk of his life: he described his brutal father, the untimely deaths that seemed to be a family curse, the crumbling abbey he had inherited, his adventures in Turkey and Greece. His life was indeed as gothic as that of Childe Harold.

We eternally chafe at restrictions, covet \ Whatever's forbidden. (Look how a sick man who's told \ No immersion hangs round the bath-house.) \ . . . Desire \ Mounts for what's kept out of reach. A thief's attracted \ By burglar-proof premises. How often will love \ Thrive on a rival's approval? It's not your wife's beauty, but your own \ Passion for her that gets us—she must \ Have something, just to have hooked you. A girl locked up by her \ Husband's not chaste but pursued, her fear's \ A bigger draw than her figure. Illicit passion—like it \ Or not—is sweeter. It only turns me on \ When the girl says, "I'm frightened."

—Ovid, *The Amores*, translated by Peter Green

Within days the two became lovers. Now, though, the tables turned: Lady Caroline pursued Byron with unladylike aggression. She dressed as a page and sneaked into his carriage, wrote him extravagantly emotional letters, flaunted the affair. At last, a chance to play the grand romantic role of her girlhood fantasies. Byron began to turn against her. He already loved to shock; now he confessed to her the nature of the secret sin he had alluded to in *Childe Harold*—his homosexual affairs during his travels. He made cruel remarks, grew indifferent. But this only seemed to push her further. She sent him the customary lock of hair, but from her pubis; she followed him in the street, made public scenes—finally her family sent her abroad to avoid further scandal. After Byron made it clear the affair was over, she descended into a madness that would last several years.

In 1813, an old friend of Byron's, James Webster, invited the poet to stay at his country estate. Webster had a young and beautiful wife, Lady Frances, and he knew Byron's reputation as a seducer, but his wife was quiet and chaste—surely she would resist the temptation of a man such as Byron. To Webster's relief, Byron barely spoke to Frances, who seemed equally uninterested in him. Yet several days into Byron's stay, she contrived to be alone with him in the billiards room, where she asked him a question: how could a woman who liked a man inform him of it when he did not perceive it? Byron scribbled a racy reply on a piece of paper, which made her blush as she read it. Soon thereafter he invited the couple to stay with him at his infamous abbey. There, the prim and proper Lady Frances saw him drink wine from a human skull. They stayed up late in one of the abbey's secret chambers, reading poetry and kissing. With Byron, it seemed, Lady Frances was only too eager to explore adultery.

It is often not possible for [women] later on to undo the connection thus formed in their minds between sensual activities and something forbidden, and they turn out to be psychically impotent, i.e. frigid, when at last such activities do become permissible. This is the source of the desire in so many women to keep even legitimate relations secret for a time; and of the appearance of the capacity for normal sensation in others as soon as the condition of prohibition is restored by a secret intrigue—untrue to the husband, they can keep a second order of faith with the lover. • In my opinion the necessary condition of forbiddenness in the erotic life of women holds the same place as the man's

That same year, Lord Byron's half sister Augusta arrived in London to get away from her husband, who was having money troubles. Byron had not seen Augusta for some time. The two were physically similar—the same face, the same mannerisms; she was Lord Byron as a woman. And his behavior toward her was more than brotherly. He took her to the theater, to dances, received her at home, treating her with an intimate spirit that Augusta soon returned. Indeed the kind and tender attention that Byron showered on her soon became physical.

Augusta was a devoted wife with three children, yet she yielded to her half brother's advances. How could she help herself? He stirred up a strange passion in her, a stronger passion than she felt for any other man, including her husband. For Byron, his relationship with Augusta was the ultimate and crowning sin of his career. And soon he was writing to his friends, openly confessing it. Indeed he delighted in their shocked responses, and his long narrative poem, *The Bride of Abydos*, takes brother-sister incest as its theme. Rumors began to spread of Byron's relations with Augusta, who was now pregnant with his child. Polite society shunned him—but women were more drawn to him than before, and his books were more popular than ever.

Annabella Milbanke, Lady Caroline Lamb's cousin, had met Byron in those first months of 1812 when he was the toast of London. Annabella was sober and down to earth, and her interests were science and religion. But there was something about Byron that attracted her. And the feeling seemed to be returned: not only did the two become friends, to her bewilderment he showed another kind of interest in her, even at one point proposing marriage. This was in the midst of the scandal over Byron and Caroline Lamb, and Annabella did not take the proposal seriously. Over the next few months she followed his career from a distance, and heard the troubling rumors of incest. Yet in 1813, she wrote her aunt, "I consider his acquaintance as so desirable that I would incur the risk of being called a Flirt for the sake of enjoying it." Reading his new poems, she wrote that his "description of Love almost makes *me* in love." She was developing an obsession with Byron, of which word soon reached him. They renewed their friendship, and in 1814 he proposed again; this time she accepted. Byron was a fallen angel and she would be the one to reform him.

It did not turn out that way. Byron had hoped that married life would calm him down, but after the ceremony he realized it was a mistake. He told Annabella, "Now you will find that you have married a devil." Within a few years the marriage fell apart.

In 1816, Byron left England, never to return. He traveled through Italy for a while; everyone knew his story—the affairs, the incest, the cruelty to his lovers. But wherever he went, Italian women, particularly married noblewomen, pursued him, making it clear in their own way how prepared they were to be the next Byronic victim. In truth, the women had become the aggressors. As Byron told the poet Shelley, "No one has been more carried off than poor dear me—I've been ravished more often than anyone since the Trojan war."

Interpretation. Women of Byron's time were longing to play a different role than society allowed them. They were supposed to be the decent, moralizing force in culture; only men had outlets for their darker impulses. Underlying the social restrictions on women, perhaps, was a fear of the more amoral and unbridled part of the female psyche.

Feeling repressed and restless, women of the time devoured gothic novels and romances, stories in which women were adventurous, and had the same capacity for good and evil as men. Books like these helped to trigger a revolt, with women like Lady Caroline playing out a little of the fantasy life they had had in their girlhood, where it had to some extent been permit-

need to lower his sexual object. . . . Women belonging to the higher levels of civilization do not usually transgress the prohibition against sexual activities during the period of waiting, and thus they acquire this close association between the forbidden and the sexual. . . . • The injurious results of the deprivation of sexual enjoyment at the beginning manifest themselves in lack of full satisfaction when sexual desire is later given free rein in marriage. But, on the other hand, unrestrained sexual liberty from the beginning leads to no better result. It is easy to show that the value the mind sets on erotic needs instantly sinks as soon as satisfaction becomes readily obtainable. Some obstacle is necessary to swell the tide of the libido to its height; and at all periods of history, wherever natural barriers in the way of satisfaction have not sufficed, mankind has erected conventional ones in order to be able to enjoy love. This is true both of individuals and of nations. In times during which no obstacles to sexual satisfaction existed, such as, maybe, during the decline of the civilizations of antiquity, love became worthless, life became empty, and strong reaction-formations were necessary before the indispensable emotional value of love could be recovered.

—Sigmund Freud, "Contributions to the Psychology of Love," *Sexuality and the Psychology of Love*, translated by Joan Rivière

ted. Byron arrived on the scene at the right time. He became the lightning rod for women's unexpressed desires; with him they could go beyond the limits society had imposed. For some the lure was adultery, for others it was romantic rebellion, or a chance to become irrational and uncivilized. (The desire to reform him merely covered up the truth—the desire to be overwhelmed by him.) In all cases it was the lure of the forbidden, which in this case was more than merely a superficial temptation: once you became involved with Lord Byron, he took you further than you had imagined or wanted, since he recognized no limits. Women did not just fall in love with him, they let him turn their lives upside down, even ruin them. They preferred that fate to the safe confines of marriage.

This is how Monsieur Mauclair analyzed men's attitude toward prostitutes: "Neither the love of a passionate but well-brought-up mistress, nor his marriage to a woman whom he respects, can replace the prostitute for the human animal in those perverse moments when he covets the pleasure of debasing himself without affecting his social prestige. Nothing can replace this bizarre and powerful pleasure of being able to say everything, do everything, profane and parody without any fear of retribution, remorse, or responsibility. It is a complete revolt against organized society, his organized, educated self and especially his religion." Monsieur Mauclair hears the call of the Devil in this dark passion poetized by Baudelaire. "The prostitute represents the unconscious which enables us to put aside our responsibilities."

—Nina Epton, *Love and the French*

In some ways, the situation of women in the early nineteenth century has become generalized in the early twenty-first. The outlets for male bad behavior—war, dirty politics, the institution of mistresses and courtesans—have faded away; today, not just women but men are supposed to be eminently civilized and reasonable. And many have a hard time living up to this. As children we are able to vent the darker side of our characters, a side that all of us have. But under pressure from society (at first in the form of our parents), we slowly repress the naughty, rebellious, perverse streaks in our characters. To get along, we learn to repress our dark sides, which become a kind of lost self, a part of our psyche buried beneath our polite appearance.

As adults, we secretly want to recapture that lost self—the more adventurous, less respectful, childhood part of us. We are drawn to those who live out their lost selves as adults, even if it involves some evil or destruction. Like Byron, you can become the lightning rod for such desires. You must learn, however, to keep this potential under control, and to use it strategically. As the aura of the forbidden around you is drawing targets into your web, do not overplay your dangerousness, or they will be frightened away. Once you feel them falling under your spell, you have freer rein. If they begin to imitate you, as Lady Caroline imitated Byron, then take it further—mix in some cruelty, involve them in sin, crime, taboo activity, whatever it takes. Unleash the lost self within them; the more they act it out, the deeper your hold over them. Going halfway will break the spell and create self-consciousness. Take it as far as you can.

Baseness attracts everybody.

—Johann Wolfgang Goethe

Hearts and eye go traveling along the paths that have always brought them joy; and if anyone attempts to spoil their game, he only makes them the more passionate about it, God knows. . . . so it was with Tristan and Isolde. As soon as they were forbidden their desires, and prevented from enjoying one another by spies and guards, they began to suffer intensely. Desire now seriously tormented them by its magic, many times worse than before; their need for one another was more

Keys to Seduction

Society and culture are based on limits—this kind of behavior is acceptable, that is not. The limits are fluid and change with time, but there are always limits. The alternative is anarchy, the lawlessness of nature, which we dread. But we are strange animals: the moment any kind of limit is imposed, physically or psychologically, we are instantly curious. A part of us wants to go beyond that limit, to explore what is forbidden.

If, as children, we are told not to go past a certain point in the woods, that is precisely where we want to go. But we grow older, and become polite and deferential; more and more boundaries encumber our lives. Do not confuse politeness with happiness, however. It covers up frustration, unwanted compromise. How can we explore the shadow side of our personality without incurring punishment or ostracism? It seeps out in our dreams. We sometimes wake up with a sense of guilt at the murder, incest, adultery, and mayhem that goes on in our dreams, until we realize no one needs to know about it but ourselves. But give a person the sense that with you they will have a chance to explore the outer reaches of acceptable, polite behavior, that with you they can vent some of their closeted personality, and you create the ingredients for a deep and powerful seduction.

You will have to go beyond the point of merely teasing them with an elusive fantasy. The shock and seductive power will come from the reality of what you are offering them. Like Byron, at a certain point you can even press it further than they may want to go. If they have followed you merely out of curiosity, they may feel some fear and hesitation, but once they are hooked, they will find you hard to resist, for it is hard to return to a limit once you have transgressed and gone past it. The human cries out for more, and does not know when to stop. You will determine for them when it is time to stop.

The moment people feel that something is prohibited, a part of them will want it. That is what makes a married man or woman such a delicious target—the more someone is prohibited, the greater the desire. George Villiers, the Earl of Buckingham, was the favorite first of King James I, then of James's son, King Charles I. Nothing was ever denied him. In 1625, on a visit to France, he met the beautiful Queen Anne and fell hopelessly in love. What could be more impossible, more out of reach, than the queen of a rival power? He could have had almost any other woman, but the prohibited nature of the queen completely enflamed him, until he embarrassed himself and his country by trying to kiss her in public.

Since what is forbidden is desired, somehow you must make yourself seem forbidden. The most blatant way to do this is to engage in behavior that gives you a dark and forbidden aura. Theoretically you are someone to avoid; in fact you are too seductive to resist. That was the allure of the actor Errol Flynn, who, like Byron, often found himself the pursued rather than the pursuer. Flynn was devilishly handsome, but he also had something else: a definite criminal streak. In his wild youth he engaged in all kinds of shady activities. In the 1950s he was charged with rape, a permanent stain on his reputation even though he was acquitted; but his popularity among women only increased. Play up your dark side and you will have a similar effect. For your targets to be involved with you means going beyond their limits, doing something naughty and unacceptable—to society, to their peers. For many that is reason to bite the bait.

painful and urgent than it had ever been. • *. . . Women do lots of things just because they are forbidden, which they would certainly not do if they were not forbidden. . . . Our Lord God gave Eve the freedom to do what she would with all the fruits, flowers, and plants there were in Paradise, except for only one, which he forbade her to touch on pain of death. . . . She took the fruit and broke God's commandment . . . but it is my firm belief now that Eve would never have done this, if she had not been forbidden to.*

—GOTTFRIED VON STRASSBURG, *TRISTAN UND ISOLDE*, QUOTED IN ANDREA HOPKINS, *THE BOOK OF COURTLY LOVE*

One of Monsieur Leopold Stern's friends rented a bachelor's pied-à-terre where he received his wife as a mistress, served her with port and petits-fours and "experienced all the tingling excitement of adultery." He told Stern that it was a delightful sensation to cuckold himself.

—NINA EPTON, *LOVE AND THE FRENCH*

In Junichiro Tanazaki's 1928 novel *Quicksand,* Sonoko Kakiuchi, the wife of a respectable lawyer, is bored and decides to take art classes to wile away the time. There, she finds herself fascinated with a fellow female student, the beautiful Mitsuko, who befriends her, then seduces her. Kakiuchi is forced to tell endless lies to her husband about her involvement with Mitsuko and their frequent trysts. Mitsuko slowly involves her in all kinds of nefarious activities, including a love triangle with a bizarre young man. Each time Kakiuchi is made to explore some forbidden pleasure, Mitsuko challenges her to go further and further. Kakiuchi hesitates, feels remorse—she knows she is in the clutches of a devilish young seductress who has played on her boredom to lead her astray. But in the end, she cannot help following Mitsuko's lead—each transgressive act makes her want more. Once your targets are drawn by the lure of the forbidden, dare them to match you in transgressive behavior. Any kind of challenge is seductive. Take it slowly, heightening the challenge only after they show signs of yielding to you. Once they are under your spell, they may not even notice how far out on a limb you have taken them.

The great eighteenth-century rake Duc de Richelieu had a prediliction for young girls and he would often heighten the seduction by enveloping them in transgressive behavior, to which the young are particularly susceptible. For instance, he would find a way into the young girl's house and lure her into her bed; the parents would be just down the hall, adding the proper spice. Sometimes he would act as if they were about to be discovered, the momentary fright sharpening the overall thrill. In all cases, he would try to turn the young girl against her parents, ridiculing their religious zeal or prudery or pious behavior. The duke's stategy was to attack the values that his targets held dearest—precisely the values that represent a limit. In a young person, family ties, religious ties, and the like are useful to the seducer; young people barely need a reason to rebel against them. The strategy, though, can be applied to a person of any age: for every deeply held value there is a shadow side, a doubt, a desire to explore what those values forbid.

In Renaissance Italy, a prostitute would dress as a lady and go to church. Nothing was more exciting to a man than to exchange glances with a woman whom he knew to be a whore as he was surrounded by his wife, family, peers, and church officials. Every religion or value system creates a dark side, the shadow realm of everything it prohibits. Tease your targets, get them to flirt with whatever transgresses their family values, which are often emotional yet superficial, since they are imposed from the outside.

One of the most seductive men of the twentieth century, Rudolph Valentino, was known as the Sex Menace. His appeal for women was twofold: he could be tender and attentive, but he also hinted of cruelty. At any moment he could become dangerously bold, perhaps even a little violent. The studios played up this double image as much as possible—when it was reported that he had been abusive to his wife, for example, they exploited the story. A mix of the masculine and the feminine, the violent and the tender, will always seem transgressive and appealing. Love is supposed to be tender and delicate, but in fact it can release violent and destructive emotions; and the possible violence of love, the way it breaks down our normal reasonableness, is just what attracts us. Approach romance's violent side by mixing a cruel streak into your tender attentions, particularly in the latter stages of the seduction, when the target is in your clutches. The courtesan Lola Montez was known to turn to violence, using a whip now and then, and Lou Andreas-Salomé could be exceptionally cruel to her men, playing coquettish games, turning alternately icy and demanding. Her cruelty only kept her targets coming back for more. A masochistic involvement can represent a great transgressive release.

The more illicit your seduction feels, the more powerful its effect. Give your targets the feeling that they are committing a kind of crime, a deed whose guilt they share with you. Create public moments in which the two of you know something that those around you do not. It could be phrases and looks that only you recognize, a secret. Byron's seductive appeal to Lady Frances was connected to the nearness of her husband—in his company, for example, she had a love letter of Byron's hidden in her bosom. Johannes, the protagonist of Søren Kierkegaard's *The Seducer's Diary*, sent a message to his target, the young Cordelia, in the middle of a dinner party they were both attending; she could not reveal to the other guests that it was from him, for then she would have to do some explaining. He might also say something in public that would have a special meaning for her, since it referred to something in one of his letters. All of this added spice to the affair by giving it a feeling of a shared secret, even a guilty crime. It is critical to play on tensions like these in public, creating a sense of complicity and collusion against the world.

In the Tristan and Isolde legend, the famous lovers reach the heights of bliss and exhilaration exactly *because* of the taboos they break. Isolde is engaged to King Mark; she will soon be a married woman. Tristan is a loyal subject and warrior in the service of King Mark, who is his father's age. The whole affair has a feeling of stealing away the bride from the father. Epitomizing the concept of love in the Western world, the legend has had immense influence over the ages, and a crucial part of it is the idea that without obstacles, without a feeling of transgression, love is weak and flavorless.

People may be straining to remove restrictions on private behavior, to make everything freer, in the world today, but that only makes seduction more difficult and less exciting. Do what you can to reintroduce a feeling of transgression and crime, even if it is only psychological or illusory. There must be obstacles to overcome, social norms to flout, laws to break, before the seduction can be consummated. It might seem that a permissive society imposes few limits; find some. There will always be limits, sacred cows, behavioral standards—endless ammunition for stirring up the transgressive and taboo.

Symbol: *The Forest. The children are told not to go into the forest that lies just beyond the safe confines of their home. There is no law there, only wilderness, wild animals, and criminals. But the chance to explore, the alluring darkness, and the fact that it is prohibited are impossible to resist. And once inside, they want to go farther and farther.*

Reversal

The reversal of stirring up taboos would be to stay within the limits of acceptable behavior. That would make for a very tepid seduction. Which is not to say that only evil or wild behavior is seductive; goodness, kindness, and an aura of spirituality can be tremendously attractive, since they are rare qualities. But notice that the game is the same. A person who is kind or good or spiritual within the limits that society prescribes has a weak appeal. It is those who go to the extreme—the Gandhis, the Krishnamurtis—who seduce us. They do not merely expound a spiritual lifestyle, they do away with all personal material comfort to live out their ascetic ideals. They too go beyond the limits, transgressing acceptable behavior, because societies would find it hard to function if everyone went to such lengths. In seduction, there is absolutely no power in respecting boundaries and limits.

19
Use Spiritual Lures

Everyone has doubts and insecurities—about their body, their self-worth, their sexuality. If your seduction appeals exclusively to the physical, you will stir up these doubts and make your targets self-conscious. Instead, lure them out of their insecurities by making them focus on something sublime and spiritual: a religious experience, a lofty work of art, the occult. Play up your divine qualities; affect an air of discontent with worldly things; speak of the stars, destiny, the hidden threads that unite you and the object of the seduction. Lost in a spiritual mist, the target will feel light and uninhibited. Deepen the effect of your seduction by making its sexual culmination seem like the spiritual union of two souls.

Object of Worship

Liane de Pougy was the reigning courtesan of 1890s Paris. Slender and androgynous, she was a novelty, and the wealthiest men in Europe vied to possess her. By late in the decade, however, she had grown tired of it all. "What a sterile life," she wrote a friend. "Always the same routine: the *Bois,* the races, fittings; and to end an insipid day: dinner!" What wearied the courtesan most was the constant attention of her male admirers, who sought to monopolize her physical charms.

One spring day in 1899, Liane was riding in an open carriage through the Bois de Boulogne. As usual, men tipped their hats at her as she passed by. But one of these admirers caught her by surprise: a young woman with long blond hair, who gave her an intense, worshipful stare. Liane smiled at the woman, who smiled and bowed in return.

A few days later Liane began to receive cards and flowers from a twenty-three-year-old American named Natalie Barney, who identified herself as the blond admirer in the Bois de Boulogne, and asked for a rendezvous. Liane invited Natalie to visit, but to amuse herself she decided to play a little joke: a friend would take her place, lounging on her bed in the dark boudoir, while Liane would hide behind a screen. Natalie arrived at the appointed hour. She wore the costume of a Florentine page and carried a bouquet of flowers. Kneeling before the bed, she began to praise the courtesan, comparing her to a Fra Angelico painting. All too soon, she heard someone laugh—and standing up she realized the joke that had been played on her. She blushed and made for the door. When Liane hurried out from behind the screen, Natalie chastised her: the courtesan had the face of an angel, but apparently not the spirit. Contrite, Liane whispered, "Come back tomorrow morning. I'll be alone."

The young American showed up the next day, wearing the same outfit. She was witty and spirited; Liane relaxed in her presence, and invited her to stay for the courtesan's morning ritual—the elaborate makeup, clothes, and jewelry she put on before heading out into the world. Watching reverently, Natalie remarked that she worshiped beauty, and that Liane was the most beautiful woman she had ever seen. Playing the part of the page, she followed Liane to the carriage, opened the door for her with a bow, and accompanied her on her habitual ride through the Bois de Boulogne. Once inside the park, Natalie knelt on the floor, out of sight of the passing gentlemen who tipped their hats to Liane. She recited poems she had writ-

Ah! always to be able to freely love the one whom one loves! To spend my life at your feet like our last days together. To protect you against imaginary satyrs so that I can be the only one to throw you on this bed of moss. . . . We'll find each other again in Lesbos, and when dusk falls, we'll go deep in the woods to lose the paths leading to this century. I want to imagine us in this enchanted island of immortals. I picture it as being so beautiful. Come, I'll describe for you those delicate female couples, and far from the cities and the din, we'll forget everything but the Ethics of Beauty.

—Natalie Barney, letter to Liane de Pougy, quoted in Jean Chalon, *Portrait of a Seductress: The World of Natalie Barney,* translated by Carol Barko

Terrible Natalie, who used to ravage the land of love. Formidable Natalie, feared by husbands since no one could resist her seductiveness. And one could see how women

ten in Liane's honor, and she told the courtesan she considered it a mission to rescue her from the seamy career into which she had fallen.

That evening Natalie took her to the theater to see Sarah Bernhardt play Hamlet. During the intermission, she told Liane that she identified with Hamlet—his hunger for the sublime, his hatred of tyranny—which, for her, was the tyranny of men over women. Over the next few days Liane received a steady flow of flowers from Natalie, and telegrams with little poems in her honor. Slowly the worshipful words and looks became more physical, with the occasional touch, then a caress, even a kiss—and a kiss that felt different from any in Liane's experience. One morning, with Natalie in attendance, Liane prepared to take a bath. As she slipped out of her nightgown, Natalie suddenly flung herself at her friend's feet, kissing her ankles. The courtesan freed herself and hurried into the bath, only for Natalie to throw off her clothes and join her. Within a few days, all Paris knew that Liane de Pougy had a new lover: Natalie Barney.

Liane made no effort to disguise her new affair, publishing a novel, *Idylle Saphique*, detailing every aspect of Natalie's seduction. She had never had an affair with a woman before, and she described her involvement with Natalie as something like a mystical experience. Even at the end of her long life, she remembered the affair as by far her most intense.

Renée Vivien was a young Englishwoman who had come to Paris to write poetry and flee the marriage that her father was trying to arrange for her. Renée was obsessed with death; she also felt there was something wrong with her, experiencing moments of intense self-loathing. In 1900, Renée met Natalie at the theater. Something about the American's kind eyes melted Renée's normal reserve, and she began sending poems to Natalie, who responded with poems of her own. They soon became friends. Renée confessed that she had had an intense friendship with another woman, but that it remained platonic—the thought of physical involvement repulsed her. Natalie told her about the ancient Greek poet Sappho, who celebrated love between women as the only love that is innocent and pure. One night Renée, inspired by their discussions, invited Natalie to her apartment, which she had transformed into a kind of chapel. The room was filled with candles and with white lilies, the flowers she associated with Natalie. That night the two women became lovers. They soon moved in together, but when Renée realized that Natalie could not be faithful to her, her love turned into hatred. She broke off the relationship, moved out, and vowed to never see her again.

Over the next few months Natalie sent her letters and poems, and showed up at her new home—all to no avail. Renée would have nothing to do with her. One evening at the opera, though, Natalie sat down beside her and gave her a poem she had written in her honor. She expressed her regrets for the past, and also a simple request: the two women should go on a pilgrimage to the Greek island of Lesbos, Sappho's home. Only there could they purify themselves and their relationship. Renée could not resist.

would abandon their husbands, homes, children, to follow this Circe of Lesbos. • Circe's method was to concoct magic potions. Natalie preferred writing poems; she always knew how to blend the physical and the spiritual.

—Jean Chalon, *Portrait of a Seductress: The World of Natalie Barney*, translated by Carol Barko

There once lived in the town of Gafsa, in Barbary, a very rich man who had numerous children, among them a lovely and graceful young daughter called Alibech. She was not herself a Christian, but there were many Christians in the town, and one day, having on occasion heard them extol the Christian faith and the service of God, she asked one of them for his opinion on the best and easiest way for a person to "serve God," as they put it. He answered her by saying that the ones who served God best were those who put the greatest distance between themselves and earthly goods, as happened in the case of people who had gone to live in the remoter parts of the Sahara. • She said no more about it to anyone, but next morning, being a very simple-natured creature of fourteen or thereabouts, Alibech set out all alone, in secret, and made her way toward the desert, prompted by nothing more logical than a strong adolescent impulse. A few days later, exhausted from fatigue and hunger, she arrived in the heart of the wilderness,

On the island they retraced the poetess's steps, imagining they were transported back into the pagan, innocent days of ancient Greece. For Renée, Natalie had become Sappho herself. When they finally returned to Paris, Renée wrote her, "My blond Siren, I don't want you to become like those who dwell on earth. . . . I want you to stay yourself, for this is the way you cast your spell over me." Their affair lasted until Renée's death, in 1909.

Interpretation. Liane de Pougy and Renée Vivien both suffered a similar oppression: they were self-absorbed, hyperaware of themselves. The source of this habit in Liane was men's constant attention to her body. She could never escape their looks, which plagued her with a feeling of heaviness. Renée, meanwhile, thought too much about her own problems—her repression of her lesbianism, her mortality. She felt consumed with self-hatred.

Natalie Barney, on the other hand, was buoyant, lighthearted, absorbed in the world around her. Her seductions—and by the end of her life they numbered well into the hundreds—all had a similar quality: she took the victim outside herself, directing her attention toward beauty, poetry, the innocence of Sapphic love. She invited her women to participate in a kind of cult in which they would worship these sublimities. To heighten the cult-like feeling, she involved them in little rituals: they would call each other by new names, send each other poems in daily telegrams, wear costumes, make pilgrimages to holy sites. Two things would inevitably happen: the women would start to direct some of the worshipful feelings they were experiencing toward Natalie, who seemed as lofty and beautiful as the things she held up to be adored; and, pleasantly diverted into this spiritualized realm, they would also lose any heaviness they had felt about their bodies, their selves, their identities. Their repression of their sexuality would melt away. By the time Natalie kissed or caressed them, it would feel like something innocent, pure, as if they had returned to the Garden of Eden before the fall.

Religion is the great balm of existence because it takes us outside ourselves, connects us to something larger. As we contemplate the object of worship (God, nature), our burdens are lifted away. It is wonderful to feel raised up from the earth, to experience that kind of lightness. No matter how progressive the times, many of us feel uncomfortable with our bodies, our animal drives. A seducer who focuses too much attention on the physical will stir up self-consciousness, and a residue of disgust. So focus attention on something else. Invite the other person to worship something beautiful in the world. It could be nature, a work of art, even God (or gods—paganism never goes out of fashion); people are dying to believe in something. Add some rituals. If you can make yourself seem to resemble the thing you are worshiping—you are natural, aesthetic, noble, and sublime—your targets will transfer their worship to you. Religion and

where, catching sight of a small hut in the distance, she stumbled toward it, and in the doorway she found a holy man, who was astonished to see her in those parts and asked her what she was doing there. She told him that she had been inspired by God, and that she was trying, not only to serve Him, but also to find someone who could teach her how she should go about it. • On observing how young and exceedingly pretty she was, the good man was afraid to take her under his wing lest the devil should catch him unawares. So he praised her for her good intentions, and having given her a quantity of herb roots, wild apples, and dates to eat, and some water to drink, he said to her: • "My daughter, not very far from here there is a holy man who is much more capable than I of teaching you what you want to know. Go along to him." And he sent her upon her way. • When she came to this second man, she was told precisely the same thing, and so she went on until she arrived at the cell of a young hermit, a very devout and kindly fellow called Rustico, to whom she put the same inquiry as she had addressed to the others. Being anxious to prove to himself that he possessed a will of iron, he did not, like the others, send her away or direct her elsewhere, but kept her with him in his cell, in a corner of which, when night descended, he prepared a makeshift bed out of palm leaves, upon which he invited her to lie down and rest. • Once he had taken this step, very little time elapsed before temptation went to war against his willpower, and after the first few assaults, finding himself outmaneuvered on all fronts, he laid down his arms and surrendered. Casting aside pious thoughts, prayers, and penitential exercises, he began to concentrate his mental faculties upon the youth and beauty of the girl, and to devise suitable ways and means for approaching her in such a fashion that she should not think it lewd of him to make the sort of proposal he had in mind. By putting certain questions to her, he soon discovered that she had never been intimate with the opposite sex and was every bit as innocent as she seemed; and he therefore thought of a possible way to persuade her, with the pretext of serving God, to grant his desires. He began by delivering a long speech in which he showed her how powerful an enemy the devil was to the Lord God, and followed this up by impressing upon her that of all the ways of serving God, the one that He most appreciated consisted in putting the devil back in Hell, to which the Almighty had consigned him in the first place. • The girl asked him how this was done, and Rustico replied: • "You will soon find out, but just do whatever you see me doing for the present." And so saying, he began to divest himself of the few clothes he was wearing, leaving himself completely naked. The girl followed his example, and he sank to his knees as though he

spirituality are full of sexual undertones that can be brought to the surface once you have made your targets lose their self-awareness. From spiritual ecstasy to sexual ecstasy is but one small step.

> *Come back to take me, quickly, and lead me far away. Purify me with a great fire of divine love, none of the animal kind. You are all soul when you want to be, when you feel it, take me far away from my body.*
>
> —Liane de Pougy

Keys to Seduction

Religion is the most seductive system that mankind has created. Death is our greatest fear, and religion offers us the illusion that we are immortal, that something about us will live on. The idea that we are an infinitesimal part of a vast and indifferent universe is terrifying; religion humanizes this universe, makes us feel important and loved. We are not animals governed by uncontrollable drives, animals that die for no apparent reason, but creatures made in the image of a supreme being. We too can be sublime, rational, and good. Anything that feeds a desire or a wished-for illusion is seductive, and nothing can match religion in this arena.

Pleasure is the bait that you use to lure a person into your web. But no matter how clever a seducer you are, in the back of your targets' mind they are aware of the endgame, the physical conclusion toward which you are heading. You may think your target is unrepressed and hungry for pleasure, but almost all of us are plagued by an underlying unease with our animal nature. Unless you deal with this unease, your seduction, even when successful in the short term, will be superficial and temporary. Instead, like Natalie Barney, try to capture your target's soul, to build the foundation of a deep and lasting seduction. Lure the victim deep into your web with spirituality, making physical pleasure seem sublime and transcendent. Spirituality will disguise your manipulations, suggesting that your relationship is timeless, and creating a space for ecstasy in the victim's mind. Remember that seduction is a mental process, and nothing is more mentally intoxicating than religion, spirituality, and the occult.

In Gustave Flaubert's novel *Madame Bovary*, Rodolphe Boulanger visits the country doctor Bovary and finds himself interested in the doctor's beautiful wife, Emma. Boulanger "was brutal and shrewd. He was something of a connoisseur: there had been many women in his life." He senses that Emma is bored. A few weeks later he manages to run into her at a county fair, where he gets her alone. He affects an air of sadness and gloom: "Many's the time I've passed a cemetery in the moonlight and asked myself if I wouldn't be better off lying there with the rest. . . . " He mentions his bad reputation; he deserves it, he says, but is it his fault? "Do you really not know that there exist souls that are ceaselessly in torment?" Several times he takes Emma's hand, but she politely withdraws it. He talks of love, the magnetic force that draws two people together. Perhaps it has roots in some earlier existence, some previous incarnation of their souls. "Take us, for example. Why should we have met? How did it happen? It can only be that something in our particular inclinations made us come closer and closer across the distance that separated us, the way two rivers flow together." He takes her hand again and this time she lets him hold it. After the fair, he avoids her for a few weeks, then suddenly shows up, claiming that he tried to stay away but that fate, destiny, has pulled him back. He takes Emma riding. When he finally makes his move, in the woods, she seems frightened and rejects his advances. "You must have some mistaken idea," he protests. "I have you in my heart like a Madonna on a pedestal. . . . I beseech you: be my friend, my sister, my angel!" Under the spell of his words, she lets him hold her and lead her deeper into the woods, where she succumbs.

Rodolphe's strategy is threefold. First he talks of sadness, melancholy, discontent, talk that makes him seem nobler than other people, as if life's common material pursuits could not satisfy him. Next he talks of destiny, the magnetic attraction of two souls. This makes his interest in Emma seem not so much a momentary impulse as something timeless, linked to the movement of the stars. Finally he talks of angels, the elevated and the sublime. By placing everything on the spiritual plane, he distracts Emma from the physical, makes her feel giddy, and packs a seduction that could have taken months into a matter of a few encounters.

The references Rodolphe uses might seem clichéd by today's standards, but the strategy itself will never grow old. Simply adapt it to the occult fads of the day. Affect a spiritual air by displaying a discontent with the banalities of life. It is not money or sex or success that moves you; your drives are never so base. No, something much deeper motivates you. Whatever this is, keep it vague, letting the target imagine your hidden depths. The stars, astrology, fate, are always appealing; create the sense that destiny has brought you and your target together. That will make your seduction feel more natural. In a world where too much is controlled and manufactured, the sense that fate, necessity, or some higher power is guiding your relationship is doubly seductive. If you want to weave religious motifs into your seduction, it is always best to choose some distant, exotic religion with a slightly pagan air. It is easy to move from pagan spirituality to pagan earthiness. Timing counts: once you have stirred your targets' souls, move quickly to the physical, making sexuality seem merely an extension of the spiritual vibrations you are experiencing. In other words, employ the spiritual strategy as close to the time for your bold move as possible.

The spiritual is not exclusively the religious or the occult. It is anything that will add a sublime, timeless quality to your seduction. In the modern world, culture and art have in some ways taken the place of religion. There are two ways to use art in your seduction: first, create it yourself, in the target's honor. Natalie Barney wrote poems, and barraged her targets with

were about to pray, getting her to kneel directly opposite. • In this posture, the girl's beauty was displayed to Rustico in all its glory, and his longings blazed more fiercely than ever, bringing about the resurrection of the flesh. Alibech stared at this in amazement and said: • "Rustico, what is that I see sticking out in front of you, which I do not possess?" • "Oh, my daughter," said Rustico, "this is the devil I was telling you about. Do you see what he's doing? He's hurting me so much that I can hardly endure it." • "Oh, praise be to God," said the girl, "I can see that I am better off than you are, for I have no such devil to contend with." • "You're right there," said Rustico. "But you have something else instead, that I haven't." • "Oh?" said Alibech. "And what's that?" • "You have Hell," said Rustico. "And I honestly believe that God has sent you here for the salvation of my soul, because if this devil continues to plague the life out of me, and if you are prepared to take sufficient pity upon me to let me put him back into Hell, you will be giving me marvelous relief, as well as rendering incalculable service and pleasure to God, which is what you say you came here for in the first place." • "Oh, Father," replied the girl in all innocence, "if I really do have Hell, let's do as you suggest just as soon as you are ready." • "God bless you, my daughter," said Rustico. "Let's go and put him back, and then perhaps he'll leave me alone." • At which point

them. Half of Picasso's appeal to many women was the hope that he would immortalize them in his paintings—for *Ars longa, vita brevis* (Art is long, life is short), as they used to say in Rome. Even if your love is a passing fancy, by capturing it in a work of art you give it a seductive illusion of eternity. The second way to use art is to make it ennoble the affair, giving your seduction an elevated edge. Natalie Barney took her targets to the theater, to the opera, to museums, to places full of history and atmosphere. In such places your souls can vibrate to the same spiritual wavelength. Of course you should avoid works of art that are earthy or vulgar, calling attention to your intentions. The play, movie, or book can be contemporary, even a little raw, as long as it contains a noble message and is tied to some just cause. Even a political movement can be spiritually uplifting. Remember to tailor your spiritual lures to the target. If the target is earthy and cynical, paganism or art will be more productive than the occult or religious piety.

The Russian mystic Rasputin was revered for his saintliness and his healing powers. Women in particular were fascinated with Rasputin and would visit him in his St. Petersburg apartment for spiritual guidance. He would talk to them of the simple goodness of the Russian peasantry, God's forgiveness, and other lofty matters. But after a few minutes of this, he would inject a comment or two that were of a much different nature—something about the woman's beauty, her lips that were so inviting, the desires she could inspire in a man. He would talk of different kinds of love—love of God, love between friends, love between a man and a woman—but mix them all up as if they were one. Then as he returned to discussing spiritual matters, he would suddenly take the woman's hand, or whisper into her ear. All this would have an intoxicating effect—women would find themselves dragged into a kind of maelstrom, both spiritually uplifted and sexually excited. Hundreds of women succumbed during these spiritual visits, for he would also tell them that they could not repent until they had sinned, and who better to sin with than Rasputin.

Rasputin understood the intimate connection between the sexual and the spiritual. Spirituality, the love of God, is a sublimated version of sexual love. The language of the religious mystics of the Middle Ages is full of erotic images; the contemplation of God and of the sublime can offer a kind of mental orgasm. There is no more seductive brew than the combination of the spiritual and the sexual, the high and the low. When you talk of spiritual matters, then, let your looks and physical presence hint of sexuality at the same time. Make the harmony of the universe and union with God seem to confuse with physical harmony and the union between two people. If you can make the endgame of your seduction appear as a spiritual experience, you will heighten the physical pleasure and create a seduction with a deep and lasting effect.

he conveyed the girl to one of their beds, where he instructed her in the art of incarcerating that accursed fiend. • Never having put a single devil into Hell before, the girl found the first experience a little painful, and she said to Rustico: • "This devil must certainly be a bad lot, Father, and a true enemy of God, for as well as plaguing mankind, he even hurts Hell when he's driven back inside it." • "Daughter," said Rustico, "it will not always be like that." And in order to ensure that it wouldn't, before moving from the bed they put him back half a dozen times, curbing his arrogance to such good effect that he was positively glad to keep still for the rest of the day. • During the next few days, however, the devil's pride frequently reared its head again, and the girl, ever ready to obey the call to duty and bring him under control, happened to develop a taste for the sport, and began saying to Rustico: • "I can certainly see what those worthy men in Gafsa meant when they said that serving God was so agreeable. I don't honestly recall ever having done anything that gave me so much pleasure and satisfaction as I get from putting the devil back in Hell. To my way of thinking, anyone who devotes his energies to anything but the service of God is a complete blockhead." • . . . And so, young ladies, if you stand in need of God's grace, see

***Symbol**: The Stars in the sky. Objects of worship for centuries, and symbols of the sublime and divine. In contemplating them, we are momentarily distracted from everything mundane and mortal. We feel lightness. Lift your targets' minds up to the stars and they will not notice what is happening here on earth.*

that you learn to put the devil back in Hell, for it is greatly to His liking and pleasurable to the parties concerned, and a great deal of good can arise and flow in the process.

—Giovanni Boccaccio, *The Decameron*, translated by G. H. McWilliam

Reversal

Letting your targets feel that your affection is neither temporary nor superficial will often make them fall deeper under your spell. In some, though, it can arouse an anxiety: the fear of commitment, of a claustrophobic relationship with no exits. Never let your spiritual lures seem to be leading in that direction, then. To focus attention on the distant future may implicitly constrict their freedom; you should be seducing them, not offering to marry them. What you want is to make them lose themselves in the moment, experiencing the timeless depth of your feelings in the present tense. Religious ecstasy is about intensity, not temporal extensity.

Giovanni Casanova used many spiritual lures in his seductions—the occult, anything that would inspire lofty sentiments. For the time that he was involved with a woman, she would feel that he would do anything for her, that he was not just using her only to abandon her. But she also knew that when it became convenient to end the affair, he would cry, give her a magnificent gift, then quietly leave. This was just what many young women wanted—a temporary diversion from marriage or an oppressive family. Sometimes pleasure is best when we know it is fleeting.

20

Mix Pleasure with Pain

The greatest mistake in seduction is being too nice. At first, perhaps, your kindness is charming, but it soon grows monotonous; you are trying too hard to please, and seem insecure. Instead of overwhelming your targets with niceness, try inflicting some pain. Lure them in with focused attention, then change direction, appearing suddenly uninterested. Make them feel guilty and insecure. Even instigate a breakup, subjecting them to an emptiness and pain that will give you room to maneuver—now a rapprochement, an apology, a return to your earlier kindness, will turn them weak at the knees. The lower the lows you create, the greater the highs. To heighten the erotic charge, create the excitement of fear.

The Emotional Roller Coaster

One hot summer afternoon in 1894, Don Mateo Díaz, a thirty-eight-year-old resident of Seville, decided to visit a local tobacco factory. Because of his connections Don Mateo was allowed to tour the place, but his interest was not in the business side. Don Mateo liked young girls, and hundreds of them worked in the factory. Just as he had expected, that day many of them were in a state of near undress because of the heat—it was quite a spectacle. He enjoyed the sights for a while, but the noise and the temperature soon got to him. As he was heading for the door, though, a worker of no more than sixteen called out to him: "*Caballero*, if you will give me a penny I will sing you a little song."

The more one pleases generally, the less one pleases profoundly.

—Stendhal, *Love*, translated by Gilbert and Suzanne Sale

The girl's name was Conchita Pérez, and she looked young and innocent, in fact beautiful, with a sparkle in her eye that suggested a taste for adventure. The perfect prey. He listened to her song (which seemed vaguely suggestive), tossed her a coin that was equal to a month's salary, tipped his hat, then left. It was never good to come on too strong too early. As he walked along the street, he plotted how he would lure her into an affair. Suddenly he felt a hand on his arm and he turned to see her walking alongside him. It was too hot to work—would he be a gentleman and escort her home? Of course. Do you have a lover? he asked her. No, she said, "I am *mozita*"—pure, a virgin.

You should mix in the odd rebuff \ With your cheerful fun. Shut him out of the house, let him wait there Cursing that locked front door, let him plead \ And threaten all he's a mind to. Sweetness cloys the palate, \ Bitter juice is a freshener. Often a small skiff \ Is sunk by favoring winds: it's their husbands' access to them, \ At will, that deprives so many wives of love. \ Let her put in a door, with a hard-faced porter to tell him \ "Keep out," and he'll soon be touched with desire \ Through frustration. Put down your blunt foils, fight with sharpened weapons \ (I don't doubt that my own shafts \ Will be turned against me). When a new-captured lover \ Is stumbling into the toils, then let him believe \ He alone has rights to your bed—but later, make him

Conchita lived with her mother in a rundown part of town. Don Mateo exchanged pleasantries, slipped the mother some money (he knew from experience how important it was to keep the mother happy), then left. He considered waiting a few days, but he was impatient, and returned the following morning. The mother was out. He and Conchita resumed their playful banter from the day before, and to his surprise she suddenly sat in his lap, put her arms around him, and kissed him. His strategy flying out the window, he took hold of her and returned the kiss. She immediately jumped up, her eyes flashing with anger: you are trifling with me, she said, using me for a quick thrill. Don Mateo denied having any such intentions, and apologized for going too far. When he left, he felt confused: she had started it all; why should he feel guilty? And yet he did. Young girls can be so unpredictable; it is best to break them in slowly.

Over the next few days Don Mateo was the perfect gentleman. He visited every day, showered mother and daughter with gifts, made no advances—at least not at first. The damned girl had become so familiar

conscious \ Of rivals, of shared delights. Neglect \ These devices—his ardor will wane. A racehorse runs most strongly \ When the field's ahead, to be paced \ And passed. So the dying embers of passion can be fanned to \ Fresh flame by some outrage—I can only love, \ Myself, I confess it, when wronged. But don't let the cause of \ Pain be too obvious: let a lover suspect \ More than he knows. Invent a slave who watches your every \ Movement, make clear what a jealous martinet \ That man of yours is—such things will excite him. Pleasure \ Too safely enjoyed lacks zest. You want to be free \ As Thaïs? Act scared. Though the door's quite safe, let him in by \ The window. Look nervous. Have a smart \ Maid rush in, scream "We're caught!" while you bundle the quaking \ Youth out of sight. But be sure \ To offset his fright with some moments of carefree pleasure— \ Or he'll think a night with you isn't worth the risk.

—Ovid, *The Art of Love*, translated by Peter Green

"Certainly," I said, "I have often told you that pain holds a peculiar attraction for me, and that nothing kindles my passion quite so much as tyranny, cruelty and above all unfaithfulness in a beautiful woman."

—Leopold von Sacher-Masoch, *Venus in Furs*, translated by Jean McNeil

with him that she would dress in front of him, or greet him in her nightgown. These glimpses of her body drove him crazy, and he would sometimes try to steal a kiss or caress, only to have her push him away and scold him. Weeks went by; clearly he had shown that his was not a passing fancy. Tired of the endless courtship, he took Conchita's mother aside one day and proposed that he set the girl up in a house of her own. He would treat her like a queen; she would have everything she wanted. (So, of course, would her mother.) Surely his proposal would satisfy the two women—but the next day, a note came from Conchita, expressing not gratitude but recrimination: he was trying to buy her love. "You shall never see me again," she concluded. He hurried to the house only to discover that the women had moved out that very morning, without leaving word where they were going.

Don Mateo felt terrible. Yes, he had acted like a boor. Next time he would wait months, or years if need be, before being so bold. Soon, however, another thought assailed him: he would never see Conchita again. Only then did he realize how much he loved her.

The winter passed, the worst of Mateo's life. One spring day he was walking down the street when he heard someone calling his name. He looked up: Conchita was standing in an open window, beaming with excitement. She bent down toward him and he kissed her hand, beside himself with joy. Why had she disappeared so suddenly? It was all going too quickly, she said. She had been afraid—of his intentions, and of her own feelings. But seeing him again, she was certain that she loved him. Yes, she was ready to be his mistress. She would prove it, she would come to him. Being apart had changed them both, he thought.

A few nights later, as promised, she appeared at his house. They kissed and began to undress. He wanted to savor every minute, to take it slowly, but he felt like a caged bull finally set free. He followed her into bed, his hands all over her. He started to take off her underwear but it was laced up in some complicated way. Eventually he had to sit up and take a look: she was wearing some elaborate canvas contraption, of a kind he had never seen. No matter how hard he tugged and pulled, it would not come off. He felt like hitting Conchita, he was so distraught, but instead he started to cry. She explained: she wanted to do everything with him, yet to remain a *mozita*. This was her protection. Exasperated, he sent her home.

Over the next few weeks, Don Mateo began to reassess his opinion of Conchita. He saw her flirting with other men, and dancing a suggestive flamenco in a bar: she was not a *mozita,* he decided, she was playing him for money. And yet he could not leave her. Another man would take his place—an unbearable thought. She would invite him to spend the night in her bed, as long as he promised not to force himself on her; and then, as if to torture him beyond reason, she would get into bed naked (supposedly because of the heat). All this he put up with on the grounds that no other man had such privileges. But one night, pushed to the limits of frustration, he exploded with anger, and issued an ultimatum: either give me what I want or you will never see me again. Suddenly Conchita started to cry. He had never seen her cry, and it moved him. She too was tired of all this, she said, her voice trembling; if it was not too late, she was ready to accept the proposal she had once turned down. Set her up in a house, and he would see what a devoted mistress she would be.

Don Mateo wasted no time. He bought her a villa, gave her plenty of money to decorate it. After eight days the house was ready. She would receive him there at midnight. What joys awaited him.

Don Mateo showed up at the appointed hour. The barred door to the courtyard was closed. He rang the bell. She came to the other side of the door. "Kiss my hands," she said through the bars. "Now kiss the hem of my skirt, and the tip of my foot in its slipper." He did as she requested. "That is good," she said. "Now you may go." His shocked expression just made her laugh. She ridiculed him, then made a confession: she was repulsed by him. Now that she had a villa in her name, she was free of him at last. She called out, and a young man appeared from the shadows of the courtyard. As Don Mateo watched, too stunned to move, they began to make love on the floor, right before his eyes.

The next morning Conchita appeared at Don Mateo's house, supposedly to see if he had committed suicide. To her surprise, he hadn't—in fact he slapped her so hard she fell to the ground. "Conchita," he said, "you have made me suffer beyond all human strength. You have invented moral tortures to try them on the only man who loved you passionately. I now declare that I am going to possess you by force." Conchita screamed she would never be his, but he hit her again and again. Finally, moved by her tears, he stopped. Now she looked up at him lovingly. Forget the past, she said, forget all that I have done. Now that he hit her, now that she could see his pain, she felt certain he truly loved her. She was still a *mozita*—the affair with the young man the night before had been only for show, ending as soon as he had left—and she still belonged to him. "You are not going to take me by force. I await you in my arms." Finally she was sincere. To his supreme delight, he discovered that she was indeed still a virgin.

Interpretation. Don Mateo and Conchita Pérez are characters in the 1896 novella *Woman and Puppet*, by Pierre Louÿs. Based on a true story—the "Miss Charpillon" episode in Casanova's *Memoirs*—the novella has served as the basis for two films: Josef von Sternberg's *Devil Is a Woman*, with Marlene Dietrich, and Luis Buñuel's *That Obscure Object of Desire*. In Louÿs's story, Conchita takes a proud and aggressive older man and in the space of a few months turns him into an abject slave. Her method is simple: she stimulates as many emotions as possible, including heavy doses of pain. She excites his lust, then makes him feel base for taking advantage of her. She gets him to play the protector, then makes him feel guilty for trying to buy her. Her sudden disappearance anguishes him—he has lost her—so that when she reappears (never by accident) he feels intense joy; which, however, she

Oderint, dum metuant [Let them hate me so long as they fear me], as if only fear and hate belong together, whereas fear and love have nothing to do with each other, as if it were not fear that makes love interesting. With what kind of love do we embrace nature? Is there not a secretive anxiety and horror in it, because its beautiful harmony works its way out of lawlessness and wild confusion, its security out of perfidy? But precisely this anxiety captivates the most. So also with love, if it is to be interesting. Behind it ought to brood the deep, anxious night from which springs the flower of love.

—Søren Kierkegaard, *The Seducer's Diary*, translated by Howard V. Hong and Edna H. Hong

The lovely marble creature coughed and rearranged the sable around her shoulders. • "Thank you for the lesson in classics," I replied, "but I cannot deny that in your peaceful and sunny world just as in our misty climate man and woman are natural enemies. Love may unite them briefly to form one mind, one heart, one will, but all too soon they are torn asunder. And this you know better than I: either one of them must bend the other to his will, or else he must let himself be trampled underfoot." • "Under the woman's foot, of course," said Lady Venus impertinently. "And that you know better than I." • "Of course, that is why I have no illusions." • "In other words you are now my slave without illusions, and I shall

quickly turns back into tears. Jealousy and humiliation then precede the final moment when she gives him her virginity. (Even after this, according to the story, she finds ways to continue to torment him.) Each low she inspires—guilt, despair, jealousy, emptiness—creates the space for a more intense high. He becomes an addict, hooked on the alternation of charge and withdrawal.

Your seduction should never follow a simple course upward toward pleasure and harmony. The climax will come too soon, and the pleasure will be weak. What makes us intensely appreciate something is previous suffering. A brush with death makes us fall in love with life; a long journey makes a return home that much more pleasurable. Your task is to create moments of sadness, despair, and anguish, to create the tension that allows for a great release. Do not worry about making people angry; anger is a sure sign that you have your hooks in them. Nor should you be afraid that if you make yourself difficult people will flee—we only abandon those who bore us. The ride on which you take your victims can be tortuous but never dull. At all costs, keep your targets emotional and on edge. Create enough highs and lows and you will wear away the last vestiges of their willpower.

trample you mercilessly." • "Madam!" • "You do not know me yet. I admit that I am cruel—since the word gives you so much delight—but am I not entitled to be so? It is man who desires, woman who is desired; this is woman's only advantage, but it is a decisive one. By making man so vulnerable to passion, nature has placed him at woman's mercy, and she who has not the sense to treat him like a humble subject, a slave, a plaything, and finally to betray him with a laugh—well, she is a woman of little wisdom." • "My dear, your principles . . ." I protested. • "Are founded on the experience of a thousand years," she replied mischievously, running her white fingers through the dark fur. "The more submissive woman is, the more readily man recovers his self-possession and becomes domineering; but the more cruel and faithless she is, the more she ill-treats him, the more wantonly she toys with him and the harsher she is, the more she quickens his desire and secures his love and admiration. It has always been so, from the time of Helen and Delilah all the way to Catherine the Great and Lola Montez."

—Leopold von Sacher-Masoch, *Venus in Furs*, translated by Jean McNeil

Harshness and Kindness

In 1972, Henry Kissinger, then President Richard Nixon's assistant for national security affairs, received a request for an interview from the famous Italian journalist Oriana Fallaci. Kissinger rarely gave interviews; he had no control over the final product, and he was a man who needed to be in control. But he had read Fallaci's interview with a North Vietnamese general, and it had been instructive. She was extremely well informed on the Vietnam War; perhaps he could gather some information of his own, pick her brain. He decided to ask for a preinterview, a preliminary meeting. He would grill her on different subjects; if she passed the test, he would grant her an interview proper. They met, and he was impressed; she was extremely intelligent—and tough. It would be an enjoyable challenge to outwit her and prove that he was tougher. He agreed to a short interview a few days later.

To Kissinger's annoyance, Fallaci began the interview by asking him whether he was disappointed by the slow pace of the peace negotiations with North Vietnam. He would not discuss the negotiations—he had made that clear in the preinterview. Yet she continued the same line of questioning. He grew a little angry. "That's enough," he said. "I don't want to talk any more about Vietnam." Although she didn't immediately abandon the subject, her questions became gentler: what were his personal feelings toward the leaders of South and North Vietnam? Still, he ducked: "I'm not the kind of person to be swayed by emotion. Emotions serve no purpose." She moved to grander philosophical issues—war, peace. She

In essence, the domain of eroticism is the domain of violence, of violation. . . . The whole business of eroticism is to strike to the inmost core of the living being, so that the heart stands still. . . . The

praised him for his role in the rapprochement with China. Without realizing it, Kissinger began to open up. He talked of the pain he felt in dealing with Vietnam, the pleasures of wielding power. Then suddenly the harsher questions returned—was he simply Nixon's lackey, as many suspected? Up and down she went, alternately baiting and flattering him. His goal had been to pump her for information while revealing nothing about himself; by the end, though, she had given him nothing, while he had revealed a range of embarrassing opinions—his view of women as playthings, for instance, and his belief that he was popular with the public because people saw him as a kind of lonesome cowboy, the hero who cleans things up by himself. When the interview was published, Nixon, Kissinger's boss, was livid about it.

In 1973, the Shah of Iran, Mohammed Riza Pahlavi, granted Fallaci an interview. He knew how to handle the press—be noncommittal, speak in generalities, seem firm, yet polite. This approach had worked a thousand times before. Fallaci began the interview on a personal level, asking how it felt to be a king, to be the target of assassination attempts, and why the shah always seemed so sad. He talked of the burdens of his position, the pain and loneliness he felt. It seemed a release of sorts to talk about his professional problems. As he talked, Fallaci said little, her silence goading him on. Then she suddenly changed the subject: he was having difficulties with his second wife. Surely that must hurt him? This was a sore spot, and Pahlavi got angry. He tried to change the subject, but she kept returning to it. Why waste time talking about wives and women, he said. He then went so far as to criticize women in general—their lack of creativity, their cruelty. Fallaci kept at him: he had dictatorial tendencies and his country lacked basic freedoms. Fallaci's own books were on his government's blacklist. Hearing this, the shah seemed somewhat taken aback—perhaps he was dealing with a subversive writer. But then she softened her tone again, asked him about his many achievements. The pattern repeated: the moment he relaxed, she blindsided him with a sharp question; when he grew bitter, she lightened the mood. Like Kissinger, he found himself opening up despite himself and mentioning things he would later regret, such as his intention to raise the price of oil. Slowly he fell under her spell, even began to flirt with her. "Even if you're on the blacklist of my authorities," he said at the end of the interview, "I'll put you on the white list of my heart."

Interpretation. Most of Fallaci's interviews were with powerful leaders, men and women with an overwhelming need to control the situation, to avoid revealing anything embarrassing. This put her and her subjects in conflict, since getting them to open up—grow emotional, give up control—was exactly what she wanted. The classic seductive approach of charm and flattery would get her nowhere with these people; they would see right through it. Instead, Fallaci preyed on their emotions, alternating harshness and kindness. She would ask a cruel question that touched on the deepest

whole business of eroticism is to destroy the self-contained character of the participators as they are in their normal lives. . . . We ought never to forget that in spite of the bliss love promises its first effect is one of turmoil and distress. Passion fulfilled itself provokes such violent agitation that the happiness involved, before being a happiness to be enjoyed, is so great as to be more like its opposite, suffering. . . . The likelihood of suffering is all the greater since suffering alone reveals the total significance of the beloved object.

—Georges Bataille, *Erotism: Death and Sensuality*, translated by Mary Dalwood

Always a little doubt to set at rest—that's what keeps one craving in passionate love. Because the keenest misgivings are always there, its pleasures never become tedious. • Saint-Simon, the only historian France has ever possessed, says: "After many passing fancies the Duchesse de Berry had fallen deeply in love with Riom, a junior member of the d'Aydie family, the son of one of Madame de Biron's sisters. He had neither looks nor brains; he was fat, short, chubby-cheeked, pale, and had such a crop of pimples that he seemed one large abscess; he had beautiful teeth, but not the least idea that he was going to inspire a passion which quickly got out of control, a passion which lasted a lifetime, notwithstanding a number of subsidiary flirtations and affairs. . . . • He would

insecurities of the subject, who would get emotional and defensive; deep down, though, something else would stir inside them—the desire to prove to Fallaci that they did not deserve her implicit criticisms. Unconsciously they wanted to please her, to make her like them. When she then shifted tone, indirectly praising them, they felt they were winning her over and were encouraged to open up. Without realizing it, they would give freer rein to their emotions.

In social situations we all wear masks, and keep our defenses up. It is embarrassing, after all, to reveal one's true feelings. As a seducer you must find a way to lower these resistances. The Charmer's approach of flattery and attention can be effective here, particularly with the insecure, but it can take months of work, and can also backfire. To get a quicker result, and to break down more inaccessible people, it is often better to alternate harshness and kindness. By being harsh you create inner tensions—your targets may be upset with you, but they are also asking themselves questions. What have they done to earn your dislike? When you then are kind, they feel relieved, but also concerned that at any moment they might somehow displease you again. Make use of this pattern to keep them in suspense—dreading your harshness and keen to keep you kind. Your kindness and harshness should be subtle; indirect digs and compliments are best. Play the psychoanalyst: make cutting comments concerning their unconscious motives (you are only being truthful), then sit back and listen. Your silence will goad them into embarrassing admissions. Leaven your judgments with occasional praise and they will strive to please you, like dogs.

> *Love is a costly flower, but one must have the desire to pluck it from the edge of a precipice.*
>
> —Stendhal

excite but not requite the desire of the princess; he delighted in making her jealous, or pretending to be jealous himself. He would often drive her to tears. Gradually he forced her into the position of doing nothing without his leave, even trifles of no importance. Sometimes, when she was ready to go to the Opéra, he insisted that she stay at home; and sometimes he made her go there against her will. He obliged her to grant favours to ladies she did not like or of whom she was jealous. She was not even free to dress as she chose; he would amuse himself by making her change her coiffure or her dress at the last minute; he did this so often and so publicly that she became accustomed to take his orders in the evening for what she would do and wear the following day; then the next day he would alter everything, and the princess would cry all the more. In the end she took to sending him messages by trusted footmen, for from the first he had taken up residence in Luxembourg; messages which continued throughout her toilette, to know what ribbons she would wear, what gown and other ornaments; almost invariably he made her wear something she did not wish to. When she occasionally dared to do anything, however small, without his leave, he treated her like a servant, and she was in tears for several days. • . . . Before assembled company he would give her such brusque replies that everyone lowered their eyes, and the Duchess would blush, though her passion

Keys to Seduction

Almost everyone is more or less polite. We learn early on not to tell people what we really think of them; we smile at their jokes, act interested in their stories and problems. It is the only way to live with them. Eventually this becomes a habit; we are nice, even when it isn't really necessary. We try to please other people, to not step on their toes, to avoid disagreements and conflict.

Niceness in seduction, however, though it may at first draw someone to you (it is soothing and comforting), soon loses all effect. Being too nice can literally push the target away from you. Erotic feeling depends on the creation of tension. Without tension, without anxiety and suspense, there can be no feeling of release, of true pleasure and joy. It is your task to create that tension in the target, to stimulate feelings of anxiety, to lead them to and fro, so that the culmination of the seduction has real weight and intensity. So rid yourself of your nasty habit of avoiding conflict, which is in any case unnatural. You are most often nice not out of your own inner goodness but out of fear of displeasing, out of insecurity. Go beyond that fear and you suddenly have options—the freedom to create pain, then magically dissolve it. Your seductive powers will increase tenfold.

for him was in no way curtailed." • For the princess, Riom was a sovereign remedy against boredom.

—STENDHAL, *LOVE*, TRANSLATED BY GILBERT AND SUZANNE SALE

People will be less upset by your hurtful actions than you might imagine. In the world today, we often feel starved for experience. We crave emotion, even if it is negative. The pain you cause your targets, then, is bracing—it makes them feel more alive. They have something to complain about, they get to play the victim. As a result, once you have turned the pain into pleasure they will readily forgive you. Stir up their jealousy, make them feel insecure, and the validation you later give their ego by preferring them over their rivals is doubly delightful. Remember: you have more to fear by boring your targets than by shaking them up. Wounding people binds them to you more deeply than kindness. Create tension so you can release it. If you need inspiration, find the part of the target that most irritates you and use it as a springboard for some therapeutic conflict. The more real your cruelty, the more effective it is.

In 1818, the French writer Stendhal, then living in Milan, met the Countess Metilda Viscontini. For him, it was love at first sight. She was a proud, somewhat difficult woman, and she intimidated Stendhal, who was terribly afraid of displeasing her with a stupid comment or undignified act. Finally, unable to take it any longer, he one day took her hand and confessed his love. Horrified, the countess told him to leave and never come back.

Stendhal flooded Viscontini with letters, begging her to forgive him. At last, she relented: she would see him again, but under one condition—he could visit only once every two weeks, for no more than an hour, and only in the presence of company. Stendhal agreed; he had no choice. He now lived for those short fortnightly visits, which became occasions of intense anxiety and fear, since he was never quite sure whether she would change her mind and banish him forever. This went on for over two years, during which the countess never showed him the slightest sign of favor. Stendhal never found out why she had insisted on this arrangement—perhaps she wanted to toy with him or keep him at a distance. All he knew was that his love for her only grew stronger, became unbearably intense, until finally he had to leave Milan.

To get over this sad affair, Stendhal wrote his famous book *On Love*, in which he described the effect of fear on desire. First, if you fear the loved one, you can never get too close or familiar with him or her. The beloved then retains an element of mystery, which only intensifies your love. Second, there is something bracing about fear. It makes you vibrate with sensation, heightens your awareness, is intensely erotic. According to Stendhal, the closer the loved one brings you to the edge of the precipice, to the feeling that they could abandon you, the dizzier and more lost you will become. Falling in love means literally falling—losing control, a mix of fear and excitement.

Apply this wisdom in reverse: never let your targets get too comfortable with you. They need to feel fear and anxiety. Show them some coldness, a flash of anger they did not expect. Be irrational if necessary. There is always the trump card: a breakup. Let them feel they have lost you forever, make them fear that they have lost the power to charm you. Let these feelings sit with them for a while, then pull them back from the precipice. The reconciliation will be intense.

In 33 B.C., Mark Antony heard a rumor that Cleopatra, his lover of several years, had decided to seduce his rival, Octavius, and that she was planning to poison Antony. Cleopatra had poisoned people before; in fact she was an expert in the art. Antony grew paranoid, and finally one day confronted her. Cleopatra did not protest her innocence. Yes, that was true, it was quite within her power to poison Antony at any moment; there were no precautions he could take. Only the love she felt for him could protect him. To demonstrate, she took some flowers and dropped them into his wine. Antony hesitated, then raised the cup to his lips; Cleopatra grabbed his arm and stopped him. She had a prisoner brought in to drink the wine, and the prisoner promptly dropped dead. Falling at Cleopatra's feet, Antony professed that he loved her now more than ever. He did not speak out of cowardice; there was no man braver than he, and if Cleopatra could have poisoned him, he for his part could have left her and gone back to Rome. No, what pushed him over the edge was the feeling that she had control over his emotions, over life and death. He was her slave. Her demonstration of her power over him was not only effective but erotic.

Like Antony, many of us have masochistic yearnings without realizing it. It takes someone to inflict some pain on us for these deeply repressed desires to come to the surface. You must learn to recognize the types of hidden masochists out there, for each one enjoys a particular kind of pain. For instance, there are people who feel that they deserve nothing good in life, and who, unable to deal with success, sabotage themselves constantly. Be nice to them, admit that you admire them, and they are uncomfortable, since they feel that they cannot possibly match up to the ideal figure you have clearly imagined them to be. Such self-saboteurs do better with a little punishment; scold them, make them aware of their inadequacies. They feel they deserve such criticism and when it comes it is with a sense of relief. It is also easy to make them feel guilty, a feeling that deep down they enjoy.

Other people experience the responsibilities and duties of modern life as such a heavy burden, they long to give it all up. These people are often looking for someone or something to worship—a cause, a religion, a guru. Make them worship you. And then there are those who want to play the martyr. Recognize them by the joy they take in complaining, in feeling righteous and wronged; then give them a reason to complain. Remember: appearances deceive. Often the strongest-looking people—the Kissingers and Don Mateos—may secretly want to be punished. In any event, follow up pain with pleasure and you will create a state of dependency that will last for a long time.

Symbol: *The Precipice. At the edge of a cliff, people often feel lightheaded, both fearful and dizzy. For a moment they can imagine themselves falling headlong. At the same time, a part of them is tempted. Lead your targets as close to the edge as possible, then pull them back. No thrill without fear.*

Reversal

People who have recently experienced a lot of pain or a loss will flee if you try to inflict more on them. They have enough in their lives already. Far better to surround these types with pleasure—that will put them under your spell. The technique of inflicting pain works best on those who have it easy, who have power and few problems. People with comfortable lives may also feel a gnawing sense of guilt, as if they had gotten away with something. They may not consciously know it, but secretly they long for some punishment, a good mental thrashing, something that will bring them back down to earth.

Also, remember to not use the pleasure-through-pain tactic too early on. Some of the greatest seducers in history—Byron, Jiang Qing (Madame Mao), Picasso—had a sadistic streak, an ability to inflict mental torture. If their victims had known in advance what they were getting themselves into, they would have run for the hills. In truth, most of these seducers lured their targets into their webs by appearing to be paragons of sweetness and affection. Even Byron seemed like an angel when he first met a woman, so that she tended to doubt his devilish reputation—a seductive doubt, for it allowed her to think of herself as the only one who really understood him. His cruelty would come out later on, but by then it would be too late. The victim's emotions were engaged, and his harshness would only intensify her feelings.

In the beginning, then, wear the mask of a lamb, making pleasure and attentiveness your bait. First get under their skin, then lead them on a wild ride.

Phase Four

Moving In for the Kill

First you worked on their mind—the mental seduction. Then you confused and stirred them up—the emotional seduction. Now the time has come for hand-to-hand combat—the physical seduction. At this point, your victims are weak and ripe with desire: by showing a little coldness or uninterest, you will spark panic—they will come after you with impatience and erotic energy (21: Give them space to fall—the pursuer is pursued). To bring them to a boil, you need to put their minds to sleep and heat up their senses. It is best to lure them into lust by sending certain loaded signals that will get under their skin and spread sexual desire like a poison (22: Use physical lures). The moment to strike and move in for the kill is when your victim is brimming with desire, but not consciously expecting the climax to come (23: Master the art of the bold move).

Once the seduction is over, there is the danger that disenchantment will set in and ruin all your hard work (24: Beware the aftereffects). If you are after a relationship, then you must constantly re-seduce the victim, creating tension and releasing it. If your victim is to be sacrificed, then it must be done swiftly and cleanly, leaving you free (physically and psychologically) to move on to the next victim. Then the game begins all over.

21

Give Them Space to Fall— The Pursuer Is Pursued

If your targets become too used to you as the aggressor, they will give less of their own energy, and the tension will slacken. You need to wake them up, turn the tables. Once they are under your spell, take a step back and they will start to come after you. Begin with a touch of aloofness, an unexpected nonappearance, a hint that you are growing bored. Stir the pot by seeming interested in someone else. Make none of this explicit; let them only sense it and their imagination will do the rest, creating the doubt you desire. Soon they will want to possess you physically, and restraint will go out the window. The goal is to have them fall into your arms of their own will. Create the illusion that the seducer is being seduced.

Seductive Gravity

In the early 1840s, the center of attention in the French art world was a young woman named Apollonie Sabatier. She was so much the natural beauty that sculptors and painters vied to immortalize her in their works, and she was also charming, easy to talk to, and seductively self-sufficient—men were drawn to her. Her Paris apartment became a gathering spot for writers and artists, and soon Madame Sabatier—as she came to be known, although she was not married—was hosting one of the most important literary salons in France. Writers such as Gustave Flaubert, the elder Alexandre Dumas, and Théophile Gautier were among her regular guests.

Near the end of 1852, when she was thirty, Madame Sabatier received an anonymous letter. The writer confessed that he loved her deeply. Worried that she would find his sentiments ridiculous, he would not reveal his name; yet he had to let her know that he adored her. Sabatier was used to such attentions—one man after another had fallen in love with her—but this letter was different: in this man she seemed to have inspired a quasi-religious ardor. The letter, written in a disguised handwriting, contained a poem dedicated to her; titled "To One Who Is Too Gay," it began by praising her beauty, yet ended with the lines

> And so, one night, I'd like to sneak,
> When darkness tolls the hour of pleasure,
> A craven thief, toward the treasure
> Which is your person, plump and sleek. . . .
> And, most vertiginous delight!
> Into those lips, so freshly striking
> And daily lovelier to my liking—
> Infuse the venom of my spite.

Mixed in with her admirer's adoration, clearly, was a strange kind of lust, with a touch of cruelty to it. The poem both intrigued and disturbed her—and she had no idea who had written it.

A few weeks later another letter arrived. As before, the writer enveloped Sabatier in cultlike worship, mixing the physical and the spiritual. And as before, there was a poem, "All in One," in which he wrote,

Omissions, denials, deflections, deceptions, diversions, and humility—all aimed at provoking this second state, the secret of true seduction. Vulgar seduction might proceed by persistence, but true seduction proceeds by absence. . . . It is like fencing: one needs a field for the feint. Throughout this period, the seducer [Johannes], far from seeking to close in on her, seeks to maintain his distance by various ploys: he does not speak directly to her but only to her aunt, and then about trivial or stupid subjects; he neutralizes everything by irony and feigned pedanticism; he fails to respond to any feminine or erotic movement, and even finds her a sitcom suitor to disenchant and deceive her, to the point where she herself takes the initiative and breaks off her engagement, thus completing the seduction and creating the ideal situation for her total abandon.

—Jean Baudrillard, *Seduction*, translated by Brian Singer

The rumor spread everywhere. It was even told to the queen [Guinevere], who was seated at dinner. She nearly killed herself when she heard the perfidious rumor of Lancelot's death. She thought it was true and was so greatly perturbed that she was scarcely able to speak. . . . She arose at once from the table, and was able to give vent to her grief without being noticed or overheard. She was so crazed with the thought of killing herself that she repeatedly grabbed at her throat. Yet first she confessed in conscience, repented and asked God's pardon; she accused herself of having sinned against the one she knew had always been hers, and who would still be, were he alive. . . . She counted all of the unkindnesses and recalled each individual unkindness; she noted every one, and repeated often: "Oh misery! What was I thinking, when my lover came before me and I did not deign to welcome him, nor even care to listen! Was I not a fool to refuse to speak or even look at him? A fool? No, so help me God, I was cruel and deceitful! . . . I believe that it was I alone who struck him that mortal blow. When he came happily before me expecting me to receive him joyfully and I shunned him and would never even look at him, was this not a mortal blow? At that moment, when I refused to speak, I believe I severed both his heart and his life. Those two blows killed him, I think, and not any hired killers. • "Ah God! Will I be forgiven this murder, this sin? Never! All the rivers

No single beauty is the best,
Since she is all one flower divine....
O mystic metamorphosis!
My senses into one sense flow—
Her voice makes perfume when she speaks,
Her breath is music faint and low!

Clearly the author was haunted by Sabatier's presence, and thought of her constantly—but now she began to be haunted by *him,* thinking of him night and day, and wondering who he was. His subsequent letters only deepened the spell. It was flattering to hear that he was enchanted by more than her beauty, yet also flattering to know that he was not immune to her physical charms.

One day an idea occurred to Madame Sabatier as to who the writer might be: a young poet who had frequented her salon for several years, Charles Baudelaire. He seemed shy, in fact had hardly spoken to her, but she had read some of his poetry, and although the poems in the letters were more polished, the style was similar. At her apartment Baudelaire would always sit politely in a corner, but now that she thought of it, he would smile at her strangely, nervously. It was the look of a young man in love. Now when he visited she watched him carefully, and the more she watched, the surer she was that he was the writer, but she never confirmed her intuition, because she did not want to confront him—he might be shy, but he was a man, and at some point he would have to come to her. And she felt certain that he would. Then, suddenly the letters stopped coming—and Madame Sabatier could not understand why, since the last one had been even more adoring than all of the others before.

Several years went by, in which she often thought of her anonymous admirer's letters, but they were never renewed. In 1857, however, Baudelaire published a book of poetry, *The Flowers of Evil*, and Madame Sabatier recognized several of the verses—they were the ones he had written for her. Now they were out in the open for everyone to see. A little while later the poet sent her a gift: a specially bound copy of the book, and a letter, this time signed with his name. Yes, he wrote, he was the anonymous writer—would she forgive him for being so mysterious in the past? Furthermore, his feelings for her were as strong as ever: "You didn't think for a moment that I could have forgotten you? . . . You to me are more than a cherished image conjured up in dream, you're my superstition . . . my constant companion, my secret! Farewell, dear Madame. I kiss your hands with profound devotion."

This letter had a stronger effect on Madame Sabatier than the others had. Perhaps it was his childlike sincerity, and the fact that he had finally written to her directly; perhaps it was that he loved her but asked nothing of her, unlike all the other men she knew who at some point had always turned out to want something. Whatever it was, she had an uncontrollable desire to see him. The next day she invited him to her apartment, alone.

Baudelaire appeared at the appointed hour. He sat nervously in his seat, gazing at her with his large eyes, saying little, and what he did say was formal and polite. He seemed aloof. After he left a kind of panic seized Madame Sabatier, and the next day she wrote him a first letter of her own: "Today I'm more calm, and I can feel more clearly the impression of our Tuesday evening together. I can tell you, without the danger of your thinking I'm exaggerating, that I'm the happiest woman on the face of the earth, that I've never felt more truly that I love you, and that I've never seen you look more beautiful, more adorable, my divine friend!"

Madame Sabatier had never before written such a letter; she had always been the one who was pursued. Now she had lost her usual self-possession. And it only got worse: Baudelaire did not answer right away. When she saw him next, he was colder than before. She had the feeling there was someone else, that his old mistress, Jeanne Duval, had suddenly reappeared in his life and was pulling him away from her. One night she turned aggressive, embracing him, trying to kiss him, but he did not respond, and quickly found an excuse to leave. Why was he suddenly inaccessible? She began to flood him with letters, begging him to come to her. Unable to sleep, she would wait all night for him to show up. She had never experienced such desperation. Somehow she had to seduce him, possess him, have him all to herself. She tried everything—letters, coquetry, all kinds of promises—until he finally wrote that he was no longer in love with her and that was that.

and the seas will dry up first! Oh, misery! How it would have brought me comfort and healing if I had held him in my arms once before he died. How? Yes, quite naked next to him, in order to enjoy him fully. . . ." • . . . When they came within six or seven leagues of the castle where King Bademagu was staying, news that was pleasing came to him about Lancelot—news that he was glad to hear; Lancelot was alive and was returning, hale and hearty. He behaved most properly in going to inform the queen. "Good sir," she told him, "I believe it, since you have told me. But were he dead, I assure you that I could never again be happy." • . . . Now Lancelot had his every wish: the queen willingly sought his company and affection as he held her in his arms and she held him in hers. Her love-play seemed so gentle and good to him, both her kisses and caresses, that in truth the two of them felt a joy and wonder of which has never been heard or known. But I shall let it remain a secret for ever, since it should not be written of: the most delightful and choicest pleasure is that which is hinted at, but never told.

—Chrétien de Troyes, *Arthurian Romances*, translated by William W. Kibler

Interpretation. Baudelaire was an intellectual seducer. He wanted to overwhelm Madame Sabatier with words, dominate her thoughts, make her fall in love with him. Physically, he knew, he could not compete with her many other admirers—he was shy, awkward, not particularly handsome. So he resorted to his one strength, poetry. Haunting her with anonymous letters gave him a perverse thrill. He had to know she would realize, eventually, that he was her correspondent—no one else wrote like him—but he wanted her to figure this out on her own. He stopped writing to her because he had become interested in someone else, but he knew she would be thinking of him, wondering, perhaps waiting for him. And when he published his book, he decided to write to her again, this time directly, stirring up the old venom he had injected in her. When they were alone, he could see she was waiting for him to do something, to take hold of her, but he was not that kind of seducer. Besides, it gave him pleasure to hold himself back, to sense his power over a woman whom so many desired. By the time she turned physical and aggressive, the seduction was over for him. He had made her fall in love; that was enough.

The devastating effect of Baudelaire's push-and-pull on Madame Sabatier teaches us a great lesson in seduction. First, it is always best to keep at some distance from your targets. You do not have to go as far as remaining anonymous, but you do not want to be seen too often, or to be seen as

He was sometimes so intellectual that I felt myself annihilated as a woman; at other times he was so wild and passionate, so desiring, that I almost trembled

intrusive. If you are always in their face, always the aggressor, they will become used to being passive, and the tension in your seduction will flag. Use letters to make them think about you all the time, to feed their imagination. Cultivate mystery—stop them from figuring you out. Baudelaire's letters were delightfully ambiguous, mixing the physical and the spiritual, teasing Sabatier with their multiplicity of possible interpretations.

before him. At times I was like a stranger to him; at times he surrendered completely. Then when I threw my arms around him, everything changed, and I embraced a cloud.

—Cordelia describing Johannes, in Søren Kierkegaard, *The Seducer's Diary*, translated by Howard V. Hong and Edna V. Hong

Then, at the point when they are ripe with desire and interest, when perhaps they are expecting you to make a move—as Madame Sabatier expected that day in her apartment—take a step back. You are unexpectedly distant, friendly but no more than that—certainly not sexual. Let this sink in for a day or two. Your withdrawal will trigger anxiety; the only way to relieve this anxiety is to pursue and possess you. Step back now and you make your targets fall into your arms like ripe fruit, blind to the force of gravity that is drawing them to you. The more they participate, the more their willpower is engaged, the deeper the erotic effect. You have challenged them to use their own seductive powers on you, and when they respond, the tables will turn and they will pursue you with desperate energy.

> *I retreat and thereby teach her to be victorious as she pursues me. I continually fall back, and in this backward movement I teach her to know through me all the powers of erotic love, its turbulent thoughts, its passion, what longing is, and hope, and impatient expectancy.*
>
> —Søren Kierkegaard

It is true that we could not love if there were not some memory in us—to the greatest extent an unconscious memory—that we were once loved. But neither could we love if this feeling of being loved had not at some time suffered doubt; if we had always been sure of it. In other words, love would not be possible without having been loved and then having missed the certainty of being loved. . . . • The need to be loved is not elementary. This need is certainly acquired by experience in later childhood. It would be better to say: by many experiences or by a repetition of similar ones. I believe that these experiences are of a negative kind. The child becomes aware that he is not loved or that his mother's love is not unconditional. The baby learns that his mother can be dissatisfied with him, that she can withdraw her affection if he does not behave as she wishes, that she can be angry or cross. I believe that this experience arouses feelings of anxiety in the infant. The possibility of losing his mother's love certainly strikes the child with a force which can no more be

Keys to Seduction

Since humans are naturally obstinate and willful creatures, and prone to suspicions of people's motives, it is only natural, in the course of any seduction, that in some ways your target will resist you. Seductions, then, are rarely easy or without setbacks. But once your victims overcome some of their doubts, and begin to fall under your spell, they will reach a point where they start to let go. They may sense that you are leading them along, but they are enjoying it. No one likes things to be complicated and difficult, and your target will expect the conclusion to come quickly. That is the point, however, where you must train yourself to hold back. Deliver the pleasurable climax they are so greedily awaiting, succumb to the natural tendency to bring the seduction to a rapid end, and you will have missed an opportunity to ratchet up the tension, to make the affair more heated. After all, you don't want a passive little victim to toy with; you want the seduced to engage their will in all its force, to become active participants in the seduction. You want them to pursue you, hopelessly ensnaring themselves in your web in the process. The only way to accomplish this is to take a step back and make them anxious.

You have strategically retreated before (see chapter 12), but this is different. The target is falling for you now, and your retreat will lead to panicky thoughts: you are losing interest, it is somehow my fault, perhaps it is something I have done. Rather than think you are rejecting them on your own, your targets will want to make this interpretation, since if the cause of the problem is something they have done, they have the power to win you back by changing their behavior. If you are simply rejecting them, on the other hand, they have no control. People always want to preserve hope. Now they will come to you, turn aggressive, thinking that will do the trick. They will raise the erotic temperature. Understand: a person's willpower is directly linked to their libido, their erotic desire. When your victims are passively waiting for you, their erotic level is low. When they turn pursuer, getting involved in the process, brimming with tension and anxiety, the temperature is raised. So raise it as high as you can.

When you withdraw, make it subtle; you are instilling unease. Your coldness or distance should dawn on your targets when they are alone, in the form of a poisonous doubt creeping into their mind. Their paranoia will become self-generating. Your subtle step back will make them want to possess you, so they will willingly advance into your arms without being pushed. This is different from the strategy in chapter 20, in which you are inflicting deep wounds, creating a pattern of pain and pleasure. There the goal is to make your victims weak and dependent, here it is to make them active and aggressive. Which strategy you prefer to use (the two cannot be combined) depends on what you want and the proclivities of your victim.

In Søren Kierkegaard's *The Seducer's Diary*, Johannes aims to seduce the young and beautiful Cordelia. He begins by being rather intellectual with her, and slowly intriguing her. Then he sends her letters that are romantic and seductive. Now her fascination blossoms into love. Although in person he remains a little distant, she senses in him great depths and is certain that he loves her. Then one day, while they're talking, Cordelia has a strange sensation: something about him is different. He seems more interested in ideas than in her. Over the next few days, this doubt gets stronger—the letters are a little less romantic, something is missing. Feeling anxious, she slowly turns aggressive, becomes the pursuer instead of the pursued. The seduction is now much more exciting, at least for Johannes.

Johannes's step back is subtle; he merely gives Cordelia the impression that his interest is a little less romantic than the day before. He returns to being the intellectual. This stirs the worrisome thought that her natural charms and beauty no longer have as much effect on him. She must try harder, provoke him sexually, prove to herself that she has some power over him. She is now brimming with erotic desire, brought to that point by Johannes's subtle withdrawal of affection.

Each gender has its own seductive lures, which come naturally to them. When you seem interested in someone but do not respond sexually, it is disturbing, and presents a challenge: they will find a way to seduce you. To produce this effect, first reveal an interest in your targets, through letters or subtle insinuation. But when you are in their presence, assume a kind of

coped with than an earthquake. . . . • The child who experiences his mother's dissatisfaction and apparent withdrawal of affection reacts to this menace at first with fear. He tries to regain what seems lost by expressing hostility and aggressiveness. . . . The change of its character comes about only after failure; when the child realizes that the effort is a failure. And now something very strange takes place, something which is foreign to our conscious thinking but which is very near to the infantile way. Instead of grasping the object directly and taking possession of it in an aggressive way, the child identifies with the object as it was before. The child does the same that the mother did to him in that happy time which has passed. The process is very illuminating because it shapes the pattern of love in general. The little boy thus demonstrates in his own behavior what he wants his mother to do to him, how she should behave to him. He announces this wish by displaying his tenderness and affection toward his mother who gave these before to him. It is an attempt to overcome the despair and sense of loss in taking over the role of the mother. The boy tries to demonstrate what he wishes by doing it himself: look, I would like you to act thus toward me, to be thus tender and loving to me. Of course this attitude is not the result of consideration or reasoned planning but an emotional process by identification, a natural exchange of roles with the unconscious aim of seducing the mother into fulfilling his wish. He demonstrates by his own actions how he wants to be loved. It is a primitive presentation through reversal, an example of how to do the thing which he wishes done by her. In this presentation lives the memory of the attentions, tendernesses, and endearments once received from the mother or loving persons.

—Theodor Reik, *Of Love and Lust*

sexless neutrality. Be friendly, even warm, but no more. You are pushing them into arming themselves with the seductive charms that are natural to their sex—exactly what you want.

In the latter stages of the seduction, let your targets feel that you are becoming interested in another person—this is another form of taking a step back. When Napoleon Bonaparte first met the young widow Josephine de Beauharnais in 1795, he was excited by her exotic beauty and the looks she gave him. He began to attend her weekly soirees and, to his delight, she would ignore the other men and remain at his side, listening to him so attentively. He found himself falling in love with Josephine, and had every reason to believe she felt the same.

Then, at one soiree, she was friendly and attentive, as usual—except that she was equally friendly to another man there, a former aristocrat, like Josephine, the kind of man that Napoleon could never compete with when it came to manners and wit. Doubts and jealousies began to stir within. As a military man, he knew the value of going on the offensive, and after a few weeks of a swift and aggressive campaign he had her all to himself, eventually marrying her. Of course Josephine, a clever seductress, had set it all up. She did not say she was interested in another man, but his mere presence at her house, a look here and there, subtle gestures, made it seem that way. There is no more powerful way to hint that you are losing your desire. Make your interest in another too obvious, though, and it could backfire. This is not the situation in which you want to seem cruel; doubt and anxiety are the effects you are after. Make your possible interest in another barely perceptible to the naked eye.

Once someone has fallen for you, any physical absence will create unease. You are literally creating space. The Russian seductress Lou Andreas-Salomé had an intense presence; when a man was with her, he felt her eyes boring into him, and often became entranced with her coquettish ways and spirit. But then, almost invariably, something would come up—she would have to leave town for a while, or would be too busy to see him. It was during her absences that men fell hopelessly in love with her, and vowed to be more aggressive next time they were with her. Your absences at this latter point of the seduction should seem at least somewhat justified. You are insinuating not a blatant brush-off but a slight doubt: perhaps you could have found some reason to stay, perhaps you are losing interest, perhaps there is someone else. In your absence, their appreciation of you will grow. They will forget your faults, forgive your sins. The moment you return, they will chase after you as you desire. It will be as if you had come back from the dead.

According to the psychologist Theodor Reik, we learn to love only through rejection. As infants, we are showered with love by our mother—we know nothing else. But when we get a little older, we begin to sense that her love is not unconditional. If we do not behave, if we do not please her, she can withdraw it. The idea that she will withdraw her affection fills us with anxiety, and, at first, with anger—we will show her, we will throw a tantrum. But that never works, and we slowly realize that the only way to keep her from rejecting us again is to imitate her—to be as loving, kind, and affectionate as she is. This will bond her to us in the deepest way. The pattern is ingrained in us for the rest of our lives: by experiencing a rejection or a coldness, we learn to court and pursue, to love.

Re-create this primal pattern in your seduction. First, shower your targets with affection. They will not be sure where this is coming from, but it is a delightful feeling, and they will never want to lose it. When it does go away, in your strategic step back, they will have moments of anxiety and anger, perhaps throwing a tantrum, and then the same childlike reaction: the only way to win you back, to have you for sure, will be to reverse the pattern, to imitate you, to be the affectionate, giving one. It is the terror of rejection that turns the tables.

This pattern will often repeat itself naturally in an affair or relationship. One person goes cold, the other pursues, then goes cold in turn, making the first person the pursuer, and on and on. As a seducer, do not leave this to chance. Make it happen. You are teaching the other person to become a seducer, just as the mother in her own way taught the child to return her love by turning her back. For your own sake learn to relish this reversal of roles. Do not merely play at being the pursued, but enjoy it, give in to it. The pleasure of being pursued by your victim can often surpass the thrill of the hunt.

Symbol: *The Pomegranate. Carefully cultivated and tended, the pomegranate begins to ripen. Do not gather it too early or force it off the stem—it will be hard and bitter. Let the fruit grow heavy and full of juice, then stand back—it will fall on its own. That is when its pulp is most delicious.*

Reversal

There are moments when creating space and absence will blow up in your face. An absence at a critical moment in the seduction can make the target lose interest in you. It also leaves too much to chance—while you are away, they could find another person, who will distract their thoughts from you. Cleopatra easily seduced Mark Antony, but after their first encounters, he returned to Rome. Cleopatra was mysterious and alluring, but if she let too much time pass, he would forget her charms. So she let go of her usual coquetry and came after him when he was on one of his military campaigns. She knew that once he saw her, he would fall under her spell again and pursue her.

Use absence only when you are sure of the target's affection, and never let it go on too long. It is most effective later in the seduction. Also, never create too much space—don't write too rarely, don't act too cold, don't show too much interest in someone else. That is the strategy of mixing pleasure with pain, detailed in chapter 20, and will create a dependent victim, or will even make him or her give up completely. Some people, too, are inveterately passive: they are waiting for you to make the bold move, and if you don't, they will think you are weak. The pleasure to be had from such a victim is less than the pleasure you will get from someone more active. But if you are involved with such a type, do what you need to if you are to have your way, then end the affair and move on.

22

Use Physical Lures

Targets with active minds are dangerous: if they see through your manipulations, they may suddenly develop doubts. Put their minds gently to rest, and waken their dormant senses, by combining a nondefensive attitude with a charged sexual presence. While your cool, nonchalant air is calming their minds and lowering their inhibitions, your glances, voice, and bearing—oozing sex and desire—are getting under their skin, agitating their senses and raising their temperature. Never force the physical; instead infect your targets with heat, lure them into lust. Lead them into the moment—an intensified present in which morality, judgment, and concern for the future all melt away and the body succumbs to pleasure.

Raising the Temperature

In 1889, the top New York theatrical manager Ernest Jurgens visited France on one of his many scouting trips. Jurgens was known for his honesty, a rare commodity in the shady entertainment world, and for his ability to find unusual acts. He had to spend the night in Marseilles, and while wandering along the quay of the old harbor, he heard excited catcalls issuing from a working-class cabaret, and decided to go in. A twenty-one-year-old Spanish dancer named Caroline Otero was performing, and the minute Jurgens laid eyes on her he was a changed man. Her appearance was startling—five foot ten, fiery dark eyes, black waist-length hair, her body corseted into a perfect hourglass figure. But it was the way she danced that made his heart pound—her whole body alive, writhing like an animal in heat, as she performed a fandango. Her dancing was hardly professional, but she enjoyed herself so much and was so unrestrained that none of that mattered. Jurgens also could not help but notice the men in the cabaret watching her, their mouths agape.

After the show, Jurgens went backstage to introduce himself. Otero's eyes came alive as he spoke of his job and of New York. He felt a heat, a twitching, in his body as she looked him up and down. Her voice was deep and raspy, the tongue constantly in play as she rolled her Rs. Closing the door, Otero ignored the knocks and pleas of the admirers dying to speak to her. She said that her way of dancing was natural—her mother was a gypsy. Soon she asked Jurgens to be her escort that evening, and as he helped her with her coat, she leaned back toward him slightly, as if she had lost her balance. As they walked around the city, her arm in his, she would occasionally whisper in his ear. Jurgens felt his usual reserve melt away. He held her tighter. He was a family man, had never considered cheating on his wife, but without thinking, he brought Otero back to his hotel room. She began to take off some of her clothes—coat, gloves, hat—a perfectly normal thing to do, but the way she did it made him lose all restraint. The normally timid Jurgens went on the attack.

The next morning Jurgens signed Otero to a lucrative contract—a great risk, considering that she was an amateur at best. He brought her to Paris and assigned a top theatrical coach to her. Hurrying back to New York, he fed the newspapers with reports of this mysterious Spanish beauty poised to conquer the city. Soon rival papers were claiming she was an Andalusian countess, an escaped harem girl, the widow of a sheik, on and on. He

The year was 1907 and La Belle [Otero], by then, had been an international figure for over a dozen years. The story was told by M. Maurice Chevalier. • "I was a young star about to make my first appearance at the Folies. Otero had been the headliner there for several weeks and although I knew who she was I had never seen her before on stage or off. • "I was scurrying along, head bent, thinking of something or other, when I looked up. There was La Belle, in the company of another woman, walking in my direction. Otero was then nearly forty and I was not yet out of my teens but—ah!—she was so beautiful! • "She was tall, dark-haired, with a magnificent body, like the bodies of the women of those days, not like the lightweight ones of today." • Chevalier smiled. • "Of course I like modern women, too, but there was something of a fatal charm about Otero. We three stood there for a moment or two, not saying a word, I staring at La Belle, not so young as she once was and maybe not so beautiful, but still quite a woman. • "She looked right at me, then turned to the lady she was with—some friend, I guess—and spoke to her in English, which she thought I didn't understand. However, I did. • " 'Who's the very handsome young man?' Otero asked. • "The other one answered, 'He's Chevalier.' • " 'He has such beautiful eyes,' La Belle said, looking straight at me, right up and down. • "Then she almost floored me with her frankness. • " 'I wonder if he'd like to go to bed with me. I think I'll ask him!' Only she didn't say it so delicately. She was much cruder and more to the point. • "It was at this moment I had to make up my mind rather quickly. La Belle moved toward me. Instead of introducing myself and succumbing to the consequences, I pretended I didn't understand what she'd said, uttered some pleasantry in French and moved away to my dressing room. • "I could see La Belle smile in an odd fashion as I passed her; like a sleek tigress watching its dinner go away. For a fleeting second I thought she might turn around and follow me." • What would Chevalier have done had she pursued him? His lower lip dropped into that half pout which is the Frenchman's exclusive possession. Then he grinned. • "I'd have slowed down and let her catch up."

—Arthur H. Lewis, *La Belle Otero*

made frequent trips to Paris to be with her, forgetting about his family, lavishing money and gifts on her.

Otero's New York debut, in October of 1890, was an astounding success. "Otero dances with abandon," read an article in *The New York Times*. "Her lithe and supple body looks like that of a serpent writhing in quick, graceful curves." In a few short weeks she became the toast of New York society, performing at private parties late into the night. The tycoon William Vanderbilt courted her with expensive jewels and evenings on his yacht. Other millionaires vied for her attention. Meanwhile Jurgens was dipping into the company till to pay for presents for her—he would do anything to keep her, a task in which he was facing heavy competition. A few months later, after his embezzling became public, he was a ruined man. He eventually committed suicide.

Otero went back to France, to Paris, and over the next few years rose to become the most infamous courtesan of the Belle Epoque. Word spread quickly: a night with La Belle Otero (as she was now known) was more effective than all the aphrodisiacs in the world. She had a temper, and was demanding, but that was to be expected. Prince Albert of Monaco, a man who had been plagued by doubts of his virility, felt like an insatiable tiger after a night with Otero. She became his mistress. Other royalty followed—Prince Albert of Wales (later King Edward VII), the Shah of Persia, Grand Duke Nicholas of Russia. Less wealthy men emptied their bank accounts, and Jurgens was only the first of many whom Otero drove to suicide.

During World War I, a twenty-nine-year-old American soldier named Frederick, stationed in France, won $37,000 in a four-day crap game. On his next leave he went to Nice and checked himself into the finest hotel. On his first night in the hotel restaurant, he recognized Otero sitting alone at a table. He had seen her perform in Paris ten years before, and had become obsessed with her. She was now close to fifty, but was more alluring than ever. He greased some palms and was able to sit at her table. He could hardly talk: the way her eyes bored into him, a simple readjustment in her chair, her body brushing up against him as she got up, the way she managed to walk in front of him and display herself. Later, strolling along a boulevard, they passed a jewelry store. He went inside, and moments later found himself plopping down $31,000 for a diamond necklace. For three nights La Belle Otero was his. Never in his life had he felt so masculine and impetuous. Years later, he still believed it was well worth the price he had paid.

Interpretation. Although La Belle Otero was beautiful, hundreds of women were more so, or were more charming and talented. But Otero was constantly on fire. Men could read it in her eyes, the way her body moved, a dozen other signs. The heat that radiated out from her came from her own inner desires: she was insatiably sexual. But she was also a practiced and calculating courtesan, and knew how to put her sexuality to effect.

Onstage she made every man in the audience come alive, abandoning herself in dance. In person she was cooler, or slightly so. A man likes to feel that a woman is enflamed not because she has an insatiable appetite but because of him; so Otero personalized her sexuality, using glances, a brushing of skin, a more languorous tone of voice, a saucy comment, to suggest that the man was heating her up. In her memoirs she revealed that Prince Albert was a most inept lover. Yet he believed, along with many other men, that with her he was Hercules himself. Her sexuality actually originated from her, but she created the illusion that the man was the aggressor.

The key to luring the target into the final act of your seduction is not to make it obvious, not to announce that you are ready (to pounce or be pounced upon). Everything should be geared, not to the conscious mind, but to the senses. You want your target to read cues not from your words or actions but from your body. You must make your body glow with desire—for the target. Your desire should be read in your eyes, in a trembling in your voice, in your reaction when your bodies draw near.

You cannot train your body to act this way, but by choosing a victim (see chapter 1) who has this effect on you, it will all flow naturally. During the seduction, you will have had to hold yourself back, to intrigue and frustrate the victim. You will have frustrated yourself in the process, and will already be champing at the bit. Once you sense that the target has fallen for you and cannot turn back, let those frustrated desires course through your blood and warm you up. You do not need to touch your targets, or become physical. As La Belle Otero understood, sexual desire is contagious. They will catch your heat and glow in return. Let them make the first move. It will cover your tracks. The second and third moves are yours.

> *Spell SEX with capital letters when you talk about Otero. She exuded it.*
>
> —Maurice Chevalier

Lowering Inhibitions

One day in 1931, in a village in New Guinea, a young girl named Tuperselai heard some happy news: her father, Allaman, who had left some months before to work on a tobacco plantation, had returned for a visit. Tuperselai ran to greet him. Accompanying her father was a white man, an unusual sight in these parts. He was a twenty-two-year-old Australian from Tasmania, and he was the owner of the plantation. His name was Errol Flynn.

Flynn smiled warmly at Tuperselai, seeming particularly interested in her bare breasts. (As was the custom in New Guinea then, she wore only a grass skirt.) He said in pidgin English how beautiful she was, and kept repeating her name, which he pronounced remarkably well. He did not say

You're anxiously expecting me to escort you \ To parties: here too solicit my advice. \ Arrive late, when the lamps are lit; make a graceful entrance— \ Delay enhances charm, delay's a great bawd. \ Plain you may be, but at night you'll look fine to the tipsy: \ Soft lights and shadows will mask your faults. \ Take your food with dainty fingers: good table manners matter: \ Don't besmear your whole face with a greasy paw. \ Don't eat first at home, and nibble—but equally, don't indulge your \ Appetite to the full, leave something in hand. \ If Paris saw Helen stuffing herself to the eyeballs \ He'd detest her, he'd feel her abduction had been \ A stupid mistake. . . . \ Each woman should know herself, pick methods \ To suit her body: one fashion won't do for all. \ Let the girl with a pretty face lie supine, let the lady \ Who boasts a good back be viewed \ From behind. Milanion bore Atalanta's legs on \ His shoulders: nice legs should always be used this way. \ The petite should ride a horse (Andromache, Hector's Theban \ Bride, was too tall for these games: no jockey she); \ If you're built like a fashion model, with a willowy figure, \ Then kneel on the bed, your neck \ A little arched; the girl who has perfect legs and bosom \ Should lie sideways on, and make her lover stand. \ Don't blush to unbind your hair like some ecstatic maenad \ And tumble long tresses about \ Your uncurved throat.

—Ovid, *The Art of Love*, translated by Peter Green

much else, mind you—he did not speak her language—so she said goodbye and walked away with her father. But later that day she discovered, to her dismay, that Mr. Flynn had taken a liking to her and had purchased her from her father for two pigs, some English coins, and some seashell money. The family was poor and the father liked the price. Tuperselai had a boyfriend in the village whom she did not want to leave, but she did not dare disobey her father, and she left with Mr. Flynn for the tobacco plantation. On the other hand, she had no intention of being friendly with this man, from whom she expected the worst kind of treatment.

"How do you attract a man," the Paris correspondent of the Stockholm Aftonbladet *asked La Belle on July 3, 1910. • "Make yourself as feminine as possible; dress so that the most interesting portions of your anatomy are emphasized; and subtly allow the gentleman to know you are willing to yield at the proper time. . . ." • "The way to hold a man," Otero revealed a little later to a staff writer from the Johannesburg* Morning Journal, *"is to keep acting as though every time you meet him you are overcome with fresh enthusiasm and, with barely restrained eagerness, you await his impetuosity."*

—Arthur H. Lewis, *La Belle Otero*

In the first few days, Tuperselai missed her village terribly, and felt nervous and out of sorts. But Mr. Flynn was polite, and talked in a soothing voice. She began to relax, and since he kept his distance, she decided it was safe to approach him. His white skin was tasty to the mosquitoes, so she began to wash him every night with scented bush herbs to keep them away. Soon she had a thought: Mr. Flynn was lonely, and wanted a companion. That was why he had bought her. At night he usually read; instead, she began to entertain him by singing and dancing. Sometimes he tried to communicate in words and gestures, struggling in pidgin. She had no idea what he was trying to say, but he made her laugh. And one day she did understand something: the word "swim." He was inviting her to go swimming with him in the Laloki River. She was happy to go along, but the river was full of crocodiles, so she brought along her spear just in case.

At the sight of the river, Mr. Flynn seemed to come alive—he tore off his clothes and dove in. She followed and swam after him. He put his arms around her and kissed her. They drifted downstream, and she clung to him. She had forgotten about the crocodiles; she had also forgotten about her father, her boyfriend, her village, and everything else there was to forget. Around a bend of the river, he picked her up and carried her to a secluded grove near the river's edge. It all happened rather suddenly, which was fine with Tuperselai. From then on this was a daily ritual—the river, the grove—until the time came when the tobacco plantation was no longer doing so well, and Mr. Flynn left New Guinea.

"I missed the mental stimulation when I was younger," he answered. "But from the time I began to have women, shall we say, on the assembly-line basis, I discovered that the only thing you need, want, or should have is the absolutely physical. Simply the physical. No mind at all. A woman's mind will get in the way." • "Really?" • "For me . . . I am speaking of myself. I don't speak for male humankind. I am speaking for what I've discovered or what I need: the body, the face, the physical motion, the voice, the femaleness, the female presence . . . totally that, nothing else. That's the best. There's no possessiveness in that." • I watched him closely. • "I'm serious," he said. "That's my view and feeling. Just the elementary

One day some ten years later, a young girl named Blanca Rosa Welter went to a party at the Ritz Hotel in Mexico City. As she wandered through the bar, looking for her friends, a tall older man blocked her path and said in a charming accent, "You must be Blanca Rosa." He did not have to introduce himself—he was the famous Hollywood actor Errol Flynn. His face was plastered on posters everywhere, and he was friends of the party's hosts, the Davises, and had heard them praise the beauty of Blanca Rosa, who was turning eighteen the following day. He led her to a table in the corner. His manner was graceful and confident, and listening to him talk, she forgot about her friends. He spoke of her beauty, repeated her name, said he could make her a star. Before she knew what was happening, he had invited her to join him in Acapulco, where he was vacationing. The Davises, their mutual friends, could come along as chaperones. That would be wonderful, she said, but her mother would never agree. Don't worry about that, Flynn replied; and the following day he showed up at their house with a beautiful gift for Blanca, a ring with her birthstone. Melting under his charming smile, Blanca's mother agreed to his plan. Later that day, Blanca found herself on a plane to Acapulco. It was all like a dream.

The Davises, under orders from Blanca's mother, tried not to let her out of their sight, so Flynn put her on a raft and they drifted out into the ocean, far from the shore. His flattering words filled her ears, and she let him hold her hand and kiss her cheek. That night they danced together, and when the evening was over he escorted her to her room and serenaded her with a song as they finally parted. It was the end of a perfect day. In the middle of the night, she woke up to hear him calling her name, from her hotel-room balcony. How had he gotten there? His room was a floor above; he must have somehow jumped or swung down, a dangerous maneuver. She approached, not at all afraid, but curious. He pulled her gently into his arms and kissed her. Her body convulsed; overwhelmed with new sensations, totally at sea, she began to cry—out of happiness, she said. Flynn comforted her with a kiss and returned to his room above, in the same inexplicable way he had arrived. Now Blanca was hopelessly in love with him and would do anything he asked of her. A few weeks later, in fact, she followed him to Hollywood, where she went on to become a successful actress, known as Linda Christian.

In 1942, an eighteen-year-old girl named Nora Eddington had a temporary job selling cigarettes at the Los Angeles County courthouse. The place was a madhouse at the time, teeming with tabloid journalists: two young girls had charged Errol Flynn with rape. Nora of course noticed Flynn, a tall, dashing man who occasionally bought cigarettes from her, but her thoughts were with her boyfriend, a young Marine. A few weeks later Flynn was acquitted, the trial ended, and the place settled down. A man she had met during the trial called her up one day: he was Flynn's right-hand man, and on Flynn's behalf, he wanted to invite her up to the actor's house on Mulholland Drive. Nora had no interest in Flynn, and in fact she was a little afraid of him, but a girlfriend who was dying to meet him talked her into going and bringing her along. What did she have to lose? Nora agreed to go. On the day, Flynn's friend showed up and drove them to a splendid house on top of a hill. When they arrived, Flynn was standing shirtless by his swimming pool. He came to greet her and her girlfriend, moving so gracefully—like a lithe cat—and his manner so relaxed, she felt her jitters melt away. He gave them a tour of the house, which was full of artifacts of his various sea voyages. He talked so delightfully of his love of adventure that she wished she had had adventures of her own. He was the perfect gentleman, and even let her talk about her boyfriend without the slightest sign of jealousy.

Nora had a visit from her boyfriend the next day. Somehow he didn't seem so interesting anymore; they had a fight and broke up on the spot. That night, Flynn took her out on the town, to the famous Mocambo nightclub. He was drinking and joking, and she fell into the spirit, and hap-

physical female. Nothing more than that. When you get hold of that—hang on to it, for a short while."

—Earl Conrad, *Errol Flynn: A Memoir*

A sweet disorder in the dress \ Kindles in clothes a wantonness: \ A lawn about the shoulders thrown \ Into a fine distraction: \ An erring lace, which here and there \ Enthralls the crimson stomacher: \ A cuff neglectful, and thereby \ Ribbands to flow confusedly: \ A winning wave (deserving note) \ In the tempestuous petticoat: \ A careless shoestring, in whose tie \ I see a wild civility: \ Do more bewitch me, than when art \ Is too precise in every part.

—Robert Herrick, "Delight in Disorder," quoted in Peter Washington, ed., *Erotic Poems*

Satni, the son of Pharaoh Usimares, saw a very beautiful woman on the plain-stones of the temple. He called his page, and said, "Go and tell her that I, Pharaoh's son, shall give her ten pieces of gold to spend an hour with me." "I am a Pure One, I am not a low person," answers the Lady Thubuit. "If you wish to have your pleasure with me, you will come to my house at Bubastis. Everything will be ready there." Satni went to Bubastis by boat. "By my life," said Thubuit, "come upstairs with me." On the upper floor, sanded with dust of lapis lazuli and turquoise, Satni saw several beds covered with royal linen and many gold bowls on a table. "Please take your meal," said Thubuit. "That is not what I have come to do," answered Satni, while the slaves put aromatic wood on the fire and scattered scent about. "Do that for which we have come here," Satni repeated. "First you will make out a deed for my maintenance," Thubuit replied, "and you will establish a dowry for me of all the things and goods which belong to you, in writing." Satni acquiesced, saying, "Bring me the scribe of the school." • When he had done what she asked, Thubuit rose and dressed herself in a robe of fine linen, through which Satni could see all her limbs. His passion increased, but she said, "If it is true that you desire to have your pleasure of me, you will make your children subscribe to my deed, that they may not seek a quarrel with my children." Satni sent for his children. "If it is true that you desire to have your pleasure of me, you will cause your children to be killed, that they may not seek a quarrel with my children." Satni consented again: "Let any crime be done to them which your heart desires." "Go into that room," said Thubuit; and while the little corpses were thrown out to the stray dogs and cats, Satni at last lay on a bed of ivory and ebony, that his love might be rewarded, and Thubuit lay down at his side. "Then," the texts modestly say, "magic and the god Amen did much." • The charms of the Divine Women must have been irresistible, if even "the wisest men" were

pily let him touch her hand. Then suddenly she panicked. "I'm a Catholic and a virgin," she blurted out, "and some day I'm going to walk down the church aisle wearing a veil—and if you think you're going to sleep with me, you're mistaken." Totally calm and unruffled, Flynn said she had nothing to fear. He simply liked being with her. She relaxed, and politely asked him to put his hand back. Over the next few weeks she saw him almost every day. She became his secretary. Soon she was spending weekend nights as his house guest. He took her on skiing and boating trips. He remained the perfect gentleman, but when he looked at her or touched her hand, she felt overwhelmed by an exhilarating sensation, a tingling on her skin that she compared to stepping into a cold-needle shower on a red-hot day. Soon she was going to church less often, drifting away from the life she had known. Although outwardly nothing had changed between them, inwardly all semblance of resistance to him had melted away. One night, after a party, she succumbed. She and Flynn eventually engaged in a stormy marriage that lasted seven years.

Interpretation. The women who became involved with Errol Flynn (and by the end of his life they numbered in the thousands) had every reason in the world to feel suspicious of him: he was real life's closest thing to a Don Juan. (In fact he had played the legendary seducer in a film.) He was constantly surrounded by women, who knew that no involvement with him could last. And then there were the rumors of his temper, and his love of danger and adventure. No woman had greater reason to resist him than Nora Eddington: when she met him he stood accused of rape; she was involved with another man; she was a God-fearing Catholic. Yet she fell under his spell, just like all the rest. Some seducers—D. H. Lawrence for instance—operate mostly on the mind, creating fascination, stirring up the need to possess them. Flynn operated on the body. His cool, nonchalant manner infected women, lowering their resistance. This happened almost the minute they met him, like a drug: he was at ease around women, graceful and confident. They fell into this spirit, drifting along on a current he created, leaving the world and its heaviness behind—it was only you and him. Then—perhaps that same day, perhaps a few weeks later—there would come a touch of his hand, a certain look, that would make them feel a tingling, a vibration, a dangerously physical excitement. They would betray that moment in their eyes, a blush, a nervous laugh, and he would swoop in for the kill. No one moved faster than Errol Flynn.

The greatest obstacle to the physical part of the seduction is the target's education, the degree to which he or she has been civilized and socialized. Such education conspires to constrain the body, dull the senses, fill the mind with doubts and worries. Flynn had the ability to return a woman to a more natural state, in which desire, pleasure, and sex had nothing negative attached to them. He lured women into adventure not with arguments but with an open, unrestrained attitude that infected their minds. Understand: it all starts from you. When the time comes to make the seduction physical, train yourself to let go of your own inhibitions, your doubts, your lingering feelings of guilt and anxiety. Your confidence and ease will have more power to intoxicate the victim than all the alcohol you could apply. Exhibit a lightness of spirit—nothing bothers you, nothing daunts you, you take nothing personally. You are inviting your targets to shed the burdens of civilization, to follow your lead and drift. Do not talk of work, duty, marriage, the past or future. Plenty of other people will do that. Instead, offer the rare thrill of losing oneself in the moment, where the senses come alive and the mind is left behind.

ready to do anything in their desire to abandon themselves, even for a few moments, to their trained embraces.

—G. R. Tabouis, *The Private Life of Tutankhamen*, translated by M. R. Dobie

> *When he kissed me, it evoked a response I had never known or imagined before, a giddying of all my senses. It was instinctive joy, against which no warning, reasoning monitor within me availed. It was new and irresistible and finally overpowering. Seduction—the word implies being led—and so gently, so tenderly.*
>
> —Linda Christian

Célie: What is the moment, and how do you define it? Because I must say in all good honesty that I do not understand you. • The Duke: A certain disposition of the senses, as unexpected as it is involuntary, which a woman can conceal, but which, should it be perceived or sensed by someone who might profit from it, puts her in the greatest danger of being a little more willing than she thought she ever should or could be.

—Crébillon fils, *Le Hasard au coin du feu*, quoted in Michel Feher, ed., *The Libertine Reader*

Keys to Seduction

Now more than ever, our minds are in a state of constant distraction, barraged with endless information, pulled in every direction. Many of us recognize the problem: articles are written, studies are completed, but they simply become more information to digest. It is almost impossible to turn off an overactive mind; the attempt simply triggers more thoughts—an inescapable hall of mirrors. Perhaps we turn to alcohol, to drugs, to physical activity—anything to help us slow the mind, be more present in the moment. Our discontent presents the crafty seducer with infinite opportunity. The waters around you are teeming with people seeking some kind of release from mental overstimulation. The lure of unencumbered physical pleasure will make them take your bait, but as you prowl the waters, understand: the only way to relax a distracted mind is to make it focus on one thing. A hypnotist asks the patient to focus on a watch swinging back and forth. Once the patient focuses, the mind relaxes, the senses awaken, the body becomes prone to all kinds of novel sensations and suggestions. As a seducer, you are a hypnotist, and what you are making the target focus on is you.

Throughout the seductive process you have been filling the target's mind. Letters, mementos, shared experiences keep you constantly present, even when you are not there. Now, as you shift to the physical part of the seduction, you must see your targets more often. Your attention must become more intense. Errol Flynn was a master at this game. When he

When, on an autumn evening, with closed eyes, \ I breathe the warm dark fragrance of your breast, \ Before me blissful shores unfold, caressed \ By dazzling fires from blue unchanging skies. \ And there, upon that calm and drowsing isle, \ Grow luscious fruits amid fantastic trees: \ There, men are lithe: the women of those seas \ Amaze one with their gaze that knows no guile. \ Your perfume wafts me thither like a wind: \ I see a harbor thronged with masts and sails \ Still weary from the tumult of the gales; \ And *with the sailors' song that drifts to me \ Are mingled odors of the tamarind, \ —And all my soul is scent and melody.*

—Charles Baudelaire, "Exotic Perfume," *The Flowers of Evil*, translated by Alan Conder

homed in on a victim, he dropped everything else. The woman was made to feel that everything came second to her—his career, his friends, everything. Then he would take her on a little trip, preferably with water around. Slowly the rest of the world would fade into the background, and Flynn would take center stage. The more your targets think of you, the less they are distracted by thoughts of work and duty. When the mind focuses on one thing it relaxes, and when the mind relaxes, all the little paranoid thoughts that we are prone to—do you really like me, am I intelligent or beautiful enough, what does the future hold—vanish from the surface. Remember: it all starts with you. Be undistracted, present in the moment, and the target will follow suit. The intense gaze of the hypnotist creates a similar reaction in the patient.

Once the target's overactive mind starts to slow down, their senses will come to life, and your physical lures will have double their power. Now a heated glance will give them flush. You will have a tendency to employ physical lures that work primarily on the eyes, the sense we most rely on in our culture. Physical appearances are critical, but you are after a general agitation of the senses. La Belle Otero made sure men noticed her breasts, her figure, her perfume, her walk; no part was allowed to predominate. The senses are interconnected—an appeal to smell will trigger touch, an appeal to touch will trigger vision: casual or "accidental" contact—better a brushing of the skin than something more forceful right now—will create a jolt and activate the eyes. Subtly modulate the voice, make it slower and deeper. Living senses will crowd out rational thought.

In the eighteenth-century libertine novel *The Wayward Head and Heart*, by Crébillon fils, Madame de Lursay is trying to seduce a younger man, Meilcour. Her weapons are several. One night at a party she is hosting, she wears a revealing gown; her hair is slightly tousled; she throws him heated glances; her voice trembles a bit. When they are alone, she innocently gets him to sit close to her, and talks more slowly; at one point she starts to cry. Meilcour has many reasons to resist her; he has fallen in love with a girl his own age, and he has heard rumors about Madame de Lursay that should make him distrust her. But the clothes, the looks, the perfume, the voice, the closeness of her body, the tears—it all begins to overwhelm him. "An indescribable agitation stirred my senses." Meilcour succumbs.

The French libertines of the eighteenth century called this "the moment." The seducer leads the victim to a point where he or she reveals involuntary signs of physical excitation that can be read in various symptoms. Once those signs are detected, the seducer must work quickly, applying pressure on the target to get lost in the moment—the past, the future, all moral scruples vanishing in air. Once your victims lose themselves in the moment, it is all over—their mind, their conscience, no longer holds them back. The body gives in to pleasure. Madame de Lursay lures Meilcour into the moment by creating a generalized disorder of the senses, rendering him incapable of thinking straight.

In leading your victims into the moment, remember a few things. First, a disordered look (Madame de Lursay's tousled hair, her ruffled dress) has more effect on the senses than a neat appearance. It suggests the bedroom. Second, be alert to the signs of physical excitation. Blushing, trembling of the voice, tears, unusually forceful laughter, relaxing movements of the body (any kind of involuntary mirroring, their gestures imitating yours), a revealing slip of the tongue—these are signs that the victim is slipping into the moment and pressure is to be applied.

In 1934, a Chinese football player named Li met a young actress named Lan Ping in Shanghai. He began to see her often at his matches, cheering him on. They would meet at public affairs, and he would notice her glancing at him with her "strange, yearning eyes," then looking away. One evening he found her seated next to him at a reception. Her leg brushed up against his. They chatted, and she asked him to see a movie with her at a nearby cinema. Once they were there, her head found its way onto his shoulder; she whispered into his ear, something about the film. Later they strolled the streets, and she put her arm around his waist. She brought him to a restaurant where they drank some wine. Li took her to his hotel room, and there he found himself overwhelmed by caresses and sweet words. She gave him no room to retreat, no time to cool down. Three years later Lan Ping—soon to be renamed Jiang Qing—played a similar game on Mao Zedong. She was to become Mao's wife—the infamous Madame Mao, leader of the Gang of Four.

Seduction, like warfare, is often a game of distance and closeness. At first you track your enemy from a distance. Your main weapons are your eyes, and a mysterious manner. Byron had his famous underlook, Madame Mao her yearning eyes. The key is to make the look short and to the point, then look away, like a rapier glancing the flesh. Make your eyes reveal desire, and keep the rest of the face still. (A smile will spoil the effect.) Once the victim is heated up, you quickly bridge the distance, turning to hand-to-hand combat in which you give the enemy no room to withdraw, no time to think or to consider the position in which you have placed him or her. To take the element of fear out of this, use flattery, make the target feel more masculine or feminine, praise their charms. It is *their* fault that you have become so physical and aggressive. There is no greater physical lure than to make the target feel alluring. Remember: the girdle of Aphrodite, which gave her untold seductive powers, included that of sweet flattery.

Shared physical activity is always an excellent lure. The Russian mystic Rasputin would begin his seductions with a spiritual lure—the promise of a shared religious experience. But then his eyes would bore into his target at a party, and inevitably he would lead her in a dance, which would become more and more suggestive as he moved closer to her. Hundreds of women succumbed to this technique. For Flynn it was swimming or sailing. In such physical activity, the mind turns off and the body operates according to its own laws. The target's body will follow your lead, will mirror your moves, as far as you want it to go.

In the moment, all moral considerations fade away, and the body returns to a state of innocence. You can partly create that feeling through a devil-may-care attitude. You do not worry about the world, or what people think of you; you do not judge your target in any way. Part of Flynn's appeal was his total acceptance of a woman. He was not interested in a particular body type, a woman's race, her level of education, her political beliefs. He was in love with her feminine presence. He was luring her into an adventure, free of society's strictures and moral judgments. With him she could act out a fantasy—which, for many, was the chance to be aggressive or transgressive, to experience danger. So empty yourself of your tendency to moralize and judge. You have lured your targets into a momentary world of pleasure—soft and accommodating, all rules and taboos thrown out the window.

Symbol: *The Raft. Floating out to sea, drifting with the current. Soon the shoreline disappears from sight, and the two of you are alone. The water invites you to forget all cares and worries, to submerge yourself. Without anchor or direction, cut off from the past, you give in to the drifting sensation and slowly lose all restraint.*

Reversal

Some people panic when they sense they are falling into the moment. Often, using spiritual lures will help disguise the increasingly physical nature of the seduction. That is how the lesbian seductress Natalie Barney operated. In her heyday, at the turn of the twentieth century, lesbian sex was immensely transgressive, and women new to it often felt a sense of shame or dirtiness. Barney led them into the physical, but so enveloped it in poetry and mysticism that they relaxed and felt purified by the experience. Today, few people feel repulsed by their sexual nature, but many are uncomfortable with their bodies. A purely physical approach will frighten and disturb them. Instead, make it seem a spiritual, mystical union, and they will take less notice of your physical manipulations.

23

Master the Art of the Bold Move

A moment has arrived: your victim clearly desires you, but is not ready to admit it openly, let alone act on it. This is the time to throw aside chivalry, kindness, and coquetry and to overwhelm with a bold move. Don't give the victim time to consider the consequences; create conflict, stir up tension, so that the bold move comes as a great release. Showing hesitation or awkwardness means you are thinking of yourself, as opposed to being overwhelmed by the victim's charms. Never hold back or meet the target halfway, under the belief that you are being correct and considerate; you must be seductive now, not political. One person must go on the offensive, and it is you.

The Perfect Climax

Through a campaign of deception—the misleading appearance of a transformation into goodness—the rake Valmont laid siege to the virtuous young Présidente de Tourvel until the day came when, disturbed by his confession of love for her, she insisted he leave the château where both of them were staying as guests. He complied. From Paris, however, he flooded her with letters, describing his love for her in the most intense terms; she begged him to stop, and once again he complied. Then, several weeks later, he paid a surprise visit to the château. In his company Tourvel was flushed and jumpy, and kept her eyes averted—all signs of his effect on her. Again she asked him to leave. What have you to fear? he replied, I have always done what you have asked, I have never forced myself on you. He kept his distance and she slowly relaxed. She no longer left the room when he entered, and she could look at him directly. When he offered to accompany her on a walk, she did not refuse. They were friends, she said. She even put her arm in his as they strolled, a friendly gesture.

One rainy day they could not take their usual walk. He met her in the hallway as she was entering her room; for the first time, she invited him in. She seemed relaxed, and Valmont sat near her on a sofa. He talked of his love for her. She gave the faintest protest. He took her hand; she left it there and leaned against his arm. Her voice trembled. She looked at him, and he felt his heart flutter—it was a tender, loving look. She started to speak—"Well! yes, I . . ."—then suddenly collapsed into his arms, crying. It was a moment of weakness, yet Valmont held himself back. Her crying became convulsive; she begged him to help her, to leave the room before something terrible happened. He did so. The following morning he awoke to some surprising news: in the middle of the night, claiming she was feeling ill, Tourvel had suddenly left the château and returned home.

Valmont did not follow her to Paris. Instead he began staying up late, and using no powder to hide the peaked looks that soon ensued. He went to the chapel every day, and dragged himself despondently around the château. He knew that his hostess would be writing to the Présidente, who would hear of his sad state. Next he wrote to a church father in Paris, and asked him to pass along a message to Tourvel: he was ready to change his life for good. He wanted one last meeting, to say goodbye and to return the letters she had written him over the last few months. The father arranged a

It afforded, moreover, another advantage: that of observing at my leisure her charming face, more beautiful than ever, as it proffered the powerful enticement of tears. My blood was on fire, and I was so little in control of myself that I was tempted to make the most of the occasion. • How weak we must be, how strong the dominion of circumstance, if even I, without a thought for my plans, could risk losing all the charm of a prolonged struggle, all the fascination of a laboriously administered defeat, by concluding a premature victory; if, distracted by the most puerile of desires, I could be willing that the conqueror of Madame de Tourvel should take nothing for the fruit of his labors but the tasteless distinction of having added one more name to the roll. Ah, let her surrender, but let her fight! Let her be too weak to prevail but strong enough to resist; let her savor the knowledge of her weakness at her leisure, but let her be unwilling to admit defeat. Leave the humble poacher to kill the stag where he has surprised it in its hiding place; the true hunter will bring it to bay.

—Vicomte de Valmont, in Choderlos de Laclos, *Dangerous Liaisons*, translated by P.W.K. Stone, in Michel Feher, ed., *The Libertine Reader*

meeting, and so, one late afternoon in Paris, Valmont found himself once again alone with Tourvel, in a room in her house.

The Présidente was clearly on edge; she could not look him in the eye. They exchanged pleasantries, but then Valmont turned harsh: she had treated him cruelly, had apparently been determined to make him unhappy. Well, this was the end, they were separating for good, since that was how she wanted it. Tourvel argued back: she was a married woman, she had no choice. Valmont softened his tone and apologized: he was unused to having such strong feelings, he said, and could not control himself. Still, he would never trouble her again. Then he laid on a table the letters he had come to return.

Don't you know that however willing, however eager we are to give ourselves, we must nevertheless have an excuse? And is there any more convenient than an appearance of yielding to force? As for me, I shall admit that one thing that most flatters me is a lively and well-executed attack, when everything happens in quick but orderly succession; which never puts us in the painfully embarrassing position of having to cover up some blunder of which, on the contrary, we ought to be taking advantage; which keeps up an appearance of taking by storm even that which we are quite prepared to surrender; and adroitly flatters our two favorite passions—the pride of defense and the pleasure of defeat.

—Marquise de Merteuil in Choderlos de Laclos, *Dangerous Liaisons*, translated by P.W.K. Stone in Michel Feher, ed., *The Libertine Reader*

Tourvel came closer: the sight of her letters, and the memory of all the turmoil they represented, affected her powerfully. She had thought his decision to renounce his libertine way of life was voluntary, she said—with a touch of bitterness in her voice, as if she resented being abandoned. No, it was not voluntary, he replied, it was because she had spurned him. Then he suddenly stepped closer and took her in his arms. She did not resist. "Adorable woman!" he cried. "You have no idea of the love you inspire. You will never know how I have worshipped you, how much dearer my feelings have been to me than life! . . . May [your days] be blessed with all of the happiness of which you have deprived me!" Then he let her go and turned to leave.

Tourvel suddenly snapped. "You shall listen to me. I insist," she said, and grabbed his arm. He turned around and they embraced. This time he waited no longer, picking her up, carrying her to an ottoman, overwhelming her with kisses and sweet words of the happiness he now felt. Before this sudden flood of caresses, all her resistance gave way. "From this moment on I am yours," she said, "and you will hear neither refusals nor regrets from my lips." Tourvel was true to her word, and Valmont's suspicions were to prove correct: the pleasures he won from her were far greater than with any other woman he had seduced.

Interpretation. Valmont—a character in Choderlos de Laclos's eighteenth-century novel *Dangerous Liaisons*—can sense several things about the Présidente at first glance. She is timid and nervous. Her husband almost certainly treats her with respect—probably too much of it. Beneath her interest in God, religion, and virtue is a passionate woman, vulnerable to the lure of a romance and to the flattering attention of an ardent suitor. No one, not even her husband, has given her this feeling, because they have all been so daunted by her prudish exterior.

What sensible man will not intersperse his coaxing \ With kisses? Even if she doesn't kiss back, \ Still force on regardless! She may struggle, cry "Naughty!" \ Yet she wants to be overcome. Just

Valmont begins his seduction, then, by being indirect. He knows Tourvel is secretly fascinated with his bad reputation. By acting as if he is contemplating a change in his life, he can make her want to reform him—a desire that is unconsciously a desire to love him. Once she has opened up ever so slightly to his influence, he strikes at her vanity: she has never felt desired as a woman, and on some level cannot help but enjoy his love for her. Of course she struggles and resists, but that is only a sign that her emotions are engaged. (Indifference is the single most effective deterrent to seduction.) By taking his time, by making no bold moves even when he has the opportunity for them, he instills in her a false sense of security and proves himself by being patient. On what he pretends is his last visit to her, however, he can sense she is ready—weak, confused, more afraid of losing the addictive feeling of being desired than of suffering the consequences of adultery. He deliberately makes her emotional, dramatically displays her letters, creates some tension by playing a game of push-and-pull, and when she takes his arm, he knows it is the time to strike. Now he moves quickly, allowing her no time for doubts or second thoughts. But his move seems to arise out of love, not lust. After so much resistance and tension, what a pleasure to finally surrender. The climax now comes as a great release.

take care \ Not to bruise her tender lips with such hard-snatched kisses, \ Don't give her a chance to protest \ You're too rough. Those who grab their kisses, but not what follows, \ Deserve to lose all they've gained. How short were you \ Of the ultimate goal after all your kissing? That was \ Gaucheness, not modesty, I'm afraid . . .

—Ovid, *The Art of Love*, translated by Peter Green

Never underestimate the role of vanity in love and seduction. If you seem impatient, champing at the bit for sex, you signal that it is all about libido, and that it has little to do with the target's own charms. That is why you must defer the climax. A lengthier courtship will feed the target's vanity, and will make the effect of your bold move all the more powerful and enduring. Wait *too* long, though—showing desire, but then proving too timid to make your move—and you will stir up a different kind of insecurity: "You found me desirable, but you are not acting on your desires; maybe you're not so interested." Doubts like these affront your target's vanity (if you're not interested, maybe I'm not so interesting), and are fatal in the latter stages of seduction; awkwardness and misunderstandings will spring up everywhere. Once you read in your targets' gestures that they are ready and open—a look in the eye, mirroring behavior, a strange nervousness in your presence—you must go on the offensive, make them feel that their charms have unhinged you and pushed you into the bold move. They will then have the ultimate pleasure: physical surrender and a psychological boost to their vanity.

I have tested all manner of pleasures, and known every variety of joy; and I have found that neither intimacy with princes, nor wealth acquired, nor finding after lacking, nor returning after long absence, nor security after fear and repose in a safe refuge—none of these things so powerfully affects the soul as union with the beloved, especially if it come after long denial and continual banishment. For then the flame of passion waxes exceeding hot, and the furnace of yearning blazes up, and the fire of eager hope rages ever more fiercely.

—Ibn Hazm, *The Ring of the Dove: A Treatise on the Art and Practice of Arab Love*, translated by A. J. Arberry

> *The more timidity a lover shows with us the more it concerns our pride to goad him on; the more respect he has for our resistance, the more respect we demand of him. We would willingly say to you men: "Ah, in pity's name do not suppose us to be so very virtuous; you are forcing us to have too much of it."*
>
> —Ninon de l'Enclos

Keys to Seduction

Think of seduction as a world you enter, a world that is separate and distinct from the real world. The rules are different here; what works in daily life can have the opposite effect in seduction. The real world fea-

I knew once two great lords, brothers, both of them highly bred and highly accomplished gentlemen which did love two ladies, but the one of these was of much higher quality and more account than the other in all respects. Now being entered both into the chamber of

tures a democratizing, leveling impulse, in which everything has to seem at least something like equal. An overt imbalance of power, an overt desire for power, will stir envy and resentment; we learn to be kind and polite, at least on the surface. Even those who have power generally try to act humble and modest—they do not want to offend. In seduction, on the other hand, you can throw all of that out, revel in your dark side, inflict a little pain—in some ways be more yourself. Your naturalness in this respect will prove seductive in itself. The problem is that after years of living in the real world, we lose the ability to be ourselves. We become timid, humble, overpolite. Your task is to regain some of your childhood qualities, to root out all this false humility. And the most important quality to recapture is boldness.

No one is born timid; timidity is a protection we develop. If we never stick our necks out, if we never try, we will never have to suffer the consequences of failure or success. If we are kind and unobtrusive, no one will be offended—in fact we will seem saintly and likable. In truth, timid people are often self-absorbed, obsessed with the way people see them, and not at all saintly. And humility may have its social uses, but it is deadly in seduction. You need to be able to play the humble saint at times; it is a mask you wear. But in seduction, take it off. Boldness is bracing, erotic, and absolutely necessary to bring the seduction to its conclusion. Done right, it tells your targets that they have made you lose your normal restraint, and gives them license to do so as well. People are yearning to have a chance to play out the repressed sides of their personality. At the final stage of a seduction, boldness eliminates any awkwardness or doubts. In a dance, two people cannot lead. One takes over, sweeping the other along. Seduction is not egalitarian; it is not a harmonic convergence. Holding back at the end out of fear of offending, or thinking it correct to share the power, is a recipe for disaster. This is an arena not for politics but for pleasure. It can be by the man or woman, but a bold move is required. If you are so concerned about the other person, console yourself with the thought that the pleasure of the one who surrenders is often greater than that of the aggressor.

As a young man, the actor Errol Flynn was uncontrollably bold. This often got him into trouble; he became too aggressive around desirable women. Then, while traveling through the Far East, he became interested in the Asian practice of tantric sex, in which the male must train himself not to ejaculate, preserving his potency and heightening both partners' pleasure in the process. Flynn later applied this principle to his seductions as well, teaching himself to restrain his natural boldness and delay the end of the seduction as long as possible. So, while boldness can work wonders, uncontrollable boldness is not seductive but frightening; you need to be able to turn it on and off at will, know when to use it. As in Tantrism, you can create more pleasure by delaying the inevitable.

In the 1720s, the Duc de Richelieu developed an infatuation with a certain duchess. The woman was exceptionally beautiful, and was desired by one and all, but she was far too virtuous to take a lover, although she

this great lady, who for the time being was keeping her bed, each did withdraw apart for to entertain his mistress. The one did converse with the high-born dame with every possible respect and humble salutation and kissing of hands, with words of honor and stately compliment, without making ever an attempt to come near and try to force the place. The other brother, without any ceremony of words or fine phrases, did take his fair one to a recessed window, and incontinently making free with her (for he was very strong), he did soon show her 'twas not his way to love à l'espagnole, with eyes and tricks of face and words, but in the genuine fashion and proper mode every true lover should desire. Presently having finished his task, he doth quit the chamber; but as he goes, saith to his brother, loud enough for his lady to hear the words: "Do you as I have done, brother mine; else you do naught at all. Be you as brave and hardy as you will elsewhere, yet if you show not your hardihood here and now, you are disgraced; for here is no place of ceremony and respect, but one where you do see your lady before you, which doth but wait your attack." So with this he did leave his brother, which yet for that while did refrain him and put it off to another time. But for this the lady did by no means esteem him more highly, whether it was she did put it down to an overchilliness in love, or a lack of courage, or a defect of bodily vigor.

—SEIGNEUR DE BRANTÔME, *LIVES OF FAIR & GALLANT LADIES*, TRANSLATED BY A. R. ALLINSON

could be quite coquettish. Richelieu bided his time. He befriended her, charming her with the wit that had made him the favorite of the ladies. One night a group of such women, including the duchess, decided to play a practical joke on him, in which he was to be forced naked out of his room at the palace of Versailles. The joke worked to perfection, the ladies all got to see him in his native glory, and had a good chuckle watching him run away. There were many places Richelieu could have hidden; the place he chose was the duchess's bedroom. Minutes later he watched her enter and undress, and once the candles were extinguished, he crept into bed with her. She protested, tried to scream. He covered her mouth with kisses, and she eventually and happily relented. Richelieu had decided to make his bold move then for several reasons. First, the duchess had come to like him, and even to harbor a secret desire for him. She would never act upon it or admit it, but he was certain it existed. Second, she had seen him naked, and could not help but be impressed. Third, she would feel a touch of pity for his predicament, and for the joke played on him. Richelieu, a consummate seducer, would find no more perfect moment.

The bold move should come as a pleasant surprise, but not too much of a surprise. Learn to read the signs that the target is falling for you. His or her manner toward you will have changed—it will be more pliant, with more words and gestures mirroring yours—yet there will still be a touch of nervousness and uncertainty. Inwardly they have given in to you, but they do not expect a bold move. This is the time to strike. If you wait too long, to the point where they consciously desire and expect you to make a move, it loses the piquancy of coming as a surprise. You want a degree of tension and ambivalence, so that the move represents a great release. Their surrender will relieve tension like a long-awaited summer storm. Don't plan your bold move in advance; it cannot seem calculated. Wait for the opportune moment, as Richelieu did. Be attentive to favorable circumstances. This will give you room to improvise and go with the moment, which will heighten the impression you want to create of being suddenly overwhelmed by desire. If you ever sense that the victim is expecting the bold move, take a step back, lull them into a false sense of security, then strike.

Sometime in the fifteenth century, the writer Bandello relates, a young Venetian widow had a sudden lust for a handsome nobleman. She had her father invite him to their palace to discuss business, but during the meeting the father had to leave, and she offered to give the young man a tour of the place. His curiosity was piqued by her bedroom, which she described as the most splendid room in the palace, but which she also passed by without letting him enter. He begged to be shown the room, and she granted his wish. He was spellbound: the velvets, the rare *objets,* the suggestive paintings, the delicate white candles. A beguiling scent filled the room. The widow put out all of the candles but one, then led the man to the bed, which had been heated with a warming pan. He quickly succumbed to her caresses. Follow the widow's example: your bold move should have a theatrical quality to it. That will make it memorable, and make your aggressiveness seem pleasant,

A man should proceed to enjoy any woman when she gives him an opportunity and makes her own love manifest to him by the following signs: she calls out to a man without first being addressed by him; she shows herself to him in secret places; she speaks to him tremblingly and inarticulately; her face blooms with delight and her fingers or toes perspire; and sometimes she remains with both hands placed on his body as if she had been surprised by something, or as if overcome with fatigue. • After a woman has manifested her love to him by outward signs, and by the motions of her body, the man should make every possible attempt to conquer her. There should be no indecision or hesitancy: if an opening is found the man should make the most of it. The woman, indeed, becomes disgusted with the man if he is timid about his chances and throws them away. Boldness is the rule, for everything is to be gained, and nothing lost.

—The Hindu Art of Love, collected and edited by Edward Windsor

part of the drama. The theatricality can come from the setting—an exotic or sensual location. It can also come from your actions. The widow piqued her victim's curiosity by creating the suspense about her bedroom. An element of fear—someone might find you, say—will heighten the tension. Remember: you are creating a moment that must stand out from the sameness of daily life.

Keeping your targets emotional will both weaken them and heighten the drama of the moment. And the best way to keep them at an emotional pitch is by infecting them with emotions of your own. When Valmont wanted the Présidente to become calm, angry, or tender, he showed that emotion first, and she mirrored it. People are very susceptible to the moods of those around them; this is particularly acute at the latter stages of a seduction, when resistance is low and the target has fallen under your spell. At the point of the bold move, learn to infect your target with whatever emotional mood you require, as opposed to suggesting the mood with words. You want access to the target's unconscious, which is best obtained by infecting them with emotions, bypassing their conscious ability to resist.

It may seem expected for the male to make the bold move, but history is full of successfully bold females. There are two main forms of feminine boldness. In the first, more traditional form, the coquettish woman stirs male desire, is completely in control, then at the last minute, after bringing her victim to a boil, steps back and lets him make the bold move. She sets it up, then signals with her eyes, her gestures, that she is ready for him. Courtesans have used this method throughout history; it is how Cleopatra worked on Antony, how Josephine seduced Napoleon, how La Belle Otero amassed a fortune during the Belle Epoque. It lets the man maintain his masculine illusions, although the woman is really the aggressor.

The second form of feminine boldness does not bother with such illusions: the woman simply takes charge, initiates the first kiss, pounces on her victim. This is how Marguerite de Valois, Lou Andreas-Salomé, and Madame Mao operated, and many men find it not emasculating at all but very exciting. It all depends on the insecurities and proclivities of the victim. This kind of feminine boldness has its allure because it is more rare than the first kind, but then all boldness is somewhat rare. A bold move will always stand out compared to the usual treatment afforded by the tepid husband, the timid lover, the hesitant suitor. That is how you want it. If everyone were bold, boldness would quickly lose its allure.

Symbol: *The Summer Storm. The hot days follow one another, with no end in sight. The earth is parched and dry. Then there comes a stillness in the air, thick and oppressive—the calm before the storm. Suddenly gusts of wind arrive, and flashes of lightning, exciting and frightening. Allowing no time to react or run for shelter, the rain comes, and brings with it a sense of release. At last.*

Reversal

If two people come together by mutual consent, that is not a seduction. There is no reversal.

24

Beware the Aftereffects

Danger follows in the aftermath of a successful seduction. After emotions have reached a pitch, they often swing in the opposite direction—toward lassitude, distrust, disappointment. Beware of the long, drawn-out goodbye; insecure, the victim will cling and claw, and both sides will suffer. If you are to part, make the sacrifice swift and sudden. If necessary, deliberately break the spell you have created. If you are to stay in a relationship, beware a flagging of energy, a creeping familiarity that will spoil the fantasy. If the game is to go on, a second seduction is required. Never let the other person take you for granted—use absence, create pain and conflict, to keep the seduced on tenterhooks.

Disenchantment

Seduction is a kind of spell, an *enchantment.* When you seduce, you are not quite your normal self; your presence is heightened, you are playing more than one role, you are strategically concealing your tics and insecurities. You have deliberately created mystery and suspense to make the victim experience a real-life drama. Under your spell, the seduced gets to feel transported away from the world of work and responsibility.

You will keep this going for as long as you want or can, heightening the tension, stirring the emotions, until the time finally comes to complete the seduction. After that, *disenchantment* almost inevitably sets in. The release of tension is followed by a letdown—of excitement, of energy—that can even materialize as a kind of disgust directed at you by your victim, even though what is happening is really a natural emotional course. It is as if a drug were wearing off, allowing the target to see you as you are—and being disappointed by the flaws that are inevitably there. On your side, you too have probably tended to idealize your targets somewhat, and once your desire is satisfied, you may see them as weak. (After all, they have given in to you.) You too may feel disappointed. Even in the best of circumstances, you are dealing now with the reality rather than the fantasy, and the flames will slowly die down—unless you start up a second seduction.

You may think that if the victim is to be sacrificed, none of this matters. But sometimes your effort to break off the relationship will inadvertently revive the spell for the other person, causing him or her to cling to you tenaciously. No, in either direction—sacrifice, or the integration of the two of you into a couple—you must take disenchantment into account. There is an art to the post-seduction as well.

Master the following tactics to avoid undesired aftereffects.

In a word, woe to the woman of too monotonous a temperament; her monotony satiates and disgusts. She is always the same statue, with her a man is always right. She is so good, so gentle, that she takes away from people the privilege of quarreling with her, and this is often such a great pleasure! Put in her place a vivacious woman, capricious, decided, to a certain limit, however, and things assume a different aspect. The lover will find in the same person the pleasure of variety. Temper is the salt, the quality which prevents it from becoming stale. Restlessness, jealousy, quarrels, making friends again, spitefulness, all are the food of love. Enchanting variety? . . . Too constant a peace is productive of a deadly ennui. Uniformity kills love, for as soon as the spirit of method mingles in an affair of the heart, the passion disappears, languor supervenes, weariness begins to wear, and disgust ends the chapter.

—Ninon de l'Enclos, *Life, Letters and Epicurean Philosophy of Ninon de l'Enclos*

Fight against inertia. The sense that you are trying less hard is often enough to disenchant your victims. Reflecting back on what you did during the seduction, they will see you as manipulative: you wanted something then, and so you worked at it, but now you are taking them for granted. After the first seduction is over, then, show that it isn't really over—that you want to keep proving yourself, focusing your attention on them, luring them. That is often enough to keep them enchanted. Fight the tendency to let things settle into comfort and routine. Stir the pot, even if that means a return to inflicting pain and pulling back. Never rely on your physical charms; even beauty loses its appeal with repeated exposure. Only strategy and effort will fight off inertia.

Age cannot wither her, nor custom stale \ Her infinite variety: other women cloy \ The appetites they feed; but she makes hungry \ Where most she satisfies.

—William Shakespeare, *Antony and Cleopatra*

Maintain mystery. Familiarity is the death of seduction. If the target knows everything about you, the relationship gains a level of comfort but loses the elements of fantasy and anxiety. Without anxiety and a touch of fear, the erotic tension is dissolved. Remember: reality is not seductive. Keep some dark corners in your character, flout expectations, use absences to fragment the clinging, possessive pull that allows familiarity to creep in. Maintain some mystery or be taken for granted. You will have only yourself to blame for what follows.

Cry hurrah, and hurrah again, for a splendid triumph— \ The quarry I sought has fallen into my toils. . . . \ Why hurry, young man? Your ship's still in mid-passage, \ And the harbor I seek is far away. \ Through my verses, it's true, you may have acquired a mistress, \ But that's not enough. If my art \ Caught her, my art must keep her. To guard a conquest's \ As tricky as making it. There was luck in the chase, \ But this task will call for skill. If ever I needed support from \ Venus and Son, and Erato—the Muse \ Erotic by name—it's now, for my too-ambitious project \ To relate some techniques that might restrain \ That fickle young globetrotter, Love. . . . \ To be loved you must show yourself lovable— \ Something good looks alone \ Can never achieve. You may be handsome as Homer's Nireus, \ Or young Hylas, snatched by those bad \ Naiads; but all the same, to avoid a surprise desertion \ And keep your girl, it's best you have gifts of mind \ In addition to physical charms. Beauty's fragile, the passing \ Years diminish its substance, eat it away. \ Violets and bell-mouthed lilies do not bloom for ever, \ Hard thorns are all that's left of the blown rose. \ So with you, my handsome youth:

Maintain lightness. Seduction is a game, not a matter of life and death. There will be a tendency in the "post" phase to take things more seriously and personally, and to whine about behavior that does not please you. Fight this as much as possible, for it will create exactly the effect you do not want. You cannot control the other person by nagging and complaining; it will make them defensive, exacerbating the problem. You will have more control if you maintain the proper spirit. Your playfulness, the little ruses you employ to please and delight them, your indulgence of their faults, will make your victims compliant and easy to handle. Never try to change your victims; instead, induce them to follow your lead.

Avoid the slow burnout. Often, one person becomes disenchanted but lacks the courage to make the break. Instead, he or she withdraws inside. As an absence, this psychological step back may inadvertently reignite the other person's desire, and a frustrating cycle begins of pursuit and retreat. Everything unravels, slowly. Once you feel disenchanted and know it is over, end it quickly, without apology. That would only insult the other person. A quick separation is often easier to get over—it is as if you had a problem being faithful, as opposed to your feeling that the seduced was no longer being desirable. Once you are truly disenchanted, there is no going back, so don't hang on out of false pity. It is more compassionate to make a clean break. If that seems inappropriate or too ugly, then deliberately disenchant the victim with anti-seductive behavior.

Examples of Sacrifice and Integration

1. In the 1770s, the handsome Chevalier de Belleroche began an affair with an older woman, the Marquise de Merteuil. He saw a lot of her, but soon she began to pick quarrels with him. Entranced by her unpredictable moods, he worked hard to please her, showering her with attention and tenderness. Eventually the quarreling stopped, and as the days went by, de Belleroche felt confident that Merteuil loved him—until one day, when he came to visit, and found that she was not at home. Her footman greeted him at the door, and said he would take the chevalier to a secret house of Merteuil's outside Paris. There the marquise was waiting for him, in a renewed mood of coquettishness: she acted as if this were their first tryst. The chevalier had never seen her so ardent. He left at daybreak more in love than ever, but a few days later they quarreled again. The marquise seemed cold after that, and he saw her flirt with another man at a party. He felt horribly jealous, but as before, his solution was to become more attentive and loving. This, he thought, was the way to appease a difficult woman.

Now Merteuil had to spend a few weeks at her country home to handle some business there. She invited de Belleroche to join her for an extended stay, and he happily agreed, remembering the new life an earlier stay there had brought to their affair. Once again she surprised him: her affection and desire to please him were rejuvenated. This time, though, he did not have to leave the next morning. Days went by, and she refused to entertain any guests. The world would not intrude on them. And this time there was no coldness or quarreling, only good cheer and love. Yet now de Belleroche began to grow a little tired of the marquise. He thought of Paris and the balls he was missing; a week later he cut short his stay on some business pretext and hurried back to the city. Somehow the marquise did not seem so charming anymore.

soon wrinkles will furrow \ Your body; soon, too soon, your hair turn gray. \ Then build an enduring mind, add that to your beauty: \ It alone will last till the flames \ Consume you. Keep your wits sharp, explore the liberal \ Arts, win mastery over Greek \ As well as Latin. Ulysses was eloquent, not handsome— \ Yet he filled sea-goddesses' hearts \ With aching passion. . . . \ Nothing works on a mood like tactful tolerance: harshness \ Provokes hatred, makes nasty rows. \ We detest the hawk and the wolf, those natural hunters, \ Always preying on timid flocks; \ But the gentle swallow goes safe from man's snares, we fashion \ Little turreted houses for doves. \ Keep clear of all quarrels, sharp-tongued recriminations— \ Love's sensitive, needs to be fed \ With gentle words. Leave nagging to wives and husbands, \ Let them, if they want, think it a natural law, \ A permanent state of feud. Wives thrive on wrangling, \ That's their dowry. A mistress should always hear \ What she wants to be told. . . . \ Use tender blandishments, language that caresses \ The ear, make her glad you came.

—OVID, *THE ART OF LOVE*, TRANSLATED BY PETER GREEN

Interpretation. The Marquise de Merteuil, a character in Choderlos de Laclos's novel *Dangerous Liaisons*, is a practiced seductress who never lets her affairs drag on too long. De Belleroche is young and handsome but that is all. As her interest in him wanes, she decides to bring him to the secret house to try to inject some novelty into the affair. This works for a while, but it isn't enough. The chevalier must be gotten rid of. She tries coldness, anger (hoping to start a fight), even a show of interest in another man. All this only intensifies his attachment. She can't just leave him—he might become vengeful, or try even harder to win her back. The solution: she deliberately breaks the spell by overwhelming him with attention. Abandoning the pattern of alternating warmth with coldness, she acts hopelessly in love. Alone with her day after day, with no space to fantasize, he no longer sees her as enchanting and breaks off the affair. This was her goal all along.

If a break with the victim is too messy or difficult (or you lack the nerve), then do the next best thing: deliberately break the spell that ties him or her to you. Aloofness or anger will only stir the other person's insecurity, producing a clinging horror. Instead, try suffocating them with love and attention: be clinging and possessive yourself, moon over the lover's every action and character trait, create the sense that this monotonous affection will

In Paris the band played a concert at the Palais Chaleux. They played the first half, and then there was an hour interval—intermission, we call it—during which there was a fabulous buffet on a great long table laden with delicious foods and cognac,

go on forever. No more mystery, no more coquetry, no more retreats—just endless love. Few can endure such a threat. A few weeks of it and they will be gone.

champagne, wine and that rarity in Paris . . . Scotch. The people, aristocrats and servants, some on their hands and knees, were busily searching for something on the floor. A duchess, who was one of the hostesses, had lost one of her larger diamonds. . . . The duchess finally got bored seeing people looking all over the floor for the ring. She looked around haughtily, then took Duke by the arm, saying, "It doesn't mean anything. I can always get diamonds, but how often can I get a man like Duke Ellington?" • She disappeared with Duke. The band started the second half by themselves, and eventually Duke smilingly reappeared to finish the concert.

—DON GEORGE, *SWEET MAN: THE REAL DUKE ELLINGTON*

2. King Charles II of England was a devoted libertine. He kept a stable of lovers: there was always a favorite mistress from the aristocracy, and countless other less important women. He craved variety. One evening in 1668, the king spent an evening at the theater, where he conceived a sudden desire for a young actress called Nell Gwyn. She was pretty and innocent looking (only eighteen at the time), with a girlish glow in her cheeks, but the lines she recited onstage were so impudent and saucy. Deeply excited, the king decided he had to have her. After the performance he took her out for a night of drinking and merriment, then led her to his royal bed.

Nell was the daughter of a fishmonger, and had begun by selling oranges in the theater. She rose to the status of actress by sleeping with writers and other theater men. She had no shame about this. (When a footman of hers got into a fight with someone who said he worked for a whore, she broke it up by saying, "I am a whore. Find something better to fight about.") Nell's humor and sass amused the king greatly, but she was lowborn, and an actress, and he could hardly make her a favorite. After several nights with "pretty, witty Nell," he returned to his principal mistress, Louise Keroualle, a well-born Frenchwoman.

Keroualle was a clever seductress. She played hard to get, and made it clear she would not give the king her virginity until he had promised her a title. It was the kind of chase Charles enjoyed, and he made her the Duchess of Portsmouth. But soon her greed and difficultness began to wear on his nerves. To divert himself, he turned back to Nell. Whenever he visited her, he was royally entertained with food, drink, and her great good humor. The king was bored or melancholy? She took him drinking or gambling, or out to the country, where she taught him to fish. She always had a pleasant surprise up her sleeve. What he loved most of all was her wit, the way she mocked the pretentious Keroualle. The duchess had the habit of going into mourning whenever a nobleman of another country died, as if he were a relation. Nell, too, would show up at the palace on these occasions dressed in black, and would sorrowfully say that she was mourning for the "Cham of Tartary" or the "Boog of Oronooko"—grand relatives of her own. To her face, she called the duchess "Squintabella" and the "Weeping Willow," because of her simpering manners and melancholic airs. Soon the king was spending more time with Nell than with the duchess. By the time Keroualle fell out of favor, Nell had in essence become the king's favorite, which she remained until his death, in 1685.

I do know, however, that men become bigger-hearted and better lovers once they get the suspicion that their mistresses care less about them. When a man believes himself to be the one and only lover in a woman's life, he'll whistle and go his way. • I ought to know; I have followed this profession for the last twenty years. If you want me to, I will tell you what happened to me a few years ago. • At that time I had a steady lover, a certain Demophantos, a usurer living near Poikile. He had never given me more than five drachmas and he pretended to be my man. But his love was only superficial, Chrysis. He never sighed, he never shed tears for me and he never spent the night waiting at

Interpretation. Nell Gwyn was ambitious. She wanted power and fame, but in the seventeenth century the only way a woman could get those things was through a man—and who better than the king? But to get involved with Charles was a dangerous game. A man like him, easily bored and in need of variety, would use her for a fling, then find someone else.

Nell's strategy for the problem was simple: she let the king have his other girls, and never complained. Every time he saw her, though, she made sure he was entertained and diverted. She filled his senses with pleasure, acting as if his position had nothing to do with her love for him. Variety in women could wear on the nerves, tiring a busy king. They all made so many demands. If one woman could provide the same variety (and Nell, as an actress, knew how to play different roles), she had a big advantage. Nell never asked for money, so Charles plied her with wealth. She never asked to be the favorite—how could she? She was a commoner—but he elevated her to the position.

Many of your targets will be like kings and queens, particularly those who are easily bored. Once the seduction is over they will not only have trouble idealizing you, they may also turn to another man or woman whose unfamiliarity seems exciting and poetic. Needing other people to divert them, they often satisfy this need through variety. Do not play into the hands of these bored royals by complaining, becoming self-pitying, or demanding privileges. That would only further their natural disenchantment once the seduction is over. Instead, make them see that you are not the person they thought you were. Make it a delightful game to play new roles, to surprise them, to be an endless source of entertainment. It is almost impossible to resist a person who provides pleasure with no strings attached. When they are with you, keep the spirit light and playful. Play up the parts of your character they find delightful, but never let them feel they know you too well. In the end you will control the dynamic, and a haughty king or queen will become your abject slave.

my door. One day he came to see me, knocked at my door, but I did not open it. You see, I had the painter, Callides, in my room; Callides had given me ten drachmas. Demophantos swore and beat his fists on the door and left cursing me. Several days passed without my sending for him; Callides was still in my house. Thereupon Demophantos, who was already quite excited, went wild. He broke open my door, wept, pulled me about, threatened to kill me, tore my tunic, and did everything, in fact, that a jealous man would do, and finally presented me with six thousand drachmas. In consideration of this sum, I was his for a period of eight months. His wife used to say that I had bewitched him with some powder. That bewitching powder, to be sure, was jealousy. That is why, Chrysis, I advise you to act likewise with Gorgias.

—LUCIAN, *DIALOGUES OF THE COURTESANS*, TRANSLATED BY A.L.H.

3. When the great jazz composer Duke Ellington came to town, he and his band were always a big attraction, but especially so for the ladies of the area. They came to hear his music, of course, but once there they were mesmerized by "the Duke" himself. Onstage, Ellington was relaxed and elegant, and seemed to be having such a good time. His face was very handsome, and his bedroom eyes were infamous. (He slept very little, and his eyes had permanent pouches under them.) After the performance, some woman would inevitably invite him to her table, another would sneak into his dressing room, yet another would approach him on his way out. Duke made a point of being accessible, and when he kissed a woman's hand, his eyes and hers would meet for a moment. Sometimes she would signal an interest in him, and his glance in return would say he was more than ready. Sometimes his eyes were the first to speak; few women could resist that look, even the most happily married.

With the night's music still ringing in her ears, the woman would show up at Ellington's hotel room. He would be dressed in a stylish suit—he

"A wife is someone on whom one gazes all one's life; yet it is just as well if she be not beautiful"—so spake Jinta of the Gion. This may be the flippant saying of a go-between, but it is not to be dismissed too lightly. . . . Besides, it is with beautiful women as with beautiful views: if one is forever looking at them, one soon tires of their charm. This I can judge from my own experience. One year I went to Matsushima, and, though at first I was moved by the beauty of the place and clapped my hands with

loved good clothes—and the room would be full of flowers; there would be a piano in the corner. He would play some music. His playing, and his elegant, nonchalant manner, would come across to the woman as pure theater, a pleasant continuation of the performance she had just witnessed. And when it was over, and Ellington had to leave town, he would give her a thoughtful gift. He would make it seem that the only thing taking him away from her was his touring. A few weeks later, the woman might hear a new Ellington song on the radio, with lyrics suggesting that she had inspired it. If ever he passed through the area again, she would find a way to be there, and Ellington would often renew the affair, if only for a night.

Sometime in the 1940s, two young women from Alabama came to Chicago to attend a debutante ball. Ellington and his band were the entertainment. He was the women's favorite musician, and after the show, they asked him for an autograph. He was so charming and engaging that one of the girls found herself asking what hotel he was staying at. He told them, with a big grin. The girls switched hotels, and later that day they called up Ellington and invited him to their room for a drink. He accepted. They wore beautiful negligées that they had just bought. When Ellington arrived, he acted completely naturally, as if the warm greeting they gave him were completely usual. The three of them ended up in the bedroom, when one of the young women had an idea: her mother adored Ellington. She had to call her now and put Ellington on the phone. Not at all put out by the suggestion, Ellington played along. For several minutes he talked to the mother on the telephone, lavishing her with compliments on the charming daughter she had raised, and telling her not to worry—he was taking good care of the girl. The daughter got back on the phone and said, "We're fine because we're with Mr. Ellington and he's such a perfect gentleman." As soon as she hung up, the three of them resumed the naughtiness they had started. To the two girls, it later seemed an innocent but unforgettable night of pleasure.

Sometimes several of these far-flung mistresses would show up at the same concert. Ellington would go up and kiss each of them four times (a habit of his designed for just this dilemma). And each of the ladies would assume she was the one with whom the kisses really mattered.

Interpretation. Duke Ellington had two passions: music and women. The two were interrelated. His endless affairs were a constant inspiration for his music; he also treated them as if they were theater, a work of art in themselves. When it came time to separate, he always managed it with a theatrical touch. A clever remark and a gift would make it seem that for him the affair was hardly over. Song lyrics referring to their night together would keep up the aesthetic atmosphere long after he had left town. No wonder women kept coming back for more. This was not a sexual affair, a tawdry one-nighter, but a heightened moment in the woman's life. And his carefree attitude made it impossible to feel guilty; thoughts of one's mother or

admiration, saying to myself, "Oh, if only I could bring some poet here to show him this great wonder!"—yet, after I had been gazing at the scene from morning until night, the myriad islands began to smell unpleasantly of seaweed, the waves that beat on Matsuyama Point became obstreperous; before I knew it I had let all the cherry blossoms at Shiogama scatter; in the morning I overslept and missed the dawn snow on Mount Kinka; nor was I much impressed by the evening moon at Nagané or Oshima; and in the end I picked up a few white and black pebbles on the cove and became engrossed in a game of Six Musashi with some children.

—Ihara Saikaku, *The Life of an Amorous Woman*, translated by Ivan Morris

Men despise women who love too much and unwisely.

—Lucian, *Dialogues of the Courtesans*, translated by A.L.H.

I shall endeavor briefly to outline to you how a love when gained can be deepened. They say it can be increased in particular by making it an infrequent and difficult business for lovers to set eyes on each other, for the greater the difficulty of offering and receiving shared consolations, the greater become the desire for, and feeling of, love. Love also grows if one of the lovers shows anger to the other, for a lover is at once sorely afraid that a partner's

husband would not spoil the illusion. Ellington was never defensive or apologetic about his appetite for women; it was his nature and never the fault of the woman that he was unfaithful. And if he could not help his desires, how could she hold him responsible? It was impossible to hold a grudge against such a man or complain about his behavior.

Ellington was an Aesthetic Rake, a type whose obsession with women can only be satisfied by endless variety. A normal man's tomcatting will eventually land him in hot water, but the Aesthetic Rake rarely stirs up ugly emotions. After he seduces a woman, there is neither an integration nor a sacrifice. He keeps them hanging and hoping. The spell is not broken the next day, because the Aesthetic Rake makes the separation a pleasant, even elegant experience. The spell Ellington cast on a woman never went away.

The lesson is simple: keep the moments after the seduction and the separation in the same key as before, heightened, aesthetic, and pleasant. If you do not act guilty for your feckless behavior, it is hard for the other person to feel angry or resentful. Seduction is a lighthearted game, in which you invest all of your energy in the moment. The separation should be lighthearted and stylish as well: it is work, travel, some dreaded responsibility that calls you away. Create a memorable experience and then move on, and your victim will most likely remember the delightful seduction, not the separation. You will have made no enemies, and will have a lifelong harem of lovers to whom you can always return when you feel so inclined.

wrath when roused may harden indefinitely. Love again experiences increase when genuine jealousy preoccupies one of the lovers, for jealousy is called the nurturer of love. In fact even if the lover is oppressed not by genuine jealousy but by base suspicion, love always increases because of it, and becomes more powerful by its own strength.

—Andreas Capellanus, *On Love*, translated by P. G. Walsh

4. In 1899, twenty-year-old Baroness Frieda von Richthofen married an Englishman named Ernest Weekley, a professor at the University of Nottingham, and soon settled into the role of the professor's wife. Weekley treated her well, but she grew bored with their quiet life and his tepid lovemaking. On trips home to Germany she had a few love affairs, but this wasn't what she wanted either, and so she returned to being faithful and caring for their three children.

One day in 1912, a former student of Weekley's, David Herbert Lawrence, paid a visit to the couple's house. A struggling writer, Lawrence wanted the professor's professional advice. He was not home yet so Frieda entertained him. She had never met such an intense young man. He talked of his impoverished youth, his inability to understand women. And he listened attentively to her own complaints. He even scolded her for the bad tea she had made him—somehow, even though she was a baroness, this excited her.

Lawrence returned for later visits, but now to see Frieda, not Weekley. One day he confessed to her that he had fallen deeply in love with her. She admitted to similar feelings, and proposed they find a trysting spot. Instead Lawrence had a proposal of his own: Leave your husband tomorrow—leave him for me. What about the children? Frieda asked. If the children are more important than our love, Lawrence replied, then stay with them. But if you don't run away with me within a few days, you will never see me

You've seen the fire that smolders \ Down to nothing, grows a crown of pale ash \ Over its hidden embers (yet a sprinkling of sulphur \ Will suffice to rekindle the flame)? \ So with the heart. It grows torpid from lack of worry, \ Needs a sharp stimulus to elicit love. \ Get her anxious about you, reheat her tepid passions, \ Tell her your guilty secrets, watch her blanch. \ Thrice fortunate that man, lucky past calculation, \ Who can make some poor injured girl \ Torture herself over him, lose voice, go pale, pass out when \ The unwelcome news reaches her. Ah, may I \ Be the one whose hair she tears out in her fury, the one whose \ Soft cheeks she rips with her nails, \ Whom she sees, eyes glaring, through a rain of tears; without whom, \ Try as she will, she cannot live! \ How long (you may ask) should you leave her lamenting her wrong? A little \ While only, lest rage gather strength \ Through procrastination. By then you should have her sobbing \ All over your *chest, your arms tight around her neck. \ You want peace? Give her kisses, make love to the girl while she's crying— \ That's the only way to melt her angry mood.*

—Ovid, *The Art of Love*, translated by Peter Green

again. To Frieda the choice was horrific. She did not care at all about her husband, but the children were what she lived for. Even so, a few days later, she succumbed to Lawrence's proposal. How could she resist a man who was willing to ask for so much, to take such a gamble? If she refused she would always wonder, for such a man only passes once through your life.

The couple left England and headed for Germany. Frieda would mention sometimes how much she missed her children, but Lawrence had no patience with her: You are free to go back to them at any moment, he would say, but if you stay, don't look back. He took her on an arduous mountaineering trip in the Alps. A baroness, she had never experienced such hardship, but Lawrence was firm: if two people are in love, why should comfort matter?

In 1914, Frieda and Lawrence were married, but over the following years the same pattern repeated. He would scold her for her laziness, the nostalgia for her children, her abysmal housekeeping. He would take her on trips around the world, on very little money, never letting her settle down, although it was her fondest wish. They fought and fought. Once in New Mexico, in front of friends, he yelled at her, "Take that dirty cigarette out of your mouth! And stop sticking out that fat belly of yours!" "You'd better stop that talk or I'll tell about *your* things," she yelled back. (She had learned to give him a taste of his own medicine.) They both went outside. Their friends watched, worried it might turn violent. They disappeared from sight only to reappear moments later, arm in arm, laughing and mooning over one another. That was the most disconcerting thing about the Lawrences: married for years, they often behaved like infatuated newlyweds.

Interpretation. When Lawrence first met Frieda, he could sense right away what her weakness was: she felt trapped, in a stultifying relationship and a pampered life. Her husband, like so many husbands, was kind, but never paid enough attention to her. She craved drama and adventure, but was too lazy to get it on her own. Drama and adventure were just what Lawrence would provide. Instead of feeling trapped, she had the freedom to leave him at any moment. Instead of ignoring her, he criticized her constantly—at least he was paying attention, never taking her for granted. Instead of comfort and boredom, he gave her adventure and romance. The fights he picked with ritualistic frequency also ensured nonstop drama and the space for a powerful reconciliation. He inspired a touch of fear in her, which kept her off balance, never quite sure of him. As a result, the relationship never grew stale. It kept renewing itself.

If it is integration you are after, seduction must never stop. Otherwise boredom will creep in. And the best way to keep the process going is often to inject intermittent drama. This can be painful—opening old wounds, stirring up jealousy, withdrawing a little. (Do not confuse this behavior with nagging or carping criticism—this pain is strategic, designed to break up rigid patterns.) On the other hand it can also be pleasant: think about proving yourself all over again, paying attention to nice little details, creating new temptations. In fact you should mix the two aspects, for too much pain or pleasure will not prove seductive. You are not repeating the first seduction, for the target has already surrendered. You are simply supplying little jolts, little wake-up calls that show two things: you have not stopped trying, and they cannot take you for granted. The little jolt will stir up the old poison, stoke the embers, bring you temporarily back to the beginning, when your involvement had a most pleasant freshness and tension.

Remember: comfort and security are the death of seduction. A shared journey with a little bit of hardship will do more to create a deep bond than will expensive gifts and luxuries. The young are right to not care about comfort in matters of love, and when you return to that sentiment, a youthful spark will reignite.

5. In 1652, the famous French courtesan Ninon de l'Enclos met and fell in love with the Marquis de Villarceaux. Ninon was a libertine; philosophy and pleasure were more important to her than love. But the marquis inspired new sensations: he was so bold, so impetuous, that for once in her life she let herself lose a little control. The marquis was possessive, a trait she normally abhorred. But in him it seemed natural, almost charming: he simply could not help himself. And so Ninon accepted his conditions: there were to be no other men in her life. For her part she told him that she would accept no money or gifts from him. This was to be about love, nothing else.

She rented a house opposite his in Paris, and they saw each other daily. One afternoon the marquis suddenly burst in and accused her of having another lover. His suspicions were unfounded, his accusations absurd, and she told him so. This did not satisfy him, and he stormed out. The next day Ninon received news that he had fallen quite ill. She was deeply concerned. As a desperate recourse, a sign of her love and submission, she decided to cut off her beautiful long hair, for which she was famous, and send it to him. The gesture worked, the marquis recovered, and they resumed their affair still more passionately. Friends and former lovers complained of her sudden transformation into the devoted woman, but she did not care—she was happy.

Now Ninon suggested that they go away together. The marquis, a married man, could not take her to his château, but a friend offered his own in the country as a refuge for the lovers. Weeks became months, and their little stay turned into a prolonged honeymoon. Slowly, though, Ninon had the feeling that something was wrong: the marquis was acting more like a husband. Although he was as passionate as before, he seemed so confident, as if he had certain rights and privileges that no other man could expect. The possessiveness that once had charmed her began to seem oppressive. Nor did he stimulate her mind. She could get other men, and equally handsome ones, to satisfy her physically without all that jealousy.

Once this realization set in, Ninon wasted no time. She told the marquis that she was returning to Paris, and that it was over for good. He begged and pleaded his case with much emotion—how could she be so heartless? Although moved, Ninon was firm. Explanations would only make it worse. She returned to Paris and resumed the life of a courtesan. Her abrupt departure apparently shook up the marquis, but apparently not too badly, for a few months later word reached her that he had fallen in love with another woman.

Interpretation. A woman often spends months pondering the subtle changes in her lover's behavior. She might complain or grow angry; she might even blame herself. Under the weight of her complaints, the man may change for a while, but an ugly dynamic and endless misunderstandings will ensue. What is the point of all of this? Once you are disenchanted it is really too late. Ninon could have tried to figure out what had disenchanted her—the good looks that now bored her, the lack of mental stimulation, the feeling of being taken for granted. But why waste time figuring it out? The spell was broken, so she moved on. She did not bother to explain, to worry about de Villarceaux's feelings, to make it all soft and easy for him. She simply left. The person who seems so considerate of the other, who tries to mend things or make excuses, is really just timid. Being kind in such matters can be rather cruel. The marquis was able to blame everything on his mistress's heartless, fickle nature. His vanity and pride intact, he could easily move on to another affair and put her behind him.

Not only does the long, lingering death of a relationship cause your partner needless pain, it will have long-term consequences for you as well, making you more skittish in the future, and weighing you down with guilt. Never feel guilty, even if you were both the seducer and the one who now feels disenchanted. It is not your fault. Nothing can last forever. You have created pleasure for your victims, stirring them out of their rut. If you make a clean quick break, in the long run they will appreciate it. The more you apologize, the more you insult their pride, stirring up negative feelings that will reverberate for years. Spare them the disingenuous explanations that only complicate matters. The victim should be sacrificed, not tortured.

6. After fifteen years under the rule of Napoleon Bonaparte, the French were exhausted. Too many wars, too much drama. When Napoleon was defeated in 1814, and was imprisoned on the island of Elba, the French were more than ready for peace and quiet. The Bourbons—the royal family deposed by the revolution of 1789—returned to power. The king was Louis XVIII; he was fat, boring, and pompous, but at least there would be peace.

Then, in February of 1815, news reached France of Napoleon's dramatic escape from Elba, with seven small ships and a thousand men. He could head for America, start all over, but instead he was just crazy enough to land at Cannes. What was he thinking? A thousand men against all the armies of France? He set off toward Grenoble with his ragtag army. One at least had to admire his courage, his insatiable love of glory and of France.

Then, too, the French peasantry were spellbound at the sight of their former emperor. This man, after all, had redistributed a great deal of land to them, which the new king was trying to take back. They swooned at the sight of his famous eagle standards, revivals of symbols from the revolution. They left their fields and joined his march. Outside Grenoble, the first of the troops that the king sent to stop Napoleon caught up with him. Napoleon dismounted and walked on foot toward them. "Soldiers of the Fifth Army Corps!" he cried out. "Don't you know me? If there is one among you who wishes to kill his emperor, let him come forward and do so. Here I am!" He threw open his gray cloak, inviting them to take aim. There was a moment of silence, and then, from all sides, cries rang out of "Vive l'Empereur!" In one stroke, Napoleon's army had doubled in size.

The march continued. More soldiers, remembering the glory he had given them, changed sides. The city of Lyons fell without a battle. Generals with larger armies were dispatched to stop him, but the sight of Napoleon at the head of his troops was an overwhelmingly emotional experience for them, and they switched allegiance. King Louis fled France, abdicating in the process. On March 20, Napoleon reentered Paris and returned to the palace he had left only thirteen months before—all without having had to fire a single shot.

The peasantry and the soldiers had embraced Napoleon, but Parisians were less enthusiastic, particularly those who had served in his government. They feared the storms he would bring. Napoleon ruled the country for one hundred days, until the allies and his enemies from within defeated him. This time he was shipped off to the remote island of St. Helena, where he was to die.

Interpretation. Napoleon always thought of France, and his army, as a target to be wooed and seduced. As General de Ségur wrote of Napoleon: "In moments of sublime power, he no longer commands like a man, but seduces like a woman." In the case of his escape from Elba, he planned a bold, surprising gesture that would titillate a bored nation. He began his return to France among the people who would be most receptive to him: the peasantry who had revered him. He revived the symbols—the revolutionary colors, the eagle standards—that would stir up the old sentiments. He placed himself at the head of his army, daring his former soldiers to fire on him. The march on Paris that brought him back to power was pure theater, calculated for emotional effect every step of the way. What a contrast this former amour presented to the dolt of a king who now ruled them.

Napoleon's second seduction of France was not a classical seduction, following the usual steps, but a re-seduction. It was built on old emotions and revived an old love. Once you have seduced a person (or a nation) there is almost always a lull, a slight letdown, which sometimes leads to a separation; it is surprisingly easy, though, to re-seduce the same target. The old feelings never go away, they lie dormant, and in a flash you can take your target by surprise.

It is a rare pleasure to be able to relive the past, and one's youth—to feel the old emotions. Like Napoleon, add a dramatic flair to your re-seduction: revive the old images, the symbols, the expressions that will stir memory. Like the French, your targets will tend to forget the ugliness of the separation and will remember only the good things. You should make this second seduction bold and quick, giving your targets no time to reflect or wonder. Like Napoleon, play on the contrast to their current lover, making his or her behavior seem timid and stodgy by comparison.

Not everyone will be receptive to a re-seduction, and some moments will be inappropriate. When Napoleon came back from Elba, the Parisians were too sophisticated for him, and could see right through him. Unlike the peasants of the South, they already knew him well; and his reentry came too soon, they were too worn out by him. If you want to re-seduce someone, choose one who does not know you so well, whose memories of you are cleaner, who is less suspicious by nature, and who is dissatisfied with present circumstances. Also, you might want to let some time pass. Time will restore your luster and make your faults fade away. Never see a separation or sacrifice as final. With a little drama and planning, a victim can be retaken in no time.

***Symbol:** Embers, the remains of the fire on the morning after. Left to themselves, the embers will slowly die out. Do not leave the fire to chance and to the elements. To put it out, douse it, suffocate it, give it nothing to feed on. To bring it back to life, fan it, stoke it, until it blazes anew. Only your constant attention and vigilance will keep it burning.*

Reversal

To keep a person enchanted, you will have to re-seduce them constantly. But you can allow a little familiarity to creep in. The target wants to feel that he or she is getting to know you. Too much mystery will create doubt. It will also be tiring for you, who will have to sustain it. The point is not to remain completely unfamiliar but rather, on occasion, to jolt victims out of their complacency, surprising them as you surprised them in the past. Do this right and they will have the delightful feeling that they are constantly getting to know more about you—but never too much.

Appendix A

Seductive Environment/Seductive Time

In seduction, your victims must slowly come to feel an inner change. Under your influence, they lower their defenses, feeling free to act differently, to be a different person. Certain places, environments, and experiences will greatly aid you in your quest to change and transform the seduced. Spaces with a theatrical, heightened quality—opulence, glittering surfaces, a playful spirit—create a buoyant, childlike feeling that make it hard for the victim to think straight. The creation of an altered sense of time has a similar effect—memorable, dizzying moments that stand out, a mood of festival and play. You must make your victims feel that being with you gives them a different experience from being in the real world.

Festival Time and Place

Centuries ago, life in most cultures was filled with work and routine. But at certain moments in the year, this life was interrupted by festival. During these festivals—saturnalias of ancient Rome, the maypole festivals of Europe, the great potlatches of the Chinook Indians—work in the fields or marketplace stopped. The entire tribe or town gathered in a sacred space set apart for the festival. Temporarily relieved of duty and responsibility, people were granted license to run amok; they would wear masks or costumes, which gave them other identities, sometimes those of powerful figures reenacting the great myths of their culture. The festival was a tremendous release from the burdens of daily life. It altered people's sense of time, bringing moments in which they stepped outside of themselves. Time seemed to stand still. Something like this experience can still be found in the world's great surviving carnivals.

The festival represented a break in a person's daily life, a radically different experience from routine. On a more intimate level, that is how you must envision your seductions. As the process advances, your targets experience a radical difference from daily life—a freedom from work or responsibility. Plunged into pleasure and play, they can act differently, can become someone else, as if they were wearing a mask. The time you spend with them is devoted to them and nothing else. Instead of the usual rotation of work and rest, you are giving them grand, dramatic moments that stand out. You bring them to places unlike the places they see in daily life—heightened, theatrical places. Physical environment strongly affects people's moods; a place dedicated to pleasure and play insinuates thoughts of pleasure and play. When your victims return to their duties and to the real world, they feel the contrast strongly and they will start to crave that other place into which you have drawn them. What you are essentially creating is festival time and place, moments when the real world stops and fantasy takes over. Our culture no longer supplies such experiences, and people yearn for them. That is why almost everyone is waiting to be seduced and why they will fall into your arms if you play this right.

The following are key components to reproducing festival time and place:

Create theatrical effects. Theater creates a sense of a separate, magical world. The actors' makeup, the fake but alluring sets, the slightly unreal costumes—these heightened visuals, along with the story of the play, create illusion. To produce this effect in real life, you must fashion your clothes, makeup, and attitude to have a playful, artificial, edge—a feeling that you have dressed for the pleasure of your audience. This is the goddesslike effect of a Marlene Dietrich, or the fascinating effect of a dandy like Beau Brummel. Your encounters with your targets should also have a sense of drama, achieved through the settings you choose and through your actions. The target should not know what will happen next. Create suspense through twists and turns that lead to the happy ending; you are performing. Whenever your targets meet you, they are returned to this vague feeling of being in a play. You both have the thrill of wearing masks, of playing a different role from the one your life has allotted you.

Use the visual language of pleasure. Certain kinds of visual stimuli signal that you are not in the real world. You want to avoid images that have depth, which might provoke thought, or guilt; instead, you should work in environments that are all surface, full of glittering objects, mirrors, pools of water, a constant play of light. The sensory overload of these spaces creates an intoxicating, buoyant feeling. The more artificial, the better. Show your targets a playful world, full of the sights and sounds that excite the baby or child within them. Luxury—the sense that money has been spent or even wasted—adds to the feeling that the real world of duty and morality has been banished. Call it the brothel effect.

Keep it crowded or close. People crowding together raise the psychological temperature to hothouse levels. Festivals and carnivals depend on the contagious feeling a crowd creates. Bring your target to such environments sometimes, to lower their normal defensiveness. Similarly, any kind of situation that brings people together in a small space for a long period of time is extremely conducive to seduction. For years, Sigmund Freud had a small, tight-knit stable of disciples who attended his private lectures and who engaged in an astonishing number of love affairs. Either lead the seduced into a crowded, festivallike environment or go trolling for targets in a closed world.

Manufacture mystical effects. Spiritual or mystical effects distract people's minds from reality, making them feel elevated and euphoric. From here it is but a small step to physical pleasure. Use whatever props are at hand—astrology books, angelic imagery, mystical-sounding music from some far-off culture. The great eighteenth-century Austrian charlatan Franz Mesmer filled his salons with harp music, the perfume of exotic incense, and a female voice singing in a distant room. On the walls he put stained glass and mirrors. His dupes would feel relaxed, uplifted, and as they sat in the room where he used magnets for their healing powers, they would feel a kind of spiritual tingling pass from body to body. Anything vaguely mystical helps block out the real world, and it is easy to move from the spiritual to the sexual.

Distort their sense of time—speed and youth. Festival time has a kind of speed and frenzy that make people feel more alive. Seduction should make the heart beat faster, so that the seduced loses track of time passing. Take them to places of constant activity and movement. Embark with them on some kind of journey together, distracting their minds with new sights. Youth may fade and disappear, but seduction brings the feeling of being young, no matter the age of those involved. And youth is mostly energy. The pace of the seduction must pick up at a certain moment, creating a whirling effect in the mind. It is no wonder that Casanova did much of his seducing at balls, or that the waltz was the preferred tool of many a nineteenth-century rake.

Create moments. Everyday life is a drudgery in which the same actions endlessly repeat. The festival, on the other hand, we remember as a moment when everything was transformed—when a little bit of eternity and myth entered our lives. Your seduction must have such peaks, moments when something dramatic happens and time is experienced differently. You must give your targets such moments, whether by staging the seduction in a place—a carnival, a theater—where they naturally occur or by creating them yourself, with dramatic actions that stir up strong emotions. Those moments should be pure leisure and pleasure—no thoughts of work or morality can intrude. Madame de Pompadour, the mistress of King Louis XV, had to re-seduce her easily bored lover every few months; intensely creative, she devised parties, balls, games, a little theater at Versailles. The seduced revels in affairs like this, sensing the effort you have expended to divert and enchant them.

Scenes from Seductive Time and Place

1. Around the year 1710, a young man whose father was a prosperous wine dealer in Osaka, Japan, found himself daydreaming more and more. He worked night and day for his father, and the burden of family life and all of its duties was oppressive. Like every young man, he had heard of the pleasure districts of the city—the quarters where the normally strict laws of the shogunate could be violated. It was here that you would find the *ukiyo,* the "floating world" of transient pleasures, a place where actors and courtesans ruled. This was what the young man was daydreaming about. Biding his time, he managed to find an evening when he could slip out unnoticed. He headed straight for the pleasure quarters.

This was a cluster of buildings—restaurants, exclusive clubs, teahouses—that stood out from the rest of the city by their magnificence and color. The moment the young man stepped into it, he knew he was in a different world. Actors wandered the streets in elaborately dyed kimonos. They had such manners and attitudes, as if they were still on stage. The streets bustled with energy; the pace was fast. Bright lanterns stood out against the night, as did the colorful posters for the nearby kabuki theater. The women had a completely different air about them. They stared at him brazenly, acting with the freedom of a man. He caught sight of an *onnagata,* one of the men who played female roles in the theater—a man more beautiful than most women he had seen and whom the passersby treated like royalty.

The young man saw other young men like himself entering a teahouse, so he followed them in. Here the highest class of courtesans, the great *tayus,* plied their trade. A few minutes after the young man sat down, he heard a noise and bustle, and down the stairs came a few of the *tayus,* followed by musicians and jesters. The women's eyebrows were shaved, replaced by a thick black painted line. Their hair was swept up in a perfect fold, and he had never seen such beautiful kimonos. The *tayus* seemed to float across the floor, using different kinds of steps (suggestive, creeping, cautious, etc.), depending on whom they were approaching and what they wanted to communicate to him. They ignored the young man; he had no idea how to invite them over, but he noticed that some of the older men had a way of bantering with them that was a language all its own. The wine began to flow, music was played, and finally some lower-level courtesans came in. By then the young man's tongue was loosened. These courtesans were much friendlier and the young man began to lose all track of time. Later he managed to stagger home, and only the next morning did he realize how much money he had spent. If father ever found out . . .

Yet a few weeks later he was back. Like hundreds of such sons in Japan whose stories filled the literature of the period, he was on the path toward squandering his father's wealth on the "floating world."

Seduction is another world into which you initiate your victims. Like the *ukiyo,* it depends on a strict separation from the day-to-day world. When your victims are in your presence, the outside world—with its morality, its codes, its responsibilities—is banished. Anything is allowed, particularly anything normally repressed. The conversation is lighter and more suggestive. Clothes and places have a touch of theatricality. The license exists to act differently, to be someone else, without any heaviness or judging. It is a kind of concentrated psychological "floating world" that you create for the others, and it becomes addictive. When they leave you and return to their routines, they are doubly aware of what they are missing. The moment they crave the atmosphere you have created, the seduction is complete. As in the floating world, money is to be wasted. Generosity and luxury go hand in hand with a seductive environment.

2. It began in the early 1960s: people would come to Andy Warhol's New York studio, soak up the atmosphere, and stay awhile. Then in 1963, the artist moved into a new Manhattan space and a member of his entourage covered some of the walls and pillars in tin foil and spray-painted a brick wall and other things silver. A red quilted couch in the center, some five-foot-high plastic candy bars, a turntable that glittered with tiny mirrors, and helium-filled silver pillows that floated in the air completed the set. Now the L-shaped space became known as The Factory, and a scene began to develop. More and more people started showing up—why not just leave the door open, Andy reasoned, and come what may. During the day, while Andy would work on his paintings and films, people would gather—actors, hustlers, drug dealers, other artists. And the elevator would keep groaning all night as the beautiful people began to make the place their home. Here might be Montgomery Clift, nursing a drink by himself; over there, a beautiful young socialite chatting with a drag queen and a museum curator. They kept pouring in, all of them young and glamorously dressed. It was like one of those children's shows on TV, Andy once said to a friend, where guests keep dropping in on the endless party and there's always some new bit of entertainment. And that was indeed what it seemed like—with nothing serious happening, just lots of talk and flirting and flashbulbs popping and endless posing, as if everyone were in a film. The museum curator would begin to giggle like a teenager and the socialite would flounce about like a hooker.

By midnight everyone would be packed together. You could hardly move. The band would arrive, the light show would begin, and it would all careen in a new direction, wilder and wilder. Somehow the crowd would disperse at some point, then in the afternoon it would all start up again as the entourage trickled back. Hardly anyone went to The Factory just once.

It is oppressive always to have to act the same way, playing the same boring role that work or duty imposes on you. People yearn for a place or a moment when they can wear a mask, act differently, be someone else. That is why we glorify actors: they have the freedom and playfulness in relation to their own ego that we would love to have. Any environment that offers a chance to play a different role, to be an actor, is immensely seductive. It can be an environment that you create, like The Factory. Or a place where you take your target. In such environments you simply cannot be defensive; the playful atmosphere, the sense that anything is allowed (except seriousness), dispels any kind of reactiveness. Being in such a place becomes a drug. To re-create the effect, remember Warhol's metaphor of the children's TV show. Keep everything light and playful, full of distractions, noise, color, and a bit of chaos. No weight, responsibilities, or judgments. A place to lose yourself in.

3. In 1746, a seventeen-year-old girl named Cristina had come to the city of Venice, Italy, with her uncle, a priest, in search of a husband. Cristina was from a small village but had a substantial dowry to offer. The Venetian men who were willing to marry her, however, did not please her. So after two weeks of futile searching, she and her uncle prepared to return to their village. They were seated in their gondola, about to leave the city, when Cristina saw an elegantly dressed young man walking toward them. "There's a handsome fellow!" she said to her uncle. "I wish he was in the boat with us." The gentleman could not have heard this, yet he approached, handed the gondolier some money, and sat down beside Cristina, much to her delight. He introduced himself as Jacques Casanova. When the priest complimented him on his friendly manners, Casanova replied, "Perhaps I should not have been so friendly, my reverend father, if I had not been attracted by the beauty of your niece."

Cristina told him why they had come to Venice and why they were leaving. Casanova laughed and chided her—a man cannot decide to marry a girl after seeing her for a few days. He must know more about her character; it would take at least six months. He himself was looking for a wife, and he explained to her why he had been as disappointed by the girls he had met as she had been disappointed by the men. Casanova seemed to have no destination; he simply accompanied them, entertaining Cristina the whole way with witty conversation. When the gondola arrived at the edge of Venice, Casanova hired a carriage to the nearby city of Treviso and invited them to join him. From there they could catch a chaise to their village. The uncle accepted, and on the way to their carriage, Casanova offered his arm to Cristina. What would his mistress say if she saw them, she asked. "I have no mistress," he answered, "and I shall never have one again, for I shall never find such a pretty girl as you—no, not in Venice." His words went to her head, filling it with all kinds of strange thoughts, and she began to talk and act in a manner that was new to her, becoming almost brazen. What a pity she could not stay in Venice for the six months he needed to get to know a girl, she told Casanova. Without hesitation he offered to pay her expenses in Venice for that period while he courted her. On the carriage ride she turned this offer over in her mind, and once in Treviso she got her uncle alone and begged him to return to the village by himself, then come back for her in a few days. She was in love with Casanova; she wanted to know him better; he was a perfect gentleman, who could be trusted. The uncle agreed to do as she wished.

The following day Casanova never left her side. There was not the slightest hint of disagreement in his nature. They spent the day wandering around the city, shopping and talking. He took her to a play in the evening and to the casino after that, supplying her with a domino and a mask. He gave her money to gamble and she won. By the time the uncle returned to Treviso, she had all but forgotten about her marriage plans—all she could think of was the six months she would spend with Casanova. But she returned to her village with her uncle and waited for Casanova to visit her.

He showed up a few weeks later, bringing with him a handsome young man named Charles. Alone with Cristina, Casanova explained the situation: Charles was the most eligible bachelor in Venice, a man who would make a much better husband than he would. Cristina admitted to Casanova that she too had had her doubts. He was too exciting, had made her think of other things besides marriage, things she was ashamed of. Perhaps it was for the better. She thanked him for taking such pains to find her a husband. Over the next few days Charles courted her, and they were married several weeks later. The fantasy and allure of Casanova, however, remained in her mind forever.

Casanova could not marry—it was against everything in his nature. But it was also against his nature to force himself on a young girl. Better to leave her with the perfect fantasy image than to ruin her life. Besides, he enjoyed the courting and flirting more than anything else.

Casanova supplied a young woman with the ultimate fantasy. While he was in her orbit he devoted every moment to her. He never mentioned work, allowing no boring, mundane details to interrupt the fantasy. And he added great theater. He wore the most spectacular outfits, full of sparkling jewels. He led her to the most wonderful entertainments—carnivals, masked balls, the casinos, journeys with no destination. He was the great master at creating seductive time and environment.

Casanova is the model to aspire to. While in your presence your targets must sense a change. Time has a different rhythm—they barely notice its passing. They have the feeling that everything is stopping for them, just as all normal activity comes to a halt at a festival. The idle pleasures you provide them are contagious—one leads to another and to another, until it is too late to turn back.

Appendix B
Soft Seduction: How to Sell Anything to the Masses

The less you seem to be selling something—including yourself—the better. By being too obvious in your pitch, you will raise suspicion; you will also bore your audience, an unforgivable sin. Instead, make your approach soft, seductive, and insidious. ***Soft:*** *be indirect. Create news and events for the media to pick up, spreading your name in a way that seems spontaneous, not hard or calculated.* ***Seductive:*** *keep it entertaining. Your name and image are bathed in positive associations; you are selling pleasure and promise.* ***Insidious:*** *aim at the unconscious, using images that linger in the mind, placing your message in the visuals. Frame what you are selling as part of a new trend, and it will become one. It is almost impossible to resist the soft seduction.*

The Soft Sell

Seduction is the ultimate form of power. Those who give in to it do so willingly and happily. There is rarely any resentment on their part; they forgive you any kind of manipulation because you have brought them pleasure, a rare commodity in the world. With such power at your fingertips, though, why stop at the conquest of a man or woman? A crowd, an electorate, a nation can be brought under your sway simply by applying on a mass level the tactics that work so well on an individual. The only difference is the goal—not sex but influence, a vote, people's attention—and the degree of tension. When you are after sex, you deliberately create anxiety, a touch of pain, twists, and turns. Seduction on the mass level is more diffuse and soft. Creating a constant titillation, you fascinate the masses with what you are offering. They pay attention to you because it is pleasant to do so.

Let us say your goal is to sell yourself—as a personality, a trendsetter, a candidate for office. There are two ways to go: the hard sell (the direct approach) and the soft sell (the indirect approach). In the hard sell you state your case strongly and directly, explaining why your talents, your ideas, your political message are superior to anyone else's. You tout your achievements, quote statistics, bring in expert opinions, even go so far as to induce a bit of fear if the audience ignores your message. The approach is a tad aggressive and might have unwanted consequences: some people will be offended, resisting your message, even if what you say is true. Others will feel you are manipulating them—who can trust experts and statistics, and why are you trying so hard? You will also grate on people's nerves, becoming unpleasant to listen to. In a world in which you cannot succeed without selling to large numbers, the direct approach won't take you far.

The soft sell, on the other hand, has the potential to draw in millions because it is entertaining, gentle on the ears, and can be repeated without irritating people. The technique was invented by the great charlatans of seventeenth-century Europe. To peddle their elixirs and alchemic concoctions, they would first put on a show—clowns, music, vaudeville-type routines—that had nothing to do with what they were selling. A crowd would form, and as the audience laughed and relaxed, the charlatan would come onstage and briefly and dramatically discuss the miraculous effects of the elixir. By honing this technique, the charlatans discovered that instead of selling a few dozen bottles of the dubious medicine, they were suddenly selling scores or even hundreds.

In the centuries since, publicists, advertisers, political strategists, and others have taken this method to new heights, but the rudiments of the soft sell remain the same. First bring pleasure by creating a positive atmosphere around your name or message. Induce a warm, relaxed feeling. Never seem to be selling something—that will look manipulative and suspicious. Instead, let entertainment value and good feelings take center stage, sneaking the sale through the side door. And in that sale, you do not seem to be selling yourself or a particular idea or candidate; you are selling a life-style, a good mood, a sense of adventure, a feeling of hipness, or a neatly packaged rebellion.

Here are some of the key components of the soft sell.

Appear as news, never as publicity. First impressions are critical. If your audience first sees you in the context of an advertisement or publicity item, you instantly join the mass of other advertisements screaming for attention—and everyone knows that advertisements are artful manipulations, a kind of deception. So, for your first appearance in the public eye, manufacture an event, some kind of attention-getting situation that the media will "inadvertently" pick up as if it were news. People pay more attention to what is broadcast as news—it seems more real. You suddenly stand out from everything else, if only for a moment—but that moment has more credibility than hours of advertising time. The key is to orchestrate the details thoroughly, creating a story with dramatic impact and movement, tension and resolution. The media will cover it for days. Conceal your real purpose—to sell yourself—at any cost.

Stir basic emotions. Never promote your message through a rational, direct argument. That will take effort on your audience's part and will not gain its attention. Aim for the heart, not the head. Design your words and images to stir basic emotions—lust, patriotism, family values. It is easier to gain and hold people's attention once you have made them think of their family, their children, their future. They feel stirred, uplifted. Now you have their attention and the space to insinuate your true message. Days later the audience will remember your name, and remembering your name is half the game. Similarly, find ways to surround yourself with emotional magnets—war heroes, children, saints, small animals, whatever it takes. Make your appearance bring these emotionally positive associations to mind, giving you extra presence. Never let these associations be defined or created for you, and never leave them to chance.

Make the medium the message. Pay more attention to the form of your message than to the content. Images are more seductive than words, and visuals—soothing colors, appropriate backdrop, the suggestion of speed or movement—should actually be your real message. The audience may focus superficially on the content or moral you are preaching, but they are really absorbing the visuals, which get under their skin and stay there longer than any words or preachy pronouncements. Your visuals should have a hypnotic effect. They should make people feel happy or sad, depending on what you want to accomplish. And the more they are distracted by visual cues, the harder it will be for them to think straight or see through your manipulations.

Speak the target's language—be chummy. At all costs, avoid appearing superior to your audience. Any hint of smugness, the use of complicated words or ideas, quoting too many statistics—all that is fatal. Instead, make yourself seem equal to your targets and on intimate terms with them. You understand them, you share their spirit, their language. If people are cynical about the manipulations of advertisers and politicians, exploit their cynicism for your own purposes. Portray yourself as one of the folk, warts and all. Show that you share your audience's skepticism by revealing the tricks of the trade. Make your publicity as down-home and minimal as possible, so that your competitors look sophisticated and snobby in comparison. Your selective honesty and strategic weakness will get people to trust you. You are the audience's friend, an intimate. Enter their spirit and they will relax and listen to you.

Start a chain reaction—everyone is doing it. People who seem to be desired by others are immediately more seductive to their targets. Apply this to the soft seduction. You need to act as if you have already excited crowds of people; your behavior will become a self-fulfilling prophecy. Seem to be in the vanguard of a trend or life-style and the public will lap you up for fear of being left behind. Spread your image, with a logo, slogans, posters, so that it appears everywhere. Announce your message as a trend and it will become one. The goal is to create a kind of viral effect in which more and more people become infected with the desire to have whatever you are offering. This is the easiest and most seductive way to sell.

Tell people who they are. It is always unwise to engage an individual or the public in any kind of argument. They will resist you. Instead of trying to change people's ideas, try to change their identity, their perception of reality, and you will have far more control of them in the long run. Tell them who they are, create an image, an identity that they will want to assume. Make them dissatisfied with their current status. Making them unhappy with themselves gives you room to suggest a new life-style, a new identity. Only by listening to you can they find out who they are. At the same time, you want to change their perception of the world outside them by controlling what they look at. Use as many media as possible to create a kind of total environment for their perceptions. Your image should be seen not as an advertisement but as part of the atmosphere.

Some Soft Seductions

1. Andrew Jackson was a true American hero. In 1814, in the Battle of New Orleans, he led a ragtag band of American soldiers against a superior English army and won. He also conquered Indians in Florida. Jackson's army loved him for his rough-hewn ways: he fed on acorns when there was nothing else to eat, he slept on a hard bed, he drank hard cider, just like his men. Then, after he lost or was cheated out of the presidential election of 1824 (in fact he won the popular vote, but so narrowly that the election was thrown into the House of Representatives, which chose John Quincy Adams, after much deal making), he retired to his farm in Tennessee, where he lived the simple life, tilling the soil, reading the Bible, staying far from the corruptions of Washington. Where Adams had gone to Harvard, played billiards, drunk soda water, and relished European finery, Jackson, like many Americans of the time, had been raised in a log cabin. He was an uneducated man, a man of the earth.

This, at any rate, was what Americans read in their newspapers in the months after the controversial 1824 election. Spurred on by these articles, people in taverns and halls across the country began talking of how the war hero Andrew Jackson had been wronged, how an insidious aristocratic elite was conspiring to take over the country. So when Jackson declared that he would run again against Adams in the presidential election of 1828—but this time as the leader of a new organization, the Democratic Party—the public was thrilled. Jackson was the first major political figure to have a nickname, Old Hickory, and soon Hickory clubs were sprouting up in America's towns and cities. Their meetings resembled spiritual revivals. The hot-button issues of the day were discussed (tariffs, the abolition of slavery), and club members felt certain that Jackson was on their side. It was hard to know for sure—he was a little vague on the issues—but this election was about something larger than issues: it was about restoring democracy and restoring basic American values to the White House.

Soon the Hickory clubs were sponsoring events like town barbecues, the planting of hickory trees, dances around a hickory pole. They organized lavish public feasts, always including large quantities of liquor. In the cities there were parades, and these were stirring events. They often took place at night so that urbanites would witness a procession of Jackson supporters holding torches. Others would carry colorful banners with portraits of Jackson or caricatures of Adams and slogans ridiculing his decadent ways. And everywhere there was hickory—hickory sticks, hickory brooms, hickory canes, hickory leaves in people's hats. Men on horseback would ride through the crowd, spurring people into "huzzahs!" for Jackson. Others would lead the crowd in songs about Old Hickory.

The Democrats, for the first time in an election, conducted opinion polls, finding out what the common man thought about the candidates. These polls were published in the papers, and the overwhelming conclusion was that Jackson was ahead. Yes, a new movement was sweeping the country. It all came to a head when Jackson made a personal appearance in New Orleans as part of a celebration commemorating the battle he had fought so bravely there fourteen years earlier. This was unprecedented: no presidential candidate had ever campaigned in person before, and in fact such an appearance would have been considered improper. But Jackson was a new kind of politician, a true man of the people. Besides, he insisted that his purpose for the visit was patriotism, not politics. The spectacle was unforgettable—Jackson entering New Orleans on a steamboat as the fog lifted, cannon fire ringing out from all sides, grand speeches, endless feasts, a kind of mass delirium taking over the city. One man said it was "like a dream. The world has never witnessed so glorious, so wonderful a celebration—never have gratitude and patriotism so happily united."

This time the will of the people prevailed. Jackson was elected president. And it was not one region that brought him victory: New Englanders, Southerners, Westerners, merchants, farmers, and workers were all infected with the Jackson fever.

Interpretation. After the debacle of 1824, Jackson and his supporters were determined to do things differently in 1828. America was becoming more diverse, developing populations of immigrants, Westerners, urban laborers, and so on. To win a mandate Jackson would have to overcome new regional and class differences. One of the first and most important steps his supporters took was to found newspapers all around the country. While he himself seemed to have retired from public life, these papers promulgated an image of him as the wronged war hero, the victimized man of the people. In truth, Jackson was wealthy, as were all of his major backers. He owned one of the largest plantations in Tennessee, and he owned many slaves. He drank more fine liquor than hard cider and slept on a soft bed with European linens. And while he might have been uneducated, he was extremely shrewd, with a shrewdness built on years of army combat.

The image of the man of the earth disguised all this, and, once it was established, it could be contrasted with the aristocratic image of Adams. In this way Jackson's strategists covered up his political inexperience and made the election turn on questions of character and values. Instead of political issues they raised trivial matters like drinking habits and church attendance. To keep up the enthusiasm they staged spectacles that seemed to be spontaneous celebrations but in fact were carefully choreographed. The support for Jackson seemed to be a movement, as evidenced (and advanced) by the opinion polls. The event in New Orleans—hardly nonpolitical, and Louisiana was a swing state—bathed Jackson in an aura of patriotic, quasi-religious grandeur.

Society has fractured into smaller and smaller units. Communities are less cohesive; even individuals feel more inner conflict. To win an election or to sell anything in large numbers, you have to paper over these differences somehow—you have to unify the masses. The only way to accomplish this is to create an inclusive image, one that attracts and excites people on a basic, almost unconscious level. You are not talking about the truth, or about reality; you are forging a myth.

Myths create identification. Build a myth about yourself and the common people will identify with your character, your plight, your aspirations, just as you identify with theirs. This image should include your flaws, highlight the fact that you are not the best orator, the most educated man, the smoothest politician. Seeming human and down to earth disguises the manufactured quality of your image. To sell this image you need to have the proper vagueness. It is not that you avoid talk of issues and details—that will make you seem insubstantial—but that all your talk of issues is framed within the softer context of character, values, and vision. You want to lower taxes, say, because it will help families—and you are a family person. You must not only be inspiring but also entertaining—that is a popular, friendly touch. This strategy will infuriate your opponents, who will try to unmask you, reveal the truth behind the myth; but that will only make them seem smug, overserious, defensive, and snobbish. That now becomes part of their image, and it will help sink them.

2. On Easter Sunday, March 31, 1929, New York churchgoers began to pour onto Fifth Avenue after the morning service for the annual Easter parade. The streets were blocked off, and as had been the custom for years, people were wearing their finest outfits, women in particular showing off the latest in spring fashions. But this year the promenaders on Fifth Avenue noticed something else. Two young women were coming down the steps of Saint Thomas's Church. At the bottom they reached into their purses, took out cigarettes—Lucky Strikes—and lit up. Then they walked down the avenue with their escorts, laughing and puffing away. A buzz went through the crowd. Women had only recently begun smoking cigarettes, and it was considered improper for a lady to be seen smoking in the street. Only a certain kind of woman would do that. These two, however, were elegant and fashionable. People watched them intently, and were further astounded several minutes later when they reached the next church along the avenue. Here two more young ladies—equally elegant and well bred—left the church, approached the two holding cigarettes, and, as if suddenly inspired to join them, pulled out Lucky Strikes of their own and asked for a light.

Now the four women were marching together down the avenue. They were steadily joined by more, and soon ten young women were holding cigarettes in public, as if nothing were more natural. Photographers appeared and took pictures of this novel sight. Usually at the Easter parade, people would have been whispering about a new hat style or the new spring color. This year everyone was talking about the daring young women and their cigarettes. The next day, photographs and articles appeared in the papers about them. A United Press dispatch read, "Just as Miss Federica Freylinghusen, conspicuous in a tailored outfit of dark grey, pushed her way thru the jam in front of St. Patrick's, Miss Bertha Hunt and six colleagues struck another blow in behalf of the liberty of women. Down Fifth Avenue they strolled, puffing at cigarettes. Miss Hunt issued the following communiqué from the smoke-clouded battlefield: 'I hope that we have started something and that these torches of freedom, with no particular brand favored, will smash the discriminatory taboo on cigarettes for women and that our sex will go on breaking down all discriminations.' "

The story was picked up by newspapers around the country, and soon women in other cities began to light up in the streets. The controversy raged for weeks, some papers decrying this new habit, others coming to the women's defense. A few months later, though, public smoking by women had become a socially acceptable practice. Few people bothered to protest it anymore.

Interpretation. In January 1929, several New York debutantes received the same telegram from a Miss Bertha Hunt: "In the interests of equality of the sexes . . . I and other young women will light another torch of freedom by smoking cigarettes while strolling on Fifth Avenue Easter Sunday." The debutantes who ended up participating met beforehand in the office where Hunt worked as a secretary. They planned what churches to appear at, how to link up with each other, all the details. Hunt handed out packs of Lucky Strikes. Everything worked to perfection on the appointed day.

Little did the debutantes know, though, that the whole affair had been masterminded by a man—Miss Hunt's boss, Edward Bernays, a public relations adviser to the American Tobacco Company, makers of Lucky Strike. American Tobacco had been luring women into smoking with all kinds of clever ads, but the consumption was limited by the fact that smoking in the street was considered unladylike. The head of American Tobacco had asked Bernays for his help and Mr. Bernays had obliged him by applying a technique that was to become his trademark: gain public attention by creating an event that the media would cover as news. Orchestrate every detail but make them seem spontaneous. As more people heard of this "event," it would spark imitative behavior—in this case more women smoking in the streets.

Bernays, a nephew of Sigmund Freud and perhaps the greatest public relations genius of the twentieth century, understood a fundamental law of any kind of sell. The moment the targets know you are after something—a vote, a sale—they become resistant. But disguise your sales pitch as a news event and not only will you bypass their resistance, you can also create a social trend that does the selling for you. To make this work, the event you set up must stand out from all the other events that are covered by the media, yet it cannot stand out too far or it will seem contrived. In the case of the Easter parade, Bernays (through Bertha Hunt) chose women who would seem elegant and proper even with their cigarettes in their hands. Yet in breaking a social taboo, and doing so as a group, such women would create an image so dramatic and startling that the media would be unable to pass it up. An event that is picked up by the news has the imprimatur of reality.

It is important to give this manufactured event positive associations, as Bernays did in creating a feeling of rebellion, of women banding together. Associations that are patriotic, say, or subtly sexual, or spiritual—anything pleasant and seductive—take on a life of their own. Who can resist? People essentially persuade themselves to join the crowd without even realizing that a sale has taken place. The feeling of active participation is vital to seduction. No one wants to feel left out of a growing movement.

3. In the presidential campaign of 1984, President Ronald Reagan, running for reelection, told the public, "It's morning again in America." His presidency, he claimed, had restored American pride. The recent, successful Olympics in Los Angeles were symbolic of the country's return to strength and confidence. Who could possibly want to turn the clock back to 1980, which Reagan's predecessor, Jimmy Carter, had termed a time of malaise?

Reagan's Democratic challenger, Walter Mondale, thought Americans had had enough of the Reagan soft touch. They were ready for honesty, and that would be Mondale's appeal. Before a nationwide television audience, Mondale declared, "Let's tell the truth. Mr. Reagan will raise taxes, and so will I. He won't tell you. I just did." He repeated this straightforward approach on numerous occasions. By October his poll numbers had plunged to all-time lows.

The CBS News reporter Lesley Stahl had been covering the campaign, and as Election Day neared, she had an uneasy feeling. It wasn't so much that Reagan had focused on emotions and moods rather than hard issues. It was more that the media was giving him a free ride; he and his election team, she felt, were playing the press like a fiddle. They always managed to get him photographed in the perfect setting, looking strong and presidential. They fed the press snappy headlines along with dramatic footage of Reagan in action. They were putting on a great show.

Stahl decided to assemble a news piece that would show the public how Reagan used television to cover up the negative effects of his policies. The piece began with a montage of images that his team had orchestrated over the years: Reagan relaxing on his ranch in jeans; standing tall at the Normandy invasion tribute in France; throwing a football with his Secret Service bodyguards; sitting in an inner-city classroom. . . . Over these images Stahl asked, "How does Ronald Reagan use television? Brilliantly. He's been criticized as the rich man's president, but the TV pictures say it isn't so. At seventy-three, Mr. Reagan could have an age problem. But the TV pictures say it isn't so. Americans want to feel proud of their country again, and of their president. And the TV pictures say you can. The orchestration of television coverage absorbs the White House. Their goal? To emphasize the president's greatest asset, which, his aides say, is his personality. They provide pictures of him looking like a leader. Confident, with his Marlboro man walk."

Over images of Reagan shaking hands with handicapped athletes in wheelchairs and cutting the ribbon at a new facility for seniors, Stahl continued, "They also aim to erase the negatives. Mr. Reagan tried to counter the memory of an unpopular issue with a carefully chosen backdrop that actually contradicts the president's policy. Look at the handicapped Olympics, or the opening ceremony of an old-age home. No hint that he tried to cut the budgets for the disabled and for federally subsidized housing for the elderly." On and on went the piece, showing the gap between the feel-good images that played on the screen and the reality of Reagan's actions. "President Reagan," Stahl concluded, "is accused of running a campaign in which he highlights the images and hides from the issues. But there's no evidence that the charges will hurt him because when people see the president on television, he makes them feel good, about America, about themselves, and about him."

Stahl depended on the good will of the Reagan people in covering the White House, but her piece was strongly negative, so she braced herself for trouble. Yet a senior White House official telephoned her that evening: "Great piece," he said. "What?" asked a stunned Stahl. *"Great piece,"* he repeated. "Did you listen to what I said?" she asked. "Lesley, when you're showing four and a half minutes of great pictures of Ronald Reagan, no one listens to what you say. Don't you know that the pictures are overriding your message because they conflict with your message? The public sees those pictures and they block your message. They didn't even hear what you said. So, in our minds, it was a four-and-a-half-minute free ad for the Ronald Reagan campaign for reelection."

Interpretation. Most of the men who worked on communications for Reagan had a background in marketing. They knew the importance of telling a story crisply, sharply, and with good visuals. Each morning they went over what the headline of the day should be, and how they could shape this into a short visual piece, getting the president into a video opportunity. They paid detailed attention to the backdrop behind the president in the Oval Office, to the way the camera framed him when he was with other world leaders, and to having him filmed in motion, with his confident walk. The visuals carried the message better than any words could do. As one Reagan official said, "What are you going to believe, the facts or your eyes?"

Free yourself from the need to communicate in the normal direct manner and you will present yourself with greater opportunities for the soft sell. Make the words you say unobtrusive, vague, alluring. And pay much greater attention to your style, the visuals, the story they tell. Convey a sense of movement and progress by showing yourself in motion. Express confidence not through facts and figures but through colors and positive imagery, appealing to the infant in everyone. Let the media cover you unguided and you are at their mercy. So turn the dynamic around—the press needs drama and visuals? Provide them. It is fine to discuss issues or "truth" as long as you package it entertainingly. Remember: images linger in the mind long after words are forgotten. Do not preach to the public—that never works. Learn to express your message through visuals that insinuate positive emotions and happy feelings.

4. In 1919, the movie press agent Harry Reichenbach was asked to do advance publicity for a picture called *The Virgin of Stamboul.* It was the usual romantic potboiler in an exotic locale, and normally a publicist would mount a campaign with alluring posters and advertisements. But Harry never operated the usual way. He had begun his career as a carnival barker, and there the only way to get the public into your tent was to stand out from the other barkers. So Harry dug up eight scruffy Turks whom he found living in Manhattan, dressed them up in costumes (flowing sea-green trousers, gold-crescented turbans) provided by the movie studio, rehearsed them in every line and gesture, and checked them into an expensive hotel. Word quickly spread to the newspapers (with a little help from Harry) that a delegation of Turks had arrived in New York on a secret diplomatic mission.

Reporters converged on the hotel. Since his appearance in New York was clearly no longer a secret, the head of the mission, "Sheikh Ali Ben Mohammed," invited them up to his suite. The newspapermen were impressed by the Turks' colorful outfits, salaams, and rituals. The sheikh then explained why he had come to New York. A beautiful young woman named Sari, known as the Virgin of Stamboul, had been betrothed to the sheikh's brother. An American soldier passing through had fallen in love with her and had managed to steal her from her home and take her to America. Her mother had died from grief. The sheikh had found out she was in New York, and had come to bring her back.

Mesmerized by the sheikh's colorful language and by the romantic tale he told, the reporters filled the papers with stories of the Virgin of Stamboul for the next several days. The sheikh was filmed in Central Park and feted by the cream of New York society. Finally "Sari" was found, and the press reported the reunion between the sheikh and the hysterical girl (an actress with an exotic look). Soon after, *The Virgin of Stamboul* opened in New York. Its story was much like the "real" events reported in the papers. Was this a coincidence? A quickly made film version of the true story? No one seemed to know, but the public was too curious to care, and *The Virgin of Stamboul* broke box office records.

A year later Harry was asked to publicize a film called *The Forbidden Woman.* It was one of the worst movies he had ever seen. Theater owners had no interest in showing it. Harry went to work. For eighteen days straight he ran an ad in all of the major New York newspapers: WATCH THE SKY ON THE NIGHT OF FEBRUARY 21ST! IF IT IS GREEN—GO THE CAPITOL IF IT IS RED—GO THE RIVOLI IF IT IS PINK—GO TO THE STRAND IF IT IS BLUE—GO TO THE RIALTO FOR ON FEBRUARY 21ST THE SKY WILL TELL YOU WHERE THE BEST SHOW IN TOWN CAN BE SEEN! (The Capitol, the Rivoli, the Strand, and the Rialto were the four big first-run movie houses on Broadway.) Almost everyone saw the ad and wondered what this fabulous show was. The owner of the Capitol asked Harry if he knew anything about it, and Harry let him in on the secret: it was all a publicity stunt for an unbooked picture. The owner asked to see a screening of *The Forbidden Woman;* through most of the film, Harry yakked about the publicity campaign, distracting the man from the dullness onscreen. The theater owner decided to show the film for a week, and so, on the evening of February 21, as a heavy snowstorm blanketed the city and all eyes turned to the sky, giant rays of light poured out from the tallest buildings—a brilliant show of green. An enormous crowd flocked to the Capitol theater. Those who did not get in kept coming back. Somehow, with a packed house and an excited crowd, the film did not seem quite so bad.

The following year Harry was asked to publicize a gangster picture called *Outside the Law.* On highways across the country he set up billboards that read, in giant letters, IF YOU DANCE ON SUNDAY, YOU ARE OUTSIDE THE LAW. On other billboards the word "dance" was replaced by "play golf" or "play pool" and so on. On a top corner of the billboards was a shield bearing the initials "PD." The public assumed this meant "police department" (actually, it stood for Priscilla Dean, the star of the movie) and that the police, backed by religious organizations, were prepared to enforce decades-old blue laws prohibiting "sinful" activities on a Sunday. Suddenly a controversy was sparked. Theater owners, golfing associations, and dance organizations led a countercampaign against the blue laws; they put up their own billboards, exclaiming that if you did those things on Sunday, you were not "OUTSIDE THE LAW" and issuing a call for Americans to have some fun in their lives. For weeks the words "Outside the Law" were everywhere seen and everywhere on people's lips. In the midst of this the film opened—on a Sunday—in four New York theaters simultaneously, something that had never happened before. And it ran for months throughout the country, also on Sundays. It was one of the big hits of the year.

Interpretation. Harry Reichenbach, perhaps the greatest press agent in movie history, never forgot the lessons he had learned as a barker. The carnival is full of bright lights, color, noise, and the ebb and flow of the crowd. Such environments have profound effects on people. A clearheaded person could probably tell that the magic shows are fake, the fierce animals trained, the dangerous stunts relatively safe. But people want to be entertained; it is one of their greatest needs. Surrounded by color and excitement, they suspend their disbelief for a while and imagine that the magic and danger are real. They are fascinated by what seems to be both fake and real at the same time. Harry's publicity stunts merely re-created the carnival on a larger scale. He pulled people in with the lure of colorful costumes, a great story, irresistible spectacle. He held their attention with mystery, controversy, whatever it took. Catching a kind of fever, as they would at the carnival, they flocked without thinking to the films he publicized.

The lines between fiction and reality, news and entertainment are even more blurred today than in Harry Reichenbach's time. What opportunities that presents for soft seduction! The media is desperate for events with entertainment value, inherent drama. Feed that need. The public has a weakness for what seems both realistic and slightly fantastical—for real events with a cinematic edge. Play to that weakness. Stage events the way Bernays did, events the media can pick up as news. But here you are not starting a social trend, you are after something more short term: to win people's attention, to create a momentary stir, to lure them into your tent. Make your events and publicity stunts plausible and somewhat realistic, but make their colors a little brighter than usual, the characters larger than life, the drama higher. Provide an edge of sex and danger. You are creating a confluence of real life and fiction—the essence of any seduction.

It is not enough, however, to win people's attention: you need to hold it long enough to hook them. This can always be done by sparking controversy, the way Harry liked to stir up debates about morals. While the media argues about the effect you are having on people's values, it is broadcasting your name everywhere and inadvertently bestowing upon you the edge that will make you so attractive to the public.

Selected Bibliography

Baudrillard, Jean. *Seduction.* Trans. Brian Singer. New York: St. Martin's Press, 1990.

Bourdon, David. *Warhol.* New York: Harry N. Abrams, Inc., 1989.

Capellanus, Andreas. *Andreas Capellanus on Love.* Trans. P. G. Walsh. London: Gerald Duckworth & Co. Ltd., 1982.

Casanova, Jacques. *The Memoirs of Jacques Casanova, in eight volumes.* Trans. Arthur Machen. Edinburgh: Limited Editions Club, 1940.

Chalon, Jean. *Portrait of a Seductress: The World of Natalie Barney.* Trans. Carol Barko. New York: Crown Publishers, Inc., 1979.

Cole, Hubert. *First Gentleman of the Bedchamber: The Life of Louis-François Armand, Maréchal Duc de Richelieu.* New York: Viking, 1965.

de Troyes, Chrétien. *Arthurian Romances.* Trans. William W. Kibler. London: Penguin Books, 1991.

Feher, Michel, ed. *The Libertine Reader: Eroticism and Enlightenment in Eighteenth-Century France.* New York: Zone Books, 1997.

Flynn, Errol. *My Wicked, Wicked Ways.* New York: G. P. Putnam's Sons, 1959.

Freud, Sigmund. *Psychological Writings and Letters.* Ed. Sander L. Gilman. New York: The Continuum Publishing Company, 1995.

———. *Sexuality and the Psychology of Love.* Ed. Philip Rieff. New York: Touchstone, 1963.

Fülöp-Miller, René. *Rasputin: The Holy Devil.* New York: Viking, 1962.

George, Don. *Sweet Man: The Real Duke Ellington.* New York: G. P. Putnam's Sons, 1981.

Gleichen-Russwurm, Alexander von. *The World's Lure: Fair Women, Their Loves, Their Power, Their Fates.* Trans. Hannah Waller. New York: Alfred A. Knopf, 1927.

Hahn, Emily. *Lorenzo: D. H. Lawrence and the Women Who Loved Him.* Philadelphia: J. B. Lippincott Company, 1975.

Hellmann, John. *The Kennedy Obsession: The American Myth of JFK*. New York: Columbia University Press, 1997.

Kaus, Gina. *Catherine: The Portrait of an Empress.* Trans. June Head. New York: Viking, 1935.

Kierkegaard, Søren. *The Seducer's Diary,* in *Either/Or, Part 1.* Trans. Howard V. Hong & Edna H. Hong. Princeton, NJ: Princeton University Press, 1987.

Lao, Meri. *Sirens: Symbols of Seduction.* Trans. John Oliphant of Rossie. Rochester, VT: Park Street Press, 1998.

Lindholm, Charles. *Charisma.* Cambridge, MA: Basil Blackwell, Ltd., 1990.

Ludwig, Emil. *Napoleon.* Trans. Eden & Cedar Paul. Garden City, NY: Garden City Publishing Co., 1926.

Mandel, Oscar, ed. *The Theatre of Don Juan: A Collection of Plays and Views, 1630–1963.* Lincoln, NE: University of Nebraska Press, 1963.

Maurois, André. *Byron.* Trans. Hamish Miles. New York: D. Appleton & Company, 1930.

———. *Disraeli: A Picture of the Victorian Age.* Trans. Hamish Miles. New York: D. Appleton & Company, 1928.

Monroe, Marilyn. *My Story.* New York: Stein and Day, 1974.

Morin, Edgar. *The Stars.* Trans. Richard Howard. New York: Evergreen Profile Book, 1960.

Ortiz, Alicia Dujovne. *Eva Perón.* Trans. Shawn Fields. New York: St. Martin's Press, 1996.

Ovid. *The Erotic Poems.* Trans. Peter Green. London: Penguin Books, 1982.

———. *Metamorphoses.* Trans. Mary M. Innes. Baltimore, MD: Penguin Books, 1955.

Peters, H. F. *My Sister, My Spouse: A Biography of Lou Andreas-Salomé.* New York: W. W. Norton, 1962.

Plato. *The Symposium.* Trans. Walter Hamilton. London: Penguin Books, 1951.

Reik, Theodor. *Of Love and Lust: On the Psychoanalysis of Romantic and Sexual Emotions.* New York: Farrar, Strauss and Cudahy, 1957.

Rose, Phyllis. *Jazz Cleopatra: Josephine Baker and Her Time.* New York: Vintage Books, 1991.

Sackville-West, Vita. *Saint Joan of Arc.* London: Michael Joseph Ltd., 1936.

Shikibu, Murasaki. *The Tale of Genji.* Trans. Edward G. Seidensticker. New York: Alfred A. Knopf, 1979.

Shu-Chiung. *Yang Kuei-Fei: The Most Famous Beauty of China.* Shanghai, China: Commercial Press, Ltd., 1923.

Smith, Sally Bedell. *Reflected Glory: The Life of Pamela Churchill Harriman.* New York: Touchstone, 1996.

Stendhal. *Love.* Trans. Gilbert and Suzanne Sale. London: Penguin Books, 1957.

Terrill, Ross. *Madame Mao: The White-Boned Demon.* New York: Touchstone, 1984.

Trouncer, Margaret. *Madame Récamier.* London: Macdonald & Co., 1949.

Wadler, Joyce. *Liaison.* New York: Bantam Books, 1993.

Weber, Max. *Essays in Sociology.* Ed. Hans Gerth & C. Wright Mills. New York: Oxford University Press, 1946.

Wertheimer, Oskar von. *Cleopatra: A Royal Voluptuary.* Trans. Huntley Patterson. Philadelphia: J. B. Lippincott Company, 1931.

Index

FOR THE BEST IN PAPERBACKS, LOOK FOR THE 

In every corner of the world, on every subject under the sun, Penguin represents quality and variety—the very best in publishing today.

For complete information about books available from Penguin—including Penguin Classics and Puffins—and how to order them, write to us at the appropriate address below. Please note that for copyright reasons the selection of books varies from country to country.

In the United States: Please write to *Penguin Group (USA), P.O. Box 12289 Dept. B, Newark, New Jersey 07101-5289* or call 1-800-788-6262.

In the United Kingdom: Please write to *Dept. EP, Penguin Books Ltd, Bath Road, Harmondsworth, West Drayton, Middlesex UB7 0DA.*

In Canada: Please write to *Penguin Books Canada Ltd, 90 Eglinton Avenue East, Suite 700, Toronto, Ontario M4P 2Y3.*

In Australia: Please write to *Penguin Books Australia Ltd, P.O. Box 257, Ringwood, Victoria 3134.*

In New Zealand: Please write to *Penguin Books (NZ) Ltd, Private Bag 102902, North Shore Mail Centre, Auckland 10.*

In India: Please write to *Penguin Books India Pvt Ltd, 11 Panchsheel Shopping Centre, Panchsheel Park, New Delhi 110 017.*

In the Netherlands: Please write to *Penguin Books Netherlands bv, Postbus 3507, NL-1001 AH Amsterdam.*

In Germany: Please write to *Penguin Books Deutschland GmbH, Metzlerstrasse 26, 60594 Frankfurt am Main.*

In Spain: Please write to *Penguin Books S. A., Bravo Murillo 19, 1° B, 28015 Madrid.*

In Italy: Please write to *Penguin Italia s.r.l., Via Benedetto Croce 2, 20094 Corsico, Milano.*

In France: Please write to *Penguin France, Le Carré Wilson, 62 rue Benjamin Baillaud, 31500 Toulouse.*

In Japan: Please write to *Penguin Books Japan Ltd, Kaneko Building, 2-3-25 Koraku, Bunkyo-Ku, Tokyo 112.*

In South Africa: Please write to *Penguin Books South Africa (Pty) Ltd, Private Bag X14, Parkview, 2122 Johannesburg.*